HISTORY OF GERMANY IN THE NINETEENTH CENTURY

TREITSCHKE'S HISTORY OF GERMANY IN THE NINETEENTH CENTURY

TRANSLATED BY EDEN & CEDAR PAUL

WITH AN INTRODUCTION BY
WILLIAM HARBUTT DAWSON

VOLUME ONE

NEW YORK

McBRIDE, NAST & COMPANY

1915

INTRODUCTION.

SATISFACTION that an English translation of Heinrich von Treitschke's monumental " History of Germany in the Nineteenth Century " is at last to appear in English, even though thirty-six years have passed since the appearance of the first and twenty-one years since the appearance of the final volume, will be tempered in many minds by a feeling of regret and almost of shame that this just tribute to a great literary achievement should have been delayed so long. It cannot be pleaded in explanation of past neglect that the History is a work for scholars only, for no famous history appeals more strongly, in virtue alike of its contents and its literary style, to the suffrages of the great public.

Year by year German works of ephemeral value are reproduced in English by the score and the hundred, in response to an ever-insistent demand for the latest in caprice or sensation, yet in this country and America this literary masterpiece, one of the foremost contributions of German scholarship to historical science, has hitherto enjoyed little more than a library reputation, and has remained inaccessible to most readers unable or unwilling to make acquaintance with Treitschke in the original. The reception given to a translated edition of the History will help to decide how far this strange disregard of Treitschke has been merely the accidental result of a lack of commercial enterprise on the part of publishers, or due to a genuine want of public appreciation.

An Introduction to a standard work of so established a reputation as this can only be redeemed from impertinence by pertinence. Inasmuch as the translation will introduce Treitschke to a new circle of readers, the title to pertinence may perhaps be conceded if in these preliminary words an attempt be made to give to those readers some indication of what the History is and what it has to offer them.

The History was neither begun nor ended as Treitschke originally intended. While still engaged in his preparatory spade work, Treitschke found the plan, as he had conceived it, expanding beneath his hands. His first idea was to write only the history of the Germanic Federation, created by the Congress of Vienna in 1815, on the ruins of the Holy Roman Empire of the German Nation, which Napoleon had impiously destroyed nine years before. What scholarship and literature would have lost had he adhered to that first design may be imagined. The spectacle of Treitschke exhausting himself in the endless task of writing the dreary, uninspiring, unheroic annals of the Deutscher Bund, suggests the hardly less congruous spectacle of a Velasquez passing his days in painting Dutch interiors—in either case a fate comparable to the rigours which might have been reserved in a tenth Circle for men of genius who had misused their talents. Treitschke, as the special historian of the Bund, might have done the work better than anyone else, but there were other men able to do it well enough.

It was not, however, the unattractiveness of the task that led him to abandon the idea of concentrating upon the history of the Bund. He tells us that he had not been long at work before he recognised that a History of the Germanic Federation would be a history for students and specialists. It was not his ambition to write such a work, but to write German history for the German nation. Hence he found it necessary to carry his researches both further back and further forward. As the plan developed he came to fix on the Peace of Westphalia as his starting point. That landmark gave him just the wide perspective which his scheme, as it had now taken shape, required, for it enabled him to survey in all essential features the beginnings of modern Germany and above all to do full justice to the romantic story of the growth of the Prussian State. It was his intention to bring the narrative down to his own day.

Of the History, five portly volumes were published, carrying the story to the revolutionary movements of 1848. The History had not to win its way laboriously into favour like many great works, for it was born famous. Edition after edition has been published, and its place in the estimation—one might almost say the reverence—of the German nation is perhaps greater to-day than ever. Nor is there any great mystery about this. The immense amount of research and the stores of erudition embodied in the History, the writer's weighty authority alike as professor, publicist, and parliamentarian, and the fascination of his literary style would alone have assured a brilliant success. Yet these were not the recommendations which gave to Treitschke and the History their immense influence over the minds of modern Germany.

Two facts, I think, contributed in a special degree to bring

Introduction

about this result. The first was the fact that Treitschke wrote for the most part of events which were part of the living tradition of his day, events many of which fell within the memory and even the experience of a large section of his contemporaries. The period between 1871, when the present Empire was established, back to the time when Napoleon's power was at its zenith, spanned barely two generations, yet what a powerful drama had been played in Germany during that short period! When it opened Prussia still lay humbled and abased beneath a foreign yoke, exhausted in body, impoverished in spirit, atrophied in will; between Jena and Leipzig she lived through a passion as bitter as ever befell a nation; in that ordeal her worth and right to live were put to the test of supreme endurance and sacrifice. Redeemed by her own efforts, Prussia came out of the trial victorious, and stood again erect, secure henceforth against the enemies of her unity within no less than against those which might threaten from without. Moreover, with Prussia's stripes the rest of Germany was healed.

After the fall of Napoleon, the history of Germany for fifty years was mainly one of slow internal reorganisation and development; there was the inevitable sway of the pendulum from a sense of buoyant freedom to apathy and reaction, followed in turn, however, by the painful emergence of the German States one by one from the twilight of absolutism into the day-dawn of constitutional government. Then came the bitter " conflict " between Crown and Parliament in Prussia, in which the old system and the new fought with desperate tenacity, without decisive victory on either side, a struggle carrying for both the moral and the warning " Thus far and no farther ! " which has been the jealous watchword of Prussian parliamentary life from that day to this. And all through this period of change and transition that pompous mockery the Bund continued its futile Diet, cumbered about many things and persistently refusing to recognise that only one thing really mattered, the question whether the future of Germany was to lie with Austria or Prussia. After vainly trying to settle this question by diplomatic wrangling, the rivals fought it out in the two campaigns of 1864 and 1866, of which the natural if not necessary sequel was the gigantic war of 1870, when the diapason of the century's longing and endeavour ended full in national unity and a New Empire, with all that the rebirth meant for the political, intellectual, and material development of the German peoples.

It was to this epoch of German history that Treitschke devoted himself, and it was to contemporaries who had lived through or in it, and to whom, therefore, its events and vicissitudes were intensely real, that his History was addressed. A nation still in the first enthusiasm of military and political triumph, still dazzled by its successes, and revelling in the consciousness of proved strength and yet greater latent power, could not fail to respond to the appeal of a historian whose eloquent periods breathed a patriotic fervour even greater than its own.

Yet even here the secret and the significance of Treitschke's influence are not exhausted. From the German standpoint it is his supreme merit that he voiced the new life and self-consciousness of modern Germany in a way that no other man—no statesman, no writer of any kind, and certainly no historian—had done before. At last there stood forth a man, like to that earlier patriot-historian of Bonn, Ernst Moritz Arndt, the " deutschester Mann " of his time, as he was called, who was able and determined to do justice not only to the past of the German nation, but to its present and future, to assert its claims and rights, to formulate its aims and ambitions, and to interpret to the world its individuality and outlook. For two generations the Great Powers had regarded Germany as for practical purposes blotted out of the map of Europe. Germany had seemed to accept her fate, hardly venturing to assert a right to recognition, apologising that she dared to stand in the light of her haughty neighbours. Even after the national revival had set in, and the disunited tribes had become a nation, the old attitude of disregard and contumely continued ; to the older states, which had so long monopolised the seats of the mighty, the German Empire was still an upstart and an outsider. For the slights from which Germany suffered, Treitschke gravely blamed Germany herself. In the past there had been too much apology. Treitschke went to the other extreme. With a defiant pride and a high disdain he struck the word apology out of the German vocabulary ; his *rôle* and his mission were to be those of his country's vindicator.

Not only was the History to be a vindication of Germany's right to be a united nation and to have her own place in the sun ; it was also intended to justify Prussia's historical right to lead Germany to the promised land of her desires and to be the completer of her appointed and just destiny. That Germany was ordained, by some dispensation unsuspected by ordinary men, to direct the world in progress, as Germany understood it, and Prussia to be her spokesman and interpreter, was to Treitschke so obvious as hardly to need argument. This Ptolemaic view of history, which regards Germanism as the centre of civilisation, runs through all his political writings, and the invective of which he was a master was specially reserved for those nations which stubbornly refused to adopt this novel order of ideas. What made this attitude and advocacy of Treitschke the more remarkable was the fact that his ancestors were not Germans at all, and that he himself, until he changed his citizenship, was not a Prussian but a Saxon.

" I write for Germans." " No nation has greater cause than we to hold in honour the memory of our hard-struggling fathers, or recalls so seldom how through their blood and tears, their sweat of brain and of hand, the blessing of its unity has been won." " The narrator of German history only half achieves his task if he merely indicates the causality of events and speaks his mind with courage. He should in addition feel himself, and create in the hearts of his readers, *joy in the fatherland.*"

In passages like these, we may find the key both to Treitschke's presentation of history and to his singular hold upon the admiration and the attachment of his countrymen. His History is what he meant it to be—a clarion call to national consciousness and an inspiration to national devotion. He stung the national spirit of his countrymen into new and virile life, made pride of race a passion, patriotism a religion, and loyalty an act of worship.

This emphasis of nationality and the national standpoint caused him to set at defiance some of the most cherished canons of historical science, for it made detachment and objectivity impossible, led him into partisanship and special advocacy, and tempted the free play of prejudice. He says in one place, indeed, that it has been his aim to " speak definitely without harshness, justly without vagueness." That was a counsel of perfection which he may for formality's sake have pinned to his inkstand, like a new year's resolution, to be kept as long as possible, but he more often ignored than observed it. For moderation was not his special grace, nor was a judicial temperament his special gift. Impartiality and equanimity are not the only virtues, but they belong to the virtues which are looked for in a historian, and when they are lacking, the greatest work falls short of perfection. Treitschke's History must be read and valued and praised subject to this reservation.

" There are many ways of writing history, and each is justified so long as the style adopted is adhered to consistently and severely." To this dictum, which Treitschke laid down for his own guidance, the History is faithful. The examination of his sources must have entailed prodigious research in divers fields, but there is no suggestion of the antiquary in his pages. For him history was something more and greater than a recital of facts and completed events, if, indeed, in the seamless web of human life any single event can be said to be completed. Regarding history as life, he strove to recreate the national drama ; he put the actors upon the stage again, and made them play over their parts, not as marionettes, but as living men and women. In so doing, he at times made heroes out of commonplace men and the heroes he turned into demigods, but that was part of his deliberate plan, which was the glorification of his country. The ground covered by the History was not new, but drawing from fuller materials than had been accessible before, he was able to throw new light upon known facts, to bring these facts into new relations, to discuss them from fresh and original points of view, to challenge established verdicts, and thus to invest the most hackneyed episodes with fresh interest.

If Treitschke's temper as a historian has received much adverse criticism, his literary style has received no less praise, and deservedly so. There is something Byzantine in the structure of the History, in the conjunction of massiveness with a bewildering wealth and variety of ornament, of strength with splendour, grandeur with dignity, severity with grace. The flow of language is easy and rhythmical ; often it is impetuous ; only when the nervous pen responds to the impulses of an imagination fired by passion, does the stream break bounds. Stung into anger or indignation Treitschke's declamations are at times torrential and overwhelming. Yet the effect is never spoiled by any suggestion of forced rhetoric ; the passion may seem to be extravagant or even misplaced, but it is sincere, and free from artifice. The literary purist will rightly find fault with occasional lapses of taste due to his ardent temperament—without doubt a part, and not the least precious part, of his Slavic inheritance—and to his inability to keep prejudice under control, but these sunspots detract little if at all from the brilliancy of the total effect.

It was Treitschke's poignant regret, when the shadow of premature death fell upon him, that he was leaving the great work of his life incomplete. He was cut off at the age of sixty-two and in his intellectual prime, having scarcely brought the story of Germany in the nineteenth century to the end of the 'forties. The History ceases, therefore, at a point which to him must have been specially distressing ; for he had not left behind the revolutionary movements of 1848, an episode which he regarded as amongst the most humiliating and hateful in German and particularly in Prussian history. Not only, therefore, did the drama which he was reconstructing remain unfinished, but the still unplayed acts were, for a passionate patriot, amongst the most fascinating of all —above all, the wars of 1864 and 1866, which gave to Prussia a series of new provinces, and put that Power and Austria in their rightful places, Prussia at the head of Germany, Austria thrust out of the imperial heritage ; the formation of the North German Confederation ; and finally the war of 1870, which destroyed one empire and created another, set New Germany on a path of unexampled progress and prosperity, yet also, as events have proved, sowed seeds of infinite coming mischief. So far as it was completed, however, the History will be seen to leave no essential phase of the national life unregarded. The political history of the period naturally occupies Treitschke's principal attention, but he also passes in review the economic movements which were of such great importance for the country's later development, the intellectual awakening, and the special tendencies which came to the front in philosophy and literature, in science and art.

It is one of the greater ironies of literary history that the last and crowning part of Treitschke's task was left undone. His treatment of the events which ushered in the Empire would not have been faultless or final, but his narrative would have been an epic worthy of the master-pieces of historical literature. "Who will finish my History?" he asked pathetically of his friend and later biographer Hausrath. In putting the question he himself gave the answer. *His* History no one else could complete. Many other German writers of eminence have described the final episodes in the inspiring story of national unity, some with a knowledge and erudition, others with an intellectual grasp, a conscientiousness, or an earnestness of purpose not unworthy of his own.

Well as they have written, however, they have only supplemented and have not replaced Treitschke. For he, while uniting all these traits, added to them another, and it is this trait which gives to the History its uniqueness. It is the intimate personal element in his work, due to the close identification of the writer with his subject, of his own life with the life of his country. Therefore it is that so much of the History is the faithful reflex and utterance of his own soul. Because he felt deeply, he wrote intensely and often passionately. If often he was prejudiced, at times even ungenerous and unjust, towards other nations, the fault lay not with a deliberate intellectual perversity, but with a narrow patriotism which disenabled him to see the life of the world, even that of his own country, "truly and to see it whole." If it be conceded that this personal element in his writings was Treitschke's strength as a politician, it was no less his weakness as a historian, yet a weakness counterbalanced by so many excellences that it is easier to condone than condemn it.

WILLIAM HARBUTT DAWSON.

DEDICATORY PREFACE

TO

MAX DUNCKER.

HONOURED FRIEND, accept the dedication of these pages as a sign of our old friendship. During the lengthy preliminary labours you have so often given me ardent encouragement ; it is a pleasure to me to declare to you, first of all, what I have to say to my readers regarding the design and purpose of this book.

It was my original plan to write only the history of the Germanic Federation, and after a brief introduction to proceed immediately to the deliberations of the Congress of Vienna. I soon came to recognise, however, that a book which was not intended solely for historical experts must extend further back. The destinies of the Germanic Federation constitute no more than the conclusion of the two hundred years' struggle between the House of Austria and the newly-arising German state ; they would remain incomprehensible to the reader unless he were well-informed regarding the beginnings of the Prussian monarchy and the destruction of the Holy Empire. In our so recently reunited nation, a national historical tradition common to all cultured persons has not yet been able to develop. That unanimous sense of joyful gratitude which older nations feel towards their political heroes, is by us Germans felt only for the great names of art and science. Opinions still differ widely upon the question, which facts in the medley of our recent history have been genuinely decisive.

I therefore resolved, in an introductory book, to describe briefly how the new Germany had come into existence since the Peace of Westphalia. I need not tell a connoisseur how difficult it is to give a concise view of this enormous mass of material. The endless multifariousness and the intertwined determinations of historical life can be adequately exposed only by descriptions of an extremely detailed character. You will readily read between the lines how often in a brief sentence I express my opinion about a difficult disputed problem, how often I have had to ponder every word, so that I could speak definitely without harshness, justly without vagueness. The undertaking was all the bolder in that we already possess a comprehensive account of the last decades of the Holy Empire in Häusser's *History of Germany*, a book whose appearance had the significance of a political achievement, and which will always remain an ornament of our historical literature. But since the death of this ever-memorable man, our knowledge of the Napoleonic epoch has been notably enlarged, and not least by your own works. Moreover, the standpoint of historical criticism has changed. He who to-day desires to further the understanding of the present through a description of that epoch, must place in the foreground of his narration the internal development of the Prussian state, and the great transformations of spiritual life.

In the introductory book I have made no attempt to relate new facts. Nor have I been afraid to repeat from time to time what is already well known, for if the historian attempts always and everywhere to relate novelties he will certainly depart from truth. It has been my endeavour to extract from the confusion of events the most important points of view ; to bring vigorously forward the men and the institutions, the ideas and the changes of destiny, which have created our new nationality. Hence the internal affairs of the minor German states are dealt with very briefly. I propose in the second volume, when I come to the description of the South German constitutional struggles, to deal with these relationships in fuller detail. I trust that you, and other indulgent judges, will find that my survey gives an approximately just idea of the great contrasts which destroyed the state structure of our middle ages, and levelled the ground for the secular political formations of the new century. Within such narrow limits it was impossible to give more than the outlines of the picture.

After the destruction of the Old Empire, the description becomes gradually more detailed, and with the days of the first Peace of Paris begins the thorough narration of history which in the second volume I hope to carry forward to the year 1830. For this period, with the permission of the Chancellor and of Baron von Roggenbach, I have utilised the Berlin archives and the archives of the ministry of foreign affairs in Karlsruhe. I cannot express sufficient gratitude for the willingness with which I have always been furnished facilities by the present administration of the archives, at first under your own leadership and subsequently under that of Heinrich von Sybel. I have never misused this confidence, because it was impossible to do so. In the history of Prussia there is nothing to cloak, nothing to conceal. What errors and sins there have been in the history of this state, have long been known to all the world, thanks to the ill-favour of our neighbours and thanks to the fault-finding spirit of our own people ; honourable research leads in most cases to the recognition that even in times of weakness, Prussian statecraft was better than its reputation.

There are many ways of writing history, and each is justified so long as the style adopted is adhered to consistently and strictly. The aim of this book is simply to relate and to judge. If the representation is not to remain altogether formless, I must give to the readers no more than the completed results of the enquiry, without showing them the entire machinery of investigation, or burdening them with polemic disquisitions.

When I survey the century and a half which this volume attempts to describe, I feel once more, as I have so often felt when writing it, the wealth and the simple greatness of the history of our fatherland. No nation has greater cause than we to hold in honour the memory of its struggling fathers, or recalls so seldom how through their blood and tears, their labour of brain and of hand, the blessing of its unity has been achieved. You, my dear friend, have already, in the Paulskirche, dreamed the dream of the Prussian empire of German nationality, and have in heart remained younger than many of the precocious younger generation ; for you know how bearable seem the troubles of the present when compared with the distresses of the old days when there was no empire. You will not blame me because now and then, out of the equable peace of historic discourse there sounds a louder tone The narrator of German history fulfils but half his task when he indicates the connection of events and expresses his opinion with frankness ; he should also himself feel and should know how to awaken in the hearts of his readers—what many of our countrymen have already forgotten in the disputes and vexations of the moment—a delight in the fatherland.

HEINRICH VON TREITSCHKE.

Berlin,
February 10th, 1879.

PREFACE TO THE FIFTH EDITION.

ALTHOUGH Max Duncker has in the interim passed away, I retain this dedication in grateful memory. During the revision of this volume, I have utilised the abundant literature of recent years in order to attain to an independent judgment concerning the beginnings of the War of Liberation, based upon new researches into the archives. The emendations and additions due to this cause are, however, not extensive.

T.

BERLIN,
    September 25th, 1894.

TABLE OF CONTENTS.

VOL. I.   BOOK ONE.

INTRODUCTION. THE EXTINCTION OF THE EMPIRE.

BOOK I

Introduction

THE EXTINCTION OF THE EMPIRE

CHAPTER I.

GERMANY AFTER THE PEACE OF WESTPHALIA.

§ I.   THE IMPERIAL CONSTITUTION.

DESPITE the antiquity of her history, Germany is the youngest of the great nations of Europe. Twice has she been granted a period of youth, twice has she been through the struggle for the principles of national power and free civilisation. It is a thousand years since she created for herself the glorious kingdom of the Germans ; eight hundred years later she found it necessary to re-establish the state upon an entirely new foundation ; first in our own days did she as a unified power resume her place in the ranks of the nations.

Long ago, forced by the overwhelming power of events, she united with her own the imperial crown of Christendom, she adorned her life with all the charms of knightly art and culture, she shrank from neither risk nor sacrifice in order to maintain the leadership of the western world. In the world-wide campaigns of her great emperors the power of the German monarchy passed away. Upon the ruins of the old kingdom there immediately grew up a new structure of territorial dominions : spiritual and temporal princes, free cities, counts and knights—a formless medley of inchoate state-structures, but full of marvellous vital energy. Amid the decline of the imperial glory, the princes of Lower Saxony, the knights of the Teutonic Order, and the burghers of the Hanseatic League, completed with sword and plough the greatest work of colonisation which the world had seen since the days of the Romans. The lands between the Elbe and the Niemen were conquered and settled ; for centuries to come the Scandinavian and Slav peoples were subordinated to German commerce and to German culture. But princes and nobles, burghers and peasants, went their separate ways ; the reciprocal hatred of the estates rendered nugatory every attempt to effect the political organisation of the nation's super-abundant creative energy, to restore in federal form the lost unity of the state.

3

Then came Martin Luther, to unite once more for great ends talented men drawn from all sections of our divided people. Through the earnestness of the German spirit, the secularised Church was led back into the lofty simplicity of Protestant Christianity, and in that spirit there burgeoned the idea of freeing the State from the dominion of the Church. For the second time our people attained to one of the summits of its civilisation and entered straightway upon the most venturesome revolution ever attempted. In other Teutonic lands, the universal work of Protestantism was to strengthen the authority of the national state, to put an end to the multiplex dominion of the Middle Ages. In the land of its birth it effected merely the dissolution of the old order. During those days of joyful expectation, a foreigner wore our crown, and this was decisive in its influence upon the whole future of the German monarchy ; for the nation hailed the Monk of Wittenberg with shouts of exultation, and, moved to the depths of its being, awaited an entire transformation of the empire. The imperial power, which should have been the leader of the Germans in their struggle with the Papacy, renounced at once ecclesiastical and political reform. The empire of the Hapsburgs chose the Catholic side, led the Latin peoples of Southern Europe into the field against the German heretics, and remained henceforward, until its inglorious fall, the enemy of all that was truly German.

Protestantism turned for help to the temporal rulers. These territorial princes justified their right to existence by their work as protectors of the German faith. But the nation was unable to secure the universal victory on German soil of its own especial work, the Reformation, and was likewise unable to rejuvenate its own national state in accordance with the temporal ideas of the new time. The German spirit, inclined, as always, to excessive idealism, was alienated from the struggles of political life by the profundities of the new theology ; impassioned Lutheranism did not understand how to avail itself of the fortunate hour for the work of liberation. Germany so powerful in arms, was ignominiously beaten in the Schmalkaldian War, and had for the first time to submit to a foreign yoke. Then came the wild uprising of Maurice of Saxony to rescue German Protestantism and to destroy the Spanish dominion, but to destroy also the ultimate bonds of monarchical order which still served to unite Germany, and the freedom of the estates of the realm assumed henceforward the form of boundless licence. After a rapid succession of partial victories and partial defeats, the wearied factions concluded the premature religious peace of Augsburg. Thereupon ensued the most deplorable period of German history. The empire voluntarily quitted the circle of the great powers and renounced all share in European politics. The amorphous mass of Catholic, Lutheran, and Calvinistic principalities, immobile and yet unreconciled, passed two generations in idle dreams, whilst at our very gates the armies of the Catholic world-empire were fighting to rob the heretics of the Netherlands of the freedom of belief, and its navies were disputing the command of the sea.

Then at length the last and decisive war of the epoch, the war of the religions, broke out. The home of Protestantism became also its battle-ground. All the powers of Europe took part in the war. The scum of all nations was heaped up on German soil. In a disturbance without parallel, the old Germany passed away. Those who had once aimed at world-dominion were now, by the pitiless justice of history, placed under the feet of the stranger. The Rhine and the Ems, the Elbe and the Weser, the Oder and the Vistula, all the ways to the sea, became " captives of foreign nations " ; on the Upper Rhine were established the outposts of French rule, while the south-east became subject to the dominion of the Hapsburgs and of the Jesuits. Two-thirds of the entire nation were involved in this dreadful war ; the people, degenerating into savagery, carrying on a burdened life amid dirt and poverty, no longer displayed the old greatness of the German character, were no longer animated by the free-spirited and serene heroism of their ancestors. The dominion of an ancient civilisation, that civilisation which alone adorns and ennobles existence, had disappeared into oblivion ; forgotten were even the craft-secrets of the guilds. The nation, which once had sung of Kriemhild's revenge, and which had fortified its heart by the heroic strains of Luther's hymns, now embellished its impoverished speech with foreign tinsel, and those who still remained capable of profound thought wrote French or Latin. The entire life of Germany lay open without defence to the influence of the superior civilisation of the foreigner. Under the urgency of the Swedish distresses, amid the petty sorrows of poverty-stricken everyday life, the very memory of the glories of the wonderful centuries of old disappeared from the minds of the masses ; in the transformed world, the ancient cathedrals, witnesses to the former magnificence of German burghership, seemed strange and unfriendly. Not till a century and a half had elapsed were the treasures of ancient German poetry recovered by the

5

laborious research of learned investigators, so that all were astonished at the wealth of the former treasure-house. Never was any other nation so forcibly estranged from itself and from its own past ; not even modern France is separated by so profound a chasm from the days of the old regime.

This horrible confusion seemed to foreshadow the destruction of the German name, and yet it proved the beginning of a new life. In those days of misery, in the time of the Peace of Westphalia, our new history begins. It is to two forces that we owe the restoration of our declining nation, which since those days has transformed its life politically and economically, in faith, in art, and in science, to make that life ever richer and ever wider in its scope : the force of religious freedom, and the force of the Prussian state.

Through the sorrows and struggles of the Thirty Years' War, Germany secured the future of Protestantism in the western world, and at the same time established upon an indestructible basis the characteristics of her own civilisation. The extreme south adhered to the Catholic world of the Romans ; the northern marches touched the hard Lutheranism of Scandinavia ; but the central regions of Germany remained the common ground of three confessions. Of all the great nations, Germany was the only one in which these different creeds competed on equal terms, and Germany was therefore compelled to establish in her homes and her schools, throughout her political and social life, that ecclesiastical peace which had been attained through a long, fierce, and bloody struggle. In earlier days, when the Roman Church was still the Church Universal, bearing in its bosom no more than the germs of Protestantism, it was Catholicism which had trained our people for civilisation, and which had provided the abundant groundwork of art and science. But when Catholicism expelled from herself these powers of freedom, and when, with the assistance of the Latin peoples, she became transformed into a closely knit ecclesiastical party, she was enabled, it is true, through the talent for dominion of the House of Hapsburg, to reconquer for herself a portion of Germany ; but the spirit of our people remained ever hostile to the Jesuitic faith. The rich spiritual forces of the Neo-Roman Church flourished in their Latin homelands ; but they could strike no root upon this foreign German soil, in this nation of born heretics. Here sang no Tasso or Calderon, here painted no Rubens or Murillo. Hardly one among the slothful German monks was found to compete in zeal for learning with the diligent fathers of the Maurist Congregation. Among the Germans, the Society of Jesus educated many pious priests and many able statesmen ; it produced also many ponderous zealots, who, like Father Busenbaum, with uncouth German bluntness disclosed to the world the secret that the end justifies the means. But the entire culture of the Society of Jesus was the work of Roman brains, and Roman also were the stultifying educational methods of the Jesuits. In Germany, the new Catholicism worked only to hinder and confuse ; the spiritual possessions of Catholicism contrasted with the thought-world of Protestantism much as the barren scholasticism of our first Jesuit, Canisius, contrasted with the straightforward wisdom of the works of Luther. Despite all the wholesale conversions of the Counter-Reformation, Germany remained, as Rome well knew, the citadel of heresy. The central fibre of our spirit was Protestant.

Dearly-bought ecclesiastical tolerance prepared the towns for a restrained freedom, a circumspect boldness of thought, which could never have thrived under the uncontrolled dominion of any single Church. Upon such a soil, so soon as the exhausted people was once more able to produce men of genius, there flourished our new science and poetry, the most vigorous literature of modern history, essentially Protestant, and yet with the freedom and gentleness of the secular spirit. Upon our troubled nation this literature once more bestowed the gift of a powerful speech, restored the ideals of humanism, and reawakened self-confidence. Thus for our people even the defeats of the Reformation ultimately proved a blessing. Constrained to carry in one bosom all the great contrasts of European life, Germany became enabled to understand them all, and to control them with the might of thought. Humanity resounded from every breath of her spirit. Her classical literature became more various, bolder, and freer, than that produced by the earlier ripened culture of her neighbours. A century and a half after the decline of the ancient German civilisation it was possible for Hölderlin thus to apostrophise the new Germany :

> "O sacred heart of the peoples, O Fatherland !
> All-patient, thou, like our silent Mother Earth,
> And misunderstood, although now from thy depths
> Strangers draw all that they have of the best."

Simultaneously there awakened the state-constructive powers of the nation. Amid the disintegration of outworn imperial forms and undeveloped territories, the young Prussian state raised its head; and in Prussia, henceforward, centred the political life of Germany. Just as nearly a thousand years before, the crown of Wessex had united all the Saxon kingdoms to form the English state, and just as the Kingdom of the Franks, starting from the Isle de France, continued to enlarge throughout the Middle Ages until it had conquered and united the isolated baronies and communes, so also out of the sundered fragments of the German nation did the monarchy of the Brandenburg-Prussian Mark create once more a Fatherland. It is, as a rule, only the virile formative energy of youthful peoples that achieves success in the fierce struggle for the beginnings of national unity ; but here the change was effected in the clear noonday light of the new time, against the opposition of the whole of Europe, in a contest with the legitimate authority of the Holy Empire, and with the countless opposing forces of the complex German life, hardened and concreted by long historical tradition. This was the most arduous movement towards national unity which Europe has ever known, and nothing but the ultimate, complete, and brilliant success of that unity has finally compelled an unwilling world to believe in the reality of the work which had often before been so vainly attempted.

It was impossible that the reconstitution of the German state should now be effected by the emperor and the empire. With the rise of Protestantism, the imperial constitution, which had for long been in an extremely fragile condition, became a hateful lie. The ultimate consequences of all great human actions remain concealed from the doer. Just as Martin Luther, when he broke loose from the mediæval Church, was unaware that he was opening the road for the secular science of our days, which would have been a scandal to his piety, so also, when he freed the state from the rule of the Church, did he lay an axe to the roots of that Roman imperialism of which he was himself a faithful subject. As soon as the majority of the nation had adhered to the Protestant doctrine, the theocratic office of the emperor became as untenable as was its principal prop, the support of the spiritual princes. The crowned guardian, and the bishops of the Old Church, could not rule a heretical nation. In the first years of the Reformation, in the Reichstag of 1525, the demand made itself audible that the spiritual prerogatives should pass under the control of the temporal princes ; and at all subsequent great turning-points of the policy of the realm the necessary idea of secularisation continually recurred, springing from the very nature of things.

But the unsatisfactory balance of forces and counter-forces which interfered with every movement of the empire rendered nugatory even this irrefutable consequence of the Reformation. The majority of the spiritual princes retained their prerogatives, and the fantastic claims to dominion of the *Sacra Cesarea Majestas* were also retained, although the German kingship in which was invested this Roman imperial crown had long been devoid of all authority, and although all the prerogatives of the ancient monarchy had long since passed into the hands of the territorial princes.

Outside the limits of the imperial heritage two-thirds of the German people became Protestant, and Protestant also became all the great princely houses, with the exception of the Wittelsbachs and the Albertines. Official Germany, however, remained Catholic. Adherents of the ancient creed retained the majority in the Council of Electors and in the Council of the Princes, and the imperial dominion continued to preserve its semi-priestly character. In virtue of his coronation, the emperor became " Participator in Our Spiritual Office " and made common cause with the Pope and the Church to testify his gratitude for the appropriate ecclesiastical honours ; *ex officio*, he was prebend of several Catholic foundations, and therefore received Holy Communion in both kinds. Under this Roman theocracy, heresy could not legally exist. The first great political act of the German Lutherans was the Protest of Spires, which gave the new faith its name ; herein it was stated in set terms that the Protestants would not submit to the majority in the empire. In the struggle with the empire which was thus begun Protestantism maintained itself henceforward as an element of continuous sedition. Protestantism enforced the religious peace treaties, which were in flat contradiction with the ancient imperial oath and with the fundamental ideas of the Holy Roman Empire, and constituted a state within the state in order to safeguard the dearly gained religious freedom against the majority in the Reichstag. The *Corpus Evangelicorum*, though somewhat milder in form than the Confederations of the Polish Nobles' Republic, was, like these, an anarchistic makeshift utterly opposed to the conception of the state.

Nothing but a revolutionary change, nothing but a transformation of the Holy Empire into a federation of temporal states, could rescue the nation from such a falsification of its political life ; nothing but a national authority which honourably recognised its own temporal character could furnish justice alike for Catholics and Protestants on the common ground of the law.

This conviction forced itself upon both the great publicists of seventeenth century Germany ; the spokesman of the Swedish party, Hippolytus a Lapide, was a passionate advocate of a war of annihilation against the imperial rule ; the judicious Samuel Puffendorf regarded the realm as hastening " with the certainty of a rolling stone " towards its transformation into a confederation of states. Even official Germany had an obscure perception how senseless the old forms had become in the new time. The religious peace treaties only pretended to be truces, and encouraged the nation to hope for better times, for " by God's grace a union shall be effected in matters of belief." The Peace of Westphalia commissioned the next Reichstag to effect a comprehensive revision of the constitution, whereby the newly acquired powers of the estates of the empire should be harmonised with the ancient rights of the imperial crown. But here also the House of Austria hindered attempts at reform. The Imperial Assembly of 1654 broke up without effecting a settlement, and since the next Reichstag continued to meet in Ratisbon for a century and a half without ever attempting its most important duty, the German state remained in actuality without a constitution. In its public law were embodied the wreckage of three fundamentally diverse constitutional forms, which existed side by side and uncombined : the shadowy vestiges of the ancient monarchical unity ; the imperfect beginnings of a new confederation of states; and, finally, and endowed with far more vitality than either of these, the particularism of the territorial powers.

Throughout all changes, the imperial dominion maintained its ancient claims to autocracy, and would never admit that an imperial law could limit the prerogatives of the emperor. The imperial suzerain continued to receive the homage of his kneeling subjects, the estates of the empire, himself seated the while, and with covered head. As far as his arm could reach, he continued to exercise judicial authority through the Aulic Council of the Empire, as if he had still in reality remained what he had once been in the days of the Sachsenspiegel—the supreme judge concerning property, fiefs, and life and death. At the coronation, the herald continued to brandish the imperial sword towards the four winds of heaven, because the whole of Christendom was subordinate to the double eagle. The imperial law continued to speak solemnly of the fiefs of the empire as extending along the Riviera past Genoa and far into Tuscany ; the three chancellorships for Germany, Italy, and the Arelate were still in existence ;

Nomeny and Bisanz, and numerous other estates which had long passed to strangers, were still summoned to vote in the Reichstag ; the Duke of Savoy was regarded as the imperial vicar in Wälschland (Italy) ; and no one could say where stood the boundary-stones of the Holy Empire. To the poetic vision of the youthful Goethe it seemed that in the ancient Frankish pageant of the imperial coronation the richly coloured glories of the old empire were recalled to life ; but to one who looked at the matter with the cool vision of the man of the world, like the Ritter von Lang, this imperialism of effete memories and boundless claims seemed a preposterous mummery, as ludicrous and absurd as the sword of Charlemagne, which bore the Bohemian lion on its blade, or as the choir-boys of St. Bartholomew's, whose clear-toned *fiat !* resounding from the chancel acclaimed in the name of the German nation the choice of the ruler of the world.

The transformation of the ancient Teutonic electoral monarchy into a hereditary monarchy secured national unity for most of the peoples of Western Europe. Germany, however, remained an electoral realm, and the union of its crown with the House of Austria during three centuries served only to arouse new forces of disintegration and discord, since for our people the imperial rule of the Hapsburgs was a foreign dominion. The Old German South-eastern Mark, separated from Middle Germany by the powerful Slav realm of Bohemia, went its own way early in the Middle Ages, and became perforce involved in the confused political life of the Hungarian-Slav-Wallachian racial compost of the Lower Danubian lands. By the House of Hapsburg, this area was made the nucleus of a powerful polyglot empire, absolved by means of privileges, false and true, of all serious duties towards the German realm. As early as the sixteenth century it had acquired so secure an independence that the Hapsburgs were enabled to entertain the idea of a union of these remoter regions with their German heritage to form a kingdom of Austria. Amid the throng of foreign peoples, the valiant tribes of the Alps and the Upper Danube faithfully preserved their German type, and with their fresh and vigorous disposition took a notable part in the intellectual creative work of our Middle Age. The art of chivalry flourished at the cheerful court of the Babenbergs ; in the days of the Hohenstaufen emperors, the greatest poet of the time was a son of the Tyrolese Alps ; the beautiful market-halls of St. Stefan and of St. Marien-am-Stiegen bore witness to the pride and the artistic diligence of the German burghers of Lower Austria. In this region also, the German spirit now allied itself to the joyful awakening of the reformed doctrine; in Bohemia, the Hussites again became active; and at the opening of the century of the Reformation the greater part of the German-Austrian crown lands adhered to the faith of our people. Thereupon the religious bigotry of the imperial house let loose over Austria all the horrors of national murder, and amid frightful atrocities the dominion of the Roman Church was restored by the imperial saviours. Those of truly German spirit, those who would not bow their necks beneath the foreign yoke, the best of the Bohemians, left their country by hundreds of thousands to find a new home in the lands of the Protestant princes. Those who remained, lost in the school of the Jesuits the vital energy of the German spirit, lost their bold conscientiousness, lost their moral idealism. By ecclesiastical oppression, the profoundest roots of the national life were destroyed. The bright gaiety of Austrian Teutondom declined into a thoughtless hedonism, and the frivolous people soon habituated itself to the false bonhomie of a priestly rule which knew well how to conceal its cold contempt for humanity beneath agreeably indulgent forms.

The Peace of Westphalia gave a legal sanction to this last great victory of the Counter-Reformation. The emperor gave his assent to the equality of the three confessions, only on condition that this equality should not exist in his own hereditary dominion. From that day Austria has remained apart from the community of German life. The one thing that still gave meaning and reality to the tattered imperial constitution, the secure freedom of religious belief, did not exist in the Hapsburg lands ; and at the very time when Germany was displaying in flaunting peace-festivals its rejoicing over the final attainment of religious harmony, the emperor was affixing to the church-doors in Vienna and Prague, in Graz and Innsbruck, the Papal Bull which condemned the conclusion of peace. After the peace, the imperial house continued to work unceasingly for the eradication of heresy. For a hundred years after this date, until the death of Charles VI, the waves of Protestant emigration from Austria towards the German north continued to flow, though becoming ever smaller as the years elapsed, until all the hereditary dominions of the empire had passed into the death-slumber of religious unity. At the beginning of the Thirty Years' War, the Bohemian County of Glatz was Protestant throughout, except for one single Catholic commune. When the grenadiers of King Frederick entered this region the people were Catholic to a man, and in the centre of the freshly proselytised country there reared its head the gracious pilgrimage-church of Albendorf, a monument of victory for the battle of the White Mountain. Henceforward the German-Austrian lands pursued a life apart, alienated from their Catholic neighbours in Bavaria by tribal hatred and ancient political hostility, and jealously shut off from all contact with the North German heresy. Intercourse between Bohemia and the Lower Elbe, which in the Middle Ages was so lively that the Emperor Charles IV could hope to establish a great Elbe empire extending from Prague to Tangermünde, came to an end ; all the old fruitful interchange of influences between north-eastern and south-eastern Germany utterly ceased ; and at the frontier between Saxony and Bohemia there gradually became manifest a sharp division of nationalities, a fundamental contrast of ideas and of customs. Into this separate world of the south, hardly a murmur made its way of the spiritual strains of the reawakening German poetry, or of the free discourse of our youthful science. While the young people of Germany were weeping over the sorrows of Werther, and while they were feeling with Robber Moor a fierce contempt for the poverty in action displayed by their quill-driving age, pleasure-loving Vienna was glorifying the dull caricatures of Blumauer's travesty of the Æneid. The works of the great Austrian composers were the only things serving to show that the creative energy of the German spirit was not yet utterly extinct in the beautiful home of Walther von der Vogelweide. Not until the nineteenth century did the isolated Germans of the South-eastern Mark once more find the power enabling them to follow with a lively understanding all the work of modern German civilisation.

In this way the policy of the Danubian land, inspired by its Catholic unity of faith, was for long utterly foreign to the aims of our people. This policy cleft the old empire asunder, creating the much-deplored German dualism. So long as the Germans remained true to themselves it was impossible for them ever to abandon their resistance to the foreign dominion of the Hapsburgs. As the centuries passed, the House of Austria became so closely associated with the Roman imperial crown that in the popular estimation the two seemed almost inseparable. The one man to hold the imperial title during recent centuries who was not an Austrian, Charles VII, seemed to his contemporaries almost an anti-emperor. A profound inner kinship united the degermanised emperorship with the Papal See, its opponent of former days. The policy of Vienna, like that of Rome, exhibits that characteristic of hypocritical unction which makes theocracy the most immoral of all forms of government. In Vienna, as in Rome, there was the like incapacity to understand the rights of an opponent. All the Hapsburgs, Maria Theresa with her serene amiability no less than Leopold I, with his dull-witted pride, endured the assaults of fate in the firm conviction that their line was under the special favour of God, and that only wicked and godless men could resist the pious Archducal House of Austria. Everywhere and always they displayed the same rigid immobility amid the storms of the centuries. Every ignominious peace which the might of history forced upon the ancient imperial house was subscribed by the Hapsburgs with a tacit reservation that when the hour should come the inalienable rights of the imperial authority would be fully restored. Everywhere and at all times there was the same audacious weaving of myths and distortion of right. Whilst Maria Theresa was rising against the rightful emperor, Charles VII, she herself displayed the moral indignation of injured imperial majesty ; when, thereupon, King Frederick anticipated her threatened attack, her husband, who up to now had lived at her court as a simple private individual, assumed the imperial sceptre, and condemned the enemy of the Queen of Hungary as an enemy of the emperor and of the empire ; confidently, and as if it were a matter of course, the little House of Lorraine then revived all the claims to dominion that had been made by the ancient imperial race ; and just as the Popes, according to their own fable, sit upon the throne of the chief of the Apostles, so did the Lorrainers behave as if the Hapsburgs had never died out. In Vienna, just as in Rome, the welfare of the people was ignored with the same courtly cold-bloodedness ; and as soon as religious unity had been firmly established and the passive obedience of the subjects had been assured, the whole might of Austria was directed to without. The life of the state was concentred in European politics, whilst at home the old-established administration pursued its leisurely course in accordance with its outworn forms. Nothing was done for the development of an orderly system of government, nothing for the general well-being or for general culture ; no attempt was made to undertake those inconspicuous but arduous duties of internal politics which form the most secure foundation for the life of a healthy secular state. During centuries, the history of Austria, while it tells us of many capable diplomatists and military commanders, has no word to say of a single great administrator. First under Maria Theresa did the crown recall to mind the primary duties of the monarchy.

None the less, even in the confused compost of the Hapsburg-Burgundian heritage, the leaven of the state-constructive energy of modern history, pressing everywhere towards the consolidation of dominion, began to work. Under Leopold I, Hungary was conquered, and the crown of St. Stephen became a hereditary appanage of the House of Austria. Therewith begins the history of modern Austria as a great power, just as contemporaneously modern German history begins with the Great Elector. The Hapsburg possessions became a geographical unity, and the Danubian empire found the focus of its military power in the warlike peoples of Hungary. Henceforward strong economic and political interests associated Germany with the thronged peoples of this south German world, in which Germandom was able only with difficulty to maintain a spiritual preponderance. In the course of the long and glorious Turkish War, a sentiment of community became established between the German, Hungarian, and Slav companions-in-arms. The conquest of Hungary completed that which the policy of the Counter-Reformation had begun, the severance of Austria from Germany. As long as the Turkish pashas were massed upon the Königsburg of Buda, Austria was contending with the eastern barbarians on behalf of German civilisation ; it was only with the help of Germany, with the aid of the good swords of the men of the Mark, of Saxony, of Bavaria, that the Turks were driven out of Hungary. But when the Porte declined into weakness, this last bond which had still united our nation to the Austrian imperialism, the bond of a common danger, was torn asunder. Germany and Austria were henceforward two independent realms, connected only in an artificial union by the forms of public law. For many decades to come, the destruction of these false forms remained the chief task of German history.

Step by step the national unity of the new Austria became more firmly established. By the Pragmatic Sanction was proclaimed the indissolubility of the imperial dominions. Thereupon the greatest of all the Hapsburg rulers bestowed upon the Hapsburg heritage, hitherto united only by the imperial house, the clergy, the nobility, and the army, a scanty common constitution. Maria Theresa founded the system of the Austro-Hungarian dualism. She established the Bohemian-Austrian chancellorship as supreme authority in the Cisleithan crown-lands, whilst the dominions under the crown of St. Stephen preserved their old-established legal rights. Thus with a sure hand were designed the forms which alone could hold together these areas of excessive national contrasts.

After many vain attempts to form a unified state or a federation of states, the Austro-Hungarian monarchy has always returned to the ideas of the empress. The stresses and the glories of the Theresan days served also to give stability to the state. During eight years of fierce fighting the brave Hapsburg empress, vigorously supported by her faithful subjects, maintained the heritage of her house against a powerful coalition. During the Seven Years' War, however brightly might shine the star of King Frederick, compelling the admiration even of the conquered, the imperial army nevertheless bore away the palm of victory at Kolin and Hochkirch, rejoiced over the heroic greatness of its Loudon, and came out of the mighty struggle with a well-justified sense of satisfaction. Long before there existed an Austrian empire, it was customary in Europe to speak of the Austrian state and the Austrian army.

The possessorship of the crown of St. Stephen made it impossible for the imperial house to pursue a consistent aim in European policy. The conqueror of Hungary, Eugene of Savoy, showed to the state the road of promise towards the Black Sea. It now became the natural aim of the Danubian empire to press onward towards the mouth of the great river, and to subordinate to its own predominant civilisation the Slav-Wallachian peoples of either bank. Distant Belgium, which continually threatened to involve the state in the affairs of Western Europe, now became an inconvenient burden ; as early as the days of the Silesian War began the attempts, thenceforward continually repeated, to exchange for some nearer province this untenable and remote area of occupation. Yet the imperial house never learned, in a mood of wise concentration, to turn its united powers against the south-east. In this realm of conflicting nationalities, a national policy was simply impossible ; never, and least of all in that despotic epoch, has public opinion exercised any influence upon Austrian diplomacy. The conduct of Austria in European affairs has invariably been determined by the personal preferences of its rulers. The power of the house was originally based upon a bold and cunning family policy, greedily seeking extended influence in all directions, but without definite plan and without question as to the peculiarities or the position in the world of the conquered areas. The notions of this dynastic statecraft and the glorious memories of imperial world-dominion long remained active in the new Danubian realm. The Austrian court clung firmly to its dominant position in the German empire ; it endeavoured, by the conquest of Bavaria, to connect the upper

Austrian possessions on the Rhine with the nuclear regions of the monarchy ; from the days of Charles VI onward it revived the Italian policy of the Spanish Hapsburgs, endeavouring to maintain its ascendancy on the further side of the Alps, conducting all the while a rapid succession of rash onslaughts on the Poles and the Turks—this excessive and ill-conceived lust of dominion leading the powerful state from defeat to defeat.

Thus the imperial power was hostile to the Protestant-German culture, was indifferent to the European tasks of German policy, and regarded with the aloofness of a midland country the commercial interests of our coasts. The ill-defined authority of the imperial rule was for the Hapsburg-Lorrainers simply a welcome means for the forcible exploitation of the fighting strength of the German nation in pursuit of the aims of the House of Austria, and for the attainment of their own aggrandisement by the misuse of the forms of the imperial law. The time-honoured imperial jurisdiction became the playground of pettifogging arts, and Germany's foreign policy an incalculable game. The empire, now exposed by the court to foreign attacks, and now involved in un-German quarrels, had ever to pay the price for Austria's defeats. Mainly through the fault of the Hapsburgs, Holland and Switzerland, Schleswig-Holstein, Pomerania and the Ordensland, Alsace and Lorraine, were lost to Germany. These were irreparable losses, less shameful for the semi-foreign power which was unable to combine its imperial duty with the interests of its own house, than for the German nation, which failed always after such disasters to find energy to tear up its pact with Austria.

The imperial dominion was rooted in a lost past, and therefore found its natural opponents in the secular princes, whose energies were on the increase, while its adherents were drawn from the rotten and degenerate portions of the empire. "Ecclesiastically endowed Germany" constituted the kernel of the Austrian party—that luxuriantly flourishing spiritual province of German life which, having been restored to the Roman Church through the victories of the Counter-Reformation, henceforward led an easy life under the lax rule of the crozier, rejoicing in nepotism and sensuality. These Catholic regions, surrounded and subdivided by Protestant areas, could not remain so utterly estranged from the national life as were the hereditary dominions of the imperial house. To many a gentle-spirited and learned prince of the Church, the ideas of the age of enlightenment were welcome. But the political energy of the spiritual states remained lost beyond hope of rescue ;

and in Cologne, Mainz, and Treves the mass of the people were so untouched by the thought of the new century that the subsequent loss of the left bank of the Rhine seemed to cause hardly a perceptible wound to the spiritual life of Germany. The powerful Catholic nobility likewise adhered to the emperor, exercising control through its prince-bishoprics over three of the electorates and a number of the princely thrones of the empire, and finding in the service of the Archducal House of Austria comfortable sinecures for its sons. Even the diets of the temporal principalities looked for help to the emperor when they wished to defend their own individual privileges against the common rights of the new monarchy. Unquestionably the Catholic majority turned a favourable eye towards the imperial court, what time the factions of the realm were tearing one another to pieces, and while their mutual suspicions were stifling all possibilities of reform, and while every power that might threaten the imperial rule was held in check by other opposing forces. The traditional reverence of the smaller princes for the Archducal House of Austria, their mutual envies, the influence of the father-confessors upon the numerous princely converts, and the abundance of honours and privileges with which the Hofburg rewarded the faithful, secured support at this epoch even from the Protestant courts ; in many of the princedoms the chancellor was simultaneously an imperial minister entrusted with the task of attending to Austrian interests in his own court. So extensive a use of these indirect means for the control of the German nobility was made by a power regardless of the laws of the empire and the duties of German policy, that an able partisan of the imperial house, Baron von Gemmingen, wrote in an unguarded moment : " The House of Austria must either be the ruler or the enemy of the German realm."

Side by side with these ruins of a declining monarchical authority used to further foreign ends, the imperial constitution also contained the beginnings of a federal order. These were an inheritance from that great period of reform when Berthold of Mainz, Frederick of Saxony, and Eitelfritz of Zollern, as leaders of the state of princes, had made a bold attempt to transform the German community into a powerful federal state. From this time date the organisation of local government, and also the imperial chamber or federal court of justice formed by the estates of the empire. But as the emperor weakened the efficiency of this tribunal of the estates by the competitive authority of his own monarchical aulic council, the majority of the more powerful princes of the empire were able to withdraw their domains from the jurisdiction of the federal court of justice. In Swabia, Franconia, and on the Rhine, where a crowd of bishops and imperial knights, of princes and free cities, of abbots and counts, were massed together in extraordinary complexity, respect for the prefects and for the provincial assemblies still sufficed at times to maintain a degree of order, and to unite the pigmy military contingents of the estates into larger units. In the north and the east, however, the change of administration never became firmly rooted. Here, since the Peace of Westphalia, the spiritual privileges had been almost entirely destroyed, and the powerful temporal princes were sufficient unto themselves. As out of an enlightened modern world, the North German looked boldly over the confused medley of little states in the south-west, of which he spoke mockingly as " the empire." All that was young and vigorous in Old Germany was in revolt against the constricting forms of the imperial constitution.

The particularism of the temporal princes remained, however, the most vigorous political force in the realm. The Holy Empire was, in fact, what Frederick the Great termed it—the illustrious republic of the German princes. From the time of the Peace of Westphalia onward, its estates possessed the power of contracting alliances, and wielded a real sovereignty alike in spiritual and in temporal affairs. Only the name of sovereignty was lacking. The princes disregarded the imperial authority just as life disregards death. Not one of the temporal states which had arisen upon the ruins of the ancient tribal dukedoms comprised a well-rounded area, not one of them represented a self-contained German tribe ; they all owed their existence to dynastic political arts which, by war and marriage, by purchase and exchange, by services and treasons, had assembled isolated fragments of the disintegrated empire and knew how to retain these in a firm grip. This domestic policy was a necessary outcome of the imperial constitution. The nation was mediatised, only the master-castes were directly represented in the empire ; at the Reichstag it was not the states but the princely houses that were represented ; it was the creed of the princely house and not that of the people which determined whether an estate of the empire should be reckoned Protestant or Catholic ; in a word, the imperial law knew nothing of states, but recognised only the land and the scions of princely houses. The changing events of a tumultuous history had led to an extraordinary confusion of territorial boundaries, and had destroyed in the members of the German princely order, all brotherly sense of justice and all respect for the possessions of their fellows. Each coveted his neighbour's land, and was always ready to seize it with the help of foreign power. The land-hunger and the dynastic pride of the great princely houses threatened the utter destruction of the empire. Long did Saxony and Bavaria strive to attain the kingly crown ; the Palatinate desired to raise to the dignity of a Kingdom of the Rhine its dominions on the Lower Rhine, and thus to obtain supremacy in the empire.

Nevertheless, in the life of these temporal princedoms there was comprised almost all which we denote to-day by the name of German statecraft. It remains the historic glory of our great nobility that the princes of Germany did not, as did the Polish magnates, use the power they had snatched from the national monarchy solely to increase the renown of their own houses, but expressly endeavoured to fulfil, within the limits of their narrow opportunities, the political duties which the empire had failed to undertake. The imperial house pursued its European schemes, and the Reichstag quarrelled about empty forms, but in the territorial areas there was governorship. Here alone were found care and protection for the laws, for the well-being, and for the culture of the German people. In their struggle with the House of Hapsburg our princes had formerly saved the treasure of German spiritual freedom. In the subsequent prolonged period of inglorious peace, there flourished that faithful electoral policy which, devoid of all great ideas, and anxiously shrinking from the hazards of the European struggle, devoted its benevolent attention to the prosperity of its own narrow area of domestic rule. The territorial fragments, pieced together by miraculous chances, gradually grew to form an exiguous political community. The territories became states. In the narrows of their separate lives a new particularism came into being. The subjects of the Elector of Saxony, the inhabitants of the Palatinate, the Brunswick-Lüneburgers, adhered faithfully to their respective princely houses, which so long had shared joy and sorrow with their little peoples. Their own happiness and that of their children was in the hands of their prince, while the great fatherland became to them no more than an obscure saga. After the Thirty Years' War it was, once more, not the emperor and the empire that helped the burghers and the peasants to reconstruct their devastated habitations and to save out of the great destruction scanty fragments of their ancient well-being ; it was to their own Karl Ludwig that the Palatiners owed the return of happier days. The temporal princedom, whose unrestrained egoism threatened the destruction of all the bonds of national unity, yet remained an active and efficient element in the life of the nation. If a reconstruction of united Germany were to be at all possible it must be on the foundation of these territorial authorities.

In this chaos of contradictions every institution of the empire had lost its meaning and every law had lost its safeguards. The imperial house pursued its own aggrandisement at the cost of Germany. The honourable office of the imperial chancellorship, whose holders had formerly been the natural leaders of the nation in every constitutional struggle, gradually became in the hands of the Archbishops of Mainz a pliable instrument of Austrian Catholic party policy. The electoral capitulations, originally designed to check any dynastic misuse of the imperial authority, now served to free from all restraint the dynastic ambitions of the territorial chiefs. Like the States General of the Netherlands, the Reichstag had effected its own transformation from an assembly of the estates into a Bundestag or federal diet, but never proved itself able, as did the States General, to construct a healthy federal life. Everywhere the forms of law were in conflict with the living power of history. The imperial constitution bestowed the right of the majority upon the weakest estates and forced upon the more powerful the conviction that what was given to the empire was taken from their own freedom. A thick fog of phrases and lies enveloped the Gothic ornamentation of the ancient imperial structure ; in no state of the modern world was there so much pertinacious and solemn falsehood. The pious imperial and fatherly intimations of the degermanised imperial majesty, the ardent patriotic asseverations of the estates of the empire at a time when they were leagued with the foreigner, the boastful talk of German liberty and of the unbowed neck of the nation—everything in this activity at Ratisbon seems to us a colossal lie.

After those weary days following the Peace of Augsburg, in which the ancient German pride was transformed into a timorous philistinism, there made itself manifest in our people a mean-spirited tendency to seek consolation for the intolerable and the painful, and German patience did not disdain to provide scientific explanation and justification even for the absurdity of this imperial constitution. Vainly did Samuel Puffendorf raise his warning voice and describe the empire truthfully as a political monstrosity. As the passions of the wars of religions gradually subsided, and the falsity of the theocratic imperial forms ceased to be felt to any considerable extent in daily life, there was no disturbance in the passively obedient spirit of learned legalism. Certain Cesarians of the school of Reinkingk continued to maintain that the Holy Empire was an absolute monarchy and that its emperor was the true successor of the divine Augustus. Others, again, regarded with favour the weakness of the empire and the undisciplined state of its members as the Palladium of German freedom. The majority considered happy Germany to be the realisation of the ideal of the composite state, combining all the advantages of other constitutional forms. Not even a Leibnitz could free himself from the dominion of this world of dreams.

In the sloth of a national life of this character the well-grounded sense of proportion, characteristic of the national genius, had begun to disappear. An epoch of intolerable troubles had broken the courage of the burghers and had accustomed the common man to prostrate himself before the powerful. Our free-spirited tongue learned to decline into a slavish obedience, and adopted that cringing phraseology which has not to this day been entirely discarded. The unprincipled *raison d'état* of the age exercised its pernicious influence even on civic life. A people greedy of money competed, in corruption and intrigue, to secure the favour of the great ; hardly even in the quiet of domestic life were there preserved any traces of true-hearted kindliness. The nobleman, who was no longer able in the diet to maintain his influence against the rising power of the monarchy, endeavoured to secure it in other ways—by influence at court and by misuse of the common people. Never in our history was the nobility more powerful, and never was it more injurious to the life of the nation. The conspicuous example of the Bourbon kingship had befooled the senses of our petty territorial chiefs, so that the estate of princes forgot its ancient fatherly care for the common people. The larger courts misemployed the newly acquired right of forming alliances ; they became involved in European intrigues ; they founded splendid armies with marshals and generals ; and distinguished among them was the Elector Palatine, who was able to have an admiral upon his revenue-boats on the Rhine. All of them, great or small, endeavoured to vie in splendour with the *Grand Monarque ;* the poorest country of Western Europe soon outshone all its neighbours in the multitude of its flaunting princely castles. There was not a count of the empire who could get on without his Versailles, his Trianon ; in the castle-garden at Weikersheim the entrance to the seat of the realm of Hohenlohe was guarded by statues of the conquerors of the world—Ninus, Cyrus, Alexander, and Cæsar. Neither a sense of duty towards the monarchy, nor a spirit of responsibility towards their own order, could impose moral restraints upon the German princelings. Many of them regarded their empty and purposeless existence as a curse, and many dissipated their energies in unrestrained license.

There was no place in the Old German state for a co-operation between the nobles and the commons, for an English Lower House. The Hansa League had fallen as soon as the unified national powers of the peoples of the west had conquered the two Indies ; the glorious flag which in the Middle Ages had waved victoriously over all the northern seas was hardly to be seen among the fleets of the new transatlantic traffic. The nation was as completely estranged from the ocean as was its imperial house. Among all the German writers of the eighteenth century there is but one, Eustace Möser, who voices the love of the sea and who knows how to prize the liberating power of that commerce which binds the nations together. In the motionless atmosphere of our quiet midland life the joyful sea-proverb which was still to be read on the Navigation House in Bremen, "Navigare necesse est, vivere non necesse," sounded like a mockery. Colonial wares were brought up the Elbe and the Rhine in English and Dutch bottoms, and almost the only German goods in the world-market were linen and metal wares. None of the anciently celebrated imperial cities could maintain their historic position. The waters of the Trave lay idle, the overland trade came to an end, the history of Lübeck architecture ceased with the decline of Gothic, that of Augsburg architecture with the epoch of the Renaissance. Only in a few younger trade centres, such as Hamburg and Leipzig, did a new commerce slowly become established. The old imperial towns shut themselves up within their walls, anxiously cherishing their municipal privileges and their guild customs, not venturing to express their views in the Reichstag, full of alarm at the increasing power of their princely neighbours. During long decades we find hardly an intimation in our history that these once proud communities were still alive. In the servile atmosphere of the new princely residences civic pride could not thrive, and for this reason the country, whose Hanseatic heroes had once had in their gift the kingly crowns of Scandinavia, now grew proverbial for all that was petty and poor-spirited. Germany became the spectacle, previously unknown in history, of an ancient nation without a capital city. Nowhere was there a focus of the national life such as was possessed by the neighbouring nations in London, Paris, Madrid, and even in Copenhagen, Stockholm, and Amsterdam. Nowhere was there a site upon which the party struggles of a state-guiding nobility and the culture and wealth of a self-conscious burgherdom could come into contact with a reciprocally fertilising influence. The energies of the nation were dispersed in endless subdivisions, breaking up like the German River into a thousand petty channels : each estate, each city, each territorial area was a world by itself.

The full disgrace of this subdivision was manifested in the defencelessness of the realm. In the days of her greatness Germany had encircled her threatened eastern frontier with the iron girdle of the marches ever ready for war. Now, when attack was ever imminent from the west, the weakest, because the unarmed regions of the empire, lay within the grasp of the greedy hands of France. All along this "priests' quarter" of the Rhine, from Münster and Osnabrück below to Constance above, was a confusion of petty states, unfitted for any serious military preparation, forced into treason by the recognition of their own weakness. Almost all the courts of the Rhineland were pensioners of Versailles ; the first Rhenish federation of 1658 was esteemed by inspired patriots a glorious under-taking for the safeguarding of German freedom. An area of nearly three thousand six hundred square miles was composed of these tiny states, not one of which extended over more than one hundred and thirty square miles. The popular wit made a mock of the soldiers of Cologne, who knitted their own stockings, and of the fierce warriors of the Bishop of Hildesheim, whose hats bore the inscription, " Give peace in our time, O Lord ! " This region of Germany—a third of the land, and its richest portion—was simply a burden in the wars of the empire. It remains a striking testimony to the valour of Germany that, despite this self-mutilation, the nation was never completely overthrown by the rulers of France or of Sweden. But the German realm as a whole hardly took a place in the second rank of the powers ; whilst its own limbs, more powerful than itself, were playing independent parts on the stage of European politics.

The imperial constitution has the aspect of a carefully con-ceived system especially designed to enchain the energies of the most warlike of all the nations. This unnatural state of affairs was, in fact, only maintained in its integrity by the watchful care of the entire Continent. As once by reason of its strength, so now by reason of its weakness, the Holy Empire remained the centre and the foundation of the European system of states. Upon the impotence of Germany and Italy were established the new powers of Austria, France, Sweden, Denmark, and Poland ; thereupon were grounded also the British command of the sea and the independence of Switzerland and the Netherlands. The centre of the Continent was kept enchained by a tacit conspiracy of all the other nations. Foreigners made a mock of *les querelles allemandes* and of *la misère allemande,* and the Frenchman Bouhours asked scornfully whether it were possible for a German to be a man of spirit. Never before had the nation been so profoundly despised by its neighbours ; it was only the ancient renown of the German warriors which could not be disputed. The political state, however, which was responsible for this general contempt of Germany was everywhere regarded as the essential safeguard of European peace ; and our people, whose reputation for national arrogance had once been as bad as is that of the British to-day, repeated in parrot phrases the accusations of their jealous neighbours, and accustomed themselves to look upon their fatherland with the eyes of the stranger. The German political science of the eighteenth century enriched the old illusions of German freedom with the new rallying cry of the freedom of Europe. All our publicists, not excepting Pütter and Johannes Müller, warn the peace-loving world of the destructive power of German unity, and conclude their praise of the Holy Empire with the zealous exhortation : Woe to the freedom of this quarter of the world if the hundreds of thousands of German bayonets should ever learn to obey a single master !

A dispensation unsearchable in its wisdom chastises the nations by those very gifts which they have so scandalously misused. From very early days a many-sided and cosmopolitan broadmindedness was secured for our people by its position in the world, by its inborn disposition, and by the course of history. The German nation was endowed with a natural understanding of the Latin world ; the Romance nationalities were established by German conquerors upon the ruins of Roman civilisation ; the Germans were closely akin by blood to the English and to the Scandinavians, and had been from of old made intimately acquainted with the Slavs by war and commerce ; during the Middle Ages, as a midland people, they received civilisation from the south and the west, and handed it on to the north and the east. Thus the Germans became the most cosmopolitan of all the nations, even more receptive of foreign ideas than their companions in fate, the Italians. The impulse towards what was afar off became for us a destiny, wherein lay at once the curse and the greatness of German life. The centuries of plans for German world-dominion were succeeded by an epoch of passive cosmopolitanism. The midland people received the commands of all the world. As estates of the empire, or as sponsors of peace, the great princes of Europe belonged to the German empire and thus controlled its life. But the nation, becoming familiarised with foreign dominion, cleaved with German fidelity to the foreign flags. Particularist obscurity, a preference for the foreign neighbour over the neighbour who was akin by blood, flourished nowhere so luxuriantly as in the German provinces belonging to foreign princes. The Holsteiner prided himself upon his Danebrog ; the Stralsunder rejoiced in the glory of the three crowns, and compassionated the Pomeranian of Brandenburg whose ruler wore a mere electoral hat ; the successors of the conquerors of the Vistula region, the proud families of the Huttens, the Oppens, and the Rosenbergs, took Polish names, and, rejoicing in the freedom of the Sarmatian nobility, ridiculed the marchland despotism of the Prussian Duchy.

The old adventurous love of wandering remained, however, unconquerable in our active-minded race. For fully three centuries, so long as the employment of mercenary troops continued, a stream of German soldiers flowed into every country. The noise of German blows was heard on every battle-field of Europe, before the walls of Athens no less than in the green isle of Erin. The flags of France, Sweden, and Holland, and the hardly less un-German imperial service, were regarded as more honourable than the dull uniformity of garrison life at home : on his death-bed the trusty old blade adjured his son to gain glory for his house and riches for himself in the service of foreign crowns. The German regiments of Bernard of Weimar formed the nucleus of the unconquerable armies which were led to victory by Turenne and Condé; it was in the German school that our neighbours learned how to fight us. To foreign climes, also, was withdrawn a long series of German statesmen, physicians, merchants, and men of learning— vigorous offshoots of the German stock, lost for ever to the fatherland. A spectacle at once dismal and imposing was this titanic excess of energy of a people given over to the stranger. Every attempt to write our history must remain altogether defective if it fails to do justice to these workings of the German spirit and of the German arms that were dispersed throughout the world. At the very time when France was conquering the western marches of the Holy Empire, Peter the Great was creating the new Russian state with the aid of German energies. Even the princely houses were seized by the national migratory impulse ; every ambitious German court sought to establish itself on some foreign throne, and the imperial house favoured this tendency in order to promote the removal of troublesome rivals from within the empire. Ultimately all the crowns of Europe, except those of Piedmont and the Bourbon states, fell into the hands of princes of German stock ; but the acquirement of this masterful position by the leaders of our nobility served only to strengthen the centrifugal tendencies within the realm, to enslave the German state all the more firmly to the will of the outer world.

Over this decayed life of the community there was spread the glamour of a history dating back from a thousand years. A tradition, never once interrupted, connected to-day with yesterday. Anyone well versed in the history of the empire was a skilful counsel in the lawsuits of his own day ; when the young lawyer Wolfgang Goethe was gaining from Datt's folios scientific instruction concerning the public peace and the legal procedure of the empire, he could see the honest figure of the Ritter Goetz von Berlichingen, seated sturdily upon the penitent's bench. Always the imperial constitution remained the one and only bond of political unity for our disintegrated people. In the very last year of the effective life of that constitution, the Hamburg publicist Gaspari wrote : " Through the emperor alone we are free ; without him we should no longer be Germans." Through its unwieldy forms there continued to find expression that ancient Teutonic idea of the state which even in the very earliest days of our history had manifested the moral earnestness and the love of freedom of the Germans : the imperial authority was protector of the common peace, and was thus honourable even in its decay. The people could never completely lose a sense of unity so long as they continued to live under a common law, and so long as the national community of spirit was displayed at once in the science of jurisprudence and in the practice of the courts. Even when the common law became gradually overgrown by particularist legal forms, the national form of legal procedure remained established, and the empire secured for the nation the independence and high position of the judges. Every right in the empire ultimately rested upon the rights of the emperor ; one who resisted the imperial majesty had the ground cut from under his feet. " If I hold to the emperor, I shall remain elector, and my son will be elector after me ! "—such were the words with which the temporising George William of Brandenburg rejected the advances of Gustavus Adolphus. Throughout the following century the same consideration stood in the way of every bold resolution, whenever a revolutionary will declared itself, whenever there was manifest a desire to cut new paths through this overgrown wilderness of imperial law, at once so natural and so unnatural. The policy of foreign nations and that of the House of Austria, the self-interest and the mutual jealousies of the smaller courts, the balance of political forces and the interests of a social order hastening to destruction, cosmopolitanism and dreams of German freedom, the legalist spirit and ancient custom, the force of sloth and German fidelity—all these things combined to maintain the established order. In the middle of the eighteenth century, in the general opinion of the world, the Holy Empire was secure for a future of which no one could foresee the end.

§ 2. THE PRUSSIAN STATE.

Upon the foundation of this imperial law and of its structure of territorial states, and yet in sharp contrast with both, the Prussian state came into existence. The vigorous will of the North German tribes gave them from the earliest times a superiority in state-constructive energy over the softer and wealthier population of High Germany. Only so long as the crown was in Saxon hands did the German monarchy remain a vigorous kingship ; its power declined in the hands of the Franconians and of the Swabians, chiefly in consequence of the haughty disobedience of the Saxon princes. Then there arose in Low Germany the two powerful political creations of the later Middle Ages—the Hansa League and the Order of Teutonic Knights, both independent of the imperial authority and often at enmity with it. The north was the cradle of the Reformation. It was against the resistance of the North Germans that the Spanish dominion shattered itself; and, after the un-German policy of the Hapsburgs had evoked dualism in the empire, the north was the chief home of the German opposition. In the course of the seventeenth century the leadership of this opposition passed to the Hohenzollerns from the unready hands of the Wettins. The centre of gravity of German politics moved to the north-east.

There, in the marches beyond the Elbe, a new North German tribe had come into existence, consisting in part of the conquering Lower Saxon stock, in part of immigrants from all the German-speaking lands, but containing also a slight admixture of the blood of the old Wendish indigenes. Hard were they, and weather-proof, steeled by toil on a niggardly land, fortified too by the unceasing combats of a frontier life, able and independent after the manner of colonists, accustomed to regard their Slav neighbours with the contempt of a dominant race, as rugged and incisive as was compatible with the genial and jovial solidity of the Low German character. Three times had this sorely tried land begun the rough journeyman's work of civilisation : first of all, when the Ascanian conquerors cleared the pine-forests around the lakes of the Havel and built their towns, fortresses, and monasteries in the lands of the Wends ; next, at the beginning of the fifteenth century, when the first of the Hohenzollerns laboriously re-established the peace and well-being that had been destroyed by the Bavario-Lutzelburg dominion ; and now once again had Brandenburg suffered from the horrors of the Thirty Years' War, suffered more severely than the rest of Germany, so that it was necessary to begin the work of civilisation anew.

Throughout the Middle Ages the rough customs of this needy frontier-land gave it an evil reputation in the empire. The sands of the marches have provided never a saint for the Roman Calendar ; very rarely did a minnesong make itself heard in the rude courts of the Ascanian Margraves. The industrious Cistercians of Lehnin laboured rather to acquire the reputation of diligent farmers than to win fame in art and learning ; the sturdy burghers in the towns of the Mark passed their lives in rough and homely toil, and it was only the men of Prenzlau who could compare their Marienkirche with the fine buildings of the rich towns on the Baltic. It was solely in warlike energy and vigorous ambition that the state of the Brandenburgs was pre-eminent over its neighbours ; even in the days of the Ascanians and of the Lutzenburgers, plans were several times conceived for the foundation of a great north-eastern power in this favourable position between the Elbe and the Oder, between the petty states of Mecklenburg, Pomerania, and Silesia. Still more exalted seemed the prospects of the Mark when the burgraves of Nuremberg received the electoral hat ; Frederick I was the leader of the German princes in the reform movement in empire and Church, Albrecht Achill the admired leader of the knightly nobility in their struggles with the towns. At the same time within the state there began a bold and firm monarchical policy. The Mark received, at the hand of Frederick I, the gift of public peace, and enjoyed it before the Holy Empire; in the Mark earlier than in other lands of the empire the indivisibility of the state received legal expression in the laws of Albrecht Achill. The nobility and the towns bowed their stubborn necks before the will of the three first Hohenzollerns. But the early promises were not fulfilled in the immediate sequel. The successors of these heroes of lofty aims soon relapsed into the narrow comfort of German electoral policy. They lost the barely acquired sovereign authority, which for the most part passed once more to the diet ; for good or for ill they made terms with their overbearing territorial nobles ; like all the more powerful princes of the empire they endeavoured to safeguard their administration and the legal rights of their country against every onslaught of the imperial authority, remaining the while well disposed and loyal to the imperial house ; late and with hesitation did they enter the Lutheran Church, preferring to abandon the leadership of the Protestant parties to the Electorates of Saxony and of the Palatinate.

With good reason does King Frederick remark in the memoirs of his house, that, just as a river first becomes of value when it is navigable, so does the history of Brandenburg first become profoundly significant towards the beginning of the seventeenth century. Not until the days of the Elector John Sigismund were three things effected which assured for the Mark a great future, a development differing fundamentally from the life of the other lands of the empire : the union with Brandenburg of the secularised Teutonic Ordensland; the adhesion of the princely house to the Reformed Church ; and, finally, the acquirement of the frontier regions of the Lower Rhine.

Other princes of the empire, Catholics as well as Protestants, had indeed enlarged their power by acquiring the possessions of the ancient Church. But in the Ordensland the policy of the German Protestants made its boldest seizure ; on the advice of Luther, Albrecht Hohenzollern snatched from the Roman Church the greatest of its ecclesiastical territories. The whole area of the new Duchy of Prussia was spoil taken from the Church ; the rebellious princes who effected this rape incurred the ban of the Pope and of the emperor. The seizure never received the recognition of the Roman See. When the Hohenzollerns of the Mark united the ducal crown of their Prussian cousins with their own electoral hat they broke for ever with the Roman Church ; henceforward their state must stand or fall with Protestantism. At the same time John Sigismund made his personal adhesion to the reformed faith

He thus laid the foundation for the subsequent union of his house with the heroic race of Orange, emerging from the deplorable sloth of a torpid Lutheranism into the fellowship of that Church which alone pursued with warlike courage the political ideas of the Reformation. In the Mark the Calvinistic ruler held sway over a stubborn Lutheran people ; in Prussia Lutherans and Catholics, and in the lands of the Lower Rhine the adherents of all three of the great Churches of Germany, lived in a variegated assembly. Threatened by the religious hatred of its own subjects, the princely house was constrained to extend an equal tolerance to all the ecclesiastical parties. Thus originated the peculiar duplex attitude of the Hohenzollerns towards our ecclesiastical life : with the fall of the power of the Palatinate they became the leaders of militant Protestantism in the empire, but had also to represent the fundamental idea of the new German civilisation—freedom of religious belief. As early as the days of John Sigismund some of the imperial statesmen declared, with the keen insight of hatred, that it was greatly to be dreaded that the Brandenburgs would now become the leaders of the whole Protestant party.

Together with the Prussian ducal crown the House of Hohenzollern acquired that proud colony of united Germany which had been watered with the blood of all the German tribes even more richly than the Mark, and which could boast a greater and more heroic history than any other territorial region in the empire ; here, in the " New Germany," the Teutonic knights had once built up the Baltic great power of the Middle Ages. This remote frontierland, continually threatened by the enmity of the Polish nobles and by that of its Scandinavian and Muscovite neighbours, involved the state of the Hohenzollerns in the confused struggles of the northern territorial systems. Thus when John Sigismund planted his foot firmly on the shores of the Baltic, he simultaneously acquired the Duchy of Cleves as well as the counties of Mark and Ravensberg, a region of trifling extent, but one of great importance alike to the internal development and to the foreign policy of the state. These were regions of ancient and faithfully guarded yeoman and city freedoms, wealthier and more highly civilised than the needy colonies of the east, invaluable frontier posts on the weakest border of Germany. In Vienna and in Madrid it was regarded as a serious reverse that a new Protestant power should establish itself upon the Lower Rhine—where the Spaniards and the Netherlanders were fighting for the existence or non-existence of Protestantism—should establish itself under the very gates of

Cologne, the central stronghold of Romanism in the empire. In its fifteen hundred square miles the young state included almost all the ecclesiastical, territorial, and feudal contrasts which filled the Holy Empire with open strife : with legs wide-straddled, like the Colossus of Rhodes, this state stood over the German lands, its feet planted on the threatened frontiers of the Rhine and of the Niemen.

A power in such a situation could no longer remain confined within the narrow circle of German territorial policy. It was constrained to attempt to round off its dispersed provinces into a more tenable shape ; it was compelled to negotiate and to fight on behalf of the empire, for every attack upon German soil made by the foreigner involved a wound of its own flesh. And yet towards the imperial authority this state, ruling over German land alone, occupied a position of fortunate independence. For those estates of the empire, whose dominions were entirely comprised within the frontiers of the empire, it was always a matter of difficulty to conduct an independent European policy. Other princely houses, whose acquirement of foreign crowns had withdrawn them from the shackles of the imperial constitution, were lost to German life. The House of Brandenburg, too, received many alluring appeals from distant lands : opportunities for dominion in Sweden, in Poland, in the Netherlands, in England, seemed to offer. The force of circumstances, however, in every case led the reasonable discretion of the princely house to withstand these dangerous temptations. A fortunate Providence (for to the serious mind this cannot seem a matter of chance) compelled the Hohenzollerns to remain in Germany. They had no need of foreign crowns, for they owed their independent position in the community of states to the possession of the Duchy of Prussia, a German region to the core, bound to the motherland by all the roots of its life, and at the same time outside the legal union of the empire. Thus with one foot in the empire and the other outside, the Prussian state acquired the right of conducting a foreign policy which could pursue none but German ends. This state could take thought for Germany without troubling about the empire and its outworn forms.

It is not permissible to the historian to deduce the present from the past, the future from the present, after the simple manner of the natural philosopher. Man makes history. The advantages of the situation become effective in the national life only through the conscious will of those who know how to avail themselves of these advantages. Once more the state of the Hohenzollerns fell from its hardly acquired position of power ; it moved towards disaster so long as George William, the successor of John Sigismund, looked sleepily over the world out of his heavy eyes. It appeared as if this new attempt at the upbuilding of a German state was again to end in the pettiness of particularism, as had happened before, in the case of the Guelphs, the Wettins, the Palatiners, whose power had seemed to establish itself under far more favourable auspices. Then came the Elector Frederick William, a landless prince, the greatest German of his day, thrusting himself with a vigorous impetus into the desert of German life, to inspire the slumbering forces of his state with the might of his will. Never since that time has the strength of the purposive monarchical will of the developing German power known any decline. We can conceive English history without William III, we can conceive French history without Richelieu ; the Prussian state is the work of its princes. There are few other countries in which monarchy has so continually preserved the two virtues upon which its greatness depends : a bold and far-seeing idealism which sacrifices the convenience of to-day to the greatness of to-morrow ; and that strong sense of justice which ever constrains self-interest in the service of the whole. It was only the wide vision of the monarchy that could recognise in these poverty-stricken territorial fragments the foundation-stones of a new great power. It was only in the sense of duty to the crown, in the idea of the monarchical state, that the mutually hostile tribes and estates, parties and churches, which were comprised within this microcosm of German life, could find protection and peace.

Even in the earliest years of the Great Elector the peculiarities of the new German power became plainly manifest. The nephew of Gustavus Adolphus, who led his young army to battle with the ancient Protestant warcry " With God," took over the ecclesiastical policy of his uncle. He was the first to find the saving solution for the quarrels of the Churches, demanding a general and unconditional amnesty for all three confessions. This was the programme of the Peace of Westphalia. But the toleration extended by the Hohenzollerns in the interior of their own dominion went far beyond the prescriptions of this Peace. In accordance with the imperial law Brandenburg was recognised as a Protestant estate, and yet this was the first state in Europe in which complete religious freedom was secured. In the Netherlands the multiplicity of unassociated sects was dependent simply upon anarchy, upon the weakness of the state ; but here freedom of conscience rested upon the laws of a powerful state-organisation which would not allow itself to be deprived of its right to supervise the Churches. In the other territories of Germany there still everywhere existed one dominant Church, whose power was restricted only in so far as it was unable altogether to forbid the other creeds to hold religious services ; in Brandenburg the throne stood free above all the Churches and protected their equality. While Austria was forcibly expelling its best Germans, an unparalleled hospitality threw open the frontiers of Brandenburg to the toleration of every belief. How many thousand times in the Mark was uplifted the hymn of gratitude of the Bohemian exiles :

"Thy people, else in darkness, by error quite surrounded,
Finds here abundant house-room, secure, on freedom grounded!"

When Louis XIV revoked the Edict of Nantes, the Lord of Brandenburg, as spokesman of the Protestant world, set himself in bold opposition, and in his Edict of Potsdam offered protection and shelter to the children of the martyr-Church. Wherever the flames of the ancient religious hatred weie still raging among the German people, the work of the Hohenzollerns was one of guardianship and reconciliation. They summoned to the Spree the Jewry of Vienna ; *via facti*, and without asking the leave of the empire, they secured the Protestants of Heidelberg in the possession of their churches ; for the Protestants of Salzburg they provided a new home in East Prussia. Thus into the unpeopled eastern Mark there streamed year after year an abundance of young life ; the German blood which the Hapsburgs rejected fertilised the land of their rival. At the death of Frederick II about one-third of the population of the state was made up of the offspring of immigrants who had found their way into the country since the days of the Great Elector.

It was this Church policy of the Hohenzollerns which closed the epoch of the religious wars, ultimately compelling the best of the temporal princes to follow in Brandenburg's footsteps, and at the same time depriving the spiritual estates of the last justification for existence—for why should there be any more spiritual princes of the empire now that freedom was assured to the Catholic Church beneath the wings of the Prussian eagle ? By the Peace of Westphalia Frederick William acquired the great foundations of Magdeburg, Halberstadt, Minden, and Kammin. No other state in

Germany was so greatly enriched by the goods of the Roman Church; yet the seizure was justified, for therewith were also taken over the great tasks of civilisation which the Church of the Middle Ages had of old performed for the immature state—the duty of providing for the poor and the work of popular education. The same need for self-preservation which compelled the Hohenzollerns to maintain peace between Catholics and Protestants, forced them also to mediate between the antagonisms within the Protestant Church. From the time when John Sigismund first forbade the Lutheran zealots to fulminate against the Calvinists, the idea of Protestant union became characteristic of the Prussian state; and what had been begun simply from necessity became ultimately a political tradition, became a matter of principle with the princely house.

Just as the Prussian state secured for the Germans peace between the Churches and enabled Germany to take part once more in the activities of the civilised nations, so also did Prussia restore what had been lacking since the opening of the days of religious discord—a coherent will against the foreign world. Throughout Germany abundant energies were failing to find an outlet in the narrow spheres that were open to them, so that anyone with lofty ambitions hastened to some foreign country; then came Frederick William to grasp in his resolute hand the scanty resources of the poorest region in Germany, compelling his people to serve their own homeland, and showing Europe once more the might of the German sword. The empire lived upon ancient memories, preserving in the new Europe the political forms of the Middle Ages; but this North German power was firmly rooted in the modern world; its vigorous state-authority rose above the ruins of the old ecclesiastical dominion and above the ancient rights of the estates; it lived through the troubles of the present with eyes fixed on schemes for a great future. With a single blow, Frederick William made for his despised little territory a place in the ranks of the European powers, so that, after the battle of Warsaw, Brandenburg could stand side by side with the ancient military states. This strongly-unified and warlike power appeared to rise suddenly, like a new-made volcanic island, out of the raging sea of conflicting sovereignties in Germany, and before the wondering gaze of a people which had long ceased to believe in rapid resolve and high endeavour. So vigorously blew the fresh breeze of purposive political will through the history of the new Prussian state, so tensely and vigorously were all the muscles of its people turned to work, so gross appeared the disproportion between ambition and means, that to friend and foe alike it seemed for a century and a half that Prussia could be no more than an artificial venture. The world regarded as the chance creation of a few favourites of fortune, what was in reality the necessary reconstruction of the ancient national state of the Germans.

In the great struggles for power of the European world, no less than in the contests between the creeds within the German borders, Prussia maintained a difficult intermediate position. So long as Protestant Germany had remained prostrate and lacked the will to arise, Europe consisted of two distinct state-systems which rarely came into contact. The powers of the south and the west were fighting for the dominion of Italy and for the Rhenish Burgundian lands, while the powers of the north and the east disputed for the ruined fragments of the Teutonic Ordensland, and for the command of the Baltic Sea, the legacy of the Hanseatic League. There was only one desire that was common to the east and to the west, and this was to keep ever open the terrible abyss that yawned in the middle of the Continent. Now uprose the youngest power of Germany, greatly mocked as "the realm of the long borders." Belonging to the European system, its dispersed provinces touched the boundaries of all the great powers of the Continent. As soon as Prussia began to move with an independent will the powers of the west were involved in the affairs of the east, and the interests of the two state-systems became ever more frequently and closely intertwined.

The born opponent of the old order of Europe, established upon Germany's weakness, Prussia stood in a world of enemies, whose jealousies were her only salvation—stood without a single natural ally, for elsewhere in the German nation there was as yet no understanding of the significance of this young force. This, too, was in the time of that hard statecraft in which the state was the mere incorporation of power, regarding the destruction of its neighbours as a natural duty. Just as the House of Savoy won through against the preponderant power of the Hapsburgs and the Bourbons, so also, but in far more difficult circumstances, must Prussia cut a way for herself between Austria and France, between Sweden and Poland, between the sea-powers and the inert mass of the German empire, availing herself of all the means furnished by a reckless egoism, ever ready for a change of front, ever with two strings to her bow.

To its very marrow, electoral Brandenburg came to realise

the extent to which foreign elements had eaten their way into Germany. All the unbridled forces of feudal licence which strove against the strict rule of the new monarchy looked for support to foreign aid. Dutch garrisons were established along the Lower Rhine and favoured the struggle of the estates of Cleves against the German suzerain; the diets of Magdeburg and of the Electoral Mark looked for help to Austria; the nobles of Königsberg, Polish in their sympathies, appealed to the Polish overlord for help against the despotism of the Mark. In the struggle against foreign dominion, the national unity of these dispersed provinces and the repute of their ruler became established. Frederick William destroyed the barrier of the Netherlands in the German north-west, and drove the Dutch troops out of Cleves and East Frisia; he liberated Old Prussia from the Polish feudal suzerainty, and forced the diet of Königsberg to accept his own lordship. Then he made his appeal to the deaf nation in the words, " Remember that you are German!", and endeavoured to expel the Swedes from the realm. Twice the disfavour of France and Austria served to deprive the Brandenburger of the reward of his victories and to cheat him of his dominion in Pomerania; but none could rob him of the glory of the day of Fehrbellin. At length, after long decades of shame, there came a brilliant triumph of German arms over the first military power of the age, and the world learned that Germany could once more dare to assert her rights. The inheritor of the German ecclesiastical policy of Gustavus Adolphus, destroyed the daring structure of the Scandinavian Baltic Empire which had been established by the sword of the King of Sweden. The two artificial powers of the seventeenth century, Sweden and Holland, began to withdraw within their natural borders, and the new state which arose in their place displayed neither the licentious lust of conquest of the Swedish military power nor the monopoly-seeking mercantile spirit of the Netherlands. It was German; it was satisfied to protect its own domain; and to the plans of the Bourbon for world-dominion it opposed the ideas of the European balance of power and of freedom for the nations. When the Republic of the Netherlands seemed likely to succumb before the onslaught of Louis XIV, Brandenburg boldly attacked the conqueror. Frederick William conducted the one serious campaign ventured by the empire for the reconquest of Alsace; and on his death-bed he concerted with his nephew of Orange the plan for the rescue of Protestant and parliamentary England from the arbitrary rule of the Stuarts, the vassals of Louis. Wherever this young power stood alone its campaigns were victorious, but it was everywhere unfortunate when Prussia was forced to involve itself in the confusions of the imperial army.

Thus in its very inception the new structure of the state showed itself a European necessity. At length Germany had again found one who could extend the empire. With the rise of Prussia there began the long and bloody task of the liberation of Germany from foreign dominion. Despoiled by its neighbours for centuries past, the empire now saw for the first time the foreign powers yielding back a few fragments of German ground. In this single state of Prussia there reawakened, though still but half-conscious and as if drunken from prolonged slumber, the ancient stout-hearted pride in the fatherland. The faithful landsfolk of the County Mark began the little war against the French; the peasants of East Prussia put the Swedes to headlong flight. When the peasant Landwehr of the Altmark, guarding the Elbe-dike against the Swedes, wrote upon their flags, " We are peasants of little wealth, and serve our gracious elector and prince with goods and blood," the disjointed words breathed the same heroic spirit as that which of old, in days of greater freedom, was voiced by the warcry, " With God for King and Fatherland."

Whilst the power of the Hapsburgs was extending beyond the limits of Germany, by the continuous control of destiny the state of the Hohenzollerns pressed ever deeper into the inner current of German life, at times against the will of its chief. Frederick William never ceased to regret his inability to maintain, against the opposition of Austria and Sweden, his hereditary Pomeranian claims in the Peace of Westphalia. As King of the Vandals he hoped to rule the Baltic from the harbour of Stettin, but was forced to content himself with the Saxon-Westphalian Church lands as a substitute for the mouths of the Oder. Yet this diplomatic reverse was in reality advantageous to the state, which was thus preserved from a half-German separate life on the Baltic, so that its central position was strengthened, and it was forced to take part in all the negotiations of internal German policy. Moreover, the whole of North Germany was overlaid with a network of agreements respecting hereditary claims which had been concluded during past centuries by the far-seeing House of Hohenzollern. Any day the fortune of death might bring some new enlargement to the ambitious power.

The House of Hapsburg recognised, even earlier than the Hohenzollerns themselves, how dangerous to the ancient constitution of the Holy Empire was the growth of this modern North German state. Although electoral Saxony still bore the title of *Director Corporis Evangelicorum*, Prussia was the real leader of German Protestantism; its monarchical order threatened the whole structure of feudal and theocratic institutions which supported the imperial crown; its powerful army and its independent appearance in the community of states, threatened the traditional system of imperial domestic policy. In Silesia, in Pomerania, in the dispute about the Jülich-Cleves inheritance —everywhere, filled with misgivings, Austria encountered this dangerous rival. All the imperial princes regarded with as much suspicion as was felt by the court of Vienna, this restless state which threatened to embrace the whole of the German north. Whenever a bold venture was undertaken there arose throughout Germany a cry of alarm concerning "the Brandenburg dominion thrusting itself yet further into the realm." When the great Elector expelled the Swedes from Düppel and Alsen, the princes of the west combined with the crown of France to constitute the first Confederation of the Rhine, for the protection of the Swedish realm. Since the imperial house still exercised through the Breisgau and Upper Swabia a military control over the whole of Southern Germany, in the South German courts the dread of Austria's land-hunger was at times greater than anxiety regarding distant Brandenburg; but ultimately all the smaller princes came to consider the imperial court a great conservative force, whereas this newcomer in the north was separated from the ancient order of German affairs by a profound and irreconcilable opposition.

Thus the nation regarded the rise of the state of the Hohenzollerns with a hatred and alarm similar to that which had of old been inspired in the Italian tribes by the conquests of Rome. The free spirits of the time were already beginning to turn towards the ideas of modern absolutism; but the mass of the people still cleaved to the ancient and traditional feudal forms which it was the mission of the House of Brandenburg to abolish. Some of the warlike deeds of Frederick William aroused, indeed, the admiration of his contemporaries; after his bold march from the Rhine to the Rhyn he was greeted for the first time by the name of "the Great" in the Alsatian folk-song. But such exalted moods were of brief duration. The arrogant member that set itself up against the empire, and yet was unable to offer the nation a substitute for the crumbling ancient order, was regarded with rage and hatred; Leibnitz, the inspired imperial patriot, declared, in an eloquent memoir, that the Brandenburger must be punished by his peers because he had led his army single-handed against the French for the rescue of Holland. In this race, that was still lacking true political insight, no one perceived that the leadership of sundered peoples necessarily falls to that section among them which takes upon itself the duties of the whole. All the more distressing, therefore, became the vague foreboding that this active power must be destroyed if it were not to expand to the detriment of the rest ; and even as in the Middle Ages the popular wit was always directed against that German tribe which happened to be inspired by the thought of national unity, so now particularist anxiety and particularist self-complacence displayed their ridicule against the Marks.

The people mocked the poverty of the " sandbox " of a Holy Empire, mocked the Brandenburg despotism ; the burghers of Stettin fought desperately to preserve for their good town the advantages of Swedish freedom, and to protect it from the yoke of the men of blood from the Mark. The particularism of all the estates and of all the provinces learned with horror that the Great Elector forced his subjects to live as " members of one body," that he imposed upon the dispersed dominion of the diets the commands of the supreme central authority, and that he based his throne upon the two pillars of monarchical dominion, the *miles perpetuus* and permanent taxation. In the popular view, troops and taxes still seemed extraordinary burdens, for days of special need. Frederick William made the army a permanent institution, and weakened the power of the separate estates of his realm by the introduction of two taxes of general application : a general land tax in the country and an excise in the towns, a manifold system of small direct and indirect contributions, adapted to the poverty of the exhausted national economy, and impinging upon the taxable capacity to the widest possible extent. Throughout the empire there was one common voice of disapprobation against these first beginnings of the modern military and fiscal systems. From the first days of its independent history, Prussia was the best-hated of all the German states ; the imperial lands which passed under the control of this princely house entered the new community of states in almost every case amid loud complaints and violent resistance, and yet all of them soon congratulated themselves on their new lot.

The terrible and hopeless confusion of German conditions, the hereditary respect of the Hohenzollerns for the imperial house, and the domestic needs of their own state, surrounded as it was by powerful enemies, made it impossible for many decades for the old and the new Germany to come into open conflict each with the other. Frederick William lived and worked in the hope of imperial reform. With all the fiery impetuosity of his heroic nature, at the first Reichstag after the Peace of Westphalia, he pressed for that redrafting of the imperial constitution which had been promised at Osnabrück. When this plan came to nothing, George Frederick of Waldeck conceived the venturesome idea, that the Hohenzollern himself should impose a new order upon the empire. He suggested that there should be constituted a league of German princes under the hegemony of the enlarged Brandenburg state. The times, however, were not yet ripe. The Elector left his bold adviser in the lurch, for he was forced to meet a more immediate need, and to form an alliance with the emperor against the Swedes ; subsequently he even abandoned the long-cherished plan of the conquest of Silesia because he needed the help of Austria in his struggle with France. Yet the way had been disclosed, and every new disturbance of German life led the Prussian state back to the twofold idea of the enlargement of its own dominion and of a federal hegemony.

Frederick William's successor brought to his house with the kingly crown a worthy place in the society of the European powers, and he gave to his people the common name of Prussians. It was only the need and the hope of Prussia's armed help that decided the imperial court to accede the new honour to its rival. A shudder went through the theocratic world : electoral Mainz protested, the Teutonic Order demanded the restoration of the ancient possession which now gave its name to the heretic kingdom, and, for a century yet to come, the Papal Almanack continued to recognise nothing more than the " Margrave " of Brandenburg. To the grandson of Frederick I, the possession of a kingly crown, with all the claims necessarily attaching to this position, seemed a serious warning of the need for increasing the power and independence of his state. But the weak spirit of the first king knew little of such pride. A loyal imperial prince, he served the imperial house, and fought in knightly fashion on the Rhine, in the artless hope that the emperor would recover the fortress of Strasburg ; he helped the Hapsburgs to beat the Turks, allowed his army for a scanty pay to fight as an accessory force of Austria, and permitted his naval forces to take part in the war of the Spanish succession. It was then that the French first learned to dread the Prussian infantry as the nucleus of the German army ; but the Berlin court played no part in the political conduct of the war. While the brave soldiers of Prussia were gaining fruitless renown in the campaigns of Hungary, the Netherlands, High Germany, and Italy, Sweden was carrying on a struggle of despair against the powers of the north; but Prussia failed to take advantage of its central position, and thus to bring the northern war to a decisive conclusion by a bold diversion of its forces from the Rhine to the Oder. Laboriously must Frederick William I subsequently pay for his father's mistakes in order, out of the shipwreck of the Swedish empire, to save for Germany at least the mouths of the Oder.

From of old the Hohenzollerns, in accordance with the sound custom of the German princes, had paid careful attention to the ideal aims of the life of the state ; it was they who founded the universities of Frankfort and Königsberg, and re-established that of Duisburg. And now, under the tolerant rule of the free-handed Frederick and his philosophical queen, it seemed as if the re-awakening art and science of Germany were finding their home in rude Brandenburg. The four great reforming thinkers of the age, Leibnitz, Puffendorf, Thomasius, and Spener turned towards the Prussian state. The new university at Halle became the centre of free investigation, assuming for several decades the leadership of Protestant science, and filling the gap which had been left by the destruction of the old university of Heidelberg. The poverty-stricken capital became adorned with the gorgeous architectural work of Schlüter; the court, greedy of fame as a patron of the arts, endeavoured to outshine the hated Bourbons. Yet the frivolous self-glorification of courtly despotism remained ever foreign to the House of Hohenzollern ; the luxury of Frederick I lagged far behind the reckless extravagance of the Saxon Augustus. The charms of sin were not felt by the heavy North German nature ; again and again, and often in ludicrous contrast, the earnest and sober northern characteristics broke through the artificial forms imported from Versailles. Even as it was, the expenditure of the court threatened to exhaust the means of a poor country ; for a community the force of whose will had pushed it into a situation beyond the scope of its natural powers, nothing was harder to endure than a tame mediocrity. It was well for Germany that the close-fist of Frederick William I brought to a speedy close the pleasures and the glories of these early days of kingship.

The immature state contained the germs of a many-sided life, and yet with its inconsiderable powers it was hardly ever able to fulfil its tasks adequately ; rarely have its princes directly carried on the work of their fathers ; the successor, while entering the breach which his predecessor had opened, turned his own best energies to departments of the national life which that predecessor had neglected. The Great Elector had to struggle throughout his life with the pressure of hostile neighbours. In the great projects of European policy he never lost that strong domestic sense which had characterised most of his ancestors, and which even in the early days of his house had brought to many of its chiefs the cognomen of *œconomus ;* he did all in his power to restore well-being to his country, nurtured the roots of a monarchical officialdom, and began to effect the transformation of the national economy in accordance with the needs of the modern monetary system. But in the storms of this war-filled regime it was impossible to effect a thorough reform of the administration ; the shapeless bundle of territories was with difficulty held together by the personal repute of the ruler and by the unwieldy and antiquated authority of the privy council. It was by the grandson of the Great Elector that the ancient state-system was finally abolished.

The fundamental ideas of the internal order of the Prussian state were so irrevocably fixed by King Frederick William I that even the laws of Stein and Scharnhorst and the reforms of our own days could serve only to develop and not to destroy the work of the founder. He was the creator of the new German administration, of our officialdom and our military caste ; his inconspicuous and laborious activity was not less fruitful for German life than were the deeds at arms of his grandfather, for it was he who introduced into our history a new form of government, the circumscribed national unity of the modern monarchy. He gave meaning and content to the new name of Prussia, united his people in a community for the fulfilment of political duty, and stamped for all time upon the consciousness of this state the notion of duty. Only one who is familiar with the gnarly growth, with the hard edges and angles of the Low German national character, will understand this rigid disciplinarian, will understand his breathless and stormy passage through life—the scorn and the terror of his contemporaries, rough and rude, scolding and quarrelsome, ever at work, forcing his people and himself to labour, a sterling old German, essentially German in his childish frankness, his goodness of heart, his profound sense of duty, and not less so in his terrible fits of hasty anger and in his formless and unconquered solidity. In this royal burgher, the ancient hatred of the North German people for the modish refinements of Gallic manners, as expressed in Lauremberg's Low German satirical poems, became incorporated in flesh and blood ; his severity towards wife and child showed him also the true son of the classic age of German domestic tyranny—an age in which, owing to the enslavement of public life, the energies of the men could find vent only within the narrow limits of the household. Severe, joyless, terribly restricted, did life become under the close-fisted rule of this rigid disciplinarian. The hard one-sidedness of his spirit could value those simple moral and economic forces alone, which served as internal bonds of national union ; with the whole energy of his masterful will he threw himself into the province of administration, displaying here the primitive force of a creative spirit. Firmly and consistently, as of old William the Conqueror in overthrown England, did Frederick William I piece together the structure of a unified state out of the dispersed fragments of his territories. But not to him, as to William the Norman, did the unified state appear as a mere appanage of his own house. Rather, in the mind of the unlettered prince, was there conceived, clearly and vividly, a notion of the state that was accordant with the new doctrine of natural law: the notion that the state exists for the good of all, and that the king is placed at its head to administer with unbiassed justice over all the estates of the realm, to pursue the public weal regardless of all private privileges and preferences. To the development of this idea he devoted his unceasing activities ; and if, when he placed his heavy foot on the loose immorality of the paternal court he also stamped upon the germs of a more abundant culture which had begun to develop under Frederick I, he yet did but what he had to do. The firm and manly discipline of a fighting and industrious people was of greater importance for Prussia's high destiny than were the premature blossoms of art and science.

A gentler hand than his could never have succeeded in bringing the ancient feudal licence under the control of the majesty of the common law ; milder natures than Frederick William and Leopold von Dessau would never have been able to stand against the storm-wind which then blew from the Gallic quarter over the German courts. Among all the statesmen of modern history, two only can be compared as organisers of administration with this soldier king : Bonaparte and von Stein. He united to the daring of the innovator, the painfully exact sense of order of the economical householder, who measured the black and white threads with which the official documents were tied and counted the buttons on the

44

gaiters of his grenadiers; he conceived audacious plans whose realisation has become possible only in the nineteenth century, and yet retained in all his negotiations a secure grasp of the limits of the possible. His prosaic sense, directed towards that which was practically useful and could be immediately grasped, adopted other measures than those characteristic of his heroic grandfather, and yet, in the midst of his care for that which was very small and very near, he always remained conscious of the lofty destiny of his state; he was well aware that he was collecting and forming the energies of his people for the decisive hours of a great future, and he often said, " I know perfectly well that in Vienna and Dresden they call me a penny-wise pedant, but my grandchildren will reap the benefit! "

It was by the army that Prussia was raised to the rank of a European power, and it was by the army that the first breach was made in the old administrative system of the state. For the management of the new taxes which he had introduced to finance his military establishment, the Great Elector had established a number of intermediate boards, the war-commissariats; thus for some decades the tax-economy of the developing modern state existed side by side with the administration of the crown lands, the last fragments of the natural economy of the Middle Ages. Frederick William I put an end to this dualism. In the general directory he created a supreme authority, and in the war-chambers and domain-chambers intermediate authorities for the whole administration, and also endowed these bodies with judicial authority in questions of public law. The variegated and manifold characteristics of the area he controlled forced the king to establish an institution to intermediate between the provincial-system and the real-system; at the head of the subdivisions of the general directory he placed provincial ministers, who had also to conduct certain branches of the administration on behalf of the state as a whole. Speaking generally, however, a centralised administration was here earlier established than elsewhere on the Continent. Whatever still remained of the ancient feudal authorities, was either abolished or else subjected to the control of the officials of the monarchy; an unpitying current of reform swept through the profoundly corrupt administration of the towns, did away with the nepotism of the magistrature, forcibly imposed a new and juster system of taxation; threw the three towns of Königsberg into one, united into a single municipality the two communes of Brandenburg that were separated by the Havel, and placed the entire system of municipal administration under the keen supervision of royal war councillors.

Everywhere the particularism of the estates, of the territorial areas, and of the communes, presented a hostile front to the new and generally applicable order. The nobles murmured against the authority of the bourgeois officials. The proud East Prussians complained of the infringement of ancient charters, now that Pomeranians and Rhinelanders could take office in the Duchy. The law-courts, too, were still living in the circle of ideas of the old feudal state, and, just like the French parliaments, almost invariably took the side of the decaying rights of the parts against the vigorously living right of the whole. It was in the victorious struggle to secure national unity and equality before the law, that Prussia's new ruling class of officials under the crown obtained its schooling. From that homeless race of servants, which during the seventeenth century had flitted from court to court, there was gradually constructed a class of Prussians whose members devoted their lives to the service of the monarch, who found their honour in his, who were vigorous, active, and conscientious like their king. They did not, as had done the feudal lords of the old time, allow their energies to atrophy within the limited fields of territorial interest and nepotism ; they belonged to the nation, they learned to feel no less at home in Cleves than in Königsberg ; and in the class struggles of society maintained against high and against low the law of the land. By an established order of precedence, and by an assured position, the king secured for his officials a respected status in bourgeois life ; he demanded, from every candidate for office, proof of scientific knowledge, and thus founded an aristocracy of culture side by side with the old aristocracy of birth. The result showed how justly he had esteemed the living energies of German society ; the best intelligences of the nobility and of the bourgeoisie streamed to join the new ruling class. Prussian officialdom was for long years the firm support of the German national idea, just as in former days the jurists of Philip the Fair had been the pioneers of French national unity.

The Great Elector had imposed upon his subjects the general liability to taxation ; to this Frederick William I added the obligations of universal military service and compulsory education, thus establishing the threefold group of general civic duties by which the people of Prussia have been trained in an active love for the fatherland. In his mind, powerful for all its limitations, the road was unconsciously prepared for a strong national sentiment akin to the citizen-sense of antiquity. In the eastern march of Germany, ever accustomed to battle, the ancient German idea of military service for all physically fit men had never completely disappeared, even during the epoch of mercenary armies. In East Prussia there lasted on into the eighteenth century the vestiges of the old Polish Landwehr, and Frederick I undertook to constitute a territorial militia for the unified state. In the soldier eye of his son such attempts at an unregulated arming of the people found no favour. King Frederick William understood the superiority of well-disciplined standing armies ; he saw that his state could survive only through the tense employment of all its energies, and yet was unable to effect a permanent provision for the cost of his levies. Since with him every other consideration was subordinated to the demands of political duty, he came to the bold resolve that all Prussians should pass through the school of the standing army. In recent centuries there had been but two political thinkers, Machiavelli and Spinoza, who had ventured to defend the simple and great idea of universal military service ; both these thinkers revived this idea from the history of classical antiquity, and both failed to find understanding among their contemporaries. The needs of domestic economy and an instinctive recognition of the nature of his state now led the rough, practical man who occupied the throne of Prussia to adopt the same view, little as he recked of the moral force of a national army. First among the statesmen of the new Europe did he give expression to the principle : " Every subject is born to bear arms." To construct an army of the children of his country was his life-long ideal. The cantonal regulation of 1733 announced the duty of universal military service.

It was but the establishment of a principle. The notion was still unripe, for it was flatly contradicted by the long term of military service then customary. The poverty of the country and the force of adverse prejudice, compelled the king to make numerous exceptions, so that the burden of compulsory service was imposed, in actual fact, upon the shoulders of the country-folk alone ; and, even thus limited, the duty of bearing arms could not be fully enforced. Unconquerable remained the tacit resistance to the unheard-of novelty, the detestation of the people for the long and severe term of duty. It was seldom possible to make up more than half of the army with homebred cantonists, and the deficiency was made up by voluntary enlistment. Many of the masterless German soldiers of fortune who had hitherto marketed their skins in Venice and the Netherlands, in France and Sweden, now found a home under the flag of the North German power ; the south and the west of the empire were the most fertile recruiting grounds of the Prussian regiments. By such a wonderful and devious route has our nation risen to power and unity. That unarmed third of the German people whose state authorities hardly raised a finger for the defence of the empire paid the blood-tax to the fatherland in the persons of the thousands of its lost sons who fought as mercenaries in the armies of Prussia ; the petty princes of Swabia and the Rhine, who regarded Prussia as their most dreaded opponent, helped to increase the fighting strength of their enemy. As soon as the Prussian army came into existence the empire gradually ceased to be a general recruiting ground ; and, as that army gathered strength, it came to pass that Germany was no longer the battle-field of all other nations.

In the army the king found the means to reconcile the territorial nobility with the monarchical order. The repute of the war-lord had risen greatly since the rude days of the Great Elector, but it was his grandson who succeeded in bringing under his immediate control the nomination of all the officers, and in thus constituting the first truly monarchical corps of modern history. His sense of organisation, always understanding how to adapt political reform to the given social conditions, led him to perceive at once that the hardy sons of the numerous impoverished noble families of the east were the natural leaders of the peasant lads liable for military service. He placed the officers' corps, as a closed aristocracy, at the head of the rank and file ; created in the house of cadets a training school for the officers ; threw open to all who wore epaulettes the way to the highest offices in the army ; kept a strict watch over the honour of the military order ; and endeavoured in every possible way to win the nobles for this knightly caste, whilst preferring to direct the cultured members of the bourgeoisie into the civil service of the administration. How often, with prayers and threats, did he warn the arrogant nobility of East Prussia to provide for their rude sons the discipline of the house of cadets, and, practising his own precept, he made all his own boys serve in the army. Moser refers with admiration to this " hereditary maxim of the Prussian house to accustom the nobles to the military and financial system of the crown." By these means he succeeded in creating out of the semi-savage junkers a brave and loyal monarchical nobility, ready to conquer and to die for the [fatherland,

and as firmly associated with the life of the state as the parliamentary nobility of England. Everywhere else throughout the high aristocratic world of the Baltic regions feudal anarchy continued to flourish—in Sweden, Swedish Pomerania, Mecklenburg, Polish Prussia, and Livonia ; it was only in Prussia that the nobles were won for the duties of the modern state. The army seemed as if it were a state within the state, with its own courts, churches, and schools ; the burgher regarded with disgust the iron strictness of the inhuman military discipline by which the rough masses of the rank and file were forcibly held together ; he bore unwillingly the blustering arrogance of the lieutenants and their centaurian hatred for the quill-driver's pretensions to learning—a hatred which had been manifest in the officers' circles since the days of the fiery Prince Karl Emil and in the berserker roughness of the Old Dessauer. And yet this army was not merely the best-trained and best-equipped military force of the time, but was also, of all the great armies of the modern nations, the most highly endowed with the civic spirit, the only one which never broke faith with its war-lords and never endeavoured (after the Pretorian model) to set the laws of the land at defiance.

No less uncongenial than the army organisation, appeared, to the Germans, the Prussian system of compulsory education ; the ignorance of the masses was still regarded by the ruling classes as the great safeguard of public order. King Frederick William, however, like his grandfather, admired the Protestant Netherlands as the chosen land of civic welfare ; he had there learned to appreciate the moral and economic blessings of a comprehensive system of school education, and he felt obscurely that the vital energy of Protestant civilisation sprang from the elementary school. Convinced that the oppressed and brutalised masses of the north-east could have their native roughnesses removed only by the compulsion of the state, he decisively anticipated, in this respect also, the legislation of all the other great powers ; and by the educational law of 1717 he directly imposed upon all heads of families the duty of sending their children to school. Very slowly, upon the foundation of this law, the Prussian school system became established. The difficulties attendant upon its development were in part due to the poverty and inertness of the people ; but were in part also the king's own fault, for all popular culture must rest upon the prosperity of independent research and of creative art, and for these ideal activities Frederick William felt a characteristically barbarian contempt.

Thus through the community of arduous civic duties, through the unity of the officialdom and of the military system, the men of Magdeburg and Pomerania, of the Mark and of Westphalia, were welded together into a single Prussian people; and when Frederick II extended to all his subjects the Prussian nationality he did no more than give a legal sanction to his father's work. However roughly and masterfully the Prussian kingship might manifest its sovereignty against all disloyal opposition, the work of unification yet proceeded far more considerately than did, in the adjoining country, the forcible " levelling of the French soil." The state could not give the lie to its own Teutonic nature; it was permeated throughout by a powerful element of historical piety. Just as it had endeavoured to reconcile the ecclesiastical differences, so was it compelled in political life to adopt an intermediate position in order to counteract the excess of centrifugal tendencies. Towards the ancient traditions of the territorial areas a tolerant respect was everywhere exhibited; even to-day the double eagle of Austria may be seen displayed in the market place of almost every Silesian town, and the patron saint of Bohemia still looks out from the citadel of Glatz over the beautiful surrounding country. The arrogant lords who wished to forbid the Great Elector to bury his father with Calvinistic rites were finally, after a severe struggle, reduced to the common position of subjects. The diets lost their ancient rights of government and were deprived of all influence in financial and military affairs; but were permitted to retain a semblance of life as soon as these necessary changes had been effected.

Until the extinction of the Holy Empire there were only three occasions on which, throughout all the territorial areas which gradually accrued to the crown of Prussia, a local constitution was formally abolished. This occurred in Silesia, in West Prussia, and in Münster, for here the estates became the nucleus of a party hostile to the central government, seriously threatening its predominance. Everywhere else the diets lived on into the new time, remarkable vestiges of that ancient epoch in which the German north still consisted of numerous petty territories. They were the fragments of eggshell that the eaglet still carried on its head: they represented the past of the state; whereas the crown, officialdom, the army, represented the present. They represented particularism and feudal privilege, as opposed to the national unity and to the common law; their power still sufficed, at times, to render difficult the great progress of monarchical legislation,

but they were no longer able to arrest that progress completely.
The diets remained competent to allot certain taxes and to administer the territorial debts ; in this narrow sphere there persisted
unchanged the nepotism, the routine, and the empty formalism of
the old feudal order ; and the nobleman of the Mark still preferred
to speak of his Brandenburg as an independent state under the
crown of Prussia. Nor was the feudal office of Landrat abolished,
but a place was found for it in the order of monarchical officialdom ;
the Landrat, nominated by the crown after being proposed by the
estates, was at the same time representative of the knighthood ;
and a royal official subordinated to the war-chamber and to the
domain-chamber. The king cherished a thoroughly citizen mistrust of the overbearing disposition of his junkers, but he needed
the cordial support of the nobility for the establishment of his new
military constitution. He therefore sought to appease the disaffected by honours and dignities, leaving to the landed proprietors
a portion of their old privileges of taxation and of their other
seignorial rights, but always under the supervision of the royal
officials.

It was this prudent and tolerant policy which rendered it
possible for the king to carry into execution his great economic
reforms. He founded that peculiar system of monarchical organisation which for two generations harmonised the traditional
organisation of classes with the new tasks of the nation. Every
province and every class was made to undertake certain
branches of economic and political work on behalf of the crown.
In addition to agriculture (which was the principal industry of the
entire monarchy), in the electoral Mark and the Westphalian provinces, manufactures, in the coastlands, commerce, and in the
Magdeburg districts, mining, must be carried on. The nobles
remained the sole great landed proprietors, and had an almost exclusive right to become officers in the army ; the peasantry
undertook the work of agriculture and must serve in the
ranks ; the burghers engaged in commerce and industry, and
must bear the chief burden of taxation.

It was regarded as a primary duty of the royal justice to
secure these territorial rights and class privileges against all possible
attack, and nowhere was the fulfilment of this duty so difficult as
upon the old colonial soil where the excessive powers of the territorial chiefs was a danger alike to the crown and to the civic peace.
The most human of all royal duties, the protection of the poor
and of the oppressed, was for the Hohenzollerns a primary need of

self-preservation; they bore with pride the name " Kings of the Beggars," which had been assigned to them in mockery by France. The crown forbade the purchase of the peasants' lands which in Mecklenburg and Swedish Pomerania had given the nobility the absolute dominion of the countryside, thus saving the agricultural middle class from destruction; and, from the days of Frederick William I onwards, a carefully considered agrarian legislation aimed at promoting the enfranchisement of the agriculturists. It was the desire of the king to abolish hereditary serfdom, and to transform all peasant property into free ownership of the land; as early as 1719 he said: " What a fine thing it would be if my subjects were free instead of being serfs, so that they could better enjoy what is their own, could carry on their affairs with so much more zeal and diligence because they would be dealing with their own property." For long, indeed, it was impossible for the crown to carry this desire into effect. Not only had there to be faced the passionate opposition of the powerful nobles, already rendered antagonistic by the abolition of feudalism, but there must also be reckoned with the passive resistance of the rude peasantry themselves, who regarded with suspicion every change in the traditional order. Continually, however, and without pause, the king drew nearer to his goal. His " whipping decree " protected the serf from maltreatment; the services and dues that could be demanded from the peasantry were lightened; a commencement was made in the subdivision of the communal lands to form separate sections of real estate; everywhere the way was opened for the liberation of the land and of the working powers of the labourer. The reforms of Stein and Hardenberg could achieve their striking success only because they came when preparation for them had been made by the legislation of three generations. In the officialdom of the crown the small man found protection against the arrogance of the nobles, found expert advice, and found also inexorably strict supervision; to the thrifty king no sacrifice seemed too great that was for the good of his peasant-folk; the entire revenue of a year was devoted to the restoration of civilisation in East Prussia, devastated by pestilence and war, and to the repeopling with diligent workers of the wide deserts on the Niemen and the Pregel.

It was to their faithful care for the well-being of the masses, and not to their renown in war, that the Hohenzollerns owed the unshakable confidence which, through all need and all temptation, was felt by the people in the crown. Periods of torpor and exhaustion occurred in the Prussian state as elsewhere; indeed, such periods seemed in Prussian history more conspicuous and more deplorable than in other lands, because Prussia was ever regarded by a thousand hostile eyes eager to search out its weaknesses and to detect influences that might destroy it without any effort on the part of its enemies. Yet none who take a tranquil view of a considerable period of time can fail to recognise the steady progress of the monarchy towards national unity and towards the institution of equality before the law. The portraits of the Hohenzollerns do not display the spiritless and monotonous uniformity that we see in the Hapsburg princes, but they show, nevertheless, an unmistakable family likeness; and the same family likeness is seen also in their political activity. Whether strong or weak, whether intelligent or the reverse, they almost all displayed a sober understanding of the hard realities of life; not disdaining to be great in little things, and all taking a high view of their princely duty.

The mood of the first Hohenzollern of the Mark, who termed himself " God's simple officer in the princedom," prevailed in all his descendants; we find it once more in the motto of the Great Elector: " For God and the people "; we find it in the feverish zeal for service displayed by the soldier-king, who never ceased to be conscious that he must answer with his own soul's salvation for the well-being of his people; we find it, finally, given profounder and freer expression in the words of Frederick the Great: " The King is the first servant of the state." Many of the Hohenzollerns have failed in their task through an over-scientific dread of the game of hazard which is war, but very few through an unready lust of battle; the traditional policy of the house sought to establish the glory of the ruler in the maintenance of the law and in the culture of the works of peace; it was but occasionally, in great moments of history, that they directed the carefully fostered energies of the state towards an enemy without—in this respect, as in all others, offering an absolute contrast to the Hapsburgs, whose statesmanship was wholly concerned with European questions. Long ago, like the old Frankish kings, the dynasty had relinquished its domestic possessions to the state; it lived solely for the good of all. Whilst almost all other territories of the empire bore the name and the arms of their princely house, the banners of the Hohenzollerns displayed the ancient imperial eagle of the Hohenstaufen, that flag which had for centuries defended the distant eastern marches, and bore the colours of the Teutonic Knights. This severe political kingship educated a maltreated and brutalised people in the rights and duties of citizenship. Wherever we may contemplate the condition of the German territories, comparing their condition before and after their entrance into the Prussian state, be it in Pomerania, in East Prussia, in Cleves, or in the County Mark, everywhere the roll of the Prussian drums had brought freedom to the Germans, had signalised enfranchisement from foreign authority and from the tyranny of feudal polyarchy. Upon the foundation of the common law there was then erected, with severe struggles it is true, but in accordance with a natural and necessary development, a new and riper form of political freedom, involving the orderly participation of the citizens in the conduct of the state. It was not genius but character and firm discipline which gave this state its moral greatness ; and its power depended, not upon the wealth of its resources, but upon their orderliness and upon their readiness for immediate use.

Now, however, was least of all the moment in which the German nation was ready to understand the strange phenomenon of this state armed and ready to strike, youthful and immature, tough in bone and sinew, full of vigour and fire, but ungainly, its bones ill-clothed, lacking grace and nobility of aspect. The old hostility of the Germans for the upstart Brandenburg was increased to a passionate hatred by the Bœotian roughness of Frederick William I. It does not become the historian to tone down the painfully crude colours of our modern history ; it is not true that this profound hatred was merely a dissembled love. At this time there originated in the general mind that view of the nature of the Prussian state, that view strangely compounded of true and false, which for a hundred years yet to come was to remain dominant throughout the half-cultured circles of Germany, and which even now has the upper hand in German history as written by the foreigner. This land under arms seemed to the Germans no more than a magnified barrack. All the sounds that found their way into the rest of the empire from out the weary silence of this great prison-house were merely the threatening and steady tramp of the giant Guards of Potsdam, the harsh words of command of the officers, and the cry of distress of the deserters hunted through the streets ; of the blessings which the grateful Lithuanian peasant called down from heaven upon his severe king, Germany heard nothing. In the empire the nobles had fallen upon golden days. In Hanover, now that their elector passed his days in distant England, the dominion of the territorial chiefs was unrestricted ; the junkerdom of Saxony took advantage of their Polish king's conversion to the

Roman Church to struggle for new feudal privileges, and passed their days in licentious living at the shameless court of a ruler engaged in the ruin of his country. With mixed anger and contempt the proud races of the neighbouring lands contemplated the citizen-soldier despotism of the Hohenzollern, by which the joyful days of the rule of the nobles had been so forcibly disturbed.

Nor did the townsman regard the Prussian system with a cordial eye. He viewed, now with ironical sympathy, and now with dread, the iron industry and the inflexible severity of the Prussian official; it seemed to him that all the sacredness of the law was threatened when he saw the new administration, ever at war with the old courts, taking its way remorselessly across the ancient charters of the territories and the communes; and he could not grasp that the old life which was here being trampled down was only the teeming life of corruption. The hostility of the men of education was better founded. The whole academic world felt a sense of shameful injury when the rough king played his clownish tricks with the valiant J. J. Moser and the Frankfort professors. The effect produced upon rich artist natures by the contemplation of the stiff and dry military order is manifested by the excess of hatred which the greatest Prussian of those days exhibited towards his fatherland. Yearningly did Winckelmann seek to escape from the heavy and suffocating air of the accursed land, and when he finally shook from off his feet the dust of the schoolroom of Altmark and revelled with intoxicated joy in the paintings of the Dresden gallery, he continued, with the artlessness of a great Pagan, to send his curses back to the homeland : " I think with loathing of this country, which groans under the greatest despotism that the world has ever known. It is better to be a circumcised Turk than a Prussian. In such a country as Sparta [an extremely ideal description of the regime of the corporal's stick !] the arts cannot possibly thrive, and degenerate perforce." So widely divergent were then the two creative energies which in unconscious union have made the new Germany. The lesser people of the empire detested the King of Prussia on account of the universal nuisance of his enlistments. " Don't grow too tall, or the recruiters will get hold of you," said the Swabian mother anxiously to her son. Everyone along the Rhine could recount a hundred terrible tales of the inn in Frankfort which was the head-quarters of the Prussian recruiting officers ; there was no possible devilry that they failed to ascribe to these savage brutes.

All this force and cunning, all the enormous expenditure on

the army which swallowed up fully four-fifths of the Prussian revenue, served merely—such was the view in the empire—for the purposeless playing-at-soldiers of a thick-headed tyrant. A whole generation had passed away since the heroic struggle of Cassano, when the blood of the grenadiers from the Mark reddened the waters of the Ritorto, and the grateful Lombards first greeted the brave *prussiani* with the exhilarating tones of the Dessauer march ; when the wild and stimulating strain was now heard upon a peaceful drill-ground, the Germans laughed scornfully at the " Prussian bluster." The reign of Frederick William came in the poverty-stricken time of the Peace of Utrecht, a period barren of ideas ; the petty arts of Fleury, Alberoni, and Walpole dominated European politics. Perplexed was the simple-minded prince amid the crafty intrigues of diplomacy. He adhered to his emperor with ancient German fidelity ; he wished to put sabre and pistols in his children's cradles that they might help in expelling foreign nations from the imperial soil ; how often with the beer-tankard of the fatherland in his hand did he not raise his resounding shout : " Vivat Germania teutscher Nation ! " Now must the guileless man learn how the court of Vienna, in conjunction with his two ambitious neighbours of Hanover and Saxony, was secretly planning the partition of Prussia, and must witness their helping the Albertiners to the Polish crown, and their surrender of Lorraine to the French ; he must witness their attempts to sow discord in his own household between father and son ; must finally experience their perfidious attempts to deprive him of his sound hereditary right to Berg and East Frisia. Thus throughout his life he was pushed to and fro between open opponents and false friends ; not until the close of his days did he see through Austria's cunning and conjure his son to avenge the tricks played upon the father. At the foreign courts it was currently said, that the King of Prussia always stood on watch with his gun at full cock, but would never pull the trigger ; and when, within the empire, the other Germans were sometimes anxious about the Potsdam military parades, they consoled themselves by saying, " After all, the Prussians are very slow to shoot ! "

The joke missed fire when Prussia found a ruler who combined with the sense of the practicable and with the fortunate sobriety characteristic of the Hohenzollerns, the boldness and the insight of genius. The clear sunshine of youth was diffused over the beginnings of the Frederician epoch, when at length, after so prolonged an arrest, the inert mass of the German world was once more set in motion, and when the powerful opposing forces which Germany contained within its bosom broke into inevitable conflict. Since the days of the Lion of the North, Germany had not again seen a heroic figure upon which the whole nation could gaze with wondering admiration. But the figure which in proud freedom, like that of Gustavus Adolphus of old, strode among the great powers and forced the Germans to believe once again in the wonders of the heroic age, was now that of a German.

The central characteristic of this powerful nature was his pitiless and cruel German realism. Frederick presents himself as he is, and sees things as they are. Just as in the long series of his letters and writings we find not a single line wherein he endeavours to glorify his own actions or to adorn his own image for the benefit of posterity, so also do we find in his statesmanship, even though he did not despise the petty arts and cunning of the age as means to his ends, the stamp of his royal frankness. Whenever he takes the sword in hand he explains with unmistakable definiteness what he demands from the opponent, and does not lay down his weapon until he has attained his end. As soon as he awakens to self-consciousness he is filled with pride and rejoicing to be the son of a free century, which is using the torch of reason to illumine the dusty corners of a world of ancient prejudices and exanimate traditions ; on the ceiling of his bright hall at Rheinsberg was painted a picture of the sun-god, rising victoriously through the clouds of dawn. It is with the self-confident assurance of the disciple of enlightenment that he approaches the phenomena of history, examining them each by each with the judgment of his keen understanding. In the struggles for power among the states he concerns himself only about what is really alive, cares only for the power that can speedily and wisely find expression in effective action. "Negotiations without weapons are like music without instruments," he says frankly. When he is informed of the death of the last Hapsburg he says to his councillors, " I give you a problem to solve ; if one has an advantage in one's hand, should one make use of it or not ? " Never did anyone exhibit a prouder contempt for that boastful powerlessness that pretends to possess power, that immoral privilege which bases itself upon the sacredness of historic right, that dread of action which conceals its helplessness behind an empty respect for forms ; and never did this implacable realism exercise so cleansing, so destructive, so revolutionary an influence as in that great world of fable which was the Holy Empire. Nothing was more remorseless than Frederick's scorn for the sacred majesty of the Emperor Francis, tied to his wife's apron-strings, a worthy king of Jerusalem, occupied in lucrative commissariat-negotiations for the armies of the Queen of Hungary ; nothing could be more cruel than his mockery of the " phantom " of the imperial army, his scorn of the obscure nonentity of the petty courts, of the formal commercial spirit " of these accursed periwig-pates of Hanover," of the vain pride of the landless junkers of Saxony and Mecklenburg, of " this whole race of princes and people of Austria." He that bends the knee before the great ones of this world " is one who does not know them."

With an assured sense of superiority he opposes to the shadow-pictures of the imperial law the healthy reality of his modern state ; a fierce love of mischief speaks out of his letters when he brings home to " the pedants of Ratisbon " the iron necessity of war. Frederick effected in action that which the disputatious publicists of the previous century, Hippolytus and Severinus, had attempted in words alone ; he held up a mirror before the " disagreeable and corpse-like countenance of Germany," proving to all the world the hopeless corruption of the Holy Empire. Well-meaning contemporaries blamed him because he thus exposed to laughter the anciently venerable community, but posterity thanks him, in that he restored truth to a place of honour in German statecraft, as of old had done Martin Luther in the spheres of German thought and belief.

Frederick adopted early in life that strict Protestant view of German history and imperial policy which, since the days of Puffendorf and Thomasius, had dominated the freer spirits of Prussia ; amid the embittering experiences of his joyless youth he had remoulded this view with a keen independence. In the Schmalkald rising, in the Thirty Years' War, in all the confused happenings of the last two centuries, he sees nothing but the unceasing struggle of German freedom against the despotism of the House of Austria, that house which " with a rod of iron " ruled the weak princes of the empire like slaves, and allowed only the strong ones to do as they liked. Not without personal satisfaction does he interpret the facts of history in accordance with such a one-sided view, for to direct this one-sidedness towards the light and towards life seems to him the privilege of the creative hero, and he regards it as the task of the Prussian state to lead this ancient struggle to victory. In his earlier years he remained faithful to Protestantism ; he esteemed it the glorious duty of the House of Brandenburg " to work on behalf of the Protestant religion throughout the German empire and Europe," and he contemplated Heidelberg with uneasiness, seeing that here in the old leading centre of our Church the monks and the priests of Rome were once more vigorously at work. Even at a later date, when he had become estranged from religious belief, and when from the altitude of his independent philosophical enlightenment he passed a hostile judgment upon the mediocre parson-natures of Luther and Calvin, he remained actively conscious that his state must continue ever rooted in the Protestant world. He knew how all the accomplices of the Holy See were secretly working for the destruction of the new Protestant great power ; he knew that his human ideal of freedom of belief, of the right of all to seek salvation after their own fashion, was attainable only on the soil of Protestantism ; he understood that in new and secular forms he was himself carrying on the struggles of the sixteenth century ; and to his latest work, the plan for the League of German Princes, he attached the significant superscription, " Drawn up after the example of the League of Schmalkald."

The earliest of Frederick's political writings which has come down to us shows the glance of the youth of eighteen already directed towards that region of national life upon which he was to exercise the greatest and most individual forces of his genius—the great questions of statecraft. The crown prince contemplates the position of his nation in the world, finds the situation of its dispersed areas an extremely dangerous one, and draws up, still half in jest, daring plans for the rounding off of the remoter provinces, so that they may no longer remain in isolation. It is not long before these immature youthful proposals reappear as profound and powerful ideas ; three years before his ascent to the throne the great path of his life is perceived with a wonderful prophetic clearness. " It seems," he writes, " that heaven has predestined the king to make all those preparations which a wise foresight undertakes before the beginning of a war. Who can tell whether it may not be reserved for me to make a glorious use of the opportunities thus provided, and to employ these materials of war in the realisation of the designs for which my father's prevision intended them ! " He observes how his state vacillates in an untenable position between the petty territories and the great powers, and is resolved to put an end to this vacillation (*décider cet être*). To enlarge the national area, *corriger la figure de la Prusse*, has become a necessity if Prussia is to stand on her own feet and to do credit to the name of her king.

From generation to generation his ancestors had paid faithful service to the House of Austria, conscientiously refraining from turning to their own advantage the difficulties of their neighbour, but rewarded always with ingratitude, treachery, and contempt. Frederick himself, in the distressing period of his misused youth, had found it hard to endure " the arrogance, the presumption, the overbearing insolence, of the court of Vienna"; his heart was cankered with hatred " for the imperial band " which with its tricks and its lies had alienated his father's heart. His untamable pride was in revolt when at his father's court there was lacking the correct tone of cold refusal for the exacting demands of Austria ; he wrote angrily that a King of Prussia should resemble the noble palm-tree, of which the poet says, "If you wish to fell it, it rears its proud head the higher." With watchful eye he followed the varying fortunes of the European system of states, and came to the conclusion that the old policy of the balance of power was altogether outworn. After the victories of the war of the Spanish succession the time was over for fighting the Bourbon in alliance with Austria and England ; now the moment had come for the new German state " by the terror of its arms " to raise itself to such a height of power as would enable it to maintain its own freedom of will against all its neighbours and against the imperial house.

Thus in the mouth of Frederick, the old and greatly misused expression "German freedom," acquired a new and nobler meaning. It was no longer to signify that dishonourable policy of the petty princes which called in the foreigner to help them against the emperor, and which betrayed the marches of the realm into foreign hands ; it was to signify the formation of a great German power which should defend the fatherland with the strong hand in the east and in the west ; and which should do this of its own will, independently of the imperial authority. For hundreds of years it had been the rule that whoever was not a good Austrian must be a good Swede (like Hippolytus a Lapide), or a good Frenchman (like the princes of the Confederation of the Rhine), or a good Englishman (like the scions of the Guelphs). Even the Great Elector, in the press between neighbours of predominant power, was able only at intervals to maintain an independent position. It was the work of Frederick, avoiding on either hand the destructive tendencies to the acceptance of concealed or manifest foreign dominion, to institute a third tendency, a policy that was Prussian, and Prussian only. To this policy belonged Germany's future.

It was not the way of this hater of phrases to talk much of the fatherland ; and yet his soul was animated by a vigorous national pride inseparably associated with his keen sense of personal independence and with his princely sentiment. It seemed to him to touch his honour that foreign nations should play the masters upon German soil ; that this should be, was a discredit to his illustrious blood, for which the philosophic king, with the naive inconsistency of genius, had a very high respect. When the inextricable confusion of German affairs forced him at times to form an alliance with the foreigner, he never alienated an acre of German soil, and never allowed his state to be misused for foreign purposes. All his life through he was exposed to the accusation of faithless cunning, for no treaty and no alliance could ever make him renounce the right of free self-determination. All the courts of Europe spoke angrily of *travailler pour le roi de Prusse ;* accustomed from of old to dominate German life they found it hardly possible to grasp the new situation and understand that now at length the resolute egoism of an independent German state was able to set itself in successful opposition to their will. Voltaire's royal disciple began for the German states the same work of liberation that Voltaire's opponent, Lessing, effected for our poetry. Even in his youthful writings, Frederick strongly condemns the weakness of the Holy Empire, which had thrown open to the foreigner its Thermopylæ, Alsace ; he rages against the court of Vienna for its surrender of Lorraine to France ; he can never forgive the Queen of Hungary for having turned loose upon the German empire the savage mob of " those Graces of the east," the Jazyges, the Croats, and the Tolpatsches, and for having for the first time induced the barbarians of Muscovy to take part in the internal affairs of Germany. During the Seven Years' War his German pride and hatred often found vent in grim and scornful words. To the Russians, who have plundered his peasants of Neumark, he sends the greeting : " Oh ! that with one leap they could sink themselves in the Black Sea, so that they and all memory of them might pass away for ever." When the French overran Rhineland he composed (in French, it is true) an ode which recalls to our minds the strains of the War of Liberation :

> "To its uttermost sources
> Spumes the ancient Rhine with hate,
> Cursing the shame, that its waters
> Must bear a foreign yoke ! "

"Prudence teaches us how to guard what we already possess; but through intrepidity alone do we learn how to increase our possessions"—such are the words with which Frederick, in his Rheinsberg days, already betrays how his inmost nature urges him to rash resolution, to tempestuous daring. It appears to him the first duty of the statesman to avoid half measures; and of all conceivable resolutions the worst of all seems to him to resolve to do nothing. Yet in this also he displays his German blood, that from the first he knows how to control his ardent love of action by cool and sober consideration. One who felt within himself the heroic force of an Alexander determined to work for permanent ends within the narrow circle in which destiny had placed him. In war, sometimes, his fiery spirit leads him beyond the bounds of prudence; he demands the impossible from his troops, and fails through a proud under-estimation of his enemy; but as a statesman he always preserves a perfect moderation, a wise limitation, which leads him to reject at once any too adventurous design. He is never for a moment befooled by the thought of cutting his own state loose from the fallen German community; his position in the empire does not impair his freedom of action in European policy, while it gives him the right to intervene in the destiny of the empire itself, and for this reason he wishes to keep his foot in the stirrup of the German steed. Still less does he dream of aspiring to the imperial crown. Since the days of the prophecies of the court astrologers of the Great Elector there had always persisted in Hohenzollern circles the obscure premonition that the house was destined to bear the sword and sceptre of the Holy Empire; and the Hotspurs, Winterfeldt and Leopold of Dessau, sometimes ventured to greet their royal hero as the German Augustus. But Frederick knew that his temporal state could not carry the Roman crown, that the attempt to assume it would involve the newcomer among the powers in interminable intrigues, and said drily, "For us it would be no more than a fetter."

Hardly had he mounted the throne when there arrived that great crisis in German destiny which the seer's vision of Puffendorf had already indicated as likely to furnish the only possible means of thorough-going imperial reform. The old imperial house died out, and before the ardent eyes of the young king, in whose hands was the only well-ordered fighting force of Germany, there opened a world of alluring prospects, which must have led astray into overbearing dreams a spirit less profound and less firmly collected. Frederick felt the earnestness of the hour. "Day and night," he wrote, " the fate of the empire monopolises my thoughts, and to me alone is given the will and the power to secure it." He felt assured that this great moment must not be allowed to pass without bringing to the Prussian state complete freedom of movement, and without providing it with a place in the council of the great powers ; and yet he also recognised how incalculably confused would become the situation of Germany owing to the greed of its foreign neighbours, and owing to the hopeless internal dissensions of the empire, as soon as the Hapsburg monarchy fell in ruins. For this reason he desired to protect Austria, and was satisfied, out of the mass of the carefully considered ancient claims of his house, to put forward the most important alone. Single-handed, and without a word to the watching foreign powers, he broke upon Silesia in an overwhelming storm. Germany, accustomed to the solemn considerations and counter-considerations of its imperial jurists, received with astonishment and horror the doctrine that the rights of the state can be maintained by living force alone. The conqueror offered the imperial crown to the spouse of Maria Theresa and undertook to fight France on behalf of Austria. It was the resistance of the Hofburg that urged him on to comprehensive plans of imperial reform, which remind us of the daring dreams of Waldeck.

It was not Frederick who created German dualism, although he was reproached with this by his contemporaries and by posterity; dualism had existed since the days of Charles V, and Frederick was the first who seriously attempted to destroy it. As soon as he found it impossible to come to an understanding with the Viennese court, the king conceived the bold idea of removing the imperial crown for ever from the House of Austria, and thus severing the last bond which still connected this dynasty with Germany. He approached the Bavarian Wittelsbachs, the only one among the more powerful princely races of Germany which resembled the Hohenzollerns in ruling over German lands alone, and who, like the Hohenzollerns, regarded Austria as their natural enemy ; he was the first to establish that alliance between the two greatest of the purely German states which has since then been so often renewed, and always for the good of the fatherland. The Elector of Bavaria received the imperial dignity, and it was the hope of Frederick that this new emperorship, which he himself spoke of as " my work," would secure a firm support for the crown of Bohemia.

Forthwith there reawakened in Berlin and in Munich that

saving idea of secularisation which sprang to life whenever a healing hand was laid upon the sick body of the empire. The aim was to strengthen the power of the great temporal estates of the realm, which in Frederick's view were the sole really living members of the empire, at the expense of the theocratic and republican territories; a purely temporal art of statesmanship devoted itself to the realisation of the political ideas of the Reformation. Certain spiritual provinces of High Germany were to be secularised, and several of the imperial towns were to be annexed to the adjoining princely domains. With good reason did Austria complain that this Bavarian emperorship under Prussian tutelage threatened grave injury to the nobility and to the Church. Should these inchoate ideas be realised, German dualism would be practically done away with, and the imperial constitution, even should it persist in form, would be profoundly modified in substance; Germany would become a confederation of temporal princes under the dominant influence of Prussia; the spiritual states, the imperial towns, the crowd of petty counts and barons, deprived of the support of the Hapsburgs, would go down to destruction, and the German bulwark in the heart of the empire, the crown of Bohemia, would be conquered for Teutonic civilisation. Thus Germany could have effected spontaneously and by her own powers that necessary revolution which two generations later was shamefully forced upon her by the might of the foreigner. But the House of Wittelsbach, already estranged from German life by its hereditary association with France as well as by the rigidity of Catholic unity, displayed a distressing incapacity in face of this great opportunity; the nation failed to understand the significant fortune of the moment. In a tour through the empire the king gained so disheartening an insight into the dissensions, the greed of gain, and the slavish anxiety of the petty courts, that he learned to lay aside for ever his hopes for Germany; moreover, his own power did not yet suffice to overcome the valiant resistance of the Queen of Hungary. Notwithstanding the triumphs of Hohenfriedberg and Kesselsdorf, the second Silesian War ended in the restoration of the Austrian emperorship. The empire remained in its state of unconstitutional confusion, Francis of Lorraine ascended the imperial throne after the death of Charles VII, and there was reconstituted the old alliance between Austria and the Catholic majority in the Reichstag.

The attempt to do away with German dualism miscarried; sharper, more hostile than ever before, was the separation of parties in the empire. Yet one permanent gain had been secured by the king—the establishment of Prussia's position as a great power. He had saved Bavaria from destruction, had increased the strength of his own land by more than a third ; with a hardy stroke he had broken the long chain of Hapsburg-Wettin territorial areas which shut in the Prussian state to the south and east ; and for the first time the proud imperial house had suffered profound humiliation at the hands of one of the princes of the empire. It was solely his own energy that he had to thank for his victories, and he presented so brave a front in face of all the old powers, that Horace Walpole was forced to admit that this King of Prussia now held in his hands the control of the European balance. Saxony, Bavaria, Hanover, all the central states, which up till now had remained rivals of the crown of Prussia, were by the Silesian Wars permanently reduced to the second rank. High above the innumerable petty opposi- tions that flourished within the empire there arose the one dominant question : Prussia or Austria ? The problem of the future of Germany had been stated. From a free altitude the king now looked down upon the turmoil of the estates of the German empire, and to all insulting demands could jestingly reply, that those who made them must take him for a Duke of Gotha or for a Prince of the Rhine ! In relation to his smaller neighbours he was now able to assume that role of benevolent patron and protector which, in his *Anti-Machiavel*, he had pointed out as the sublime duty of the stronger ; already in the Reichstag there was forming the nucleus of a Prussian party, and the North German courts were beginning to send their sons to serve in the king's army.

Meanwhile, with astonishing rapidity, the new acquisitions became fused with the monarchy. For the first time upon any considerable area did the state exhibit that strong force of attrac- tion and that formative energy which it has since then everywhere displayed in German and half-German lands. The new energies of the modern world made their way into the neglected province, the victim of feudal and ecclesiastical oppression ; the officialdom of the monarchy overthrew the dominion of the nobles, the strength of law put an end to nepotism, toleration replaced restraint in matters of conscience, and the German school-system superseded the profound spiritual slumber of priestly education. The sluggish and servile peasant learned once again to hope for the morrow, and his king forbade him to abase himself before the officials by kneeling to kiss the hem of their garments.

In that century of struggles for power there was no other state whose working imposed such manifold and widely human tasks. It was the peaceful labour of administration which first gave a moral justification to the conquest of Silesia, and furnished the proof that this widely censured act of daring was a genuinely German deed. By the Prussian rule there was restored to the German nation this magnificent frontier-land which had already been half-overwhelmed by foreign influences. Silesia was the only one of the German-Austrian hereditary dominions in which the policy of religious unity had been unable to effect a complete victory. In the valleys of the Riesengebirge the calm and easy-going German stock had withstood with insuperable tenacity the violent deeds of the Lichtenstein dragoons and the oratorical arts of the Jesuits. The majority of the Germans remained true to the Protestant faith. The Protestant Church, oppressed and despised, despoiled of its goods, continued a poverty-stricken existence ; only the threats of the crown of Sweden secured for this Church, in addition to the small number of God's houses which still remained to it, the possession of a few sanctuary churches. The Catholic Poles of Upper Silesia and the Czech colonists whom the imperial court had summoned into the land to carry on the struggle against the German heretics, were the props of the imperial dominion. With the entry of the Prussian army the German elements once more gladly raised their heads ; joyfully there resounded through the sanctuary churches praise to the Lord, Who after showing severity to His people had now at length displayed a banner for them to follow. Under the protection of Prussian toleration, Protestantism soon regained its consciousness of spiritual superiority, the Polish elements visibly lost ground, and after a few decades the Prussian Silesians, in ideas and customs, resembled their North German neighbours more closely than they resembled the Silesians across the border. The Protestant conqueror, however, left the Roman Church in undisturbed possession of almost all the Church property of the Protestants, and whilst England was constraining its Irish Catholics to pay taxes in support of the Anglican State Church, in Silesia, the Protestant must continue now as formerly to pay taxes on behalf of the Catholic Church. It was only the treasonable practices of the Roman clergy during the Seven Years' War that forced the king to abandon this excess of toleration, which had involved injustice towards the Protestants ; and even then the situation of the Catholic Church in Prussian Silesia remained a more favourable one than in any other Protestant state.

The flourishing development of Silesia under Prussian rule

sufficed to show that the new province had found its natural master, and that the change in the destiny of the German east was unalterably established. The Viennese court, however, continued to cherish the hope of securing revenge for the past shame, and of reducing the conqueror of Silesia once again to the mediocre situation of the ordinary German prince, just as had been possible in the case of those presumptuous ones who had formerly ventured to raise their hands against the imperial authority. King Frederick knew, moreover, that the final and decisive appeal to arms still lay before him. He attempted on one occasion during the brief years of peace to exclude the son of Maria Theresa from the imperial dignity, so that for the future at least the empire should be separated from the House of Austria, but the scheme was wrecked by the hostility of the Catholic courts. The irreconcilable opposition between the two leading powers of Germany determined for a lengthy period the course of European politics and deprived the Holy Empire of its last vestiges of vital energy. In painful anticipation the nation seemed to foresee the approach of a new Thirty Years' War. That which had been slowly prepared by the quiet labours of toilsome decades appeared to the next generation merely as a wonderful chance, as the fortunate adventure of a talented spirit. Quite isolated in the diplomatic correspondence of the epoch is the far-seeing utterance of the Dane, Bernstorff, who in the year 1759 wrote sadly to Choiseul: "All that you are endeavouring to-day in the hope of preventing the uprise in central Germany of a warlike monarchy whose iron arm will soon crush the petty princes—it is all lost labour!" The neighbouring powers in the east and in the west vented their anger against the lucky one who, out of the turmoil of the war of the Austrian succession, had alone drawn the prize of victory; nor was it simply the personal hatred of powerful women that was weaving the web of the great conspiracy which now threatened to enmesh Frederick. It was the general feeling of Europe that the ancient and traditional structure of the comity of states was imperilled as soon as any victorious great power became established in the centre of the Continent. The Roman See was deeply concerned that the detested home of heresy should be once again enabled to give expression to its own independent will; it was only in consequence of the co-operation of Rome that it became possible for the two ancient enemies, the two great Catholic powers of Austria and of France, to unite against Prussia. The aim was to render the impotence of Germany eternal.

By a daring onslaught the king saved his crown from certain destruction, and when, after seven terrible years, he had defended his German state on the Rhine and on the Pregel, on the Peene and in the Riesengebirge, against foreign and semi-foreign armies, and in concluding peace had maintained the extent of his power over the last village, Prussia seemed to stand once more in the same position as at the outset of the murderous campaign. Not a hand's breadth more German soil had been added to its domain, half the country lay desolate, the abundant work of peace of three generations had been almost completely destroyed, in the unhappy Neumark the work of civilisation had to be begun at the beginning for the fourth time. The king himself could never think without bitterness of these dreadful days, when evil fortune had heaped upon his shoulders all the distresses which a man can bear, and even more ; what he then suffered seemed to him the senseless and evil caprice of a mocking fate, a tragedy without justice and without definite aim. Nevertheless there was a colossal success acquired as the outcome of this struggle, in appearance so fruitless ; the new order of German affairs, which had begun with the foundation of the Prussian power, had proved itself an irrevocable necessity, and this in face of the severest test conceivable. A hundred years earlier Germany had been able to free herself from the Hapsburg dominion only by the struggles of an entire generation, and even to effect this had been forced to pay shameful subsidies to her foreign allies ; now the poorest region of the empire was competent within seven years to repel the attacks of a world in arms, and the victory was gained by German force alone, for the sole foreign power which had come to the help of the king betrayed him in the hour of need. Germany's star was once again in the ascendant ; for the Germans those were true words which were uttered in joyful thanksgiving in all the churches of Prussia : " Many a time have they afflicted me from my youth : Yet they have not prevailed against me."

At the opening of the second campaign it had been the proud hope of Frederick to fight a battle of Pharsalia against the House of Austria, and to dictate terms of peace beneath the walls of Vienna, for this teeming time displayed everywhere the embryonic germs of the great new formations of a distant future, and plans were already on foot for an alliance between Prussia and Piedmont, Austria's other rival. But the battle of Kolin once more plunged the king in despair, and he fought now only for the existence of his state. The attempts he made to summon a counter-Reichstag to oppose a North German union to the imperial league were nullified by the unconquerable jealousy of the smaller courts, and above all by the arrogant opposition of his Guelph allies. The hour was not yet come for the abolition of German dualism, for the reconstitution of the empire ; but by the terrible reality of this war the obsolete ancient formalisms of the German community were morally annihilated, and the ultimate veil was stripped from the colossal lie of the Holy Empire. Never before had any emperor played so brainlessly with the fatherland as did this Loraine-Augustus, who threw open all the gates of Germany to foreign plunderers, surrendered the Netherlands to the Bourbons, and the eastern marches to the Muscovites. And while the emperor thus trampled his oath under foot, and himself deprived his house of all right to the German crown, there was played at Ratisbon the impudent farce of an appeal to the disciplinary powers of the imperial law. The Reichstag summoned the conqueror of Silesia in its antiquated formula, "By these presents must he, the said Elector, be guided" ; the Brandenburg envoy kicked the messenger of the illustrious assembly downstairs ; the eager but miserable imperial army assembled under the banner of the Bourbon enemy of the empire, to be instantly dispersed like chaff before the wind by the cavalry squadrons of Seydlitz. But the German nation loudly acclaimed the victor of Rossbach, the rebel against the emperor and the empire. With this barren satirical comedy the great tragedy of imperial history came in truth to its close ; what still remained of the old German community barely preserved henceforward even the semblance of life.

The victor, however, who amid the thunder of the battles had overthrown the ancient theocratic forms, was the official protector of Protestantism. However effete in this epoch of enlightenment might seem the ecclesiastical oppositions, Frederick nevertheless recognised that the essential content of the Peace of Westphalia, the equality of religious beliefs in the empire, would become untenable as soon as the two Catholic great powers should triumph ; the common cause of Protestantism afforded him the only stimulus with which he could urge the hesitating petty princes into the struggle against Austria. With a watchful eye, he followed the underground intrigues of the " prêtraille " at the Protestant courts ; it was his word of power that protected the freedom of the Protestant Church in Würtemberg and Hesse when in these states the successors to the crown went over to Rome. His smaller North German allies recognised even more clearly than did

Frederick himself the religious significance of the war. In the letters of F. A. von Hardenberg, minister of Hesse, the allies of Prussia were always spoken of plainly as the " Protestant Estates," and it is esteemed the natural policy of all the Protestant states of the empire to give their firm support to the Prussian party. The Prussian grenadier went into battle to the strains of Lutheran hymns ; the Protestant soldiers of the Swabian region dispersed with execrations, refusing to fight against their co-religionists ; in the conventicles of the English dissenters, godly ministers prayed on behalf of the Maccabeus of Holy Writ—Frederick, the free-thinker. The Pope, on the other hand, bestowed upon the empress's field-marshal a consecrated hat and sword, and every fresh news of Prussian victory aroused in the Vatican a storm of anti-pathy and fear. How crushed and fallen had the Protestant world lain before the feet of Rome a hundred and twenty years earlier, when the banners of Wallenstein were waving on the shores of the Baltic and when the Stuarts were endeavouring to subject parlia-ment to their Romish kingcraft. Now it was a Protestant great power which gave to the Holy Empire the death-blow, and by the battles on the Ohio and on the Ganges it was decided for all time that the dominion of the ocean and the colonies should belong to the Protestant Teutons.

The struggle for the existence of Prussia was the first truly European War ; it created the unity of the new comity of states and gave to that comity the aristocratic form of a pentarchy. When the new central European great power forced recognition from its neighbours the two ancient state-systems of the east and of the west were fused into an inseparable whole, and at the same time there was a decline in the importance of the less powerful states, which had formerly, at times, by their accession to a coalition, been able to decide the issue of a great war, but which were no longer competent to meet the demands of the new and more grandiose methods of war-making ; the states of the second rank must be satisfied henceforward to leave the conduct of European affairs to the great powers of land and sea. Of these five dominant powers, two were Protestant, and one was schismatic, so that it now remained unthinkable that Europe should ever pass back beneath the rule of the crowned priest. The establishment of the Protestant-German great power was the most serious reverse that the Roman See had experienced since the rise of Martin Luther. King Frederick had in truth, as the English ambassador Mitchell phrased it, been fighting for the freedom of the human race.

In the school of sorrows and of struggles the people of Prussia acquired a vivid sense of nationality, so that the king was justified in speaking of his *nation prussienne*. Before this time, to be a Prussian had been an arduous duty, but it now became an honour. The idea of the state, of the fatherland, arose in a million hearts to stimulate and to strengthen. Even the oppressed spirit of the common man could appreciate a flavour of the classical citizen-sense that was expressed in the blunt words of the king : " It is not necessary that I should live, but it is necessary that I should do my duty to the country and fight for the fatherland." Throughout Prussia, beneath the stiff forms of the absolute monarchy, there flourished the self-sacrifice and the great passion of the people's war. The army which fought Frederick's last battles was a national army ; the exigencies of the time had forbidden recruiting in foreign lands. The estates of the Mark voluntarily entered those regiments which saved for the nation the fortresses of Magdeburg, Stettin, and Küstrin ; the seamen of Pomerania assembled with their little fleet to hold the mouths of the Oder against Sweden. During six years the officials received no pay, and quietly went on with their work as if it were a matter of course. In zealous competition, all the provinces did their sworn duty and fulfilled their sworn obligations, as it was expressed in the new Prussian manner of speech—all, from the brave peasants of the Rhenish County Mörs on the one side, to the unhappy East Prussians on the other, who opposed to the Russian conqueror their tough and passive resistance, and whose loyalty was undisturbed even when the pitiless king accused them of treachery and loaded them with proofs of his disfavour.

It was the nation-building power of war which first reawakened in these North German tribes that stubborn pride which had of old animated the German invaders of the Roman empire and the mediæval conquerors of the Slavs ; the active self-satisfaction of the Prussians contrasted strangely with the harmless and amiable modesty of the other Germans. Confidently Count Hertzberg refutes Montesquieu's doctrine of republican virtue. Where, he asks, in any republic can you find a finer and more thriving civic virtue than here under the steely skies of the north, in the offspring of those heroic nations of the Goths and Vandals who long ago shattered the Roman empire ? The same sentiment animated the mass of the people, shown now in arrant boasting, in the thousand mocking anecdotes that were current of imperial stupidity and Prussian military cunning, and now in the moving lineaments of conscientious loyalty. The young seaman Joachim Nettelbeck comes to Danzig and is hired to row the King of Poland across the harbour ; there is placed upon his head a hat, bearing the monogram of King Augustus ; for a long time he refuses to put it on, for it seems to him treason to his Prussian king to bear the sign of the foreign ruler; finally he yields, but the ducat that he earns seems to burn his hand, and directly he gets back to Pomerania he gives away the wages of sin to the first Prussian wounded soldier he encounters. So sensitive had now become the political pride of this people who a few decades before were utterly absorbed in their petty household cares.

It was impossible to ignore that to the two great captains of history, to Cæsar and Alexander, a companion must now be added, and that this companion was a Prussian. In the temperament of the North German people we find side by side with a remarkable staying-power a trait of inconsiderate rashness, which leads them to love playing with danger, and the Prussians found this characteristic of their own magnified to genius in their commander Frederick. They noted how, after a hard apprenticeship, having rapidly become a master-craftsman, he threw on one side the careful rules of the laborious ancient art of war, and himself "dictated the laws of war" to the enemy, always ready to seek decision in open battle. They noted how he restored cavalry, the rashest of all the arms, to its old position, proper to the great conduct of war. They noted how after every victory and also after each one of his three defeats he continued to maintain " the proud privilege of initiative." The result proved how happy was the understanding between king and people. A crowd of heroes surrounded their commander, diffusing through all ranks of the army that joyous love of adventure, that spirit of the offensive, which in all great periods of its history has remained the strength of the Prussian army. Out of the junkers of the Mark and the peasant-lads of Pomerania, Frederick created the dreaded regiments of the Ansbach-Beyreuth dragoons and the Zieten hussars, who in the fury of their charges and the shock of their onset soon excelled the savage horsemen of Hungary. As the king proudly expressed it, such soldiers knew nothing of risk : " A general who in other armies would be regarded as insane is with us simply a man who does his duty." The twelve campaigns of the Frederician epoch have impressed their own stamp for ever upon the warlike spirit of the Prussian people and of the Prussian army ; even to-day the North German, when war is discussed, involuntarily adopts the expressions of those heroic days, and speaks like Frederick of "brilliant campaigns" and "fulminating attacks."

The good-hearted amiability of the Germans outside Prussia rendered it necessary that a longer time should elapse before they could overcome their repulsion towards the hard realism of this Frederician policy, which unchivalrously chose the precise moment to attack an enemy when that attack was least welcome. But when the great year of 1757 came, victorious attack and serious defeat, new and audacious uprising and new and brilliant victories, followed one another with perplexing speed, and out of the welter of events the image of the king continually emerged ever great and dominant, the people was moved to its very marrow by the contemplation of true human greatness. The weather-beaten and hard-bitten figure of old Fritz, as it had been forged by the hammer-blows of pitiless destiny, exercised a magical charm upon countless loyal spirits, which had regarded with no more than a confused alarm the brilliant apparition of the youthful hero of Hohenfriedberg. The Germans were, as Goethe said of his Frankforters, Fritz-possessed—"for what had we to do with Prussia?" With suspended breath they watched how, from year to year, the unconquerable man saved himself from the forces of destruction. That overwhelming harmony of undivided love and joy which at times illumines as with a golden light the history of fortunate peoples, was indeed still denied to distracted Germany. Like Luther and Gustavus Adolphus, the only two earlier heroes whose image is ineradicably imprinted upon the memories of our people, in the crozier-ridden lands on the Rhine and the Main, Frederick also was feared as the great enemy. The enormous majority of Protestants, however, wide circles among the Catholics, and above all every advocate of the young science and art of the epoch, followed his career with ardent sympathy. People treasured his witty sayings, and recounted wonder upon wonder performed by his grenadiers and hussars. Yet the alarmed generation of his contemporaries was far from realising that this German was the first man of his century, and that the renown of the great king extended to Morocco and to America.

Few were as yet aware that the Prussian renown in battle was no more than a rejuvenescence of the primeval military glory of the German nation; even Lessing sometimes speaks of the Prussians as of a half-foreign people, and remarks with wonder, that heroic courage seems in them to be inborn as it was in the Spartans. Gradually, however, even the masses began to feel that Frederick was fighting for Germany. The battle of Rossbach, the *bataille en douceur*, as he mockingly terms it, was of all his victories the one that most powerfully influenced our national life. If in this nation of private individuals there still existed any political passion whatever, it was the tacit sentiment of bitterness against French arrogance which, so often chastised by the German sword, had still always maintained itself intact, and had now once more drenched the Rhineland with blood and tears. But now came Frederick with his good sword to encounter France, which was submerged in the waters of shame ; a loud shout of rejoicing arose from all parts of Germany, and Schubart the Swabian cried : " Then impetuously I seized the golden harp, thereon to sing Frederick's praises." It was then that once again the Germans throughout the empire experienced a feeling resembling national pride, and they sang with old Ludwig Gleim : " Germans let us be, and Germans let us remain ! " The French officers who returned to Paris from the German battle-fields were open in their praises of the victor of Rossbach, for it still seemed impossible to their pride that this little Prussia could ever seriously threaten the power of France ; but in the German comic drama to the once dreaded Frenchman was now sometimes allotted the role of butt and windy adventurer.

It is true that the nation still lacked a political understanding of the nature of Prussia. Alike in respect of the decisive facts of its recent history and in respect of the institutions of its most powerful state, this well-informed people lived in remarkable ignorance. When the victories of Frederick had to some extent mitigated the ancient hatred for Prussia, even in the Protestant lands of the empire every citizen continued to regard himself as fortunate because he was not a Prussian. The industrious fables of the Austrian party found everywhere willing listeners : " This free people," wrote Frederick Nicolai in 1780 from Swabia, " looks down upon us poor Brandenburgers as slaves." The attractive energy of the powerful state exercised itself only upon strong and aspiring natures. From the Frederician days onwards there was a steady stream of youthful talent carrying men out of the empire into the Prussian service : some were impelled by admiration for the king, and some by a longing for a wider field of activity ; but many had also an obscure intimation of the significance of this throne. The monarchy had now completely outgrown the narrow-mindedness of territorial life, gladly took to itself all the healthy energies of the empire, and found among the circles of the immigrants many of its most loyal and capable servants—found there also its saviour, Stein.

With the Treaty of Hubertusburg there began for the German north a period of forty years of profound quiet, that richly blessed epoch of peace upon which Goethe in his old age so often looked back with grateful emotion. The old tradition of the poverty of Prussia began to seem fabulous. Social life, especially in the capital city, assumed richer and freer forms ; the popular well-being underwent a remarkable increase, and the great years of German literature began. The position of the empire had been at once simplified and rendered more difficult by the war. All that remained alive of the old order was the unsolved opposition of the two great powers. The premonition of a day of painful decision went through the German world ; the lesser courts engaged in busy negotiations, seeking to protect themselves by the formation of a federation of the minor powers, in the event of their being endangered by a new concussion " between the two colossi of Germany." King Frederick, however, thoroughly instructed as to the unending force of sloth in this ancient empire, was satisfied to devote himself to the reconstitution of the exhausted energies of his own state ; the aims of his German policy were henceforward merely these, to obviate the working of any foreign influence upon the empire, and to maintain an effective counterpoise against the power of Austria.

A serious danger which threatened the German power from the east disturbed his peaceful plans. Since the war the Polish republic had been subject to the will of the Czarina, and the formal union of the distracted state with the Russian empire seemed only a question of time. Thereupon Frederick conceived the idea of the partition of Poland, which ran counter to the Russian views, setting limits to Russia's ambition. It was a victory of German diplomacy at once over the unending land-hunger of Russia and over the powers of the west which were pushed relentlessly aside by the straightforward procedure of the powers of the east. The necessary deed unquestionably opened a prospect of incalculable complications, for the corrupt realm of the Sarmatian nobles now pursued its path towards hopeless extinction ; but it was necessary, for it rescued the loyal land of East Prussia from the return of the Muscovite dominion, and secured for the state that connecting link between the region of the Pregel and the region of the Oder which, as crown prince, Frederick had already recognised as indispensable for Prussia. For the second time the king was the Augmenter of the Empire, restoring to the great fatherland the nuclear region of the power of the Teutonic Knights, the beautiful valley of the Vistula which, in days long gone by, the German Knights had won from the barbarians, and the German peasantry from the rage of the elements. When the estates of West Prussia in the refectory of the High Master's castle at Marienburg " swore fealty to the re-established dominion " (to quote the phrase used on the commemorative medals), atonement was made for the wrong done to this German land by the overweening ambition of the Poles and by the treason of feudal licence. The struggle of five centuries between the Germans and the Poles for the possession of the Baltic shore was decided in favour of Germany.

The state, still bleeding from the wounds of the last war, had now to begin the arduous labour of peaceful reconquest. Horribly had the Sarmatian nobility infested the land of the Vistula, exhibiting that contemptuous disregard of foreign rights and foreign nationality which has ever distinguished the Poles from the other nations of Europe. Even more vigorously than formerly in Silesia, must the conqueror now comport himself in order to restore the German system to repute in the ancient and honourable cities once renowned for German military fame and German civic industry, in Schwetz, Kulm, and Marienburg ; to re-institute in the devastated country the first beginnings of economic life. Just as in former days the first German conqueror had wrested from the waters the corn lands of the inter-riverine district, so now there arose from the marches around the flourishing Bromberg the creation of the second conqueror, the industrious region of the Netzegau. Frederick himself had but an obscure vision of the significance to the great course of German history of this re-acquirement of the Ordensland, whilst the nation had become estranged from its own past, and hardly realised that these districts had ever been German. Some, with the acid obscurity of the moral platitudinarian, censured the diplomatic intrigue which had led to the alienation of the land ; others repeated credulously the fables circulated by the French, the ancient allies of the Poles, in order to stamp as infamous the powers that effected the partition ; most of them remained cold and indifferent, finding merely a new reason for acceptance of the current view that old Fritz was possessed by the devil. Not a soul in the empire gave him any thanks for the new benefit he had bestowed upon our people.

The restless ambition of Emperor Joseph II made it necessary for the king in the evening of his life to return to those ideas of imperial policy which had occupied his youth. The court

of Vienna abandoned the conservative attitude which alone could
preserve in the empire any regard for the imperial house and undertook to compensate itself in Bavaria for the loss of Silesia ; the
whole course of Austrian history for the last two centuries, the
continuous development of the imperial state outward from the
German realm, was suddenly to be reversed by a wild internal adventure.   Thereupon for the second time King Frederick made an
alliance with the Wittelsbachs, and with the might of the sword
forbade the House of Austria to increase its power upon German
soil ; more sharply and clearly than ever before did the contrast
between the two rivals become manifest in the light of day.   The
war of the Bavarian succession exhibits at once in its military aspects
and in its political aims many remarkable similarities with the
decisive war of 1866 ; but the former campaign was undertaken,
not to free Germany from the dominion of Austria, as was the case
when Prussia drew the sword three generations later, but merely
to repel Austrian aggression, to maintain the *status quo*.   Although
the ageing hero no longer possessed the audacity to enable him to
carry into effect his campaign on the great lines in which it was
conceived, none the less the power of Prussia was sufficient to compel
the Viennese court to give way.   For the second time Bavaria
was saved, the proud imperial court must stoop " to plead before
the tribunal of Berlin," and the embittered Prince Kaunitz uttered
that prophecy which upon the field of Königgrätz was to find
fulfilment in the opposite sense from that intended by the prophet :
if ever Austria and Prussia were again to cross swords, these swords
would not be sheathed " until the matter had been fought to a
manifest, complete, and irrevocable issue."   Hardly less valuable
than the immediate result was the powerful revolution of opinion
in the empire.   The dreaded disturber of the peace, the rebel against
emperor and empire, now seemed to the nation the wise protector
of the law ; the smaller courts, which had so often trembled before
the sword of Prussia, now terrified by the restless scheming of the
Emperor Joseph, looked for rescue to the arbiter in Sans Souci.
In the farms of the Bavarian Alps, side by side with the picture of
the popular saint Corbinian, there was hung that of the old warrior
with the three-cornered hat.   In the chorus of the Swabian and
North German poets which sang the king's fame there were now
mingled a few voices from the profoundly hostile Electoral Saxony ;
the bard Ringulph related in enraptured odes how " from the
bosom of the Almighty, King Frederick, has issued thy great soul
rejoicing in battle."   Not long before K. F. Moser had said that

it was impossible for the vision of the ordinary man to follow this eagle in his flight, but perchance there would some day arise a Newton of political science who could measure the paths of the Frederician policy. For the Germans began to perceive that this enigmatic policy had, after all, been wonderfully and essentially simple, that Frederick the statesman, devoid alike of hatred and of love, utterly free from personal feeling, had always sought that alone which was clearly demanded by the situation of his state.

When the War of Independence broke out in North America and the enlightened world joyfully hailed the new sun that was rising in the west, Frederick, too, did not conceal his pleasure. To his youthful great power a yet newer state elbowing its way into the circle of the ancient powers was heartily welcome. He was glad to see this England, which had so shamefully betrayed him in the last war, and which during the Polish negotiations had prevented his acquiring Danzig, now herself in a painful quandary. He declared openly that he would not for a second time defend Hanover for ungrateful England ; he even once forbade the passage of the English accessory troops hired in Germany, because this unclean trade in men enraged him, and still more because he needed the young men of the empire for his own army. He took advantage of the need of the Queen of the Seas to preserve, through the federation of the armed neutral powers, the rights of the navies of the second rank. After peace had been declared he was the first among the European princes to conclude a commercial treaty with the young republic, thus manifesting that free and humane conception of international law which has ever since been a traditional characteristic of the Prussian state. But neither his hatred of the " goddam government," nor the outburst of popular favour which was displayed towards him in the colonies, ever induced him to take a single step beyond what was demanded by the interest of his own state. His ancient enemy Kaunitz might continue to explain the brilliant course of the Frederician policy as the outcome of the incalculable cunning of a demoniacal nature. In the empire, however, the old mistrust gradually passed away ; the nation observed that nowhere were its opportunities considered with such calm and deliberate attention as in the palace of Sans Souci.

Thus it was that the unheard-of came to pass, that the high nobility of the empire of their own free will worked assiduously under Frederick's banner. The Emperor Joseph resumed his old Bavarian plan, intending to shatter the power of Prussia ; at the same time, by a hastily conceived design of secularisation, he threatened the status of his spiritual neighbours. A spasm of alarm seized the smaller states, who thus saw their natural protector become their enemy. There was talk of a federation of the central powers and of a league of the spiritual princes, until at length they were forced to recognise that they could do nothing without the help of Prussia. With youthful fire the aged king threw himself into the struggle. All the alluring appeals that were made to him to unite with the emperor in order to divide the ownership of Germany he scornfully rejected as appeals to " common covetousness " ; he controlled his contempt for the petty princes, recognising that it was only by strict justice that he could bind *ces gens-là* to his side. He succeeded in securing the great majority of the council of electors and most of the more powerful rulers on behalf of his league of German princes, so as to maintain against the emperor the ancient imperial constitution and the *status quo* of the estates of the empire. " It is only my love for the fatherland and my duty as a good citizen," he wrote, " which drives me in my old age into this new undertaking." The dreams of his youth were brilliantly fulfilled in the days of his old age. No longer hidden behind a Bavarian shadow-emperor as in the Silesian Wars, but with visor raised, the crown of Prussia now took the stage as the protector of Germany. All the neighbouring powers, which had counted on Germany's weakness, noted with alarm the unexpected crisis in German affairs : France and Russia drew nearer to the Viennese court, and there was danger that the alliance of 1756 would be reconstituted. The cabinet of Turin, on the other hand, hailed the League of Princes with joy as " the tutelary deity of the Italian states."

The policy of federalism had during two centuries never got beyond the stage of half-beginnings, but now that it was supported by the power of the Prussian state it suddenly achieved a striking success. The memory of the times of Maximilian I and of the reform proposals of the Elector Berthold was revived. The League of Princes was determined to preserve the ancient imperio-feudal-theocratic Germany. But as affairs progressed, and when Prussia maintained her leadership of the great estates of the empire, the old forms of the imperial law necessarily became devoid of meaning. The prospect was opened of the complete overthrow of the Austrian system. As Count Hertzberg joyfully exclaimed, there was hope of excluding the Archdukes from the great German fellowship, of transferring the imperial crown at the next election to another house, and of placing the leadership of the empire in the hands of the mightiest of all the estates. The young Charles Augustus of Weimar had already resolved to subject to the examination of the empire those ancient privileges which secured for the House of Austria its peculiar position of authority. It almost seemed as if the great problem of the future of Germany was to find a peaceful solution. But the League of Princes could not endure, and this bitter truth was manifest above all to the sober sense of the old king. Only a concatenation of fortunate circumstances, only the departure of the Emperor Joseph from the traditional methods of Austrian statecraft, had thrown the petty princes into the arms of Frederick; their confidence in Prussia extended only so far as it was forced on them by their dread of Austria. It was with the utmost reluctance that Electoral Saxony accepted the leadership of the younger and less distinguished House of Brandenburg; Hanover was hardly less distrustful; even the most devoted and the weakest of the federated estates, Weimar and Dessau, were secretly taking counsel, so we learn from Goethe, how they could best protect themselves against the dominion of their Prussian protector. Directly the Hofburg abandoned its greedy designs it was inevitable that the old and natural division of parties should be re-established, that the spiritual princes now seeking help from Berlin should once more regard Protestant Prussia as simply the sworn enemy of their rule. Since Frederick knew this, since he knew his faithful allies to the very marrow of their bones, he was under no illusions as to the prospects of the affair, and was well aware that this new League of Schmalkald was only a temporary help, a means for the momentary preservation of an equilibrium. Charles Augustus, in generous enthusiasm, was drawing up bold plans for the structure of the new imperial association, and thinking of a customs-union, of military agreements, and of a German legal code; Johannes Müller was glorifying the League of Princes in fulsome pamphlets, and Schubart was singing its praises in ardent lyric effusions; Dohm, in an inspired memoir, came to the conclusion, "there can never be any conflict between German and Prussian interests." The cool reason of the king was uninfluenced by such dreams as these; he knew that nothing but a terrible war could overthrow the Austrian rule in the empire; it sufficed him to prevent Austria from exceeding her legal power, for he needed peace for his country.

All the necessary conditions were still lacking for a serious reform of the empire; and above all there was lacking the will of the nation. The imperial-patriotic protagonists of the League of Princes did not get beyond the ancient illusions of German freedom. The Josephan policy, Hertzberg assures us in moving terms, threatened to roll together the energies of Germany into a single mass, and to subject free Europe to a universal monarchy, whilst in the eyes of Dohm it seemed a praiseworthy aim of the new league to keep open the western frontiers of Austria so that France might at any time be able to come to the aid of German freedom. The people perceived darkly that the existing order was not worthy to exist ; in the writings of Schubart the small Swabian territories are often depicted as an open dovecot, just under the claws of the princely marten. But all such views and intimations were held in check by a sentiment of hopeless resignation such as the more active-minded present finds it difficult to understand ; it seemed to the German as if an unsearchable hidden destiny had condemned this people to vegetate for all eternity in a futile state of affairs, which had long lost every right to existence. When the great king departed he left, indeed, a generation of men whose outlook on the world was happier and prouder than had been that of their fathers ; there had been an enormous increase in the power of that state which might at some future time lead Germany to a new day. But the question by what ways and means a really living order might be created for the German community, seemed at the death of Frederick almost as insoluble as it had seemed when he ascended the throne ; and indeed the great majority of Germans made no serious effort to seek a solution. There hardly existed as yet the first beginnings of a national party ; and to those without counsel it seemed as if only a miracle could bring help. The horrible confusion of everything is most conspicuously displayed by the simple fact that the hero who had once used his good sword to prove the nullity of the institutions of the empire, must now spend the evening of his days in the defence of these exanimate forms against the very head of the empire.

If it were possible to Frederick merely to pave the way for a solution of the German constitutional problem, if he were forced to leave this task unfinished, he was able, on the other hand, to exercise a deep and lasting influence upon the internal politics of the German territories, and to educate our people to a nobler sense of the state, to a worthier view of its nature. He came at the end of the great days of absolute monarchy, and seemed to his contemporaries the representative of a new conception of the state, that of benevolent despotism. Propagandist energy is the peculiar privilege of genius ; genius alone is competent to assemble a reluctant world beneath the banner of new ideas. Just as the ideas of the Revolution were first effectively diffused by Napoleon, so also was that serious conception of the duties of kingship, which since the days of the Great Elector had been dominant on the Prussian throne, transmitted first by Frederick to the general consciousness of mankind. It was the brilliant results of the Silesian Wars which had turned the attention of the world, hitherto admiringly fixed on the courtly magnificence of Versailles, to contemplate with a profounder consideration the unadorned crown of the Hohenzollerns. In war and in foreign policy the king displayed the incomparable creative force of his spirit, in internal administration he was the son of his father. He animated the traditional forms of the state with the energy of genius, completing the incomplete freely and greatly ; but he undertook no entirely new construction. Yet Frederick was able to bring into conformity with the culture of the century, those ideas of political kingship which his father had realised as a hard-handed practical man ; unceasingly he manifested his activity both to himself and others. When still crown prince he had acquired a place among the political thinkers of the age ; despite all its faults of youthful unripeness his *Anti-Machiavel* is nevertheless the best and profoundest work that has ever been penned concerning the duties of the princely office in an absolute monarchy. Subsequently, in the first flush of victory, he wrote the *Fürstenspiegel* for the young Duke of Würtemberg. Yet more powerful than all theory was the evidence of his deeds, for in the days of trial he followed his own precepts, showing the world what it means " to think, to live, to die as a king." Finally, he received also that favour at the hands of destiny which even genius needs if it is to impress its stamp on an entire generation ; he had the good fortune to live on into a ripe old age. He was now the Nestor, the accepted leader, of European princes ; his fame drew the gaze of all the thrones, and from his words and his works other kings could learn how to think greatly of their own calling.

The traditional view of the petty princeling, that land and people were the personal property of the sublimely estimable princely house, fell into disrepute after the dry remark of the king : " The prince has no relatives nearer than his state, whose interests must always take precedence of the claims of kin." The overweening dynastic egoism of the Bourbons was displayed in all its vanity when Frederick, on mounting the throne, had turned his back upon the light pleasures of life with the words, " My only

God is my duty," when for half a century he had been serving this one god with all the forces of his soul, and when to every grateful utterance of his people he made the same quiet answer, " That is why I am here." Never before had a monarch spoken so frankly of the princely dignity, as did this autocrat, who recognised without reserve the right to existence of the republic as well as of the constitutional kingdom, and who sought the greatness of absolute monarchy only in the arduousness of its duties, saying : " The prince must be the head and heart of the state ; he is the supreme chief of the civic faith of his country."

The coming generation of the high nobility formed itself after Frederick's model, and in accordance with the philanthropic ideas of the new enlightenment. The petty sultans of the days of Frederick William I were succeeded by a long series of well-disposed fathers of their country, men true to duty, such as Charles Frederick of Baden and Frederick Christian of Saxony. It became common for the princes to receive a military education after the Prussian manner ; ecclesiastical toleration, furtherance of the public well-being and of the schools, were regarded as princely duties ; in some of the smaller states, as in Brunswick, the freedom of the press became yet greater than in Prussia. Even in certain spiritual provinces there was a tendency to improvement, and Münster could value the gentle and careful administration of its Fürstenberg. Not everywhere, indeed, nor in a moment, could the ingrained errors of the petty princely despotism be eradicated ; the old immorality of the trade in soldiers reached its climax during the American War to show of what the German minor princes were capable. The Frederician system of seeking the happiness of the people as a gift from above was apt to lead in the narrow domains of the lesser states to empty play-acting or to oppressive tutelage. The Margrave of Baden spoke of his council as "The natural guardian of our subjects " ; many a well-meaning lordling maltreated his tiny state by the imposition of the new-fashioned physiocratic system of taxation, and by all kinds of unripe philanthropic experiments ; whilst the princely state-directory of Oettingen-Oettingen must provide the inquisitive ruler with precise information concerning the " name, breed, use, and outward characteristics " of all dogs within his domain, together with innumerable additional servile reports. On the whole, however, the princely generation of the eighties was the most honourable that for long had occupied the German thrones. Wherever he could, the king opposed the excesses of his fellows, liberating the aged Moser from prison, and securing the Würtembergers in the possession of their constitution. The condition of the empire as a whole was hopeless, but in many of its members a new and hopeful life began to pulsate.

Moreover, the example of Frederick exercised its influence far beyond the German borders. Maria Theresa became his aptest pupil, diffusing in the Catholic world the ideas of the Frederician monarchy. The old Austria, surrounded by weak neighbours, had hitherto passed its time in a careless slumber, and it was the growth in strength of its ambitious northern neighbour which first forced the imperial state to undertake a vigorous development of its energies. Haugwitz, the North German, transformed the Austrian administration in accordance with the Prussian model, in so far as this was possible, and from these Austrian reforms enlightened despotism elsewhere now learned its lesson, so that in all the lands of Latin civilisation, in Naples and Tuscany, in Spain and Portugal, there began restless endeavours for the forcible imposition of popular happiness. The pride of the French Bourbons held out longest against the new conception of monarchy, and with mocking laughter it was related at Versailles that at Potsdam the court chamberlain never handed the king his shirt. Not until it was too late, not until the Revolution was already knocking at the door, did the French monarchy begin to have some inkling of its duties. The Bourbons never fully emerged from the vain notion of courtly self-deification and contempt for mankind, hence their shameful fall. Among the Germans, on the other hand, the monarchical sentiment which was in our people's very blood, and which had never completely decayed during the centuries of feudal polyarchy, was reinvigorated by King Frederick. In no other nation of modern history was the task of kingship understood in so great and lofty a sense, and for this reason the German people remained, even when the time of the parliamentary struggle arrived, the most monarchical in sentiment among all the great civilised nations.

The love of peace of the House of Hohenzollern remained active even in the greatest of its warrior-princes. Power was prized by Frederick as no more than a means to secure the well-being of the nations and to spread civilisation among them. It seemed to him an injury to princely honour to conceive that power could ever become an end in itself, that the struggle for power for its own sake could ever bring historic fame. It was for this reason that he wrote his passionate polemic against Machiavelli. It was for this reason that in his writings he returned again and again to the repellent example of Charles XII of Sweden. He was perhaps secretly aware that within his own breast elemental forces were at work which might lead him to similar aberrations, was never weary of depicting the vanity of aimless warlike renown, and in the circular hall at Sans Souci he had the bust of the King of Sweden placed contemptuously at the feet of the Muses. Even in the salad days of his youth he was perfectly clear as to the moral aims of power. " This state," he then wrote, " must become strong so that it may be able to play the fine role of maintaining peace solely out of the love of justice, and not by inspiring fear. But if in Prussia it should ever happen that injustice, partisanship, and vice should gain the upper hand, I should hope to see the headlong fall of the House of Brandenburg." When, at the close of the Seven Years' War, he felt himself strong enough to maintain peace by justice, he devoted himself so zealously to the restoration of the popular well-being, that the army actually suffered in consequence.

This is literally true. The military commander, who had brought Prussia so many laurels, left the Prussian army in a worse condition than that in which he had found it on ascending the throne, and as a military organiser was not the equal of his rough father. He needed diligent workers to restore his devastated country, and it was therefore a principle with him to favour foreign recruiting for the maintenance of the army. The regimental commanders must draw up their cantonal lists in conjunction with the local administrators, and from the time this arrangement was instituted there occurred annually in every district that conflict between military demands and civic interests which, under changing forms, continued to manifest itself throughout the history of Prussia. On this occasion the contest was decided in favour of the needs of the popular economy. The civic authorities endeavoured to save every vigorous and capable youth from the red stock of the cantonist. The king himself intervened on this side, liberating from the duty of military service numerous classes of the population, such as immigrants, the families of all those engaged in industry, the servants of landlords. A number of towns, and even entire provinces, such as East Frisia, received special privileges. Soon after the peace, the army came to be more than half composed of foreigners. Frederick took a high view of the army, loved to speak of it as the Atlas which carried the state upon its strong shoulders ; the fame of the Seven Years' War still continued to produce its effect, so that service as a common soldier, although in Prussia as everywhere else it was regarded as a misfortune, was not here, as elsewhere in the empire, considered a disgrace. The king brought the great summer manœuvres on the heath of Mockerau to a degree of technical perfection which has probably never been attained in the sequel; he never ceased to urge his officers " to love detail, which is also a work of glory " ; and he wrote for their instruction his military manuals, the ripest of all his works. No advance in military matters escaped his glance ; even when a very old man he constructed the new arm of light infantry, the green fusiliers, after the model of the American riflemen. The fame of the Potsdam drill-ground drew spectators from every country ; in Turin, Victor Amadeus and his generals carefully imitated every movement of the great Prussian drill-sergeant, even to the bent position of the head ; and when the young Lieutenant Gneisenau saw the pointed morions of the grenadiers on parade sparkling in the sun, he cried out with enthusiasm, " Which among all the peoples of the world can show such a wonderful sight as this ? "

Yet it is unquestionable that in Frederick's later years the efficiency of the army declined. The flower of the old officers' corps lay upon the battle-fields; during the Seven Years' War—and this is without example in the history of warfare—with very few exceptions all the notable generals had either been killed or permanently disabled. Those who now came to the front had learned war only as subalterns, and they sought the secret of the Frederician victories in the manual exercises of the drill-ground. Among the foreign officers, there were many adventurers of dubious character. Advancement was sought by favour, and there was no place for the proud courage of a York or a Blucher. The king, less friendly towards the bourgeoisie than his father, believed that only the nobleman was a man of honour, and cashiered most of his bourgeois officers. In the noble officers' corps there arose a junker sentiment which became yet more intolerable to the people than had been the unrestrained roughness of earlier days. The enlisted veterans ultimately came to live in civic occupation, in comfort with their wives and families, and detested the thought of active service for a country in which they remained foreigners. Already in the war of the Bavarian succession Frederick noted with annoyance how little this army could do, but the explanation of the failure eluded his observation. The eudæmonism of his epoch led him to misunderstand the moral energies of the military system. At one time, in accordance with the custom of his day, he had formed

Prussian regiments of Austrian and Saxon prisoners-of-war, and not even the numerous desertions of these unfortunates could teach him that he was wrong. In the latest years of the war he had had abundant evidence of what an army of the children of the country was able to effect, and yet this powerful appeal to the united energy of the nation was always regarded by him as a temporary resource for days of especial need, " now that the protection of the fatherland is in question and that danger is extremely pressing." Among his statesmen, Hertzberg alone held sacred the bold ideas of Frederick William I, who had desired gradually to purge his army of all foreigners, " for then we shall become invincible like the Greeks and the Romans." But the venerable king saw with gratification the economic progress of his unhappy country, and he described his ideal of a military system in the extraordinary words : " The peaceful citizen should be altogether unaware of the fact when the nation is at war." Thus one of the pillars supporting the state structure, the idea of universal military service, was slowly crumbling away.

The traditional subdivision of classes, and the organisation of labour which rested thereon, were maintained by the king even more strictly than they had been by his father ; whenever the peasant, the burgher, the nobleman seemed to him no longer adequate for his part in the national economy, he gave help by instruction and by relentless coercion, by presents and by loans. The noble must remain the first estate of the realm, for " I need him for my army and for my national administration." By the mortgage institutions, and by notable contributions in hard cash, Frederick succeeded in " preserving " the landed property of the nobles after the devastation of the years of war. Hence he dared as little as his father to attempt to carry into practice that complete liberation of the country-folk to which his great mind aspired. It is true that by the common law the crude form of serfdom was abolished, but the only slightly less oppressive hereditary subordination was everywhere maintained. The administration was content to mitigate in certain details the severities of the existing class-rule. Unnoticed and undesired by the ageing prince, there was beginning a significant transformation in the relationships of social power. The new literature was producing a cultured public as a compost of all the classes ; the merchants and industrials of the great towns, the bourgeois leaseholders of the extensive crown-lands, gradually attained a secure state of well-being and a vigorous self-consciousness, and could not permanently tolerate the privileges of the nobles. The nobleman lost, little by little, at once the moral and the economic foundations of his dominant position. The structure of the ancient class-subdivisions was undermined unawares.

The administrative organisation of the father also remained unchanged under the son, the only difference being, that to the provincial departments of the general directory he added four new sections, dealing with the entire state, and concerned respectively with war, commerce, mining, and forestry, thus making a step further in the direction of the unified state. The crown continued to stand high above the people. Country dragoons were instructed to supervise the peasantry in the use of the seed potatoes presented by the king; by an order of the Landrat and of the Chamber, compulsion was used to overcome the vigorous passive resistance of those concerned, against the new communal division, against the irrigation schemes, against all advances in agricultural technique. The completely exhausted spirit of enterprise of urban industry could be re-established only by the forcible methods of the prohibitive system. The errors of the Frederician economic policy lay, not in the zeal of the administration for the happiness of the people (a zeal which made light of obstacles, but for which the time was not yet ripe), but in the fiscal artifices which were forced upon the king by his financial needs. He was compelled to utilise three-fourths of his regular expenditure upon the army, and he endeavoured to balance his budget by the use of monopolies and of indirect taxes. In its lack of elasticity, the financial system still resembled that of a private household ; nearly half of the regular income was derived from the royal demesnes and the forests. The high expenditure of the state was rendered possible only by its extensive territorial possessions, which served also for the technical education of the country people. The maximum of the principal taxes being established by law, for the extraordinary expenses of domestic colonisation and reclamation recourse must be had to the expansible yield of the public administration of utilities. The carefully guarded war-chests sufficed for a few brief campaigns ; but it was impossible for Prussia to conduct a long and arduous war without the aid of foreign subsidies, for the rights of the diets, the traditional views of officialdom, and the immaturity of the national economy, forbade recourse to governmental loans. Notable as was the increase in civic welfare, progress in this respect was less rapid than among the more fortunately situated neighbouring peoples. The Prussian state always remained the poorest of the great powers of the west, essentially an agricultural country, and one which played a very modest part in world commerce, even after Frederick, by the acquisition of East Frisia, had opened access to the North Sea. The harbours of the Ems and of the Oder lacked the possession of a wealthy industrial hinterland.

As a reformer Frederick was active in that province only of the internal life of the state which his predecessor had failed to understand. As regards the administration of justice, almost the only service rendered by Frederick William had been an apt transformation of the mortgage system. His son created the new Prussian judiciary, just as his father had brought into being the modern German executive officialdom. He knew that the administration of justice is a political duty inseparable from the state : throughout all his dominions he secured the complete independence of the imperial courts ; instituted a ministry of justice side by side with the general directory ; placed the entire administration of justice in the hands of a hierarchially ordered state officialdom, which trained its own successors, and which exercised a rigid supervision over the private judicial authorities that still existed in the lowest ranks of the magistracy. There was a promise of the unconditional independence of the courts vis-à-vis the administration, and such independence was in practice secured except as regards a few instances of judicial power arbitrarily but benevolently exercised by the royal cabinet. The new judiciary, though not very highly paid, preserved an honourable sense of its duties ; and whilst the courts of the empire displayed venality and partisanship, in Prussia the proud saying was justified (even against the king's will) *il y a des juges à Berlin* To the youth of the age of enlightenment, who regarded the state as a construction of the human will consciously working towards a definite end, it was a self-evident desire that the state must not be something fixed and traditional in character, but that it must be dominated by a consciously conceived and purposive system of law ; all through his life it was Frederick's idea to effect the first comprehensive codification of the law which had been undertaken since the time of Justinian. Not till after his death, did the system of civil law come into operation which manifests more plainly than any other work of this epoch the Janus-head of the Frederician conception of the state. On the one hand the legal code is so careful to preserve the traditional social differences that the whole system of the laws was adapted to the ancient feudal division of classes, even preserving for the nobility a feudal marriage law in conflict with the common law; on the other hand the code pushes the notion of state sovereignty so boldly to its ultimate consequences that many of its utterances anticipate the ideas of the French Revolution, leading Mirabeau to say that in this respect Prussia was a century in advance of the rest of Europe. The aim of the state is the general welfare; it is only in pursuit of this aim that the state may impose limitations upon the natural freedom of its citizens; but in pursuit of this aim it is also empowered to abolish all existing privileges. The king is no more than the chief of the state, and only as chief of the state does he possess rights and duties. Such were the views of the ruler of Prussia in the days in which Biener and other notable jurists were still maintaining as an incontestable legal principle the rights of the German princes as private owners of country and people. Consequently the authority of the state, placed above the domain of private rights, exercises an ordering and instructive influence in all private affairs, prescribes moral duties to parents and children, to masters and servants, endeavouring in its promethean legislative wisdom to provide for every possible legal dispute of the future.

This legal code marks the ultimate terms of the ancient absolutism : strict limits were imposed upon authority, and the community was raised to the level of a legal state. At the same time the code, inasmuch as it overthrew the dominion of Roman law, was unwittingly paving the way for a new legal unity of the German people. The mechanical state-idea of the Frederician days was soon superseded by a profounder and more far-seeing philosophy, the incomplete juristic culture of Carmer and Suarez was replaced by the work of historical jurisprudence ; but for many decades the civil code remained the powerful foundation upon which all further reforms of the Prussian state were erected. Among the officials, as among the people, the belief in the dominion of law, a belief which is the pre-condition of all political freedom, became a living force. If the state existed in order to secure the general well-being it followed by an inevitable necessity (although Frederick himself failed to see this) that the privileges of the dominant castes should be abrogated and that the nation should participate in the conduct of public affairs. Sooner or later this conclusion would have to be drawn, for even now, in the enlarged domains of state activity, only a supply of talented human energies could prove adequate for the severe tasks which the kingship was undertaking.

Far less effectually did Frederick work on behalf of the intellectual life of his people. We know, indeed, from Goethe's memoirs how the heroic episodes of the Seven Years' War exercised upon German culture a fertilising and liberating influence, how in those years of renown in arms a sense of national existence, an enlarging sentiment of vital energy, came to animate the exhausted field of poetry ; how the poverty-stricken speech of the country, which had long been stammeringly attempting the expression of exuberant feelings, now at length escaped from dulness and emptiness, to find the great expression for the great idea. It was within sound of the drums of the Prussian war camp that the first German comedy, *Minna von Barnhelm*, was written. In this wonderful spiritual awakening the people of Prussia took an extensive share, providing for the literary movement several of its pioneer figures, from Winckelmann to Hamann and Herder. Interpermeated with the Prussian spirit was the new and maturer form of Protestantism which ultimately emerged victoriously from the thought-struggles of this fermenting epoch to become a common heritage of the North German people—I refer to the Kantian ethics. It was only upon this soil of Protestant freedom that the categorical imperative could flourish, only here that was conceivable that work of renunciation and faithfulness to duty. Where in former days rough commands had enforced silent obedience, there was now to be seen the evocation of a free-spirited assent by the image of the king who built fearlessly upon the power of the investigating understanding, and who willingly recognised that he who reasons best goes farthest. Frederick carried on in the freest sense the ancient Prussian policy of toleration in matters of belief, incorporating in his legal code the principle, " ideas of God and of divine things cannot be the object of legal compulsion." Nor did the free-thinker abandon the attempts towards religious union that had been made by his predecessors, but insisted that the two Protestant Churches should not refuse to one another in case of need the community of the sacraments. The supreme episcopal authority which he claimed for his own crown, secured him against any state-hostile machinations on the part of the clergy, and even allowed him to tolerate that Society of Jesus which had recently been suppressed by the Pope. He secured for the press a freedom which was rarely limited, for " if newspapers are to be interesting they must work without interference." He declared all the schools to be " state institutions," and spoke gladly and with enthusiasm of the duty of the state to train the coming generation to independent thought and to self-sacrificing love of country. How often did he praise a renown for science and art as the finest ornament of the crown?

In this also he showed himself a true German and a prince of peace, in that he regarded a classical education as the source of all higher culture, whereas the soldier Napoleon preponderantly esteemed the exact sciences. Despite all this, the king exercised but little direct influence in the promotion of popular culture.

The exiguity of financial resources, the lack of efficient elementary school-teachers, and his incessant struggles, now with foreign enemies and now with domestic poverty, rendered it difficult for the king to carry his plans into execution; and ultimately the narrow utilitarianism of the father manifested itself also in the son. The thrifty-minded man found it easier to provide means for any other purpose than for that of popular instruction. When the Germans in the empire made a mock of the hungry Prussians, they thought above all of the Prussian professors. For the elementary schools the provision was extremely scanty ; for extensive areas in the country districts the rule of universal compulsory education, though continually made more stringent, remained in practice a dead letter. None of the Prussian universities attained the fame of the new Georgia Augusta University. Not until near the close of the Frederician epoch, when Zedlitz, the friend of Kant, undertook the control of the educational institutes, was a somewhat freer impulse given to the educational system. At that time the excellent Abbot Felbiger was improving the Catholic elementary schools, and found imitators in Austria and elsewhere in the empire, so that ultimately even Catholic Germany came to share in the finest blessings of the Reformation.

It seemed an easy matter to assemble in Berlin for abundant activities a brilliant circle of the best heads of Germany. Every young talent in the empire wished to develop under the eye of the national hero. Even Winckelmann, who had once in hatred shaken the dust of the Mark from his feet, now felt how strong were the bonds with which this state attached the hearts of its sons. " For the first time," he now wrote, " I hear the voice of the fatherland calling me." He burned with desire to show the Aristotle of the art of war that a native-born subject could do something worth doing, and for years was in treaty for a post at Berlin. At Frederick's French academy, however, there was no place for German thinkers. The Medicean days which had once been expected from the art-inspired prince of the Rheinsberg court of the Muses, were provided only for the foreign wits at the round table of Sans Souci ; the disciple of French culture had no understanding of the young life that was growing within the frame of his own people. Whilst Berlin society was intoxicating itself to excess in the ideas of the new literature, while mocking free-thought and artificialised pleasure-seeking were expelling the old rigid moral simplicity, the Prussian administration continued to retain its one-sided tendency towards the immediately useful. That intolerably stiff home-made and prosaic spirit which the old soldier-king had introduced into his state was mitigated by Frederick but not abolished ; it was only the baroque magnificence of the new palace and the mighty cupolas of the Gendarmenkirche which showed that there was proceeding a gradual modification in that barbaric hatred of culture which had characterised the thirties.

The Prussian state continued to give expression to one side only of our national life. The delicacy and the yearning, the profundity and the enthusiasm, of the German nature could not come to their rights in this sober-minded world. The focal centre of German policy did not become the home of the spiritual life of the nation ; the classical epoch of our poetry found its stage in the petty states. This significant fact is the key to many of the riddles of modern German history. To the cool and undetached attitude of King Frederick our literature owes the most precious of all its possessions, its incomparable freedom; but this indifference of the crown of Prussia during the days that were decisive as to the character of modern German culture, is also responsible for the fact that it long remained difficult for the heroes of German thought to understand the one truly living state of our people. After Frederick's death it was fully two decades before Prussia could give a hospitable reception to the intellectual forces of the new Germany ; and a considerably longer period must subsequently elapse before German science was able to recognise that it was of one blood with the Prussian state—that the state-constructive force of our people was rooted in the same vigorous idealism which had inspired German research and German art in its bold ventures.

Frederick's coldness towards German culture is unquestionably the most tragical, the most unnatural phenomenon in the long history of the passion of new Germany. The first man of the nation, the one who had re-awakened in the Germans the courage to believe in themselves, regarded from the outlook of a foreigner the finest and most characteristic works of his own nation ; there is surely no more expressive, no more shocking way of describing the slowness and difficulty with which this people of ours was able to shake off the dire heritage of the Thirty Years' War, the excessive power of foreign influences. Frederick was not, as had been

Henry IV of France, a loyal advocate of the national merits and defects ; he lacked Henry's understanding of the national temperament in every shade of its caprices. Two natures were at war within him. On the one hand he was the philosophical connoisseur, who rejoiced in the strains of music, in the sweet sounds of French verse, who regarded the fame of the poet as the greatest happiness on earth, who in honest admiration exclaimed to Voltaire : " To me the fortune of birth has given an empty appearance, but to thee every talent possible, and thine is the better part." On the other hand, he was the energetic North German, who stormed at his Brandenburger churls in the rough dialect of the Mark, to the hard people an image of warrior-courage, of restless labour, of iron strength. The French enlightenment of the eighteenth century suffers from the essential disease of a profound untruth, in that it possesses neither the desire nor the power to harmonise life with the ideal. People waxed enthusiastic regarding the sacred innocence of nature, whilst wallowing with delight in the most unnatural practices which had ever prevailed in the European world. They mocked the ridiculous chances of birth, dreamed of primitive freedom and equality, while indulging in the most uncontrolled contempt for mankind and in all the sweet sins of the old courtly society, satisfied with the hope that in some remote future reason would assert its sway over the ruins of the actual world of their day. At the Prussian court the talented and ill-conditioned Prince Henry was a true child of this culture : theoretically a contemner of that empty vapour which the mob term fame and greatness, but in practice a man of the hard reason of state, unscrupulous, an expert in all possible wiles and artifices.

Frederick, too, led after his own manner the double life of the men of the French enlightenment. It was his tragical destiny to think and to speak in two languages, of neither of which he had perfect command. To the youth intoxicated with beauty, the rude gibberish that was to be heard in his father's tobacco-parliament was as repugnant as were the obscure writings of over-refined pedantry with which he came into contact in the works of bigoted theologians ; for well or for ill he had to make use of this uncouth speech in discharging current affairs, now in a rough dialect, now in a stiff legal style. For the world of ideas fermenting in his head he could find worthy expression only in the tongue of cosmopolitan culture. He often admitted that his rough and bizarre muse spoke in a barbarous French, and in the recognition of this weakness he was apt to take too low an estimate of the artistic value and linguistic purity of his own verses. One thing at least among those which make the poet, a protean talent, was not lacking to him. His muse ranged over the entire gamut of moods. Now, in appropriate earnestness it could express the great and the sublime ; now again, in satiric caprice, tease and worry its victims with the malice of a Kobold—or, to say truth, with the mischievous waggery of a Berlin gutter-snipe. Yet it was a true feeling which taught him that the wealth of his soul failed to find such abundant and pure expression in his verses as in the tones of his flute ; the most tuneful expression, the ultimate profundity of sensation, were for the German unattainable in the foreign tongue.

The philosopher of Sans Souci never became truly at home in the foreign culture which he so ardently admired. In especial he was separated from his French associates by the strictness of his moral view of the world-order. The greatness of Protestantism consists in its imperious demand for the unity of thought and will, of the religious and of the moral life. Frederick's moral culture struck its roots too deeply into German Protestant life for him to escape a sense of the secret weakness of French philosophy. Frederick could adopt towards the Church an attitude more dis-passionate than was possible to Voltaire, the Catholic, who, in his *Henriade,* the evangel of the new toleration, finally comes to the conclusion that all respectable men must belong to the Roman Church. Frederick never bent his neck like Voltaire beneath religious forms which his conscience rejected, and could endure with the serene indifference of the born heretic the action of the Roman Curia in placing his works on the Index. Whilst he some-times condescends to describe philosophy as his passion, we recognise that with him consideration of the great problems of exist-ence is something of far more importance than a casual pastime ; after the manner of the ancients he seeks and finds in the thought-process the repose of the spirit at one with itself, the security of the soul that is lifted above all the vicissitudes of fate. After the aberrations of passionate youth, he early learned to exercise a forcible control over the tendency towards artistic softness and sensuality, which often impelled him to grasp at the pleasures of the moment. However boldly and disrespectfully doubt and mockery might course through his mind, he ever held firmly to the conception of the moral order of the world and to the thought of duty. The solemn earnestness of his life utterly consecrated to duty is separated by the heaven's breadth from the loose and fragile morality of the Parisian enlightenment. His writings, couched in a clear and precise style, which is sometimes trivial but never confused, are directed with persistent force of will towards a secure and determinate conclusion, and in the same way he desires to regulate his life in accordance with recognised truth. As far as is practicable in face of the resistance of a barbaric world he endeavours to secure for humaneness, which he terms the cardinal virtue of every thinking being, the dominion over state and society ; and he goes to meet death with the quiet conviction " that he leaves the world heaped over with his benefits."

Nevertheless it remained for ever impossible to him completely to overcome the division of his soul. The internal contradiction is manifest at the first glance in Frederick's mordant wit, which is so nakedly displayed because the hero, in his proud truthfulness, never dreamed of attempting to conceal it. The life of the man of genius is always impenetrable in its obscurity, and very rarely indeed is it so difficult to understand as in the wealth of this spirit thus cleft asunder. The king looks down with superior irony upon the flat ignorance of his Brandenburg nobility ; he draws a deep breath of relief when after the tedium of this dull society he can refresh himself in the company of the one man to whom he looks with admiration, the master of the tongue of the Gallic muses : yet at the same moment he feels what he owes to the trustworthy soundness of this rough race ; cannot find words enough in which to express his esteem for the high spirit, the fidelity, the honourable disposition of his nobles; and bridles his spirit of mocker when he contemplates the firm biblical faith of old Zieten. The French are his welcome guests for the pleasant hours of supper ; but his respect is given to the Germans. Not one of his foreign associates is so near to Frederick's heart as the " man of his soul," Winterfeldt, who maintained his German disposition even against his royal friend. Very frequently Frederick expresses in his letters his yearning for the new Athens on the banks of the Seine, and bewails the envy of unfavourable gods who have condemned the son of the Muses to rule over slaves in the Cimmerian region of winter ; and yet he shares without repining, just as did his father, the sorrows and labours of this poor people, glad at heart on account of the new life that was springing to existence under the hard hands of his peasants, exclaiming with pride : " I prefer our simplicity, and even our poverty, to that accursed wealth which destroys the worth of our race." Woe to the foreign poets when they take upon themselves to offer political counsel to the king ; severely and mockingly he then refers them to the limitations of their art.

However vividly, moreover, the ideas of the new France may occupy his mind, he is a great writer only when, in his French words, he is expressing German ideas, when in his political, military, and historical writings he is speaking as a German prince and commander. It was not in the school of the foreigner but through his own energy and through his own incomparable experience that Frederick became the first publicist of the eighteenth century, the one German who approached the state with creative critical faculty, and who spoke in the great style of the duties of the citizen. Never before in this denationalised race had anyone written of love of country with the same warmth and profundity as the author of the *Letters of Philopatros*. The ageing king no longer considered it worth while to descend from the altitude of his French Parnassus into the lowlands of German art, or to examine with his own eyes whether the poetic energy of his people had not at length been awakened. In his essay upon German literature, composed six years before his death, he recapitulates the ancient accusations of the ordinary Parisian critic against the undisciplined wildness of the German tongue, and dismisses with disdainful words the detestable platitudes of *Goetz von Ber-lichingen*—which he can hardly have read. And yet this very essay bears eloquent witness to the passionate national pride of the hero. He prophesies for the future of Germany an epoch of spiritual glory, the rays of whose sunrise were already illuminating those still blind to the light. Like Moses, he sees the promised land from afar off, and comes to the hopeful conclusion, " It may be that the last comers will excel all their predecessors ! " So near to his people, and yet so remote, so greatly estranged and yet so closely akin, was the great king of Germany.

The grand epoch of the old monarchy went down to its rest. Around the king it became ever quieter ; the heroes who had fought his battles, the friends who had laughed with him and shared his enthusiasms, sank one by one into the grave ; he was overwhelmed by solitude, the curse of greatness. He was accustomed to spare no human feeling ; for himself in former days all the wondrous dreams of his youth had been trampled under foot by his unpitying father. In his old age his inconsiderate strength took the form of an unyielding hardness. The serious-minded old man who in the scanty hours of his leisure walked alone with his greyhounds in the picture gallery of Sans Souci, or, heavy-hearted, in the round temple of his park, pondered memories of his dead sister, saw far below at his feet a new generation springing up of the petty children of man, ready to fear him and to obey, but not to give him their love. The excess of power of this one man lay as a heavy burden upon their spirits. When sometimes he still visited the Opera House, the opera and the singers seemed to wilt before the spectators ; everyone looked towards the place in the parterre where the lonely old man with his great severe eyes was sitting. When the news of his death came, a Swabian peasant, expressing the innermost thought of countless Germans, exclaimed: " Who is now to rule the world ? " Until his last breath was drawn all the energy of will of the Prussian monarchy continued to emanate from this single man ; the day of his death was the first rest-day of his life. His testament showed once again to the nation how different was the political kingship of the Hohenzollerns in its understanding of the kingly office from the petty courts of Germany : " In the moment of my death my last wishes will be for the happiness of this state ; may it be the happiest of all states through the mildness of its laws, the most just of all in its domestic administration, the most bravely defended of all by an army that lives only for honour and fame for noble deeds, and may this realm continue to flourish until the end of time ! "

A century and a half had passed away since, amid the ruins of the old empire, Frederick William had sought the first materials for the upbuilding of the new great power. A hundred thousand men of Prussia had found a hero's death, a colossal labour had been expended to establish in safety the new German kingship, and as the outcome of this frightful struggle there had at least been secured for the empire one abundant blessing—the nation once more found itself master on its own soil. For the Germans in the empire, life offered a consciousness of security which had long been lacking ; it seemed to them as if this Prussian had been predestined to cover with his shield against all foreign disturbers the peaceful work of the nation ; without this powerful sentiment of civic security our German poetry would not have found the joyful spirit necessary for great creation. Public opinion began gradually to reconcile itself with the state that had grown up against the public will ; people accepted it as a necessity of German life without troubling themselves much about its future. The difficult problem as to how so venturesone a state-structure was to maintain itself without the vivifying force of genius, received serious consideration from one contemporary mind alone, that of Mirabeau. The old epoch and the new were still greeting one another on friendly terms, when shortly before the death of the king the tribune of the approaching Revolution passed an hour at the table of Sans Souci. In the glowing terminology of his rhetoric Mirabeau has described the greatest man upon whom he had ever set eyes. He termed Frederick's state a truly beautiful work of art, the one state of the day which could seriously interest a talented head, but he did not fail to see that this daring structure rested unfortunately upon too slender a foundation. The Prussians of those days could not understand such doubts ; the glory of the Frederician epoch seemed so miraculous that even this most carpingly critical of all the peoples of Europe was blinded by its splendour. For the next generation, the fame of Frederick was a destructive influence ; people reposed upon that fame in specious security, and forgot that it is only by arduous labour that the work of earlier arduous toil can be maintained. Yet when the days of disgrace and trial arrived, Prussia was once more to experience the power of genius slowly working to its issue and diffusing blessings ; the memories of Rossbach and Leuthen provided the ultimate moral energy which preserved the leaky vessel of the German monarchy from submergence beneath the waters ; and when the state once again took up arms in a struggle of desperation, a South German poet saw the form of the great king descending from the clouds, and calling to his people : " Up, my Prussians, assemble under my banners, and you shall be greater even than were your forefathers ! "

§ 3. THE NEW LITERATURE.

Meanwhile the German people, with a youthful energy and speed unique in the slow history of ancient nations, had completed a revolution in its spiritual life ; barely four generations after the hopeless barbarism of the Thirty Years' War there dawned the finest days of German art and science. From the vigorous roots of religious freedom there sprouted a new secular free culture, just as hostile to the ossified forms of German society as was the Prussian State to the Holy Roman Empire. The classic literature of all other nations was the offspring of power and of wealth, the ripe fruit of a developed national civilisation ; the classical poetry of Germany served to reintroduce the German people into the circle of civilised nations, to open Germany's way to a purer civilisation. Never before in the whole course of history has a powerful literature so utterly lacked favouring external conditions. Here there was no court which cherished art as an ornament of its crown ; there was no large urban public which could at once encourage the poet and confine him within the limits of a traditional artistic form ; there were no vigorous commerce and industry to present to the natural philosopher fruitful problems for investigation ; there was no free national life to offer the historian the school of experience : even the lofty sensibility which derives from living amid great events was first provided for the Germans by the deeds of Frederick the Great. Spontaneously from the heart of this nation of idealism did its new poetry spring to life, just as formerly had originated the Reformation from the sound German conscience. The middle classes lived their lives almost entirely excluded from the conduct of the state, immured in the tedium, the compulsions, and the poverty of the life of petty towns, and yet in such tolerably secure economic conditions that the struggle for existence did not as yet monopolise all vital activities, and the savage jostle for earnings and enjoyments still remained unknown to their peaceful existence. Among these human beings in a condition of almost incredible material well-being, there now awakened the passionate yearning for the true and the beautiful. The more intelligent among them felt themselves the free children of God, and soared above the realm of petty realities into the pure world of the ideal. The note was given by men of altogether exceptional talent, and a hundred inspired voices joined in a full chorus. Each one spoke after his own heart, confidently following the joyful message of the youthful Goethe : it is an inner impulse, and therefore it is a duty ! Each one gave to the full measure of his powers, as if the creative activity of the thinker and of the poet was the only thing in the wide world worth doing for a man of free spirit. They lived their happy lives, recking little of the monetary reward of their labour, immersed in their poetry, their contemplation, and their research, rejoicing in the ever-flowing approbation of warm-hearted friends, and rejoicing even more in the consciousness of their own vision of the divine.

Thus from the year 1750 onwards three generations of Germans, working simultaneously and successively, and often striving in passionate contests, created the youngest of the great literatures of Europe. This literature, for long almost unnoticed outside the German borders, endowed with unbounded receptivity, took to itself the enduring content of the classical poetry of England, France, Spain, and Italy, reconstituting this with a new creative spirit, to find fulfilment ultimately in Goethe, the most many-sided of all poets. The movement was so perfectly free, so spontaneous an outcome of the innermost impulse of an overfilled heart, that of necessity it culminated finally in the audacious idealism of Fichte, who regarded the moral will as the sole reality, and the whole outer world as merely a creation of the thinking ego ; yet the whole process was a necessary and natural growth. The creative energy of the German spirit had long been slumbering like a chrysalis in its delicate envelope, but there now happened what the poet expresses in the words : " The moment comes for the imago to emerge, to spread its wings, and fly to the heart of the rose." A pure-minded ambition, seeking truth for the sake of truth, beauty for the sake of beauty, now animated the clear heads of the German youth. No other of the modern nations has ever devoted itself with the same earnestness, with the same undivided ardour, to the world of ideas ; no other numbers among the leading spirits of its classical literature so many fine and humanly lovable characters. Hence, for our people, whenever their star seems to be undergoing obscuration, the memory of the days of Weimar will remain an inexhaustible source of confidence and hope. To the Germans, art and science became matters of vital consequence, and were never here, as once of old among the Romans, a mere elegant play-acting, a pastime for the idle hours of the world of fashion. Not with us did the courts develop our literature, but the new culture arising from the free activity of the nation brought the courts under its own subordination, liberated them from unnatural foreign customs, and gradually won them to the adoption of a gentler and more humane civilisation.

Moreover, this new culture was German to the core. Whilst the political life of the country was subdivided into innumerable currents, in the domain of spiritual work the natural vigour of the national unity was so overwhelming that no attempt was ever made at any territorial subdivision. All the heroes of our classical literature, with the solitary exception of Kant, were migratory men, and did not find their region of richest efficiency upon the soil of their own home. All were inspired by a consciousness of the unity and originality of the German nature, and all were animated by the passionate desire to restore the peculiar gifts of this nation to their rightful place of honour in the world; they knew, every one, that the whole of Germany was hanging upon their word, and they felt it to be a proud privilege that only the poet and the thinker were competent to speak to the nation and to act on behalf of the nation. Thus it came to pass that for many decades the new literature and the new science were the mightiest bond of union for this people split into so many fragments, and literature and science ultimately determined the victory of Protestantism in German life. It was in Protestant Germany that this great intellectual movement had its original home, and only gradually did the Catholic regions of the empire submit to the same impulse. The thought-process of the philosophers gave rise to a new moral view of the world-order, to a new doctrine of humanism which, though free from all dogmatic rigidity, was yet rooted in the soil of Protestantism, and which ultimately became a common heritage of all thinking Germans, Catholic and Protestant alike. One to whom this new humanism was unknown was no longer living in the new Germany.

The middle strata of society among which this new culture sprang to life came to such an extent to occupy the foreground of the national life that Germany, more than any other country, became a land of the middle class ; the moral judgment and the artistic taste of the middle class were the determinants of public opinion. Classical education, which had hitherto been the instrument for the expert training of lawyers and divines, now became the basis of the general popular culture ; upon the ruins of the old aristocracy of birth there upbuilt itself the new aristocracy of the educated people which for a hundred years has been the leading class of our nation. In all directions the literary movement exercised its awakening and fertilising influence ; it ennobled manners, restoring to woman her due place as mistress in social intercourse ; it provided once again for an oppressed and intimidated generation the free breath of life. Building upon the written speech of Martin Luther, it developed a common tongue of intercourse for all branches of the German stock ; it was only in the final third of the eighteenth century that the cultured classes began to pay due respect to the pure High German even in daily life. Unaffected by the noise and the hurry of the great world, German poetry was able to maintain for an extraordinarily long period the blameless cheerfulness, the concentrated reflectiveness, and the fresh love of being, characteristic of youth. It was this which so greatly charmed Madame de Staël in the brilliant days of Weimar art ; she felt that on the Ilm, among the most highly cultured of the German people, she was drinking in the forest-love of a primitive human life, and was taking breath once more after the vapours and the dust of her native world-city. And as it is the right of youth to promise without restraint, and whilst receiving crowns of glory to reach out the hands once more in pursuit of further aims, the German nation, in this period of poetic rejuvenescence, displayed an extraordinarily many-sided activity, unweariedly propounding new problems, discovering new artistic forms, and devoting its energies to every possible science, with the one exception of the science of politics.

It must be admitted that side by side with the peculiar merits characteristic of its origin, our new literature exhibited also peculiar weaknesses. Since the poet was unable to create his matter directly out of the great passions of vigorously active public life, it resulted that criticism gained a preponderance that was often dangerous to the naive artistic creative energy, most of the dramatic heroes of our classical art display a morbid tendency to renunciation, to a dread of action. The unbridled freedom of creation readily led the poets to arbitrary conceits, to elaborate artifices, to ambitious beginnings which never found completion ; and it is not by mere chance that the greatest of all our poets is the one who, among the great poets of history, has left the world the largest number of fragments. Individual talent could display its primitive energies undisturbed, and was not all tuned to a single measure by the exigencies of party life. Love became stormy, friendship effeminate, and every sensation found expression to excess ; an enviably rich sense of fellowship, fertile in ideas, produced a few men of universal culture, such as had not been known in Europe since the Renaissance. But within the retired sphere of this purely private life there developed, not only what is valuable in individuality, but also the defects characteristic of the free personality. " Love, to the very marrow, love, hate, and fear, tremble, hope, and despair." This was the watchword of the new sensationalism of the epoch of *Sturm und Drang ;* an unbridled self-confidence, a faith in their power to storm the heavens became active in the young generation, reacting against the lack of freedom characteristic of public affairs. Incalculable caprices, personal hates and personal envies, were given unrestricted expression ; many of the works of this epoch are comprehensible to-day to those only who are familiar with the letters and diaries of their writers.

A literature of such an origin and such a character could not become popular in the fullest sense of the word, and could influence the masses but slowly and indirectly. Whilst the men of culture were inspiring themselves by the contemplation of the pure forms of the antique, the sense of beauty among the common people, although these were now better educated than formerly, remained much blunter than that of the same class in France and in Italy.

Once only in this northern land was there a passable cultivation of the general sense of form : in the days of the Hohenstaufen, when the palaces and the cathedrals of the late Romanesque style were constructed, and when the glorious songs of our earlier classical poetry were understood by the peasant lads and maidens in every village along the Rhine and the Main. Since those days, at every stage in the development of German civilisation, there has been displayed a hideous foundation of unrestrained barbarism. When the beautiful Renaissance facade of the Otto Heinrich building in Heidelberg was erected, the German art of poetry was in a profoundly depressed condition, and the noble edifice was defaced by lamentable doggerel verses. Similarly, when the joyful days of our second classical literature arrived, the fine arts, which flourish only in the soft atmosphere of general well-being, were hardly affected by the fresh current of the new time, and Goethe wasted the beauty of his verses upon such ridiculous buildings as that Roman house at Weimar whose pseudo-antique forms are altogether repugnant, and which offends the cultured sense by its utter vanity. We cannot, indeed, fail to be moved by the contemplation of this heroic generation of idealism, which, amid the unadorned poverty of the palaces of our petty princes, continued to aspire towards the highest good of mankind : yet there persisted an unnatural severance between the wealth of ideas and the poverty of life, between the bold flights of the imagination of the cultured and the utterly prosaic daily activities of the labouring masses. The nobility of a harmoniously developed civilisation such as that which brought happiness to the Italians in the days of Leonardo still remained denied to the Germans.

All its defects and errors notwithstanding, it was this literary revolution which determined the character of the new German civilisation. By developing the fundamental ideas of the Reformation into a right of absolutely unprejudiced free investigation, it made this country once again the central region of heresy. Awakening the ideals of a purely humanistic culture, it awakened also the national pride of country. However immature might be the political culture of the time, however wrong-headed its cosmopolitan dreams, in all the leaders of the movement there was none the less active the noble ambition to prove to the world that, as Herder says, " the German name is strong, firm, and great in its own right." The national inspiration of the War of Liberation arose, not in conflict with the ideas of humanism, but on a truly humanist foundation. When the cruel blows of destiny had again reminded the German genius of the needs to come down from the clouds to the finite conditions of existence, the nation also attained by a necessary last step to the consciousness that its new spiritual freedom could endure only in a respected and independent state; the idealism that breathed from the thoughts of Kant and the dramas of Schiller, became transfigured in the heroic wrath of the year 1813. It resulted that our classical literature, proceeding from an entirely different starting-point, aspired towards the same goal as the political labours of the Prussian monarchy. It is to these two formative energies that our people owes its position among the nations and the best features of its recent history. It is very remarkable how both for a hundred years held equal pace in their development, bearing witness to an inner connection, which for this very reason cannot be fortuitous, since an immediate and obvious reciprocal action is rarely traceable. At the very time when the Great Elector was creating the new temporal state of the Germans, there happened also in the world of literature the decisive liberation of science from the yoke of theology. When subsequently, under Frederick William I, the Prussian state was collecting its forces in a period of quiet work, the intellectual life of the nation was also in a state of self-containment, the arid prose of the Wolffian philosophy once more taught the middle classes how to think and to write logically. Finally, towards the year 1750, contemporaneously with the heroic deeds of King Frederick, there began the awakening of creative energy in literature, and the first permanent works of the new poesy made their appearance.

To the mind of the Middle Ages, the moral world appeared a closed visible unity; state and church, art and science, received the moral laws of their being from the hands of the Pope. It was the aim of the Reformation to destroy this dominion of ecclesiastical authority, and to win alike for the state and for knowledge the right to an independent moral existence. Yet the success thus attained was but a half-measure. Just as the theocracy of the Holy Empire remained established, and all the temporal states continued to support the zealotry of the Churches, so also knowledge relapsed under the theological perversion; the old queen of the sciences continued to occupy her throne, and all the teachers at the universities were compelled to avow some particular religious creed. Then began, first of all in Germany's highly cultivated neighbour-lands, the great work of the mathematical century; a strict and clear-headed research, working in a free secular spirit, elucidated the secrets of nature; and towards the end of the seventeenth century, when Newton discovered the laws of celestial mechanics, there gradually ensued a profound change in our views of the world-order. Dogmatic religious belief had hitherto been regarded as the only trustworthy guide in the insecure realm of thought, but now knowledge seemed to furnish greater security than belief. It will always remain a proud memory for our people how boldly and freely the harassed generation of the Thirty Years' War participated in this mighty movement, at first in a spirit of receptive discipleship (for Leibnitz found it necessary to say that industry was the only talent of the German nation), but subsequently in a mood of active independence. After a long and fierce struggle Puffendorf expelled the theologians from the field of political science and founded for Germany a true doctrine of the state. Other sciences followed suit and learned to stand upon their own feet; the University of Heidelberg was the first to abandon the principle of religious unity. In Leibnitz there arose a thinker whose cautiously intermediating spirit was inwardly free from the dominion of dogma, and who opened a path of unprejudiced research to German philosophy; whilst soon Thomasius could joyfully exclaim, " It is unrestricted freedom which alone gives the spirit its true life." By the secularisation of the sciences, the political power of the Churches was gradually destroyed from within outwards. By the middle of the eighteenth century there was little left of the power which the court-chaplains and consistories had formerly possessed in the Protestant lands of the empire; the new officialdom held fast to the sovereignty of the state. At this period, also, Thomasius ventured to introduce the German tongue into academic instruction, and since all the Protestant universities followed his example, the Latin learning of the Jesuits was no longer able to enter into rivalry with Protestant science; everyone in Germany who desired a living culture hastened to enrol himself at some Protestant university. Although the corporate pride of the professors and the roughness of the academic youth were not yet entirely overcome, the first bridge had been erected between science and the life of the nation.

At the same time there ensued for the Protestant Church a period of new life, centred above all in the young University of Halle, and firmly attached to the tolerant ecclesiastical policy of the Prussian state. The nation had been heartily sickened by the raging contests of dogma during the epoch of the wars of religion. The efforts of the Calixtiners towards religious union, the "religious inwardness" of the pietists, and the rationalising criticism of

Thomasius, found themselves side by side in a common struggle
with the tyranny of the theological belief in the letter of the written
word. The moral content of Christianity, which had almost been
forgotten amid the noisy struggles of the zealots, came once more
to its own, now that Francke and Spener had exhorted their congre-
gations to live the life of the gospels in mutual brotherly love.
The effective sense of Christian piety was manifested in the magnificent foundation of the Halle orphanage and in other works of
charity; the doctrine of pietism spoke to the heart, and enabled
women to feel themselves once more to be living members of the
congregation. Nor did this revival of German Protestantism lead,
like the efforts of the Dutch Arminians and of the English Latitu-
dinarians, to the formation of new sects; it effected, rather, a genuine
union of the whole Protestant name, permeating the Church once
more with the spirit of primitive Christianity, and fulfilling the
word " in My Father's house are many mansions." After many
struggles and aberrations it yet remained as a permanent acquirement that German Protestantism became the gentlest, the freest,
and the most comprehensive of all the Christian communities, and
one which was still able to find place within its bosom for the boldest
ventures of philosophy ; it resulted also that religious toleration
gradually made its way into the daily life of the Germans, and that
numerous mixed marriages, and before long also mixed schools,
gave a permanent seal to ecclesiastical peace.

It is only this revival of German Protestantism which explains
those most peculiar tendencies of the new German civilisation
which remain incomprehensible to most non-Teutons, and even to
the English ; this alone has rendered it possible for the German
to be at the same time pious and free, for his literature to be Protestant without the taint of dogma. The English and French
enlightenment has the sign written on its forehead to show how it
was effected in conflict with the tyranny of enslaved Churches and
with the obscure zealotry of an ignorant populace ; even the deism
of the British is irreligious, for the deists' god makes no appeal to
the conscience, and merely fulfils the office of the great machine-
driver of the world. The German enlightenment, on the other hand,
was firmly rooted in Protestantism ; it attacked ecclesiastical
tradition with even sharper weapons than did the philosophy of
the neighbouring peoples, but the boldness of its criticism was
mitigated by a profound veneration for religion. It awakened
the consciences which the Anglo-French materialism put to sleep ;
it preserved the belief in a personal God, and in the ultimate

purpose of the perfected world, the human immortal soul. The fanatical hatred of the Church and the mechanical view of the world-order which characterised the French philosophers, were regarded by the Germans as a sign of enslavement ; Lessing turned with repulsion from the mockeries of Voltaire, and, with the self-certainty of the young man rejoicing in the future, the student Goethe laughed at the senile tedium of the *Systéme de la Nature*. All through the eighteenth century the Protestant parsonage continued to exercise its ancient beneficial influence upon German life, while never ceasing to take an ardent part in the creation of the new literature. Even though our art could not become a possession of the whole people, we have still to thank the rejuvenation of German Protestantism for the great blessing that the most highly cultivated moral views have come to permeate the conscience of the masses, and that ultimately the ethics of Kant forced their way into the Protestant pulpits and thence into the lowermost strata of the North German people. The moral gulf between the upper and the lower strata of society was narrower in Germany than in the lands of the west.

This first epoch of modern German literature exhibits also a severe prosaic tendency. Men of learning are the leaders of the movement ; art is hardly touched as yet by the spirit of the new age ; only in Schlüter's buildings and statuary, and in the compositions of Bach and Handel, do we witness a great and free manifestation of the heroic character of the epoch. Yet to-day those notable struggles against Jesuitism and against coagulated Lutheranism seem to us as pioneer and as radical as the political deeds of the Great Elector. They laid the firm foundation for everything which we to-day speak of as German spiritual freedom. From the maturer writings of Leibnitz and Thomasius, from Puffendorf's work upon the relationship of State and Church, there speaks already that spirit of unconditional toleration which in foreign lands neither Locke nor Bayle could whole-heartedly advocate.

In the succeeding generation, the creative energy was almost completely suspended. These were the empty days in which the crown prince Frederick was experiencing the decisive impressions of his youth. The market of learning was under the dominance of a sterile polymathy, and the ambitious works of the day were lacking precisely in those qualities of measure, precision, and definiteness of expression, which were especially prized at the Rheinsberg court of the Muses. Gottsched's poetry slavishly followed the rigid rules of French poetry without ever rising out of the level of bumptious platitude to attain the rhetorical pathos of the romance world. Electoral Saxony was the only German land which could boast of tasteful culture and of a fertile artistic activity ; but the splendid operas and the fine baroque buildings of the Dresden court are no more than the signs of the fantastic late blossoming of Gallic art, and by no means indicate a progress in our national life. Yet even now the growth of the German spirit was far from being arrested. The more generally comprehensible products of the intellectual work of the highly talented previous generation became gradually current among the people. The philosophy of Christian Wolff effected a reconciliation between faith and knowledge sufficient for the needs of the epoch, and thus provided for the coming generation a consistent and harmonious view of the universe. The average culture of the middle classes found peace in the belief that God operates in accordance with natural laws. Wolff deliberately transcended the limits of the learned world, awakened in wide circles a desire for thinking and writing, and accustomed men of learning to contribute their quota to the work of general enlightenment. Simultaneously, pietism was working its influence in society. The rough tone of tyrannical hardness disappeared from family life. In the sentimental assemblies of the finer spirits there began the cult of personality. The life of every individual acquired an unexpected new value and content ; the Germans came to recognise once more how rich is the world of the heart, and became capable of understanding profoundly conceived works of art.

Now there appeared in the arena, as suddenly as the might of the Frederician state, and exhibiting the same overwhelming strength, those forces of German genius which had been quietly maturing in the long years of anticipation. In 1747 were published the first cantos of Klopstock's *Messiah*. The warmth and intimacy of feeling which in the prayers and diaries of the revivalists had found no more than an immature and often ludicrous expression, now at length attained to a worthy poetic form ; the jejune speech gained buoyancy, nobility, and boldness ; the entire world of the sublime was reopened to the German imagination. With remarkable speed the nation understood that a new epoch in its culture had begun. A swarm of young men of talent surrounded the bard, in whose personality the loftiness of the new art also found a worthy representative ; and these admirers, in the naive self-appreciation characteristic of all periods of powerful expansion, placed the epic of the German master above that of Homer, and his odes above those of Pindar. This artistic circle was intoxicated by a fantastic enthusiasm for the fatherland, and this sentiment, propagated slowly but vigorously, found its way through all strata of the German middle class. Just as every nation, when there comes a turning-point in its existence, is accustomed to find fresh sources of enthusiasm in the great memories of the primitive homeland, so now the yearnings of these days turned back towards the simple greatness of the Teutonic primitive age, conceiving that only in the shadows of the German oak-forests, only in the land of Arminius and the bards, were truth and loyalty, strength and ardour at home. What a chorus of acclamation arose from the new Germany when the singer of the *Messiah* called upon the new contestant, the young German muse, to enter the field against the poesy of England.

Meanwhile Winckelmann made our people acquainted with ancient art, and rediscovered the simple and profound truth that art is the representation of the beautiful. At the same time he produced the first work of the new German prose that was perfect in respect of form. Clear, weighty, and inspired, sounded the words of this priest of beauty, embodying passion and great thoughts pressed together in a measured and concise form ; it was by " the illuminated brevity " of his style that the shapeless prolixity of learned pedantry was first overcome. His writings gave to the young literature its trend towards the classical ideal. In rivalry and in passionate delight, art and science sought to fulfil themselves with the spirit of antiquity ; and since man values that only which he over-values, it resulted that this generation, rejoicing in beauty, intoxicated with the joys of first awakening, could see nothing in the ancient civilisation but pure humanity, health, and nature. It was only to the Romans themselves that the world of classical Rome was truly congenial, but to the genius of Greece the Germans were attracted by a sentiment of kinship. To the Germans first among the modern nations did there come a full understanding of Greek life, and as the new culture ripened, the poet could joyfully exclaim : " The sun that smiled on Homer smiles also on us now ! " By its entry into the antique world the German tongue, which had so often been impoverished and obscure, reacquired a considerable proportion of its ancient wealth, and it now came to display an unanticipated plastic softness and flexibility. Alone among the new languages of civilisation, German showed itself competent to employ at once faithfully and vividly all the measures of the Greeks ; as soon as Voss, the German Homer, had shown the way, Germany gradually became the leading speech of the world for translations, hospitably providing a second home for the poetic figures of all peoples and all ages. Yet this charming receptivity implied neither weakness nor lack of independence : the German disciples of the classic preserved their spiritual freedom from the classical ideals, not allowing themselves, as had happened to the humanists at the close of the fifteenth century, to be led astray from the firm regulation of their own lives by the moral views of the antique world. Winckelmann, indeed, reminds us in many of his characteristics of the unrestrained heroes of the Renaissance : but the majority of poets and thinkers who followed in his footsteps remained German, taking from the Hellenic culture that only which was accordant to the German nature ; and the poem which of all the works of modern art approximates most closely to the spirit of the antique, Goethe's *Iphigenia*, was nevertheless permeated by a sentiment of loving gentleness such as was never understood by the hard-hearted heathen of antiquity.

Independent of these two tendencies, and yet at one with both in the struggle for the rights of the free artistic creator, Lessing went on his way. The most productive critic of all time, he stood in relation to the pathetic exuberance of Klopstock as once Puffendorf and Thomasius had stood in relation to pietism, at the same time divergent and bringing fulfilment. His creative criticism effected that which the enthusiasm of the new lyric poetry would never by its own unaided powers have succeeded in effecting, the permanent destruction of the strained unnaturalness of the poetic art of Gottsched, the expulsion from the German Parnassus of the bastard type of didactic poem, the liberation of the nation from the yoke of the rules of art imposed by Boileau. Little as we are justified in ascribing to the man who regarded patriotism as a heroic weakness the conscious sentiment for the fatherland characteristic of our own day, yet through those powerful controversial writings which held up the dramas of Voltaire for the laughter of the Germans there runs that same great tendency of a strengthening national life that we find in the heroic progress of Frederick. Lessing's criticism turned the German poets from the courtiers'-versification of the Bourbons to the methods of Aristotle rightly understood, to the simple examples of classic art, and he taught them to esteem that truth which is true to nature more than all highly elaborated rules. That criticism displayed to them in the plays of Shakespeare a source of primitive Teutonic life which became a fountain of youth for German art ; the poet of the merry England of old soon found in the free secular sense of the Germans a fuller understanding than in his own fatherland sterilised by puritanism. Lessing, above all, educated the new public ; he was the first German man of letters, the first who by his own personal worth raised to honour the profession of the free author, and the first who understood how to make an effective appeal to all the cultured minds of the nation. The most obscure problems of theology, of æsthetics, of archæology, seemed luminously clear when treated by him in the light tones of the lively speech of Upper Saxony, in that prose that was simple and yet so full of art, which everywhere reflected his own inmost nature, the serenity of his own understanding.

And here, even in the earliest youth of the classic German prose, it became manifest that our free tongue was suited to every individuality of style, that it permitted each creative mind to work after its own fashion. The style of Lessing, plainly modelled on French examples, was no less German than were the majestic periods of Winckelmann—for both these authors wrote as they had to write. But the security of the literary sense of self-sufficiency first came to the Germans when the great critic showed himself also to be an original artist, presenting to our stage the first works that were not shamed by contrast with the rich reality of the Frederician epoch, and that could bear comparison with the dramas of foreign lands. These were works displaying the keenest understanding of art, and yet full of passionate dramatic movement ; apt for the stage, and yet composed in perfect freedom ; works of imperishable human content and yet taking their figures with a vigorous hand from the animated life of the immediate present. Thus he rose higher and higher, dispersing in all directions the seed of free culture. By his *Emilia* he gave our young literature the courage to raise its voice against the lack of freedom in the state and in society. His theological controversial writings laid the foundations for a new epoch in theological science, for the biblical criticism of the nineteenth century. The last of his poetic works established the forms for the drama of lofty style which was subsequently to undergo further development at the hands of Schiller, and manifested at the same time that comprehending faith in enlightenment whose serene mildness was not to become apparent to other nations until after the storms of the Revolution.

In the seventies, a new and still richer generation came upon the stage. The universal spirit of Herder united at once the

vigorous understanding of Lessing and the rich emotional nature
of Klopstock. He rediscovered that truth which had been lost
in the long centuries overlaid by barbarism, that art is not the
exclusive possession of particular peoples or ages, but is a common
gift of all nations and all times ; and he led back our German
lyric poetry to the ancient forms and subjects of the folk-songs.
The moving tones of German rhyme came once more to their
own, and emotional feeling found a warm, profound, and natural
expression in songs and ballads. A thoroughly unhistoric epoch,
one which had acquired its fame in the destruction of a decaying
world of historical ruins, was awakened by Herder to an understanding of historical life. His free spirit despised the poverty of
that self-satisfied illusion which regards all the children of men as
created only " for that which we term civilisation." He recognised that each nation has its own measure of happiness, its own
golden age ; and with wonderful insight he discerned the peculiar
characteristics of the spiritual life of the peoples. It was through
his work that the contrast between the naive civilisation of antiquity and the sentimental culture of the modern world first became
apparent. To his prophetic glance there was already revealed
the interconnection between nature and history ; he conceived the
magnificent idea of " following the footsteps of the Creator, of
thinking after His manner," of seeking the revelation of God at once
in the constructive energies of the world-all and in the transformations of human history ; he gave a new profundity to the idea of
humanity when he thought of mankind as a " tone in the chorus
of creation, a living wheel in the works of nature." No writer of
the eighteenth century passed a severer judgment than Herder
upon the late manifestations of Christianity, and yet none displayed a profounder understanding of faith than did this intrinsic-
ally religious spirit. The highest goal of his endeavour was to
purify religion from all that was despiritualised and enslaved.
Every one of his writings breathes an air of intense piety, an
intimate and joyful faith in the wisdom and goodness of God, a
faith that ultimately overcomes all the caprices of a self-tormenting
nature inclined to get out of tune. Thus it was that an unsparing
opponent of the errors of the Church could without hypocrisy
remain a great divine and an ecclesiastical official—a striking
testimony to the sober-minded freedom of the age.

The new universal culture for which the bold anticipations of
Herder had merely paved the way, now received their definitive
artistic form in the work of the poet of mighty speech to whom a

God gave power to express in song what he had learned in suffering. It was this mysterious power of conveying an immediate environment that his contemporaries first learnt to marvel at in the young Goethe. Soon, too, they felt the influence of his unending love, of his unsurpassed receptiveness for all that is human. It seemed like a personal revelation of himself when he made his Son of God exclaim : " Oh, my generation, how I yearn towards thee ! And how dost thou, too, pitiful in heart, supplicate Me in thy deep distress ! " Like the bards of all ages when art was naive, he sang only what he had himself experienced ; yet his spirit was so rich and multiform that his poetry gradually encompassed the wide circle of German life, and during many decades almost every new idea which this time of restless creation conceived, found its most profound and most powerful expression in the work of Goethe ; until at length the entire world of nature and of human life was reflected in the old man's quiet eyes. By his early poems he brought to German lyric poetry that new life which Herder had merely foreshadowed. All the charming and tender, sweet and yearning feelings of the German heart, which had been obscured in the pathetic style of Klopstock, the writer of odes, now found expression ; the ancient songs, such as *Röslein auf der Heide*, delighted once more the cultured youth of the day, now that Goethe had borrowed them from the herdsman and the hunter, had ennobled their simplicity by the magic of his art. The Germans learnt once more, from his genial poems, to be unrestrainedly joyful, to give themselves up without reserve to the heavenly delight of the moment. Then came *Goetz* to reproduce before the eyes of the nation the rough, untamed energy and greatness of the ancient German life ; then did the *Sorrows of Werther* furnish satisfying expression for the storm and stress of passion which filled the hearts of the young generation. It was also politically significant that even in this dispersed and distracted nation, a poet should attain an irresistible general success, like that which of old had been attained elsewhere by Cervantes ; and all that was vigorously youthful drew together in glowing enthusiasm. At the close of the Frederician epoch, the poet emerged from those struggles of the heart to which we owe the most beautiful love poems in the German tongue, to become, after ten years of life at court that were full of work and of distraction, once more an artist. He hastened to " that land where for every receptive mind the most individual culture begins." There, in the south, he learnt to reconcile northern passion and emotional profundity with classical purity of form. However great he was, and however powerful his influence, he never claimed dominion over our poetry, and German freedom would never have permitted any such claim. Even after the appearance of this almighty genius, the literary movement went on its course in joyful unrestraint. Hundreds of independent minds continued to work after their own fashion. Everywhere in the Poets' Associations and in the Freemasons' Lodges there was an ardent search for pure humanity, for knowledge of the eternal ; and everywhere in this life of activity there was a joyful foreshadowing of a wonderful future. This generation felt itself raised above the common reality of things, carried as if on the wings of the wind towards the dawning of the light, towards the perfection of humanity. The thoughtless masses, it is true, then as at all times, asked merely for comfortable amusement. Wieland's roguish liveliness was more agreeable to them than the pathos of Klopstock, just as subsequently Kotzebue was more pleasing than Schiller or Goethe. But in the best circles of society, a joyful idealism was dominant, and it was this which gave its stamp to the culture of the age.

Meanwhile the nation discovered that it possessed, not merely the greatest poet, but also the greatest philosopher of the day. The opposition between the German and the Anglo-French views of the world-order was described by Goethe in the simple words : " The French do not understand that there is anything in human beings unless it has come into them from outside." To the German idealism, it seemed, on the contrary, a problem for solution, how anything at all could enter a soul from outside. To the enlightenment of the West, the world of sensuous experience appeared the one incontestable reality. Then Kant undertook to throw light on the facts of human cognition, and asked the profound question, how is the scientific cognition of nature in any way possible ? This was the great turning point of the new philosophy. With the same royal self-confidence as Goethe, Kant had begun the work of his life : " Nothing shall hold me back from my course." He started from the ideas of the mathematical century, and faithfully followed with independent mind every movement of the new decades. Towards the end of the Frederician epoch, he produced those works which for a long time to come were to establish the fundamental moral ideas of the ripened Protestantism. More boldly than any of the atheists of the Encyclopædia, he contested the illusion that a science could ever be derived from the supra-sensual, yet in the domain of the practical reason he found once more the idea of freedom. From the necessities of moral action, he derived the great conception (not based upon theological crutches, and therefore invincibly victorious) that the most incomprehensible is of all things the most certain : the empirical ego is subordinated to the laws of causality, the intelligible ego acts with freedom. For free activity, he propounded that imperative in which simple-mindedness and the highest culture could both find peace : " Act as if the maxims in accordance with which you are acting must become natural laws." Kant's ideas, moreover, like everything that was written in this blossoming time, first came to full fruition through the power of personality. The serene wisdom of the thinker of Königsberg, which demanded from men that they should even die in a good humour, the simple greatness of this life utterly filled with the ideal, profoundly moved the minds of his contemporaries. Kant was the architect of his Old Prussian home, he reintroduced the remote Eastern Mark as an active member of the community of German intellectual workers, and the uprising of 1813 showed how profoundly this valiant people had taken to heart the saying that nothing anywhere in the world could be esteemed except a good will.

Now there appeared upon the scene the young poet who was destined to diffuse the ideas of the Kantian ethics through the widest circles of the nation. Rough and formless seemed the youthful writings of Schiller, the product of an invincible energy of will in conflict with the control of petty enslaving circumstances ; but the bold conception of his story-telling, his powerful pathos, his sustained passion, and the vigorously ascending course of his technique, already sufficed to herald Germany's discovery of her greatest dramatist—a dictatorial spirit, born to mastership and victory, who now in his days of youthful fermentation irresistibly forced upon his audience the savage and the horrible, and who subsequently, matured and refined, lifted thousands with himself above the common miseries of life. Out of the clamorous rhetoric of these tragedies, there spoke a wealth of new ideas, a glowing yearning for freedom, and the hatred of a great soul for the rigid forms of the ancient society. The writings of Rousseau and the political movement of the neighbouring lands were already throwing their first sparks over Germany. One who despised everything that was dull, narrow, and commonplace, this son of the petty-bourgeois land of Swabia, reached out into the great circles of a historical world ; he was the first to bind the cothurni on to the feet of our sons. He first led them among kings and heroes, into the greatest altitudes of humanity.

Beside such a wealth of art and science a purely political literature appears small and mean. Just as every great transformation of our intellectual life has reflected itself in the destinies of a German university, so on this occasion also we can trace the connection between the beginnings of our classical literature and the first blossoming of the Georgia Augusta University. There proceed from Göttingen a zealous care for jurisprudence and the science of the state, and this movement was reciprocally interconnected with the great thought-current of the century which was everywhere drawing its sources from the exact sciences and streaming towards the freedom of the historical world. It was a living law which was expounded by the publicists of Göttingen ; it was a point of honour in the anti-imperial professors to define the rights of Protestantism and of the temporal estates of the empire against the shadowy claims of the Emperorship. Yet neither the rough candour of Schlözer nor the industry of Pütter, neither the learnedness of the two Mosers nor any other of the remarkable manifestations of political and publicist science characteristic of that day, bears the stamp of genius. There is not a trace of the bold, universal grasp of Puffendorf, not a trace of that creative criticism which found expression in the ardent voice of the poets, there is nothing of that inconceivable wealth of expression which delights us in the belletristic literature of the time. Beside the silvery tones of the prose of Lessing and Goethe the language of Pütter has the flat sound of base metal.

Whilst German poetry and philosophy were soaring above the work of the neighbouring nations, in political science the English and the French took the lead. It was only in the actions and in the writings of the great king, himself untouched by the literary revival of his own nation, that Germany took an effective part in the great political thought-movement of the century. In Herder's *Ideas*, how weak are the political sections when compared with the richness of those that deal with the history of civilisation. The one vigorous and peculiarly endowed political thinker, belonging to the younger political life of Germany, Justus Möser, exercises a real influence upon his contemporaries only in the sphere of æsthetics, by his spirited description of German antiquity ; it was not until much later, in the days of the revival of historical jurisprudence, that his profound historical view of the state was understood by the nation. The German readers brought to the publicists a richer abundance of historical knowledge than was brought by the British and by the French, but they had not a glimmer of political passion or of political understanding. This utterly unpolitical age understood how to feel its way to art under conditions whose absolute contradiction was perceived by all. But while the research of German thinkers was boldly directed towards the solution of the most obscure riddles of the universe, there did not, even after the terrible teaching of the Seven Years' War, appear a single man who could lay his finger upon the wounds of the German state, or could with unsparing courage ask the decisive question : What is the significance for the future of our country of this uprising of a new German great power ? German life failed to discover the exhaustive expression either in the wealth of ideas of its literature or in the activities of the Prussian state. There were moments, indeed, when the two creative energies of our new history appeared to come into contact and to attain to a mutual understanding. We of this later generation are moved to learn how the gruff officers of Frederick's army sought counsel and edification in Leipzig from the pious Gellert. The poet of the Spring, Ewald Kleist, the Prussian recruiting officer, who in Zurich sought refreshment from the hardships of his man-hunting career in the circle of the artistic disciples of Klopstock, and who then found a soldier's death at Kunnersdorf, appears to us to-day a more significant figure than many a more highly gifted poet, because he united in a single personality a heroic sense of the poetic yearning of this teeming time. On the whole, however, it is certain that the Prussia of that day was no less unæsthetic than the German literature of the time was unpolitical. In the days of Lessing, the Prussian capital was for some years the Acropolis of German criticism ; since the seventies, its public had possessed the most developed artistic sense in Germany and there had prevailed in the town a refined and intellectual sociability ; but in respect of creative capacity it was poorly equipped. A shallow eudæmonism was dominant. For the dull understanding of Nicolai, the flight of the young German poetry was too lofty; while the critics of Berlin were thus lamenting, elsewhere in the empire were being fought the battles of the new German culture. The firm foundation of national power was lacking to our classical literature. This literature has proved for all time that the proud freedom of poesy can dispense with the sun of good fortune ; that a new wealth of ideas must inevitably find form and expression as soon as it springs up in the soul of a nation. There was danger, however, that the nation would morbidly over-value the intellectual goods for the very reason that its literary life was so much more magnificent than its political. The patriotism of our poets remained too subjective to exercise a direct influence upon the popular sentiment. The cosmopolitan tendency which inspired the entire literature of the eighteenth century, did not find in Germany, as it found in France, a counterpoise in a highly developed national pride, and it therefore threatened to alienate the Germans from their own state.

Never since the time of Luther had Germany occupied so shining a position in the European world as to-day, when the greatest heroes and the greatest poets of their age and century belonged to our nation. And this abundance of life came but a hundred years after the disgrace of the Swedish distresses. Anyone who at this time made a journey through the leading states of Central and Northern Germany, gained the impression that here was a noble people peacefully developing towards a beautiful future. The humanistic culture of the time was actively engaged upon innumerable institutions of general utility. The old curse of mendicity disappeared from our highways, and the great towns provided with a free hand for poor-houses and hospitals. Zealous pedagogues laboured to transform the education of youth in accordance with new-found systems, without depriving them of the innocence of the " natural " human beings of Rousseau. Everywhere the newly enlightened world was straining at the bonds imposed by the old feudal order. There were nobles here and there who voluntarily freed their serfs. Philosophers noted with satisfaction that the son of a knacker had in Leipzig become a doctor, and that in caste-ridden Weimar a young Frankfort doctor had risen above the heads of the native nobility to become a minister of state. A cheerful enthusiasm for nature drove out the old anxiety regarding the evils of fresh air, put an end to the philistine customs of a close indoor life : the men of learning began once more to feel themselves at home upon God's earth. Yet this people of ours was sick within. Motionless and unreconciled, the great lie of the imperial law stood contrasted with the new culture and the new state of the Germans. In the petty territories of the south and of the west, all the sloth, all the inertia of German life lay like a great unlighted bonfire, awaiting the firebrand which the restless neighbour-nation was to hurl across the frontier. The glory of the Frederician age had hardly begun to pale when the Holy Roman Empire fell into shameful ruin.

CHAPTER II.

REVOLUTION AND FOREIGN DOMINION.

§I.   THE REVOLUTIONARY WAR TO THE PEACE OF BASLE.

ONLY a royal commander or a reforming legislator could maintain undiminished the heritage of Frederick. The old form of the Frederician monarchy had two strings to its bow.   Unless it could engage the warlike energies of this people on a bold venture, and could provide the Holy Empire with a new constitution by the arms of Prussia, it was impossible that the forcible concentration of the entire state-authority in a single hand should be permanently maintained.   The enlarged area of the state-territory, the increased claims upon the functional activity of the state, and the greatly increased self-confidence of the well-to-do classes, involved demands for a comprehensive reform, which should transmute the national economy so as to make it more elastic, should abolish the old class divisions which had become untenable, and should permit subjects to take an active part in the administration of the districts and the communes.   If this reconstruction were not effected, illness and rigidity threatened the monarchy.   That spirit of criticism, which had been awakened by Ferderick himself, but which had been held within bounds by the dread of his genius, might readily destroy the moral security of the state, which was based upon the ancient Prussian loyalty and discipline.

It was Germany's misfortune that Frederick's successor was equally unfitted to undertake either of these tasks.   Frederick William II possessed the knightly bravery of his ancestors and a lively sense of his royal dignity and of the position of his state as a great power, but he was devoid of the expert knowledge, the enduring industry, the security of judgment, and the firm vigour of will, which were demanded by his difficult office.   He was as mild and benevolent as his uncle, in old age, had been misanthropic, readily impressible, rich in good ideas, receptive for lofty proposals; but what he had rashly and ardently undertaken was soon allowed to drop when he became wearied by any difficult obstacles, or when sly opponents knew how to play upon his generosity. Human pettiness breathed more freely when the oppressive weight of the old hero had been removed ; and the greatly loved man who so confidently and warmly associated with his people, was greeted with a chorus of acclamation. As in the days of Frederick I, the people once more spoke with approval of the free hand of the king, and talk was long current in the country of the gifts and the patents of nobility of the great year of grace 1787. Many of the severities of the Frederician regime were done away with ; the detested governmental administration of public utilities was abolished ; the recruiting officers received orders that " for the general advantage of humanity " they should do their harsh work with moderation. Yet in essentials the old administration remained unchanged, and all that was lacking was the master-spirit that had animated it. The military system declined under its senile leaders ; the king did not venture to dismiss the veterans who still wore the laurels of the Seven Years' War. The philanthropic ideas of the age, and a well-meaning but weakly compliancy towards the interests of the bourgeoisie, carried the state far from the Spartan stringency of Frederick William I. It is true that by the cantonal regulation of 1792 the old Prussian principle of universal military service was maintained ; and yet at the same time the exceptions to the obligation, already far too numerous, were legally recognised and enlarged so that the duty to bear arms pressed almost exclusively upon the sons of the peasantry.

The gay court was by no means grossly extravagant. The expenses of the court, which now provided liberal subsidies to artists and men of learning, averaged per year no more than 580,000 thalers—not more than was needed by the thrifty successor of Frederick William. The king's lack of economy was shown only in his frivolous waste of the goods of the state, and it was yet more disastrous that his good-natured humour rendered him unable to resolve to replace by new and just taxes the oppressive taxes that had been repealed. The surpluses which this national economy could not do without, soon dried up. Courage was lacking to overcome the difficult obstacles which the feudal constitution opposed to every increase in the burden of taxation ; the king was glad to take credit to himself for the alleviation he had brought to his dearly loved people. As soon as one mobilisation and two campaigns had almost completely emptied the

Frederician war-chest, the monarchy found itself in the humiliating position of having to maintain its power with the aid of foreign gold. In the city, immorality became rife now that it was able to excuse itself by the example of the court, and flourished still more luxuriantly when there ensued the inevitable reaction against the superficial freethought of the Frederician days, and when a morbidly mystical piety became the fashion in court circles. The extraordinary power of the new literary idealism is shown by the fact that public opinion has always judged the Prussian ruling system by the spirit it has displayed in the conduct of ecclesiastical and educational affairs. The whole of Germany simmered with anger when the distinguished Zedlitz was dismissed from office and the dull hypocrite Wöllner endeavoured to repress the free speculation of the century by his Religious and Censorial Edicts. It proved difficult to promulgate the civil code against the obstinate resistance of the devotees at court. The healthy nucleus of the officialdom remained indeed indestructible, but the laborious course of the administration was no longer able to keep pace with the quicker movement of bourgeois intercourse, and the general relaxation of discipline was manifested by many defalcations and instances of corruption which would have been unthinkable under the two previous kings.

And now, in these days without renown, it became clear how weak was the footing upon which had been established that sense of the state which Frederick had awakened in his people. For the most part the national pride of the Prussian was a sentiment of honour towards the great king, and that pride waned with the hero's death. To the majority of East Prussians and Silesians, Berlin was altogether out of the world; the particularism of the territorial areas found the foci of its interests in Königsberg, Breslau, and Magdeburg. An earnest and comprehensive participation in the destiny of the state was found only in narrow circles. All the louder became the chorus of criticism. The political impulse which in the officialised state found no stage for work on behalf of the Commonwealth, threw itself into literature. A flood of lampoons was spread over Germany, regaling uncritical and credulous readers with colossal fables about the Asiatic debauchery of " Saul II, King of Cannonland." This was an unwholesome and very dangerous activity, because in an absolute monarchy every censure is arrowed directly against the personality of the king, and still more dangerous because out of this abundance of censorious criticism not a single fruitful idea emerged. never an intimation of the real infirmity of the community. It was a tragical change of scene. The world continued to tell stories of the brilliant sayings of the round table of Sans Souci, whilst now close at hand in Charlottenburg and in the Marble Palace at the Heilige See, Reitz, the groom of the chambers, talked platitudes with the Countess Lichtenau, and the successor of Frederick regarded with wonder the spirits manifested in the magic mirror of Colonel Bischofswerder.

Frederick's last work, the League of German Princes, fell to pieces in the hands of his heir. The old king had indeed never had any doubt as to the real sentiments of his petty federal associates, nor of the untrustworthiness of the friendship of Hanover and Saxony. His contemptuous phrase is on record, " There is nothing to be done with these fellows." None the less he had left this League of Princes as an inheritance to posterity. As long as the extraordinary favour of the situation persisted, as long as the fear of Austria forced the high nobility of Germany to place themselves under the banner of Prussia, it was inevitable that a strong will should know how to make use of the conspicuous position at the head of the League of German Princes as a means for the permanent increase of power. The vacancy of the imperial throne was imminent, for the Emperor Joseph was seriously ill. By a secret article in the constitution of the League, it was agreed among the associated princes that the new imperial election should be decided in accordance with a common understanding. Prussia controlled the majority in the Electoral Council; in the most important of the spiritual states, Electoral Mainz, the choice of a coadjutor had just been decided in Prussia's favour. At least the attempt must be ventured to renew the policy of the second Silesian War, in circumstances that were incomparably more favourable, and, under the leadership of Prussia, to animate the dead mass of the central states of Germany until they should form a living power. Once more it seemed that it would be possible to transfer the German crown to a German house, or else to abolish the Emperorship entirely and to reconstitute in federal form the Illustrious Republic of the German Princes. The smaller associates must necessarily, however unwillingly, obey a victorious Prussia. The sceptical views of his experienced predecessor were remote from the more trivial and more trusting nature of the new king. As a prince he had already built great hopes upon the idea of the League of Princes, but now for a time he left the conduct of his German policy in the hands of Charles Augustus of Weimar.

In the head of this great-hearted patriot there blossomed bold and vastly conceived schemes of reform. Unweariedly he travelled from court to court as the courier of the League of Princes. He regarded this defensive alliance as a permanent institution, and as the solid nucleus of a new imperial constitution; he thought of creating a standing army for the League and of providing a great parade-ground in Mainz; the Bundestag, summoned to Mainz, was to undertake the task of imperial reform and to do away with the inveracities of the existing law. Prospects seemed favourable. All the petty states of Europe felt themselves threatened by the adventurous plans of conquest of the Hofburg, and were inclined to look upon Prussia as the protector of the balance of power. In Piedmont and in Switzerland, the question had already been mooted whether it would not be well to join the League of Princes, in order thus to secure protection against Austria. When Belgium took up arms against the innovations of the Emperor Joseph, the proposal was made that this imperial crown-land should also be admitted, as an independent state, into the imperial association.

Meanwhile Prussia had once more consciously assumed the role of the leading power of Central Europe. Count Hertzberg had conceived the happy thought of delivering from the dominion of the patriotic party, or in other words, from the influence of France, the Republic of the Netherlands, distracted by internal struggles. The king's troops entered Holland, gained an easy victory over the patriots, and restored the repute of the House of Orange. Now came the time to enjoy the fruits of victory and to attach to the Prussian system this royal house akin to Prussia by blood and re-established by the force of Prussian arms. It was the advice of Charles Augustus that the republic should join the League of Princes, and that by regular subsidies to the smaller princes of the empire, the maintenance of a standing army should be rendered possible. But here, for the first time, became manifest the disastrous instability of the king, who was unable to put any of his good ideas into effective operation. His zeal for the League of Princes had long had time to cool. The gentle disposition of Frederick William led him to honour, with imperial-princely devotion, the anciently consecrated forms of the German constitution, and his piety was shocked by the thought of any radical reform. The statesmen of Berlin barely concealed their contempt for the League of German petty princes, and Count Hertzberg frequently called it "the great affliction of high policy." Since

Saxony and Hanover proved antagonistic, the summoning of the Bundestag to Mainz never took place. None of the proposals of Charles Augustus were realised, and within two years of the death of Frederick there was no longer any talk of the development and firmer establishment of the League of Princes. The army of Prussia evacuated the Netherlands, and the frivolous spirit of the king was willing to leave the payment of the costs of the war to the rich neighbour peoples. The undertaking that had been so brilliantly begun, terminated in a diplomatic reverse. It was not Prussia but England that won the upper hand at the Hague, and the ancient alliance between the two naval powers was re-established. More than 6,000,000 thalers had been wasted, and from that time the government began to suffer from a disastrous lack of money. In the army, moreover, the effect of the bloodless triumphs in Holland were most unfortunate, and the professional soldier conceived a boundless contempt for the idea of an armed nation.

Even yet, however, the wonderful favour of fortune was not exhausted. The king was provided with still another opportunity to strengthen his power at once in Germany and in Europe. The Emperor Joseph could not reconcile himself to the defeats of the Silesian and Bavarian Wars. Dominated by a passionate desire to revenge the honour of his house upon the Prussian opponent, and to restore his dominant position in the empire, he abandoned the interests of Austria in the east ; he came to an understanding with Russia and acceded to the designs of Catherine upon Constantinople, in return for great expansions of territory in Bavaria, Italy, and the Turkish frontier regions. Whilst the armies of the two imperial powers now began in the Danubian region a laborious campaign against the Turks, in the hereditary dominions of Austria there was everywhere manifested a resistance to the hasty reforms of the emperor and to the forcible attempts he made in the direction of centralisation. Belgium was in open rebellion ; the Magyars were so profoundly disaffected that the Hungarian nobles were already sending messages to the King of Prussia, asking him to propose a new King of Hungary. There was an uproar in all the cabinets when the plans of aggrandisement of the imperial court came to light. King Frederick William concluded with the naval powers a triple alliance for the preservation of the *status quo* in the Orient. Sweden had already declared war against Russia ; even the Poles were thinking of taking up arms against the Empress Catherine, and formed an alliance with Prussia. France, which since the days of Choiseul had been allied with Austria, was now compelled by the outbreak of the Revolution to abandon all thought of a bold foreign policy ; the court of Berlin greeted with joy the beginnings of the Great Revolution because it endangered the Austro-French Alliance ; the Prussian diplomatists were careful to keep on good terms with Pétion and the other spokesmen of the National Assembly. Never before had the general situation been so favourable for a campaign against Austria. If the Prussian army, which was assembled on the Silesian frontier, should venture to strike a blow into the heart of the Austrian power, there was nothing between the Prussians and Vienna that could offer any serious resistance, for almost the entire fighting force of the emperor was engaged upon the distant Turkish War. Now or never was the moment to end German dualism with the sword. Now was the time to put the question which had once before been proudly asked by Frederick when he stood between enemies and doubtful friends—to ask of Destiny the question, " Prussia or Austria ? "

But neither the king nor his minister Hertzberg fully understood the significance of this great moment in relation to the future of Germany. This doctrinaire man of learning, a great Prussian, full of love for the fatherland, entirely convinced that the irreconcilable opposition between the two great powers of Germany, was the inevitable outcome of geographical necessity, had been a valuable assistant to the old king, active alike as publicist and as writer of despatches in all the diplomatic negotiations that had taken place from the beginning of the Seven Years' War until the foundation of the League of Princes ; but he was not competent to undertake the independent continuation of the Frederician policy in its simple greatness. Although King Frederick had used him merely as an instrument and had seldom listened to his advice, he was in his own mind the true heir of the great king and of all " the ancient and powerful Brandenburger system," and he considered himself to be the leading connoisseur of the diplomatic relationships of Europe. He thought that so long as his hand was on the tiller, no mistake could possibly be made, and that Prussia would continue to play the leading part in European affairs. Instead of the simple plans which the old hero had pursued with relentless openness, his pupil loved to think out elaborate and artificial combinations for the preservation of the balance of power ; and it seemed to him that an alliance between the three northern powers, Prussia, England, and Russia, was the philosopher's stone of the situation, although suitable conditions for such an alliance were altogether lacking. Whereas Frederick ever held it as a sober opinion that in the wide world Prussia had only enemies, open or concealed, Hertzberg built with unshaken self-conceit upon the victorious force of his reasoning. He dreamed that he had found an unfailing way for the solution of the eastern problem : the separation of the northern provinces from Turkey and the reunion of Galicia with Poland were to provide the means for a comprehensive territorial redistribution in Eastern Europe which would be accepted with joy by all the powers of the east ; the Prussian go-between was to be rewarded with Swedish Pomerania, Danzig and Thorn, Kalisz and Posen—in a word, all the gaps on the northern and eastern frontiers of Prussia were to be filled in. This was to be effected without any need for un-sheathing the sword, by the magic of the pen of a diplomatist.

To Hertzberg's astonishment this over-elaborated plan was rejected by the two imperial powers ; and he soon encountered also the veto of the allies of Prussia. The naval powers feared an open breach with the imperial courts because they were afraid of losing the lucrative Russian trade. It was for this reason that as long ago as the Seven Years' War England had refused to Prussia the one really valuable help she could give as an ally, namely, the sending of a strong fleet into the Baltic. The Poles, too, were unwilling to consent to the withdrawal from Danzig and Posen, which might perhaps have rendered possible the continuance of the Polish Republic. The Porte, finally, would not hear of any reduction of its dominion, for its armies were making a good resist-ance to the attacks of the imperial powers. In this emergency, Prussia dropped her demands and asked merely for the restoration of the *status quo* in the east. Even now the negotiations might have led to a decisive reckoning with Austria, if the Prussian tone had been strengthened so that Austria might have seriously feared war. But Hertzberg refused to go as far as this, whereas the king with a wiser judgment demanded a decision by recourse to arms. In the middle of this momentous development the Emperor Joseph died, and now payment had to be made for the arrogant contempt which Hertzberg had displayed for the League of Princes. The League had already been weakened, because the sentiment of the smaller courts was so unstable that to them the great question of the election of the emperor no longer seemed a matter of import-ance. With his usual fickleness, King Frederick William soon abandoned his warlike schemes, consoling himself with the reflection that even his uncle had never wished to acquire the imperial honour for his own house ; and when the successor of King Joseph, Leopold II, approached him in a yielding spirit he, without further consideration, offered Leopold the imperial dignity. Content with a half victory, he concluded on July 26, 1790, the unlucky Reichenbach Convention, which merely restored the *status quo* before the Oriental War.

It was so far a success that the threatening attitude of Prussia compelled the House of Lorraine to abandon its conquest of Belgrade, and to bring to an inglorious close that Turkish War which had been undertaken with such extravagant hopes and with such a great beating of drums. And yet Leopold quite understood the situation when, drawing a breath of relief, he wrote : " This is the least bad peace we could hope to conclude." The death of Joseph II was as disastrous to Prussia's German policy as had formerly been the death of Charles VII. Joseph's prudent successor rescued Austria's position of power in the empire by giving up his brother's oriental plans. As he himself admitted, he received the imperial crown without conditions, as a generous gift from the King of Prussia. The diplomatic defeat of Austria was advantageous solely to the Turks and to the maritime powers. By the intervention of Prussia, the Porte was relieved of a dangerous opponent ; and to the excessive prudence of Hertzberg, the rigidly conservative oriental policy of England owed an easy triumph. Soon, however, the court of Berlin saw the world-situation altered to its disadvantage. By the skilled compliancy of Leopold, the rebellious crown-lands were rendered once more obedient, were kept quiet by his Florentine secret policy. In Poland, Austria soon acquired a dominant influence. Sweden concluded a disadvantageous peace with Russia. England openly refused to co-operate in Hertzberg's Polish schemes. Above all, the Convention of Reichenbach was the death of the League of Princes, was the end of the German policy of the great king. The smaller princes, when they saw that in Berlin there was now lacking a proud and dominant will, and that from Leopold's moderation there was nothing more to fear, relapsed one after another to their natural party position ; they reconciled themselves with Austria ; the League of Princes vanished without leaving a trace ; there was not even effected a serious reform of the electoral capitulation.

The last favourable hour in which Prussia might perhaps have done something to relieve the hopeless confusion of imperial policy had passed beyond recall. Without guidance, the shapeless

German community drifted hopelessly towards its destruction by foreign power. Charles Augustus complained bitterly of the slumbering spirit of the Germans, which regarded this chaos as the sacrosanct ideal of a good constitution. Whilst in the west the storm was already gathering which threatened to destroy all the ancient forms of the European world, the well-meaning Elector of Cologne expressed the heartfelt wish of the German high nobility for the future of the fatherland. "We need a peaceful Emperor, one who will economically maintain the German system; but we must leave to the pigmies their illusion that they also are running the machine." The people, too, were totally without understanding of the seriousness of the time. Isolated intelligent publicists, such as George Forster, esteemed the triumph of Prussian statecraft, but the sins of omission of that statecraft passed unmarked. The mass of the nation rejoiced over the re-establishment of peace. When during the Reichenbach negotiations the king paid homage to the fashionable Nature-cult and climbed to the summit of the Heuscheuer, the loyal Silesians erected a monument to him upon the frontier mountains, with the grateful inscription, "His shield is the safeguard of our peace."

A necessary consequence of this pusillanimous maintenance of peace was that before long Hertzberg was thrust aside by the already powerful favourite Bischofswerder. However unfortunate he had been in his choice of means, Hertzberg had at least never abandoned one of the fundamental principles of the Frederician statecraft, for he had always endeavoured to maintain the proud independence of Prussian policy from the commands of the Hofburg. But with the accession to power of Bischofswerder, an entirely new tendency came into operation—the policy of peaceful dualism. In sharp contrast with the glorious fifty years that had just closed, it was hoped by this policy to safeguard the existence of the state by an alliance with Austria, directed especially against Russia. The idea of imperial reform was utterly renounced, it being considered that the best hope for German affairs lay in a loyal understanding with the imperial house. In the spring of 1791, Bischofswerder began the negotiations for the Austro-Prussian Alliance. Nothing could have been more unfortunate for the fate of Germany. This alliance between two irreconcilable enemies was an essential falsehood. On both sides confidence was wholly lacking. The great majority of the Prussian statesmen still adhered firmly to the Frederician traditions, and followed with lively suspicion every step taken by the Vienna cabinet ; in the Hofburg neither the conquest of Silesia nor the humiliation of Reichenbach had been forgiven, and there was no inclination whatever to recognise the northern newcomer as an equal associate. Of all the great questions of power which were in dispute between the two rivals, not a single one had been solved. Contrary to the expectations of Berlin, the alliance between Austria and Russia remained established. The pliant disposition of the king towards the imperial house did not change in the mind of the emperor the old conviction that every increase of Prussian power in the empire was disastrous to Austria ; the Court of Vienna marked with great anxiety the union with Prussia of the some-time Hohenzollern territory of Ansbach-Bayreuth whereby Prussia for the first time planted her feet firmly in South Germany and won a threatening position on the flank of Bohemia. Still sharper was the contrast of interests between the two allies in respect of the Polish question.

Both the powers desired to maintain the Republic of Polish Nobles as a bulwark against Catherine's restless policy of conquest. The mechanical conception of the state characteristic of the age found pleasure in artificialities. Whereas peace can be established only through the sound internal health of vigorous national states, it was then hoped to secure peace by a carefully maintained system of balances ; by the arbitrary construction of petty states, which should act as buffers between the great powers. Neither in Vienna nor in Berlin did anyone come to understand that this Polish state of unbridled Junkerdom was doomed to destruction, that the freedom of Poland was nothing more than the foreign domination of Sarmatian nobles and landed gentry over millions of Slav, Lithuanian, German, Jewish, and Wallachian subjects, who had no rights and no sentiments in common with their cruel masters. Austria, intimately akin to the Catholic State of Nobles, and for hundreds of years past in continuous alliance with that state, had nothing more to expect from a new partition, and hoped rather to find in a strong Polish realm protection against Russia and Prussia. The Prussian state, on the other hand, had grown up in conflict with its Sarmatian neighbours, and had reason to dread that a revival of the Polish power would greatly endanger the German Vistula region. The results of the first partition could prove satisfactory to Prussia only on the condition that Poland should remain a harmless power of intermediate importance, and that at least Thorn and Danzig should be united with West Prussia. Now that the two most important places in the German section of the Vistula were surrounded by Prussian territory, it was impossible that they should be permanently left in the hands of a foreign conqueror who was no longer able to keep his old plunder in his grasp. Every consideration of prudence impelled the Polish notables to gain the friendship of Prussia by a yielding disposition. But not even the terrible experience of the year 1772 had brought the stupid and arrogant nobles to their senses. Now, as before, the unhappy people was racked by party struggles. In Warsaw the hope was still cherished of unfurling the white eagle once again upon the Green Bridge of Königsberg.

After a brief attempt at friendliness, the Polish policy became once more decisively hostile towards the western neighbour, the old deadly hate against the Germans, the Protestants, the conquerors of the mouth of the Vistula, broke out once more. The *coup d'état* of the victorious party on May 3, 1791, led to the creation of a new constitution which to Prussia was necessarily equivalent to a declaration of war ; the crown of Poland was to be furnished with enhanced power and was to be the hereditary appanage of the House of the Albertines. The unnatural alliance between Saxons and Poles which once before had for long decades, as Frederick William I was accustomed to say, shut up the Prussian state in a " cage," was now to be renewed for all time. A Slav-Catholic power with a population twice as large as that of Prussia, hostile to the German nation by race, creed, and ancient memories, ruled by a princely house which must inevitably fall under the influence of the Roman nuncio and of the Austrian ambassador, threatened to spring into existence in the centre of Germany and to enclose the Prussian state in the south as in the east. This plan, which once more put in question the very existence of the Prussian great power, the entire work of the Hohenzollerns since the days of the Great Elector, received the eager support of the Emperor Leopold, the ally of the King of Prussia. Though the king, in a wave of generous caprice, had accepted the new Polish constitution, yet the moment must soon come in which he would recognise his error, and would understand that the policy of the Hofburg was equally hostile to Prussian interests in Poland and in Germany.

Such was the state of affairs. The constitution of the Holy Empire was hopelessly disorganised ; every possibility of a reform from within outwards had been lost ; the two leading powers were allied in appearance but within were separated more sharply than ever by ancient hatred and conflicting interests. Whilst in this posture, Germany was influenced by that elemental movement which had shaken France to its vitals. Goethe has depicted for us how this ingenuous race of ours, free from envy and ever appreciative of the great deeds of the foreigner, rejoiced " when the first rays of the new sun began to shine, when we heard of the Rights of Man, the rights common to all." A joyful belief in the unending progress of humanity, this cherished idea of the philosophical century, appeared to be established ; it seemed as if " the highest that man can conceive was now near and attainable." The æsthetic impulse towards freedom characteristic of the young poet had long intoxicated him with the idea of the free individuality, which, liberated from all compulsion, should obey only the voice of its own heart. The preference of genius threw aside all traditional morals, even the bonds of domestic fidelity ; in artistic circles, adultery and easy-going divorce became exceedingly common, and could reckon upon the smiling tolerance of free spirits. And now, since the night of the fourth of August, the detested compulsory authority of the state also appeared to be no more than a construction of human arbitrariness, no more than a soft clay which the will of freemen could always knead into new forms. The artist, yearning for freedom from the state, saw his most cherished dreams overwhelmingly fulfilled by the Declaration of the Rights of Man ; to the æsthetic view of the world-order characteristic of this generation there seemed no need to seek freedom within the state, to think of the duties which bind the citizen to the community. The one of the existing political institutions which in literary circles aroused the most passionate hostility was the legal inequality of the classes, which was felt to be all the more abhorrent because in the free social intercourse of cultured circles it had long been in fact disregarded. What joy was now felt when France announced the equality of all who bear the human form ; when the prophecies of Rousseau, who more than any other Frenchman appealed to the enthusiastic idealism of the German youth, seemed on the point of realisation. All the yearnings of the time, the noble impulse towards the recognition of human dignity and of the heaven-storming confidence of the sovereign ego, now found satisfaction in the audacious paradox of the Genevese philosopher, that in a state of complete freedom each man would obey himself alone.

To the guileless German theorists, the sins of the Revolution seemed hardly less seductive than its greatness. To the taste that had been schooled upon Plutarch's *Lives*, the stilted Catonism of the new apostles of freedom made a powerful appeal; the unhistorical abstractions of their doctrine of the state corresponded to the philosophical self-complacency of the age. The enthusiastic youth, in whose ears were still ringing the words of power of the Robber Moor, was powerfully moved by the rhetorical pathos of the French enthusiast, admired the republican virtue of the school of the Girondists, at the very time that this party was with a reckless light-heartedness planning war against Germany. The romantic glorification of the old Emperordom which during recent years had been in vogue among the Swabian poets, now came altogether to an end. Even Klopstock turned away from his Cheruscan oak-groves to direct his eyes towards the new capital of the world, to sing the praises of the hundred-armed, hundred-eyed giant, and to exclaim, " Had I a hundred voices, I could not celebrate the liberation of Gallia with loud enough tones, if the divine voices did not join in the chorus." Cosmopolitan enthusiasm for freedom dreamed of a brotherhood of all the nations, declaimed in verse and in prose against tyrants and slaves, " to whom the sound of chains is sweet !" In Hamburg and other towns, on the anniversary of the storming of the Bastille, the Festival of Fraternity was celebrated and the tree of liberty was erected. The whole circle of those who surrounded Klopstock—Henning, the embodiment of the spirit of the age, Frau Reimarus and the Stolbergs—was intoxicated with this new spirit. Campe and the other advocates of the new doctrines of education saw with delight how the over-cultured world seemed to be turning back once more to the innocence of primitive humanity. For High Germany, Strasburg was the centre of the revolutionary ideas ; thither went the young hotheads from Swabia in order to learn the new French evangel. In the street-talk of the students, in Tübingen, Mainz, and Jena, there could sometimes be heard political appeals ; here and there there were brawls with the *emigrés*, the arrogant and undisciplined behaviour of these traitors to their country seeming to justify all the violence of the Revolution. Even in Berlin, women of the upper classes were seen adorned with the tricolor, and the rector of the Joachimstal Gymnasium took occasion on the king's birthday to celebrate in an official speech the glories of the Revolution, doing this with the lively approval of the minister Hertzberg.

Among the leaders of the nation none was more profoundly impressed by the great movement of the neighbour country than was Kant. In his quiet way he had attentively followed the political thought-movement of the age. More especially, he was intimately acquainted with the works of Rousseau and Adam Smith, and he now summed up in scientific phrase the metaphysical struggles for freedom of the century in the great saying : " In every man we must honour the dignity of the whole race, and no human being must be used as a means to the ends of others." What he had discovered in his solitary reflection he now saw realised in the deeds of the French, and since in the serene quiet of his life he had absolutely no intimation of the elemental energies of the French populace, not even the horrors of the Reign of Terror disturbed his admiration for the Revolution, for the men-of-blood of the guillotine were also appealing to the rights of the ideal. In the school of Kant the true content of the ideas of the revolutionary epoch is most faithfully displayed.

This enthusiasm of the German cultured world for revolutionary France remained purely theoretical. Just as the jurists of Göttingen and Halle, in the more general part of their discourses, had built up a system of rational law out of the ideal in order subsequently, in the special part of these discourses, to expound dispassionately the precise opposite of the rational state, the labyrinth of the imperial German constitution, so now the German admirers of the Revolution never asked themselves how their ideas were to be realised in flesh and blood. The sage of Königsberg unconditionally rejected all right of resistance. Fichte, himself the most radical of Kant's pupils, who ventured to defend French liberty even in the days of Robespierre, uttered an express warning against the attempt to carry out his own ideas ; he saw no bridge between " the level highroad of natural right " and " the obscure by-ways of a semi-barbarous policy," and came to the regretful conclusion that " worthiness for liberty can come only from below, but liberty can be installed without disorder only from above." As long as the blows of the Revolution affected only the nobility and the Old Church, the theoretical admiration of the Germans was unaffected ; it was their naive belief that the Jacobins were engaged by dire necessity in the struggle with a rout of dangerous traitors, and that " whoever fell, fell because he had done wrong." But when the party-struggle became continually fiercer, and when the fanatical rage for equality undertook to annihilate even the ultimate aristocracy, that of life itself, it was no longer possible for the leal and severe German sentiment to follow the capricious development of Gallic passion. The German enthusiasts turned with tears from the barbarians who had desecrated their sanctuary. Klopstock complained " Our golden dream is shattered " : people were horrified and disillusioned. The sentiment of cold contempt which the cruelty of the Reign of Terror must necessarily arouse in a politically mature nation, was not produced in the good-natured Germans ; they noticed merely that the mass-murders of the Committee of Public Safety were imposed by an infinitesimal minority upon a slavishly obedient people. Those who had been thus disillusioned, sank back into the ancient political indifference, and devoted their whole activity once more to the work of art and science. Goethe expressed the heartfelt view of the great majority of cultured Germans when he laid it to the charge of France that that country had to-day, as had Lutheranism of old, disturbed peaceful culture. Schiller, too, voiced the general feeling when he introduced the " Hours " with the words : " The poet and philosopher belongs in the body to his own age, because he cannot help it, but in the spirit he is a contemporary of all the ages."

The most noble literary work which in Germany was the outcome of the Revolution, came from the opposite camp. It was inevitable that the forces of conservatism should draw together in order to counteract the revolutionary ideas. Among the Prussian officers, it was especially the perjury of the French troops which aroused profound disgust ; there was formed a Royalist Club, upon whose members was strictly impressed the sacred character of their oath to the flag. Brandes and Rehberg expressed the sentiment of the old society in well-meaning and well-informed writings, which lacked however both energy and profundity ; Spittler judged the blessings and the curses of the great movement with the impartial security of the historian. The insight of Captain Gneisenau recognised as early as the year 1790 that the French were ripe for enslavement, and foresaw that an unparalleled revolution threatened the frontiers of all the nations. It was somewhat longer before Frederick Gentz came to a full understanding of the signs of the times. In April, 1791, he dissented from Burke's attacks upon the Revolution ; but a year and a half later he translated the Englishman's book into German, and appended those valuable essays which constitute a turning-point in the history of our political culture. In these it was recognised for the first time that the great age of our literature was destined to rejuvenate and enlighten the political thinking also of the nation. A disciple of the new culture, equipped with the wealth of ideas of the Kantian philosophy and with the pure sense of form of classical poetry, he was the first to exhibit that energy of productive criticism which owed a new life to art and science, devoting himself not to abstract speculation upon natural law, but to the criticism of the living facts of contemporary history. He understood how to see reality, how, in the inchoate structure of the moment, to recognise the foreshadowings of future development. With a power and wealth of speech which Germany had hitherto known in its poets alone, he chastised the folly that characterised the mob, and prophesied, " France will pass from form to form, from catastrophe to catastrophe." It was indeed already evident that in strength of character this first publicist of the age was not the equal of his own talents ; his hatred for the Revolution was not free from nervous anxiety ; he trembled before the excess of knowledge, before this wild century " which begins to need the bridle," and yet from his work there springs sharply and clearly the ground-ideas of a new and vigorous view of the state, one closely connected with the awakening of the historical sense of German science. The historical doctrine of the state is here opposed to the cosmopolitan radicalism of the Revolution ; it attacks the pleasing illusion of soft-headed people who wish to introduce into politics the discarded claims of a Church in which alone can be found salvation, who think of limiting the rich multiplicity of national culture, political and legal, by a catechism of commonplaces concerning natural rights. It dispelled superstitious belief in the right reason of the majority by the incisive saying, " It is not majority rule, but the *liberum veto*, which is a natural right." It defended the power of the state against the unbridled individualism of the age, and maintained against the grasping demands of the sovereign ego the profound truth that " political freedom is politically limited freedom."

Many years of hard experience were to pass away before the cultured members of the nation could learn to understand this saying. For the moment, their happy peace remained undisturbed ; and still less in the lower strata of the people was any dangerous political excitement to be noted. The curse of Germany was in its system of petty states and in the torpor of the imperial constitution. And how was it possible for the quietly satisfied particularism of the masses to recognise these essential disorders of German life ? The internal conditions of the greater temporal states, in so far as these had been affected by the spirit of the Frederician epoch, gave no occasion for passionate unrest. Many of the political ideas which the half-culture of to-day is apt to celebrate as " the ideas of '89," had in Prussia long been realised or were approaching realisation. Freedom of conscience had been established for generations ; freedom of the press was but little curtailed ; almost everywhere in the Protestant North the churches were subordinated to the authority of the state, and their goods had been secularised ; a benevolent agrarian administration imposed strict limits upon the feudal rights of the nobles ; what still remained in existence of the vestiges of an outworn social order could be peacefully abolished by a firm reforming will. It was only in the petty states, where the justice of the monarchy was lacking, that there was still to be found a counterpart of the sins of the French aristocracy under the old regime. In the ecclesiastical states of Germany, there yet flourished a Catholic unity of belief ; in the arrogant aristocratic cathedral-capitals, in the imperial towns, there still prevailed the sloth and the corruption of the old civic nepotism ; in the territories of the princes, the counts, and the imperial knights, there was still active the arbitrary spirit of hole-and-corner tyrants. The whole existence of these corrupt and ossified administrations was a scandal to the ideas of the century.

It was almost exclusively in these inconsiderable sections of the empire, when the joyful tidings came from France of the liberation of the peasantry, that there was manifest a certain fermentation among the people. It resulted that the Abbess of Frauenalb was chased out of the country by her subjects, while to her colleague in Elten the oath of allegiance was refused. Minor disturbances among the peasantry broke out in the district of Treves, in the territories of some of the imperial knights, and above all in Spires, the most notorious of the German bishoprics, where since the days of the Peasant War there had prevailed a rigid priestly dominion, and where the Table of Laws for the temporal servants of the state held up before the officials as their highest aim " the fulfilling of the will of the Lord, which is best for all." In Mecklenburg, ill-treated serfs assembled and threatened to put their feudal chief to death. The wretched local quarrels, which for most of the imperial towns formed the essential fabric of life, now assumed an exceptionally fierce tone ; the language used against the suzerainty became louder and more virulent ; the spiritual princes all along the Rhine betrayed their serious anxiety by the issue of threats of punishment against the rebellious spirit of their subjects.

All this had very little significance. In truth, nowhere else in the empire was the political slumber so profound as here ; and even the literary movement of Protestant Germany had barely touched the demoralised little peoples of the lands of the crozier. But whilst there was no serious danger of uprising from below, whilst even Forster in the days of his radical enthusiasm had to admit that Germany was not ripe for a revolution, it was also true that in this region of feckless and unarmed petty states there was lacking all power of resistance to foreign force. The slowly-dying members of the empire were neighbours to France, and had been accustomed for two centuries past to obey the orders of the court of Versailles ; such regions were interspersed among the domains of the more vigorous temporal states. Should revolutionary France endeavour to establish in some new form the old dominion of the Bourbons upon the German Rhine, ecclesiastical Germany might easily go to pieces at a touch, and might bring down with it in its fall the last ruins of the Holy Empire.

This danger threatened already in the very earliest, in the reputedly blameless, days of the Revolution. It was the greatness and the curse of this movement that it tended inevitably to over-flow the borders of France. The horrible Peasants' War of the summer of 1789 and the new laws to countenance the results of this mass-movement, served merely to realise a whole world of desires and thoughts which during a century past had undergone diffusion through all the nations of the west ; what wonder, then, that the French now regarded themselves as the Messiahs of freedom. The sudden collapse of the Bourbon rule was ascribed, not to the fact that the old order was enormously more degenerate in France than in other lands, but to the superiority of the French genius. Among the causes of the Revolution, a considerable one was undoubtedly the general discontent regarding the profound decline in the standing of France in Europe ; and now that the power of this people had after all displayed itself so gloriously, and when foreign nations were looking admiringly towards Paris as the capital of the world, the French felt that it was their mission to impose laws on all the earth. The nation was accustomed to despise every foreign power ; it dreamt that its culture must always serve as an example to the entire world as it had in earlier days, in the time of Louis XIV ; of the new and original culture which had sprung to life in Germany, the French knew nothing. The Declaration of the Rights of Man had set an example to all other peoples, and Lafayette hailed the new tricolor with the prophecy that the flag should wave round the world. Since then, the force of the revolutionary propaganda had increased; the internal disorders of all the neighbouring countries, of Italy and Spain, of Holland and Belgium, of Switzerland and the German petty states, promised an easy victory to France. A world-war such as had been unknown in Europe since the days of the wars of religion was imminent when all the horrible corruption which had characterised France under the rule of the Bourbons (dependent upon the immorality of the higher classes and the rude ignorance of the lower), in association with the elemental energy of the ideas of a new epoch, rose like a flood to overwhelm this world of defenceless states.

The first blow against the rights of the German empire had already been struck; the estates of the empire in Alsace had been deprived of their territorial rights, and the ecclesiastical princes had been robbed of their spiritual goods in defiance of public agreements and without asking the empire. Thus the old question of power which had so long been disputed between the two neighbouring peoples, the struggle for the region of the Rhine that had never been fought to a conclusive issue, was forced upon the Germans in a wonderfully complicated form. It was impossible to contest the need for an appeal to force. Everyone knew the unhappy situation of the unfortunate peasants of Alsace, who had to pay taxes to the crown of France and at the same time feudal dues to the petty German lords. Through the liberating act of the Revolution, the hearts of the kindly people in this German area had been completely won for France. Should Prussia, should the intelligent temporal imperial princes who had themselves long ago made free with the goods of the Church, and who worked considerably to secure the liberation of their own peasantry, now intervene with the strong hand to secure the tithes of the Bishops of Treves and Spires, intervene on behalf of the feudal exactions of the overlords of Worms and of Leiningen, take action in support of this compost of petty princes and lords who in the Reichstag were in the habit of voting obediently *in omnibus sicut Austria,* and who in the north were regarded only with contempt? The struggle against France might very readily become war against the Revolution, for the radicalism of war tolerates no half measures. The *emigrés* were thronging and agitating in all the courts; the danger was imminent that if the sword were once drawn, these sworn foes of the Revolution would gain the upper hand, and that the German powers would be led on to the mad undertaking of attempting to restore the old Bourbon regime. But the privileges of the Alsatian estates of the realm formed the one bond of international law which still connected the *avulsa imperii* with the whole empire. To hand them over unconditionally to the sovereignty of the Paris National Assembly would be to abandon the last claims of the empire upon Alsace. The German state had not yet sunk so low as of its own free will to put the finishing touches to the work of Louis XIV—least of all now, when France broke out into ominous threats, and yet had neither money nor an army ready for war.

Thus alike in the west and in the east the storm was threatening, and for long the great enemy of Germany had been on the watch reckoning the hour when these two tempests should break simultaneously over our fatherland, when the destruction of Poland and the French War occurring coincidently might completely paralyse the leading German power. The Empress Catherine bore a grudge against the Prussian court because King Frederick had brought her Polish schemes to naught and because Frederick's successor, half involuntarily, had nullified her dreams of Byzantine imperialism. She had seen with regret Prussia and Austria come to an understanding, but soon found means to make these allies harmless to Russia. Could she only succeed in involving the German powers in the incalculable risks of a war with France, she would be mistress in Poland, and could carry out the inevitable destruction of the Nobles'-State as best she pleased. She hardly took the trouble to conceal her wishes, declaring openly to her councillors, "I want to have my elbows free, and to keep the German courts busy with French affairs." For this reason she hastened to bring the Turkish War to an end, and for this reason also she, the friend of Diderot, now appeared as a fanatical opponent of the Revolution. She protected the *emigrés*, and continually warned her neighbours of the common duty of all sovereigns to restore the ancient crown of France ; she desired to bring about a counter-revolution through the agency of the brothers of King Louis ; she pledged, in indefinite terms, the arms of Russia in aid of the great campaign of Royalism, keeping the power in her own hands of withdrawing her assistance as soon as she pleased. This course of conduct on the part of the court of St. Petersburg was so necessary a consequence of Russia's well-secured geographical position that the Prussian minister, Alvensleben, a man of by no means exceptional talent, immediately saw through the designs of the czarina, and foreshadowed to the king the policy of his restless neighbour.

Neither the emperor nor the statesmen of Prussia failed altogether to understand the incalculable dangers of a war in so confused a situation. Leopold's sober judgment long remained unaffected by the letters demanding help sent by his unfortunate sister, Marie Antoinette, who, filled with feminine passion and suffering from injured pride, went to the verge of treason in her machinations. The Prussian cabinet was at first well satisfied by the demeanour of the constitutional parties. The Prussian ambassador, von der Goltz, frankly recognised that the Revolution was justified, and did not shut his eyes to the accumulated follies of the unfortunate court. In Vienna and in Berlin the plots of the *emigrés* were severely censured. It was not until the spring of 1791, after King Louis had already had to atone for his ill-conceived attempt at flight by incredible personal humiliations, that the two courts began seriously to think of taking up arms against the Revolution. The exciting news came at a most momentous instant, for Bischofswerder had just taken the first steps towards the permanent union of the two powers. Frederick William's knightly sense was inspired by the idea of revenging the injury of the majesty of France with his own royal sword. Certain clever heads among the *emigrés* gradually acquired secret influence at the court ; it was not by chance that just at this moment a new and un-Prussian manner came over the administration ; that there was a departure from the proud free-spiritedness of the great king ; that pinpricks were directed against the leaders of the enlightenment. The powerful favourite was the book-keeper of all the demagogues and conspirators in Prussia. When the man of ill omen visited Austria for the second time in the summer of 1791, in order to confirm the understanding initiated in the spring, he found the emperor at Milan in an excited mood ; threatening expressions were let fall, to the effect that it was time for the bane of revolution to be uprooted—time for the disturbers of the peace to be attacked everywhere, not excepting Germany. Shortly afterwards in a circular letter from Padua, Leopold demanded of the European powers that they should come to the help of his misused brother-in-law ; that they should revenge the injury done to the honour of the king by recourse to powerful measures, and that they should refuse to recognise any French constitution which was not freely adopted by the crown. Bischofswerder, of his own initiative and against his instructions, signed the Vienna Convention of July 25th, whereby both powers guaranteed each other's possessions and promised one another help in case of internal disorders.

Therewith was the descending path which had been entered at Reichenbach pursued to its end. The cunning of Leopold had

completely overreached the king's favourite. Prussia abandoned
the proud independence of the Frederician policy, undertaking,
without receiving any corresponding advantage, to help the imperial
court in its need, for only Austria, and not Prussia, was threatened in its possessions. In Belgium the fires of discontent were
still smouldering, and an attack by the French might readily lead
them to break into open flame. The negotiator who had thus
exceeded his instructions was received with reproaches in Berlin:
several of the ministers entered vigorous protests against this
momentous change in the political system, contending that the most
effective means against revolution were careful husbandry of the
energies of the state, that the Vienna Convention involved incalculable responsiblities which might easily prove destructive to
the army and to the finances. Public opinion in Prussia was also
profoundly suspicious of the Austrian friendship. The memories
of the Seven Years' War had not yet passed away ; the rights of
the estates of the empire in Alsace and the fate of the left bank of
the Rhine were so remote from the thoughts of the North Germans
that even later, when the imperial war on the Rhine had already
lasted a year and a half, one of the first political intelligences of the
time, Spittler, wrote naively, " We Germans are enjoying a happy
repose ! " King Frederick William, however, approved the arbitrary steps of his friend. Soon afterwards he met Leopold at
Pillnitz, was attracted by the dignified personal conduct of the sly
Florentine, and exclaimed with rejoicing that the alliance between
the two great powers of Germany would endure to all eternity
for the blessing of future generations. There was, indeed, in
all this ill-will no immediate danger to France. Whilst Frederick
William himself ardently desired the campaign against the French
rebels, his minister was as decisively opposed to the thought of
an offensive war as was the entirely peaceful emperor. In Pillnitz, the *emigrés* who clamoured for war were ignored, and all
that resulted was the meaningless Declaration of August 27th,
in which the two powers stated that they regarded King Louis's
plight as the common concern of all sovereigns, and that intervention in the internal affairs of France would ensue as soon as all the
powers of Europe were in agreement upon the matter. This
amounted to nothing at all, for everyone was well aware that
England would never take part in an armed intervention. Even
these vague intimations came to nothing in Vienna when King
Louis was in the autumn restored to his dignities and when he
voluntarily accepted the new constitution. It seemed that the

Revolution had come to a standstill. The emperor was completely pacified, and even the old Prince Kaunitz, who had earnestly desired a European War against "the rabid fools" of France, now admitted that all danger of war was over. The negotiations concerning the rights of the empire in Alsace were conducted by Leopold, in accordance with ancient imperial custom, with a moderation that was tantamount to weakness ; he disregarded all measures of military security, and demanded merely an indemnity, but not restoration of what had been stolen. Austria and Prussia, upon the request of France, demanded of the Electoral Prince of Treves that he should forbid the equipment of the army of *emigrés* at Coblenz—this poor little army which, considering the deadly hate of the French against the traitor nobles, could never have been a danger to the new France. When Leopold added that he would use his Belgian troops to protect the men of Treves against the attacks of French levies, he did no more than promise to undertake what was already his inalienable duty as overlord of the empire.

It was France and France alone that forced war upon the German powers, notwithstanding their peaceful disposition. The fundamental law of the constitutional monarchy had been hardly established when the doctrinaires of the Gironde were already working for its destruction. They desired a republic, and speedily recognised that a declaration of war against the king's brother-in-law would irreparably undermine the repute of the throne, that the last poor vestiges of the old kingship must inevitably crumble as soon as the flood of the revolutionary propaganda began to flow over the whole of Europe. The antagonism to the republic of the enormous majority of the nation was to be overcome by glory and success in war, by the cherished ancient dream of the natural frontier ; and the financial need of the state was to be relieved by abundant booty. In view of the sensitive pride of the profoundly moved nation, and of its utter ignorance of foreign affairs, it was not difficult for the wild oratory of Brissot, Guadet, and Gensonné to weave out of true and false an attractive web of illusion, to assimilate the insane letters of the unhappy court and the open treason of the *emigrés* with the heedless words of the Declarations of Padua and Pillnitz. The nation began to believe that its new freedom was endangered by an obscure conspiracy of all the old powers, that the sword must be drawn in order to maintain the right of national self-government against the tutelage of Europe. Since the warlike mood gained ground from day to day in the legislative assembly, extreme arrogance was shown in the negotiations with the emperor, and no definite indemnity was offered to the estates of the empire in Alsace. Then the assembly, carried away by the flaming speeches of the Girondists, demanded of the emperor a formal declaration that he would abandon the plan of a European coalition, and that he would hold himself ready to support France in accordance with the old alliance with the Bourbons, and all this under pain of instant war. Since Leopold returned a dignified and temperate answer, war was declared against Austria upon April 20, 1792. Not more wantonly were begun the robber campaigns of Louis XIV than this struggle which, as far as all human expectation could show, must involve unprepared France in a shameful defeat. The doctrinaire speech of Condorcet then announced to the world that the principle of republican freedom was uprising against despotism. The gauntlet was thrown down to the whole of old Europe. As regards Prussia, the Vienna Convention now came into operation, and was reinforced by a formal defensive alliance.

The war was forced upon the German powers. Almost at the same moment, Russian troops, making light of all resistance, entered Poland, extending the control of the czarina as far as the Vistula. Once again, as so often before, the central power of the Continent stood between two fires. The statesmen of Prussia had now to choose whether they should offer a stout resistance to the hardly functional army of the Revolution, while devoting the main forces of the state to safeguarding German interests in the east, or whether conversely they should for a time let the Polish matter await decision, in order first to settle the French War with speedy and powerful strokes. Since France had herself torn up the old treaties by her declaration of war, a heroic sentiment might now conceive the hope of restoring to the empire the Vosges, so often mourned by King Frederick as the German Thermopylæ. Whichever might be the choice, the hour was pressing. It was essential that the entire might of Prussia should at once be put into the field in order, either in the east or in the west, to attain to a decisive issue with overwhelming speed. But the eagle eye of the great king was no longer watching over his state, and the pigmies who surrounded his successor advised the adoption of the stupidest course possible ; they began an offensive war against France, and devoted to this venturesome undertaking barely the half of the Prussian army.

The war of the first coalition was lost by diplomatic mistakes, not in consequence of reverses in the field. It was decisive for the course of the war that in Vienna and in Berlin all the sins and all the lies of the covetous and uninspired cabinet-policy of the eighteenth century were now revived, the policy which had failed to understand the level sense of Frederick William I and had despised the heroic pride of his son. The Emperor Leopold died at the very outset of the war. His youthful successor, Francis II, believed in the old Hapsburg 𝔄 𝔈 𝔍 𝔒 𝔘 [the initials of *Austria Est Imperare Orbi Universo*] with all the stiff obstinacy of a head empty of ideas, inclining always to the simple view that his archducal house could never possess land enough. He revived the Josephan plans of conquest, hoping by means of the French War ultimately to be able to effect the exchange of Belgium for Bavaria. Nor did Prussian statecraft any longer display the ancient character of sober self-restraint. Since the conclusion of the Austrian alliance, Prussia had also been affected with the insatiate greed of the Hapsburg-Lorraine policy, and vacillated in vain pursuit of the illimitable, instead of following, in accordance with the good old Hohenzollern manner, a firmly restricted aim pursued with iron persistency. The aim of the court intriguers, Haugwitz and Lucchesini, was to obtain the greatest possible gain in land and people with the smallest possible sacrifice. They perceived that the Vienna Convention, which pledged Prussia to come unconditionally to the support of the emperor, had been a deplorable folly ; and now, before Austria had disclosed her Bavarian plans, they demanded, in return for military help, a portion of Poland and the Palatinate territories on the Lower Rhine—the Bavarian Palatinate could seek compensation in Alsace. They thus had in view the reconquest of the German Western Mark, and imagined at the same time that the old dispute concerning the Jülich-Cleves succession could be brought to a conclusion entirely to the advantage of Prussia. It is undeniable that this plan had a sound kernel ; but how could it be hoped that so striking a gain, a simultaneous acquirement of Posen and the Rhine provinces, could be effected, except by the use of all the powers of the monarchy ? It was a loathsome sight, how the greedy desires of the two courts now led them to bargain with one another. To be sure of compensation in Poland, Prussia now agreed that Austria should enlarge her dominion with plunder from Bavaria ; the prime principle of the Frederician policy, the old king's resolution which he so often maintained with sword and with pen, that on no condition whatever was the House of

Austria to be allowed to enlarge its power in the empire, was abandoned with lamentable weakness—" from cowardly greed," as Frederick had once said in relation to similar proposals. And yet, after all, a loyal friendship between the two allies was far from being secured.

In July, 1792, the high nobility of the German nation assembled at Mainz around their new emperor Francis. It was the farewell supper of the doomed Holy Empire. Once more there flaunted through the narrow alleys of Mainz the golden chariots of the spiritual electors, the brilliant array of retainers of hundreds of princes, counts, and barons of the empire, all the splendour of the good old days—the last display of the kind before the new century was to tread down with its iron heels the antediluvian Rhenish frippery of bishops' mitres and princely crowns. While this splendid festival was in progress, the two great powers were secretly in treaty concerning the spoils of victory. The fate of Bavaria seemed to be decided. Prussia completely abandoned its old ward, the House of Wittelsbach, and considering the military weakness of the South German state, it seemed beyond question that Austria could immediately enforce the Bavario-Belgian exchange. But thereupon the imperial negotiators explained that their chief did not demand Bavaria alone but also Ansbach-Bayreuth, which Prussia had just legally acquired, and this left no doubt that the Hofburg aimed at the partition of Germany, at the subjection of the whole of the south. The ministers in Berlin were " seriously enraged," and the king regarded as a personal injury the demand for the Franconian lands which had been the ancient appanage of his house. Nor could a clear understanding be arrived at concerning the Polish question. Although Austria did not absolutely forbid Prussia to increase her dominion in the east, both parties to the negotiations felt that there was a wide divergence in their views as to the future of Poland. The court of Berlin had at length become convinced that the May constitution of Poland, which was favoured by Vienna, was strictly contrary to Prussian interests.

In a mood of depression, grumbling at one another, and without any clear agreement as to the aims of the war, the two allies took the field. The imperial court engaged in the campaign unwillingly, regarding it as a war of defence which had been forced upon it ; the Prussian statesmen played just as unwillingly their part in rendering a help which, in accordance with the treaties they had made, it was impossible to refuse ; both the powers consoled themselves with the vague hope that the uncongenial undertaking would in one way or another provide them with an extension of territory. King Frederick William alone was inspired by a knightly sentiment. He regarded himself as the defender of the rightful kingship, and through his dreams there passed the figures of Arminius and other saviours of the German Fatherland. But even in him there was lacking any clear understanding of what kind of order he was to impose upon conquered France.

Even before the armies met there became manifest not only the dissentient aims of the allies but also the other elements of hopeless untruth by which the coalition was affected. Since the orators of the Gironde were preaching a war of principle on behalf of revolutionary freedom, it was impossible for their enemies completely to escape the influence of the counter-revolutionary party. In Paris, Austria was regarded as the protector and advocate of all those ancient political ideas which were tolerantly spoken of by the general name of feudalism ; and against this power of darkness the spokesmen of the Revolution fought with joyful zeal. But that the state of the philosopher of Sans Souci, the rebel against emperor and empire, should now protect the old-time Europe with its armies, seemed to them almost incredible ; they could not abandon the hope that they would still be able to win this kingdom over to the side of enlightenment. Yet at the Prussian head-quarters it was impossible to keep away the *emigrés* who were offering their services ever more loudly and more confidently. In a moment of unintelligent weakness, the Duke of Brunswick, the commander-in-chief, penned a fanatical war-manifesto which was coloured with the sentiments of the Hotspurs among the *emigré* nobles, and which aroused disgust in the Prussian cabinet : the talented disciple of the French philosophy, to whom the Minister of War in Paris had recently offered the leadership of the revolutionary army, now threatened revolutionary France with utter destruction. The Gironde exulted, for it seemed proved beyond question that the plans of the allied despots were counter-revolutionary.

Not less unhappy than the policy which had led to the struggle was the conduct of the war. For a long time, it is true, the well-drilled regiments of Austria and Prussia maintained an advantage over the haphazard and bewildered mass of the revolutionary army. Whenever it came to the issue of battle, the French were regularly defeated by the Frederician troops ; they never dared to make a stand against the Prussian cavalry, and especially against the dreaded "red king," Colonel Blucher of the Red Hussars. For years to come, the peasant of the Mark joked about the French blockheads, the "katzköppe," as he nicknamed the chasseurs. At the close of the three Rhine campaigns, Blucher published his journal, describing modestly and yet with cordial self-approval how often he had "smashed" the enemy. The officers returned home from the war with the consciousness of duty gloriously fulfilled. And yet these three campaigns, which brought to the Prussian flag so many magnificent and isolated successes, closed in a shameful peace. The conduct of war is everywhere determined, and especially in wars conducted by a coalition, by the aims of the statecraft which the war is to subserve, and a policy that dreads victory cannot endure great military commanders. The vacillations of Prussian policy found their true expression in the weakness of will and in the circumspect hesitation of the Duke of Brunswick. In the last days of the Seven Years' War, King Frederick had been forced by the overwhelming power of his enemies to adopt a caution which was altogether foreign to his own inclination and principles. What had thus been imposed upon him by necessity seemed to the generals of the years of peace to be the fine flower of military wisdom. They considered it the commander's task to deploy their troops in a widely extended cordon, to cover every threatened point, to protect the mountain by the battalion and the battalion by the mountain ; that spirit of initiative which Frederick had so often declared to be the very nerve of war, had been completely lost in this peace-loving generation. The artificiality of this circumspect method of conducting war corresponded at once to the temperament of the Brunswicker and to his political views, for he alone among the generals of the allied army dreaded the elemental energies of the Revolution and shunned the venture of open battle.

In accordance with ancient Austrian custom, of the auxiliary forces summoned by the empire only a small proportion put in an appearance. The commander-in-chief first acquired the fortresses along the Meuse, and then, unwillingly obeying the king's orders, advanced westwards towards Paris, although his army was far too weak to attempt the conquest of the hostile capital. The campaign was already decided by September 20th. The Duke did not dare to attack the French upon the heights of Valmy, abandoned certain victory, and evacuated French soil on the approach of French reinforcements. Goethe perceived the consequences of this great change of front with the seer's vision of the poet ; beside the watch-fire he said to the Prussian officers, " To-day there begins a new epoch in world history." Meanwhile, by the revolt of the tenth of August the throne of the Capets had been overthrown ; a French Republic arose out of the horrible blood-bath of the September massacres ; and the rulers of the New France could bring to the convention as a wedding-gift the great tidings that the Frederician army had ingloriously fled before the troops of freedom.

The surprises of this wild year of 1792 were not even yet at an end ; it seemed as if an inscrutable destiny were to prove the folly of all human foresight. A French volunteer-corps under an incompetent leader pressed forward in a mad adventure upon the flank of the Prussian army until close to Mainz ; the first fortress of Germany opened its gates without resistance. The glories of the Rhenish system of petty states collapsed like a house of cards ; princes and bishops fled in wild disorder. In accordance with the ancient treacherous custom of the Wittelsbachs, the Bavarian Palatinate declared itself neutral ; the Holy Roman Empire sensed the beginning of the end. The weak-willed population of the spiritual territories allowed themselves to be seduced by a handful of noisy hotheads into the play-acting of a Rhenish Republic, imitating in reverent awe all the brave words of the Parisian dispensers of happiness, although " the phlegm which nature has imposed upon us allows us only to regard the French with wondering admiration." The contemplation of this caricature of freedom broke the unstable heart of the most intelligent of the Rhenish enthusiasts, George Forster. Meanwhile, Savoy and Belgium, badly defended, fell into the hands of the ragged troops of the Republic. Wonderful and brilliant results were these, which might even have intoxicated a sober people. A measureless self-confidence now animated the leaders of the new Republic ; they demanded that all the nations who wished to rise on behalf of freedom should follow the French example. The campaign of the revolutionary propagandists was ceremoniously announced ; war to the palaces, peace to the huts ! In this fanatical assurance of victory there resided an immeasurable moral force. Moreover, the military power of the Republic was increasing, although everything in its military system was still disorderly and confused. The extraordinary mobs which the Convention led into the field were certainly unable in open battle to secure victory in face of the methodical conduct of war of the Frederician generals, and yet to the little armies of the old days it was quite impossible completely to overthrow such a national uprising. Among the volunteers of 1792, there was an abundance of youthful talent, a great proportion of the marshals and generals of the subsequent empire ; the new equality gave an open road to all aspiring spirits, and the terror of the guillotine spurred everyone on to venture the highest.

There were thus manifested a new art of war and a new state-craft combining the land-hunger of the old cabinet policy with unheard-of contempt for all the traditional forms of international law. If the empire was to withstand the attack of this incalculable young power, it was essential that the Rhineland above all should receive a more vigorous political order and should be rendered capable of offering resistance. Through the fault of the petty courts, the fortress of Mainz had fallen into the hands of Custine, and, after the defeat, could offer nothing to the oppressed fatherland beyond pitiful complaints, appeals to precedent, and a few passionate pamphlets which were to incite loyal subjects to revolt against the " petty-bourgeois Custine." Was it desirable to reinstate these outworn political authorities which had collapsed at the first touch of the enemy ? Once more the idea of secularism inevitably sprang to life ; if effected promptly and by the sole hand of the German powers, it would have offered the last means of saving the existence of the imperial domain. In Berlin, as in Paris, the abolition of the spiritual cities was then seriously considered, but in face of Austria's veto, the Prussian statesmen abandoned the plan, and there recommenced the deplorable bargaining for a cheap advantage.

It was finally resolved, after the Prussians had already driven the French out of Frankfort and well across the Rhine, that in the next year Belgium and Mainz should be reconquered, whilst the emperor should be compensated with Bavarian, and the Prussians with Polish, territory. Both powers were continuing the unhappy war in the sole hope of securing a rounding-off of their dominions. The plan of a royalist counter-movement, which still dominated the honourable mind of the King of Prussia, lost all foundation as soon as the Republic had been founded, and when, not long after, King Louis XVI went to the guillotine.

Meanwhile the Russians established their power on the Vistula. By the Peace of Jassy, Catherine had been disembarrassed of the Turkish War, and as she now threw herself upon the Polish prey with all her forces she once more found an ally in the party passion of the Sarmatian nobility. With the aid of the Confederation of Targowitz, she abolished all the reforms of 1791 and restored the old constitution—restored, in a word, her own dominion over the crown of Poland. For thirty years past she had been working incessantly to bring Russia into direct contact with the civilisation of the west by means of the conquest of Poland ; now she seemed to attain the goal of her desires, for she ruled over the land of the Vistula, and could decide as she wished when and in what manner she could effect the complete absorption of the conquered domain. Who could withstand her ? By the dissensions among her German neighbours, by the decay of the Western European comity of nations, the power of Russia had been enormously increased, and was, moreover, over-estimated by all its contemporaries ; no one perceived that this thinly populated land had lost a million men in the wars of its restless empress, and that its means for a war of offence were inconsiderable. The diplomatic arts of Catherine rendered it impossible for the German courts to take the side of the Polish patriots. Since the court of St. Petersburg condemned in passionate terms the murder of the king by the Jacobins, the patriotic party at Warsaw rallied to the help of the French ; whoever was the enemy of France could not possibly be the ally of Poland.

Thus it was owing to the carefully planned and unscrupulous policy of the empress that King Frederick William found himself surrounded by enemies, exactly as had been his predecessor twenty years earlier. He was forced to decide whether he would tolerate the sole dominion of the Russians in Poland, or whether he would limit the increase of the Muscovite power by a new partition. The choice could not be long in doubt. The Prusso-Polish alliance was torn up by the Poles themselves when they offered the House of Wettin the hereditary crown. The court of Berlin finally took the step which had long been demanded by Prussian interests. It declared openly against the constitution of May, 1791, and did so in terms of artificial anger which were detestably inconsistent with its former attitude. It assembled half the army on the eastern frontier, and as Catherine, in view of the sinister fermentation with which Poland was filled, did not feel secure of her position, she unwillingly agreed in January, 1793, to the second partition of Poland. Then the world witnessed the suicide of a once mighty people. All the horror of the rule of the Convention in Paris seemed innocence itself when compared with the detestable spectacle of the mute sitting of the Reichstag of Grodno. By a preconcerted trickery, by the appearance of acting under compulsion, the suborned delegates and magnates agreed to the partition. Prussia acquired, in addition to Thorn and Danzig, the extensive

Polish areas of Posen and Gnesen, whose lack in the Seven Years' War had involved such difficulties for Frederick. They constituted a natural connecting link between Silesia and Old Prussia. Since they already possessed a considerable proportion of German inhabitants, and since they were in vigorous communication with the empire, it seemed probable that in the course of years they might be altogether won over to Teutonic civilisation. The great gap in our eastern frontier was at length closed ; all the injustice that the Polish nobility had for centuries past done to the pioneers of German civilisation was now to be atoned for. If, however, the partition itself was a deed of just necessity, the choice of the means displayed the moral decay of the Prussian state. By breach of faith and by lies, by corruption and by trickery, was the goal attained. Not satisfied with securing the frontier, Prussia took more than was necessary, extending its dominion as far as the Bzura, deep into the interior of a purely Polish region. Poland thus mutilated could no longer maintain its existence ; the second partition led inevitably and speedily to a final overthrow which could not fail to be injurious to Germany.

The immediate consequence of the treaty of partition was the destruction of the Prusso-Austrian alliance. It was true that the Emperor Francis had at first agreed to the enlargement of Prussia because he was unable to subdue Belgium without the assistance of the North German power ; but he was disquieted to learn that his ally had independently, and earlier than himself, secured the reward of victory ; it seemed to him as if he were mocked when Catherine wrote that he might crown his work by agreeing to the new partition of Poland. He angrily dismissed his ministers and entrusted the conduct of foreign affairs to the minister Thugut. This man was the most hateful of all the enemies of Prussia, far excelling the statesmen of Berlin in emotional slyness and unscrupulous activity. He hoped to follow Catherine's example and to take advantage of the terrible confusion of the European situation to carry out a plan of conquest in the grand style. His greedy desires extended in all directions, to Flanders and Alsace, to Bavaria, Italy, to the Danubian regions, to Poland. His hatred of the North German allies had become even greater since the heir to the Bavarian Palatinate, the Duke of Zweibrücken, had safeguarded himself against the scheme for the Bavario-Belgian exchange, and since Prussia, at length recognising past errors, had declared in plain terms that the exchange could not be allowed to take place without the free assent of the House of Wittelsbach. The

Austrian statesman immediately attempted to attack the power of Prussia in Poland. Nothing could be more welcome to Catherine; she found it hard to accept that the Polish booty should for a second time be diminished in size by the intervention of Prussia, and she cleverly utilised the mutual hate of the German powers to weaken them by playing one neighbour off against the other. Already in the summer of 1793 the courts of Vienna and St. Petersburg were drawing together. In Berlin there could be no possible doubt as to the hostile aims of the new league of the emperors.

The decay of the coalition was immediately reflected in the events of the war. The Prussians crossed the Rhine at Caub, near the old Palatinate, in the same place where two decades later they recommenced the struggle for the German River; they drove the enemy from the left bank, besieged and conquered Mainz. Under the protection of their arms, the refugee high nobility returned, and reconstituted unhindered all the old nuisance of the system of petty states, although the hopeless corruption of that system was well understood in Berlin. The Prussian army then remained for a long time in the mountains of the Palatinate, fronting southward toward Alsace, everywhere victorious when the enemy attempted an attack; but the Prussians did not venture to advance, for the cabinet of Berlin distrusted the intentions of its ally. The imperial general Wurmser, in command of the left wing of the army at the front of the Weissenburg " Lines," demanded an advance into Alsace, in order to restore there, as had been done along the central Rhine, the rule of his fellows of the imperial nobility, and defied the Prussian commander-in-chief with open disobedience. Towards the end of the war, General Hoche was appointed to the command of the French troops, the finest man among the young military leaders of the Republic. Defeated by the Prussians at Kaiserslautern, with the impetuosity of the born commander he turned against Wurmser's army, defeated the imperial troops at Gaisberg, Wörth, and Fröschweiler, in those foot-hills where were subsequently to be fought the first battles of the great war of retaliation, liberated Landau from its siege by the allies and forced Wurmser to retreat. After the defeat of the Austrians, the Prussian army could no longer hold the mountain, and evacuated the Palatinate. In the horrors of the " winter of rapine " the unhappy country learnt to experience the advantages of French liberty. In a valiant army, severe defeats awaken moral energy; but this campaign, which had been lost by the fault of others, disordered the discipline of the Prussian officers. They grumbled, broke into open complaint, and demanded that the army should be recalled from this useless war. The un-Prussian spirit which paralysed the administration had penetrated to the army ; it was like a military republic ; the anger against Austria displayed itself in a hundred detestable ways. In the theatre of war in the Netherlands, the coalition, now strengthened by the accession of England, had also but little good fortune. Belgium had been won back, and in the summer, after the taking of Valenciennes and Mainz, the road to Paris lay open before the allied armies, if resolution could only be found to unite forces for a common forward movement. But the English commercial policy demanded the possession of Dunkirk, while Thugut insisted upon the conquest of Picardy ; owing to the quarrels of diplomacy the favourable moment was lost, and at the close of the campaign the armies found themselves once more on the defensive upon the southern frontier of Belgium. Meanwhile the military strength of the Republic was steadily increasing. The Jacobin Reign of Terror subjected the entire country to the dictatorship of the capital ; war was a necessity, for economic prosperity was utterly disturbed. The idea of the revolutionary propagandists became a terrible truth : an unresting conspiracy extended its nets over half Europe, to Warsaw and Turin, to Amsterdam and Ireland, endeavouring to disturb the frontiers of every country. Tremblingly the people made the incredible sacrifices which were imposed upon them by the demands of the government in Paris. Although in the German provinces of France, and in Catholic Alsace, the terrorism of the commissaries of the Convention awakened, here and there, old Austrian memories, in the east the mass of the populace remained faithful to the tricolor because they dreaded that a victory of the coalition would involve the reimposition of tithes and the revival of forced labour. In Strasburg, people chanted the Song of the Revolution. The genius of Carnot gave the army a new organisation, introducing troops of the line and national guards into the tactical unity of the half-brigade. He dismissed the useless elected leaders, and constituted out of the best energies of the old Bourbon officers, and out of new volunteers, a capable officers' corps. To those trained in the old and cautious art of war, the wild venturesomeness of the Republican generals, who hurled themselves upon the enemy with a reckless expenditure of human life and of the munitions of war, proved irresistible ; moreover, in the long campaign the conduct of the French troops underwent a steady improvement.

Thus the enemy gained strength; whereas Prussia, at the beginning of the third campaign, was completely paralysed by the exhaustion of her financial resources. The Treasury was almost entirely depleted. Already in the second year of the war, the king had not been able to dispense with the aid of English gold. It was to him and to his army alone that the empire owed the reconquest of a dominant position on the Rhine. He would be able to carry on the imperial war in the years to come if the other estates of the empire, which had hitherto put into the field for the defence of the western frontier a force of barely twenty thousand men, were to help him out in his financial need, and to undertake the support of his army on the Rhine. But to the penetrating vision of petty particularism it seemed that the Prussian proposals involved a revival of the ideas of the League of Princes. Everywhere was faint-heartedness and self-seeking. In many of the courts there was even open treason, for France had long been at work to bring the petty lords under her influence. Nor was Austria in favour of a change which would have made the King of Prussia appear as the imperial military commander, and his troops as the imperial army. The attempts at a loan which Hardenberg strove to raise among the smaller courts of the west, had no notable result. Thus deserted by his co-estates, Frederick William finally resolved to place his entire army of the Rhine at the disposal of the naval power, for hire. This state of affairs, *per se* hardly tolerable for a great state, involved in addition the most invidious disputes, for the agreement regarding the subsidies contained a number of ambiguous sentences. The naval power held that it could dispose of the troops of its ally as it pleased, and desired to assemble all the armies of the coalition in the Netherlands in pursuit of the interests of English commercial policy. Prussia, on the other hand, contended that the choice of the theatre of war was reserved to herself, and still endeavoured to defend the imperial frontier along the central Rhine. Austria hoped once more to secure conquests in Flanders and in Lorraine. Field-Marshal Möllendorff opened the campaign with a second victory at Kaiserslautern. After being compelled in the summer to withdraw from the mountains, he advanced once more in the autumn, and for the third time the Prussian regiments victoriously occupied the bloodstained heights above the Lauter. Even in the Netherlands, the North German accessory troops did not lack conspicuous success. The heroic sally from Menin made by the Hanoverian General Hammerstein and his adjutant Scharnhorst, proved that the old Prussian valiancy in arms was not yet extinct. But the courage of individuals could not atone for the disastrous effects of the weakness of the leadership and of the ambiguous character of the imperial policy. In October, the Austrian army withdrew from Belgium over the Rhine. The enemy pushed after it, occupied the Rhineland as far as Coblenz ; and the Prussians, since their rear was then threatened, were also forced to evacuate the left bank of the river.

At the same time the king experienced the evil consequences of his dependence upon the naval power. England, embittered by the independent attitude of the Prussian generals, refused the payment of the monetary subsidy, thus making it impossible for the king to continue the campaign. Thus it happened that the best army of the coalition was lost to the European War through England's selfish arrogance. Towards Christmas, Pichegru entered Holland, crossing the great rivers on the ice, and the navy of this state, which had once ruled the seas, lowered its flag to a troop of French cavalry. The Batavian Republic was proclaimed, for the great free state of the west now began to surround itself with a wall of daughter-republics. Thus the third Rhenish campaign had been fought in vain, and next summer the Westphalian territories must expect attack from the French by way of Holland. Prussia was completely isolated, and it was soon learnt that the rupture between Prussia and England had been hailed with delight both in St. Petersburg and in Vienna. But in the Prussian nation no one had any understanding of how profoundly the power of the state had been damaged by a policy of half-measures and confused aims. The capital rejoiced over the three victories of Kaiserslautern ; the minds of the people were intoxicated with patriotic pride and royalist devotion. Then for the first time, in the years 1793 and 1794, there was heard at Berlin the song " Hail to thee in the victor's crown," the new Prussian words set to the old melody of Handel. The beautiful monument of victory of the old monarchy, the Brandenburg Gate, was unveiled ; with enthusiastic delight the people assembled in crowds to see the bride of the young crown prince make her entry through this gate of triumph. Prussian writers, in a well-meaning infatuation, compared the undisturbed good fortune of their loyal and victorious nation with the confusion and powerlessness of the state of the French regicides.

Meanwhile the shaky accord of the coalition was completely disturbed by the Polish negotiations. In Easter week, 1794, a sanguinary revolt took place at Warsaw, and the Russians were driven

out of the country. With the support of Paris, the area of disturbance continually widened, reaching far into Prussian Poland.
This time also, in the last struggle of despair, the Polish nobility
still displayed its ancient sins of dissension and undiscipline. Yet
the unhappy nation manifested more strength than the partitioning powers had expected, and a gracious destiny bestowed upon
Poland the good fortune of reinvigorating her heart at the prospect
of a true hero. Kosciuszko possessed neither the genius of the
great commander nor the world-wide vision of the statesman, but
his pure spirit, animated with all the knightly virtues of his people,
was endowed also with an invincible uprightness, with a genuine
devotion for his fatherland, such as had been unknown in
Poland for centuries past. To the rough levies of the Polish peasantry, when the sober-minded hero, clad in a white frieze countryman's coat, rode through the ranks of his men, Father Thaddeus
seemed like a guardian angel. In Russia, on the other hand, there
now flamed up the ancient hatred of the Byzantine Christians
against the Latins, of the Eastern Slavs against the Western. Like
one man, the empire demanded the annihilation of Poland in atonement for the affront that had been offered. Never was any war
more sacred to the Russian people. It was obvious that in the
bloody day of Warsaw, the Poles' last hour had begun. It was
therefore the duty of Prussia to take immediate action, and before
the Russian armies could be assembled from the remote corners
of the empire, it was essential that Prussia should herself subdue
the revolt in order thereafter, in the inevitable final partition, to
be able to speak the decisive word. The king understood all that
was at stake. He sent his army over the frontier, defeated the
Poles at Rawka, subdued Cracow, and then turned against Warsaw,
which was badly equipped, torn by faction-fights, and by no
means prepared to resist the Prussian attack. But that unlucky
over-carefulness and over-refinement which had ruined the
Rhenish campaigns, served also to deprive the king of the fruits
of his Polish victories. The royal-minded man wished to take
Praga by storm, and then, like his ancestor the Great Elector, to
enter the Polish capital as a conqueror. Bischofswerder, however,
warned him to husband his forces for the reckoning with Russia ;
one of Catherine's agents, the Prince of Nassau-Siegena, eagerly
joined in this cowardly advice. A regular siege was begun and
was discontinued after a few days. Whilst the Prussian army,
depressed and embittered, withdrew from Warsaw, Souvòroff, the
barbarian of genius, in whom the savage national temperament of

the Muscovites found vigorous expression, came to the attack with the bulk of Catherine's forces. His devotion to the White Czar and to the Orthodox Church was as blind as that of any Russian peasant, and yet he was a master in the western art of war, a great warrior, born to command, accustomed to expect the impossible from the courage of his soldiers, accustomed to act up to his motto, " The bullet is a foolish woman, but the bayonet is every inch a man." He carried out what the Prussian commanders had failed to effect, defeated the army of Kosciuszko, and took Praga by storm after murderous battles. Warsaw lay at the feet of Catherine, her troops held the commanding position between the Bug and the Vistula. The revolt had been suppressed, not by Prussia but by Russia ; and the court of St. Petersburg announced boastingly, " Poland has been completely overthrown by the armies of the Empress."

The sins of omission of the Prussian generalship must be paid for when the three eastern powers came to negotiate at St. Petersburg concerning the last partition. Prussia demanded the line of the Vistula, with Warsaw, Sandomierz, and Cracow. Since Austria, which had done very little towards the suppression of the revolt, coveted these last two districts for herself, General Tauentzien returned an answer which showed the complete decay of the coalition. He said : " These two provinces in your hands would give us more trouble than all the democracies of the world." Russia, however, took Austria's side, since for more than a year Thugut had been successfully engaged in acquiring the favour of Catherine. The two imperial courts were at one in the intention of controlling Prussian ambition by all the means in their power, and since Prussia would not give way, on January 3, 1795, Austria and Russia signed a secret treaty against their ally. By this it was arranged that Poland should be partitioned in such a way that Russia and Austria should receive the preponderant part of the country, while Prussia must remain content with Warsaw and a narrow strip on the eastern Prussian frontier. In addition, a comprehensive plan of conquest was laid down. In the Danubian provinces, Russia was to enjoy the right of a younger son, while Austria received a free hand for the annexation of Bavaria, Bosnia, and Serbia, and also the Venetian Republic. Indeed, the empress gave her assent to all other conquests which her ally might still consider necessary. Should Prussia offer any opposition, this was to be overpowered by the full might of the Russian and Austrian armies. Thus all the immoderate desires of the Emperor

Joseph were revived. On the Lower Danube, in the heart of South Germany, and above all on the Adriatic, Thugut hoped to enlarge the power of his state, and Catherine gladly acceded to these desires because in the general disturbance she hoped to attain the second great goal of her statecraft, the control of Constantinople.

To this had the Prussian state come in the five years since the days of Reichenbach. By the naval power and by the German empire, means for the conduct of the war were refused, while Russia and Austria threatened an onslaught. For some months, the treaty of January 3 still remained unknown in Berlin, but there could be no possible doubt as to the sentiments of the imperial court. Thugut had long ago assembled troops in Bohemia in order to use them in the attack upon his Prussian allies. Was it possible for Prussia, without money, and with the aid of such allies as these, to prosecute the French War, whose aims in the confused quarrels of diplomacy became ever obscurer and more questionable ? For a long time all the king's advisers had been demanding peace or an alliance with France—even Hardenberg, the talented minister who by his skilful administration had won the Franconian Margravates for the monarchy, and who now began to exercise an influence upon foreign affairs. Charles Augustus of Weimar, who from the first had been strongly opposed to the war with France, now renewed his efforts for peace. The army, and even the valiant Blucher, were altogether averse to continuing the war in alliance with the Austrians ; and not less eager for peace was the nation, which considered that enough laurels had been won. Young Vincke voiced the heart-felt sentiments of all enlightened Prussians when he asked bitterly, " How long are we to remain a voluntary sacrifice for Austrian double-dealing ? " Hans von Held, whose tongue was the sharpest among those of the literary opposition, wrote the moving exhortation : " Frederick William, give the signal, call thy valiant army back ! Let us be the Frenchmen's brothers, thus commands the voice of Fate." In the empire, too, everything was calling for peace, for the condition was one of general exhaustion. Thugut, on the other hand, passionately embittered, threatened that he would himself come to terms with France if he were not allowed to have Cracow. The hasty withdrawal of the Austrians from the Netherlands, and many serious reports that were received concerning the activity of Carletti, the Tuscan minister in Paris, served to increase the suspicion of the Prussian court against the Hofburg.

In France the need for peace was hardly less pressing, and there was an earnest desire for an understanding at least with Prussia. With the fall of the Terror, the moderate parties came into control at Paris, and the statesmen of Berlin flattered themselves with the expectation that if Prussia were to conclude a separate peace, this would pave the way for a general peace and would restore the *status quo* in the empire. Against his will, the king at length gave permission for the opening of peace negotiations; in the bottom of his soul, as a faithful prince of the empire, he still wished to carry on the Rhenish campaign. Notwithstanding the diplomatic skill of Hardenberg, the course of the Basle negotiations proved unfortunate, because the ministers in Berlin lacked courage to threaten their opponents with a resumption of hostilities. Nor did the Prussian diplomats venture seriously to entertain the idea of secularisation, which was once more brought up by the French, and which might perhaps have furnished a passable way out of the difficulty. They were content with half-measures, and on April 5, 1795, they concluded the Peace of Basle, in virtue of which Prussia simply withdrew from the coalition ; if the French proved unable to maintain their position on the left bank of the Rhine, the king was to be indemnified for his possessions in this region, and it was a tacit understanding between the parties to the bargain that the indemnity was to take the form of secularised ecclesiastical lands.

In view of the state of affairs and personalities in Prussia, the conclusion of peace was the last despairing means for the rescue of the state from an untenable situation. It was the necessary consequence of the errors and misfortunes of many years, of a lying alliance which carried within itself the germs of treachery, of a policy without energy oscillating ever between Poland and the Rhine, and never venturing to strike a decisive blow. The responsibility did not attach to individual men, but to the entire nation, which, after having been once awakened by a great man from its political slumber, had lapsed into a waking dream, and had learned once more with a slack self-content, to despair of its political future. Notwithstanding all excuses and explanations, it was the gravest political error of our new history, a disloyalty of the Prussian state to itself, which had to be atoned for by two decades of dishonour and stress, by unexampled sacrifices and struggles.

In its position as augmenter of the empire, Prussia had outgrown the futility of the system of petty states. No defeat in the open field could abase it more profoundly than it was abased by its own action when without compulsion it drew its hand from the German Western Mark, and when it abandoned to an unknown destiny the region of Mainz, which Prussia's own army had so recently restored to the empire. Amid powerful neighbours, Prussia had always maintained itself by the energy of its own will. More unbecoming than even an open alliance with the enemy of the empire was the slothful pusillanimity of spirit which was content to wait upon events to see if perchance the Austrians might still be able to drive the French out of the empire. An honourable sentiment of imperial pride led the king to refuse to the last possible minute his consent to the Peace of Basle. He was the heir of that Great Elector who had been betrayed no less shamefully by Austria and yet had ever and again ventured to renew the struggle for the Rhenish land; moreover, he perceived obscurely, as did the brave old minister Finkenstein, that for the position of Prussia in the world, the maintenance of the western frontier of the empire was far more important than the possession of Sandomierz and Cracow. Betrayed by his allies, he was unquestionably justified in withdrawing from the coalition as soon as France offered honourable terms of peace and recognised the ancient frontiers of the empire, but peace on such terms was attainable only by the hazard of a fourth Rhenish campaign. The war had left untouched the kernel of the monarchy. Although the misfortunes of the year 1794 had caused momentary difficulties, there was everywhere visible a general condition of well-being. There could be no question of the people being overburdened with taxation. The domain which was now enlarged by thousands of square miles provided its amiable ruler with an annual income greater by barely a million thalers than that yielded in former days by the little state of Frederick II. In such a situation, a great statesman would have known how to find means for a new campaign, notwithstanding all financial difficulties and notwithstanding the unfortunate outcome of the recent attempt at raising a foreign loan. But in the king's council there was no man of creative mind; the unhappy prince saw no way out and pacified his conscience with the gloomy consolation that the peace at least involved no formal surrender of German land.

All the reckonings and expectations of his cunning advisers soon showed themselves to have been erroneous. They had expected to bring the imperial war to a close. Hardenberg believed that France would voluntarily renounce the Rhine frontier simply in order to come to terms with the empire, and naively expected that there would result a permanent friendly relationship between Prussia and the Republic. How little did they understand the character of revolutionary France ! Soon after the Basle Treaty had been signed, the war party at Paris once more gained the ascendancy, expected armed help from Prussia, and, disappointed in this expectation, treated the peaceful neutral neighbour with unconcealed contempt. It became ever clearer that a peace with this revolutionary-minded state would not become possible until the old European system lay in ruins. Haugwitz and Alvensleben had hoped that the conclusion of peace would give them a free hand for the Polish negotiations, but were compelled ultimately to accept with trifling modifications the partition proposed by the two imperial courts, for it was only as the ally of France that Prussia could oppose the masterful will of Thugut and Catherine, whilst the sense of honour of the king and the inertia of most of his advisers rendered impossible an open alliance with the Revolution. None the less, by the Treaty of Basle, Prussia had already become an accomplice, a secret ally of the French policy of conquest. It was known in Berlin that the Republic would retain the left bank of the Rhine ; compensation was expected from French friendship for the lands of Cleves, and thus Prussia, however repugnant the idea might seem, was chained to the victorious chariot wheels of France.

The first step led to others. On August 5, 1796, a supplementary treaty was concluded which placed in prospect certain definite acquisitions. If the left bank of the Rhine should be lost, the king was to receive the Bishopric of Münster, and his brother-in-law of Orange was also to be indemnified with certain spiritual territories of the empire. Thus the great idea of secularisation lost its true significance. King Frederick had understood it as a means for the reform of the empire, but now it was to serve merely for the spoliation of Germany. By the peace, Prussia apparently won a great extension of its power. The petty states of North Germany quickly followed the example of their powerful colleague. A line of demarcation was drawn along the Rhine and then straight across Central Germany ; behind it lay the neutral north, guarded by the arms of Prussia against the terrors of war. The canny folk of Berlin rejoiced ; the rule of the black eagle over the whole of North Germany was now established by the peaceful arts of diplomacy. And yet the brilliancy of this position was utterly illusory. The Rhine did not form a tenable frontier, the Republic could hold the left bank only if it controlled also the right bank directly or indirectly. Inevitably the war extended far into High Germany ; for all the South German states had already concluded treaties of submission to France, the precursors of the Confederation of the Rhine. Surrounded by France and its vassals to the south and to the west, North Germany could maintain its independence only so long as France found it necessary to safeguard this in her own interests. It was nothing but a peace-loving inertia which held together the German alliance on behalf of neutrality ; should the protector of North Germany become involved in a new war with France, this league, which was devoid alike of moral content and of positive aim, must immediately break up, for it was inevitable that the smaller associates would fall away from a conquered Prussia. From the egoism of these courts it was useless even to expect a permanent subordination of the minor North German contingents under the leadership of Prussia. The policy of Berlin, poor in ideas, hardly even made an earnest attempt to transform into a legally established hegemony, the dominant position which Prussia in fact occupied in the north ; and yet the peace could have been justified only if it had been utilised to revive in North Germany the policy of the League of Princes.

The old king had always inexorably opposed the separation of the north from the south, whenever the Emperor Joseph had wished to effect this in the interest of Austria, but now the partition of Germany was realised for the advantage of France. Since Prussia withdrew into the retired life of North German neutrality, the best of the political gains which the re-acquirement of the Franconian family lands had brought to the Hohenzollerns was irrecoverably lost ; the powerful step forward into the centre of High German life had been vainly effected. Among the South Germans there existed henceforward two parties only, the French and the Austrian—existed so far as this outworn race still possessed any political sentiment whatever. The unsatisfied provincial diets of Würtemberg and a few hotheads in Bavaria and Swabia admired the victorious Republic as the protector of liberty. The people in general knew nothing of the secret designs of the Hofburg ; they saw that the imperial troops continued for years to fight against the enemies of the empire, while Prussia stood inactive on one side ; and they honoured the empire as the last loyal protector of their native soil. In the autumn of 1795 the Bavarian Landsturm united with the Austrian forces, and fought the plundering and undisciplined troops of the Sansculottes in the Taunus and the Westerwald. Since in the person of the young Archduke Charles, Austria had found a new hero, the long almost discredited name of the imperial house now acquired a new esteem among the High

Germans. Even to-day in the farms of the Black Forest we find old wood-cuts commemorating the battles fought by the imperial commander-in-chief. In these years there was constituted among the best Germans of the southern highlands an Austrian historical tradition which continued to exercise a powerful influence for decades to come. It was at this time that the Szeklers and Kroats were in the Neckar valley, and that the young Uhland received the decisive political impressions of his life. Prussia, however, which had never really acquired the confidence of the High Germans, was now, and for a long time to come, the object of general contempt. Thus the consequences of the Basle Treaty were disastrous in every direction, and while Hardenberg had hoped that the peace would pave the way for his state to effect a long series of internal reforms and to introduce the sound ideas of the Revolution, this hope also was doomed to disappointment. It rather resulted that the newly acquired territory remained for years a hindrance to internal progress.

The Basle Treaty, which was to have brought for the king the honourable position of the intermediator of European peace, resulted only in alienating from Prussia the whole comity of states. At the two imperial courts, the news from Basle awakened passionate anger. What was merely empty-headed weakness was regarded in St. Petersburg and Vienna as black treachery—and naturally so, for Prussia could now only derive advantage from the victory of the Republic. Both the courts remained firmly convinced that Prussia was secretly intriguing with France ; and they attributed the worst possible designs to the king's councillors, seriously believing that Prussia was meditating a war of offence, was secretly endeavouring to egg on the Turks and the Swedes to attack Catherine. Thugut assembled an army on the Silesian frontier, and incited the Russian cabinet in violent despatches to undertake a war of destruction against their " natural enemy." He drew up an adventurous plan by which Prussia was to be deprived of all her Polish provinces and also of West Prussia. Souvòroff was to lead the Russian armies against the Prussian capital. The military preparations against the North German power brought the Rhenish campaign to a standstill throughout the summer. It was not until the autumn that the two imperial courts became convinced that there was nothing to be feared from Prussian weakness, and at the same time Thugut came to recognise that an understanding with the Republic was impossible. The idea of the preservation of the frontiers of the empire lay remote from his hard policy of interest. He was ready to sacrifice the left bank of the Rhine if Austria could acquire the Bavarian hereditary dominion. No one in the Hofburg thought of the duties of the emperorship. The court of St. Petersburg was expressly assured that the Russian troops might enter Germany as freely as they pleased in order to chastise the estates of the realm that had fallen away from Austria. It was only in respect of Italian affairs that no agreement could be effected. Thugut hoped to annex to Lombardy the domain of the neutral Republic of Venice, whilst France did not wish to leave Milan, the key to Italy, in Austria's hands. The result was that once again in the autumn of 1795 the swords were unsheathed, the court of Vienna hoping to conquer Venice on the Rhine. Since the war was renewed for the sake of Italy, a decisive issue must be fought out in Italy as well. United with Russia and England more firmly than ever by the new triple alliance, supported by Pitt with abundant monetary subsidies, Thugut rushed into the incalculable struggle. On all hands simple greed was dominant, everywhere was manifest contempt for all rights. Whether France or Austria should prove victorious, the one thing that would necessarily be overthrown was the old-established international law. And while this disastrous struggle was in progress there remained neutral that state whose boast that it held the balance of European power had once been echoed alike by friend and foe !

It was astonishing to observe that in North Germany no one seemed to dream of how dire was the penalty which Prussia had to pay in the loss of general repute for this mean-spirited peace ; no one seemed to understand the devastating effect of the loss of all good feeling and all sense of justice which must inevitably result in Germany now that the one truly living German state had abandoned the empire. All over North Germany, a general approval was given to the wise men who had made peace. Trade and commerce were flourishing ; the shipping and the grain-trade of Prussia enjoyed the advantage of neutral flags and received an altogether unexpected expansion owing to the general naval war. The energies of the new literature developed in undisturbed security ; now were the golden days of Weimar. Half in contempt and half in indifference, Saxony, proud of its culture, looked down out of the fullness of its intellectual life into the desolate disorder of war across the line of demarcation. By the joyful news from Basle, Kant was incited to the composition of his essay upon *Perpetual Peace*, and dreamed that the barbarism of war was soon to be done away with—at the very moment that a new age of blood and iron was dawning for enlightened Europe. The king, too, who had so long resisted the peace, soon consoled himself with the contemplation of the general satisfaction. Learning to make a virtue of necessity, he wrote, filled with self-approval, to Catherine, that it was his hope to follow the example of his predecessor, who had first enlarged the boundaries of his state, and had then devoted himself systematically to maintaining his newly-acquired dominion and to ruling it in peace.

In actual fact, except John Sigismund and Frederick II no other Hohenzollern had brought the monarchy so remarkable an extension of territory ; in the ten years of this reign the domain grew from 3,500 to nearly 5,600 square miles [German]. With the accession of the Franconian Margravates, another happy land of ancient civilisation was added to the needy trans-Elbian colonies. Under the guidance of Hardenberg there was formed a Franconian school of Prussian officials ; Alexander Humboldt presided over the mining development of the Fichtelgebirge. Altenstein, Kircheisen, and Nagler learnt there to adapt the stricter principles of the ancient Prussian administration to the comfortable circum stances of free peasants and well-to-do townsmen of the lower middle classes. These men of Franconia, and the philosophical East Prussians who, like young Schön, had sat at the feet of Kant in Königsberg, and who had become acquainted with the ideas of Adam Smith through the instrumentality of the excellent Kraus, were subsequently the founders of the reform party of the officialdom. From the military and economic points of view, the new frontier on the Bug and the Pilitza was most advantageous, since it opened free intercourse between the harbours of the province of Prussia and the internal regions of Poland that were rich in wood and grain, while it gave to the state an admirable and impregnable position, between the Vistula, the Bug, and the Narew. The unhappy inhabitants of Great Poland and Masovia learnt for the first time for centuries the blessings of a just and benevolent administration. Misfortune was respected by a lenient treatment of the insurgents, whereas in Russian Poland a cruel system of punishments was enforced. The noble became at length a subject, was forced to respect the law ; the peasants and the Jews could once more provide for the future and devote themselves to peaceful labour without trembling before the horsewhip of the landed gentry. Security before the law, hitherto unknown in Poland, attracted numerous settlers, and led to an influx of capital from the German provinces into this rich virgin soil. There was a notable expansion of agriculture; the regulation of mortgages rendered possible a more vigorous agrarian development, new roads and new canals were built; with astonishing rapidity Warsaw assumed the character of a German town. No one could fail to recognise the general blossoming of improved economic conditions.

But it soon became manifest that the power and happiness of states do not depend upon military and commercio-political conditions alone. The justice of historical destiny remains ever inscrutable, and becomes acceptable only in a spirit of reflective devotion, because neither to people nor to individuals does it mete out justice with equal measure. Among nations, as among individuals, there are favourites of fortune, in whose hands everything thrives without effort; and there are others of harder metal for whom only that which is obtained by prolonged struggle turns to advantage. What the Prussian state had hitherto gained had been the reward of serious work; but this new and large extension of territory was acquired by ineffective campaigns and inglorious undertakings, and upon the orderly domesticity of the country it had the effect of a gambling gain. Often had the Hohenzollerns resisted alluring appeals from abroad, but this time they gave way to temptation. Of the ten and a half million inhabitants of Prussia, four millions were now Slavs, so that there was serious danger that the country would be alienated from its great German future. The acquisition of Warsaw and Pultusk was indeed a necessary step, unconditionally demanded in accordance with the views of the time, since it was impossible for Prussia to abandon either to Austria or to Russia the key of its eastern frontier. It cannot be made a matter of personal reproach to the king that he failed to look beyond the doctrines of his epoch relating to the balance of power, and that he understood no better than his contemporaries the force of national contrasts. It remained, however, impossible to reconcile with the Protestant German state these thousands of hostile gentry and these stupid peasants who blindly obeyed their priests. During the Rhenish Wars, Polish recruits could be seen in fetters marching towards the west, and it happened sometimes that as many as half of these escaped upon the way. The Polish provinces weakened the moral energy of the state, which cannot exist without the free consent of its citizens, and they brought its internal development to a standstill. The partition of Poland stands first among the manifold causes of that deplorable torpor which affected the administration and the army for the next few decades. The energies of the German officialdom barely sufficed to ensure the beginnings of a civilised human life for these semi-barbarous lands which were not yet ripe for Prussian administration. How was it possible to think of reforms and of the introduction of self-government, which in two-fifths of the monarchy would have been simply to the advantage of the tyrannous Polish Junkers? Or how could anyone dream of the formation of a truly national army in which among ten soldiers four would have been Poles?

Whereas formerly, in newly acquired provinces, the state had immediately introduced with a wholesome severity all its institutions, and especially its system of taxation, there now prevailed at court a deliberate mildness, an excessive readiness to listen to every desire expressed by the children of the new land, to allow for every peculiarity, justified or unjustified. Instead of simply including the new provinces in the organisation of the ancient Prussian authorities, they were given a provisional administration. Hardenberg ruled in Franconia, and Count Hoym in South Prussia, with the powers of a viceroy. The old system of taxation remained in operation. Even in the confused and disastrous Polish system of taxation all that was done was to remedy a few crying defects, and the incredible result was that the extensive Polish domains provided to the general revenue of the state the trifling sum of 200,000 thalers, whilst the rich region of Franconia actually required a financial supplement from the national revenue. It seemed as if the exhausted state no longer ventured to breathe its own spirit into its new acquisitions. To the soft philanthropy of the age it appeared cruel to apply the old manly principle of the relentless straining of every possible nerve. Moreover, the acquirement in Poland of the landed property of the starosts and of the Church offered an irresistible temptation to the generosity of the king; instead of dividing up these estates and distributing them among German immigrants, he disposed of the greater part of them by favour and caprice. The greedy competition for the Southern Prussian crown-lands severely affected the already slackened discipline of the officialdom; and the Polish peasant, when he saw the scandalous gift of lands to the new lords, forgot to return thanks for the good deeds of the Prussian administration.

Among all the sins of omission of these weary years, there was none so disastrous as the neglect of the army. The goodheartedness of the king, the false economy of a lax policy of peace, and the tacit mistrust of the loyalty of the Polish soldiers, resulted in a failure to undertake the necessary strengthening of the army. Whilst the population had been almost doubled, the troops were increased by no more than 35,000 men; the army estimates, which at the death of Frederick had been from 11,000,000 to 12,000,000 thalers, rose only to 14,000,000. Meanwhile the armies of all the neighbouring realms increased enormously, while the position of the nation in the world had been rendered more difficult than ever by the extension of the frontiers in the east and in the west.

When Frederick William II died, Prussia's power, both internal and external, was less than it had been at the close of his uncle's reign. From a compact German state capable of the incredible under the impulse of a vigorous and talented will, Prussia had become a motley and unwieldy German-Slav realm, possessing neither military strength nor financial resources sufficient for the defence of its wide domains, and requiring a prolonged term of peace in order to regain internal unity. The great penal judgments of history seem strange to weak spirits, for the executioner of the judgment is almost always partisan, almost always himself tainted with crime. Thus the destruction of the Polish state, merited as it was by accumulated misdeeds, was now carried out by unclean hands. The blame which had to be apportioned for the necessary deed was punished in Russia by a long series of internal struggles, and in Austria by the misfortunes of the French War; but by none of the three partitioning powers was the sin so severely atoned as by Prussia, for in the conquest of purely Polish territory none had strayed so far from the paths of a natural policy as had this German state. The mean-spiritedness of Basle and the quarrels of Grodno, had been turned by Prussia to her account in such a way that henceforward there became supreme in Europe that reckless land-hunger which recognised no right but the right of the stronger and which found in Napoleon its supreme representative. Germany herself, now that all her states had recognised that reform was inevitable, was once more in the same situation as in the days of Gustavus Adolphus; as then the equality of the Churches, so now the secularisation of the Holy Empire, the destruction of theocracy, could be effected only by the intervention of foreign forces.

§ 2. FREDERICK WILLIAM III. THE PRINCIPAL RESOLUTION OF THE DIET OF DEPUTATION. CLASSICAL POETRY.

Such was the situation of affairs when King Frederick William III ascended the throne. Serious-minded and with a strong sense of duty, pious and upright, just and veracious, a thorough German alike in his merits and in his defects, he possessed all the virtues which form a good and pure-hearted man, and seemed created to lead a well-ordered state of intermediate strength honourably through a period of quiet ; it was a need to this profoundly affectionate spirit to be loved by his subjects. His intelligence comprehended only a narrow area ; and yet in all questions which came within his scope, his judgment was clear and sound, formed after profound and thorough consideration, and he always retained an inborn and fortunate comprehension of the forces of reality. In his education, everything had been neglected which might have led this noble but inelastic and essentially unpolitical nature to the freedom of a royal view of the world-order. First of all, the artless cheerfulness of the boy so forcibly repressed by the morose temperament of a pedantic tutor, the theologian Behnisch ; next the strict prince had to look on at the light-minded activities of the paternal court and was forced shyly to conceal the profound disgust which the spectacle aroused in his mind. He thus learned to withdraw into himself and to shun the world. His active powers were paralysed by an invincible diffidence ; it was his misfortune that he was never able to take life lightly and to look around among his fellows with serene self-command. Every appearance in public, and even speaking to any large number of people, was a burden to him. When he had to do it, he expressed his intelligent judgment and his tender sensibilities in bare, curt phrases ; his compressed and bald manner never furnished a true expression for this fine knightly figure with the beautiful and honest blue eyes. Accustomed from youth upwards to associate with persons of mediocre intelligence, he was seldom able to overcome his aversion to genius, to boldness, to anything that was out of the ordinary. He was alarmed by that inconsiderate freedom of speech which is characteristic of the great among the Teutons. Among all the talented men who served him, one only became truly dear to him, Scharnhorst, the man of simple nature, whose greatness imposed no claims.

It is the strength and the weakness of staunch natures that they find it difficult to forget. Frederick William was always ready to pardon, but he never forgot. Whilst he remembered with gratitude every service and every trifling obligation, and whilst he was profoundly pained by separation from faithful subjects, he could harbour a sentiment of anger for years until at length he plucked up sufficient courage " to give his opinion in good German"; and then the good-natured prince, violent in his anger, was unjust and petty in good German. Least of all was he able to forgive any arbitrary conduct on the part of his servants. He wished to be king, and was king. No one ever controlled him. Incredibly difficult was it for him to make any great resolution; he hesitated and procrastinated, let things slide, tolerated for a long time anything that displeased him, because he lacked confidence in his own judgment; yet once he was forced to come to a decision he always and everywhere followed his own conscience. From lack of resolution he left much undone to which his own level reasoning urged him, but he never did anything except as the outcome of his own well-weighed conviction. His slow moving but firm and vigorous spirit would accept from the ideas of great intelligences no more than what his own nature approved; no force of persuasion ever induced him to abandon the moral and political principles he held sacred. The blame and the glory of his long reign belongs to himself far more than his contemporaries were aware, for amid the brilliant figures of his generals and statesmen they were apt to lose sight of the inconspicuous prince. He chiefly was responsible for that lax policy of peace which prepared the destruction of the old state, but to him also belonged the credit that after ten years of hesitation and after the cruel assaults of destiny, he at length dared to be altogether himself, freely and spontaneously resolving to undertake the reconstruction of the state, carrying out the reforming ideas of his councillors just as far as they seemed to him right, and not undertaking the long-prepared War of Liberation until he himself saw that the right moment had come. In the second half of his reign he was responsible for the association of Prussian policy with Austrian, for the persecution of the demagogues, and for the non-appearance of the promised constitution; but he also conducted the reconstruction of the Prussian unified state with resolute patience, recognising with true insight the right moment for this undertaking, when the oriental confusion of the struggles of German commercial policy allowed the state once more to resume its independent way. Without him, and without the general confidence in his uprightness, the reconciliation of the innumerable contrasts of the new Prussia would have been as impossible as the peaceful creation of that customs-union which inseparably connected non-Austrian Germany with the Prussian state, and which laid the foundations of the new German Empire.

This king was not able, like the first Frederick William and his son, to stamp his own nature upon the state, but must derive his creative ideas from other and more brilliant intelligences. Yet he remained the master. During his reign, for good or for evil, the monarchical character of the Prussian state was ever maintained. In need and in disgrace, under discouragements by which a freer and bolder spirit might well have been plunged in despair, he pursued the course of duty without ever turning aside. Thus his name is inseparably associated at once with the gloomiest and the purest memories of our new history. His faithfulness to duty and his natural feeling for the honour of the throne gave him the energy to attain by gradual growth to a competent understanding of his position. By degrees he learned to value those domains of the national life which to his sober and domesticated nature had at first seemed alien. He learned to make himself at home in foreign policy ; and this prosaic man, who in his youth had found pleasure in the deplorable insipidity of the *Contes* of La Fontaine, became ultimately the Mæcenas of his house, a patron of the arts and sciences to a wider extent than had been any other of the Hohenzollerns. One who wished to see him in his human lovableness must seek him out in the lonely castle at Paretz. There under the ancient trees, beside the blue waters of the Havel, the young prince passed his happiest days by the side of his beloved consort Louise, in the lively circle of the pretty little flaxen-heads who grew up around him ; there he unbent, and by his humorous sallies he even provoked to disrespectful laughter that strict guardian of etiquette, the Countess Voss. It was a blessing for his somewhat heavy nature, inclined to melancholy, that he could cheer himself in the society of his serene-minded and high-spirited wife and breathe there the whole breath of life ; and yet for him, as for so many Teutons of deep feeling, the happiness of marriage exercised for a time a narrowing rather than an expanding influence. As a young husband he found full satisfaction in the innocent joys of his home, and gave to the state no more than an honourable diligence, not the free sacrifice of his entire intelligence which was demanded by the princely office ; entangled in the unconscious egoism of content, it was unwillingly that he left the pure atmosphere of his home, and he was satisfied to keep far from his personal environment the corruption which was eating up the state and society, instead of making it his kingly duty to fight it without pity.

By his candid tutor Sack, the crown prince was early introduced to the old Hohenzollern idea of Protestant union, and was habituated to a profound and yet free conception of the Christian faith. From Engel, he learnt the philanthropic ideas of the age of enlightenment ; from Suarez the political doctrines of the masters of common law ; in the campaigns on the Rhine and in Poland, as well as in military manœuvres in times of peace, he showed himself to be a valiant and well-informed officer. But, as he often himself complained, he was kept far from all affairs of state. When he entered upon the twenty-seven years of his reign, he found himself in an unknown world. Filled with a profound veneration for the works of his great-uncle, he was surrounded by elderly and opinionated masters who encountered the timid young man with the obscurity of the Frederician omniscience. Nothing was more remote from his mind than a fantastical over-estimation of the royal dignity. As the term " state " had gradually found its way into the customary terminology of the people from the laws of Frederick II, it had long been taken as a matter of course that every King of Prussia should conceive his high office as a grave political duty. The young king had a cordial feeling for the common man ; his inclinations were simply bourgeois like those of his great-grandfather, he had no preference for the nobility. It was his desire to complete that liberation of the agricultural workers which his ancestors for hundreds of years past had been effecting step by step. In the same sense as the first Frederick William, he was able to say, " I think as a Republican." Not that he was bewitched by the ideas of the French Revolution ; to his peace-loving nature and to his sense of justice alike, the bloody spectacle of the forcible popular uprising was repulsive. But his natural fair-mindedness, the traditions of his house, and the political ideas he had imbibed in the school of Suarez, impelled him in the direction of social reform. By philanthropic sentiment he was a free-trader ; an opponent of those laws which tended to make the necessaries of life dearer for the common people, or which rendered it more difficult to get a fair value for the energies of labour. His sound understanding soon discovered almost all the defects from which the benumbed state was suffering. When the disturbances broke over Prussia, the king spoke with a clearness, which to his environment seemed actually uncanny, about the causes of the crash. Concerning the ways and means of improvement, he often reflected with impressive understanding ; and it was with perfect truth that in respect of most of the proposals for reform put forward by Stein and Scharnhorst he was later accustomed to remark, " I have had this idea for a long time." There was only one essential idea, which he failed to grasp—the impossiblity of effecting important changes in the Frederician state by isolated reforms. Lacking this essential idea, all else was useless.

That rigid system of monarchical division of labour which the first Frederick William and his son had brought into being, was the creation of a deliberately conscious will, and was the outcome of the one-sided greatness characteristic of Old Prussia. The whole structure was cast in a single mould, and as if held together by iron clamps ; one pillar supported the others ; the divisions of the classes and the arrangement of the administration were inseparably connected ; if one stone were torn away, the whole building would collapse. If it was desired to abolish the privileges of the nobles in the army, the nobleman must be allowed to carry on bourgeois occupations and to buy land of the peasants. If the peasants were to be freed from the obligation to forced labour, the separation between town and country, the guild-system, and the excise, could no longer be maintained. The monarchy needed reform through and through as soon as it was recognised that the ancient forms of society were outworn. But no one in Prussia had yet attained to this degree of insight, not even Baron von Stein.

The first decade of the reign of Frederick William III, the most decried and the least-known epoch of Prussian history, was a period of well-meaning but utterly unfruitful attempts at reform. A few years earlier this state had still ranked, with good reason, as the best-ruled on the Continent ; in the opinion of the whole of North Germany it had faithfully guarded its vital energies in the struggle against the Revolution. Thus it happened that even the critical candour of the North German hardly noted how everything was going wrong in the community. The new century was hastening forward on the wings of the wind ; now in a few brief years important historical changes were to be effected which before this had taken decades to mature ; in such days as these who did not go forward went backward. But of this great transformation of the times there was no intimation whatever in the peaceful people that stayed in philosophic calm within its own boundaries, merely observing with languid interest that two powerful nations were struggling for the conquest of the world.

German good-nature is always inclined to expect the highest from a new ruler, but seldom have there been such exaggerated hopes as those which hailed the advent of this unassuming prince. His strict morality sufficed to win the hearts of the middle classes, and these intermediate strata of society became more and more the exponents of our public opinion. In practice the enlightened epoch rejoiced in an unrestrained good-fellowship, filled with the warm pleasures of the senses, and yet in theory it retained a lively enthusiasm for abstract " virtue "; this term had not yet acquired the connotation of philistine vacuousness which it bears to-day. Since the days of the Great Elector, the Prussian people had not again witnessed connubial happiness on the throne. What a delight it was to these German family men when the " throne became a shrine and the court a family," as Novalis sang with worthy enthusiasm. The pitiless severity of the two powerful kings of the eighteenth century had held the masses remote from the throne, imposing upon them sentiments of timid respect ; but now, through the cheerful cordiality of Queen Louise, the relationship between the Hohenzollerns and their loyal people acquired that homely characteristic of confidence which was elsewhere displayed only in the quiet life of the petty states.

The Prussians felt proud as Royalists, as opponents of the Revolution. Not alone the Hotspur among the youth of the Mark, young Marwitz, but also other members of the nobility and of the officers' corps, encountered the regicide Sieyès, the envoy of the Republic, with angry glances when he made his appearance with unpowdered hair and wearing a tricolor sash, at the gorgeous old-fashioned ceremony of the oath of allegiance. The enlightened society of Berlin, however, held a position of conscious opposition to Austria and to the Holy Empire. The French were given to understand that the king was a democrat after his own fashion, that he would effect with due measure and in an orderly manner what they had done so stormily, and it was soon reported that a Jacobin had complained, " this king is stealing our thunder." When the young king now made a clean sweep of the dubious members of his father's environment, and when in an eloquent address to his cabinet he gave utterance to an abundance of excellent proposals and humane views, Marquis Herz exclaimed with delight : " Pure reason has come down from Heaven and is established upon our throne." An authors' club of Berlin published " Annals of the Prussian Monarchy," which were to describe the performances of the royal reformer step by step. This mood of hope endured for a considerable period. When in the year 1800 Hufeland was summoned to Berlin, he wrote with satisfaction : " I am going to a liberal state, one which is blossoming under a new government." Schiller, too, and Johannes Müller, spoke with cordial approbation of the essential freedom of Prussian life, and expressed their satisfaction at the speed with which Berlin was becoming a centre of German art and culture.

But the king was soon to learn how limited was in truth his absolute authority, limited by the inertia of the adminstration, by the passive resistance of public opinion, by feudal prejudices, and by the military and bureaucratic spirit of caste. In the enlarged monarchy, even a Frederick had hardly found it possible to retain in a single hand the immediate conduct of all the affairs of state. Personal government had become an impossibility, but its forms persisted in an altered sense. Under Frederick, the cabinet councillors had been mere secretaries, whose duty it was to transmit to the executive authorities the commands of the king ; under his two successors they acquired a dangerous power. Since the prince could not himself supervise the enormous mass of reports, the secretaries became advisers. The cabinet councillors were chosen for the most part from the ranks of the bourgeois judges ; they alone held regular intercourse with the monarch and soon came to regard themselves as tribunes of the people, as representatives of the peaceful bourgeoisie against the nobility and the army. Between the crown and its ministers there was a throng of incalculable subaltern influences at work. Among these trusted councillors, there was not a single one whom the young prince could raise out of the slothful atmosphere or tepid resolves into the fresh air of vigorous determination. The most notable among them, Mencken, was of value to the royal pair through the benevolence of his enlightened moral and philosophical views. He did all he could to institute numerous reforms in matters of detail, but he lacked the comprehensive insight of the statesman. Subsequently Beyme had control of the most important internal affairs, and Lombard of foreign affairs ; the former was an able lawyer and a man of humane views, but was great in little things only, whilst Lombard was an empty-headed and frivolous debauchee. The personality of the adjutants-general was also in harmony with the spirit of trivial mediocrity which dominated the whole circle. Colonel Zastrow was a conceited opponent of all reform ; Colonel Köckritz was a man of narrow philistine spirit, pleasing to his young master by his phlegmatic good nature, happy when he could recreate himself after the labours of the day over a pipe and a quiet game of cards, but extremely testy at a young gentleman among his subordinates who allowed himself " to make verses," as did poor Heinrich von Kleist. Although the king's views extended far beyond those of these petty-minded men, he nevertheless gradually allowed himself to be lowered to the level of their smallness and pusillanimity.

Just as in former days the reconstruction of the state had proceeded from the army, so now it was in military affairs that it first became apparent that the new epoch had need of new forms. The most important acquisition of the old monarchy was lost when the left bank of the Rhine was ceded to France, and when, not long after, the new middle states of the south-west founded their own little armies. Thus at the very outset of his reign the king was forced to institute a more extensive levying of the native Prussians who were liable to military service, " owing to a decline of the enlistment in other parts of the empire." This first step had to be followed by others. Henceforward the army depended upon Prussian strength alone. If it were to be furnished with that accession of numbers which was so urgently required, at least a portion of the privileged classes must be summoned to bear arms. This was impossible so long as the officers' corps remained a closed caste placed at an inaccessible height above the rank and file, and so long as the cruel old discipline still persisted, that discipline which had become utterly repugnant to that philanthropic temperament which the age cultivated to the extreme of softness. As soon as the old stock of recruited foreigners died out, a radical reconstruction of the army became unavoidable, a complete change of the old caste relationships and, above all, a change in the position of the nobility in the state and in society.

Numerous proposals for reform were made. A few enlightened spirits among the younger officials, such as Hippel and Vincke, went so far as to demand that the old Prussian idea of universal military service should be put into complete execution. Knesebeck, Rüchel, and other officers recommended the formation of a territorial militia. But the ignorant pride of the old generals was hostile to every proposed change. They still believed that the Frederician army was unsurpassable. Even Frederick Gentz, who, to the scandal of the poor-spirited time, ventured to send an open letter of admonition to the new monarch, said of the army, " as far as this is concerned, no change is needed " ; and Blucher, who was afraid of no one, continued as late as the spring of 1806 to speak of " our invincible army." Since to every proposal for reform the proud old Field-Marshal Möllendorff made answer with a snarl, " This is altogether above my head," the king determined, to his bitter subsequent regret, not to show himself any wiser than these old men of established reputation. On the other hand, in the enlightened world there prevailed a doctrinaire belief in the blessings of peace, which formed a ludicrous contrast to the bloody practice of the states of the new century, but which harmonised well with the German good-nature. In unctuous pamphlets the question was asked, "Are standing armies necessary in time of peace?" The decline of rigid absolutism is manifested by the fact that such expressions of public opinion now began to exercise an influence with which the government had to reckon. At the court, Mencken ardently advocated the old view of the officialdom, that the military expenditure was too heavy ; and the king himself wished to do no more than was absolutely indispensable, for he desired to reduce the burden of debt he had inherited from his father. Last of all, the serious question had to be faced of how trustworthy regiments could possibly be formed out of the disaffected Poles.

In view of these conflicting considerations, despite innumerable proposals and much consideration, no important reform was effected. A trifling increase was made in the army, raising its total strength to 250,000 ; but this involved a notable increase in the army-expenses until they attained the figure of 16,000,000 or 17,000,000 thalers, for the king at length undertook to provide for the troops on a more liberal scale, although still quite inadequately. For the reinforcement of this insufficient army, there was to be a territorial reserve of 50,000 men, constituted chiefly out of the privileged classes ; this reserve was actually in process of formation when the confusions of the war of 1805 brought to a premature conclusion this policy of half reforms. No support was given to a brilliant plan of Scharnhorst, who, in the spring of 1806, proposed to form a great militia of 3,000,000 men. Even the reduction of the cumbersome equipment and other technical improvements which seemed necessary to the clear soldier's insight of the king, had to encounter the obstinate resistance of the pompous old gentlemen with the long waistcoat-flaps. The affable prince was greatly disturbed by the arrogance of his officers, and warned them sharply that they should not dare to be rude to the meanest of the citizens, "for it is the citizens, not I myself, who maintain the army." Yet he failed to understand that such admonitions could bear no fruit so long as the ancient forms of the army-constitution persisted, and so long as the officers' corps continued to be recognised as the first class in the state.

How strange, however, had been the metamorphosis effected in that army of the Silesian wars, then so harmonious despite its severity and roughness. A new and over-talented generation was growing up ; all the heroes of the future War of Liberation had for some time been in the army, and most of them were already staff officers. In many of the circles of the officers' corps there prevailed a fresh and scientific sentiment, a lively understanding of the present age. In the new military academy, Colonel Scharnhorst gave his lectures—Scharnhorst, son of a peasant of Lower Saxony, who had found no field for his energies in noble-ridden Hanover, and who had finally answered the king's summons to Berlin. He was already teaching that which to the wisdom of men of the old cautious military school seemed rank heresy, that one " should never remain on the defensive in concentration, but should always attack in concentration." He illustrated his doctrines by the wars of Frederick, and by those of young Bonaparte, whom the Frederician veterans would hardly admit to be even a bourgeois general. Forgotten in his little Silesian garrison there lived Gneisenau, the born commander, poring over his maps, following with attentive gaze every step taken by the Corsican from the days of the first Italian campaign ; endeavouring to grasp all the peculiarities of this new elemental force, as if foreseeing that he himself was some day to encounter the unconquerable man. The new spiritual life of the nation began at length to exercise its influence even upon this military circle which had hitherto been completely unaffected. All the literary tendencies had certain representatives among the young officers, not excepting even the peace-loving cosmopolitanism of the Kantian philosophy ; Lieutenant Heinrich Kleist complained bitterly that he had to waste his time so immorally in the Rhenish campaigns.

The dominant tone, however, remained extremely unspiritual. Most of the old officers assiduously manifested their hatred for culture and did not conceal their contempt for the schoolmaster Scharnhorst. Since in each company only four or five new recruits were introduced annually, the difficult and grateful task of the military education of the people, which forms the chief work of the infantry officers of the modern popular army, did not exist at all for the officers of that day, and to high-spirited natures the perpetual repetition of the same parades, with the same veteran professional soldiers, became quite unbearable. The timid citizens of Berlin were terrified, and the king intervened with severe punishments, when the young officers of the notorious Regiment of Gensdarmes made the streets hideous with noisy masquerades, and when the overgrown Charles Nostitz, dressed up as Katharina von Bora, brandished his riding whip behind Doctor Luther. The hot young blood, unable to accommodate itself to the tedium of perpetual pipeclay and perpetual drill, broke out in such rough sports as these. The whole tragedy of this army of peace was incorporated in the tragic fate of Prince Louis Ferdinand ; it was dreadful to see how the free and bold young hero, born for all that was glorious, dissipated his energies in wild enjoyment and mad adventures because he could not bear an empty existence. More and more the true purpose of the military system was forgotten. The orders " pour le mérite," previously given only on the field of battle, now became rewards for the heroic deeds performed in peaceful manœuvres. A pettifogging spirit supervised the length of the pigtails, the shape of the trusses of hay, the clash of the presented arms ; but, for the sake of economy, the artillery had no teams to draw it. To the Frederician army nothing seemed of any importance but a majestic slowness ; it happened on one occasion that an artillery regiment took four days to march from Berlin to Breslau. The common soldier, who did not wish to lose his customary skill in his manual occupation, was as peace-loving in his thoughts as were the majority of the grey-headed captains, for whom the furloughs of the years of peace brought many savings for their private purse. It seemed as if the sword of Prussia was never more to be drawn from the scabbard. The foreboding of Frederick, in which he had warned " the favourites of Mars " that they should never allow their manhood to be corrupted by sloth, arrogance, and softness, was now literally fulfilled.

Just as little was there effected any comprehensive reform of the administration. The king did not venture to follow the example of his great-uncle, who had decided everything for himself. His fair-mindedness shrank from the acceptance of the hard Frederician principle which was inseparable from such omnipotence, that the monarch must never admit error. Wherever possible, therefore, he referred all petitions to the appropriate permanent authorities. In this way there was added much work to the already oppressive labours of the officials. Since the new provinces in Poland and Franconia had at length been placed under the control of the General Directory, the central authority, which formerly and in simpler circumstances had been so thoroughly efficient, proved altogether incompetent ; each department went its own way, and all unity of control was lacking. The members of the official bureaucracy remained far superior to those of the neighbouring German states ; they were active, full of patriotic pride, and highly cultured, although here and there isolated presidents endeavoured to rival the generals in their hatred of culture. But the antiquated organisation of the authorities which were interpolated between the provincial system and the real system, resulted in this, that no one was in reality minister and able to supervise the course of the administration. The simplest matter could not be carried out without distressing disputes about competence, the delimitation of authority, and the increase of the number of ministerial appointments served only to increase the evil. In the old official families which had now been attached to the service of the state for many decades, there was indeed handed down from father to son a lively sentiment of the honour of their order, but there was also transmitted a considerable measure of official arrogance ; newcomers like Baron von Stein, who found their way into this bureaucratic world from the fresh and natural activities of the country house, noted with regret that the writing of official orders threatened to become an end in itself. A formalised documentary activity gained the upper hand and could not be overcome by the mild admonitions of the royal decrees, because there was lacking at the head of affairs that far-sighted statesmanship which might have imposed new positive duties upon the officialdom. An additional difficulty was to be found in the distressing inertia of the Polish provinces, which weighed as heavy as lead upon the administration. It was an intolerable misfortune that the ruling classes received hardly any young accession of strength from the wide Slav dominions. The mocking saying of its opponents that the Prussian state was a purely fortuitous structure, seemed now to be justified by the facts.

Soon after ascending the throne, the king expressed, in opposition to Struensee, the Minister of Finance, his disapproval of the untenable prohibitive system which was perpetually violated. It was not till seven years later that he was able to make the first breach in this old order of affairs, and (through the intermediation of Struensee's successor, Stein) almost entirely repealed the internal duties. The introduction of uniform frontier tariffs was still everywhere regarded as a foolhardy venture. In his Budget Reports of 1781, Necker said that there was little hope that it would be possible to abolish the *constitution barbare* of the provincial tolls. The fiscal unity of France was first established by the Revolution. When now in Prussia it was ventured to abolish the internal customs dues, it was soon realised that this reform was no more than a half measure. For there still remained the excise with its sixty-seven different tariffs, and a cabinet decree of the king vainly attempted to bring clearness into this confusion. There still existed the industrial compulsion which distinguished the towns from the open country ; only in the County Mark had Stein already ventured to abolish this limited distinction. Together with the provincial customs dues there was abolished also the freedom from tolls of the privileged classes, and this first moderate invasion of the privileges of the nobility in matters of taxation immediately raised the question whether the far more oppressive inequality of direct taxation would still be suffered to continue. In the Electoral Mark, in the year 1806, the towns paid nearly 2,500,000, the peasants 644,000, and the whole of the landed proprietors only 21,000 thalers, in taxes to the state. But the time had not yet come for a radical transformation of the national economy. There was a terrible conflict of economic views. Most of the more intelligent among the younger officials, like Vincke, were enthusiasts for the " divine Adam Smith," but the landed proprietors inclined to the ideas of the physiocrats.

The greatest hindrance to reform lay, however, in the opposition of the diets. The strong passive resistance of the old orders had always turned the edge of the agrarian laws of the eighteenth century ; now, under a government that was far too considerate, this resistance displayed an altogether unexpected strength. One of the first steps taken by the king was to give to certain free peasants, known as the Köllmers, the right to representation among the estates of East Prussia. Thus rejuvenated, the Diet of Königsberg became the only tolerably healthy body among the decayed feudal corporations of the monarchy ; with some reason it described itself as the " representative of the nation." But when the king further proposed to abolish patrimonial jurisdiction, even the Diet of East Prussia offered repeated and open opposition. Another cherished plan of the peasant-loving prince, the abolition of forced labour for the peasantry and the transformation of all peasant land held on terms of feudal subservience into free property, also had to encounter the resistance of the nobles. This idea was by no means the outcome of the French Revolution, but was a necessary development of the earlier legislation of the Hohenzollerns, who for two hundred years had been working for the liberation of the country folk ; simultaneously, and altogether independently of one another, such officials as Stein and Hippel, and such writers as Leopold Krug, recommended the abolition of hereditary servitude. On the crown-lands of West Prussia and East Prussia, the valiant president Auerswald succeeded in abolishing statute labour, and wherever any one of the nobles was willing of his own initiative to undertake the same reform, he received all possible encouragement from the king ; but it was thought too venturesome to attempt a comprehensive law for the entire monarchy. The opposition was offered not by the landed proprietors alone, but also by the rude peasants, who regarded with a vigorous mistrust every attempt to alter the established order ; even the trees planted along the new high roads were not safe from the hands of these barbarians.

The same unteachable hostility was displayed also when the king, impelled solely by the goodness of his own heart, undertook the improvement of the elementary schools and made a serious attempt to enforce the universal duty of school attendance. The government still stood high above the people. Whilst the detestable lampoons of the opposition were now, as formerly, characterised by a deplorable poverty of ideas, in official circles all the great social reforms of the subsequent century already received a thoroughly intelligent advocacy ; J. G. Hoffmann even recommended the complete abolition of the guild system. But energy was lacking to constrain the hostile people to the acceptance of these good ideas. In deference to " public opinion," the tobacco monopoly was repealed, and yet this, properly administered, would have been a very lucrative source of national income and one interfering very little with the natural course of trade. When Struensee, in the year 1798, proposed the issue of a moderate amount of paper money, a trifling expression of dissatisfaction on the part of the commercial classes of Berlin induced all the ministers to declare with one voice that they felt it was impossible to carry out so odious a measure. The weakness of the throne was displayed especially in the moral condition of the capital. Whilst at the court an ancient and inexpensive simplicity of manners was strictly observed, the fashionable world of Berlin lived in complete disregard of this admirable example of domestic virtue. The population of the town now numbered 182,000 ; the upper classes already showed all the freedom of metropolitan life, whilst among the middle classes a dull surburbanism still prevailed. Sociability became a fine art such as it had never before been in Germany. Wit and criticism developed without restraint. Profligacy and intellectual arrogance became so conspicuous that even Goethe spoke with some aversion of this dangerous society. In such an atmosphere there grew up natures of illimitable receptivity and sensitiveness, such as Schleiermacher ; virtuosi of pleasure and of thought, such as

William Humboldt and Frederick Gentz; but also the empty-headed imitators and idea-brokers the circle of Varnhagens, and such virtuosi of crime as the murderess Ursinus.

During this decade of half beginnings and well-meaning attempts there was on the whole a great deal of good effected. In agrarian economy there was real progress; in the twenty years following the death of Frederick, the price of grain doubled, whilst the price of land rose still faster, almost giddily. Thaer was the first to draw the attention of the North Germans to the example of English agriculture, and after the skilled advocate of free labour had opened his educational institute in Möglin, among the younger agriculturists there was a great increase in technical insight and knowledge of agriculture. Without the influence of Thaer it would hardly have been possible to carry into effect the Stein-Hardenberg laws. Now for the first time the roads and waterways, which had been terribly neglected throughout the empire, received serious attention. Through the work of Stein, the Ruhr was opened to navigation. The king himself devoted his earnest attention to the valley of the Vistula, where, under the Polish regime, the mighty dikes of the Teutonic Knights had completely fallen into decay. The mining industry, which had already received a considerable impetus under Heinitz, Stein's teacher, now underwent a further advance when Count Reden instituted the great mining works in Upper Silesia. Krug and Hoffmann were actively engaged in the newly founded Statistical Bureau, while Niebuhr was summoned from Denmark to take charge of the Bank.

In the general opinion there was nothing for which the new Government was so highly esteemed as for the dismissal of the detested Wöllner and for the repeal of his severe Edict of Religions. The young prince's contention that reason and philosophy are the inseparable accompaniments of religion, went straight to the heart of the enlightened world, for everyone could interpret the phrase in accordance with his own pleasure. But when the king recommended the ecclesiastical authorities to unite for a common Protestant liturgy—a proposal he owed to his tutor, Sack—it appeared once more that the crown was considerably in advance of the people. He had to defer this plan of union till better days, for in delicate questions of ecclesiastical policy he wished to work even more cautiously than in matters of ordinary statecraft. The same excess of caution was responsible for his temporary failure to carry into effect that reform of the educational system which had been discussed in so many memorials and treatises; no satisfactory choice had been effected from among all the diverse methods of education which the age of Pestalozzi was unweariedly producing. A zeal hitherto unknown in Prussia was displayed for learning, and the barrier was at length removed which had so long cut off this state from German science. Alexander Humboldt, Johannes Müller, Hufeland, and a long series of distinguished professors, were summoned to Berlin; even Fichte, who had been driven out of Jena by the bigotry of the Lutherans of Electoral Saxony, found an asylum on the Spree. The intellectual life of the capital began to advance with giant strides. As early as the winter of 1786, twenty-one courses of public lectures were announced in the town, and since that date they had become even more numerous and important. In Berlin, A. W. Schlegel gave lectures on literary history embodying the programme of the Romantic School. The collections of the Royal House, which the young king was the first to open to the public, and above all the theatre, which, under the direction of Iffland, was still a great national institute of culture, favoured a lively interchange of ideas, and thus, quite spontaneously, the question came to the fore whether this wealth of intellectual life should not be centred in a university. No other German university arose by so natural a development as that of Berlin; it was really in existence before it was formally constituted. But for the moment not even this plan got beyond the stage of cabinet discussion. The whole age seemed bewitched, and no important matter could be brought to a conclusion.

The philistine indifference of the state to the fine arts was at length overcome. Public picture-galleries were now opened, and Berlin already possessed an independent school of aspiring artists. Contrasted with the work of Langhans, a man of classical spirit, who designed the Brandenburg Gate, was the robust realism of Schadow. When the queen went out driving, there stood, hat in hand, at the door of her carriage, the young lackey, Christian Rauch, who was subsequently to outdo all others when his benevolent mistress had smoothed his path to great artistic creation. But in these respects also there was the same distressing phenomenon of costly energies that were not utilised and of extensive beginnings that were never brought to a conclusion. After a number of plans had been taken up and discarded, only one great public building was completed, the new Mint, adorned by Schadow with admirable reliefs, and yet the building itself was repulsively bald, a true image of this barren time.

Similarly in all the spheres of political life, the old was not yet swept away and the new was not yet properly developed. The state had lost in character what it had gained in humane mildness. It resembled a Gothic building still mighty in decay, upon which shaky hands had here and there erected basely-designed turrets. Yet the loyal people was happy in these incredible conditions. It was unquestionable that the childlike manifestations of joy which greeted the king and the queen whenever they made a progress through the country, and which were loudest among the warm-blooded Franconians, came just as sincerely from the heart as did later the tragical letters of farewell from the lost provinces.

The king's ideas in matters of reform went no further than social improvements. Not even Hardenberg had any thought of more than the institution of civic equality in accordance with the French example. There was but one man in Prussia who conceived generous plans of political reform. As president of the chamber in Westphalia, Baron von Stein had become acquainted with the old municipal freedom of the County Mark, and from his experience there, and from his study of English history, he had formed the opinion that a sound political order exists only where the people itself learns to put its hand to the work of government. When the feudal constitution was abolished in the newly acquired Münster territories, he wrote to the king : [1] " These diets, which hitherto have been abused by the officials as the enemies of all reform, might, if rightly handled, become the pillars of social order. They check those arbitrary breaches of the constitution and of the laws, of which in the pressure of affairs the territorial councils are not infrequently guilty ; and by property and by dependence on the fatherland they are chained to those interests of the country which the foreign public officials often fail to recognise, towards which they are apt to be indifferent, and which they sometimes regard with hatred and contempt. Rulers have nothing to fear from the propertied classes ; but they have much to fear from the innovating tendencies of the younger officials, from the luke-warmness and the mercenary spirit of the older ones, and from the flabbiness and the egoism making light of all morality which invade all classes alike." Such ideas were at present altogether beyond the king's understanding. He did not, indeed, share the detestation of the Revolution which was felt by the bigoted Royalists of his court, for he fully recognised the justice of the liberation of the French peasantry ; but owing to the bloody deeds of the

---

[1] Report to the King, Münster, October 30, 1804.

French revolutionists he was suspicious of anything that savoured of constitutional monarchy. In view of the general contentment of his people, how could it occur to him that the absolutism which had brought his state into existence, now belonged to the past ? Not even Stein himself knew how rotten had become the old order, and how urgently necessary was a reconstruction. In all classes there prevailed the same incredible illusion. Historical criticism can offer no suggestion how the disgraces of 1806 might have been spared to the old monarchy. Only the incisive demonstration of war could display to this blinded generation the inward decay of those Frederician forms which paralysed all activity by the magic of ancient renown. Only a defeat could put an end to the unnatural episode of the German rule in Warsaw, could restore the state to itself, and could revive its true German nature.

Originally Frederick William was as little prepared for his royal duties as for the conduct of foreign policy ; of a slow and cautious temperament, he needed long training in a severe school before his soft disposition became accustomed to the hardness of the great questions of political power. By inclination and by his sense of duty he was a man of peace. He would have regarded it as criminal folly, in the absence of urgent necessity, to introduce to the hazard of war this industrious North Germany, whose quiet happiness was esteemed by all, even by Frederick Gentz ; he was loath to expose the heavily-burdened state to new confusions ; he could be forced to draw the sword only by direct attack. The general peace-loving character of the North Germans found no more ardent representative than at the Prussian court ; here pacifism had even become a constitutional doctrine. "A king," said Colonel Köckritz to his royal friend, "has no right to stake the existence of his state in a war ; such a right is reserved for a Re-public." But there was no doubt in the sound sense of the king about the dangerous intentions of France. His father had ever remained faithful to the old hostility to the Republic. On his death-bed he had rejected the offer of an alliance with France, and he would not allow himself to be led astray when Caillard held out to him the prospect of acquiring the German imperial crown. Count Haugwitz, also, was now full of mistrust of the rulers of Paris. Consequently the relations between the two powers remained extremely cool, and the young king sometimes declared that he wished to save up the energies of his state for the time when perhaps a decisive struggle with this robber neighbour might become necessary. It is probable that he himself did not know whether he meant this seriously, or whether he was merely seeking a cloak for his own pacifism. As a good German, he desired the contentment of the whole empire and the restoration of the ancient frontiers; he approved the position of the French neither in Mainz, which had been conquered by his own troops, nor yet in his own hereditary dominions on the Lower Rhine.

The prince under whose rule the greatest and most extensive changes of territorial area occurred that were ever effected in Prussian history, was one with a constitutional dislike to any trafficking in lands and people ; even trifling rectifications of frontier were repugnant to his conscience. He had at length agreed to the cession of Cleves and Guelderland only because these territories, temporarily occupied by the French, had not yet paid him homage. Throughout Germany the relationship between a prince and his subjects was still regarded as a matter of personal duty ; as soon as a ruler died the gates of the towns were immediately closed and the troops were at once sworn in to their new master. The sober sense of the son was not illusioned by the romantic honour which the father had paid to the ancient and honourable forms of the imperial constitution ; he recognised the irrevocable decay of the empire, and as a faithful Protestant he had but little sympathy with the troubles of the spiritual states. But since he had not as yet paid any serious attention to the possibility of imperial reform, the simple re-establishment of the *status quo* in Germany would have been most agreeable to his sense of justice and to his love of peace. If this should prove impossible, he desired at least to preserve a balance between Austria and Prussia, to compensate every enlargement of Austrian power by a corresponding increase of his own state. Without any personal rancour against the Hofburg, he revived the Bavarian policy of his great-uncle, working on behalf of the rights of the Wittelsbachs against the imperial plans of conquest. It is true that the leading thought of his German policy remained the preservation of peace in the north. In his view the power of the monarchy, at once against France and against Austria, must be maintained by diplomatic means alone.

It was with this sentiment of a just paterfamilias that the inexperienced young prince went to encounter the elemental energies which during recent months had transformed the aspect of the world. The leaders of the Reign of Terror had once boasted that the Revolution was to plough deep furrows ; and this prophecy had been horribly fulfilled. In the nine years since the storming of the Bastille, 22,331 new laws had been passed in unhappy France; every bridge between the past and the present had been destroyed; of all the institutions of the Bourbon state the only one that still remained was the Academy of Paris. A third of the soil of France had been forcibly torn from its old possessors. Depreciated paper money had been issued to the amount of 47,000,000 francs. All the rights of property were in a state of hopeless confusion. For years the country had been despoiled by the practical communism of the Paris mob. Well-being and security before the law had disappeared, and therewith had disappeared also all the nobility of its culture. The Goddess of Reason had been enthroned upon the altars of the defiled churches; the most tasteful people of Europe paid honour to the red cap of the convicted prisoner as the emblem of its new freedom, and renamed the days of the calendar after the pig, the donkey, and the potato. The hideous work of the guillotine had at length come to an end, but the cruel penal laws against priests and *emigrés* were still enforced with pitiless rancour. The goods and the civic existence of thousands were still at the mercy of the incalculable caprices of the dominant party. Nine years of incredible misery had extinguished the last sparks of political idealism, and had deprived of all meaning the struggles of public life; the disputes between parties were, as they have ever since remained in France, nothing more than a contest for the possession of power.

The French nation demanded peace, legal security for the new distribution of property, and the restoration of the ancient Church. If matters were left to themselves, the recall of the royal house seemed inevitable, not because the wearied people still retained any sentiment of loyalty to the dynasty, but because it was only the monarchical order which seemed to promise an epoch of peaceful well-being. In the general decay, the army alone preserved some degree of virile discipline; in the general exhaustion, it alone retained moral aims. Numerous successes, deserved and undeserved, had awakened warlike ambition and pride in the unconquered tricolor, and this especially among the young generals. It was through this army, the one orderly and enthusiastic power in the new France, that the radical parties of the Convention retained their dominion against the will of the nation. On the 13th of Vendémiaire, 1795, General Bonaparte suppressed the Royalist rising and forcibly secured the entry of two-thirds of the members of the Convention into the popular assembly of the new directorial constitution. But this involved a continuance of the war, for it was only in war-time that the victorious minority could hope to retain a secure possession of power.

With the Italian campaign of the year 1796 began the second epoch of the period of the Revolution, and the epoch most important to the history of Europe. Now for the first time the revolutionary propaganda became really effective. A new order of affairs made an end of the old territorial distribution, abolished the traditional forms of state and society in Central Europe. It was through the victories of Bonaparte that the arms of France first obtained an incontestable superiority. When the young hero, passing round the Alps, invaded Northern Italy from the south, he at once showed himself to be master of a new and bolder method of warfare, of a method which was able to make war pay for war, to nourish it upon the resources of the conquered land ; he was not afraid to accept the risk of annihilation, but offered battle to the enemy after a sudden change of front. No longer, as in the day of the old linear tactics, were battles a simple struggle between two compact lines, either army endeavouring to break through the line of the other. Bonaparte gave to the course of war a dramatic movement ; he forced a decisive issue by the infliction of overwhelming blows with his carefully saved reserves as soon as the forces of his first lines of attack had been used up ; and no one ever knew as well as he how to make the best possible use of the favour of fortune. Not to him, as to the commanders of the costly old mercenary armies, did it seem to be the first duty of the general to spare his own troops—for all losses could be readily made good by conscription. His primary aim was to destroy the forces of the enemy. Marching rapidly through the country, he endeavoured to strike a vital blow at the heart of his opponent, to rob him of his capital city. With an enthusiastic belief in himself and in the power of his sword, his spirit glowing with the obscure and majestic poetry of war, he educated his troops to believe with a blind confidence in his destiny, taught them that " honour, glory and wealth " are the highest arms of war, and filled them through and through with a restless, adventurous military spirit which despised as empty chatter all talk of popular happiness and popular freedom. He christened the French with the cleverly chosen name of *la grande nation*, and induced in the people, who were sickened of party struggles, an intoxicated sentiment of overweening belief in themselves and in the fortune of war—a spirit which proved stronger and more enduring than had been the enthusiasm for freedom of the early days of the Revolution.

The victor of Montenotte and Rivoli imposed a change of character upon the European policy of France no less than upon the conduct of war. Notwithstanding the cosmopolitan catchwords with which the government was accustomed to deck its actions, its designs were not notably different from those that had characterised the national policy of the House of Bourbon. The desire was to extend the boundary of the nation towards the east, and by the weakening of Germany to give to France a preponderant influence in the counsels of Europe and to secure for her the leadership of the Latin peoples ; the direct control of Europe was not the French ambition. But the insatiable man who now held his Byzantine court in Italy, who at his caprice carved the conquered regions into vassal states, who overcame all opposition on the part of the Directory, now by threats and now by sending abundant plunder, was a man without a fatherland. As a youth he had once been an enthusiast for the liberation of his Corsican home, but his precocious wisdom in the things of the world soon dissipated these youthful dreams ; with never a regret he entered the service of the conquerors of Corsica because he saw that the dissolution of the old order in revolutionary France offered the highest possibilities to a man of supreme endowments. He now felt himself to be the born conqueror, superior to all other mortals in the energy of his will and in his ability to carry out his designs. He luxuriated in the feeling of being the one power of the time which was able to undertake the impossible, and rejoiced in the proud consciousness that to him alone was it given to carry into effect the determinations of a terrible destiny. Before him was extended the old Europe, split up by contesting interests, paralysed by a cumbersome military system and by antiquated constitutions—a world of petrified states, appealing to historical precedent alone in justification of their right to existence. At his back were the powerful warlike energies of the French nation, a nation that had broken with its own past, and regarded itself as endowed with the mission to impose new laws on the whole earth.

Thus there arose in the mind of this man without a fatherland to whom the spiritual life of the nations and the world of ideas always remained incomprehensible, the detestable thought of a new world-empire. The images of the Cæsars and of the Carlovingians loomed before his mind ; the rich history of a millennium was to be annihilated by a giant adventure ; the many-sided culture-world of the west was to obey the orders of a single Colossus. With a marvellous sureness of aim, and with unexampled freedom from conscientious scruples, this new and utterly un-French policy of world-conquest advanced towards its goal. The insight of Bonaparte at once recognised by what means Austria, victorious in Germany but beaten in Italy, was to be forced to a transitory peace. He saw through the plans of Thugut in the Adriatic ; with unprecedented treachery he made an excuse for the conquest of the neutral Republic of Venice ; easily overthrew the undefended Venetians ; and then offered the imperial court to exchange Venice for Milan, Belgium, and the left bank of the Rhine, knowing that the rounding-off of her dominion with Venice would be more grateful to Austria than the retention of the lost and untenable outposts. In addition, to the emperor were promised the secularised ecclesiastical lands of Salzburg and Bavaria as far as the Inn, whilst to his cousin, who had been driven out of Modena, was to be given the Breisgau. It was on these terms that the Peace of Campo Formio was concluded on October 7, 1797.

Once again had the Holy Empire to pay the price for Austrian defeats ; and once again, and more hypocritically than ever before, there were heard in the Reichstag those consecrated imperial and fatherly phrases with which the German imperial power was accustomed to veil the aims of its own self-seeking policy. Whilst in the secret articles of the Treaty of Campo Formio the mutilation of the German western frontier, the secularisation of the spiritual domains, and the indemnification of foreign princes at the expense of the empire, had been arranged, in the open phrasing of the Treaty of Peace allusion was made to the retention of the perfect integrity of the empire. A decree of the imperial court invited the estates of the empire to a Congress at Rastatt, in order that "upon the basis of integrity, Germany's constitution and welfare may be established for centuries to come, to the permanent ecstasy of peace-loving humanity." At the Congress of Rastatt, the envoys of the Republic appeared as the masterful umpires of German affairs. Nearly three hundred German diplomats were assembled ; among them were many men of learning, eager to enrich the great collection of riddles known as the imperial law by the addition of some new prodigies. By flattery and by corruption they rivalled one another to secure the favours of the arrogant strangers. The French language and French ways were dominant. Every evening, official Germany applauded French play-actors when these were doing their best to amuse *les bêtes Allemandes*. It was the task of the Austrian statesmen to keep secret from the envoys of the estates of the empire the real character of the conversations of Campo Formio. For a time this deceit was successful, for the emperor was represented by three different embassies : as Emperor, as Archduke of Austria, and as King of Hungary, and always one of his envoys could skilfully hide himself behind the others.

At length, however, the unhallowed secret had to be made public. At Christmas, 1797, Mainz was evacuated by the imperial troops. The hopelessly confused situation of the two nations of central Europe whose destinies had been intertwined by fate, now came to light, for on the same day the French occupied the unconquered bulwark of the Rhineland, and the conquered Austrians entered the town of St. Mark. Soon afterwards, the French plenipotentiaries in Rastatt openly demanded the left bank of the Rhine. This was the first official announcement of the annihilation of the Holy Empire. For in accordance with the patrimonial conception of the imperial law it was regarded as self-evident that the houses of the temporal hereditary princes must be compensated for the losses they sustained on the left bank of the Rhine, whilst the spiritual electoral princes (in the French documents of state they received the descriptive name of *princes usufruitiers*) were to be indemnified for their right of usufruct by pensions. General secularisation, of which for years past the idea had continually and inevitably recurred, now seemed to be the last possible means of satisfying the dynastic wishes of the German estate of princes. The plunder of the goods of the Church by the high nobility now began. The emperor himself had opened the floodgates by the deliberate annexation of the Salzburg ecclesiastical lands. In savage greed, the princely envoys thronged round the plenipotentiaries of the Directory in order to obtain from the favour of the enemies of the empire a rich share in the domains of their spiritual co-estates.

It was the intention of Thugut that in this robbery of the spiritual princes Prussia should come off empty-handed. In the secret articles of the Treaty of Campo Formio, the cession of the left bank of the Rhine from Basle to the Nette was approved on the express understanding that in this way Prussia would retain its possessions on the Lower Rhine, and thus would have no claim to indemnity. This understanding was in open contradiction with the Treaty of August, 1796, which had promised the court of Berlin an advantageous rounding-off of Prussian dominion in the event of the cession of the left bank of the Rhine. Thus by two contradictory secret treaties, France had tied to her side the two mutually hostile great powers of Germany, one of which hoped to secure advantage out of its defeats, and the other out of its inaction. Inevitably, the third power, which based its claims upon the victorious use of the sword, would derive the maximum advantage from these contradictory negotiations.

Even after all that had happened, the way was open for a resolute Prussian policy. The Prussian possessions on the Lower Rhine became untenable, now that the emperor had ceded to France Belgium, Mainz, and the region of the Moselle. The whole left bank of the Rhine had been lost to Germany through the Treaties of Campo Formio. These facts would have to be accepted ; and an endeavour must be made to give to Germany a tenable secular constitution at least on the right bank of the Rhine. It was for Prussia, the natural opponent of the spiritual states, to undertake with her own hands the now unavoidable task of the general secularisation of the Holy Empire, the task of breaking the power of the Hofburg in Germany by the annihilation of the spiritual dependencies of Austria, of transforming the empire into a League of Princes under the leadership of Prussia. The smaller temporal princes must receive their indemnification at the hands of Prussia, not at the hands of France. It must be the aim to win them over to the Prussian side by the one influence that was sacred to them, by the influence of their dynastic interests. Dohm, the Prussian envoy in Rastatt, had in fact advised the king thus to undertake secularisation in the grand style, as a means to carrying out a comprehensive reform in the empire, and not for the gratification of petty greeds. But to the poor-spirited blindness of the court of Berlin, no bold resolution was possible. During the war, Prussian policy had been animated by the benevolent aim of establishing peace between Austria and France upon the basis of the integrity of the empire ; but the proposed intermediation of Prussia was roughly rejected because Thugut could not overcome his gloomy mistrust of the North German power, and also because a state which under no circumstances was willing to strike a blow was not able to play the part of intermediator in a world-war. Now that the cession of the Rhineland had been decided against the wishes of the king, his envoys in Rastatt endeavoured, in accordance with the natural policy of Prussia, to bring about an indemnification of the temporal princes on as liberal a scale as possible, whilst the court of Vienna desired to limit the extent of the secularisation, and, above all, protect the established pillars of the Hapsburg empire, the three spiritual electoral states. From Berlin a strong opposition was also offered to the Hapsburg plans of Bavarian conquest.

Prussia and Bavaria now appeared, as formerly in the days of Frederick, as the leaders of the anti-Austrian party ; but not now, as of old, was this opposition dictated by the proud consciousness of their own power. It soon became evident how insecure was that apparently brilliant position of strength which the Prussian state had acquired through its policy of North German neutrality. Its small protégés soon realised that the fulfilment of their greedy wishes was to be expected only from the conscienceless activities of the young Republic and not from the pacifism of Berlin. The French envoys dominated the Congress, and Prussia herself in reality was playing only the deplorable role of the first among the petty states on the look-out for plunder, and she did not even venture to propose a thorough-going reorganisation of the German constitution. To this abasement had the empire sunk when the dreaded Corsican paid a flying visit to Rastatt, thus obtaining his first glance into German life. It was in the bitter quarrels of this fruitless Congress that Bonaparte formed his judgment of our fatherland. He saw through the absolute nullity of the imperial law, and was satisfied to feel that if the imperial constitution could no longer be maintained, its fall could only redound to the advantage of France. With the malicious joy of the plebeian he noted with contempt the slavish abasement of the German estate of princes. Yet it did not escape his notice that in consequence of the weakness of its territorial authorities this country was over-ripe for national unity, and it seemed to him urgently necessary that by the satisfaction of their land-hunger the smaller dynasties should be won over entirely to the side of France, and that divided Germany should thus be robbed of its nationality (*dépayser l'Allemagne*).

The Congress of Rastatt was broken up by a recommencement of the war. Thugut had accepted the Treaties of Campo Formio unwillingly, for he had hoped to acquire the Papal States in addition to Venice. When France refused to accede to this desire, and when, contrary to the agreement, he worked for the general secularisation of Germany, that is to say, for the annihilation of the old emperordom, the Hofburg felt that the foundations of its power were threatened ; for, so wrote the minister to St. Petersburg, " not only does Germany subsist through Italy, but also Italy subsists through Germany." Meanwhile there ensued new arbitrary acts of French statecraft. In the midst of the peace, the Pontifical State was transformed into a Roman Republic, and the Swiss Unified State was established. The old powers had the view forced upon them that no peaceful common life was compatible with this restless policy of world-conquest. As early as the summer of 1798, Austria, England, and the new Czar Paul were working for the formation of the second coalition. The allies took the matter very seriously, utilising all their energies. It was their intention to attack the revolutionary state and its daughter-republics, along the whole extended line from the Texel to Calabria, along all its frontiers simultaneously. There was a better prospect for the success of their gigantic armaments because, of the two most notable commanders of the Republic, one, Hoche, had just died, while the other, Bonaparte, was far away in Egypt. The young hero had conceived the grandiose idea of striking at the power of England, which he hated as the most dangerous enemy of his plans of world-conquest, in her most vulnerable spot, the east.

For Prussia, the question of joining the new coalition was not one to be decided inconsiderately, for every one of the allied powers was pursuing aims which were foreign to German policy, or were even directly hostile to Germany. Russia desired to maintain the *status quo* in the east, in order subsequently to solve the eastern question according to her own wishes. In the English Parliament, there were manifested always more plainly and arrogantly the designs of an active commercial policy, which, as it was phrased by the German poet, "desired to lock up the domain of free Amphitrite as if it were a private house." To the naval powers of the second rank, it was impossible that either England's sole dominion in the Mediterranean, or yet the complete destruction of the French and Dutch colonial possessions, could be welcome. Finally, the court of Vienna hoped for great conquests in Italy, and also for the re-establishment within the empire of the supreme imperial authority. Its paid writers once more adopted a threatening tone of Ferdinandian arrogance, warning the German high nobility to fulfil their duties of feudal allegiance towards the imperial majesty. Above all, the second coalition displayed a marked reactionary character which had little in common with the moderate views of the Prussian court. The Czar Paul spoke in his fantastical manner of the restoration of the ancient French kingship. Fanatical pamphlets preached a war of annihilation against the godless men of new France, declaring that all the *roturiers* of Europe were looking towards Paris. The embassy-murder at Rastatt at the beginning of the war already served to show how blindly embittered were the advocates of the traditional law, although the deed of blood was not directly ordered by the Hofburg. The cruel re-establishment of the Bourbon tyranny in Naples showed still more plainly what intense passion the fury of the Jacobins had awakened, and what confusion Europe had to expect if through the victory of this most powerful of all alliances the forces of the counter-revolution gained free sway.

Yet there were overpowering reasons why Prussia should join the Triple Alliance. The statesmen of Berlin were at one with the three powers in the intention to impose limits upon the floods of the world conquest. Count Haugwitz had at length clearly recognised the character of French policy. Moreover, if every one of the allied powers pursued her own immediate aims, it would be all the more possible for Prussia to establish her own dominance in Germany by resolute action. England was preparing for a landing on the coast of Holland, while Austria assembled her army in High Germany and Italy. If Prussia, whose eastern frontier was no longer threatened, threw all her military forces into the wide gap between these two theatres of war, it seemed to all human foresight that the honourable and heartfelt desire of the young king, the reconquest of the Rhineland, must be fulfilled, and that the victorious state would by German deeds acquire the hegemony of the north which it had hitherto possessed only in appearance. It was the fault of the king, and of his generals weakened by old age, that the great hour remained unutilised. The hesitating prince considered that the moment had not yet come for the overthrow of the Revolution ; he wished to wait upon events, to save up his energies for a possible last blow. North Germany, in love with peace, joyfully agreed to this poor-spirited determination ; its princes and its peoples delighted in the return to the Basle policy of neutrality.

Thus the colossal struggle began without Prussian co-operation. The battle of Aboukir founded the Mediterranean rule of the British, and brought Bonaparte's oriental schemes to naught ; the victories of Souvòroff and Melas snatched Italy from the French ; the Archduke Charles pressed victoriously forward into High Germany, and once more the peasantry of the German south threw in their lot with the imperial troops ; the domain of the Republic lay open before the armies of the coalition, but once again the dissensions of the allies proved the salvation of France. To the Hofburg the arrogance of the Russian commanders seemed as intolerable as the policy of the czar, who in Italy demanded the restoration of the legitimate governments and seized Corfu and Malta for himself. Whilst Thugut was endeavouring to subject the Peninsula to the dominion of Austria, Souvòroff counteracted his endeavours in every possible way, and finally refused to take full advantage of victory and to conquer Genoa, the last position of the French in Italy. Upon the proposal of England, from the open road of victory the great Russian was diverted to Switzerland, where he wasted time and energy in that heroic march over the Alps which displayed to the astonished world the extraordinary staying-power of the Russian soldiers, but which was fruitless from a military point of view. When the end of the year 1799, which had opened with such glowing hopes, was approaching, the powerful Triple Alliance broke up in fierce hostility. The czar summoned his troops home, and there was no longer any talk of threatening the domain of the Republic.

The idea of world-conquest had already struck so deep a root in the life of the new France, that the French nation regarded the loss of its Italian conquests as an intolerable disgrace, and greeted the Corsican hero on his return from Egypt with rejoicing, regarding him as a saviour. The *coup d'état* of the 18th Brumaire, the outcome of an internal necessity, brought the whole authority of the state into the hands of the commander-in-chief who, for the past three years, had, by the terror of his arms, maintained the radical war-party in power, and this change gave to the new France the constitution which, with trifling alterations, has persisted to the present day. The only two new political ideas which had really permeated the nation, the idea of national unity and the idea of social equality, were carried out to their ultimate consequences ; the altered distribution of property was recognised, and was secured by a strict legal system. Above the undifferentiated mass of this people of equals there now arose *l'homme peuple*, the democratic autocrat in whose boundless authority the one and indivisible nation found a satisfactory realisation of its own greatness. The compact hierarchy of the active new officialdom obeyed his will, since for those who, while accepting subordination to the autocrat, formed part of this hierarchy, there was promise for the satisfaction of every ambition ; while the hierarchy relieved the ruled of all care and all labour for the nation's weal. The army of taxpayers of the lower classes obeyed him blindly ; whilst the military organisation, happily adapted to the aims of a policy of conquest, placed at the disposal of the First Consul at the same time the

masses of the national levies and the technical efficiency of bodies
of mercenary troops employed for a long term of service. The
possessing classes, on the other hand, liberated from the burden
of compulsory military service, enjoyed, in comfortable security,
the triumphs of the tricolor, and learnt to value the exciting news
of war and victory as an indispensable pastime.

This was at once the greatest triumph and the self-annihila-
tion of popular sovereignty. It was the proudest, the cleverest,
and the best-ordered despotism of modern history, the necessary
conclusion of the course of development in which the French state
had been engaged since the accession of the Bourbons to power.
Even the ancient traditional catholic character of French culture
was now re-established by the Concordat. All the fruitful new
ideas which the legislation of the National Assembly and the Convention had realised or prepared, found in the prefectoral system,
in the legal code, and in the fiscal and military systems of the new
autocracy a talented realisation, in so far as they correspond to
the two aims of the democratisation of society and the centralisation of the state. On the other hand, of the desires of the Revolution for liberty, of the participation of the nation in the conduct
of affairs, there remained nothing but the empty spectacle of
worthless parliamentary forms. The constitution of Napoleonic
France, like that of the old Bourbon regime, was in reality no more
than a method of administration. Commerce, which had been
almost completely ruined in the party struggles of the last decade,
now rapidly revived, thanks to the legal security and to the freedom of movement which the new laws provided for the economic
energies of the nation. But the new ruler neither desired nor was
able to effect any change in the other tragical heritage of the
Revolution, in the spiritual desolation of French life. His
mind was filled with common human ambition ; freedom of
thought and independent creative activity in art and science were
regarded by him as vain ideology, partly ludicrous and partly open
to suspicion.

Thus there entered upon the stage that strange two-edged
system of Bonapartism which, in self-consciousness, readiness for
activity, and organising energy, was enormously superior to the
ossified states of the neighbour country. It was a structure of the
Revolution, democratic from the foundation upwards, the natural
opponent of the historical state-authorities and social forms of old
Europe ; but it was also despotic from the foundation upwards,
the sworn enemy of all freedom, of all national peculiarity in popular

life. Napoleon's first task was to make good the losses of the last year, to re-establish the *status quo* of Campo Formio. His brilliant attempt to shake the naval dominion of England by the alliance of all the sea-powers of the north and of the south, was a complete failure; but in war upon land, fortune was kind to him. His dramatic march across the St. Bernard showed to the delighted French that the laurels of Souvòroff could be worn also by French soldiers. The victory of Marengo restored the dominion of Italy to Bonaparte; the dismissal of Thugut showed that the tough staying-power of the court of Vienna was beginning to fail. But there was still required one last blow, the battle of Hohenlinden, to compel exhausted Austria to make peace. On February 9, 1801, the Peace of Lunéville recognised publicly and unmistakably what the Treaty of Campo Formio had established secretly and obscurely, that henceforward the Rhine was to be the boundary of Germany.

A domain of 1,150 square miles [German], and of almost 4,000,000 inhabitants, had been lost to Germany, nearly one-seventh of the population of the old empire, which, without Silesia, had been estimated at 28,000,000. The German nation accepted this terrible blow with an uncanny cold-bloodedness. Hardly a sign of patriotic anger was manifested when Mainz and Cologne, Aix-la-Chapelle and Treves, the broad and beautiful homelands of our most ancient history, passed to the foreigner. Yet the stunted generation of the Thirty Years' War had once shed an abundance of bitter tears over a Strasburg.

It was the fault of the rule of the crozier that the country of the left bank of the Rhine had become so foreign to the nation. The ecclesiastical domain had taken no part whatever in the victories of Frederick and in the poems of Goethe, no part in anything which had filled the life of the new Germany. This region now accepted its fate with dull resignation; it was only the Lower Rhenish provinces of Prussia which loudly bewailed their separation from an honourable state. It was natural that the moving propaganda of the Revolution had not been entirely without effect during the long years of the French occupation. Here and there might be witnessed a modest copy of the revolutionary societies of the people of Mainz. For a time the young men were intoxicated with the hope that their home would become an independent daughter-republic under the protection of France. In Coblenz, the federates of the Cis-Rhenish Republic danced round the red, white, and green tree of freedom. Biergans, the Brutus of Cologne, diligently endeavoured to imitate the fierce eloquence of Marat and Desmoulins ; but the copy was hardly more successful than was the German Marseillaise, the tame, philistine league-song of the Rhenish Republicans : " Rejoice, brothers all, Reason has conquered." It was only young Joseph Görres who understood how to speak this fanatical speech which was foreign to the German nature. With all the impetuosity of his fantastic intelligence and with all the unripeness of his half culture, acquired in the conventual schools of the episcopal lands, the honourable and enthusiastic youth threw himself into the whirlpool of the revolutionary movement, celebrating in speeches and in pamphlets the wonders of Gallic freedom. When the evacuation of Mainz had decided the fate of the Rhineland he delivered the funeral oration of the Holy Empire, exclaiming : " Nature created the Rhine for the boundary of France : woe to the weak mortal who shall attempt to move her boundaries, and who shall prefer mud and heaps of stones to her sharply-drawn natural outlines." Such was the scorn with which the most gifted son of the Rhineland took leave of his fatherland ; such were the sentiments which experience of the ecclesiastical rule had aroused in the hot spirit of the man who, not long after, was to become the most enthusiastic apostle of Germanism on the Rhine !

Among the masses of the Rhenish people the activity of the Jacobins had no effect. They groaned under the burdens imposed by the war and under the insecurity of the endless provisional conditions ; they saw with discontent how the foreign officials plundered the country, rudely destroyed the monuments of antiquity, deforested the mountains, carried off to Paris the old pillars from the grave of Charlemagne. It was only with the completion of the annexation that they learnt also to esteem the advantages of the new administration. For the spiritual domains of the Rhineland, as for Italy, the French Government was the pioneer of the modern state-life ; it brought the beginnings of civic equality, which in Prussia, and in many of the neighbouring temporal states, had long existed ; and it brought also numerous other political reforms which were still lacking elsewhere in Germany. Under this regime, moreover, the homeless and unarmed people of the lands of the crozier learnt for the first time the glory of war and the self-satisfaction that comes from forming part of a great community.

The region that consisted of a confused assembly of ninety-seven bishoprics, abbacies, princedoms, counties, and estates of the empire, and that had nourished an innumerable body of Imperial

Knights, was divided into four well-rounded departments. A strict police broke up the bands of oppressors, and established in the mountain-districts of the Eifel and of the Hunsrücken a state of peaceful security which had been unknown in the days of the dispersed rule of powerless petty states. In these lands of ancient peasant freedom the abolition of hereditary serfdom had but little significance. But all the more profound and valuable was the effect of abolishing the feudal burdens of the ecclesiastical tithes ; and still more valuable was the result of the sale of the national goods ; upon the ruins of the ancient spiritual landed domains there came into existence a new and well-to-do system of petty proprietorship. The gates of the ghetto of Benn were opened and the Protestants of Cologne and Aix-la-Chapelle built their first churches. The public procedure of the Courts of Assize put an end to the extraordinary forms of legal procedure which had previously been characteristic of the thirteen courts of the good town of Cologne and of the innumerable tribunals of spiritual and temporal lords. Instead of the Lords of Council, to whom the people had given the nickname of the " Cologne Clique," instead of the highly noble and all-wise patricians who once ruled the "realm of Aix," prefects and mayors were everywhere at work as obedient servants of the First Consul. All local independence had been abolished ; and yet the new official Government showed itself, not only more kindly, but also, more honourable and more just, than the ancient nepotist dominion.

It is true that the Rhinelanders stoutly defended their German speech and German customs against all attempts at forcible Gallification. The arbitrary unnaturalness of the new river boundary was felt as a great grievance. All along the river the people carried on a petty warfare against the detested customs-officers, and refused to abandon neighbourly intercourse with their fellow-countrymen on the right bank of the Rhine. Yet it was soon realised how powerful are the bonds with which a vigorous state attaches its members. Free trade with the extensive western hinterland, the abolition of the old guild rights and boundary rights, called into existence new industrial undertakings and new relationships of intercourse. The good French gold, which had been current in France since the plunder-campaigns and the fiscal reforms of Bonaparte, looked very different from the *Petermannchen* and the *Kastemannchen* and all the other variegated coinage of the episcopal days. The people of the middle and lower Rhine never became so whole-heartedly French as did the soldier-race of Alsace.

Notwithstanding the enfranchisement of agriculture and industry, the increasing pressure of taxation and the terrible sacrifice of men that resulted from the Napoleonic wars, rendered impossible a sense of genuine economic well-being. But still it was generally held in these regions that they belonged for ever to France. The Rhinelanders had broken with their past, and of all their old traditions they had taken with them into the new time only the Catholic faith, hence the feeling of inner kinship which for a long period to come bound them to the new French culture. The old order had vanished without leaving a trace behind, and all possibility of its restoration had passed away ; soon there disappeared the very memory of particularism. For the rising generation of the Rhineland, a living history really began with the entry of the French. It was only men of exceptionally deep nature, such as Görres and the brothers Boisserée who gradually came to recognise the curse of all foreign dominion, the atrophy and disorder which that dominion imposes upon spiritual life. They turned their longing gaze towards the centuries of the Middle Age when the Rhineland was still a living member of the German Empire, and amid tears and repentance they rediscovered their lost fatherland. To the great majority, what had happened seemed an unalterable necessity, especially in view of the fact that the condition of affairs in the empire was not such as to tempt any thought of reunion. Even upon the right bank of the Rhine, everyone believed that the new western frontier of Germany had been established for all time.

It was now the task of the imperial authorities to carry out the great work of indemnification which was a necessary outcome of the diminution of the empire. By the Seventh Article of the Peace of Lunéville, it was agreed that the hereditary princes of the left bank of the Rhine should receive compensation in the interior of Germany (*dans le sein de l'Empire*) ; the conversations of Rastatt were here to serve as a guide. Thus by the sword of the foreign conqueror there was imposed upon the Reichstag the duty of secularising the Holy Empire and destroying the spiritual states. What in the days of the Silesian War had led to the salvation and rejuvenescence of the German state, now led to the partition of Germany. During the confused negotiations which for the next two years were proceeding between Paris and Ratisbon, between Berlin, St. Petersburg, and Vienna, there spontaneously resulted that grouping of German parties, of which anticipations had already been manifested at the Congress of Rastatt. The court of Vienna remained for long a prey to the extraordinary illusion that Bonaparte would not trouble himself about the reconstitution of Germany, and endeavoured to save as many as possible of the theocratic authorities of the ancient empire, and above all to save the spiritual electoral princes. In one of the Austrian state-papers we read : " It is not the amount of their income but their very existence which is of value to the German constitution." Prussia and Bavaria, on the other hand, the most powerful of the temporal states, fought on behalf of the common interests of the hereditary princes, favoured general secularisation, and were therefore considered by the world to be the allies of France.

Not even at this time, however, did there exist an unconditional understanding between the First Consul and the Crown of Prussia. Bonaparte could not endure as an ally anyone who claimed the independence of a great power ; the new " federal system " which he proposed to institute in place of the old comity of states, gave room only for a dominant France and for powerless vassals. He was the enemy of every independent power, and he never had any good feeling towards Prussia. In the life of Bonaparte, there was no development. He did not, like the true heroes of history, learn from experience, but unmoved and untaught, he worked to the end of his career for the realisation of his original plan of world-conquest. It is for this reason that he seems greatest in the days of the consulate, when these dreams of power first became revealed. In four neighbour countries at once he appeared as the intermediator of peace and as the great organiser. In Switzerland he threw on to the dust-heap the old structure of the Unified State and gave to the Confederates a reasonable federal constitution, for, as he put it, " Nature herself has predestined you to be a federation of states, and no reasonable man seeks to force Nature from her path." With the same penetrating insight he recognised that in Holland the federal form of state was out of date ; he allowed the Batavian Unified State to persist, and imposed a constitution which facilitated the transition to monarchy. For the Italians, he awakened a world of brilliant memories and expectations, bringing once more into honour the ancient name of the country, and raising the vassal state on the Po to become an Italian republic ; here also the train was carefully laid for monarchy and for a veiled foreign dominion. Finally, in the matter of his German policy he had long indicated the way which was to lead to the destruction of the German name. Never was an impossible scheme undertaken with more crafty consideration, and never was it put into operation with a more vigorous activity.

Revolution and Foreign Dominion

When in speeches and state-papers the First Consul described the German Empire as indispensable to the balance of European power, all that he had in mind was the anarchy of German particularism and he was thinking not at all of the theocratic forms of the imperial constitution. The Carlovingian traditions of the Holy Empire were not less hostile to the Corsican's plans of world-dominion than were the medieval institutions of ancient Germany in conflict with the modern democratic character of the new tyranny. As the *Moniteur* wrote, the German constitution was " the centre of all the feudal prejudices of Europe," and was at the same time one of the chief pillars of the Austrian power. But in Paris the court of Vienna was considered, next to England, to be the bitterest enemy of the Revolution ; the destruction of Austrian power in Germany had been long determined. As early as the summer of 1800, one of the hired scribes of Talleyrand was writing the *Letter of a German Patriot,* a first *ballon d'essai* in the direction of those devilish half truths by means of which Bonapartism exercised so misleading an influence upon our people. The pamphlet related in eloquent words the long tale of Austria's sins against the Holy Empire, and urged all enlightened Germans to overthrow the Hapsburg dominion. The First Consul revived the plan which already in the year 1798 Sieyés had suggested when he was ambassador in Berlin. He prepared the tri-partition of Germany, and in order to bring the defenceless petty states as far as possible under his own authority, he wished first to push back towards the east the two German great powers. It was for this reason that the Breisgau was given to the Duke of Modena ; it was for this reason that France, for the moment in unison with the court of Vienna, offered a decisive objection when Hardenberg ventured to propose that Prussia should seek her indemnification in Franconia. It was for this reason that the wishes of Bavaria, which was already casting greedy eyes upon Ansbach-Bayreuth, received gracious approval in Paris. It was for this reason, finally, that the First Consul enquired of Berlin whether Mecklenburg might not conveniently round off the Prussian dominion, while the ancient ducal house might be compensated in the Prussian Rhineland. In this respect Bonaparte had no more than a partial success, for King Frederick William firmly refused to take possession of Mecklenburg against the will of the dukes ; but Bonaparte succeeded to this extent, that Prussia was not allowed to increase her Franconian possessions, and lost all influence in the south.

The great despiser of men now found an infallible means for

the control of these southern and western German domains. It was not in vain that at the Congress of Rastatt he had seen into the innermost souls of the German high nobility. It was in order to secure for ever the dissociation of Germany that he became the creator of our new middle states. The little people of princes, counts, and imperial knights, was a nuisance to him, for most of them belonged to the Austrian party and were useless in war. Among the electoral princes and the dukes, on the other hand, he saw sufficient utilizable material for the creation of a crowd of vassals to France. They were too weak to stand upon their own feet, too vain to yield to the authority of a national state, but they were powerful enough to constitute a number of small contingents which, under the leadership of the conqueror of the world, might once more exhibit the ancient German valiancy in arms. During the last war they had almost all concluded separate peaces with the enemy of the empire, had left the path of legality as rebels against the emperor and the empire, and had broken down the bridges behind them. When the man of power took under his protection these political hermaphrodites which could neither live nor die, when he gratified their greed by throwing them a few fragments taken from the possessions of their pettier co-estates, when he flattered their vanity by resounding titles and the appearance of independence ; when, that is to say, he compacted together the hundreds of tiny territories into a few dozen new casually constructed states, which without a history and with no legal title to existence, existed solely by the grace of France ; when he then induced his satraps to wage insolent wars against the fatherland, leading them from one felony to another, and rewarding every new crime by new booty—they had signed away their souls to him, and he could henceforward confidently reckon that they would rather kiss the shoes of the foreigner than ever again voluntarily subject themselves to a German community. He was not the man to leave to his protégés a debt of gratitude. " France," he wrote to the Elector of Bavaria, " and France alone, can secure you in your power " ; and once more, " to us alone does Bavaria owe her enlargement, and at our hands alone can she receive protection."

Up to this point Bonaparte's German policy seems no more than a grandly conceived further development of the old French statecraft, which since the days of Henry IV had continually aimed at the establishment of a protective suzerainty over the German petty states. In the state-papers of the First Consul there now recurs the seductive word " sovereignty," which in the Peace of

Westphalia the diplomats of France had first applied to the German territorial suzerainty. But the ideas of this restless spirit now sought to push far beyond these goals. As soon as Western Germany had been subjected, Austria and Prussia were to be enchained. Bonaparte's friendship for Prussia was never anything more than an adroit double game. Although he cherished a profound and justified contempt for the timid policy of the court of Berlin, he none the less shared an error then universal, and overestimated the might of Prussia. It was true that the man who despised all ideology had no vision for the inexhaustible moral energies which slumbered in the inert state ; but he was well aware of what the Prussian soldier had been able to achieve in the Rhenish campaigns, and was not sufficiently well informed with regard to the progressive decay of the Frederician army. With such an opponent, he wished to fight only under favourable circumstances, and with all the rest of Germany on his side. During the war he had several times hoped, through the intermediation of the most peace-loving of the great powers, to attain to a general peace, and subsequently to allay the awakening mistrust of the court of Berlin by indefinite concessions. After the peace, he regarded the destruction of the Austrian party in the empire as his most immediate task, and for this end the help of the Lorrainer's old rival was indispensable. The letters of the First Consul to the young king overflowed with terms of endearment. He wrote that every wish of his royal friend would be regarded by the French Cabinet as a command ; he said that both he and William, one the admirer and the other the successor of Frederick, should continue to walk hand in hand in the footsteps of the great king. To the mightiest of the temporal estates of the empire it was impossible to refuse abundant indemnification ; but it was essential to avoid any strengthening of the Prussian party. Hence Talleyrand was given instructions that the Prussophile House of Mecklenburg was to be excluded from the new Electoral Council, but the minister did not venture to propose this exclusion.

The court of Berlin, upon its side, was far from convinced of the good faith of France. In Berlin, as almost everywhere else, the *coup d'état* of the 18th Brumaire had been welcome because the establishment of an orderly government in France seemed to offer promise of a general peace. Once again, as so often before, it was hoped that the integrity of the empire would be preserved by diplomatic methods. But how could a German state which even after the declaration of the imperial war in the year 1799 had failed to draw its sword, attain so high an aim ? The sundering of the Rhineland from Germany had been completed, and Prussia had not ventured upon any serious step to ward off the blow. At length, indeed, a bold move was made, when France and Russia threatened, in the year 1801, to occupy Hanover and to force the closing of the German ports ; thereupon Prussia stepped forward and herself occupied the German land—a resolute measure which England valued at its true worth but which Bonaparte never forgave. Meanwhile, however, the king observed with regret how isolated was his state, but he mistrusted the incalculable aims of Bonaparte, and to the enquiries of the First Consul whether Prussia would not seek compensation in Hanover, he repeatedly refused to do this, not only on grounds of justice, but because he recognised the ulterior designs of French policy. On the other hand, he saw that the interests of Prussian shipping were seriously interfered with by the commercial policy of England. Finally he was separated from the court of Vienna by the old unteachable mutual mistrust ; so recently as the war of 1799, Austria had sent a considerable proportion of its army into Bohemia in order to hold Prussia in check.

Thus the king determined to seek an understanding with Russia ; it seemed to him that this state was by geographical position a power mainly defensive. Now for the first time the young monarch took part in foreign policy with an independent idea ; he now began in these questions also to find a sphere for his peculiar deliberative method. Since there had always been a strong Prussian party at the court of St. Petersburg it was soon possible to come to a good understanding with the Czar Paul. It was Prussia which in the year 1800 endeavoured to bring about peace between France and Russia. The drawing together of Prussia and Russia became a friendship when the young Czar Alexander ascended the throne over the corpse of his father. On June 10, 1802, the two neighbour princes had that memorable meeting in Memel which was to have such weighty consequences for the reign of Frederick William. Both were young men, both were full of the philanthropic ideas of the age of enlightenment which aimed at popular happiness, so that they were soon on common ground ; they discussed the danger which was threatening both from the world power of the west, and they swore mutual fealty. Upon the czar, who was still little more than a boy, the knightly and serious behaviour of the king and the bewitching grace of the queen made a lively impression, so far as his character, with its strange admixture of enthusiasm, self-deception, and slyness, was capable of profound sensations. Again and again his Polish friend Czartoryski, an irreconcilable opponent of Prussia, complained that this day of Memel had been the beginning of all evil. But Frederick William cleaved to his new friend with the unchangeable loyalty of his honourable heart. A personal inclination strengthened him in the resolve which had been formed through the working of his sober reason. He would venture upon a war with France only in alliance with Russia. He urged the Russian court to participate in the negotiations about the German indemnity questions, in order that France might not be the only arbiter in the empire.

Whilst the king thus secretly endeavoured to protect his rear in the case of a possible war with France, in his German policy he was also pursuing ideas which were in flat opposition to the designs of the First Consul ; it was solely in consequence of the confused party involvements of the moment that the Prussian court seemed for a time to walk hand in hand with the French government. The general secularisation could be welcome to the Prussian state only as soon as the cession of the Rhinelands was decided. All the Prussian Protestant traditions combined to lead the king to work towards this end. Moreover, in the enlightened world there was then dominant the doctrine of the unrestricted power of the state, which by right controlled all the goods of the Church on behalf of the nation. Stephani's book upon *The Absolute Unity of State and Church* was now going the round of North Germany. The King of Prussia was himself permeated by these views, and was now making his cabinet work out a comprehensive plan for the confiscation of all the ecclesiastical goods in Prussia. In like manner he believed that he would be acting altogether in the spirit of his great-uncle if he placed himself on the side of Bavaria and the new middle states ; Frederick, in his plans for imperial reform, had always had in mind the strengthening of the great temporal estates of the empire. Bonaparte favoured the middle states, because he desired to construct out of them the nucleus of a French party. The Prussian court, conversely, supported this policy in the hope that by the destruction of the most futile of the petty states the force of resistance of the empire against France could be enhanced. Haugwitz declared frankly to the Austrian ambassador Stadion, that such had for years been the persistent view of his court. Russia spoke in the same sense to the court of Vienna, for from the Prussian state-papers the conviction had been gained that a general secularisation was necessary to strengthen the German west. Once more with the same grounds the king justified himself to the czar for Prussia's own demands for indemnification : he must strengthen himself for the eventuality of a great German war against Bonaparte.

Behind all these schemes and wishes there remained the shy and indefinite hope that it would be possible to reorganise the secularised empire, or at least the north, in federal form. The recognition that the old emperordom was no longer tenable gradually found a wider acceptation. Already a year after the death of Frederick a pamphlet had put the question in plain terms, "*Why should Germany have an Emperor?*" During the war of the second coalition there appeared another pamphlet, *Hints concerning the State Constitution of Germany,* and in this the admonition was uttered, " Germans ! unite to form a strongly united German Federation ! " Similar federalist ideas were discussed among the Prussian statesmen. In the year 1800, the indefatigable Dohm, after a conversation with the Duke of Brunswick, carried a stage further the proposals he had already announced in Rastatt, and drew up a plan for a North German Federation. The aim of this was to check the overgrowth of the power of France, already threatening all her neighbours. For this reason, the Basle league of neutrality must be transformed to constitute a vigorous and permanent federation. There were to be four sections, under the leadership of the more powerful of the middle states and the supreme leadership of Prussia. There were to be a Bundestag and permanent federal courts. The army was to be under Prussian command and was to be trained on the Prussian model. Such plans were freely discussed at the court of Berlin but no one ventured to attempt to carry them out. Not even Dohm could free himself from that deplorable error which tainted all the old ideas of Prussian policy. He also was under the illusion that the re-establishment of the German power could be effected by pacific means ; the First Consul would offer no opposition so long as the idea of " national independence " was not expressly avowed !

The wisdom of the statesmen of Berlin failed to see how profoundly relationships in the empire had been modified since the days of Frederick. It was not Prussia, but France, which now held in its hands the balance of German power. France divided in accordance with her own favour and caprice the ruins of the spiritual states. As things were, the co-operation of Russia in the negotiations could be no more than apparent ; the sole result of this co-operation was, that in the distribution of lands, some princes

who were related to the court of St. Petersburg received preferential
treatment. When in such conditions the Prussian state demanded
the constitution of the new middle states, this could serve only
to strengthen the French party in the empire without securing any
loyal support for Prussia. Prussia became Bonaparte's accomplice
without securing for herself any permanent alliance with the man
of power.

How much more adroitly than by this well-meaning policy of
half-measures and self-deception did the straightfoward unconscientiousness of the new court of Munich know how to turn matters
to its own advantage. Here the House of Pfalz-Zweibrücken had
just attained to the throne which had been so often contested by
the greed of Austria. The Prime Minister, Count Montgelas, never
failed for a moment to recognise that the young dynasty had everything to fear from the Hofburg and everything to hope from Bonaparte. Quickly making up his mind, he appeared soon after the
peace at the head of the French party in Germany, and for this was
rewarded by the grateful assurance of the First Consul that the
high-minded nobility of France would forget the earlier vacillations of the Bavarian court. The unscrupulous realist saw in
Bavaria's past no more than a history of lost opportunities ; now
at length, when the world was out of joint, was the time to grasp
at the skirts of happy chance, to get into the victorious chariot of
the conqueror of the world, and by faithful vassal's service and
unwearied haggling to secure just as much booty as the conqueror
was willing to spare. To this policy of logical particularism, anything that remained to the empire of the millennial union of the
German nation seemed frankly ludicrous ; all shame, all affection,
all sentiment for law, were here unknown. Greedily it seized the idea
of a German Trias, which had once before emerged after the Peace
of Hubertusburg, and which was now revived when Prussia abandoned the South German petty states whilst Austria threatened
them. Gagern, the minister of Nassau, a well-meaning imperial
patriot, who, after the dilettantist manner of the petty-state diplomatists, was always full of slight, readily conceived, and obscure
projects, had as long ago as the time of the Treaty of Campo Formio
naively urged upon the imperial court the formation of a league
of the smaller states, under Russian guarantees. In a similar
sense the honourable Swabian publicist, Pahl, wrote an appella-
tion to the Lunéville Peace Congress. But now that the writers
of the Bavarian Palatinate urged a separate alliance of all the lesser
German powers, without Austria and Prussia, it was not their wish,

as it had been the wish of these eloquent dreamers, to rescue the national independence of the German south. What they desired was the subjection of the middle states under the arbitrary dominion of France, the annihilation of Germany. Temporarily, so long as it was still necessary to fight the Austrian party, the Zweibrücken dynasty remained on good terms with its ancient protector, Prussia. Bonaparte did not interfere, for he knew how easy it would be to break up this friendship, since the Franconian margravates of the King of Prussia were at the very gates of Bavarian greed.

During this most difficult crisis which had ever affected the ancient German state, Austria deprived herself of all possible influence, endeavouring to rescue an untenable position by a policy of stupid rigidity. At the Prussian court, there was no failure to recognise the need for the destruction of the old order, but the desire for the reconstruction of the empire merely took the form of a weak and indefinite hope. Thus the decision as to the future of Germany was inevitably left in the hands of the foreign conqueror, who boasted, " I alone know what I have to do." Even during these troubled years, the Reichstag of Ratisbon had remained so true to the sleepy customs of its spectral existence that a warm-hearted imperial patriot was able in the middle of the imperial war, to write with all seriousness upon the problem of what the distinguished Imperial Assembly was to consider in the near future. The empire accepted the Peace of Lunéville, and the spiritual estates did not find the courage to protest against their death-sentence. Almost the whole of the year 1801 had passed before Austria and Prussia finally succeeded in constituting a Diet of Deputation, and even at the end of eight months more, the deliberations of this committee had not yet been begun. The decayed body of the Holy Empire no longer possessed the power to carry out its intentions without assistance. The struggle of all against all and the infatuation of the Austrian court rendered every resolution impossible.

The Hofburg was still unable to understand that in the Peace of Lunéville it had abandoned the spiritual estates ; it did everything it could to avoid the inevitable consequences of its own actions, and even arranged for the election by its own adherents of an archduke to fill the vacant prince-bishoprics of Cologne and Münster. At the same time the Hofburg exhibited its ancient hostility to all enlargement of Prussia. It would be better, so the phrase ran at the court of Vienna, to renounce three rich Turkish provinces than to yield up Münster and Hildesheim to the Protestant great power. Meanwhile the Bavarian neighbour was continually rendered anxious by Austrian plans of exchange and enlargement. This emperor, who could not find words strong enough to express his anger at the forcible dispossession of the spiritual estates, would freely permit the court of Munich to appropriate in the south-west the dominions of neighbouring imperial towns, counts, and barons, if only Austria should receive in exchange the eastern part of Bavaria. It was Austria which first uttered the momentous phrase, " destruction of the smaller temporal estates," whereas hitherto in official documents there had been references only to the secularisation of the spiritual states. It was owing to this rigidly conservative and recklessly greedy conduct of the imperial court that Prussia and Bavaria found it necessary to secure their own indemnification by separate treaties with France. The Prusso-French Treaty contained the expressive sentence that the crown of Prussia acquired its compensatory territory " with unlimited suzerainty and sovereignty, upon the same footing as that occupied by Prussia in her other German possessions "— whereas the imperial law did not recognise the sovereignty of the imperial estates. It was not regarded as any longer worth the trouble of even keeping up a pretence of the imperial over-lordship. Without consulting the empire, Prussia, on August 3, 1802, took possession of the new acquisitions allowed by Bonaparte.

Meanwhile the Parisians made a mock of the aspect of the princes and statesmen of the Holy Empire who were hastening in crowds to the First Consul's seat of dominion. The light-minded city had speedily recovered its ancient Celtic cheerfulness after the terrible years of the Revolution. Bonaparte understood the Parisians' insatiable desire for nervous excitement, and knew how to satisfy Paris by the brilliant spectacle of his campaigns of triumph and booty. But even more entertaining than all these festivals was the unexampled drama of the voluntary humiliation of the German high nobility. How often, during all these heavy years, must it have come home to the souls of the German petty princes that an end had come to all their ancient glories. Again and again they had fled before the armies of the Revolution, and they had turned into money anything they could get together of the possessions of their state. Now came the decisive hour ; it still seemed possible to save their thrones. In their anxiety, all pride and all shame were lost. Every noble conception of princely duties, such as had gained ground at the German courts in the days of Frederick, was destroyed by the tyranny of Bonaparte ; once more the sentiments of the princely dealers-in-soldiers of the good old time gained the upper hand.

The high nobility of Germany settled upon the open wounds of the fatherland like a swarm of hungry flies. With cynical composure Talleyrand opened the great market for the land and people of Germany, and said equably that if any German nobleman still experiences any trace of shame, *il faut étouffer les regrets.* The highborn opponents of the Revolution begged for his favour, paid court to his mistresses, tenderly carried about his lap-dog, mounted, eager for service, to the little attic where lived his assistant Matthieu—the most cunning among that long series of talented Alsatians, whose powers of work and knowledge of affairs were gladly utilised by Bonaparte in his dealings with Germany. The gold of the little courts, which they had never been able to find when the empire needed money for the defence of the fatherland, now ran in streams. In the diplomatic world everyone knew the tariff of the French negotiators, and knew to a thaler the cost of a vote in the princely council of the Reichstag. The Prince of Löwenstein, a successor of the victorious Frederick of the Palatinate, played the broker in this unclean traffic. Even the rascality of Paris was not slow to avail itself of the new opportunities ; many of the greedy German princes, countrified in their simplicity, were caught in the toils of a false agent of Talleyrand, until Bonaparte himself took steps to put an end to the scandal.

All were drawn into this unwholesome activity, the good as well as the bad, for nothing was to be expected of the Ratisbon negotiations, and anyone in Paris who failed to look after his own interests was remorselessly trodden under foot amid the throng. Even the most valiant of the German petty princes, Charles Frederick of Baden, must have his chaffering negotiator. Amid the throng of the begging and offering smaller men, there stood with self-conscious and patronising mien, the much-courted Prussian envoy, Lucchesini, who believed himself able to outdo all others in his cunning, and who failed to see how greatly Prussia was injuring her repute by favouring an unsavoury game at chess which recalled the Reichstag of Grodno and the shameful self-destruction of the Polish nobility. This rivalry of dynastic greed destroyed what still remained to the empire of loyalty, of faith, of duty, of honour. Bonaparte rejoiced that there was no longer any moral bond to hold the old German state together. Each court demanded unashamedly what suited its own convenience ; hardly any attempt was now made to offer compensation for actual loss as an excuse.

It soon became evident that the spiritual domains on the right bank of the Rhine would not suffice to satisfy all these greedy desires, and there was a general agreement that the imperial towns should also form part of the spoil, as soon as the imperial towns of the left bank had similarly been destroyed without compensation. Finally the great land-auction came to an end. The goods were knocked down, sometimes to the highest bidder, sometimes to the Prussian and Russian favourites, but for the most part to those courts which Bonaparte had selected as props to his German policy. When the negotiations were finished, he wrote openly to the Margrave Charles Frederick, a near relative of the Czar, that the House of Baden had now attained the rank " which is demanded by its distinguished kinship and by the true interests of France."

After the most essential matters had been arranged in Paris, France and Russia appeared in Ratisbon as intermediaries. Bonaparte permitted the czar an apparent co-operation, to satisfy his avarice and to meet the wishes of Prussia. The mediators declared, with good reason, that jealousy and opposition of interests in the Reichstag made their intermediation essential. They disclosed their plan of indemnification, and concluded masterfully that it was their will that this plan should be accepted without alteration. The emperor offered a resistance even now, and did not yield until Prussia and Bavaria had concluded a formal alliance with France, and until a threatening note had been despatched from St. Petersburg ; but then the disinterested protector of the spiritual states showed no hesitation in rounding-off his own hereditary dominion by the bishoprics of Trent and Brixen. In the Diet of Deputation, the customary quarrels still continued for a time. The Russian statesmen complained with disgust how tedious and wearisome was this German disputatiousness, seeing that for every trifling change in the ownership of lands a special courier must be sent to investigate. But the die had been cast, and the more powerful princes had already secured their booty.

On February 25, 1803, the Diet of Deputation terminated its deliberations, and on April 27, by the last of the imperial decrees, the annihilation of one hundred and twelve German states was declared. Of the spiritual estates three only were left ; the two Knightly Orders, these being spared because it was wished to leave the Catholic nobility, so severely affected by the changes, a last refuge for their sons ; and the Imperial Chancellor in Germania, because Bonaparte recognised a useful tool for French designs in the unstable vanity of the Mainz Coadjutor, Dalberg. All the imperial towns disappeared except the six largest. More than two thousand square miles of territory, supporting over three million inhabitants, were divided among the temporal princes. Prussia received fivefold compensation for her losses on the left bank of the Rhine ; Bavaria gained three hundred thousand heads ; Darmstadt was compensated eightfold, and Baden tenfold. Some, also, of the foreign princely houses took part in the great spoliation, such as Tuscany and Modena, cousins to Austria, and Nassau-Orange, the protégé of Prussia. Quite forgotten was the Frederician principle that Germany belonged to herself alone. To the foreigner, central Europe seemed, as it had seemed in the sixteenth century, a masterless mass, a place of spoil for the princes of all nations. The Holy Empire was annihilated ; nothing but its disgraced name still continued to exist for three distressing years.

Few among the great state-transformations of modern history seem so detestable, so base, and so mean as this Princes' Revolution of 1803. It was a triumph of hard and material self-seeking. Not a glimmer of a bold idea, not a spark of noble passion illuminated the colossal breach of public law. And yet the overthrow was a great necessity. All that was buried was already dead ; all that was disturbed was that upon which the history of three centuries had already passed judgment. The ancient forms of the state vanished in an instant, as if they had been swallowed up by the earth, and never has anyone seriously thought of reviving them. The ridiculous falsehood of theocracy was at length done away with. With the spiritual princes fell also the Holy Empire itself and the claims of the Holy Roman emperor to world-dominion. Even the ancient ally of the Hapsburg emperor, the Papal See, would now recognise no more than the *imperium Germanicum*. The Italian's fine sense of power recognised that the protectorate over the Roman Church had now been transferred to France, and the Pope wrote to his " beloved son " Bonaparte that Rome would turn to him whenever help was needed. The Holy Empire became transformed into a League of Princes, and it was with justice that Talleyrand now spoke officially of the *Fédération Germanique*. This loose association of temporal princedoms was at first held together solely by the name of Germany, and it seemed as if in the near future a break up of the German community might be expected, rather than its federative reconstruction. But with the disappearance of the theocratic forms there had disappeared also that spirit of rigid immobility which had hitherto held in thrall

all the political energies of the nation. The new temporal Germany was capable of movement, of development. If liberation from foreign tutelage could once be effected, there might result upon the soil of temporal territorialism the uprising of a national unified state which would be less of a falsehood than had been the Holy Empire.

With the effecting of secularisation there came an end to that artificial distribution of votes which had hitherto given to Catholicism an inequitable preponderance in the imperial assembly. Henceforward the majority in the Reichstag was Protestant, like the majority of the German nation outside Austria. In the electoral council there appeared in place of Cologne and Treves, the new electors of Salzburg, Würtemberg, Baden, and Hesse; in this body there were six Protestant votes among ten. The still remaining members among the imperial towns were all Protestant, including Augsburg, where religious equality prevailed. In the Council of Princes there remained fifty-three Protestant estates beside twenty-nine Catholic estates. When, in accordance with the imperial law, the new lords of the secularised lands claimed the votes of the dispossessed estates, the last great dispute of the Ratisbon assembly broke forth. The course of this struggle manifested the great modification of influences and the radical change in the old relationships of power in the empire. At one time it had been necessary for the Protestants to protect themselves against the preponderant Catholic majority with the aid of the *Corpus evangelicorum ;* now, in the name of the Catholics, the emperor appealed to the principle of religious equality, and demanded for his co-religionists a sufficient number of new votes to establish equality in the council. But the contemporaries of Kant had outgrown the hatreds of the religious wars. The great majority of the Reichstag, and, above all, Prussia and Bavaria, would not admit that the essence of religious equality was to be found in equality of votes. It was openly said that the old difference between Catholic and Protestant votes had lost its meaning now that a rational system of tolerance prevailed in every German state. The Emperor Francis, on the other hand, hoped to re-establish the power of the Austrian party at all costs. In opposition to the constitution, he employed for the last time the ultimate right of the imperial majesty, imposing his veto, and the dispute remained unsettled until the formal dissolution of the empire. A partisan misuse of the rights of the crown for the advantage of the House of Austria and of the Catholic party—such was

the last act of imperial rule performed by the Hapsburg Lorrainers : a worthy conclusion to the long series of historical sins
of the Ferdinands and the Leopolds.

In the Roman camp there was unending complaint. With a
single blow the last theocracies of the Christian world, outside
the Pontifical State, had been destroyed, and the German clergy
lost its ecclesiastical wealth at the same time as its political power.
It was not only the goods of the spiritual lords who were immediates
of the empire that were subjected to secularisation, but the mediate
endowments and cloisters were, by the decision of the Imperial
Deputation, placed at the free disposal of the temporal lords. All
the world believed that this was the end of Romanism in the empire ;
no one had the least idea that secularisation would ultimately bring
as much gain as loss to the Papal See. The noble ecclesiastical
princes of the eighteenth century were for the most part practical
children of this world, slack in the performance of their ecclesiastical duties, and by their aristocratic class-feeling and by their
obligations as territorial suzerains were closely associated with the
national state. If only on account of neighbourly association, they
were unable completely to escape the spirit of toleration which filled
this people of ours devoted to religious equality ; they accepted the
principles of the Peace of Westphalia, which had been condemned
by the Pope ; and it was unwillingly that they bowed their stiff
necks beneath the feet of the Italian priest. At all times the idea
of a German national church found among them a few supporters,
and in Hontheim-Febronius a talented advocate. The result of
secularisation was to give the nobles a dislike for the service of the
Church. So far as is known, during the Napoleonic epoch, not a
single young nobleman of ancient lineage entered the priesthood.
The plebeian clergy which now came into existence was remote from
bourgeois society. It had a grudge against the new Germany on
account of the great spoliation of the Church ; it regarded the
Church as its only home ; and at a later date, when the Roman
designs for world-dominion were renewed, this clergy obeyed the
orders of the Pope with a blind zeal which was hardly less valuable
to the Roman curia than had been the territorial and princely power
of the opinionated prelates of the old regime.

The Catholic nobility suffered even more severely. By the
confiscation of seven hundred and twenty benefices it lost, not
merely a considerable proportion of its wealth, but also its whole
political authority. The last vestiges of an independent aristocracy
disappeared from the empire ; the days were over in which the

power of the Westphalian counts could be esteemed equal to that of two electors. It was the curse of these old stocks that they lacked the consciousness of political duty. Like the Bourbon court nobility, they had sought the good of their order in the luxuries of an easy life, and they had never learned, in accordance with the example of the old Prussian Junkerdom, to assimilate themselves to modern monarchical forms, but withdrew in rancour from the life of the nation. It was only to the Archducal House of Austria that they would, in accordance with ancient custom, devote the services of their sons. From the circles of this Catholic nobility there came into existence an embittered opposition to the new temporal Germany. Passively influential, disturbing the internal peace of the country even down to our own day, this opposition has yet in the end, by its fruitless obstruction, served merely to accentuate the democratic tendencies of our recent history.

It was the mediatised imperial towns which most readily adapted themselves to the new order of things. Here and there, indeed, the obstinate pride of the honourable patricians came into sharp conflict with the efficient arbitrariness of the bureaucracy ; and many even of the younger generation, like Frederick List, for instance, preserved throughout life the proud self-confidence of the old imperial burghers. But the consciousness of hopeless weakness made serious resistance everywhere impossible. In the Reichstag hardly any disturbance was noticeable on the part of the Third College, which at one time had been as powerful as the First and Second Colleges together. The few imperial towns which were still inclined temporarily to offer any resistance carried no weight against the power of the princes ; indeed, by the decision of the Imperial Deputation, they were excluded from political influence ; they could take no part in the discussions concerning peace and war, and in the imperial war they were to enjoy an unconditional neutrality. The pacifist generation felt no annoyance at this extraordinary decision. The shippers of Hamburg found an old wish of their heart fulfilled, and one which honest Büsch had often expressed. Even the inland press gave cordial approval, contending that such a wise favouring of commerce was in accordance with the enlightenment of the day.

Thus it came to pass, as the outcome of the political struggles that had continued in the empire for many hundreds of years, that the princely authority emerged as sole conqueror. The hierarchical, municipal, and aristocratic state-structures of ancient Germany had been destroyed except for a few vestiges. All that was not of princely blood became absorbed into the mass of subjects ; the gulf between princes and people, which had become ever greater in the period of absolute monarchy, was now widened even more. How powerful, too, appeared the influence of the estate of princes upon our national life. Just as in former days the reformation of the Church had found protection and salvation among the territorial magnates, so now the political revolution was imposed from above upon an inert and silent people. That which implanted in our soil the fundamental principles of revolutionary France was not the propoganda of the trans-Rhenish Republicans but the dynastic policy of the German courts. This policy marched forward with the same all-embracing recklessness that had characterised the parties of the French Convention, inconsiderately destroying all historical right in the name of public safety.

The Princes' Revolution was a severe defeat for Austria. The old imperial party was destroyed, the imperial dignity became an empty name ; and it seemed that it might be desirable to abandon even this name, for the new council of electors was strongly inclined to choose a simple archduke when the time for a new election should arrive. It was true that the monarchy attained a notable rounding-off in the south-east in compensation for the sacrifice of its western provinces ; and the diplomats of the Hofburg congratulated themselves upon having at length been delivered from a dangerous and difficult situation. The courts of Münich and Stuttgart had no longer any reason to tremble before the Austrian lust of conquest, as it seemed possible that friendly relations might again be opened. But the military dominion over the German south-west had been lost, and in reality Austria left the empire. Her policy would have to pursue an entirely new course if she was still to exercise any kind of influence upon Germany, for the means of power employed by the old emperorship had been annihilated.

Nor had the power of Prussia been enhanced by the decision of the Imperial Deputation. It was certainly an advantage that the Austrian party had disappeared, and that in the Reichstag there had become established a working balance between the north and the south. Hitherto, the states of the south and of the west, controlling a majority, had exercised a decisive influence, but now the votes of North Germany had come into their own. None the less, the prestige of Prussia in the empire had greatly diminished. Her policy, devoid of energy, had everywhere attained to the precise opposite of her good intentions. Instead of an increase in the German power of resistance, there had resulted rather a confirmation of French preponderance ; instead of a reconstruction of the imperial constitution, there had rather been produced an absolute anarchy which drifted towards utter dissolution. Even the new acquisitions of territory seemed more brilliant than they really were. Prussia had lost the dominions on the Lower Rhine, which were loyal, and were of value at once to Prussian power and to Prussian civilisation, and had acquired in place of these, in addition to Hildesheim, Erfurt, and a few other small imperial towns and ecclesiastical foundations, the Münsterland, which was the tower of strength of the dissatisfied Catholic nobility. Here, for the first time upon German soil, had the Prussian conqueror to encounter, not merely a transient particularist hostility, but a profound and enduring hatred, such as had been encountered in the Slav provinces. The cumbersome new administration aroused little respect in this refractory country ; three years were required before Prussia could make up its mind to abolish the cathedral chapter, the centre of all disaffection. The increase in territory did not bring with it any increase in national revenue, for here, as formerly in Franconia and in Poland, Prussia was over-considerate towards the taxable capacity of its new subjects. Even the army received only the trifling increase of about three regiments. In addition, by the new treaties there had not even been acquired a defensible frontier ; as the mocking phrsae ran in Berlin, it was merely the Prussian archipelago of the west that had been enriched by a few new islands. The king perceived very clearly that in so disturbed a time the Westphalian provinces could not be maintained without Hanover. It might soon become absolutely necessary to annex the Guelph lands, and yet nothing was done to prepare the state for this serious future possibility. The lax system of paternal mildness and economy persisted as if the day of eternal peace had already dawned.

Meanwhile the German south effected with one vigorous blow what Prussia had effected by the work of two centuries. In North Germany, the spiritual domains had for the most part been united with the neighbouring temporal states during the sixteenth and seventeenth centuries ; the resolution of the Imperial Deputation gave to these states no more than a moderate enlargement, without altering their historical character. In the southwest, on the other hand, the whole traditional territorial status was completely overthrown ; even the Palatinate, the most celebrated of the High German territories, was divided up among its neighbours. In this respect the Princes' Revolution led not merely to a change in territorial distribution but to a new construction of states. The arbitrarily assembled fragments of land which now received the names of Baden, Nassau, and Hesse-Darmstadt, possessed no community of historical recollections, and even in Bavaria and Würtemberg the old hereditary territory of the dynasty was far from being strong enough to fulfil with its spirit the newly acquired areas. Thus it happened that our multiform national life was enriched by a new contrast which has not completely disappeared even in our own day. The new Germany fell into three sharply differentiated groups. First of all, came the smaller North German states with their old feudal order and their hereditary princely houses ; secondly, the new creations of Bonapartism, the bureaucratic state-structures of High Germany, states without a history ; in between these, was Prussia, whose continuous development had led to the overthrow of the old feudal order without completing the abolition of feudal forms. Suddenly, and with revolutionary roughness, the modern state now invaded the south. An arrogant, vigorous, and busy bureaucracy, which took Bonaparte's prefects as its example, tore down the double eagles from the council-halls of the imperial towns, removed the ancient coats of arms from the gates of the episcopal castles, threw on to the dustheap the constitutions of the towns and of the territories, and out of the chaos of multiform areas created strongly-centralised administrative districts. In these unarmed regions they created a young and not inconsiderable military power, which could easily threaten Prussia ; they endeavoured by all the means at their disposal to foster a new sentiment of Bavarian, Würtemberger, and Nassauer nationality.

In its ultimate consequences, however, this great transformation redounded to the advantage, not of particularism, but of national unity. It was a long stride further upon the way which our history had taken for the past three hundred years. Throughout this period it had again and again happened that a pitiless necessity had destroyed outworn petty states, and had compacted these together to form larger areas ; and now, in a moment, more than a hundred of such petty states were swept away. It was inevitable that from such an experience the German people should sooner or later come to recognise that even the new territorial distribution was but a temporary one, that it was the destiny of Germany to march unceasingly forward towards the annihilation of particularism, towards the construction of the truly national state. The Princes' Revolution destroyed for ever that charm of historical venerability which had made the Holy Empire seem so invincible. The old law had been broken ; the new conditions aroused respect nowhere, and they made the arbitrary unnaturalness of the subdivision of German forces plain to every healthy mind. It seemed nonsensical that in Bamberg the Franconians and in Memmingen the Swabians should henceforward have to call themselves Bavarians, while in the valley of the Neckar the Palatiners were to feel themselves to be men of Baden. The profound falsity of this new and artificial particularism came at length, as a sense of political self-consciousness awakened in the nation, to arouse a feeling of passionate hatred in Germans of free and noble spirit, and to lead them towards the conception of national unity. Even among the unthinking masses, many detestable particularist prejudices disappeared, now that people had been forcibly shaken out of the ancient tradition of their lives. Just as in the new chance-made states of Italy, Lombardy and Romagnola now found themselves side by side, so also in the middle states of Germany, burghers of the imperial cities and inhabitants of electoral and episcopal territories were forcibly thrown together, and learnt to value as a loyal fellow-countryman a previously detested and despised neighbour. In Italy, as in Germany, the arbitrary force of foreign dominion had uprooted the naive belief in the eternity of the existing order, and had thus prepared the ground for new catastrophic changes which Bonaparte himself had never foreseen.

With the revolution of 1803, there began for Germany that new century which in France dated from fourteen years earlier. The great nineteenth century was in its inception, the richest century of modern history. It was the destiny of this century to reap the harvest that had been sown in the epoch of the Reformation, to transform and to realise in popular life, the bold ideas and foreshadowings of that thought-pregnant period. First in this new century were the last traces of mediæval civilisation to disappear and the characteristics of modern civilisation to develop. The freedom of belief, of thought, of economic work, which in the days of Luther existed merely in name, was to become a secure possession of western Europe. The work of Columbus was to be completed, and the trans-Atlantic world was to be united with the old civilised peoples for a vigorous community of world-historical labour. Even the dream of the Huttens and the Machiavellis, the unity of the two great nations of central Europe, was to find incorporation in flesh and blood. Germany was entering this epoch of fulfilment when the theocratic state-structure of its middle age fell to pieces, and when the political testament of the sixteenth century was thus at length fulfilled.

Yet how many were the battles and the storms before all the transformations of the new age could be completed! At first the German realm exhibited an aspect of hopeless confusion. No seer could imagine that a glorious young life was ultimately to arise out of these ruins. One thing alone was unmistakable —that a profound transformation was at hand. The Revolution had done but half its work, for Bonaparte intended from the first to keep German affairs in a flux. Since the fortunate issue of the campaign of plunder, the ancient land-hunger of the German estate of princes exceeded all bounds ; this rage seized the protégés of Bonapartism like an epidemic of madness, and during the next decade dominated the entire policy of the new middle states. In this restless monarchical world, the imperial knights, counts, and barons could no longer maintain themselves ; by the fall of their colleagues on the left bank of the Rhine, and by the abolition of the cathedral chapters, they had had the ground cut from under their feet, and they themselves had been spared only because French policy was not yet in a position to carry all its designs into effect. The resolution of the Imperial Deputation had hardly been subscribed, when several of the princes began to " mediatise " the domains of the neighbouring imperial knights (for to " mediatise " was the fashionable phrase). The emperor attempted at Ratisbon to espouse the cause of his persecuted followers, but Prussia once more took the side of the princes, and one imperial knight after another was swallowed up by greedy neighbours.

The conduct of the new Reichstag was in no respect distinguished from that of the old. Jean Paul wittily compared this body to a great polyp, whose shapeless form undergoes no alteration however much it may have swallowed. With the ancient and customary fruitless disputes, there was also transmitted into the new time the old established imperial-patriotic phraseology. The envoy of the Archducal Chancellor Dalberg, welcomed the representatives of the new electors with the pompous words : " The ancient and honourable imperial structure, which seemed so near to its complete overthrow, is to-day supported by four new main pillars." But in reality no one shared this confidence. Dull, vain, and heavy was the course of the proceedings. Not one of the envoys ventured even to propose the question whether the old constitution could still be maintained in an empire whose essential basis had thus been altered. Everyone felt that in reality all was at an end : looking on with folded arms they all recognised that the hour was approaching when this misery of Ratisbon would come to an end for ever.

Among the people all remained tranquil. Not a hand was raised to resist the new authorities ; even the complaints regarding the loss of the much-prized ancient liberty, sounded dull and timid. The imperial-patriotic jurist, Gaspari, found even in his distress a good-natured word of gratitude for the Imperial Deputation, because by its pensions this body " had at least brought consolation to the unfortunate"; and even the conservative Barthold Niebuhr was unwilling to lament over the dead or to contest the necessity of this breach of law. The few among the cultured cosmopolitans of North Germany who still at times looked down out of the heaven of ideas into the low world of political life, greeted the triumph of the princely order as a victory of modern civilisation ; they hoped, as Harl of Erlangen expressed it in his work upon the latest state-changes in Germany, that the " beautiful dawn of enlightenment would at length expel obscurity from the spiritual lands." A sounder view than that of most of his contemporaries was taken by young Hegel concerning the situation of the empire. He saw in this chaos " the juxtaposition of two contradictions, that a state is at the same time to be and not to be," and he found the ultimate cause of the trouble in the vaunted German freedom. But his insight appears merely as the uncannily clear vision of one who is hopelessly diseased ; no breath of passion inspires his wise words ; for this reason, after scientifically discussing the problem, he allowed his essay to remain unpublished. To the arrogance of the Berliners, which seemed to increase with the increasing weakness of their state, it appeared that the Princes' Revolution had not done enough for Prussia. In the carping circles of the capital, where such men as Held and Buchholz were the loudest talkers, the king was blamed because he had not grabbed enough in the general scramble. " Why," it was asked, " did not Prussia swallow all the North German territory, without paying so many compliments, and without troubling itself about copybook morality and so-called legality ? " The great majority of the nation was equally unconcerned with such frivolous boastings, as with the quiet distresses of the dethroned, for the nation continued to maintain its unshaken indifference.

One man alone, with moral earnestness and statesmanlike insight, ventured to speak openly of the disgrace of the fatherland.

When the Prince of Nassau endeavoured to deprive the ancient imperial knightly house of Stein of its territorial suzerainty, the Baron Karl von Stein sent an open letter to the petty despot, referring him in pithy phrases to the judgment of his own conscience and to the punishments that would be inflicted by an offended Deity, and concluded : " If the great and beneficial aims of independence and self-sufficiency of Germany are to be attained, the petty states must be united with the two great monarchies upon whose existence depends the endurance of the German name, and may Providence allow me to live to see this fortunate event." It was through this letter that the name of the president of the Westphalian Chamber first became known outside the bounds of Prussia. His proud spirit was admired, but the nation was not yet competent to understand the ideas of the most valiant of its sons.

Yet this land of ours was not a Poland, and there still lived in our people, which received so equably the blows of the stranger, the joyful consciousness of a great destiny. The same decade which witnessed the burial of the ancient German state brought to the new poetry its purest successes. How remote now seemed those days when Klopstock had, with a beating heart, seen the German Muse start on her uncertain course. Schiller was singing with quiet pride : " We may freely display the laurels that have bloomed on the German Pindus ! " The Germans had long been aware that they had enriched with new and independent ideals the treasures of European culture that had been handed down to them, and that they occupied a place in the great community of civilised nations which no one else in the world could fill. It was with enthusiasm that the youth of our nation spoke of German profundity, of German idealism, of German universality. To look freely forth over all the dividing limits of finite existence, to regard nothing human as foreign, to traverse the realm of ideas in living community with the best of all nations and all times— this was regarded as German, this was esteemed the special privilege of German culture. The national pride of this idealist generation was gratified with the idea that no other people was able to follow to the uttermost the bold flight of German genius, to attain to the freedom of our cosmopolitan sense.

In fact our classical literature bore the definite stamp of national peculiarity. Madame de Staël herself admitted that those only who, like herself, were half German by blood, could adequately grasp of the wonderful peculiarity of German thought. All the activity, all the passion of our youth became involved in these literary struggles which had now for three generations enticed German men into their charmed circle. An incomparable mass of new ideas was springing up. As the talented Frenchwoman put it, " an ingenuous foreigner might easily regard as a genius any skilled German talker, who is merely echoing the ideas of others." The insatiable impulse towards the communication of ideas, which is characteristic of all spiritually productive epochs, now found vent in an extraordinarily rich interchange of letters. Just as in former days Hutten had joyfully communicated to his humanist friends every new revelation which came to his mind, so now the invisible Church of the German thinkers joined in happy mutual devotion. In the law court, behind a pile of legal documents, the father of Theodor Körner eagerly read the works of his friends at Weimar ; and how often did Prince Louis Ferdinand, when in Westphalia with his regiment, ride over early in the morning to Lemgo, after a night spent in feasting, in order to talk with the Rector Reinert about Sophocles and Homer. Every poem was an event, was discussed, dissected, admired, in detailed letters and criticisms. All the unavoidable defects of literary epochs, tittle-tattle and party spirit, sentimentality, paradox, and even self-deception, had free play. Yet out of the very weakness of the time there spoke the vital force and the joy of life of a talented and high-thinking generation, to whom the world of ideas was the only reality. Unashamedly William Humboldt praised the divine anarchy of Papal Rome because it left thinkers undisturbed to experience and to contemplate. What did he care for the Romans of flesh and blood, as compared with those spiritual voices which spoke to him from the marble statues of the Vatican ? In the same sense, Schiller complains of the emptiness of his revolutionary age which stimulates the spirit without giving to it any object upon which to work, without, that is to say, any æsthetic image to contemplate.

One who does full justice to the profound earnestness of this idealism, and to the abundance of intellectual energy which is required to carry it through, will no longer find puzzling the political incapacity of the epoch we are considering. The parsimony of nature imposes upon the creative activity of nations, just as of individuals, strict limits, and to every great human activity attaches the evil of one-sidedness. It was impossible that a generation characterised by such energy of intellectual creation should at the same time possess the astute sense of worldly values, the resolute unanimity, and the hard national hatred, which alone would have saved the country from the unparalleled dangers of the political situation. Just as Luther, full of his ideas of God, had no glance to spare for works of art in the Rome of Leo X, so the heroes of the new German culture deliberately turned their gaze away from the desolation they saw spreading over the German south-west, and joined with Goethe in thanking destiny that they themselves were safe in the impassive northern region which it was not so easy to injure.

In the friendship between Schiller and Goethe, the human amiability and the creative power of the new culture found their most finished expression. From ancient days it had been a glory of the Germans to claim that no other people had so often exhibited the finest blossoms of friendship between men, the ungrudging and faithful co-operation of great men for great ends ; and among the numerous fine friendships of German history, this was the finest of all. During ten fruitful years, these two friends never ceased to provide new gifts for their nation, fulfilling Goethe's own saying that genius is that human power which furnishes laws and rules by its own spontaneous activity. And yet it was only a part of their natures that they devoted to this abundant poietic activity, for they were well aware that no one wins permanent fame who is not himself greater than his works.

In the hearts of the youth of the time there was preserved, beyond the possibility of oblivion, this unique picture of artistic and human greatness : how these two, so long separated by destiny, by the course of their education, and by the nature of their respective gifts, at length found one another, and thenceforward, during the prime of their lives, stood firmly side by side in true German fealty, working so harmoniously together that neither knew which of them had written many of the individual epigrams in the *Xenien*, and yet each of them fully conscious of his own worth, giving and receiving in perfect freedom, and without the least inclination to interfere with his friend's individuality. On the one side, the favourite of fortune, brought up in luxury, liberally endowed with rank and wealth, beauty and health ; on the other side, the man sorely tried, who had for years contended with sickness and privation, and who had yet remained so proud and free in spirit that not a single line of his writings displays the common needs of his everyday life. The one was unrestrainedly himself, living for the moment only and indifferent to the future. He allowed the golden fruits of his poetry to ripen at their leisure until at the approved hour he could easily pluck them from the branch. To him, the German tongue revealed her most cherished secrets, following like a diligent pupil every hint of the master. From the depths of an ever fresh and clear imagination, from the wide extent of an immeasurable knowledge, there flowed spontaneously into his mind an unsought stream of images and ideas. In the mind of the other there glowed a nobler ambition. He wished to conquer here and now ; he wished to transfigure in great and beautiful lineaments the luminous thoughts which moved his heart, to force the dull world to believe in them and to shake off " all the rubbish of reality." He made full use of every hour, as if he had a premonition of the near approach of death, he knew how to compensate by untiring industry the deficiencies of his less many-sided culture ; and he knew how, like a careful steward, to make a secure and effective use of every word in his less wealthy verbal treasury. He availed himself to the utmost of the force of his ardent will, until he had attained to a finished and forcible conclusion ; whereas Goethe, in his easy way, was so often content to leave his work rough-hewn.

Goethe's genius was predominantly lyrical, and to him all poetic activity had the fervour of a religious creed ; and yet in the midst of the excitement of subjective sensibility, he never failed to retain that " kindly restraint in love with the real " which he so greatly esteemed as the true productive state of the born poet. When he came to an end of his inner experiences he always produced in his readers the lofty illusion that he had himself completely disappeared behind imaginary figures which had been nourished upon the blood of his own heart. The dramatic genius of Schiller trod more firmly in the objective world. Seeking and choosing, he often reached out for materials which originally had nothing in common with his own inner life ; but when he had warmed these foreign figures with his formative hands, he breathed upon them with the breath of his heroic nature, and furnished them so directly and so powerfully with the lofty pathos of his ardent sensibility, that his hearers always came to imagine that it was Schiller's own voice they were hearing, and regarded him as a subjective poet. In addition to the secure foothold of genius walking amid visions, both these poets were endowed with that clarity of consciousness which was characteristic of the whole epoch, and they loved to give to themselves and to others an account of the laws of their art. Neither of them considered that in æsthetic culture alone was to be found the true task of their epoch. One worked as statesman, natural philosopher, and psychologist, the other as historian and philosopher, to render a many-sided culture more profound and more luminous. Both felt at one with their nation. They did not fail to recognise that their works would prove fruitful on foreign soil, but they knew that it was to German life that they owed all that was most characteristic in their activities, and that they could find an intimate and spontaneous understanding only where German hearts were beating : " In the Fatherland write what pleases thee ! There are the bonds of thy affection, there is thy world ! "

It is, however, to the honour of German uprightness that even in this age of æsthetic contemplation, Schiller stood higher in the favour of the people than did his great friend. The average man does not rise beyond the material stimulus of poetry, and for this reason he cannot accept the one-sided moral estimate characteristic of art. It was only richly endowed spirits that could really understand the profound stream of the later poetry of Goethe. Only to the experts in life was the inner significance of his figures apparent ; only natures with insight were able amid his protean transformations to recognise the figure of the genius who always remained true to himself. Over the most highly cultured members of the nation the life and works of Goethe gradually came to exercise a quiet but irresistible power, which became ever greater as the years passed. We owe it to Goethe that William Humboldt was able to say that nowhere else was the true essence of poetry so profoundly understood as in Germany. From *The Table Talk* of Luther, the Germans had once learnt what it means to live wholly in God ; how to sense the omnipotence and the love of the Creator in every simple event of the twenty-four hours. Now the new humanism incorporated itself in a powerful and original human existence. From the life of Goethe, the happy circle of those with insight learned how, to the spirit of the artist, every experience becomes an image, how the freest culture returns to Nature, how distinguished pride harmonises with cordial simplicity and democratic love for mankind. As is the dramatist's right, Schiller's influence was more in the direction of width ; to him belonged the hearts of the enthusiastic youth of his time ; his moral earnestness touched the conscience ; his joyful belief in the nobility of mankind was as easily comprehensible to all as was the sparkling beauty of his ever-perspicuous speech. It is he whom we have to thank for the fact that the delight in the new culture became diffused through the widest circles, in so far as it was possible for this literature to become popular ; by the powerful rhetoric of his *Jungfrau von Orleans* even the courts of Berlin and Dresden were shaken out of their essential prosiness. Goethe, as a youth, had been inspired with enthusiasm for the Strasburg cathedral, and had been the first among his contemporaries to gain an insight into the life of mediæval Germany ; it was a delight to him to incorporate the archaic into the wealth of his speech and to reanimate it with life. Schiller, on the other hand, was a modern of the moderns, modern in sensibility and in speech, devoid of all sentiment for German antiquity, and for this reason all the more popular ; for the nation which had forgotten its own past demanded novelty and plainness.

In Italy, Goethe enjoyed a second youth, living himself into the classical world, so that he became at home in antiquity as had no one since Winckelmann. Having assimilated the new views which flowed into his mind in Italy, he now astonished the nation by a series of poems which, in contrast with the obviousness and vital warmth of his youthful writings, displayed to the Germans a loftiness of style and a pregnant worth which had hitherto been unknown. But he had to learn that the mass of his readers could not follow his new style, and that they were unable to understand either the tender sensuous beauty of his *Iphigenia,* or the restrained but profound passion of his *Tasso.* The Germans lost sight of the poet now that he had buried himself " in his badger's earth," and year after year through research and contemplation became the confidant of nature. He ventured upon the titanic undertaking, proceeding step by step from the simplest to the highest organisation, to gain an understanding of Nature as a whole, and in that understanding to live at one with nature. And this scientific cognition was at the same time artistic contemplation ; he gave himself up to nature with all the energies of his soul, so intimately and so lovingly that he could with justice speak of his geological studies as his " friendship with the earth." Research did not lead him astray, but strengthened in him the naive contemplative attitude of the poet who always seeks the centre of gravity of the world in the heart of humanity. To his seeing gaze, the all became alive ; and inasmuch as he recognised how the eternal is active throughout all nature, he cleaved all the more joyfully to the belief in the independent conscience, the sun of our moral system. Since he had come to sense the God which is the intimate motive energy of the world, the serene joy of his poet's spirit seemed explicable through the consecration of a pious and holy conception : " The joy of life streams out of all things, from the smallest as from the greatest star ; all advance and all struggle is eternal peace in God our Lord ! "

Schiller, meanwhile, as he himself tells us, had in his poetic activity become a completely new man, and by earnest philosophical research had acquired the knowledge that through art alone will our race attain to harmonious perfection, that in art alone is man at once active and free, operating effectively upon externals and at the same time altogether himself. Thus was the most intimate secret of the age given bold enunciation. A thousand delighted voices answered his rousing appeal, " from the narrow and dull life of every day, flee to the refuge of the ideal," and welcomed the happy message that the artist is the complete man, that everything beautiful is good, and that that alone is good which is beautiful. At the same time the poet passed a severe and even a harsh judgment upon the shapelessness of his own youthful writings, and attained to a mastery of the classical purity of form. It was by Schiller that the work of Winckelmann was first completed ; only after Schiller had brilliantly glorified the Gods of Greece, did the longing for the sublime simplicity of the antique, the cult of the classical ideal, become a common possession of cultured Germans. With wonderful speed did Schiller make himself at home in this world from which his youth had been so remote. With the certainty of genius he discovered the motive energy of ancient history, the last and highest thought of Hellenism : " Even though the body be fallen into dust, the great name lives on ! "

The two great poets having thus formed an alliance, the next thing was to permeate the world with this new idealism, to make a clean sweep of the spurious wisdom of prosy everyday morality, of dull utilitarianism and fantastical obscurity, to drive them out of the temple of the German Muses, to provide an open road for all that was truly significant and creative, to convince mediocrity that art offers no place for it. The Xenien-dispute subserved this purpose. It was a party struggle in the grand style which, in spite of all its roughness and animosity, was yet necessary to the development of our national life ; the Germans were well aware that in this there was being fought a question vital to their civilisation. Inspired by his active-minded friend to fresh creative work, Goethe continued to show himself in ever new manifestations. Intoxicated with beauty, with the pagan frankness of a rose-crowned poet of antiquity, he sang in Roman elegies the joys of the love-warmed camp, and only on occasions when he was furnishing a majestic view of eternal Rome did he allow the reader to perceive that the intellectual wealth of a spirit overlooking all the centuries was hidden behind the cordial sensuality of these delightful verses. Soon afterwards he stood once more in the midst of the German present, describing with Homeric simplicity the healthy energy of our middle classes, the straightforward greatness which dwells amid the small things of the contented home; and exhorted our people to remain true to themselves, in a time of stress to hold fast to their own. The ardent and faithful love for the fatherland which spoke from *Hermann und Dorothea* made but slight impression upon Goethe's contemporaries in their pride of culture. But with delight did they recognise their own personalities in the figures of *Wilhelm Meister*—in these men without fatherland, without family, without calling, free from all the bonds of the historical present, and knowing only life itself, knowing only the passionate impulse for human culture. In this Odyssey of culture Goethe held up the mirror to his age, delineating with wonderful clearness all the characteristics of that literary epoch, alike its weakness and its fullness of life; and he fulfilled the highest task of the romantic poet, succeeding where none had succeeded before in showing how life itself educates striving and erring men.

Schiller, meanwhile, less many-sided, ceaselessly making the most of his natural gifts, acquired the mastery of the German stage. To him was essential that vigorous dramatic stimulus which Goethe was glad to keep at a distance. Brilliant pictures of battle and victory passed through his dreams. The sound of the trumpets, the rustle of the banners, and the clash of the swords, followed him even to his death-bed. The passions of public life, the struggles for the great purposes of mankind, for dominion and for liberty, those mighty changes of destiny which decide the issues of national suffering and national greatness, furnished the natural soil for his dramatic genius. His smaller poems, too, deal, by preference, with the beginnings of national life, displaying in manifold applications how the sacred compulsion of the law binds unpeaceful men together in the bonds of humanity. Never has the intertwining of the simple life of mankind with the great controlling powers of the state and of society been more beautifully described than in the *Lay of the Bell*.

However profoundly he might despise this "prosaic" age, however proudly he might reject any attempt at writing poetry with a purpose, nevertheless, this mind wholly directed towards the historic world was yet fulfilled with an intense political passion,

which was fully understood only by those of a later generation.
It was not by mere chance that he so long cherished the idea of celebrating in an epic the deeds of Frederick the Great. When the
Germans took up arms for the liberation of their own land, the
glowing picture of the popular uprising in Schiller's *Maid of
Orleans* first became truly comprehensible. When under the
pressure of foreign dominion they once again came to realise themselves, they were first able to do full justice to the greatness of the
poet who in his two most powerful dramas had brought the history
of the fatherland so near to their understanding. In his poetry
the most deplorable period of our past regained so fresh and
joyful a life that even to-day the German finds himself almost more
at home in the camp of Wallenstein than among the soldiers of
Frederick. From the battles of the sturdy German peasants of
the Alps he composed a luminous picture of a great war of liberation, incorporating in this poem everything that alone such a high
spirit as his could say concerning the eternal rights of humanity,
concerning the fortitude and unanimity of free peoples. In
political life, *Wilhelm Tell* was soon to become more significant than
had formerly been Klopstock's *Ballads of the Bards*. It was upon
this poem in especial that the rising generation nourished its inspiration for liberty and fatherland. To the young enthusiasts, the
dramatically voiced exhortation, " Unite, unite, unite ! " seemed
a sacred legacy from the poet to his own people.

It is true that it was not possible for Schiller to give to the
Germans that national theatre for which ever since Lessing all our
dramatists had longed. This could be created by no single man.
Schiller endeavoured to attain to a national style, which should
consciously and independently unite in itself the genuine greatness
of the older drama ; the richness in figures, the activity of movement, and the profound characterisation, of Shakespeare ; the
lyrical tendency of classical, and the strict composition of French
tragedy ; and which should thus express the character of our new
culture. But there was lacking to the poet a vigorous intercourse
with the people. It is only the loud acclamations of the audience
in a great town that can show the dramatist when he has found that
which is common to all, that which is truly popular. The handful
of dull petty bourgeois in the parterre of the theatre at Weimar
were not the *people ;* and the distinguished wits in the court boxes
gave the same applause, and even a more lively applause, to the
experiments of talented caprice as to what was simply great. What
was above all lacking in the Germans, as Goethe complains, was

" a national culture, which should constrain the poet to adapt to that culture the peculiarities of his genius." Giving bounteously, but receiving very little, stood the dioscuri of Weimar over against their people, which by them was first raised to a loftier culture. It is for this reason that both of them, after many attempts with trilogies and single dramas, with iambics and couplets, with choruses and melodramatic interludes, did not after all succeed in creating an artistic form for our drama, a form which could be generally recognised as national. Just as the ceremonious and exaggeratedly pathetic declamation of the Weimar actors was not copied by the rest of Germany, so the dramatists themselves worked arbitrarily and capriciously, each beginning anew, each endeavouring by new arts and new artifices to outshine all the others. Our stage offered a picture of anarchy, which yet displayed all the charms of unrestrained freedom. No one was more painfully aware than Goethe himself of the petty dispersal of German life, and of the disastrous influence of this dispersal upon art. Of his own *Wilhelm Meister* he said that he had been forced to choose, " a most wretched kind of matter, comedians, country gentry and such stuff," because German society had nothing better to offer to the poet ; and in his *Tasso*, with a bitterness which must have been the outcome of personal experience, he described the oppressive narrowness of life at petty courts—oppressive and narrow despite all the refinement of its culture.

It was not only the natural tendency of the German spirit (which finds more satisfaction in the depiction of character than in the discovery of tense situations), that was responsible for the rare appearance, in this blossoming time of German poetry, of that humour which was brilliant enough in our merry sixteenth century. Another, and indeed the chief, reason of this failure was the atrophy of our public life. Comedy could not follow the bold advance of tragedy. Comedy is rooted always in the present, and flourishes only amongst people who possess an ingenuous belief in themselves, who feel perfectly at home in their own skins ; it needs firmly established national customs and ideas of decorous behaviour, unless it is to occupy itself with arbitrarily chosen and commonplace social struggles and interests, unless it is to become insipid. In the slowly reviving German nation there were as yet but weak beginnings of all this. The most popular comic dramatist of the time, Kotzebue, whose talent in this direction was unquestionable, repelled nobler natures not only by the inborn commonness of a thoroughly superficial spirit, but even more by the pettiness of the circumstances he described, and by the insecurity of his moral sentiment which oscillated between lamentable weakness and smirking looseness. Even Jean Paul, *der Einzige*, who was then, with high artistic aims, devoting himself to the service of the comic Muse, was defeated by the desultory unreadiness of German social life. His figures moved, now in the heavy and suffocating atmosphere of the confined and poor-spirited life of the little town, and now in the tenuous ether of an ideal freedom, where man can no longer breathe. The enthusiasm of his warm-hearted love of humanity fails, nevertheless, to furnish him with any firm moral grasp ; he capriciously plays with the eternal laws of the moral world, in order subsequently to luxuriate in glorified sentimentality, and to leave his lovers " to dwell in the brief and blessed elysium of the first kiss." His readers had no definite sense of style, and consequently he could permit to his humour all possible manifestations of caprice ; unashamedly he gives free rein to the lack of form then natural to the German spirit, twisting language out of its proper channels, and overloading it with inflated artificialities.

The moral dangers of the æsthetic view of the world-order did not escape the keen sight of Goethe. He warned the youth of his time that they should " know how to accompany the Muses, but should not take the Muses for their leaders " ! Yet it was a rich generation which so unrestrainedly followed its own impulses. All the sluices of the German genius seemed to have been raised ; our music attained its most classical development ; in philology, F. A. Wolf, and in the fine arts, Asmus Karstens, were adventurously breaking new ground. Even social charm, which is apt to be lacking to German straightforwardness, was brilliantly developed in the circles of the elect ; seldom have woman's love and woman's naughtiness been described in a more delightful and seductive manner than in the letters of Caroline Schelling. Nor can we fail to rejoice in the contemplation of the noble prince who allowed all these great men to work as they pleased, who understood them, and who at the same time was himself so firm-hearted and so stately. Unrestrainedly Charles Augustus shared in this young and vigorous life, until at length he was taught, not by foreign counsel but by personal experience, " gradually to impose limits upon his free soul."

Men of the old French nobility, such as Talleyrand, Ségur and Ligne, were accustomed to maintain that no one could really know what life was who had not had experience of the last days of the old regime ; but with much better reason could the poets and thinkers of Germany say the like of their golden age. A wonderful compactness of spiritual existence enabled each one to effect the harmonious development of his gifts in every direction ; and it merely corresponded to the actual circumstances of the day if this fine sociability was more highly esteemed than the dull life of the state, if again and again in the letters of Schiller and of Goethe we find expression given to the ancient desire that above all the state must not encroach upon " the freedom of the individual." The attitude of this artistic world to the state was brilliantly displayed by William Humboldt in his treatise upon the limits to the effective power of the state. He contends that the highest aim of life, the education of human beings to individuality of energy and culture, can be attained only when the individual moves freely amid manifold situations. For this reason the state, which is an institute of compulsion, must confine itself to securing life and property, but must leave the kingly human being to act freely in all other respects. The state stands on a higher level in proportion as the individuality of the persons who combine to make it a state is higher, richer, and more independent. In this way was the Kantian doctrine of the constitutional state in the æsthetic sense carried a stage further ; the barren doctrine of individualism based on natural right gained ground when it became associated with the cult of the free personality. The admirers of classical antiquity were preaching the flight from the state, the precise opposite of Hellenic virtue.

All too soon was to come a terrible awakening from these joyful dreams ; all too soon was the pride of culture to learn that for noble peoples there is something even more terrible than vulgarity—disgrace. Nevertheless, the heroes of German poetry are by no means exposed to the reproach of being accomplices in the disgrace of their fatherland. The destruction of the old German state had been determined ; the participation of our poets in the political events of the time could not have sufficed to avert this destiny, and could only have diverted them from the contemplation of the eternal. They cherished the most peculiar gift of our nation, the sacred fire of idealism. It is to them in especial that we owe it that there still continued to exist a Germany when the German Empire had disappeared ; that even in the midst of need and servitude the Germans could still continue to believe in themselves, in the imperishability of the German essence. Out of the culture of the free personality issued our political freedom and the independence of the German state.

In the poem which more proudly and more firmly than any other voiced the contempt of the idealists for vulgar reality, in Schiller's *Reich der Schatten*, we find the words :

> "Incorporate the Godhead into your own wills,
> Then will it descend from its lofty throne !"

The poet left them unaltered, although Humboldt aptly remarked that they failed to render satisfactorily the fundamental æsthetic ideas of the poem. But Schiller knew what he was about. For the culture which he and his friends were announcing was not contemplative enjoyment but joyful activity. Surrender of the whole personality to the service of the ideal did not weaken the energy of the will, but strengthened it, fulfilling its disciples with that steadfastness of soul which regards " everything which we term destiny as simply a matter of indifference," as Gentz said of Humboldt himself. This active humanism was neither soft, nor yet hostile to the state ; but it had not yet grasped the nature of the state, and needed the schooling of experience to develop all the virtues of the citizen and of the hero. When Humboldt, who was now preaching that people should turn their backs upon the state, subsequently served his own state with the greatest fidelity, he was not contradicting himself, but was simply marching a few steps further along the same road : he had learned that the nobility of free human culture cannot exist in an oppressed and dishonoured people.

Meanwhile there began in literature a new tendency which was to lead the Germans to a profounder understanding of the state and of the fatherland. The first manifestations of the young Romantic School seemed at the outset to bear witness to a moral and artistic decline. Whereas the last two literary generations had been extraordinarily rich in noble and lovable figures, now the number of the empty-headed, the lascivious, and the over-cultured, underwent an enormous increase. The Storm and Stress Movement upon which the rising generation of poets plumed itself, was no longer naïve youthful passion, but already displayed the characters of decadence. Simple delight in the beautiful was replaced by a morbid ambition which wished at all costs to furnish forth novelties, and Goethe says aptly of his successors, " they seem to be like knights who, endeavouring to outshine their predecessors, look for a guerdon outside the lists."

The poetic faculty of the romanticists fell far below their

intentions. Even to contemporaries it was obvious that their imaginations worked vigorously in the void. Their leaders, despite stormy claims to genius, were rather finely-cultured connoisseurs than creative artists ; their art was rather a deliberate experimentation than an instinctive creation. Goethe's " living absorption into reality " was to be replaced by irony (the deadly enemy of all naivety) as the true poetic mood. The fine saying that " all noble natures pay with what they themselves are," served to their arrogant sterility as an excuse for idleness. Arbitrary caprice confused the boundaries of all artistic form, corrupted the chaste simplicity of tragedy with operatic songs, introduced the onlookers as participators in dramatic action, brought upon the stage the incomprehensible experiences of remote nations and times—whereas the stage should always remain contemporary in the best sense of the word, and should represent nothing but what the audience can sympathetically understand. As Schiller puts it, language had now been so highly cultivated by great masters that it saved the writer the trouble of philosophising and thinking for himself ; the younger generation stretched its signification beyond the limits of the possible, speaking of " sounding colours " and " aromatic tones." The boundaries between poetry and prose were destroyed, poetry taking the form of discussions about art, whilst criticism concerned itself with fantastic pictures. Art was science, science was art ; all the manifestations of the spiritual life of mankind, belief and knowledge, prophecy and poetry, music and the fine arts, emerged from the single ocean of poesy to return to it once again.

The result was that the romanticists, while they continually spoke of popular poetry, attained to a fantastic and artificialised view of the world-order which was comprehensible to none but a few initiates, and to these comprehensible only in scant measure. Frederick Schlegel's *Lucinde* furnishes a tragical testimony at once to the lack of discipline and to the incapacity of this school. Here we have an artificially heated imagination luxuriating in " dithyrambs over the most beautiful situation," without ever becoming sensuously warm and comprehensible, but resembling the loquacious ramblings of a drunken pedant. Even philosophy became infected by the presumptuousness and the obscurity of romanticism. Hitherto it had escaped the cosmopolitan influences which had invaded all the other branches of literature, but had created for itself an independent world of ideas which had remained as incomprehensible to the foreigner as was the terminology of the German philosophers. The genius of our speech, whose tendency was in the direction of brilliant and verbose indefiniteness, lent itself only too readily to the mystical bent of the German nature; and to these inclinations, romantic enthusiasm was to prove altogether disastrous. When young Schelling, inspired by the ideas of Goethe, determined to follow nature as it is displayed in all that lives, it is true that with astonishing boldness he opened to philosophic thought a completely new domain; but he utterly lacked that profound modesty which Kant had never failed to display in his boldest speculations. The inspiration of the "intellectual outlook," which in the domain of the experimental sciences will no more than furnish brilliant hypotheses, which always need verification by empirical proof, was to serve him in place of observation and comparison. He imagined that by arbitrary interpretations, drawn from the realms of his own fancy, he could force from nature those secrets which nature will reveal to none but those who search for them with a loving and self-renouncing diligence. For the sober investigators there were contemptuously reserved the spiritless handicrafts. Good society displayed an enthusiasm for natural philosophy, or learned with satisfaction from Gall's doctrine of the skull how easy it is for the man of genius to solve the most obscure problems of psychology and natural science. All the deplorable effects of over-education began to manifest themselves. Intellectual pride capriciously questioned the world-saving laws of the moral life, looking down with contemptuous laughter upon Schiller, the moral pedant. Weaker natures became the prey of an over-intellectual faint-heartedness, learning to contemplate everything from all sides, whilst losing sight of the contrasted view-points which the intellectual wealth of the times offered to all, and losing the energy for independent thought and will. Everyone who had given a theoretical explanation of a historical phenomenon, and had learned to explain its origin, imagined that he had also thereby provided a justification for its existence.

None the less, the romantic poetry bore most valuable fruit in our life, not so much through the works of art which it produced, as in consequence of the stimulus it imparted to science through the new and wider outlook it provided for the general feeling and thought of the nation. It refined the sentiment of nature, and rendered that sentiment more profound; it awakened an understanding for the soul of the countryside, for the magical charm of the lonely forests, of the rocky wildernesses, of the moss-grown springs. The eighteenth century, like the ancients, had felt itself at home in the richly cultivated and fertile plain, but the new time sought for the romantic stimulus of nature : our youths learned to prize once more the blameless joys of the fresh and free life of the wanderer, and our people, down into the lower strata of the middle class, gradually became enriched by an abundance of new outlooks upon life. The world of fairy tale, of the mysterious, of chiaroscuro, was now for the first time fully opened to German poetry. Its visionary figures were less vivid, less sharply defined, less complete, than were those of the classical period of our art ; and yet they rose in relief out of a distant background, seeming to carry with them unending significance, and they were surrounded with the atmosphere of the " moonlit night which bewitches our senses with its charm." Primevally old and long forgotten sensations of the Teutonic mentality were once more revived.

The romanticists felt that the classical ideals had completely failed to represent the innermost life of our people ; they sought for new materials, overrunning, in the spirit of adventurous conquistadors, the whole world as far as the cradle of humanity in India, and further yet to the nature-races in the forgotten corners of the world. Wherever the all-engendering poetry had incorporated itself in language, art, and religion, its manifestations were sought with intention to wed them to the German genius. Just as of old the Romans had placed in their Pantheon the images of the gods of the subject races, so now should the new race that was victorious in the realm of the spirit, that conceived itself as penetrating and overlooking all other nations with its gaze, take to itself, in faithful reproduction, the poetry of all lands. The fine sense of form and the graceful feminine receptivity of A. W. Schlegel brought the German translator's art to its finest blossom. One after another there speedily appeared German versions of Shakespeare, Cervantes, Calderon, and a number of other happy translations. The German art of poetry proved itself adequate for all these strange tasks, and there was even a danger of its succumbing to an over-elaborated formalism which was contrary to its innermost nature ; for in all epochs of their greatness the Teutons have ever prized content far above form. Nevertheless, the bold voyages of discovery made by the romanticists brought an invaluable and permanent gain. It was in their circles that there first awoke the historical sense which had always been lacking throughout the philosophical century. A. W. Schlegal, in his lectures on the history of literature, following the foreshadowings of Herder, developed the great idea that art is rooted in the soil of nationality, that in every people their language, their religion, and their art can be understood only as a necessary unfolding of the popular spirit. Thus was the foundation laid upon which subsequently was to be erected the magnificent structure of comparative philology, comparative literature, and the comparative history of the arts.

Moreover, this free voyaging into great distances led the romanticists home again. Since everywhere in history they were searching for national characteristics and for the primitive peculiarities of the peoples, they were ultimately led to ask themselves the question, how this new German people had itself come into existence. It occurred to them to look the antiquity of their own fatherland once more in the face, and the new generation found the image a strange one, as to a grown man is apt to seem strange his own likeness as a boy. With delighted shamefacedness the Germans discovered how ludicrously little they knew of the wealth of their own land. The much-abused, obscure night of the Middle Ages became illuminated once more with a cheerful light. A multicoloured turmoil of strange figures, of monks and minnesingers, of saintly women and glorious champions, moved before their enchanted gaze ; the Hohenstaufen emperors, whose name was still known in Swabia among the common people, reappeared as the knightly heroes of the nation. The dealers at the annual fairs, who sold to humble readers the coarse-paper editions of old folk-books, now sometimes ventured to offer his wares to men of learning. Educated people gave attentive ear when the servant-maid was telling the children fairy tales, and word was passed round among initiates that in the myths of the ancient Teutonic heathendom there still lay concealed an inexhaustible treasure of profound and moving sentiment. Johannes Müller gave for the first time a detailed description of mediæval life in his *History of Switzerland*, which, despite its tortuous and artificial rhetoric, was none the less profound and vivid, and brought forward an abundance of new historical points of view. This, too, was the first book to refer to the heroic greatness of the *Nibelungenlied*. In the year 1803 was published Tieck's collection of German minnesongs. Three years later Schenkendorf issued his appeal against the utilitarian barbarians who wished to lay hands on the old High-Master's castle at Marienburg : the despised Gothic now came to its own, under the name of the Old German architectural art.

Thus there began on all sides a re-entry into German life ; a great transformation was manifesting itself, and before long this transformation was accelerated by the pressure of the foreign yoke, by the awakening of national hatred. Their æsthetic delight in the antique and the popular, made the romanticists opponents of the Revolution ; they detested the " clean-shaven aspect " of modern equality before the law ; they detested the natural right which would impose its bald rules upon the beautiful multiplicity of historical phenomena ; they loathed the new world-empire which threatened to destroy the abundance of national states and national legal developments. There happened now for the first time in history what could happen only in so thoroughly idealistic a nation, that a movement which in its origin was purely æsthetic, rejuvenated and transformed political views. For this generation, poetry was, in actual fact the ocean into which all rivers flowed. If science, faith, and art were to be understood as the necessary outcome of the folk-spirit, no less certain was it that the law and the state owed their origin to the same spirit. Sooner or later it was inevitable that this necessary conclusion should be drawn, and that the idea of the national state should be conquered for German science. The connection between Frederick Gentz and the romantic school rested upon the feeling of a profound inner kinship, and it was directly from the ideas and foreshadowings of the romanticists in the domain of the philosophy of history that was subsequently derived the historico-political doctrine of Niebuhr and Savigny.

No less weighty with consequences was the revival of religious sentiment now preparing in the younger generation. Our classical poetry held aloof from the life of the church. Although it was in intimate harmony with the fundamental moral ideas of Protestantism, it would not recognise any of the existing religions as " religion." To Kant it seemed that religion was the recognition of our duties as the laws of God, the acceptance of the divine element in will ; his sublime strictness did not do full justice to the sentiments of the believing heart, to the impulse towards elevation and submission. It was this wonderful world of feeling, of mysterious yearning, which irresistibly drew the glances of the romanticists. Whilst the most enthusiastic spirits among them were becoming intoxicated with the sensuous beauty of the Catholic cult, or were reaching out towards the discovery of a new æsthetic world-religion, young Schleiermacher remained firmly planted upon the soil of Protestantism. His spirit was too closely directed towards the world of affairs for it to be possible for him like the poets of Weimar, to forget reality for art ; and yet he was too much of an artist to find satisfaction in the pitiless general rule of the categorical imperative. To him the individual form of the general moral law was to be found in the personality which at once freely develops its own individuality and at the same time consciously harmonises itself to the great objective orderings of the state and of society. In his lectures concerning religion, he opposes to the cultured despisers of religion the warning, " religion hates solitude : " and he showed how religion has its roots in feeling, how it possesses a primitive life precedent to all intercourse and all doctrine, a moral energy which is effective in all mankind. Only through religion can the human being, immersed in the finite, make himself at one with the infinite and become eternal in every moment. With patriotic pride, which gave anticipations of the moods of later years, he referred to the invincible might of the home of Protestantism, " for Germany is still always here, and its invisible energy is unweakened." Just as he appealed to a philosophical self-sufficiency on behalf of the common religious life, so also did he wish to enforce the value of the state. The state, he taught, is the finest of all human works of art ; it first gave to the individual life in the highest degree ; and for this reason the coercion exercised by the state must never be felt as a burdensome restraint.

Similar views were reached by Fichte, that rigid and stiff-necked thinker to whom the emotional wealth of Schleiermacher appeared to be womanish weakness ; for the literary movement, which to us who look back upon it to-day seems so simple and so necessary, fulfilled itself only amid the continuous conflicts of self-confident and strongly individual personalities. The philosophy of Fichte was the last word of transcendental idealism. To the world of experience, he flatly denied all reality. It was only because moral activity demands a stage, that the spirit was forced to look out of itself into an outer world, and to assume this world to be real. In his political writings also, this venturesome man appeared to despise all the limits of historical reality. He wished to realise perpetual peace, the ideal of the age, by the complete abolition of international trade, so that the " closed commercial states " should have intercourse with one another only through the interchange of scientific ideas ; and in his speeches upon the elements of the present age, he proclaimed it as the privilege of the sun-like spirit to soar above the crowd, and as a cosmopolitan to find its fatherland " where light is and justice." None the less there speaks through these lectures an active mind which reached out beyond the world of theories. Every sentence preaches the strict service of duty : there is only one virtue, to forget oneself ; and only one vice, to think of oneself. Without knowing it, in his harsh admonitions, directed against the slackness of his contemporaries, he was glorifying the manly virtues of Old Prussia. It was merely as a bold suggestion that he expressed a thought in sharp contradiction with his cosmopolitan dreams. In the end, he said, the state is the vehicle of all civilisation, and is therefore justified in claiming all the energies of the individual.

Thus within the bosom of the literary movement there was preparing a new political tendency. One who cast even a casual glance upon the distressing contradiction in German affairs, one who saw in close juxtaposition so flourishing an intellectual, and so miserable a political life, might well be reminded of the times of Philip of Macedon, when upon the grave of Grecian freedom, upon the battle-field of Chæronæa, the Thebans erected the beautiful lion monument, and Lycurgus adorned conquered Athens with magnificent buildings. Just as Hellas had once stood insecurely between Persia and Macedonia, so now Germany, pregnant with thought, stood between Austria and France. Yet in truth, the position of affairs in Germany was by no means so hopeless ; the melancholy proverb that the owl of Minerva begins her flight only in the twilight, applied to Hellas but not to Germany. Our classical literature was not the expiring flicker of an ancient civilisation, but the significant beginning of a new development. Not among us was an Aristotle making a comprehensive survey of the last data of civilisation on its way down to the grave ; for in Germany a youthful generation, one which amid all its errors was filled with the joy of life and with a sense of security in the future, was astonishing the world with ever new discoveries. Never for a moment among the intellectual leaders of the nation was there any failure to believe in the great destiny of Germany. "Despite their miserable constitution," writes A. W. Schlegel, "and despite their defeats, the Germans remain the salvation of Europe." In the same sense writes Novalis, that whilst other nations were dissipating their energies in party struggles, or in the pursuit of wealth, the Germans were building up, with all possible diligence, a higher epoch of civilisation, and would in course of time gain an enormous preponderance over the other civilised nations. Even the gloomy Hölderlin, who was profoundly affected by the impotence of the Germans, "poor in deed, though rich in thought," still exclaimed in joyful prophecy :

"Shall there come as lightning comes from the clouds
Action out of thought ? Will the books soon come to life ? "

Servile sentiment was ever far from this generation of poets and thinkers. It is true that Germany sent her pilgrims to take their place upon that great foreign stream which, during the Consulate and the first years of the Empire, was setting towards Paris from all the ends of Europe. In Paris, as once of old in imperial Rome, the finest artistic treasures of the world were now stored, and once again, as in the days of Augustus, there was assembled in a capital city a cosmopolitan public, whose critical judgment determined which among many beautiful things was the most beautiful. It was in the galleries of the Louvre that the overwhelming greatness of Raphael was first recognised. The German intellectuals found the petty towns of the homeland too narrow : they hastened to the Seine to intoxicate themselves alike in the noble and in the ignoble joys of the capital of the world. Yet even in the dazzling splendour of their new quarters they did not lose the sense of their own superiority ; they did not forget that in the production of all these stolen glories the French themselves had no share, but had first through the works of Laplace slowly begun to rise out of barbarism towards civilisation. While Frederick Schlegel was marvelling at the turtle-soup and the naked actresses of the new Babylon, he wrote, " Paris has only one fault, that there are so many French there " ; and his Dorothea adds, " it seems almost incredible how stupid are the French." More finely than these mocking cosmopolitans did Schiller voice the national pride of his own nation of thinkers. He knew that the victories of Kant and of Goethe were of greater significance than the laurels of Marengo, that the Germans always had the right to remind their boastful neighbours of the eternal good of humanity, and he writes proudly and grandly concerning the Pantheon of the Parisian plunderers :

> "He alone possesses the Muses,
> Who bears them warm in his bosom ;
> To the Vandal, they are stone ! "

§ 3. DISSOLUTION OF THE EMPIRE. THE WAR OF 1806

Matters had now arrived at such a juncture that the only thing which could hold over-powerful France within bounds was an alliance of the four Great Powers. Austria, however, had not yet recovered from the blows received in the last war. Since the spring of 1803, the young czar had been growing seriously alarmed regarding the insatiability of the Napoleonic policy, with which he had become sufficiently acquainted in the German indemnity-negotiations ; but in his boyish instability he came to no definite decision. Prussia was anxiously endeavouring to maintain the balance between the two dreaded colossi of the east and of the west, to preserve the friendship of Russia without offending France. It was only in the happy security of the insular kingdom of Britain that people felt strong enough to look things in the face. The Peace of Amiens which had concluded the war between the two deadly enemies, soon proved no more than an unstable truce. In Italy, in Holland, in Switzerland, in Germany, everywhere the First Consul was pressing arrogantly forward, regardless of all treaties. But more serious than all this, in the eyes of commercial-minded England, was the injury to the economic interests of the island. When France, Spain, Italy and Holland were closed by Bonaparte to English trade, the nation felt that the very foundations of its power were threatened. In full accord with the people, the court of St. James's refused to evacuate Malta so long as Holland and Switzerland were occupied by French troops. Meanwhile Bonaparte had long ago determined to resume the war against the inaccessible enemy. As early as March, 1803, long before the breach between the two western powers, he sent his confidant, Duroc, to Berlin, with the intimation that he found it necessary to take possession of Hanover. Since he was unable to overcome the sea power of England, he thought that by the occupation of Taranto and of Hanover he would close to British trade the entrance to Italy and the German North.

In this manner the ultimate and sole pride of Prussian policy, the neutrality of North Germany, was put in question. To avert such a blow from the German Empire, Frederick had long ago concluded the Treaty of Westminster, and had taken upon his shoulders the dangerous burden of the Seven Years' War ; and this at a time when the left bank of the Rhine was still German, and when the power of France was far less to be dreaded. Even Count Haugwitz urgently advised that the First Consul should be fore-stalled by a resolute invasion of France. It is true that the situation was by no means simple. The perplexity of Prussia was a source of manifest satisfaction in Vienna ; an appeal for help from the Hanoverian Government was bluntly rejected, and there was no longer any talk of the duties of the suzerain of the empire. England did nothing to secure against attack the hereditary dominion of its kings and the nursery of its best soldiers. In

Hanover itself, the occupation which Prussia had two years earlier undertaken for the advantage of the country, had produced a great deal of ill-feeling ; instead of the friendship and neighbourly sentiment of the Frederician times, moodiness and mistrust were now dominant. But what were such considerations when compared with the pressing demands of honour and self-preservation ? The last vestiges of Prussian prestige would be overthrown should French troops enter without hindrance between the eastern and the western provinces, should they press on to the very walls of the principal fortress of Magdeburg. From subsequent revelations of Napoleon it appears that a well-timed and vigorous remonstrance on the part of the Berlin court would not at this moment have brought about a war with France. The First Consul was then wholly immersed in his ambitious plans for the conquest of England. He had assembled his army on the coast in the neighbourhood of Boulogne, and there in the strict military school of a two years' training-camp had brought its technical efficiency to perfection. The national hatred of the fifteenth century was revived ; a fleet of transports, notably increased by voluntary contributions, was ready to carry the army across to the enemy's coasts. If he could only gain control of the channel for twelve hours, the landing would be attempted, and, as Bonaparte said in his letters, " then England would cease to exist." The independence of Ireland and the destruction of the wealth of Britain would for ever destroy the power of the island kingdom. Lost in such dreams as these, it was impossible that Bonaparte should now desire a breach with Prussia.

King Frederick William, faithful to the leading idea of his foreign policy, did not wish to undertake this venture unless he knew that his back was guarded by Russia. After having despatched to Paris and London timid counsels in favour of peace, he demanded of the czar whether Prussia could count upon the help of Russia. In St. Petersburg, however, the blind Prussophobe sentiments of the Hanoverian Junkerdom proved decisive. Count Münster, Anglo-Hanoverian ambassador at the Russian court, shared with the English high tories their inextinguishable hatred against the heirs of the Revolution, but he shared also the profound detestation of the Hanoverian nobles for equality before the law, and for the plain bourgeois military character of the Prussian State. In the request of Prussia, he could see nothing but a trap, a hostile attack upon the independence of Hanover. Upon the advice of Münster, the czar Alexander answered his royal friend with a refusal ; and since, in addition, England refused to modify its severe navigation laws in favour of the Prussian flag, the result was that when, at the eleventh hour, the Hanoverian Government spontaneously appealed for help from Prussia, the answer was a rebuff.

In the midst of the peace of the empire, the army corps of Mortier entered undisturbed into the imperial land of Hanover, a land which in accordance with international law had nothing to do with the war between England and France. The incapacity of the old state authorities made them an easy prey for the Bonapartist armies. The loyal people detested the French as a hereditary foe, and had done so since the victories of Ferdinand of Brunswick; the Hanoverians were once again prepared to exercise the ancient warrior spirit of the Lower Saxons in a conflict with this never-resting Frenchman. But the cowardly nobles' government in Havover ordered the troops to make no kind of disturbance; and without any serious attempt at resistance, by the Treaty of Suhlingen they handed over the whole country to the foreign commander. For the second time within fifty years, the brave Hanoverian army was forced into capitulation by a dishonourable policy. Nor did there on this occasion, as formerly upon the day of Kloster-Zeven, ensue a saving intervention of the British Government. England allowed the French to do as they liked. On June 4, 1803, the birthday of George III, the French troops entered the town of Hanover. Mortier closed the Elbe and the Weser, and demanded taxes from the Hansa towns. The occupation and exploitation of the Hanoverian territory lasted for two years; Bonaparte gave autograph directions how the royal stud was to be sent to Paris, and how the forests could best be used for the advantage of the French fleet. Then a second and still more disgraceful capitulation led to the disarming of the little army. With death in their hearts, and cursing " the cowardly curs of the Government and the Diets," the betrayed soldiers accepted their disgrace. Hundreds of them got away singly on board English ships, and entered the German legion of the king of England. Everyone in the country helped the fugitives on their way; the people held together as if in a great conspiracy. The unhappy men who had capitulated at Suhlingen formed the nucleus of those glorious regiments which subsequently in Spain resumed the struggle against France, and proudly inscribed upon their banners the word *Peninsula*. There thus persisted in the German nation its old stout-heartedness; all that was lacking was the great will which should know how to make a worthy use of such magnificent energies.

R

When it was too late Alexander recognised that a mistake had been made. The cabinet of Berlin engaged in vain negotiations to induce the First Consul to evacuate the Hanoverian territory. The fine illusions which the credulous Lombard brought back from Brussels, after a conversation with Bonaparte, were soon dissipated. Before long it was learnt that France demanded an alliance with Prussia without offering any *quid pro quo*. The king felt that he could not make himself responsible for such a step, and turned once more to Russia to ask help in saving the state from an intolerable oppression. It was thanks to him that on May 4, 1804, Prussia and Russia undertook to furnish reciprocal assistance in case Bonaparte should seize any other of the imperial lands. At the same time negotiating with France, they received an indefinite assurance that French troops should not pass beyond the Hanoverian borders, and guarantees of respect were given for North German neutrality. In Berlin there was still no lack of good plans and good intentions. Enquiries were made in Weimar as to the possibility of a renewal of the League of Princes, and Hardenberg, who, since April, 1804, had been a member of the Ministry, was already giving expression to the idea which subsequently, in the latter half of his public life, came to form the fundamental element of his German policy—the plan to combine the whole of Germany into a federation of states under the joint leadership of Austria and Prussia. But all these good plans crumbled to pieces in face of the pacifist anxiety of the cabinet. The statesmen of Prussia flattered themselves with the illusion which was the outcome of the experiences of the last fifteen years, the illusion that the state could secure a gain by peaceful negotiations, could thereby strengthen its untenable position. Even the able new Minister of Foreign Affairs was still far from recognising that salvation could come only from a European alliance against France, and he hoped to secure an enlargement of the Prussian domain through friendship with France.

Meanwhile the Holy Empire was forced to drain the goblet of shame to the dregs. When Bonaparte had the Duc d'Enghien arrested and killed on Badenese territory, it was only the foreign powers of Russia, Sweden, and England that ventured in Ratisbon to demand satisfaction for this criminal disregard of the peace of the empire. Baden, acting on the orders of Napoleon, earnestly begged that the distressing matter should not be followed up, while the other envoys, taking their holidays before the proper time, sought to avoid further discussion by flight. In May, 1804, the Napoleonic Empire was founded, and it was obvious that the new crown, which was assumed by this usurper with the blessing of the Pope, was the diadem of the Cæsars and of the Carlovingians. The Roman Empire passed from the Hapsburg-Lorrainers to the Napoleons. Unashamedly the man of might already spoke of the Empire of the West; he revived all the ancient Roman recollections which had been preserved in the mingled civilisation of France. The eagles of imperial Rome waved in the field before his legions. Soon he was using threats in his letters, in view of the possibility that Austria or Russia should dream of being so foolish as to raise the standard of revolt.

In vain did Gentz assure the court of Vienna that the recognition of this crown would serve merely to incite to new excesses the insatiable man who had become great only through the pettiness of his slaves. The talented advocate of the old comity of states found ready to his hand the orphic formula which was subsequently to prove the guiding principle of the courts in their contest with Bonapartism. It was necessary, he said, to maintain historic rights against the right of revolt, against the idea of popular sovereignty. The outwearied Austrian policy remained quite unreceptive for such ideas. The legal wearers of the crown of Charlemagne had long taken a dislike to the burden of that crown, more especially since the House of Lorraine could no longer count securely upon the votes of the electors. The emperor Francis therefore seized the opportunity of the establishment of Napoleon on the throne, to secure the high rank of his own house for all time to come. With the approval of Napoleon he assumed the style of Emperor of Austria, and the usurper received in return the recognition of the ancient imperial house. In this manner was the empire of Austria, which had in reality existed since the days of Leopold I, formally established; the domestic policy of the Hapsburg-Lorrainers, which for three centuries had concerned itself solely with the preservation of the hereditary dominions of the house, attained to its natural goal. The head of the House of Hapsburg continued to hold the title of Roman Emperor, but it was impossible that this "bizarre duplex emperorship," as Talleyrand mockingly called it, could be permanently maintained. The ancient and sacred name, now deprived of all meaning, must sooner or later disappear; the power of the Carlovingian imperial crown was henceforward vested in Napoleon.

In Berlin, the Bonapartist empire was greeted as a new guarantee for the bourgeois ordering of France, and it soon gained recognition; but Frederick William's modest good sense would hear nothing of the North German imperial crown, which the diplomatists of Napoleon offered him in dubious terms. The smaller estates of the empire, good and bad alike, Baden and Hesse Rothenburg, Fürstenberg and Leiningen, Bremen and Augsburg, sent humble congratulations to the crowned plebeian, in terms whose Byzantine abasement outdid even the flatteries of the French. They described themselves as His Majesty's most submissive and obedient of servants, they congratulated the protector of the German constitution, the hero and the peace-bringer, towards whose brilliant and benevolent genius the whole Continent was looking in dumb astonishment; they described in moving terms the joy with which all German hearts were inspired at the aspect of this new Cæsar ,who was so like their first emperor, Charles ; thanked him most cordially for the benefits they had received in the German indemnity-negotiations ; and commended themselves, in conclusion, to his kindly consideration in the event of a new distribution of lands[1].

To fill the measure of German degradation, in the autumn of 1804 Napoleon made a tour through the newly acquired Rhenish territories. In the ancient imperial town of Aix-la-Chapelle, the ambassador of the Emperor Francis presented his new credentials ; in all the towns of the Rhine the prince of peace was received by the people with loud rejoicings. He established his court at Mainz, in the same halls where twelve years earlier the ancient empire had celebrated its last festivals. The princes of the south and of the west assembled in haste to pay homage to the successor of Charlemagne. Everything suggested memories of Carlovingian times ; there were already plans on foot for a second Rhenish league. But in a lonely room, the eloquent old Charles Frederick of Baden fell sobbing into the arms of the Chancellor Dalberg, bewailing the destruction of his fatherland. What had this stranger in common with the old royal peasant of the Germans, who in the night blessed the trellises of the Rhenish vine-growers ? What did he know of that ancient magic ring which had formerly drawn the German Charles to the German River ? A severe and mistrustful foreign dominion overshadowed Germany even before its princes had formally submitted themselves to the Imperator. Napoleon had his spies throughout the empire : " Ten spies," he wrote, " are

[1] I have published these letters in the twenty-ninth volume of the *Preussische Jahrbucher*, 1872, pp. 103 et seq.

hardly enough for such a town as Hamburg." No one was safe from the claws of his police. The English agent, Rumbold, arrested in Hamburg by the French, was, indeed, set at liberty upon the demand of the king of Prussia, but the confidants of Napoleon were well aware that he would treasure up this reverse against the Hohenzollerns.

Whilst the German powers were recognising the new imperial crown, there prevailed at the court of St. Petersburg a lively and warlike mood. Since the murder of the Duc d'Enghien, the young czar had completely broken with France ; he saw that Napoleon wanted a new continental war, began negotiations with Vienna and London, and gave himself up once more to the enthusiastic dreams of a great war of popular liberation which he was to resume eight years later. He wished to strike a blow for the freedom of Europe, fighting not France, but the person of the usurper ; he wished to gratify the restored ancient states by liberal constitutions, and to unite a peaceful Europe in a permanent holy league of the peoples. After long hesitation, Austria advanced a step to meet Alexander's urgent demands, and in November, 1804, agreed upon a defensive alliance with Russia in the event of a further attack of Napoleon upon Italy.

If Prussian policy truly understood the signs of the times, it was necessary that the warlike zeal of Alexander should be at once utilised and bridled. It was not by an untimely war that the peace of Europe could be saved, but only by a carefully prepared and timely armed movement of the three great powers of the east. Napoleon's thoughts were still chiefly concerned with his *armée navale*, and upon his plans for an invasion of England. He burned with desire "to take vengeance for six centuries of injury and insult ; if only this greatest of aims can be achieved, all else will follow of itself." It was with deliberate intent that in the summer of 1805, he travelled for some time in Italy, in order to withdraw the eyes of the world from the coasts of the Channel ; and then suddenly appeared once more in Boulogne, "to complete the great event before which all Europe trembles." But in accordance with his usual manner he continued to hold two doors open. The army of Boulogne could also be utilised for a sudden attack upon Austria ; and the more plainly there became manifest the enormous difficulties of landing in England, the more vigorously did Napoleon come to occupy himself with plans for a new continental war.

It seemed prudent to await the probable miscarriage of an

attempt at an English invasion, to offer the threatening opponent no excuse for an attack, and meanwhile to prepare as quietly as possible the armaments required for a new war of coalition, even though the army and finances of Austria were in so pitiful a condition that the most notable man in the imperial army, the Archduke Charles, urgently advocated peace. A reconciliation between the courts of Berlin and Vienna seemed no longer impossible. The Archduke John, and the patriotic circle which surrounded him, had long advocated the view that nothing could be done without the aid of Prussia. Even Gentz, who became more and more embittered in his hatred for the Revolution, and who was already referring all the sins of modern history to Protestantism, still remained statesman enough to urge an understanding with Prussia. However profound the mistrust of the northern rival, it was impossible for the Hofburg not to recognise how indispensable was the aid of Prussian arms ; in the course of the secret negotiations of 1805, Austria seriously proposed to Berlin a reconstruction of the German constitution, so that the north should come under the dominion of Prussia, while the south should remain under Austrian suzerainty. But at the Prussian court there was still dominant the paternal wish for assured tranquillity ; it was hoped that peace could be maintained on the Continent, and that if this were impossible, the neutrality of North Germany might at least be secured. Even Hardenberg still cherished optimistic dreams ; he considered that the power of France was generally overestimated, and he wished to keep the hands of Prussia free, so that, should the circumstances demand it, by an alliance with France the strengthening of the monarchy and, above all, the annexation of Hanover, might be effected. It was through Hardenberg's influence that Prussia returned no satisfactory answer to the demands of the two imperial courts.

Thus it happened that the young czar, controlled by no will superior to his own, was left to the fancies of his restless imagination. The great statesman who for ten years had almost uninterruptedly been conducting the obstinate struggle of England against France, lacked, like all the British diplomats, a thorough understanding of continental conditions. Inconsiderately, William Pitt shared the confused plans of Alexander ; already in April, 1805, a secret treaty of war between Russia and England was signed. Meanwhile, Napoleon assumed the royal crown of Italy, and wrote to the czar, as if in defiance, that only the wish of the Italian nation compelled him to make this sacrifice of his greatness. Then the

Republic of Liguria was annexed to the empire, and therewith even hesitating Austria was forced to join the Third Coalition. The allied courts were occupied in far-reaching plans. The boundaries of France were to be pushed back to the Rhine and to the Moselle ; complete independence were to be regained for Germany, Holland, and Switzerland ; the crowns of France and Italy were to be for ever separated. It was hoped, altogether in the sense of the ancient Anglo-Dutch Barrier Treaty, to control the grasping power of the French state by strengthening Holland, Piedmont, and Switzerland. If Prussia should join the coalition, she was to receive Fulda in Orange-Nassau, and the Lower Rhineland, from the Moselle down to the Netherland frontier. A general congress was to decide the new territorial distribution when victory had been secured ; it was hoped that even the dethronement of the Corsican might be effected. But the slow and weak preparation of armaments was in crying disproportion with these bold resolves.

Among the numerous failures of the impatient and impetuous Russian policy, there was none which must be so severely atoned as the arrogant contempt for Prussia. The league of friendship concluded at Memel was now destroyed by the Polish plans of the czar, which long continued to threaten the good understanding between the two neighbouring powers. Educated in the views of the fashionable enlightenment, Alexander had from the first, like his tutor Laharpe, regarded the partition of Poland from the outlook of the French philosopher. In the terrible catastrophe he saw, not an inexorable historical necessity, but simply a deplorable deed of violence, and one which justified all the horrors of the Revolution. The thought that this bloodstained heritage was one he was forced to receive at the hands of his grandmother, was a heavy burden to his feeble spirit. In such a mood as this, when he was still no more than grand duke, he made the acquaintance of Prince Adam Czartoryski, the son of that old prince who had been hailed by a party of the Polish nobles as King Adam I. To the son of the czar, the versatile Pole was irresistible ; he was talented, highly cultured, older in years and experience than the grand duke, a master in the arts of Sarmatian flattery and subtleness. To strangers he seemed to resemble a knight-errant seeking his lost fatherland, and to be illumined and ennobled by a flavour of patriotic sadness. For many years the two friends were engaged in secret plans for the atonement of Catherine's misdeeds and for the restoration of Poland. In the mind of Alexander the calculation was coloured by the feeling that his philanthropic intentions coincided precisely with his personal advantage ; if he dreamed of the liberation of Poland, he saw the crown of the Jagellons upon his own head.

Czartoryski pursued his Sarmatian plans with a vigour which to every Russian must have seemed equivalent to high treason, and misused his position as curator of the University of Vilna on behalf of a Polish-Catholic culture, and for the encouragement of a deadly hatred of the Russians. Now, when the conduct of foreign affairs was entrusted to him, he hailed the War of the Coalition as a welcome means for forcing Prussia over to Napoleon's side and then robbing the detested neighbour state of its Polish provinces. It was known that the Polish patriots continued to look hopefully towards their old ally France. For many years a Polish legion had fought under the tricolour ; Napoleon had already realised how this unhappy people might be utilised as a weapon against the eastern powers. For this reason, Czartoryski advised that the czar should forestall the Frenchman, and himself proclaim the freedom of Poland. To Polish levity it seemed a favourable opportunity for simultaneously arranging for a war against Prussia ; then Austria might secure, in Silesia and Bavaria, indemnity for her Galician possessions. The czar had not yet been completely won over to these nebulous plans, but the clever Pole had moved him to this extent, that his imperial friend, quite recklessly, was willing to side against Prussia. The ardent friendship of Memel seemed forgotten ; the negotiations in Berlin were conducted on the Russian side with insufferable arrogance, as if there was a deliberate intention to drive Prussia out of the coalition. Since King Frederick William continued steadfastly to observe neutrality, Alexander had determined that he would lead the Russian army into Austria through Prussian territory, even against the king's will.

Meanwhile the success of the Napoleonic designs against England became ever more questionable ; the elaborate plan to lure Nelson's fleet away to the West Indies and meanwhile to sweep the Channel, was defeated by the watchfulness of the British naval hero. Napoleon was already weighing the question whether it was not desirable, if not to abandon the whole undertaking (over five years later Arthur Wellesley still had good reason to fear a new attempt at invasion), yet to postpone the matter to a more favourable opportunity. In such a situation, nothing could be more welcome to the Imperator than the news of the military preparations of the Coalition. Eagerly he took up the challenge which his opponents had thrown down, and was delighted at the prospect of driving out of the German Empire "this skeleton Francis II who has been placed upon the throne by the service of his ancestors"; and he said, "Germany will see more soldiers than ever before!" Whilst the *grande armée* hastened unnoticed and in wonderful order from Boulogne to the Rhine, the theatre of war on the Upper Danube was carefully surveyed by French spies, and at the same time the most brilliant of the Napoleonic campaigns was prepared by a prudent diplomatic activity.

There was no reason to fear opposition from the Holy Empire. The Reichstag of Ratisbon was at the moment profoundly immersed in important negotiations concerning a petty question of communal pasture-lands, and in this matter worthily occupied the brief respite which was still allowed. The Imperator now addressed his old protégés, the courts of the South German Middle States, speaking as protector of dynastic particularism. He was coming to rescue German liberty, and never again should German princes be treated as subjects of the German Emperor. Upon Napoleon's orders, the elector Max Joseph of Bavaria put off the Austrian negotiators, who were masterfully and threateningly demanding his adhesion to the Coalition, by hypocritical peace-declarations. The German prince gave his sacred word of honour that his troops should not undertake any military operations; he begged, in desperate paternal anxiety, that a little patience should be granted, because his son, who was travelling in France, would be exposed to the revenge of the Corsican; and he then hastened with his army, from the betrayed Austrians, to join the French. The Bavarian people paid no heed to the infamous conduct of the court. The old tribal hatred for the empire, the old and justified mistrust of the greed of the Hofburg, reawakened. With rejoicing, the brave little army responded to the appeal of the Imperator, who said, "You are fighting for the first goods of the nation, for independence and political existence." Baden and Darmstadt joined the movement, and, after some hesitation, Würtemberg also; all four of the Middle States, which Napoleon was already speaking of as "the pillars of my future German federation," joined his camp.

He hoped to gain over Prussia also by deliberate deception. He offered Hanover to Prussia, if Prussia in return would cede Cleves on the right bank of the Rhine with Wesel, and would join the war against the Coalition. Thus the Prussian monarchy was to break with Austria and Russia, was to evacuate her last position on the Rhine, was to allow herself to be pushed back towards the east, was to surrender Italy, Switzerland, and Holland to the conqueror of the world. Napoleon expressly retained in his own hands the free disposal of these countries ; he saw that the time was approaching when the Dutch would weary of their isolation, and would demand union with France. And for all these sacrifices nothing was offered to the king beyond that Hanover which, acquired under such conditions, could be maintained as a possession only by a long war against England. With irresponsible levity, Hardenberg yielded to the French persuasions and urgently advised that the French terms should be accepted. All that was wrong in his view was that the price was not high enough, and he hoped with the help of Napoleon to gain Bohemia and Saxony in addition to Hanover. It was only the sober good sense of the king which preserved the state from a disastrous step, one which threatened for ever to destroy the possibility of an understanding with the eastern powers, to prevent a common uprising against the Napoleonic empire of the world. Frederick William rejected the French offer of alliance, but he was soon to learn the truth of the words of the Great Elector that "for this state, neutrality is the most thankless of all political systems." For whilst Napoleon was endeavouring by new negotiations to secure neutrality on terms that would be advantageous to France, Prussia was simultaneously threatened from the east. The czar Alexander announced in open plain terms that his troops would march through Prussia. The king did what his honour demanded, put a large proportion of his army upon a war footing, and assembled his troops on the Warthe. The czar was astonished and alarmed at the breach of the peace, to the despair of Czartoryski ; and his foolish conduct had as its only consequence that the junction of his army with his Austrian allies, was more and more delayed.

In this untenable situation, out of accord with France, in a state of tension with Russia approximating to open hostility, with anger and mistrust arising on all sides, the Prussian court contemplated the outbreak of this war of Titans, as the cowardly Lombard was accustomed to describe it in his anxiety of soul. With crushing blows, Napoleon overthrew the Austrian army on the Upper Danube before the Russians arrived on the scene. The world learnt for the first time what it signified for the military power of France to be reinforced by the warlike energy of the Rhineland and of the German south. The glory of the great day of Trafalgar, at which Napoleon's fleet was annihilated, almost vanished before the terrible news which came from High Germany. It was related how individual sections of the Austrian army had been defeated in a series of brilliant victories ; how the main body of the Austrians under Mack had been forced to a disgraceful capitulation at Ulm ; how the frenzy of despair had seized the imperial troops, how everywhere amongst the army and the officials there were signs of panic, weakness, and cowardice, all the sins of a profoundly corrupted state system, how the *grande armée* had at length pressed forward upon its irresistible march towards the Austrian capital.

But fortunately for the Allies, at the very beginning of the campaign, the victor had permitted himself a deed of arrogance, which, rightly utilised, might have given another turning to the hopeless struggle of the Coalition, and which necessarily put an end to the untenable neutrality of Prussia. In order to bring Bernadotte's army-corps to Ulm at the proper time, Napoleon did unreflectingly what the czar was merely threatening to do, and sent his troops into Franconia, across neutral Prussian territory. To Prussia, he thought, he could do anything he liked, for, as he had written at an earlier date, " Prussia has sunk to the level of a power of the second rank." But at this news the anger of the king flamed up, and his Hohenzollern blood began to boil. He proclaimed his rights in a courageous Declaration, broke off all his agreements with Napoleon, permitted the Russians to pass through Silesia, ordered the mobilisation of the whole army ; to his level sense it seemed self-evident that all diplomatic relations with France must immediately be broken off. The people, too, displayed a lively excitement at the outrage. In the theatre at Berlin there was ardent applause at the warlike notes of the *Reiterlied der Wallensteiner*, and the populace made a disturbance beneath the windows of the French ambassador, Laforest ; the estates of the Mark declared themselves ready to provide levies for the army, at their own expense; the young officers went to the frontier in the assurance of Frederician invincibility. It was only in secret that Lombard and the French party ventured to carry on their usual intercourse with Laforest.

Hardenberg, too, recognised the necessity for vigorous defence, but he did not realise in its entirety the pressing danger of the moment. He was unable to grasp that the king's latest steps made altogether impossible any honourable understanding with the revengeful Corsican ; nor did he recognise that this hero was not accustomed to allow negotiations to prevent him from following up his victories. The sanguine man continued to believe in the possibility of a peaceful issue, and therefore advised, although salvation might still have come from a rapid participation in the war, that there should rather be an armed intermediation which might readily be rendered useless by further warlike successes of the French. Meanwhile the czar Alexander came in person to Berlin, and on November 3rd the Treaty of Potsdam was signed. Prussia undertook to engage Napoleon, by diplomatic negotiations, to recognise the *status quo* of the Peace of Lunéville. If he refused, as it was obvious he would, the intermediating power of the Coalition was to come into action, and was to receive as the reward of victory an enlargement of territory ; Russia agreed to use her services in London to secure the cession of Hanover, whilst the English statesmen would as soon have given Holland to Prussia ! The great European warlike alliance appeared to be concluded. The czar renounced his Polish plans, saying remorsefully, " I shall not be beguiled in that way again." The alliance between the reconciled friends was cemented by a tender embrace over the grave of Frederick the Great, one of those touching incidents dear to the dramatic nature of Alexander.

According to the calculations of the duke of Brunswick, the Prussian army could not intervene in the struggle before December 15th; for the troops assembled on the eastern frontier were not to be led directly to Moravia for a junction with the Russo-Austrian army, but were to go by a wide circuitous route to Thuringia, in order thence to attack the French in the rear. This evolution corresponded to the wishes of Austria, and expressed the preference of the Brunswicker for such artificial methods ; and it is unquestionable that in the mind of the cautious old duke, the idea still persisted that perhaps the war might after all be avoided. The king cherished the same opinion ; he still hoped to enforce peace without drawing the sword, simply by the display of his military forces. He had ordered a march into Hanover, and he won Hesse and Saxony for the Coalition. An army of 200,000 men assembled on the southern frontier of the monarchy in order to defend the independence of the German north ; there were also the English and Russian troops which had landed in Hanover, and the Swedes of King Gustavus IV, the deadly enemy of the Revolution. At the same time the Russian reserve-army passed through Silesia towards Moravia, and the archduke Charles led the Austrian southern army out of Hungary.

The fate of the world hung upon a wise postponement of the battle. If the allies could hold Napoleon in Moravia by a careful defensive strategy until all their supports arrived, until with the coming of the momentous December 15th, the Prussian army would also be ready to come into action, Napoleon's defeat seemed inevitable. He was more than one hundred miles from the French border, could expect no reinforcements, and even now his army was hardly so strong as that of the enemy. But he was again to be saved by the blunders of his opponents. During the negotiations, he had appeared to be in a yielding mood and inclined for peace, in order to arouse the belief that he was afraid. Alexander saw through the game, and insisted again and again that the cunning of the enemy should never lure him to a premature attack; all the experienced officers urged him to caution. But a brilliant review of the army overthrew all the good resolutions of the czar. His arrogant pride was awakened at the sight of these fine regiments, still crowned with the laurels of the campaigns of Souvòroff. The young Hotspur was fascinated by the idea of astonishing the world by a decisive war, even before Prussia was ready to take part in it. The young court generals, who had so often in Russian history been to blame for light-minded resolutions, vehemently applauded the idea of an imprudent attack. It was determined that an attack should be delivered upon Napoleon's well-secured position in a direction from east to west, in such a way that the army, if beaten, would have to retreat into Hungary, and would be cut off from communication with Silesia, where, at Neisse, 40,000 Prussians were standing ready. On the anniversary of the day of Napoleon's crowning as emperor, Alexander received, in the battle of Austerlitz, the reward for the greatest folly of his life, and now Emperor Francis also lost his head and begged the victor for a truce. Napoleon agreed, on condition that the Hofburg should abandon the alliance with the czar, that the Russian troops should proceed homeward by way of Hungary, and that no foreign army should remain on Austrian soil.

Thus was the great European war-alliance broken in its inception by the fault of the two emperors. Yet the military situation of Prussia still remained advantageous. The czar did not completely abandon the war, but placed at the king's disposal the Russian forces still in Silesia and Prussian Poland. Frederick William had command of 300,000 fresh troops ready for war; with such a force he might well hope to protect the liberty of North Germany, and to assist oppressed Austria to a tolerable peace. That this hope also came to nothing was chiefly the fault of the Prussian negotiator, Count Haugwitz, but in the last analysis it was the fault of the king himself. Prussian armed intermediation was meaningless unless the Prussian negotiator was prepared to present a plain alternative, demanding of the conqueror that he should either accept the conditions of peace imposed by Prussia, or else try the fortune of war. But the pacifist king could not summon up sufficient resolution. From the first he took the edge off the negotiations, inasmuch as he gave his envoy secret instructions that at all hazards he was to maintain peace with France.[1] During recent years Haugwitz had given many proofs of diplomatic insight, and had often formed a sounder judgment of Napoleon's hostile intentions than had his colleague Hardenberg, but in the present complication neutrality seemed to him the only possible policy. He had therefore no idea of going beyond the peaceful instructions he had received from the king. He travelled slowly, as he had been ordered, in order that the 15th of December might pass. When at length he encountered Napoleon, in the course of a conversation lasting several hours he said not a word of the king's conditions of peace, not a word of armed intermediation or threats of war, but allowed himself to be put off with empty phrases, and went to Vienna to wait upon events. There he received the news of the battle of Austerlitz, and immediately resolved to secure at all costs a reconciliation with the man of power. In his anxiety of soul, he persuaded himself that Austria was already thinking of joining Napoleon in order to fight Prussia. Subsequently, on his own initiative, and without any adequate authority, he signed at Schönbrunn, on December 15th an offensive and defensive alliance with France, in which Prussia recognised in advance all the concessions which Napoleon hoped to force from the Emperor Francis, abandoned Cleves on the right bank of the Rhine to France, abandoned loyal Ansbach to Bavaria, and received in return Hanover.

The victor rejoiced, saying, " If I am sure of Prussia, Austria must do whatever I want ! " With the Treaty of Schönbrunn in his hand, he compelled the unhappy court of Vienna, on December 26th, to accept the oppressive conditions of the Peace of Pressburg. The House of Austria lost Venice, Tyrol, and the remains of its Swabian possessions ; the ceded German provinces were divided among the South German satraps of France. By the grace of Napoleon, Bavaria and Würtemberg received kingly crowns, and therewith the greatest of all goods, the last goal of two centuries of treason and felony, full and unrestricted sovereignty. Emperor Francis had to accede in advance to all the consequences that might arise out of these new rights. Therewith disappeared the last

---

[1] Recently proved by M. Lehmann, *Scharnhorst*, I, 354.

shadows of the ancient national monarchy; the German kingship could no longer be maintained over sovereign kings. In the announcement of peace, the realm was already spoken of as the German Federation. For a long time past the Imperator had been discussing with the South German courts, what could best be established in place of the " miserable monkey play " of the Reichstag of Ratisbon. Now, in affable letters, he announced to his loyal followers their new glories: Baden had entered the sphere of the great powers, and Bavaria at the first opportunity was to receive still further enlargement. He stood now at the climax of his successes. No misfortune had as yet tarnished the wonderful triumphs of his fortunate flags. France regarded the invincible one with astonishment; the German city of Strasburg was proud to allow itself to be used by the new empire as a gate of entry into its old fatherland, and rechristened the Metzgertor after the battle of the three emperors; in Paris, a Trajan's column was to celebrate the fame of the Imperator.

On the return journey Napoleon received in Munich the obedient gratitude of the new King of Bavaria, celebrated the nuptials of his stepson with the daughter of the Wittelsbacher, and was gratified to learn how Max Joseph was announcing to his rejoicing people the " restoration " of the ancient Bavarian royal dignity. All Bavarians were now to wear blue and white cockades, "that they might know one another mutually as brothers and that they might secure from foreigners proper recognition as Bavarians." Chancellor Dalberg hastened to the wedding. The man of many abilities had issued during the war, in a wave of patriotic sentiment, a confused appeal to the German Reichstag, plaintively asking: " Shall the name of Germany, the name of German Nation, the name of a Race, become extinct, the name of the people that once conquered the Roman colossus ? " He had to listen to a severe reprimand, because he had " endeavoured to reawaken the German spirit." To secure complete reconciliation with those in authority he shortly afterwards nominated Cardinal Fesch, Napoleon's uncle, to be his coadjutor; this man was a worthless offshoot of the House of Bonaparte, a Corsican who understood not a single word of German, and who accepted the offered honour unwillingly, only on the understanding that he was soon to mount the most distinguished princely throne of Germany. At the same time the heir to the Baden throne was married to Stephanie Beauharnais. To his brother-in-law Murat, Napoleon gave the Prussian Cleves and the Duchy of Berg, which latter (in accordance with an old Bavarian design) was now exchanged for Ansbach. Thus the Bonaparte family made its joyful entry into the ranks of the high nobility of the German nation ; the German estate of Princes formally recognised the just claim of equality " of the fourth dynasty of France."

Meanwhile Napoleon took all possible measures to force the crown of Prussia to accept the Treaty of Schönbrunn. The *grande armée* and the South German troops advanced to the Main ; other army corps were pushed forward in Nassau and in Holland, up to the Prussian border. When the Imperator returned to France, he left Berthier in Munich, and his horses in Strasburg. It was his intention to return " as quick as lightning " in order to arrange for his armies to invade Prussia simultaneously from the west and from the south. Such was the position of affairs when Haugwitz returned after a tedious journey, flattering himself that by the Treaty of Schönbrunn he had saved the state. Was the king to punish by shameful dismissal the negotiator who had forgotten his duty and had exceeded his instructions to such an incredible extent, and was he to maintain, sword in hand, that dominion over North Germany, including Hanover (which in actual fact belonged to Prussia) ; or was he to receive this same Hanover as a gift at the hands of Napoleon and to give in exchange Cleves and Ansbach, to conclude a defensive and offensive alliance with France, and to allow himself to be involved in the war against England ? For an honourable state there could be no hesitation between these two alternatives. And yet Hardenberg advised a middle course. He counselled that the Treaty of Schönbrunn should be accepted, but under reservations which should prevent a breach with England ; for although he strongly condemned the conduct of his opponent Haugwitz, he hoped, even now, that it might be possible to secure further accessions of territory by new negotiations with Napoleon. In this way the cunning enemy was given the desired excuse to refuse on his side to be bound any longer by the Treaty of Schönbrunn. This serious mistake was immediately followed by a second and even greater one. Whilst Napoleon wrapped himself in a dubious silence and advanced his armies from all sides against Prussia, the demobilisation of the Prussian army was determined. Deceived by the ambiguous utterances of Laforest, Prussia believed that the attitude of France was friendly, and wished to escape the continued burden upon the finances, To meet the costs of the mobilisation, a loan had been floated and the issue of currency notes to the amount of 5,000,000 thalers had been authorised.

The state was to pay dearly for this pusillanimous economy. Napoleon had merely waited for the return home of the Prussian army in order to force Prussia " to yet another treaty." Now that Prussia stood before him disarmed, he at once removed the mask. Hardenberg continued ingenuously to hope that he would come to a friendly understanding with the Imperator concerning the reconstitution of Germany ; he thought of a German trias, that is to say, that Austria should keep to her own affairs, while Prussia acquired predominant influence in the north and France in the south, and he believed that it would still be possible in such an intolerable situation as this to retain a certain political community for the German nation. Then Haugwitz, who was to conclude the negotiations in Paris, sent the shattering news that Napoleon would no longer recognise the Treaty of Schönbrunn. On February 15, 1806, the perturbed negotiator signed the Treaty of Paris, whose conditions were even more severe than those of Schönbrunn. Prussia undertook to close the Hanoverian rivers, to begin at once a war against England which would completely paralyse Prussian trade, whilst not a word was said in the new Treaty of the compensation for Ansbach which had been promised in the Treaty of Schönbrunn. What a situation ! The regiments had long been on a peace footing and were dispersed in their garrisons ; the French armies, invading from the Main and from the Rhine simultaneously, could overrun the country in a few weeks. Austria had concluded peace ; the czar held back, advising his friend secretly to come to terms as best he could, for good or for evil, with the preponderant power. Nor could any speedy help be expected from England. By the disaster of Austerlitz, the heart of the great Pitt had been broken, and after his death for a considerable time the British policy was a vacillating one. All the generals, even Rüchel the fierce enemy of France, declared that resistance was impossible ; but Hardenberg, moved to the depths of his soul, left the decision to the king, since the ministers did not as yet possess any independent responsibility. Frederick William decided as he was compelled to decide, and accepted the Treaty of Paris.

Such was the lamentable ending of the first attempt to abandon the easy-going Basle policy of neutrality. Through the meddlesomeness of the czar and the pusillanimity of Emperor Francis, the coalition had been destroyed. Prussia having been thus isolated, had been lured by Napoleon out of one false position into another, and had finally been subdued for good or evil. Despite the ill-will of the Hanoverians, the black eagles were affixed to the gates of the old Guelph towns. The lamentations of the faithful Ansbachers remained unheard although they sent despairing petitions to the king that he would not abandon them. Yet even in the midst of this humiliation there became manifest the first glimmer of a moral power of resistance, which during the heavy years of peace seemed to have altogether disappeared. During the winter the old unteachable self-satisfaction had often been boastfully manifested; as late as January, so talented and active an officer as young Bardeleben wrote triumphantly, "We have attained to the happiness of peace with great and true glory!" but after the Treaty of Paris there was a change of mood. Among the enlightened publicists of the capital, there were, indeed, a few emptyheads who praised the king because without a single blow he had gained a fine province; but the nobles and the army felt with dissatisfaction that the glories of the Frederician times had passed away. Profounder natures, such as Gneisenau, saw that the decisive hour was rapidly approaching, and placed their hopes upon an alliance between the two German great powers. No one felt the disgrace more painfully than the high-minded king. He plainly declared his hopes: the Treaty of Paris was not binding for it had been secured by fraud and untruth; his duty demanded that at the very next offence committed by France, Prussia should unsheathe the sword.

Whilst Napoleon's protégé Haugwitz took over the official conduct of foreign affairs, and steered the state in the narrow waters of the French alliance, Hardenberg remained the king's trusted adviser, and in view of the near prospect of war secretly revived the treaty with Russia. The eyes even of this over-sanguine man had at length been opened. He had had a large share in the political sins of the last two years, and yet was regarded in Paris as the leader of the anti-French party because he was an opponent of Haugwitz, and because he had again and again urged the king to rid himself of this "homme sans foi et sans loi."[1] The keen intelligence of Napoleon recognised in Hardenberg a high-minded statesman: he wished to revenge himself for the troubles of the previous autumn, loaded the minister with vituperation, which received dignified answers, and ultimately demanded his dismissal. It was to these attacks of Napoleon that Hardenberg owed a reputation which his actions had not deserved; all men of standing looked hopefully towards him, and the valiant patriot Marwitz, the leader of the nobles of the Mark, honoured him as having

---

[1] Hardenberg's *Journal*, September 6, 1806.

been " since the autumn of 1805 the ideal of the man who should rescue the state." [1] But it was in these terrible weeks of the spring of 1806 that Hardenberg first really became that which the world held him to be. He saw with horror the abyss on the edge of which Prussia was tottering ; all that was noble and high-minded in this richly endowed nature sprang to active life, and henceforward until the end he was the unwearied enemy of the Napoleonic world-empire.

The last hope of Haugwitz in concluding the Treaty of Paris was that the French troops would soon be recalled. But this expectation proved vain. The *grande armée* remained in Germany, threatening Austria from the Inn, and Prussia from the Rhine and the Main. The Hofburg was to be forced to accept the formal dissolution of the Holy Empire, which had been planned by the Imperator ; and at the same time Napoleon had determined that in case of need peace with England was to be secured by the surrender of Hanover, which was to be taken from Prussia for the purpose. Should the Prussian court resist this new injury, the French army was ready for invasion. Meanwhile the fortified places of Kehl, Kastel, and Wesel were occupied by France ; the fortress on the Lower Rhine was intended to constitute a *point d'appui* for an attack upon Prussia.

Thus prepared, Napoleon proceeded to realise after his own manner the idea of the German trias with which Hardenberg had lately been playing. " La troisième Allemagne " was to be politically constituted as a protégé of France, not in alliance with Austria and Prussia but independently and in opposition to both. The fantastic memorial of Dalberg, which talked of the re-establishment of the Carlovingian empire and of a rejuvenation of the honourable German nation, and also the short and futile preliminary negotiations in Munich with the greater South German States, convinced the Imperator how difficult it would be " to make these Germans work in unison." For this reason he determined to impose the new order offhand, just as of old Charles V had constrained the Italian princes to his will by treaties which were practically forced upon them. He knew that he could do anything he liked with the Middle States if he offered them new booty at the expense of their smaller co-estates. There had, indeed, been no lack of submission among these petty lords of the south. The majority had come together to form the Frankfort Union, and they sustained a common ambassador in Paris. Again and again was the man

---

[1] Expression used by Marwitz in a letter to Hardenberg, dated February 11, 1811.

of power deafened with requests and proposals from the anxious petty princes. When he was in a good mood, he allowed Talleyrand to tell him " ce que c'est que ce prince-là," and gave a gracious answer. But the conqueror had no use for unarmed vassals ; moreover, he was suspicious of the friendship which some of these petty lords exhibited for Prussia, and which the majority among them showed for Austria. His resolution was taken : " It lies in the very nature of existing circumstances that the petty princes must be destroyed." There was already rising upon the ruins of the old comity of states the new federative system ; the central sun of France surrounded by satellite states. Two of the Imperator's brothers ascended the thrones of Holland and of Naples ; the rest of Italy, and Switzerland, were under his orders. For the German Federation, which was to strengthen the ranks of these satellite peoples, he counted first of all upon the four South German Middle States, and upon the new Lower Rhenish Grand Duchy of Joachim Murat. Of the smaller states, he had in mind to spare only a few, which had commended themselves to him by extreme servility or by dynastic ties.

In the spring of 1806 there spread through the German courts a rumour that a new and comprehensive mediatisation was in prospect. Then, as four years earlier, the envoys of our high nobility hastened to Paris, in order by flattery and corruption to secure a good share of booty for their masters. Then, as before, an Alsatian was in charge of the business of the German territorial distribution ; on this occasion the negotiations were conducted by the old imperial publicist Pfeffel, under the guidance of Talleyrand and La Besnardière. Meanwhile, however, the constitution of the Confederation of the Rhine was decided upon in Napoleon's cabinet. But no negotiations were undertaken with any of the German courts, and of the envoys in Paris four only had been allowed to read the Charter before Talleyrand, on July 12, summoned the faithful to a session. Here he displayed to them their hopeless situation ; how as rebels against the empire they could no longer deal in half measures ; thereupon the Charter was accepted without any discussion. The Rhenish Federation of Louis XIV was revived, but in an incomparably stronger form. Sixteen German princes separated themselves from the empire, declared themselves to be sovereign, and further declared that every law of the ancient and honourable national comity was null and inoperative ; they recognised Napoleon as their Protector, and placed at his disposal for every continental war in which

France might be engaged, an army of 63,000 men. Unconditional subordination in matters of European policy and equally unconditional sovereignty in internal affairs : such were the two leading thoughts of the constitution of the Confederation of the Rhine, dictated by a thorough knowledge of the German estate of princes. The courts tolerated their subordination because, standing between Austria and France, they needed a protector, and because they hoped for new marks of Napoleon's favour. Some secretly consoled themselves with the thought that the French dominion would not last for ever ; but the sovereignty they all regarded as a treasure that was to endure to all eternity. German particularism was blossoming in all its sins.

Napoleon, in a letter to Dalberg, did not deny himself the pleasure of making a mocking reference to the time-honoured treason of the petty princes; he called the policy of the Confederation of the Rhine conservative, since it merely gave legal sanction to a protectorate which had existed in fact for several centuries. At the same time he prudently flattered dynastic arrogance. No lord paramount was any longer to be imposed upon the German princes. No foreign court could interfere in their internal affairs ; he himself was merely to exercise the duty of a Protector, and his protectorate had no ulterior aim beyond securing complete sovereignty for the allies. The promised fundamental statute for the Confederation of the Rhine never appeared ; the Bundestag, with its two councils, never assembled. For this piece of work, which was the outcome of rude force, there was lacking from the very outset all capacity for further development. It was far from the mind of the Protector, who had already scolded his own tame legislative body in Paris with the words, " Vous chicanez le pouvoir ! " to allow himself to be bothered by the tedious deliberations of a Rhenish Bundestag. It sufficed him that he had now under his command 150,000 German soldiers, regiments from the left bank of the Rhine. The two kings in the Confederation of the Rhine, however, did not conceal their hostility to any idea of their subordination to the Confederation, and they flatly rejected all the plans for federal development which the new prince-primate, Dalberg, brought forward with inexhaustible enthusiasm.

The domain of the Confederation extended over the whole of the south-west, from the Inn to the Rhine, and then stretched northward far towards Westphalia, surrounding the Prussian State and its smaller allies in a wide curve ; the thirty-ninth Article of its Charter threateningly announced that for these other

German States the right of entry was reserved. Those of the smaller estates of the empire that still remained in the south and in the west, were subjected to the suzerainty of the sixteen members of the Confederation : this was the fate of all the princes and counts, of all the imperial knights (as many of them as had still kept their heads above water in the storms of recent years), of the two knightly orders, of the imperial towns of Nuremberg and Frankfort—in all, a domain of 550 square miles [German] and containing about 1,250,000 inhabitants. All the sordidness attaching to the principal resolution of the Diet of Deputation seem trifling in comparison with the detestable brutality of this new exercise of arbitrary power ; for what had happened was not on this occasion initiated by the empire itself, and was not justified by the excuse of indemnification, but was the outcome of the arbitrariness of a handful of perjured princes. Moreover, under the protection of the Napoleonic army, the destruction was now threatened of Lobkowitz and Schwarzenberg, and of all those Austrian territorial lords who had so long constituted the nucleus of the imperial party among the temporal princes. With them fell also the old and celebrated races of the Furstenbergs and the Hohenlohes, which, but a few decades before had been almost as powerful as their fortunate neighbours in Carlsruhe and Stuttgart—and one at least among those thus mediatised allowed his doom to be proclaimed for honour's sake, and of his own deliberate will. Prince Frederick Louis of Hohenlohe-Oehringen proudly rejected all the alluring offers which Napoleon made to the celebrated Prussian general in order to win him over to the Confederation of the Rhine. He would not break the faith which had for centuries united his house with the Hohenzollerns, but lost his territorial suzerainty because he courageously placed himself on Prussia's side. Even more directly was the court of Berlin injured by the spoliation of the House of Nassau-Orange, for this house had provided for the crown of Prussia an indemnification on German soil for the lost possessions in the Netherlands, and it was now deprived of a part of its German lands, without its being thought necessary even to notify Berlin of the fact. Chance and caprice decided which of the petty states were to remain in existence and which were to be destroyed. Count von der Leyen was allowed to enter the Confederation of the Rhine as a sovereign prince because he was the nephew of Dalberg. But, unknown to these malefactors, there yet presided over this arbitrary proceeding a great necessity. Once more there disappeared a whole crowd of those sterile state-structures which had once enriched themselves with the spoils of the ancient German monarchy ; the soil was being levelled upon which subsequently was to rise a new structure of German unity.

Until far into the summer Napoleon remained convinced that the rightful emperor would refuse to accept the destruction of the ancient empire ; for the Peace of Pressburg expressly stated that the new kings were not to cease to belong to the German league. But Austria was utterly exhausted by unsuccessful war ; the Archduke Charles and the new Minister of Foreign Affairs, Count Philip Stadion, hoped that the energies of the monarchy might be re-established in peace. In addition, in the Treaty of Pressburg, all the consequences of the Bavario-Würtemberg sovereignty had been accepted, and the imperial suzerainty had therefore been indirectly abandoned. But if the will and the power to maintain the claims of the old emperordom by force of arms were lacking, the honour of the imperial house still demanded that the worthless title should be abandoned in good time, freely and voluntarily, before Napoleon enforced its renunciation. Such was the advice of Stadion ; but even in these gloomy days, in which a history dating from a thousand years was moving to its tragic conclusion, the ancient greed of the Hapsburg dynastic policy could not rest. Just as his ancestors had always regarded the occupancy of the imperial throne as no more than a means for the increase of their immediate territorial dominion, so Emperor Francis regarded the abandonment of the imperial crown simply as a possibility for a good stroke of business. " The time for discarding the imperial title," so he wrote, " is that in which the advantages which would thus be derived for my monarchy outweigh the disadvantages which its further retention might entail." For this reason Metternich was to hasten to Paris, in order there " to put a good value upon the imperial dignity," and not to refuse to resign it, but rather to display a conciliatory spirit in return for " some great advantages to be received by my monarchy." Such was the mood in which the last of the Roman-German emperors took leave of the purple of the Salii and the Hohenstauffen. The customary phrases of imperial and paternal loyalty and suzerain care were no longer heard ; the policy of the House of Austria at length displayed in plain words its attitude towards Germany. But the proposed commercial transaction miscarried. When Metternich reached Paris, the Charter of the Confederation of the Rhine had already been drawn up. The German emperor was confronted with an accomplished fact, and had only to look on whilst at Ratisbon Napoleon and his vassals decreed the formal dissolution of the empire.

Meanwhile the ultimate disgrace was inflicted on the Reichstag by one of the most loyal of the estates of the empire. The Hotspur of royalism, King Gustavus of Sweden, recalled his envoy because he regarded it as beneath his dignity to participate in deliberations which were under the influence of usurpation and egoism. When in Paris the preparations were in progress for the foundation of the Confederation of the Rhine, Dalberg was careful to give a holiday to the Assembly at Ratisbon. Then on August 1st, eight envoys declared in the names of the Rhenish federal princes that their honourable lords found it "comported with their dignity and with the purity of their aims" to separate themselves formally from the Holy Empire, which was in fact dissolved; they placed themselves under the "powerful protection of the monarch whose intentions had always proved themselves to be in harmony with the true interests of Germany." Simultaneously the French ambassador announced that Napoleon would no longer recognise the empire, which had long been merely a shadow of itself.

In the ancient centuries of force and roughness there had always been preserved among the Germans a last sentiment of shame; the murderer avoided the neighbourhood of his victim because he dreaded lest he should see the red blood burst once more from the wounds of the corpse. But this new and unprejudiced generation had no sentiments of this kind; when the declaration of the first of August was read, there were present in the Reichstag hardly any envoys beyond those from the members of the Confederation of the Rhine which had destroyed the ancient German state. The Reichstag broke up without any further proceedings. Thereupon, on August 6th, in a cool and colourless manifesto, Emperor Francis laid aside the German crown, and at the same time declared, in opposition to the law, that "the office and dignity of lord paramount" was extinct, and that the empire of Austria was exonerated of all German imperial duties. The alliance between Germany and the imperial hereditary dominions had, however, been for long so loose, that the formal separation had hardly any influence upon Austrian internal conditions. Thus by a *coup d'état* of the last Hapsburg emperor was that crown destroyed which had for a thousand years been intimately associated at once with the proudest and with the most painful memories of the German people; among these memories was the heroic fame of the Othos, but also

the horror of the Thirty Years' War and the ludicrous disgrace
of Rossbach. The empire had traversed the whole circle of earthly
destiny ; after being an ornament of Germany it had become a
detestable caricature ; and when it at length collapsed it seemed as
if a ghost had been laid. The nation remained silent and cold.
It was not until the shame of the period without an emperor had
been experienced to the full that the dream of emperor and empire
once again was awakened in the German heart.

In the camp of Bonapartism there was manifest ill-natured
rejoicing. The *Mainzer Zeitung* wrote : " There is no longer a
Germany. What some are inclined to regard as the efforts of a
nation fighting against its dissolution are no more than the lamentations of a few persons beside the grave of a people which has out-
lived its destiny. It is not now that Germany has perished. That
which gives content and life to the history of nations is the spirit
of a few great and leading men "—whereupon there followed
the customary genuflection before the hero of the century. In
the highlands and along the Rhine, the opinion was widely diffused
that England's gold and Austria's arrogance were alone responsible
for the latest war, and for the destruction of the emperordom ;
but in the north the masses hardly knew even the name of the empire
and had no sense of the seriousness of the times. Under the protection of the *grande armée*, the princes of the Confederation of
the Rhine took possession of their spoils, and just as had happened
three years before, the people suffered everything with no more
than a few trifling complaints. All the courts of the Confederation
considered that in virtue of their new sovereignty they were justified in destroying the last vestiges of the ancient rights of the
estates ; Napoleon's word of power, " C'est commandé par les
circonstances," was the justification for every arbitrary act.
Frederick of Würtemberg, immediately after he had succeeded
to the kingly crown, demanded from the Committee of the Diet the
key of the estate treasury, and abolished the old territorial constitution which had been defended in the battles of three hundred
years by the valiant Swabians, and which was the one living energy
in the German south, saying that it was " an institution no longer
adapted to the circumstances of the day " ; his ministers rejoiced,
for now at length had been overcome the stubbornness of the
estates. Even the crown of Denmark took the opportunity of the
dissolution of the empire to incorporate Holstein into its state ;
King Gustavus deprived Swedish Pomerania of its ancient territorial rights, and introduced the Swedish constitution.

The anarchy of a new interregnum broke over Germany; clublaw prevailed. The clubs were no longer in the hands of medieval brigand nobles, but in those of modern princes. Napoleon suspiciously persecuted all displays of national feeling in the subordinated lands. He wrote to Talleyrand that the interests of France demanded that German public opinion should remain divided. When at Ansbach there was published an anonymous pamphlet entitled *Germany in Her Profound Abasement*, a well-meant sentimental essay which in this time of iron could only give utterance to the peaceful counsel, " Weep, weep all noble and loyal Germans ! " to the Imperator even this groan of German philistinism seemed alarming, and he had the bookseller, Palm, who was said to have circulated the pamphlet, tried by court-martial, and shot. This was the first of Bonaparte's judicial murders on German soil, and the prudent folk of Bavaria began to doubt whether the Confederation of the Rhine had really brought about the victory of peace and enlightenment.

How differently from this tearful Ansbacher did Frederick Gentz know how to speak to his people. The finest of his writings, the fragments from the recent history of the balance of power, showed, it is true, that the talented man was now writing in the pay of Austria : for the noble archducal house he could find words of praise alone, and he flatly denied the manifest designs of the Hofburg against Bavaria. But these extenuations signified little in comparison with the magnificent frankness, with the flaming words, with which he probed the ultimate causes of the German disgrace. The old balance of power had been disturbed by a new worlddominion ; " it is not the genius of Napoleon, but the defencelessness of Germany, for which Germany is herself responsible, that has brought about her doom." The great question of the future is, whether the whole of Germany is to become what the half of Germany has become to-day, what Holland and Switzerland, Spain and Italy have become. Europe has been overthrown by Germany's fault, and by Germany must Europe be re-established. He calls for a saviour and an avenger, who shall restore us to our eternal rights, who shall build up Germany and Europe once again. With all the might of his scorn he lashes the fools who expect the salvation of the world from France. " The avenging fate which, for the punishment of Germany's arrogant stupidity has flogged her through the whole weary cycle of political insanity, has at length metamorphosed the enthusiasts of freedom—for a timid and febrile freedom—into eulogists of the most atrocious slavery which has ever oppressed the nations."

From the quiet north there at length resounded powerful words of patriotic wrath. Ernst Moritz Arndt, the valiant son of the isle of Rügen, had hitherto passed his days as an obedient subject of the three crowns of Sweden ; it was only when the disgrace of the Germans came home to him, that his German blood boiled and he came to understand which was his fatherland. During the war of 1805 he wrote the first portion of his *Geist der Zeit*, and from that time onwards he remained firmly attached to his unhappy people, playing the part of a faithful Eckart, of an awakener of consciences. There were at his disposal neither the comprehensive knowledge of Gentz, nor the insight and the logical powers of the great publicists. A child of nature, he needed many years before he could throw off the provincial prejudices of his Swedish-Pomeranian home, and get rid of the obscure enthusiasm for the land of the forests and of freedom, Scandinavia, and could overcome his hostility towards poor, sober Prussia, which, with its coldly calculating Frederick, was alone responsible for the splitting up of Germany. But fresh and powerful, like the waves of his ocean home, endowed with a primitive and immediate force of sensibility, such as was possessed by no other political writer of the age, his eloquence flowed from an overfilled heart glowing with love. His every word was true and courageous. Whilst the hard political ideas of the Viennese publicists were comprehensible to very few in this generation without a state, Arndt concluded his book with the simple appeal, " I love humanity " ; he moved emotions because he preached politics from the human side. He was the first to recognise and to chastise the moral evils of intellectual over-culture, and to the clever century he exclaimed that it was " better to live than to chatter about life." " Without the people, there is no humanity ; and without free citizens, there if no free man. A man is seldom of so strong a fibre that he can endure servitude and contempt without deterioration ; a people, never." Similar sentiments found expression in the younger literary circles of Berlin ; since the unhappy Ansbach negotiations, the old feeling of comfortable self-satisfaction was no longer possible. In the entourage of Schleiermacher, ideas were entertained of a northern federation, which by freedom of trade and intercourse, and by a common military system, was once more to restore brotherhood to the Germans of the north.

Such ideas as these, the only ones which promised salvation, had lately begun to influence even the Prussian Government. Whilst the Holy Empire went down towards destruction, and the South and the West bowed beneath the French yoke, King Frederick William, as we learn from his subsequent war-manifesto, undertook to assemble the last Germans under the flag of Prussia. Two years earlier he had bluntly rejected the North German imperial crown which Napoleon had offered him, because he mistrusted Greek gifts ; and it was with honest regret that he saw the empire abolished. Not until the old legal community of the German nation had completely disappeared, did the conscientious prince at length determine to carry out those plans of federal reform which, since the days of the League of Princes, had continually been revived at the court of Berlin ; not until then did he determine to give a firm legal form to the protectorate of Prussia over the north, which had existed in fact since the Peace of Basle. It was his desire, as he wrote to Frederick Augustus of Saxony, to oppose to the Confederation of the Rhine, a federative system which might save the north of Germany. Prussia at length re-entered the paths of a healthy German policy, and it was this very return to its great traditions which was to entail terrible humiliation, and punishment for past sins. The king no longer believed a single word of the smooth flatteries which Napoleon had continued to shower upon him throughout the winter. Since the Treaty of Paris, he had been prepared for the worst ; he considered the foundation of the Confederation of the Rhine, of which no notification whatever had been given to the allied court of Berlin, to be a revolution, and to be a manifestation of hostility towards Prussia. He felt by no means secure in the possession of Hanover, which he regarded as the bulwark of the independence of the north. The union of this country with the great power of North Germany was in such close correspondence with European interest, that even in England a few far-sighted persons advised a friendly understanding with the cabinet of Berlin ; but the Guelph pride of George III obstinately resisted such an idea. Thus while, on account of Hanover, England was carrying on a fruitless war with Prussia, the king had to fear that the trickery of his ally might once more deprive him of the dearly-bought country.

It was full time that the last countries which still remained German and free should be put in a state of military preparation. That tri-partition of Germany of which Hardenberg had dreamed in the spring, was now almost completed, although in a very different sense from that which the credulous man had foreseen. All that remained possible to the court of Prussia was to proceed independently of Austria and France, and to take independent action with regard to the third of Germany that lay within its own sphere of influence. Since even Haugwitz had long obtained a clear understanding of the intentions of Napoleon, Prussia began already in July, even before the Confederation of the Rhine had been formed, to negotiate with the courts of Dresden and Cassel regarding the constitution of a North German Federation. The Prussian plan closely resembled the old-established constitution of the empire, and demanded from the smaller courts no more than the absolutely essential military provisions. Prussia was to have the imperial dignity, whilst the two Electors were to receive the long-desired kingly crowns ; there was to be a congress of envoys, under the leadership of these three states, and each of them was to have supreme military command in one of the three regions of the federation ; finally, there were to be a federal court of justice, and a federal army of 240,000 men which in time of war was to remain under the supreme command in Prussia. Everything was anxiously avoided which might hurt the pride of the members of the federation. The congress and the tribunal were not to sit in Berlin, but, in accordance with ancient imperial custom, in two minor towns. To satisfy the ambition of Saxony and Hesse, it was arranged to mediatise the imperial knighthood and some of the pettiest counts and barons, and the two Middle States were to receive the lion's share of the spoil.

Once more, however, it was to become manifest that there was no success obtainable for this state without arduous toil. It was not as a last resort, nor yet by peaceful negotiations, that the bold idea of the Prussian emperordom could be realised. The obscure vacillations of Berlin statecraft had aroused profound distrust in all the courts ; the hesitating embarrassment of Prussia was regarded by the world as deliberate calculation. Even at the friendly court of St. Petersburg there was for some time a doubt whether this North German Federation was not a Napoleonic intrigue. It was impossible that Austria should regard with a favourable eye a policy which endeavoured to transfer to Prussia a fragment of the old imperial glory. The Emperor Francis remained full of suspicion, especially since Prussia kept the negotiations strictly secret. It was through the intermediation of the Austrian ambassador in Paris that the Elector of Saxony first heard the news that Napoleon wished to warn him against the ambitions of Berlin. In such circumstances, what could be expected from the good sentiments of those petty states which for so long had been accustomed to will the end without willing the means, to claim the protection of Prussia without offering any service in return.

The elector of Hesse had first carried on secret negotiations on behalf of his accession to the Confederation of the Rhine, and had only failed to conclude a bargain with France because Napoleon would not present to the greedy elector the territory of his cousins of Darmstadt. Now, always in the hope of fresh accessions of territory, he joyfully accepted the plan of the North German Federation, but his zeal soon cooled when it became clear that Frederick William's sense of justice intended to limit the mediatisation within narrow bounds. The Saxon cabinet displayed that stiff arrogance which had before characterised the negotiations concerning the Frederician League of Princes. There could be no question of subordinating the Saxon crown to a Prussian emperordom. Since Prussia yielded in the matter of the imperial dignity, the court of Dresden demanded the constitution of a Federal Directory, which should circulate between Prussia, Saxony, and Hesse ; and instead of a federal army and federal court of justice, there were to be three district armies, and three district tribunals under the separate guidance of the three leading powers. The old longing of the Albertines for the annexation of the Ernestine lands was revived, and from that time for two generations to come, remained the principal aim of Dresden statecraft. The Hansa towns also showed themselves averse to the scheme, although the North German Federation asked them for no more than a monetary payment instead of a supply of men for the army ; they secretly determined to form a separate Hanseatic Federation. When the danger of war now became more imminent, and Prussia demanded from the smaller protégés a contribution to the upkeep of the army, the court of Schwerin manifested the patriotic sentiments of the German petty princes in the ever-memorable declaration : " However thankful His Serene Highness the Duke would be to accept your Exalted Royal Protection if His Serene Highness believed himself to be in danger, yet in existing circumstances he must urgently excuse himself from making the proposed contribution." The upright Lord of Schwerin did, indeed, give way when Prussia recalled to his mind " the national honour of the oppressed fatherland," and threatened an invasion. Meanwhile the whole course of the tedious negotiations showed that a firm alliance with these courts could be based upon the pressure of arms alone.

The resistance of the petty states was supported in Paris, and by the faithlessness of Napoleon the North German Federation was destroyed in the germ. On July 22nd Talleyrand had written to the Berlin court suggesting that Prussia should derive advantage from the foundation of the Confederation of the Rhine, and should found a North German Empire for itself. It was manifest that this friendly invitation aimed only to secure Prussia's assent to the dissolution of the ancient empire. The Confederation of the Rhine had been from the first intended, as was plainly shown by the concluding article of its constitution, to provide for the adhesion of all the German petty states. Hardly had it been concluded when it was enlarged by the entry of the new Grand Duchy of Würzburg. At the very moment when Napoleon was offering his ally the North German imperial crown, he warned the courts of Dresden and Cassel against the Prussian alliance, and secretly encouraged the plans for the aggrandisement of Saxony, and the attempts of the Hansa towns to form a separate league. On August 13th he came more plainly into the open, transmitting by the mouth of Dalberg to the two electors his assurance of protection against the ill-will of Prussia should they wish to join the Confederation of the Rhine. Four weeks later he declared to the Prince-Primate that he had recognised the full sovereignty of all the German princes, and that he would tolerate no lord paramount over them. Nowhere did these French intrigues produce a profounder impression than at the court of Dresden. As soon as war became imminent, the alarmed elector endeavoured to carry on a double game between Prussia and France, similar to that which Bavaria a year before had carried on between France and Austria. Too timid and too honourable to refuse his neighbour his federal help, he still hoped to secure himself against all eventualities, and begged that the Prussian troops should enter his territory suddenly, because he wished to make Napoleon believe that it was unwillingly that he had become the federal ally of Prussia.

After all the lamentable humiliations of recent months, was Prussia now to endure, in addition, that Napoleon should forbid her to preserve against foreign dominion the last vestiges of Germany ? Were the Prussians to dally until the faithless man who had surrounded the monarchy with his armies, and who carried on unceasing preparations in his fortresses on the Rhine, offered to the king on the point of his sword a new and still more shameful treaty of subjection ? " Napoleon strikes at our heart,"

wrote General Rüchel, " he threatens Saxony and Hesse in viola-
tion of his most sacred assurances." Nothing but the sword could
find a way out of this intolerable situation. Since the winter,
the one-sided patriots at the court had already foreseen that the
decisive struggle was inevitably approaching. In anticipation
of the oncoming catastrophe, Stein, the Minister of Finance,
endeavoured during the spring to deliver the king from the influence
of his subordinate advisers. He drew up a memorial upon the errors
of the Government, the first programme of his great policy of reform.
" Since Prussia has no state constitution, and since the supreme
authority is not divided between the Chief of the State and the
Representatives of the Nation, there seems to be all the greater
need for a governmental constitution ; authority has become the
spoil of a subordinate influence ; for this reason the secret cabinet
government must be abolished, and in its place there must be constituted a Council of State with five expert ministers who must be
in immediate relations with the king ; moreover, these must be
new and energetic persons, for when measures are changed there
must be a change also in those who are to carry them out."
Blucher, too, boldly denounced the rout of base loungers which
surrounded the noble king. In September, just before the fall of
the dice, a number of the princes of the royal house, together with
Stein, Blucher, and Rüchel, addressed a common memorial to the
throne, informing the king of that which " all Prussia, all Germany,
all Europe knows," and imploring him to dismiss Haugwitz, Beyme,
and Lombard. How profoundly must the old and solid framework
of absolutism have been shattered when royal princes could venture
such a step ! Frederick William was not inclined to allow the
prestige of his crown to be endangered ; he called this undertaking
a mutiny, and gave the petitioners an ungracious reception. Thus
it happened that in the most important offices, the old time and the
new remained side by side and in direct contact. In the
army, the general-quartermaster Scharnhorst stood beside the
commander-in-chief the duke of Brunswick ; in the ministry,
Stein sat beside Haugwitz ; in the cabinet, Lombard acted after
his own nature, whilst Hardenberg was giving the monarch trustworthy counsel. Under such leadership as this, the shapeless old
monarchy resumed the struggle with the man of power, of whom
the French said with timid wonder : " He knows everything, he
wills everything, he can do everything ! "

The unavoidable war was at length precipitated by a new act
of treachery on the part of Napoleon. How often and how

ceremoniously had France undertaken to guarantee her Prussian ally in the possession of Hanover. Now it was suddenly learned in Berlin that the Imperator, who throughout the summer had been conducting a great peace negotiation with England and Russia, had inconsiderately offered to restore to the Guelphs their hereditary dominions. Upon recept of this news, Frederick William immediately wrote to the czar (August 9th) : " If Napoleon is treating with London about Hanover, he will destroy me." The king foresaw that before long the unworthy conditions of February would be renewed, that Prussia would have as sole alternative either to endure in silence a shameful act of robbery or to resist the invasion of the *grande armée* by force of arms. The Prussian army was therefore placed upon a war footing and assembled at Magdeburg. By this absolutely necessary step, the war was determined. For although the negotiations between France and England fell through, and the proposed deal with Hanover was temporarily abandoned, it still remained certain, in view of the secret intrigues of French diplomacy in Dresden and Cassel, that Napoleon would joyfully seize any convenient opportunity to overthrow the one state that still prevented the extension of the Confederation of the Rhine over the whole of Germany. As the king must have expected, within the next few days France threateningly demanded the demobilisation of the Prussian army, and the dissolution of the proposed North German Federation. With full justice he wrote to his Russian friend that peace was possible on two conditions only, if Napoleon should withdraw his troops from Germany and should undertake to offer no further obstacles to the North German Federation ; otherwise war was inevitable, for who could impose laws upon this man ?

Although the Imperator did not immediately send an ultimatum, the delay was dependent merely upon his desire to await the issue of the peace negotiations he was conducting with Russia. With complete foresight, and calculating every step, he had for months been engaged in diplomatic and military preparations for the Prussian war. Not one of his other campaigns of conquest had been initiated with such extreme caution, for he still had a considerable respect for the Frederician army. He succeeded in detaching his opponent almost completely from the other great powers, and he had hidden his game so cleverly that his contemporaries and posterity believed his falsehood that this war of defence he had thus forced upon the Prussian State was a desperate chance venture wantonly undertaken by the king. The fable found acceptance even in Prussia, for after the unfortunate issue of the previous passage at arms, everyone execrated the policy of 1806.

By the cession of Hanover, Napoleon had sown enmity between the Prussian court and England ; now he advised the Russian plenipotentiary, Oubril, to conclude a separate peace. Should the czar refuse to ratify the step undertaken by his envoy, there was still another weapon available which might have kept the St. Petersburg court out of the Prussian War. As long before as August, the Corsican Sebastiani had gone to Constantinople, in order to induce the Sultan Selim to declare war against Russia. He found the Divan in a state of angry excitement, for the uncertain and meddlesome policy of Czartoryski had secretly encouraged the Servians to revolt, had brought the hospodars of the Danubian provinces under Russian influence, and had sowed dissension in the isles of Greece. It was not difficult to urge the Porte onwards. When the czar Alexander rejected the separate peace proposed by Oubril, it was already known in Paris that Russia would be unable to place more than half her army at the disposal of Prussia. Soon after the battles in Thuringia, the war on the Danube broke out, and Napoleon exhorted the Sultan, "Now is the time to secure your independence ! " With the rejection of Oubril's peace proposals, there was no longer any choice open for the court of Berlin, for now a war between France and Russia was unavoidable, and this was a war which could not be carried out without Prussia's co-operation. By the oriental negotiations Napoleon simultaneously secured the neutrality of Austria. In Vienna the hatred against the victor of Austerlitz was stronger than the mistrust of Haugwitz, even stronger than the gratification which was felt at the plight of the North German rival. But in the last war the power of Austria had been so profoundly shaken, that in the complication of the moment Austria hardly counted, and now this country was completely paralyzed by the incalculable Turkish confusion. As soon as the troops of Alexander invaded Wallachia, Archduke Charles advised his imperial brother to occupy Belgrade ; for months the cabinet of Vienna remained resolved upon a war against Russia. Hence the Hofburg received no less coolly the Prussian demands for help than it received Napoleon's suggestions of an alliance for the protection of the independence of Saxony. But to secure the favour of the Imperator, the Hofburg went so far as to betray to the court of the Tuileries a war-despatch of the Prussian minister.

Thus Haugwitz was enmeshed by the diplomatic mastery of his opponent, and was, in truth, already beaten, although he continued to foster happy anticipations. He continued to reckon trustfully upon the co-operation of Austria, which there was really no reason whatever to expect ; and he believed that the people of the Confederation of the Rhine would voluntarily serve under the king's banner, whereas everywhere mistrust and coldness were exhibited towards Prussia. It was only the help of Russia which the king had been able to secure for his state by secret negotiations in St. Petersburg. But not even the czar realised the greatness of the danger, thinking that it would suffice to send to Prussia's assistance an army of 70,000 men ; and he allowed himself to be drawn into the war in the east at the very time that the struggle for Prussia's existence began. Moreover, there was a revival of the old troubles concerning the untrustworthy Polish provinces. The well-meaning Prince Radziwill advised the king to assume the title of King of Poland, and the czar, that of King of Lithuania, saying "these titles would obliterate all adverse sentiment." Frederick William was careful to avoid following this two-edged counsel ; but meanwhile in Paris a manifesto was issued summoning the Poles to fight for freedom by the side of their old French ally. For the opening of the campaign Prussia could count upon the co-operation of Electoral Saxony alone, and the loyalty of this one and only friend had long been vacillating. More than once Napoleon let the court of Dresden know that he regarded Saxony's participation in the war as compulsory ; the anxious elector did not yet venture upon open treachery, but he allowed his envoy to remain in Paris, and even before the news of the battle of Jena he sent thanks to the French emperor for his friendly attitude. Count Schönfeld, the Saxon representative in Vienna, received instructions to declare to the French ambassador that the elector had only joined Prussia under the force of circumstances, and hoped that Napoleon would not regard the behaviour of the court of Saxony as dictated by hostility against France. Napoleon could count with certainty upon the desertion of Electoral Saxony. The elector of Hesse remained neutral, since his avarice could expect nothing out of this war, and Haugwitz did not interfere with him.

Such was the isolation of Prussia when this country took up arms against the whole of western Europe. Nothing but a careful defensive could ensure even a tolerable issue for the unequal struggle. With the support of that triangle of fortresses between the Elbe and the Oder which had so often proved the salvation of the threatened state, it might perhaps be possible to withstand the overwhelming power of the enemy for such a time as would be necessary for the arrival of the auxiliary army from the interior of Russia. But Haugwitz wished to prove to the mistrustful world that he was engaged in this war in earnest. He advised an attack, and the Frederician traditions of the army also spoke on behalf of a bold offensive. The resolution was therefore taken to advance through Thuringia against South Germany, and for this madly venturesome undertaking not even the whole of the army was engaged. All the East Prussian regiments and the majority of the South Prussian regiments, nearly 40,000 men in all, remained at home. How differently did Napoleon know how to arm for battle and for victory. As early as August he had pushed forward the troops of the Confederation of the Rhine to the borders of Thuringia. In the first days of September he despatched marching orders to the *grande armée*, prescribing each days' march with detailed precision. His spies swarmed on the roads from Bamberg to Berlin : a war chest of 24,000 francs was enough for him, for any more that he wanted would be a spontaneous fruit of the anticipated victory.

Now, even more definitely than in the previous year, the Imperator indicated as the aim of the war the partition of Germany and the independence of all the German crowns ; it was for this aim that in a circular he demanded the armed help of the courts of the Confederation of the Rhine. An imperial embassy explained to the Senate how Napoleon had pledged himself to safeguard invaded Saxony from the ambitions of an unjust neighbour, and after the outbreak of the war a manifesto " to the peoples of Saxony " announced that France was coming to liberate them. The French, so far as in this dull generation there still existed any to trouble themselves about political questions, joyfully agreed with their ruler. Since Henry II had first presented himself in the guise of the eternal defender of German liberty, the protection of the German system of petty states was generally regarded as one of the tasks of French national policy. Just as readily did the princes of the Confederation of the Rhine follow the protector of German particularism. Frederick of Würtemberg exhibited all the wrath of offended majesty when the Duke of Brunswick exhorted him on behalf of the common fatherland and called to his mind the duties of German princes. The South German officers were delighted with the idea that now at length this arrogant Prussia was to be repaid for the disgraces of Rossbach and Leuthen.

Yet it was a holy war, for by this war and by its terrible miscarriage, the old order of German life was utterly destroyed. What had collapsed at Ratisbon was an empty shadow; but that which was destroyed on the battle-fields of Thuringia and East Prussia was the living German State, the only one which had given a content and an aim to the political existence of this people. It was going down to destruction when, after long years of aberration, it once more came to itself, and began to wage war against the enforced dominion of the foreigner and against the felony of its own princes. Nothing could be more honourable than the open and upright letter of defiance sent by the king to Napoleon; nothing could be better justified than were the three demands of the Prussian ultimatum of October 1st : the withdrawal of the French from Germany; the recognition of the North German Federation; a peaceful understanding concerning the other two questions still in dispute between the two powers. Even in the diffuse and ill-drafted war-manifesto we still find, here and there, a tone of worthy national pride. The king takes up arms, " in order to free unhappy Germany from the yoke now imposed upon the country; nations have rights which are greater than all treaties ! "

Neither in the people nor yet in the army was there as yet any idea of the great significance of the war. With the voice of one crying in the wilderness, Schleiermacher stood in the pulpit of the Ulrichskirche in Halle to interpret to the blind the signs of the times : " All our life is rooted in German freedom and German sentiment ; that is all that matters ! " Fichte, too, still remained solitary, and understood by but few. As soon as the serious significance of the war became manifest, there awakened in this valiant man a lively sense of the state. He resolutely discarded all his cosmopolitan dreams, and with flaming words he praised the occupation of those who were fighting on behalf of the fatherland. " What is the character of the warrior ? He must be capable of sacrifice. It is impossible for him to escape a soundness of sentiment, a genuine love of honour, an elevation towards something which is greater than life and its enjoyments." In the self-satisfied circles of the officers' corps, there was heard hardly so much as a laugh at the inspired speeches of the strange enthusiast ; here there was still dominant the stiff obscurity of the Frederician times, and in addition a spirit of carping criticism, which exercised its wit upon every command issued by those in authority. No one as yet fully understood how severely the army had been affected by the profound slumber of the last decade. The king himself, perhaps, had the clearest vision. His insight recognised the disorder, the self-sufficiency, the dullness which everywhere prevailed; but how would it have been possible for this retiring individual to make his own views felt in opposition to those of the world-renowned old Brunswicker ? The common soldier did his duties mechanically. The masses of the people remained cold and indifferent. Only the older ones who still remembered the great king trusted firmly in the sharp talons of the Prussian eagle and spoke boastfully of the march on Paris.

Thus began the only utterly disastrous campaign of the fortunate history of Prussian warfare. Unexampled as had been the rise of this state, equally unexampled was now to be its defeat, as ever memorable to all subsequent generations as a personally experienced sorrow, a warning to all towards watchfulness, humility, and loyalty. Napoleon was animated by a savage and malicious joy when he saw the most distinguished of the ancient powers helpless beneath his claws. Insults poured from his lips ; never before had he been so passionate, so full of hatred and cruelty. He felt that the last hope of Germany rested upon Prussia ; with the insight of the mean-minded man he recognised that these Hohenzollerns were made of other metal than the Emperor Francis and the satraps of the Confederation of the Rhine. In his addresses to the army it was the noble queen, above all, against whom he uttered the most malicious abuse. She, who had taken absolutely no part in the decisive negotiations of August, was to bear the blame for " the burghers' war " which had overtaken guileless France so unexpectedly ; she thirsted for blood, and like another Armida was madly setting her own castle in flames. Even before the swords were crossed, it was already decided that it was impossible for an honourable peace ever to be arranged between Napoleon and the Hohenzollerns. The Imperator scornfully concluded his war-manifesto with the words : " May Prussia learn, that while it is easy to gain territory and people by the friendship of France, her enmity is more terrible than the storms of the ocean ! "

Just as by the abuses of power of the previous winter Haugwitz had brought his state into its desperate diplomatic situation, so now he was responsible for the mistaken beginnings of the campaign. Notwithstanding its enormously heavy baggage, the Prussian army had completed the invasion of Thuringia earlier than the enemy ; but the intended invasion of France was not carried out, because Haugwitz wished first to await the issue of his ultimatum. A few invaluable days were lost in purposeless idling to the north of the Thuringian forest. Then came the news that the enemy were hurrying along the Nuremburg-Leipzig road to eastern Thuringia, threatening the Prussian left flank. The Duke of Brunswick feared for his line of communications, and ordered a withdrawal to the Elbe. While thus engaged, the army was simultaneously attacked from the south and from the east. The Imperator himself advanced northwards through the valley of the Saal. The advance guard of the Prussians was defeated at Saalfield; the death of the high-minded Prince Louis Ferdinand profoundly disturbed the morale of the troops, being regarded by them as an evil omen; and with disgust the officers heard the cry arise from the dispersed bodies of the Prussian army, the cry never heard in that army before, "We are cut off!" Prince Hohenlohe, ill-advised by the empty talker Massenbach, now forfeited in a single day the fame he had formerly acquired in knightly fashion on the Rhine. With his Prusso-Saxon corps, he withdrew past Jena to the table-land on the left bank of the Saal, and since he had received orders not to undertake any serious fighting, not only did he fail to cross the river, but failed also to occupy the valley and the heights overlooking the table-land. Napoleon immediately took advantage of the blunder, at once himself occupied the heights, torch in hand led the artillery up the steep slopes, and when the grey morning of October 14th broke, the Imperator was already secure of victory. How could this fraction of the Prussian army hold the position of Vierzehnheiligen against the French main body, which now began to attack from the commanding heights with an overwhelming preponderance of force? The German soldier fought bravely in a manner worthy of his ancient fame, now as always the Prussian cavalry showed itself superior to the French; it was only in dispersed fighting that the heavy infantry was unable to contend with the nimble tirailleurs of Napoleon. The French were inspired by the warlike ardour of young leaders accustomed to victory, whilst the allies were paralysed by the caution of their helpless old staff-officers. "Voyez donc le pauvre papa saxon!" cried the French soldier with mocking wonder to an old grey-headed colonel who had been taken prisoner. It would still have been possible for General Rüchel with his fresh troops to secure an orderly retreat for the beaten army, but he led his regiments in isolation to useless struggles. Thus it happened that the reserve was involved in the defeat, and when now in the early autumn night the retreat to Weimar was undertaken, the last moral bands which still held the army together were ruptured. Deaf to the exhortations of unloved leaders, the soldier thought only of himself. In formless masses the vestiges of the battalions and the batteries, interspersed with portions of the unending baggage-train, hastened across the table-land. Every bugle-call of the pursuing enemy increased the panic and confusion. "This was a horrible experience," writes Gneisenau referring to this dreadful night. "It would be a thousand times better to die than to live through it again!" In vain did he collect a few troops of the fugitives at the edge of the woods of Webicht, just in front of Weimar, in order to cover the retreat of the corps. He was to learn how great is the elemental might of terror over a stricken army ; a last random attack of the French cavalry, carried out in the obscurity of the night, once more led to a dispersal in wild confusion. Inextinguishably there remained in the spirit of the hero this picture of horror, an inheritance for the days of reprisal.

Simultaneously, a few miles lower down the river, Davoust gained an incomparably more difficult victory over the Prussian main body. He marched westward along the road from Naumberg in order to cut off the Prussians from the way to the Elbe. When on the morning of the 14th his columns emerged from the narrow pass of Kösen upon the undulating table-land which rises steeply above the left bank of the Saal, between Hessenhausen and Auerstedt, the two armies suddenly encountered one another in the thick fog, both of them on the march, neither of them expecting this battle, and the Prussians in this case greatly outnumbering the enemy. During the first hours of the battle the Duke of Brunswick was fatally wounded ; in the decisive moment the Prussian army was without a leader, for the king did not venture to take over the supreme command himself and had not yet nominated a commander-in-chief. Scharnhorst, indeed, pressed forward victoriously with the left wing, and believed that he had already saved the honour of the day ; but the cavalry of the right wing was unskilfully employed, and the second division under Kalckreuth took no part in the fight, for in this peace army no general dared to act on his own initiative. Thus the enemy succeeded, by using its ultimate reserves, in defeating the right wing of the Prussians, and now Scharnhorst, too, had to give way. The army retreated in tolerable order intending to turn northward at a point further to the west, near Buttstedt, and to take the road past Sangerhausen to Magdeburg. Hohenlohe had taken the same line of retreat from Weimar, and when, in the darkness of the night, the two beaten armies now encountered one another, the alarm became general, and the main army was involved in the disorder of the force of

Hohenlohe. The men were dull and unaffected in the face of the destruction of Old Prussia ; numbers of them lost their flags ; some even, who had been taken prisoner by the enemy and who were then rescued by a spirited troop of cavalry, refused to take up arms again. When the army drew nearer home, many of the soldiers deserted, those of long service saying to themselves that they had carried the musket long enough, that the king had plenty of young fellows, and that they might fight it out. The magic of the Frederician invulnerability had been destroyed, and a warlike fame beyond compare had been lost.

On October 15th Napoleon imposed upon all the Prussian provinces on the hither side of the Vistula a tax of 159,000,000 francs, on the ground that the battle of the day before had signified the conquest of the whole of this region. Never had the favourite of fortune boasted more audaciously, and yet, through a remarkable fatality, the most criminal of lies was to become a literal truth. Immediately after the defeat the Court of Dresden carried out its long-planned desertion, and went over to Napoleon. A week later, the Prussian domains on the left bank of the Elbe, as well as the possessions of the House of Orange and the House of Hesse, were temporarily annexed to the French empire. The system of ambiguous neutrality, which, with Napoleon's consent, had been adopted by the elector of Hesse, was now punished ; the conqueror would no longer tolerate a secret enemy at his back. In Münster, the devotees of the ancient liberty of the estates rejoiced in the throwing off of the Prussian yoke ; the black-and-white turnpikes were torn down, the French and Münsterland flags waved to cele-brate the entry of the Napoleonic troops. In Hanover, too, the black eagles were hastily removed, and the dismissal of the Prussian officials was greeted with unconcealed delight.

Whilst the new provinces were thus lost, the reserve army at Halle underwent a defeat ; and since it withdrew to Magdeburg instead of guarding the capital, Napoleon was able to continue unhindered his victorious march to Berlin along the chord of the wide arc which the beaten forces occupied. Terribly now had to be avenged the self-satisfied arrogance of the times of peace None of the fortresses were properly armed, for no one had regarded as conceivable the entrance of an enemy into the heart of the mon-archy ; and the unwieldy fiscal system which, after the method of a good domestic economist, measured the expenditure in accordance with the income, provided absolutely no means for extraordinary expenses. Many of the commanders of the fortresses had been valiant officers, but their sense of duty did not spring from love for the fatherland, being due simply to pride of caste. To them the army was everything, and in their invincible arrogance they calmly awaited the inevitable victory of the Frederician regiments. When the alarming intelligence of the defeat spread through the country, when the miserable remnants of this invincible army reached Magdeburg, filling the whole town with alarm and confusion, it seemed to these old officers as if the world were coming to an end ; all resistance was useless ; everything on which their life had depended for support had crumbled to pieces. After the fall of Erfurt, which capitulated disgracefully immediately after the battle, the principal fortresses of the old state, Magdeburg, Küstrin, Stettin, and a number of smaller places, opened their gates.

With a sound good sense the loyal people visited most of its wrath upon the generals, for just as the loss of the double battle was mainly due to bad leadership, so also was this last disgrace attributable to the generals. Everywhere the conduct of the garrisons showed that they were worthy of a better fate. Young officers broke their swords in despair, common soldiers placed the muzzles of their muskets against their breasts and fired, not wishing to survive the shame of the capitulation ; in Küstrin several battalions rose in mutiny against their dishonoured commanders. But so ineffective had now become the power of public censure, that subsequently not one of these old men who had thus forgotten their duty had the courage when overtaken by disgraceful punishment to atone for the stain on their honour by voluntary death. Prince Hohenlohe, even, ended in dishonour. With unspeakable privations, he had led the vestiges of his corps by a wide detour to the Uckermark, and then the French overtook him at Prenzlau, in the marshes by the Ucker See. Exhausted in body and mind, profoundly disturbed by the reports of misfortune which reached him from all sides, he allowed himself to be discouraged by the suggestions of Massenbach, and to be grossly deceived by Murat's falsehoods as to the strength of the enemy ; in the true style of the adventurer of the empire, the brother-in-law of Napoleon pledged his word of honour to a deliberate lie. A last despairing attack by Prince August failed, and the army of Hohenlohe capitulated in the open field. Such was the end of that knightly prince who had once been an ornament of the Prussian army, who amid the disorder of the days of the Confederation of the Rhine had alone among the princes of the South maintained honourable courage and German loyalty.

The army was annihilated. After the fall of Stettin and Küstrin, the line of the Oder had also become untenable, and it seemed hopeless to attempt to offer a last resistance with the aid of the East Prussian regiments on the further side of the Vistula. Napoleon wrote in a satisfied mood to the Sultan, " Prussia has vanished." Even Gentz considered that " it would be ridiculous to dream any longer of the revival of Prussia!" How many storms had passed over this State since its rulers had shown it the steep path that leads to great things ; often before had the capital seen the enemies of the country within its walls ; but now for the first time in Prussia's history was disgrace associated with misfortune. Shame and rue raged in every heart, and the coarse joy of the conqueror made him refrain from nothing which might increase these painful sensations. Designedly he displayed his contempt for everything Prussian ; in the royal castle of the Hohenzollerns he penned new and filthy libels against Queen Louise. While sending the coat and sword of Frederick the Great to the Invalides, he poured his scorn out on this people that left the grave of its greatest man so unadorned ; the Imperial Guard destroyed the obelisk on the battle-field of Rossbach ; the figure of Victory was torn down from the Brandenburg Gate, to disappear in a shed on the Seine. What a spectacle it was when the brilliant regiment of the Gensdarmes, disarmed, ragged, and almost starving, was driven up and down Unter den Linden like a drove of beasts. To the sound of drums and trumpets, in a ceremonial procession, there were carried through the streets the old banners with their aspiring eagles and whole baskets full of silver kettledrums and trumpets, witnesses of old glory and new shame. Of all the troops that had been in the field, the Garde du Corps was the only regiment that had saved all its distinctions of honour. It was soon forbidden that any Prussian uniform should be worn in Berlin ; even the pensioned officers were to lay aside the blue coat. In addition there were intolerable taxes, there were arrogance, debauchery, and the oppression of billeting. On November 21st Napoleon issued from Berlin that incredible decree which forbade all trade with England, and condemned all English goods to confiscation ; the Continental System was founded, and for years to come the well-being of Germany was forcibly repressed.

There were not lacking traits of dishonourable servitude. The baseness that is not absent from any nation appeared here more hateful than anywhere else, for German uncouthness lacks understanding of the dubious art which characterises the more refined culture of the Romans, whereby an outward respectability is preserved even amid baseness. Many a man of mean spirit crawled to offer his services to the conqueror. Lange, Buchholz, and other leaders of Berlin enlightenment, glorified the victory of reason over the prejudices of the nobles. The hatred of the people for the arrogance of the officers manifested itself in various outbreaks of rude mockery. Moreover, the cumbrous pedantry and the stupid punctiliousness of the officialdom, paralysed the powers of resistance of the state ; in this time of disorder all the authorities continued quietly to carry on their daily work, so that the conquering invader found everywhere an ordered apparatus and administration ready to his hand, and many a well-meaning old War Office clerk became, without knowing it, a tool in the hands of the enemy. Among the instances of open treachery, none appear so shameful as the desertion of Johannes Müller. The triumphs of the Imperator induced in this enthusiastic admirer of Old German and of Swiss freedom, a mood of servile admiration ; with a complete change of front, he glorified in swelling periods Napoleon and Frederick as the heroes of the modern world. His old comrade Gentz thereupon broke off their friendship in a rage, and wished for him one punishment only, that he might see the usurper overthrown and Germany free once again ! Less unworthy but no less morbid was the scientific indifference with which Hegel regarded the destruction of his fatherland. When Napoleon burst over the field of Jena, it seemed to Hegel as if the world's soul had been displayed in bodily form, and from the fall of Prussia he deduced the sagacious doctrine that spirit always gains the victory over spiritless reasoning and sophistry. Generally speaking, in Thuringia, the first overwhelming impression of misfortune was speedily dissipated, and it was only under the pitiless oppression of the following years that the people of Mid-Germany came to learn how firmly intertwined was its own life with the destiny of the Prussian State.

In the old provinces of Prussia, the change of mood began sooner, immediately after the first defeats. Napoleon's unbridled and ever-growing hatred for Prussia was nourished upon the secret suspicion that in this state, notwithstanding all the shame and the folly of recent weeks, there still slumbered an untamable force of will, such as the Imperator had never before encountered upon the Continent. What the Prussian soldier was capable of under powerful leadership was shown by the retreat of Blucher's army. In these battles several young heroes, who were subsequently to help in leading the state towards brighter days, first became known to friend and foe. With the remnants of the reserve army and some other troops, Blucher crossed the Elbe, near Magdeburg, in order to effect a junction with the forces under Hohenlohe ; and while the river was being crossed, Colonel York with his yagers held off the pursuing army for several hours in the brilliant battle of Altenzaun. When the proposed junction with Hohenlohe was rendered impossible by the news of the capitulation of Prenzlau, Scharnhorst conceived the audacious plan of turning against the flank and the rear of the French, in order to divert a portion of the hostile army from the Mark. The small force hastened towards Mecklenburg, and actually succeeded in luring three French army corps in pursuit. Even amid all the troubles and distresses of this difficult retreat, in the free spirit of Scharnhorst there began to waken the creative ideas of military reform of which he had given the first indications in the spring, in his memorial upon the militia. With convincing clearness, in a conversation with Müffling held in Gadebusch, he showed that in the defeats of the last weeks the severest and ultimate source of all the misfortunes had been the failure of the common soldier to participate in the action, and that what was above all needed was to transform the army in such a way that it should come to feel itself at one with the fatherland. [1]

Subsequently the army fought with desperate courage at the gates and in the streets of Lübeck against a superior force of the enemy, and it was only when all provisions and all munitions of war had been lost, and when further resistance was utterly impossible, that Blucher laid down his arms in Rattkau. This was a struggle full of heroic rage, such as the miserable campaign of 1805 had never seen ; and altogether different from the thought-less curiosity of the Viennese now appeared the worthy conduct of the great majority of the people of Berlin, in face of Napoleon's entry. Never before had anyone spoken so frankly to the Imperator as the preacher Erman, who at the greeting at the gate said plainly that a servant of the Gospel could not lie, and that it was therefore impossible for him to pretend that he rejoiced at the entrance of the enemy.

The pitiless reality of the war destroyed the phrases of enlightened vanity, destroyed that dream-world of the reason, in which the over-culture of the great town was accustomed to lose its way, and it forced the slack spirits once more to hate and to

[1] Recorded by Müffling in a memorial upon the Landwehr, which he transmitted to Hardenberg on July 12, 1821.

love cordially. With the well-being of intellectual sociability there disappeared also the world of literary make-believe. Now that misery dwelt in every home, even the pride of culture recognised the forcible hand of the living God ; the man of learning came to understand just as much as the man of simple mind, what this perplexing life of ours becomes without faith, and what a miserable creature is man without his nation. The longer the billeting lasted, the more serious, the more collected, the more Prussian, became the general mood, and soon the town of frivolous criticism was hardly to be recognised. All waited in breathless suspense to hear the news from the East Prussian theatre of war. The maimed veterans played upon their hurdy-gurdys the song of lament for Prince Louis Ferdinand, the one folk-song which had come into existence in the dull misery of the present war ; and on the birthday of the beloved queen, behind all the curtained windows of Berlin, lights were burned in defiance of the prohibition of the French governor. In the provinces too, there began an awakening from the slumber of the times of peace ; many a weatherproof old peasant looked with grim hope towards the picture of the great king hanging on the wall.

Thus amid distress and shame did Barthold Niebuhr first learn to know the Prussian people and cleave to it with all the passion of his great heart, recognising that noble natures appear greater in evil fortune than in good. Immediately before the battle of Jena, he had left Denmark to enter the service of the Prussian state, and when on the retreat to Königsberg he was associating with the Pomeranians and the Old Prussians, he wrote confidently : " I never expected to find in association so much energy, seriousness, loyalty, and good humour ; if they had been properly led, these people would have been unconquerable by the whole world ! " But the crowd must always feel before they can hear. As far as the masses were concerned, it was only the enduring need of the coming year that was to win them fully for the ideas of liberation ; and it was among the warlike nobles and among the men of learning that anger for the fatherland was aroused far sooner and far more easily. The military pride of ancient Prussia and the bold idealism of the new German literature suddenly encountered one another in a single idea. Amid the destruction of the old monarchy, there was already prepared the groundwork of that great change which has determined the course of our history in the nineteenth century—the reconciliation of the Prussian state with the freedom of German culture. In the old generation of soldiers there prevailed a savage bitterness against the foreign dominion, and many brave men belonging to those circles voluntarily offered their services to the king. Fichte, too, went of his own free will to Königsberg, because he could not bend his head beneath the yoke of the oppressor. Around Schleiermacher there was quietly assembling a circle of warm-hearted patriots. This loyal spirit saw " the regeneration of Germany arising out of its profound humiliation " ; he wished to play his part in speech and writing, and he considered this to be the last moment in which he ought to forsake his king. " Free speech is the sharpest poison for Napoleon," he said. Not for an instant did he believe in the permanence of the triumph of France, holding that this conqueror had " too little of the kingly spirit."

Completely overwhelmed by the unexpected defeat, King Frederick William had, immediately after the battle, offered peace under humiliating conditions. These were the most deplorable days of his life. Some of his counsellors even recommended that Prussia should join the Confederation of the Rhine. It was the arrogance of the conqueror which first restored to the unhappy prince a consciousness of his royal duties. Napoleon raised his demands in the course of the negotiations, asking not only the cession of all the territories westward of the Elbe, but also that Prussia should withdraw from the Russian alliance. This touched the king's pride. His conscience would not allow him to do what the Emperor Francis, in a far more favourable situation, had done without a thought a year before ; he could not consent to abandon the ally whose help he had so recently besought. On November 21st, in the headquarters at Osterode, a council was held concerning the acceptance of a truce which Lucchesini and Zastrow had pusillanimously subscribed. Then came the moment when the men separated themselves from the boys and from the wiseacres. Not only did Stein, who had rescued the state treasure, the means for the continuation of the war, by moving it into East Prussia, advise the rejection of the treaty, but the same course was taken by his political opponent, the high tory Count Voss, a leading noble of the Mark. The king took the same view, and here in the remote eastern Mark, the last bulwark of German freedom, he again took up arms. Immediately afterwards he dismissed Haugwitz. From this day onwards, the much misunderstood monarch, though he may often have erred and vacillated in detail, held firmly and invincibly through six terrible years to the idea that no honourable peace could be concluded with France until after the re-establishment of Prussia. Thus began the campaign in East Prussia, the first in which the sun did not shine uncloudedly upon the Imperator, the first which in despairing Europe awakened a glimmer of hope that perhaps after all this man of might was not invincible.

Napoleon's sharp gaze soon led him to recognise that in North Germany it was necessary for him to draw the reins of his dominion tighter than in the regions of the Confederation of the Rhine. In the south he was surrounded by the tried allies of France who ruled their new-formed states docilely in accordance with the principles freshly imported from France ; in the north he had to do with a tougher population, utterly refractory to the French system, and he found there a strict Protestant civilisation, cumbrous feudal institutions, and ancient princely races which were closely allied with Prussia, England, and Russia. In the north, therefore, he was from the first more severe, and retained the whole of the north-western region, the lands of the Guelphs, the Hesses, and the Oranges, at the disposal of his own relatives. One only of the established North German dynasties was welcome to him as a natural friend, and this was the House of the Albertines, the old rivals of the Hohenzollerns, and it was on behalf of the sovereignty of the Albertines that he had professedly taken up arms. On December 11th, by the Peace of Posen, the elector of Saxony was admitted into the Confederation of the Rhine, and received a royal crown. In order to detach the new king permanently from Prussia, Napoleon promised to give him Prussian Lower Lusatia and the loyal district of Kottbus in exchange for the Mansfeld territory, and bade him send an auxiliary corps into the field against his betrayed ally. The Imperator also secured the personal gratitude of the bigot Frederick Augustus, in that he ordained the equality of the Catholics and the Protestants in Saxony, an innovation which the court of Dresden had never been able to carry into effect among its rigid Lutheran population. This last step of Napoleon's was, moreover, something more than a mere diplomatic move, for from year to year there continually became plainer the inner kinship which associates every modern world-empire with the Roman world-church. Not even the heir of the Revolution could dispense with the help of Rome, just as little as could formerly Charles V. His letters to the Holy See and his embassies to the Senate, expressly drew attention to the fact that he had everywhere delivered our holy religion from its Protestant persecutors, and that he was unceasingly at war with England, the deadly enemy of the Roman Church.

German submissiveness celebrated its saturnalia even more meanly in Electoral Saxony than it had done a year earlier in Bavaria. How delighted were the Saxons to take an equal rank with their proud Prussian neighbours! In the spring of 1807, whilst the fight for the last remnants of German freedom was proceeding along the Vistula, the town of Leipzig instituted a magnificent festival in honour of the new Saxon crown. The sun of Napoleon, the boastful image which he had borrowed from his predecessor Louis XIV, shone everywhere over the decorated streets. In the market places was erected an altar to the fatherland; the students marched up in festal array, burned torches before the altar, and sang exultingly, "Our Fatherland is saved!" Even the dead bodies in the university dissecting-room were to take part in the national delight of Saxony, for an illuminated inscription over the entrance to the room announced, "Even the dead call out, Hail!"

In Napoleon's eyes, the other petty princes of the north were no more than Prussian vassals and officers, and he would gladly have got rid of them one and all. But these extraordinary state-structures were so dispersed that their annexation was difficult; moreover, in the Confederation of the Rhine there was not at the moment to be found a trustworthy king to whom they could be presented. The Imperator had more serious matters to consider; he would not devote to this question more attention than it deserved; and he wished above all to bring the negotiations to a speedy conclusion, because he desired to make immediate use of the smaller contingents in the Prussian war. For this reason, when the petty princes of Thuringia and Westphalia, some of them in person and others by proxy, besought the favour of the conqueror at the headquarters in Posen, they received a tolerably gracious reception. For the third time there began the hateful drama of the German land-chaffering, and for the third time the gold of German princes poured into the bottomless pockets of Napoleonic diplomacy; and the negotiations went on happily, for in the Nassau statesman Hans von Gagern the oppressed little princes found an alert and disinterested commission agent. This extraordinary admirer of ancient German liberty had derived from his learned historical inquiries the conclusion that pure Germanism, the true greatness of Germany, consisted in the motley disintegration of its national life. When now he heard of the anxieties of the petty lords of the north, he hastened to the scene, took the part of those who were in danger, and by his busy activities so far held in check his old admirer Talleyrand that the Frenchman, in any case a proud aristocrat and well-disposed towards the German high nobility, at length acceded to all the desires of the indefatigable German. Nor was there lacking humour worthy of such a situation. " Give me one of your petty princes," once exclaimed Talleyrand's assistant, La Besnardière ; " Not one," answered the zealous saviour of particularism, " you must swallow the whole lot of them, even if it should choke you ! "

Thus it was as sovereigns that the Ernestines and the Ascanians, the Reusses and the Schwarzburgs, the Lippes and the Waldecks, entered the Confederation of the Rhine. The count of Bückeburg at the same time acquired the princely title, for the French were carrying on the business in a spirit of contemptuous levity, and in the treaty spoke simply of the two Princes of Lippe. Subsequently, however, Napoleon complained angrily that in these negotiations he had, for the first time, been deceived, and said if he had known where Reuss, Lippe, and Waldeck really were, their princes would not have received thrones. He never forgot that these dynasts of the north had once constituted the nucleus of the Prussian party in the empire. For this reason he was always a strict master to them, would not allow them any expansion of territory, nor would admit them to kinship, whereas after his brutal manner he displayed a certain good feeling towards the rulers at Dresden and in the South German courts. It was for this reason also that the patriarchal little peoples of the North German petty states remained quite uninfluenced by the Napoleonic cult which found so many advocates in Electoral Saxony and South Germany ; the peasants of Thuringia and Mecklenburg felt themselves personally offended when they saw their tribal dukes humiliated before the foreign potentate. But the end of the matter was that even while the war continued, Prussia was thrust out of Germany (as in the previous autumn Austria had been thrust out), while the totality of the petty states of those of medium size were subjected to the Protector of the Confederation of the Rhine.

While the German allies were abandoning Prussia, this unfortunate state had to atone for the partition of Poland. The Slav domains, whose possession during the last decade had brought the internal development of the monarchy to a standstill, proved untenable in the hour of danger. Four weeks after the battle of Jena, Dombrowski raised the standard of revolt in Poland ; all the nobles hastened to place themselves beneath the banner of the white eagle, and soon the disturbance extended throughout the territory which had been annexed to Prussia in the last two partitions. The king could not endure the burden of his lofty office unless he were secure of the love and fidelity of his subjects, and he considered that the state must be held together by moral bonds. The spectacle of this great defection filled his soul with profound bitterness, but he recognised with sobriety how this national movement could not possibly be restrained, and he paid no attention to the fantastic proposals of Prince Radziwill, who dreamed of a royalist counter-movement. The revolt of the ancient ally of France was more than welcome to the Imperator. He eagerly encouraged the disturbance, distributed arms among the rebels, incited the Poles in the Prussian regiments to desert, and recorded in his bulletins that the Polish people was now showing itself in really interesting colours. At the same time he carefully guarded himself against giving the Poles any definite pledge. Coldly and distinctly did he see through these Sarmatian Junkers, recognising their stormy courage, but also their levity, their egoism, their political incapacity. The country was valuable to him as a source of excellent auxiliary troops, and as a means for preparing the long-planned humiliation of Russia; he was ready, if circumstances should make it seem desirable, to restore to the Poles the semblance of political independence.

The Polish rebellion at length made it necessary for the czar to furnish the assistance which he had promised his Prussian friend. But it was not as mere auxiliaries as had been assumed in the previous autumn, that the Russian forces appeared upon Prussian soil. The Russians had to bear the burden and heat of the day, and payment must now be made for the light-heartedness with which the Turkish War had been begun, since only a portion of the Russian army was available for Prussia. In the unhappy frontier land there were renewed the horrors of the Seven Years' War. Before long the undisciplined roughness of the Russian friends became even more detestable to the plundered Prussian countryman than was the rage of the enemy; and there had also to be endured the spectacle of the bad leadership of the Russians and the intolerable arrogance which their officers displayed towards the valiant little Prussian army of General Lestocq. Nevertheless, this campaign, which dragged on indecisively for months upon the devastated plains of Poland and Prussia, was the first which shook the victorious confidence of the Napoleonic army. The French soldiers, accustomed to rapid successes and rich booty, to the comfortable life of the vine-lands of the south, began to murmur, and to ask if their insatiable leader was never going to weary of fighting. For several

weeks in succession Lestocq's army defended, with ancient Prussian
tenacity, the crossing of the Vistula into Kulmerland ; and when at
length summoned to join the Russian army in the east, these poor
remnants of the Prussian army proved decisive in the first battle
which the conqueror failed to win. On February 7 and 8, 1807,
at Eylau, Napoleon endeavoured by a vigorous attack to drive
the army of the allies eastward. On the second day of the battle,
after a murderous struggle, the left wing of the Russian forces had
been thrown into disorder. Thereupon Scharnhorst recognised
that the decisive moment had come. He moved the troops of
Lestocq, which, after an exhausting march, had just arrived upon
the extreme right wing of the allies, against the enemy's centre.
Once again did the star of fortune of the Frederician days seem to
shine over the Germans, when the little Prussian force, with bands
playing and banners waving, advanced through the ranks of the
fleeing Russians towards the forest of Kutschitten, and then drove
the enemy before them, past Anklappen.

The French attack had failed. In opposition to all his customs,
the Imperator was compelled, after these undecisive battles, to enter
winter quarters ; and so powerful was the impression produced
by this first failure, that immediately after the battle Napoleon
approached the king with new proposals of peace. Mingling
flattery with threats, he wrote that this was the finest moment of
his life ; the Prussian nation must be restored as a protective wall
between Russia and France, either under the House of Brandenburg
or any other princely race ; he would restore all the lands on the
hither side of the Elbe ; he thought no more of Poland now that
he had come to know the country. Unmistakable, however, was
the deceiver's intention to separate Prussia from her ally, in order
subsequently, after the overthrow of Russia, to humiliate further
the king of Prussia, abandoned by all the world. Frederick William
did not hesitate for a moment, and firmly rejected the French
proposals. It was first in misfortune that the passive virtues of
loyalty and staying power in which the strength of his character
lay, came to light. The royal house, which was now carrying on
its impoverished existence in Memel on the last corner of German
territory, became for the whole country an example of honourable
resignation, of pious trust in God. More cordially, more intimately
than in the days of good fortune did the proud people of East
Prussia adhere to the ruling dynasty. Throughout the country
everyone related admiringly of the beautiful queen how, though ill
and though a terrible snow storm was raging, she had fled along

the waste of the Kurische Nerung, thinking it better to fall into God's hands than into the enemy's ; and how she subsequently stood confidently and courageously by the side of her profoundly afflicted spouse.

It was true that a free and courageous spirit was still lacking to the guidance of the state. It was not possible that in a moment should be overcome the effects of a decade of weakness and of half measures. Severe exhortations were issued to the troops, and severe punishments were inflicted upon those garrison-commanders of the fortresses who had forgotten their duty. The conduct of Lestocq's little army was exemplary ; and Scharnhorst, who in the previous year had brought about the formation of large divisions composed of all arms, now actually laid aside the old cumbrous linear tactics, and directed the movements of the army in accordance with the principles of the new and bolder conduct of war, which the king himself impressed upon his officers in a thoroughgoing course of instruction. But the equipment of nineteen reserve battalions was effected so slowly that none of them came to be utilised in the field. An appeal for the general arming of the people, already signed by the king, was never issued, because the loyal estates of East Prussia made urgent representations to the effect that the nobles could serve only in the royal army, but never in a Landsturm. Nor did the civil administration pass for many months out of a moribund state of transition. The monarch was not yet able to see that the obsolete cabinet government was irreconcilable with the independent responsibility of the ministers; and he dismissed Stein, with harsh and unjust words, when the baron openly and passionately advocated the abolition of the cabinet. Hardenberg knew better how to manage the king. His frankness, which always continued to display itself in amiable and quiet forms, at length prevailed, and on April 26, 1807, there was quietly effected a change in the constitution, the most significant in its consequences which the ancient absolutism had experienced since the days of Frederick William I. Cabinet government was abolished, and Hardenberg became prime minister and foreign secretary and was charged also with all matters concerning the conduct of the war.

Even after the partial success of Eylau, the position of the allies remained extremely serious. However successfully the toughest of Napoleon's opponents was fighting on the sea, in the management of continental affairs the shopkeeping spirit of England showed now, as formerly, a maladroitness which was already beginning to become proverbial. Whereas three years earlier not a single hand had been raised in London to defend Hanover against the French, Prussia was immediately punished by a declaration of war for her occupation of the electoral princedom ; and when, in January, 1807, peace was made between England and the Prussian court, and Prussia abandoned her claims to Hanover, the cabinet of St. James's did nothing to support her new ally against the common enemy. No treaty of subsidies was signed. Count Münster, whose advice was decisive in London regarding all German affairs, could not overcome the old Guelph mistrust of Prussia. Austria had not been shaken out of her neutrality even by the terrible news of the Polish rebellion. Both parties were eagerly wooing the Hofburg. Napoleon offered Silesia in exchange for Galicia ; the czar sent Pozzo di Borgo, the deadly enemy of the House of Bonaparte, to Vienna, with urgent exhortations ; the king of Prussia, in his great difficulties, declared himself willing to permit the temporary occupation of the Silesian forests by an army of Austrian auxiliaries. Archduke Charles, however, remained faithful to his pacifist policy. To cloak Austrian inactivity, the offer was at length made that Austria should intermediate to secure peace, but in such a situation this offer was of no avail. The friendship of the czar was the last hope of the tottering Prussian monarchy, and the enthusiastic young Russian was not sparing of fine words when, in the spring, he appeared in person upon the theatre of war. How amiably he behaved in his intercourse with the royal family, saying fervently to his unhappy friend, " It is true, is it not, neither of us can fall alone ? " and to many an honourable Prussian it seemed that he now for the first time fully understood Alexander's greatness of heart.

It is characteristic of Hardenberg's nature, of his unshaken courage, and of his happy-go-lucky instability, that at such a time, when the whole existence of Prussia was still at stake, he ventured to bring forward a profound and comprehensive plan for the re-ordering of Germany and of the entire state-system. For more than ten years he had cherished the hope that with the aid of France he might construct a North German great power, which should counterbalance the House of Austria. As soon as he came to recognise the vanity of this dream, he at once adopted a new system of German policy, to which he remained faithful until his death, the policy of a regulated dualism. Fate, however, had spoken with no uncertain voice ; both Austria and Prussia were beaten in isolation, and nothing but their faithful co-operation could liberate Germany. During the following years, all Prussian patriots without distinction of party united upon this idea ; as if by force of nature, it found simultaneous expression in a hundred troubled hearts. In the writings of Gentz, the notion returns again and again as a *ceterum censeo*. In the artistic drawings in which Colonel Knesebeck loved to represent the future of Europe, the European balance was always maintained by the alliance between Austria and Prussia. Arndt and Kleist swore to restore the two mightiest sons of Germany to mutual harmony. Queen Louise longed for the day when the reconciled German brethren should join in the holy war. The king alone quietly held to his old opinion, and when he thought of an anti-French European league, Russia always came first in his mind. Hardenberg, on the other hand, now considered the rivalry of the two German powers as an obsolete and unhappy prejudice, for their interests were identical. Simply, magnanimously, and without any ulterior motive, he prepared these plans ; not one of his state-papers shows any kind of concealed hostility towards Austria. He believed that by maintaining friendly and neighbourly relations, the ancient opposition of interests might be completely allayed, and it is undeniable that his policy corresponded to the needs of the immediate future.

It was in this spirit also that the new treaty of alliance was drawn up which was signed on April 26th at Bartenstein by Prussia and Russia. The two powers pledged themselves not to lay down their arms until Germany had been liberated, and the French had been driven back across the Rhine ; the German domain was to be safeguarded by a chain of fortresses along the left bank of the Rhine, whilst Austria was to be secured in the south-west by Tyrol and the line of the Mincio ; instead of the Confederation of the Rhine there was to be constituted a German league of sovereign states under the common leadership of the two great powers, in such a way that Austria should be supreme in the south and Prussia in the north ; as regards the dominion of Prussia, this was to be restored to the *status quo* of 1805, with rounded off and strengthened frontiers ; finally, there was to be an increase of the Guelph domain on German soil and, if at all possible, the independence of Holland was to be restored. By a special article, the door was left open for the accession of the Hofburg to the league ; the adhesion of England and Sweden was also securely counted on. With remarkable confidence there were manifested here almost all the ideas which were to be actually realised in the year 1814.

The court of Vienna, however, was alarmed by the rashness of this policy. Count Stadion's sympathies were estranged when he heard that such audacious plans had been made without the assent of the Hofburg, and would not go beyond the terms of the Peace of Pressburg. How little, too, did the Russian conduct of the war correspond to the bold flight of Hardenberg's proposals. It was only the co-operation of fortune and the valour of the soldiers which had enabled the mediocre capabilities of General Bennigsen to win the laurels of Eylau. This leader carefully guarded himself against putting his fame to further hazard, and for four long months remained almost stationary. Meanwhile Napoleon, in his winter quarters at Osterode, displayed a feverish activity. He strengthened his army, raised the conscription levies of 1808 in advance, made the princes of the Confederation of the Rhine constitute a reserve army, conducted from afar the defence of Constantinople against the English fleet, and at the same time carried on the investment of Danzig. Since this place was to serve him as a point of support for the continuation of the campaign, he determined for the second and last time in his military career to undertake the weary work of a formal siege, which he had always shunned since the battles round Mantua. The fortress was bravely defended by General Kalckreuth, and in the attempts to relieve the siege, Colonel Bülow, already a distinguished officer in the new German army, gained great renown. But since Bennigsen would venture nothing to liberate this important place, Kalckreuth was forced on May 27th into an honourable capitulation.

The fierce old General Courbiere defended himself with better success in Graudenz. In the mountains of the Silesian frontier, Count Götzen, a fiery spirit in a weak frame, also maintained a petty warfare with far-sighted boldness. But of all the deeds of the allied armies, the most conspicuous was the heroic defence of the little Farther Pomeranian fortress of Kolberg. Here, in this loyal town, which during the Seven Years' War had thrice withstood a superior force of the enemy, was the cradle of the new Prussian military renown ; here there first awakened that sacred wrath of the nation, which after six painful years was to compel the liberation of the world ; here was to appear upon the stage of history a man who better than any other embodied the true spirit of the Prussian soldier, combining incisive courage with clear insight. Twenty years of tedium in garrison-life as a subaltern had not destroyed the youthful freshness of Gneisenau. Kindly and frank, altogether free from selfishness, and a man of modest disposition though inclined to exercise an ironical wit upon stupidity and meanness, he stood on the very summit of culture. His comprehensive vision embraced the whole circle of the national history of a gigantic time, but his wealth in ideas did not lead him astray from the happy belief that the energies of a strong people are inexhaustible, and did not disturb his bold delight in adventure and fighting. In the fire of his glance, in the serene majesty of his appearance, there was to be found some of that charm which had once radiated from the young king Frederick. In the threatened fortress, everything suddenly assumed a new aspect when the unknown major came to take command of the despairing garrison; when out of the motley force in Kolberg he speedily constituted a fine body of men, inspired by a sentiment of victory; and when he induced the valiant burghers, led by the daring old seaman, Nettelbeck, to take part in the work of defence. " I took everything into my own hands," so he tells us, " behaved like an independent prince, being even somewhat despotic; I cashiered cowardly officers; lived happily among the brave fellows; did not bother myself about the future, and kept a sturdy front." The enemy's generals noted with astonishment how this man of genius was able to carry on war in a manner which placed his soldiers on an equal footing with the French. The defender changed roles wih the attacker, harassed the besiegers by surprise-sallies, threw up earthworks in the open country, which for many weeks kept the enemy away from the walls of the fortress. The high-spirited love of song characteristic of the old German soldiers, which in this melancholy war had elsewhere been in abeyance, was now revived; mockingly the men sang on their unconquered walls

> "We've plenty of cannon, we're all free from care,
> So toddle off homewards, and don't waste time here."

Simultaneously, not far from Kolberg, Schill, the bold hussar, was engaged in adventurous skirmishing, and Gneisenau learnt with a delight altogether free from envy how the masses were hailing this brave but narrow man as the hero of the fatherland. He was well satisfied as long as the oppressed soul of our people was once more hopefully aspiring, no matter upon whose image their gaze was fixed. In Hither Pomerania, Marwitz got together a volunteer corps, " for the liberation of the German fatherland," as the brave young fellow said to his men. In Westphalia, the faithful Vincke endeavoured to raise a revolt. Blucher, with a small Prussian force, with the aid of auxiliary Swedish troops, and in the hope of further help from an English army which was expected at Rügen, devoted himself to making a diversion in Napoleon's rear. To the Imperator the tenacious Prussian nature became daily more detestable. In a terrible rage, he termed Schill a robber ; in his newspapers he had the king described as a simpleton, who hardly deserved to rank as an adjutant beside Alexander ; he was resolved to destroy utterly this inconvenient state which he could no longer pardon.

Then came the decisive moment in East Prussia. In June, the general uneasiness about the fall of Danzig made it necessary for the Russian commander-in-chief at length to set his army in motion. The French attack was happily defeated at Heilsberg. When Napoleon now advanced down the Alle, in order to surround the Russians, Bennigsen, ignorant of the enemy's strength, undertook an ill-advised attack against the French columns, and at Friedland, on June 14th, was completely defeated. On the anniversary of Marengo, the Prussian War came to an end, for after this one battle, Alexander's courage collapsed, as suddenly as it had formerly after the battle of Austerlitz. His own land was still untouched by the enemy, but he dreaded a revolution in Russian Poland. His brother Constantine and the great majority of the generals were openly opposing this war for foreign ends, and even Stadion had already asked the Russian ambassador why the czar wished to sacrifice himself for Prussia. The fickle-minded man considered that he had done all that generosity demanded. Without notifying the king, who continued to believe firmly in the affectionate assurances of his friend, Alexander offered a truce. Napoleon eagerly accepted the offer. He was not now in a position to carry the war into the interior of Russia, and he was also anxious about the vacillating position of Austria, which at this time was despatching a negotiator to the allies. In a few days he succeeded in gaining over the czar for the French alliance. It was not that Alexander's shrewdness had ever trusted this ally. It was only that he hoped for a few years to derive advantage from the new friendship. If, with the help of France, two wishes dear to the heart of the young emperor could be fulfilled, if Finland could be conquered, and if a firm foot could be planted in the Balkan peninsula, Russia, thus strengthened, might hope to resume the war for the liberation of the world with better success. Blinded by such alluring prospects, Alexander hardly noticed that the Napoleonic world-empire and the Continental System could not exist without overthrowing Russia, and that by the occupation of Danzig, and the reconstruction of a Polish state, the Imperator was already preparing, long in advance, a decisive war against his new friend.

After the two emperors had united in an offensive and defensive alliance and in a common war against England, Russia's forsaken ally was summoned to the council. The king had behaved in knightly fashion, continuing the struggle until almost the last foot of his country had been lost. Now it was inevitable that he should give way, for what could an appeal to the Germans, such as Hardenberg wished him to make, avail at this hour? When upon the raft in the Memel, Frederick William met the conqueror, he could not conceal the profound antipathy in his honourable heart, whilst for the beaten enemy the conqueror could exhibit only an ill-natured contempt, and could utter only growling proposals. Even the requests of the ill-used queen, who on behalf of her country sacrificed even her woman's pride, and who personally interceded with the rude oppressor, had as much effect upon Napoleon, as he wrote himself in malicious amusement, " as water upon a duck's back."

On July 7 and 9, 1807, the Peace of Tilsit was signed, the most cruel of all the treaties of peace with France, unparalleled both in form and content. It was not to the rightful king of Prussia that the conqueror returned certain portions of land ; but out of respect for the emperor of all the Russias he restored the lesser half of the Prussian state to its king. And this ignominious phrase which, to contemporaries, seemed merely the outcome of Napoleon's ill-bred arrogance, expressed the naked truth, for it was indeed only out of regard for the czar that Napoleon consented for the moment to be content with no more than half of that destruction of Prussia upon which he had firmly resolved. He needed the Russian alliance in order to be able to undertake undisturbed his great attack upon Spain. Alexander, on his side, did not wish to allow the last narrow dam which still separated the Russian empire from the vassal lands of France to be completely demolished, and he did not conceal his uneasiness when Napoleon proposed to detach Silesia and East Prussia from the Prussian monarchy. Of the five thousand seven hundred square miles [German] which, not including Hanover, the state had possessed before the war, there were left about two thousand eight hundred ; of the twenty-three war and domain chambers only the eight largest ; of nine and three quarter million inhabitants, only four and a half million. The work of Frederick the Great seemed to have been altogether annihilated. The state was but a trifle larger than it had been in the year 1740, and was far more unfavourably situated. Pushed back to the right bank of the Elbe, and robbed of all its outposts in the west, it stood under the point of the French sword. Its rescued province, Silesia, the reduced Old Prussia, the still remaining parts of Brandenburg and Pomerania, were connected only by narrow strips, like the segments of a trefoil. At any moment, upon a nod of the Imperator, Berlin could be simultaneously attacked by the Poles from the east, the Saxons from the south, the Westphalians from Magdeburg, and the French from Mecklenburg, and the net be thus drawn together round the Hohenzollerns.

All the Polish provinces of the monarchy, with the exception of parts of West Prussia, were allotted to the king of Saxony, who assumed the title of Duke of Warsaw. Thus this fourth partition of Poland reconstituted the pernicious union between Poland and Saxony, and at the same time gave to the House of Wettin a military road through Silesia, that *via regia* which had been so often desired by the Polish Augustuses. The new duchy, following the French example, speedily constituted a vigorous army such as had never been known to the old Nobles' Republic. Beneath the feeble rule of the timid House of Wettin, the anti-German sentiments of the Sarmatian nobility were altogether unbridled, for the Wettins were quite unable to control the proud electors ; all the German officers were at once driven out of the country, in opposition to the express terms of the Treaty of Tilsit, and with the secret approval of the French Protector. To secure a fulcrum for Polish fanaticism, Napoleon made the fortress of Danzig a free town, and provided it with a strong French garrison. To separate the czar for ever from his Prussian friend, Napoleon counselled him to enrich himself at the cost of his unhappy ally, and to unite the district of Bialystock to the Russian empire. The detestable exaction thus urged by Napoleon was followed by Alexander as accommodatingly as had been the corresponding advice by Frederick Augustus of Saxony ; he consoled his conscience with the consideration that if he had refused, this territory would certainly have been united to Warsaw. Out of the Prussian lands on the left bank of the Elbe and from the territories of Electoral Hesse, with portions of the Guelph lands, a kingdom of Westphalia was constituted, and handed over to the Imperator's brother Jerome, with the intimation that he must regard obedience to France as the first of his princely duties. A " regular constitution " was here to put an end to " all those vain and ridiculous distinctions " of the estates and of the territorial jurisdictions which seemed dangerous to the bureaucratic centralisation of the world-empire.

In the courts of the Confederation of the Rhine, there was nothing but rejoicing, now that the only German state which possessed a history and a life of its own was submerged in the general German misery. The Middle States had attained the goal of their desires, for they had no longer any German power either to fear or to envy. Their officers gladly boasted how bravely they had helped in person in the humiliation of North German arrogance, and they could not tell enough of the wonders of Prussian stupidity. If one were to believe the voice of the official press in Munich and Stuttgart the battle of Jena had been the one memorable event in the history of Prussian warfare. In superficial area, the Confederation of the Rhine was twice as great as this reduced Prussia, whilst the population of the Confederation was three times as numerous ; Bavaria alone could now regard itself as the equal of the state of Frederick, for this land of the Confederation of the Rhine had a population which was only a million smaller than that of Prussia, whilst Bavaria was incomparably more prosperous. The wags of Dresden and Leipzig loved to contemplate the English humorous cartoon, representing the meeting on the raft at Tilsit. Here was seen the boastful little " Boney " embracing the young czar so vigorously that the raft was set shaking, and the onlooking Frederick William fell miserably into the water.

Of all the princes of the Confederation of the Rhine, the new king of Saxony was the most humble servant of France. The slow-minded, painfully conscientious man had grown grey in the traditions of the ancient imperial law, in the stiff formulas of a Spanish etiquette ; he alone among the greater princes of the empire had taken no part in the great spoliation of the spiritual states— which was not difficult in his case, for he had no indemnities to demand. In the previous autumn he had resolved, though with difficulty, to pay homage to the victorious plebeian. When he at length came to Berlin, the Imperator was no longer there, and all he could do in his perplexity was to ask the ever-obliging Gagern : " How can one really get on with this man ? " When subsequently his treachery to Prussia was rewarded with rich gifts, when upon the homeward journey Napoleon personally appeared in Dresden, and, speedily seeing through the thick-headedness of the king, assumed the mien of the kindly well-wisher, the weakly prince was completely blinded by the imperial grandeur of the Protector, and came to build with superstitious confidence upon the fortune of his "great ally." Contrary to all precedent in this slow-moving state system, ambitious young men were advanced to the head of the army, and they soon filled the minds of their men, who had gone over to the French side somewhat unwillingly, with the unprincipled lust of adventure of the troops of the Confederation of the Rhine ; here, as in Bavaria and Würtemberg, the red ribbon of the Legion of Honour was regarded as the highest distinction obtainable by a soldier. In everything Frederick Augustus did the will of his master, and it was hardly necessary for the Imperator to utter his warning, " What you do for Prussia you do against yourself ! "

Thus amid the rejoicings of the German particularists, the partial destruction of Prussia was effected. But the inhabitants of the older Prussian provinces had different feelings when the king notified them with the dignified words : " That which centuries of faithful forefathers, that which treaties, love, and confidence had united, must now be dismembered." With a dull inertia had the people of the hundreds of German states which in the storms of this wild time had been overwhelmed, borne their fate ; but those that were now torn asunder from Prussia, felt in the very marrow or their lives what it signified to men to belong to an honourable state. The unhappy monarch could scarcely maintain his composure when from East Prussia and Magdeburg, from Thorn and Westphalia, from all his lost German lands, there came letters full of ardent thanks, full of touching lamentations. The faithful peasants of the County Mark wrote in their rough style : " Our hearts are breaking as we take leave of you, as truly as we are alive the fault is not yours ! " So, too, the German emigrants into the Polish provinces were heavy-hearted at the separation from the old monarchy. How terribly devastated, too, was the territory that still remained to the king. A single year had destroyed the rich fruits of the peaceful work of three decades. It was first as a result of this war that the domestic life of North Germany assumed the characteristics of utter penury. Previously, some of the branches of artistic life had at least shown tolerable blossoms, but now came the epoch of general shapelessness and lack of taste. Poverty was everywhere visible. It was displayed in the unadorned buildings, in the wretched furniture, in the restricted diet ; an anxious economy dictated all the conduct of daily life. In unhappy East Prussia, whole areas of land seemed as if dead ; entire villages on the Passarge had disappeared. The preachers announced from the pulpit that anyone who wished could there reap the corn lest all should perish in the standing crop. But even after the peace the conqueror devoted himself with meticulous care to the plundering of the detested land. All the sick from the hospitals of Warsaw and Westphalia were immediately sent to Prussia ; when one of his regiments was withdrawn, a sale was first effected of all the royal stores and provisions, down to the stocks of the salt-works and the china factories. He ordered that no flintlocks and no powder should be left in the country, not even if the Prussians were willing to pay cash for them, for he said he had no longer any reason to spare Prussia. In contradiction to the plain wording of the Treaty of Tilsit, New Silesia was at once united to Warsaw. The complaints of the king were regarded as senseless and not worth a reply.

The worst remained, namely, that with all these sacrifices the quiet of peace was not even yet secured. The Prussian plenipotentiary, Field-Marshal Kalckreuth, a warm admirer of Napoleon, had conducted the negotiations at Tilsit with a trustful levity which overshadowed all the military services of the defender of Danzig, and which had to be paid for heavily by the state. The evacuation of the country and of the fortresses was to take place on the first of October, but only if the whole of the war indemnity had previously been paid, and since no definite arrangement had been made as to the amount of this sum, afterwards as before the whole Prussian domain was occupied by Napoleon's army. Thus the Imperator gained a free hand for his Spanish plans, since the *grande armée* in Prussia sufficed to keep quiet the two imperial powers of the east, whilst from the Prussian taxes he gained the money he needed for the Spanish War.

Disarmed, gagged, and mutilated, the Prussian monarchy lay at the feet of Napoleon ; with finished cunning he had prepared everything in order to destroy it completely at the chosen hour. One thing only eluded the keen insight of the contemner of ideas, namely, that this state had gained in internal unity and moral energy what it had lost in external power. Prussia was quit of the untrustworthy Poles ; such of the old German tribal lands as remained, held together like one man. It was from these lands of the eagle that formerly had proceeded the victorious plan of the Great Elector, the bold endeavour to constitute a new German state ; upon these now rested the whole future of Germany. They alone, among all the purely German territories, would have nothing to do with the Confederation of the Rhine. The honourable sentiments of Frederick William had preserved his Prussia from the ultimate disgrace of voluntary servitude. The grave errors of the last years had not only been atoned for but had been recognised; even in Tilsit, on the advice of Hardenberg, the king had resolved to entrust the reconstruction of the administration to Baron von Stein. All things that could animate a strong people to despairing resolve, pride and hatred, pain and repentance, were fermenting in a thousand valiant spirits, and every new misdeed of the foreign oppressor increased the bitterness, until at length all that was Prussian was united in the passionate desire for reprisal. If only it were possible to assemble and to organise the powerful energies of this wrathful people, if only it were possible to rejuvenate the state by the idealism of the new culture, Germany could yet be saved. Even during the war, a talented Frenchman, who had found a new home in German science, Charles de Villers, wrote warningly: "The French armies have beaten the German because they are stronger, but for the same reason the German spirit will ultimately conquer the French I believe that some indications of this development are already visible. Providence chooses its own paths."

CHAPTER III.

THE RISE OF PRUSSIA.

§ I. STEIN. SCHARNHORST. THE NEW GERMANY.

SEVERAL times before, Prussia had astonished the German world by a sudden disclosure of its hidden moral energies. This had happened when the elector, Frederick William, forced his little state into the ranks of the old powers. It had happened again when King Frederick hazarded the struggle for Silesia. But none of the great surprises of Prussian history were so unexpected by the Germans as the rapid and proud uprising of the half-destroyed great power after the profound reverse of Jena. Whilst the celebrated names of the old time were all committed to contempt and oblivion, and whilst everyone in Prussia was complaining of the complete lack of capable young men, a new generation suddenly rallied round the throne. There appeared men of powerful character, enthusiastic spirit, and clear intelligence, an unending abundance of them, a crowd of persons brilliant in camp and in council, who could take equal rank with the literary great ones of the nation. And just as formerly Frederick had merely reaped upon the battle-fields of Bohemia what his father had laboriously sown in the quiet times of peace, so now this speedy recovery of strength on the part of the humiliated monarchy was no more than the ripe fruit of long years of arduous work. When the state thus pulled itself together, it was realising all that German thinkers and poets had thought and uttered during the last decades concerning human dignity and human freedom, concerning the moral aims of life. It put its trust in the liberating power of the spirit, and let the full stream of the ideas of the new Germany flow through its life.

Now for the first time Prussia became in reality the German state. The best and the boldest of all the sons of the fatherland, the last of the Germans, assembled under the black-and-white flags. Upon the ancient Prussian valiancy and loyalty, the

X

vigorous idealism of a distinctive culture superimposed new duties and new aims ; and in the discipline of political life the Prussian spirit was quickened to activity and learned to rejoice in self-sacrifice. The state abandoned its petty preference for the immediately useful ; science recognised that it had need of the fatherland in order to become truly human. The old, hard, war-like Prussiandom, and the richness of ideas of the modern German culture, at length found themselves at one, never again to separate. The reconciliation between the two poietic powers of our new history, gives to those painful years which followed the Peace of Tilsit their historic grandeur. In this time of sorrow and self-knowledge were first formed all the political ideals for whose realisation the German nation is working to this day.

Never did the arbitrary will of the conqueror display itself more cruelly than in Prussia ; for this reason nowhere else was the great significance of the struggle which was shaking the world felt more keenly and more passionately than among the German patriots. In opposition to the adventurous plans of the Napoleonic world-empire, there arose the idea of national freedom, the same idea which the founder of the Prussian State had once defended against Louis XIV. In opposition to the cosmopolitan doctrines of the armed revolution, there displayed itself the national sentiment, the enthusiasm for fatherland, for folk-life, and for the peculi-arities of the home. In the struggle against the oppressive universal domination of Bonapartism, there came into existence a new and really living conception of the state, a conception which found the moral force of the nations in the free unfolding of personal energy. The great contrasts which here encountered one another were faithfully reflected in the persons of the leading men. On the one side was a man who believed himself to be destiny personified, that the nature of things spoke through his mouth and worked through his hands—the man of power, who, with the force of his masterful genius, oppressed all opposing wills. Far beneath him stood his servants, valiant soldiers and useful men of affairs, but hardly one of them possessed of an independent character, and hardly one whose inner life rose above the dullness of the daily commonplace. On the other side was a long series of excep-tional men, men of strongly developed and peculiar natures, each one a little world in himself, full of German defiance and German criticism, each one worthy of a biography, too independent and too full of ideas to be simply obedient, yet all united in the ardent desire to restore liberty and honour to their disgraced fatherland.

The Rise of Prussia

In this circle there was one who was not the commander but was first among equals, Baron von Stein, the pioneer of the age of reform. His ancestral castle was in Nassau, amid the motley groups of the petty particularist states ; from the bridge across the Lahn in the neighbouring town of Ems, the boy could simultaneously look upon the dominions of eight German princes and lords. Here he grew to manhood, in the free air, in the strict discipline of a proud, pious, and honourable ancient knightly house, which regarded itself as the equal of all the princes in the empire. Did not the hereditary fortresses of the Houses of Stein and Nassau stand close beside one another upon the same rock ? why then should the old coat of arms with the roses and the chevrons be regarded as of less importance than the Saxon lozenge-crown, or the antlers of the armorial bearings of the Würtemburger ? The idea of German unity, to which those born in subjection could attain only by the devious paths of historical culture, was instilled in the cradle into this proud lord who was subject to the emperor alone. He could see the matter in no other way ; " I have but one fatherland, Germany, and just as in accordance with the ancient constitution I belong to Germany alone and to no particular part of Germany, so also do I give my heart to Germany alone and to no part of Germany." But little influenced by the æsthetic enthusiasm of his contemporaries, his active spirit, concentrated upon reality, early became immersed in historical affairs. All the wonders of the history of the fatherland, from the overthrow of the Roman legions by the Germans of the Teutoburger Wald down to the grenadiers of Frederick the Great, appeared vividly before his eyes. The whole of greater Germany, as far as the German tongue is heard, was the object of his ardent love. He excluded from his affection not one of those who had ever manifested the energy and grandeur of the German nature. When in old age, in his own Nassau, he built a tower in honour of the memorable deeds of Germany, the pictures of Frederick the Great and of Maria Theresa, of Scharnhorst and of Wallenstein, hung there peaceably side by side. His ideal was the powerful German kingship of the Saxon emperors ; the newly constituted states which had since then arisen upon the ruins of the monarchy all seemed to him arbitrary structures, the product of secret treason, of foreign intrigue, ripe for destruction when anywhere and in any way the majesty of the ancient rightful kingship should come to its own again. His unsparing frankness towards crowned heads arose, not only from the inborn valiancy of a heroic spirit, but also from the pride of an imperial knight who in all these princes could see only men who had forgotten their duty, co-estates who had enriched themselves at the expense of the empire, and he could not understand why anyone should make such a fuss about these kinglets.

He had watched the Rhenish campaigns from close at hand, and had attained to the conviction, which he once expressed to the empress of Russia before the assembled court, that the German people was loyal and vigorous, and that only the poor-spiritedness of its princes was the cause of Germany's corruption. He detested the foreign dominion with the elemental power of a passionate nature which when it once broke out flowed irresistibly like a mountain torrent ; but he expected the salvation of Europe neither from the restoration of the ancient and outworn state authorities, nor yet from the artificial doctrines of the balance of power characteristic of the old diplomacy. His free and great spirit always went straight to the moral nucleus of things. With the vision of the seer he already recognised, as did Gneisenau, the elements of a permanent reconstruction of the comity of nations. In his view, the unnatural preponderance of France would stand or fall with the weakness of Germany and Italy. A new balance of power could not arise until each of the two great nations of middle Europe was united to form a powerful state. Stein was the first statesman who recognised the driving force of the new century, the impulse towards the formation of national states ; and it was not till two generations later that the course of history was to justify his brilliant vaticinations. His dream of a united Germany was still rather the conception of a high-minded enthusiast, than a clear political ideal ; he did not yet know how estranged Austria had become from the modern life of the nation, and in the struggles for Silesia he could see no more than a regrettable civil war.

Nevertheless, in recent years, he had come to recognise the living power of the Prussian state ; and, diverging in this from the ordinary views of the imperial nobles, he had devoted himself to the service of the Protestant great power. He was well suited by the fresh, natural life of the mining districts, one which was fortifying to his physical constitution ; and subsequently, when he found a second home among the free peasants and the proud, ancient nobility of the Westphalian territories, he was always personally on the spot, whatever might be the state of the weather, in order to look after affairs with his own masterful personality ; he was restless and ardent, but also good-natured and loyal ; thoroughly practical, concerned just as much about the cattle of the petty cottars, as about the aqueducts for the rich coal-mines—a true nobleman at once distinguished and affable, magnan-imous in all things, a king in his own province. He knew little of the east of the monarchy. The Rhenish Franconian was for long unable to overcome his territorial prejudice against the needy colonial lands across the Elbe. He believed himself able to recognise a furtive and lupine glance in the serious, weatherbeaten traits of the Brandenburg peasants, who did indeed bear the traces of prolonged poverty and serfdom ; and with the native pride of an imperial knight, he looked down upon the poor and needy Junkers of the Mark, who had none the less done far more for Germany's new history than all the imperial nobles put together. It was con-stitutionally difficult to this baron of the empire to receive pay and to bend his stiff neck beneath the yoke of service. When he became personally acquainted with the still vital remnants of old German communal freedom and of feudal institutions, when he observed the generally useful efficiency of the provincial diets and the peasant folk-sittings, of the town councils and church synods, and when he compared with these the stiff and formal pettiness and the ubiquitous intrusiveness of the royal officialdom, he became inspired with a profound contempt for the nullity of literalism and of red tape. With severe and even unjustified words he censures the salaried official, " a man learned in books, without interests, without property, who, whether it rains or whether the sun is shining, receives his pay regularly from the state treasury, and spends his whole life in writing, writing, writing."

Thus in vigorous activity, in lively intercourse with all classes of the people, he gradually attained to an independent view of the nature of political freedom, which bore the same relationship to the democratic doctrines of the Revolution as the German sense of the state did to the French. When he was still quite a young man, Adam Smith's doctrine of the free mobility of economic forces had made a strong and permanent impression upon his mind ; but nothing was further from the German baron than that over-estima-tion of economic goods, to which the blind followers of the Scotsman were prone, and he openly adhered to the Frederician idea that excessive wealth is the destruction of the nations. He was pro-foundly impressed by Justus Möser's vivid descriptions of the peasant freedom of ancient Germany ; the study of German and of English constitutional history, helped forward his political culture ; and there can be no doubt that the romantic conception of the world-order characteristic of the epoch, the general enthusiasm for the unbroken energy of a youthful popular life, also exercised an unconscious influence upon him. But the true source of his political convictions was a powerful moral idealism, which was steeled to a far greater extent than the baron himself was aware by the hard school of the Prussian official service.

The administration of the first Frederick William had long ago forced the people, who were then altogether estranged from public life, to take an interest in the affairs of the community. Stein recognised that those who had been thus educated were now capable, by themselves, under the supervision of the state, of looking after the affairs of the circles and communes. In place of the outworn class-differences, he wished to introduce the equality before the law characteristic of modern bourgeois society. This, however, was not to result in the creation of an undifferentiated mass of sovereign individuals, but in the production of a new and juster subdivision of society, which should impose upon the propertied members of the community, upon the well-to-do, and especially upon the landed proprietors, the burden and the honour of communal service, and which should thus furnish these with powers, constituting a young aristocracy based upon the idea of political duty. He thought that it was possible to fight the Revolution with its own weapons, to put an end to the struggle between the classes, to realise in its completeness throughout the administration the idea of the unified state. Yet with the vigorous activity of the innovator, he combined a profound affection for historical institutions, and above all for the power of the crown. " To form a constitution," he often said, " consists in developing the present out of the past." He endeavoured to pass back, from those artificial conditions of tutelage and compulsion which had formerly come into existence out of the miseries of the Thirty Years' War, to the simple and free views of our German ancestors, to whom service in arms was the honourable right of every freeman, and to whom care for the communal economy seemed to be the natural task of the burgher and of the peasant. To the greedy revolutionary sentiment, which demanded from the state unending human rights, he opposed the ancient Prussian sense of duty. To the impudent dilettantism of the political philosophers, he opposed the knowledge of affairs and knowledge of men acquired by a shrewd official who had won his insight out of the experience of life, learning that the reconstruction of the state must begin from below, and that constitutional forms are valueless if they lack the foundation of a free administration.

These ideas, however new and even rash they might appear, were the necessary outcome of the internal evolution which the Prussian State had undergone from the time of the destruction of the old feudal dominion down to the formulation of the common law. They were so closely akin at once to the moral earnestness of the Kantian philosophy and to the re-awakening historical sense of German science, that to us who come afterwards, they seem to be as it were a political precipitate from the classical age of our literature. Simultaneously, as if upon a word of command, immediately after the overthrow of the old order, the same ideas were uttered by the best men alike of the sword and of the pen, but by no one so comprehensively and with such marked individuality as by Stein. In the letters and memorials of Scharnhorst and Gneisenau, Vincke and Niebuhr, we everywhere find recurring the same leading idea. The nation must be awakened to independent and responsible political activity ; and there must thus be aroused the self-confidence, the courage, and the spirit of sacrifice characteristic of a living love of the fatherland. It was not after the manner of these practical statesmen to attempt to construct a closed system of political ideas ; they regarded it rather as a great advantage of English life that in England political theorising was so little respected. Thus the one literary work that came into existence under Stein's own eyes, Vincke's *Treatise on the British Constitution*, was devoted to the study of the real. This little work gave for the first time a faithful picture of the self-government of the English counties, which had hitherto received no attention among the wonderful subdivisions of authority in the typical constitutional state. The book contained so unmistakable a declaration of war against the French bureaucracy of the Confederation of the Rhine, that it could not be printed until after the overthrow of the Napoleonic dominion. Consequently the profundity of Stein's ideas upon statecraft were never really perceived by the baron's own contemporaries. Only in the present day has it been recognised that this great man was not merely an advocate of the conception of the national state, but that he also rescued for the European continent the ideas of self-government, and a notion o popular freedom based upon ancient and unforgotten traditions of Teutonic history. Every advance in our political life has brought the nation back to Stein's ideals.

It was the defect of his merits that he did not find himself at home in the tortuous paths of foreign policy, and that he despised as sordid trickery the indispensable arts of diplomatic astuteness.

To him were lacking cunning, caution, and gifts of hesitancy and restraint. In the domain of administration, he moved with complete certainty. But when there seemed to open a prospect for the liberation of his fatherland, his equanimity was disturbed ; and, carried away by the wild impetuosity of his patriotic enthusiasm, he readily expected the impossible.

It was not given to this hero of holy wrath and stormy veracity to steer the state cautiously through the rocks till the propitious moment arrived for the uprising. Yet no one else was born as he was born for the task of political reform. To restore to the distracted monarchy its power of direction towards high moral aims, to invigorate its slumbering magnificent energies with the awakening power of an ardent will—this was possible to Stein alone, for no other possessed the same moving and overwhelming might of a great personality. No ignoble word could be heard, no excuse for weakness or selfishness ventured to raise itself, when he expressed his serious ideas in his old-fashioned German, in a speech altogether free from artificiality, rough with the roughness of the people, in that weighty brevity which is natural to the wealth of ideas and the restrained passion of the genuine Teuton. Vulgarity trembled before the pitilessness of his thorny wit, before the crushing blows of his anger. But anyone who was really a man, and came into contact with this spirit strong in faith, always went on his way with a brighter glance and with heightened courage. The image of this baron of the empire was immovably enshrined in the hearts of the best men of Germany. His figure was firm and compact, his shoulders were powerful, as if created to wear a cuirass ; his brown eyes sparkled beneath the dominant brow, and his aquiline nose surmounted narrow and mobile lips that were full of expression ; every movement of the great hands was firm and commanding. He seemed a character out of the spirited sixteenth century, reminding us involuntarily of Dürer's picture of Ritter Franz von Sickingen, so talented and so simple, so brave among men and so humble before God, the whole man a wonderful synthesis of natural energy and of culture, of liberal-mindedness and justice, of ardent passion and equitable consideration. His was a nature which, with its incapacity for any selfish calculation, must ever remain an insoluble riddle to Napoleon and his companions in fortune. He was the man for the situation ; even his weaknesses and the one-sidedness of his views, corresponded to the needs of the moment. If he judged the officialdom and the petty nobility with undue harshness, and if he regarded the Austrians simply as

Prussia's German brethren, all the better for the state, which had now to destroy the privileges of the nobility and the sole dominion of the bureaucracy, and which must magnanimously forget everything which was a barrier between the two German great powers.

After his vain struggle against cabinet government and his contumelious dismissal, Stein had lived quietly in Nassau, and there, in a comprehensive memorial, had compiled certain sketches for the reconstitution of the state ; then came the news of the disastrous peace, which actually made the hot-blooded man seriously ill. Soon afterwards came his recall to power. He speedily recovered ; his illness was forgotten ; after three days his will mastered the fever. On September 30, 1807, he arrived at Memel, and the king, full of confidence, entrusted him with the leadership of the whole state. What a situation ! On his last birthday, Frederick William, since the French evacuation of the country had not been begun, had written an autograph letter to the Imperator, asking him the plain question whether it was his intention to annihilate Prussia. Napoleon remained dumb, deeds gave the answer. In the midst of the peace there were 160,000 Frenchmen in the fortresses and in great camps, distributed over the whole Prussian dominion, East Prussia alone excepted. The nucleus of the old Prussian army, numbering more than 15,000 men, was still held prisoner at Nancy, and whence should the plundered monarchy obtain means for the formation of a new army ? Of disposable annual income, there remained to the state only thirteen and a half million thalers, barely two-thirds of its former revenue. Everywhere where Napoleon's troops were in possession, the income of the state was impounded for France, as if the war were still in progress, so that the king received nothing, and hundreds of the officers who had been discharged on half-pay, could not be paid at all. The once greatly envied Oversea Trading Company had, like the Bank, suspended payment ; its shares fell to 25 ; the Treasury Bills fell to 27, since it was impossible to think of redeeming them, and the French authorities made use of the paper money for usurious business. Masses of depreciated small coin streamed from the ceded provinces back into the country ; and to make matters worse, the French had an additional quantity of small change, to the amount of three million thalers, coined in the Berlin mint. The state credit was so completely destroyed that a premium loan of one million, issued in small shares of twenty-five thalers each, had not been taken up at the end of three years. In the diplomatic world, Prussia was now hardly esteemed as highly as one of the kingdoms of the Confederation of the Rhine ; in the year 1808, the Dutch ambassador, a French consul, and an Austrian commercial attaché, constituted the whole foreign diplomatic corps at the court of Königsberg. The French military administration, under the brutal leadership of Daru, was even worse in peace than it had been in war, and every one of its excesses was undertaken at Napoleon's express command. One tax pressed on the heels of another, and for months it remained impossible to say how much the insatiable enemy would still demand from the exhausted country. In East and in West Prussia a progressive income-tax was imposed, rising to 20 per cent., to pay off the burdens of the war ; a certain merchant of Stettin, who was far from being a rich man, paid during the year following the peace more than fifteen thousand thalers for taxes and billeting.

Business was at a standstill. British mercantile competition had availed itself of the previous war to destroy the strongest mercantile marine of the Baltic coasts. When subsequently the war broke out with France, and peace with England had not yet been concluded, the Prussian flag was threatened simultaneously by the British cruisers and by the French. Then came the distresses of the Continental System. Within a brief space, the shipping of the Pomeranian harbours fell from a tonnage of sixty-eight thousand to forty thousand. The old, natural routes of world-commerce lay unused. The Baltic provinces, since good roads were still almost entirely wanting, had no way open for their one article of export, grain. Colonial produce was smuggled into the country from Gothenburg and Heligoland, the new Little-London ; other goods came from Malta and Corfu, by way of Bosnia and Hungary. The middle classes of Prussia could no longer pay the prices of the customary luxuries ; people drank an infusion of chicory, and smoked colt's-foot and walnut leaves. Poverty reigned in every house and in every industry. The printers of Königsberg required three weeks in order to print a law occupying six folios, for they had type enough for but one folio at a time. Schön, the able minister of finance, who prided himself on his reputation for old Prussian courage, found the posture of affairs so hopeless that, four months after the peace, he issued a memorial to the effect that the conqueror must be satisfied by the cession of the Magdeburg region on the right bank of the Elbe and portions of Upper Silesia, as otherwise the country would be absolutely ruined by the burden of taxation.

Everything recalled those lamentable days when Wallenstein had occupied the Mark and George William had passed his days in Königsberg as a prince without a country. But what an abundance of love and loyalty had come into existence in the subsequent six generations. Then the diet of Königsberg had bluntly defied the will of its elector. Now, prince and people stood together, like one great family. The poor country house at Memel and the gloomy rooms of the old castle of the Teutonic Knights at Königsberg, did not lack visitors, who wished to give pleasure to their king in his need and to say a kindly word. At the baptism of the new-born princess, the estates of East Prussia appeared as sponsors. In all the shop windows there was hanging the new picture which represented the king standing among his children, dressed in the hideous uniform of the day, and how much more royally did Frederick William know how to endure his hard lot than did the father of the Great Elector. He was filled with profound bitterness of spirit ; more than ever did he need the cordial encouragement of his spouse ; there were hours when it seemed to him as if he could succeed in nothing, as if he had been born only for misfortune. When in the cathedral of Königsberg he read the inscriptions upon the tombs of the Prussian dukes, he chose as a motto for his own hard life, " My days are passed in disquiet, my hope is in God ! " Yet this hope sustained him. He could never accept the conviction that the common souls of the family of Bonaparte who now wore the crowns of Europe were really princes, that in the reasonable world of God, this adventurer of the Napoleonic world-empire, who for all his brilliancy and glory was so inflated and so specious, could permanently continue to exist. He never allowed himself to be persuaded into any personal friendliness towards Napoleon. Even Stein once advised that the mood of the Imperator should be rendered milder by a little timely flattery, and that Napoleon should be invited to act as sponsor at the baptism of the new-born princess. The king rejected the idea unhesitatingly. But to the political proposals of his great minister, he adhered willingly and without reserve. He had a far greater share in Stein's legislation than his contemporaries were aware. Much which now came to perfection was merely the bold execution of those ideas of reform over which the irresolute prince had been brooding for a decade. Thus only do the rapid and striking successes of a single year of Stein's administration become comprehensible.

The new minister found willing helpers also among the officials. It was fortunate for him that it was on East Prussian soil that he had to begin his work of reform. Here, in especial, was keenly felt the untenability of the old division of classes, for the province possessed in its Köllmers a number of free landowners who were commoners. Here had the cultured classes, and especially the officials, long been well-acquainted with the free moral and political views which the two most efficient teachers of the University of Königsberg, Kant and the recently deceased Kraus, had diffused for many years. Most of Stein's laws were prepared in the East Prussian provincial department. At the head of this administration was the minister von Schrötter, an exemplary official of astonishing activity, who had retained even into old age a youthful receptivity for new ideas ; under him were working Friese and Wilckens.[1] Schön was completely filled with the ideas of Kant. In many respects he was a faithful representative of the vigorous, enlightened, and intelligent East Prussian character, but he was a doctrinaire advocate of unrestricted free trade, he was immeasurably vain, was incapable of modestly recognising the services of another, and, moreover, quite in conflict with the characteristics of his fine stock, was untruthful. Beside him worked Staegemann, a highly-cultured and able man of business, endowed with rare industry and rare modesty, who sometimes gave expression to his faithful affection for the Prussian state in profoundly felt, but clumsy, poems. There was also Niebuhr, the man of brilliant learning, too sensitive, too dependent upon the moods of the moment, to find himself readily at home in the equable activity of the office, but invaluable to all by the inexhaustible wealth of his living knowledge, by the width of his outlook, by the nobility of his lofty passion. There was Nicolovius, a profound spirit, strongly affected by the religious tendency of the time. There were Sack, Klewitz, and many others, a brilliant company of exceptional powers. Nearest to the views of Stein among them all, was the Westphalian, Baron von Vincke. He also had formed his views of the state in contact with the nobles and with the peasants of the countryside, but the born Prussian recognised far more frankly than did the imperial knight the services of the salaried officialdom. Vincke could not be reckoned among the poietic intelligences ; his strength lay in kinesis, in the unresting activity of the administrative official.

Hardenberg, who upon Napoleon's orders had for the second time been obliged to leave the ministry, sent from Riga a great memorial on the reorganisation of the Prussian state which he had

---

[1] Recently shown in the remarkable book by Ernst Meier, *Die Reform der Verwal.ungs-Organisation unter Stein und Hardenberg*, Leipzig, 1881.

there composed in collaboration with Altenstein. In many respects
this corresponded with the ideas of the new minister of state;
many of its proposals were taken word for word from Stein's own
utterances, such as the idea of an assembly of the estates for the
whole country. Here also, however, there was already manifest
that intimate and profound contrast which always separated the
disciples of the enlightenment from Stein's historical conception
of the state. Hardenberg was first of all a diplomatist. In
administrative affairs he was far from being so well-informed as
Stein, and for this reason in his memorial he inconsiderately incorporated certain general theoretical proposals dear also to Altenstein, the friend of Fichte. His scheme of reform was conceived
" in accordance with the highest idea of the state"; in commercial
policy the principle of *laisser-faire* was to prevail without restriction. Whereas Stein had from the first regarded the Revolution
with the mistrust of the aristocrat, and desired to transplant to
German soil a few only of its tried results, Hardenberg had been
much more strongly influenced by French ideas. He definitely
indicated as the goal of reform, " the introduction of democratic
principles in a monarchical government"; in matters of detail,
he wished to follow closely the French example, demanded for the
army conscription with right of purchasing substitutes, and would
gladly have abolished the honorary Landräte (the old-established
administrative chiefs-of-district in Prussia) to replace them by
bureaucratic district officials. He said nothing at all concerning
self-government by the commons. A point common to both these
statesmen was, however, the moral altitude of their sense of the
state. Both of them desired, as Altenstein's proposal expressed
it, " a revolution in a good sense, leading directly towards the
supreme goal of the ennoblement of humanity"; both of them
knew that France pursued a tendency of secondary importance, directed to the simple manifestation of power; and they
demanded from the rejuvenated German state that it should
protect religion, art, and science, all the ideal aims of the human
race, for their own sake, and that it should thus secure a victory
over the foreign dominion by means of moral energies.

Stein possessed in a high degree the art indispensable to the
statesman of making a good use of the ideas of others. He allowed
all the proposals which were brought to him from the circles of the
officials to influence his mind, but his ultimate decisions were determined by his own consideration. He laid down the broad line of
the leading ideas, but committed the carrying out of these to the

councils, and intervened personally only when it was necessary to push the completed work through in opposition to doubt and active resistance. When he came to Memel there was already on foot a proposal for the abolition of hereditary servitude in East and West Prussia. Schön, Staegemann, and Klewitz had worked out the plan upon the king's instructions, appealing especially to the fact that in the neighbouring duchy of Warsaw, the abolition of serfdom was imminent The new minister at once gave a wider scope to the law, demanding the extension of the reform to the whole area of the state. Since he had begun to think for himself in political matters, he had regarded the lack of freedom of the country people as the curse of north-eastern Germany. The moment seemed to him propitious for the permanent cure of the ancient evil, and with one bold step to attain the end towards which the laws of the Hohenzollerns from the time of Frerderick William I had ever advanced with partial success. The king joyfully agreed; the bold confidence of his minister awakened in him the courage to will effectively that which all his life he had merely hoped for. Thus there was promulgated on October 9, 1807, an edict concerning the facilitated ownership and the free utilisation of landed property, or, as Schön called it, the Prussian habeas corpus act. Thus in unassuming forms there was completed a far-reaching social revolution. About two-thirds of the population of the state now acquired unrestricted personal freedom. On and after Martinmas, 1810, there were to be none in Prussia but freemen. This same law destroyed at a single blow the feudal ordering of the Frederician state. The nobleman received the right to become a peasant and to carry on bourgeois industries, and this right was to be considered a compensation for the privileges previously enjoyed by the nobility in the army. Every kind of landed proprietorship, and every kind of occupation, was henceforward to be open to every Prussian.

But Stein was not inclined to discard the old national principles of the monarchy, and to allow the destruction of petty proprietorship to be effected under the cloak of free competition. It seemed to him that a free and vigorous estate of peasants was the firmest prop of the state, and the nucleus of its powers of military defence. For this reason the right to purchase the lands of the peasants was granted to the larger landed proprietors, but only under restriction; and with the consent of the authorities. Whereas Schön, faithful to the dogmas of the English free-traders, desired to accelerate the destruction of the old generation of settlers on the land, as an unavoidable economic necessity, Stein came to the rescue of the indebted great landed proprietors with a General Indulgence. Thus it became possible to assist the landed gentry through the difficulties of the immediate future, and to retain most of them in the possession of their ancient lands. No less moderate despite its boldness was the new edict which provided free property for the peasants on the domains in East and West Prussia, about forty-seven thousand families ; they were to redeem three-fourths of the services and charges attached to their lands within the space of four-and-twenty years by monetary payments. The remaining fourth was to continue as an irremovable tax. Stein rejected as too radical a disturbance of the accepted relationships of property, the idea of a complete abolition of all the encumbrances upon peasant property. He also determined upon the abolition of thirlage, of the guilds and the selling monopolies of bakers, butchers, and hucksters. His aim was to effect the transformation of all services and payments in kind into money payments, and to abolish the rights to forced labour and other manorial rights, to abolish all servitude and all communal dues ; private property was everywhere to come into its own. In sharp contrast with the Frederician system of the monarchical organisation of labour, the new laws were " to get rid of everything which had hitherto stood in the way of the individual's acquirements of such a degree of well-being as he was competent to acquire in accordance with the measure of his energies." The instructions issued to the executive authorities after Stein's resignation, expressed doubtless in a somewhat more abstract form than Stein had himself used, ran simply : " Industry must be left to take its natural course ; it is not necessary to favour trade, all that we have to do is to see that no difficulties are put in its way."

The remarkable change thus effected in the ancient social system of Prussia, was hardly noticed abroad. This quickly moving epoch had experienced a sufficient number of radical innovations, and how many of them which had been introduced with a great deal of noise had after all come to nothing. The French made fun of the caution with which in Königsberg the footsteps of the Great Revolution were being followed. In Prussia itself, however, the feeling was all the more vivid that the new legislation was profoundly affecting all the relationships of life. The cultured bourgeoisie hailed with gladness the liberation of the country folk ; in Breslau the deeds of the royal reformer were commemorated on the stage. But the nobles of the Electoral

Mark, led by the valiant Marwitz, raged against the audacious foreigner who, with his school of Franconian and East Prussian officials, was disturbing the good old Brandenburger way. No less unheard-of seemed the Jacobinical phrasing than the revolutionary content of Stein's new laws, which, in accordance with the ancient custom of Prussian absolutism, endeavoured to explain to the people the monarch's intentions in detail, and which in doing this repeatedly referred to the good of the state and to the progress of the spirit of the time. In Priegnitz, the peasants even raised a disturbance against " the new freedom," and the king had to send a force to keep them in order. In the Junkergasse at Königsberg, at the Perponcher Club, worthy gentlemen of the court, of the landed gentry, of the army, were profoundly incensed at the " viper's brood " of the reformer. No one there scolded more fiercely than General York, to whom it seemed that the severe old-time discipline was disappearing from the world, that the time was coming when every cornet would begin to stick up for the rights of man. Even Gneisenau could not follow the minister in all these bold ventures, and it seemed to him that the destruction of great landed proprietorship was imminent, until experience taught him his error. Some of the finest men of the East Prussian stocks of the Dohna, the Auerswald, and the Finkenstein, sent a petition to the king, imploring him to protect the rights of the nobility, and at least to save the noble from military service and from the patrimonial courts. Nor were justified complaints lacking, for although the legislator everywhere expressed his leading ideas with businesslike clearness and definiteness, there were nevertheless in certain matters of detail, owing to the haste with which the work was done, many obscurities and contradictions. But the prestige of the royal command was as firmly established as was the confidence in the justice of Frederick William. Even those who were personally dissatisfied could not imagine that this prince could order an open act of injustice. The reform ran its course. Once again, as so often before, it was by the will of the crown that an act of liberation was effected for the Prussian people.

The second great task which Stein undertook was the completion of the unity of the state. From the proceedings of the Paris National Assembly, he had learned the necessity for a centralised financial system, and from a study of the executive organisation of the First Consul he had come to recognise that the business of the state must be so carried on as to render a unified supervision possible. Even before the war he had recommended the appointment of departmental ministers for the whole state. The extraordinary juxtaposition of provincial ministers and departmental ministers, the intermingling of the real system with the provincial system, was no longer adequate to the needs of an active modern administration. The anxious preservation of territorial peculiarities had been carried so far during recent decades, that the officials of the old school could even speak of the Prussian monarchy as a " federal state." Yet closer examination showed how healthy and full of life was the executive organisation founded by Frederick William I. Now that the undertaking was ventured of carrying his work a stage further, full justice was for the first time done to the remarkable insight of the strict old organiser. Schön esteemed him as the greatest king of Prussia as far as internal affairs were concerned. What was resolved on was not a revolution, but the progressive development and simplification of the ancient institutions. The law of December 16, 1808, concerning the changed constitution of the supreme state authorities decreed that there should be five departmental ministers, for home affairs, finance, foreign affairs, war, and justice, at the head of the entire administration of the state, and the old general treasuries were to be united into a single general state treasury, under the charge of the minister of finance. Stein foresaw how dangerous might become the power of these five men, and he therefore intended to constitute, as the supreme authority of the monarchy, a council of state which should unite in itself all the leading energies of the state service, including the ministers, should advise as to legislative proposals, and should decide the great disputed questions of public law. But his successors failed to carry out this part of his proposals.

Through the appointment of the departmental ministers, the general directory was abolished. There remained, however, the old war chambers, and domain chambers, under the new names of " administrations." The judiciary and the executive were completely separated ; the judicial business of the old chambers was allotted to the " administrations " ; they were purged of useless members (for Stein everywhere fought against the practical irremovability of the old officialdom, and reserved to the crown the right of dismissing the executive officials at will); the course of business was simplified, and greater independence was secured for the presidents and the heads of departments in the individual branches of the executive. But the advantages of the German *collegial system*, its lack of partisanship, and its careful regard for all the circumstances of the individual case, were too highly esteemed by Stein for him to be willing to exchange that system for the readier mobility of a bureaucratic prefectural administration. The intermediate authorities of the Prussian executive remained colleges and in this form continued to work beneficially for two generations. Instead of the vain display of the general councils which stood beside the Napoleonic prefects giving diffident advice, the German statesmen demanded the active and regular participation of the nation in administrative affairs. Thus there would flow in to the men of the boardroom a wealth of views and feelings derived from the outside world, whilst the people itself would become animated with the sense of fatherland, of independence, and of national honour.

But how was this vigorous activity on the part of the ruled to be incorporated in the firmly ordered hierarchy of the paid officialdom? It was obviously impossible to transfer to the provincial diets the conduct of individual executive affairs; nepotism, cumbrousness, the commercial spirit of the old feudal committees, still gave to these bodies an evil repute. For this reason Stein and Hardenberg both conceived the remarkable idea of proposing that in every government nine of the representatives sitting in the provincial diets should be co-opted upon the boards for three years, and that these co-opted members should take full part in all the work of the boards. This idea shows very clearly how complete a breach had been made with the old views of bureaucratic self-satisfaction, but it led to nothing. The new institution came into existence in East Prussia alone; elsewhere the provincial diets showed little inclination to provide the daily allowance of money for the notables. The East Prussian representatives soon found themselves to be extremely isolated among their far more numerous bureaucratic official colleagues; they felt themselves to be dilettanti among experts; those from the country would not work long in their offices; the monetary allowances were not forthcoming; zeal soon cooled, and in the year 1812 the unlucky experiment was abandoned.[1] Nor did the new office of lord-lieutenant at first prove very satisfactory. Whereas revolutionary France had subdivided its ancient provinces into powerless departments, Stein, in deliberate contrast, wished to unite the weakly governmental areas into great and vigorous provinces. Three lords-lieutenant, for Silesia, for Old Prussia, and for the territories of Pomerania and the Mark, respectively, were

[1] Report of Minister von Schuckmann to the king, May 24, 1812.

to supervise the government, not as intermediaries but as permanent commissaries of the ministry, and as representatives of the common interests of their provinces. The institution was plainly based upon the wider relationships of a great state. In the narrow circumstances of the diminished monarchy, its only effect was to render more difficult the conduct of business ; not until after the restoration of Prussia to the position of a great power, did its utility become manifest.

The social reforms of Stein and the consolidation of the unity of the state, proceeded from the independent and peculiar working out of ideas which had been in the air since the outbreak of the revolution and which were a common possession of all clear intelligences among the Prussian officials. But a thoroughly creative action, the free work of Stein's own genius, was the Towns' Ordinance of November 19, 1808.[1] He regarded the elevation of the nation out of the dull narrowness of its domestic life, as the last and highest task of his political activity. He saw that the country was in danger of falling into a condition of sensuality, or of attributing an exaggerated worth to the speculative sciences, and he wished to lead it on towards a vigorous activity which should be of value to the community. By a happy practical insight, he was led to begin his work with the towns. Only after an independent communal life had been awakened among the cultured townsmen, would it be possible for the rude peasants who had but recently been delivered from hereditary servitude, and who still regarded their landlords with great hostility, to be awakened to the rights and duties of self-government. Wilckens played the principal part in the working out of this law. The towns were given the independent control of their finances, of their poor relief, and of their educational activities ; and on the demand of the state, they might also carry on police affairs in the state's name. They were thus to be in a position of almost complete independence *vis-à-vis* the state authority, and were even granted autonomous rights in matters of taxation, no one yet foreseeing how injurious to the community would be the effect of this last privilege. The various ancient gradations of civil right were done away with, and the privileges of the guilds were also abolished. The inhabitants of the towns consisted now of two classes only, citizens and denizens. One who had acquired the freedom of the city, and

[1] Stein always definitely described the Towns' Ordinance as his own creation. It is simply owing to the way in which the work of his office was carried on that the documents contain so few autograph comments of the minister's (E. Meier *op. cit.*, page 147)

this was not difficult to obtain, was bound to undertake all communal duties ; for whilst the freedom of property was a leading idea of Stein's law, no less important in that law was the principle that upon the property owner was imposed the duty of service to the community. An elected magistracy, whose members were partly unpaid and partly paid on a very moderate scale, with a representative assembly elected by all the burgesses (who for electoral purposes were listed in separate constituencies), conducted the administration of the town. Thus the atrophy of German communal life which had endured for two centuries came at length to an end.

This reform seems all the more remarkable in its simple clearness and directness of aim since Stein had no example to follow anywhere in Europe. The careless English municipal constitutions were of as little value to him as examples as was the patrician domination in his own beloved Westphalian towns. Now for the first time did there come into existence in Germany modern urban communities, independent corporations which, nevertheless, were at the same time trustworthy organs to fulfil the will of the central authority, and which remained subject to governmental supervision. Hitherto some of the towns had been completely deprived of independence. Others, like the baronial country-towns, constituted petty states within the state, with their own patrimonial jurisdiction and their own police, and only too often had the commands of the king to "our vassals, officials, magistrates, and beloved subjects " been thwarted by the passive resistance of these ancient municipal dominions. Now at length in the administration of the towns the centralised authority obtained a powerful prop, and one which corresponded to its own national characteristics.

This reform also had to be imposed upon the nation by the king's command. The gentry of the Mark, and the officers of the old school, complained of the republican principles of the Towns' Ordinance. What horror was felt in these circles when it was learned that one of the first state officials, the president von Gerlach, had accepted the election to the position of chief burgomaster of Berlin ! The exhausted communal sentiment of the bourgeoisie showed at first very little inclination for the enforced honorary services ; and it soon became apparent that self-government is expensive ; whereas Stein and his friends had rather anticipated a diminution in the cost. The towns, which under the rule of Frederick William I had been accustomed to strict economy, were for the most part better disposed towards the new ordinance than were the old rural communes, which were accustomed to the nepotist rule of independent magistrates. It was only during the War of Liberation that a true understanding of the blessings of freedom awakened among the townsfolk, when the central authority had almost everywhere to discontinue its work, and when every town was forced to look after itself. Since then there has become manifest in our municipal life a second flowering, less brilliant, but not less honourable than the great epoch of the Hanseatic League. In educational matters, in the relief of destitution, in foundations of general utility, the German bourgeoisie once more endeavoured to compete with the older and richer urban culture of the Romans. Just as Frederick William I had created the modern German executive officialdom, so did Stein's Towns' Ordinance prove the starting-point for German municipal self-government. Upon this were based the new by-laws, which for two generations, so long as parliamentarism still remained immature, constituted the best and the most secure element of German national freedom. Through Stein's reforms there was reawakened in the German bourgeoisie a lively communal sense and a delight in responsible political activity. It is to these reforms that we owe the fact that the German constitutional state is to-day established upon a firm foundation, that our views as to the nature of political freedom, however erroneous they may at times have been, have never become so vain and formalised as were the doctrines of the French Revolution.

Through the losses of the Treaty of Tilsit, Prussia had once more become a mainly agricultural country. For this reason it was Stein's intention that the Towns' Ordinance should be followed as soon as possible by a Rural Districts' Ordinance. A proposal by von Schrötter and the East Prussian provincial department had already been drafted. Stein demanded free rural communes with village-mayors and village-courts. The last and strongest props of the old feudal order of society, the territorial police and patrimonial courts, must be abolished, for power must be derived only from the highest authority. Stein's plans involved no alteration in the ancient historical character of the office of Landrat ; as formerly, so now, the Landrat was to be a servant of the state, but he was to be at the same time a moderately paid official, a landlord resident in the circles, and the trusted adviser of its inhabitants. But to the experienced eye of the minister, the existing circles seemed too large for the energies of a single man, and he was already considering, in conjunction with his friend

Vincke, the appointment of several Landrats in each district ; like the English justices of the peace, they were from time to time to assemble to hold quarter sessions. In addition to the Landrats, there was to be a provincial assembly, constituted of all the principal landowners and of a number of representatives from the towns and villages. The strong representation given to landed property was obviously necessary, for no one yet knew whether the rude peasantry, who had only just become freemen, were competent for representation in the provincial assembly. For this reform also the indefatigable Schrötter had already drawn up a detailed plan which in essential respects proceeded from the same principles as the Circle Ordinance of 1872.

Stein desired that the lord-lieutenant should be assisted by a provincial diet, so that the peculiarities and the separate interests of the great territories should be properly represented within the unified state. He gladly boasted that his scheme for this institution was based upon free property ; he gave the suffrage to all "property holders," and in his mouth this term meant exclusively or chiefly those who held real property in town or country. With a bold hand he had overthrown the legal barriers between the ancient classes. There no longer existed in Prussia any hereditary class differences ; and yet he did not wish in any spirit of levity to overthrow the distinction between the professional classes on the one hand and groups of interests on the other, for this distinction was still a marked one in the popular consciousness. For this reason he demanded a class representation for the provincial diets, in such a way that the country gentry, the towns, and the peasantry, were to name their representatives separately ; and he rejected the proposals of his Silesian friend, Rhediger, who wished to do away completely with the old division of classes. It was enough for Stein if the totality of the burgesses of the town and of the peasants obtained class representation, whereas only a few privileged towns that were immediates of the empire, and among the peasantry only the Köllmers, had taken part in the old feudal diets. Whilst he was still in power the first step was taken towards this end. "In order that the government may be supported by general assent," East Prussia received a new Territorial Ordinance, which secured for the Köllmers equal political rights with the nobles, and gave them the right to representation on the territorial committees.

Finally, over these new provincial estates were to be superposed the Prussian estates of the realm, as a support for the throne,

and as an indispensable means for awakening and invigorating
the national spirit. In these disordered times, the old absolutism
was everywhere feeling its powerlessness. When the stringency
of the national finances made it necessary to sell the domains, the
king was unwilling to take upon his own shoulders the responsibility for so venturesome a step, and he therefore had the new
domestic law concerning the sale of the domains laid before the
estates of all the provinces for their acceptance, although he
expressly declared that he did this as an act of grace and not as a
duty. (In Silesia, which had no estates, the proposal was laid
before the representatives of the mortgage institute and of some of
the towns.) It was impossible that such a state of insecurity in
public law should persist. Stein cherished the idea of a great
reform of taxation ; he desired to break with the anxious domestic
economy which measured the expenses in accordance with the
income, and he wished to introduce for Prussia the bold principle
which applies to every national fiscal system which is run on broad
lines, that the income must be regulated in accordance with the
expenditure. For this reform, and for all the other sacrifices which
seemed to him to be required of the reawakening nation, he considered that the approval of an assembly of the estates of the realm
was indispensable. For the moment, however, owing to the immaturity of the people, the powers of this body must be deliberative
merely.

Such, in essentials, were Stein's proposals for a thorough-going
reform, the greatest and the boldest which the political idealism
of the Germans had ever conceived. By similar plans Turgot had
once hoped to avert the approaching Revolution, but the proposals
of the German statesman far transcended the ideas of the Frenchman, in modest greatness, in logical definiteness, and in regard for
that which was historically extant. The king was in agreement
with all these proposals, but that to which he was least inclined
was the summoning of the estates of the realm. It was not that
he feared a limitation of his power ; but to his retiring nature, the
noise of the debates, the passion of the parliamentary struggle, the
necessity for his own public appearance, were repugnant. Brought
up in the traditions of a mild absolutism, full of antipathy to the
sins of the Revolution, he could not yet completely convince himself that the representative system had become indispensable. It
was in fact questionable, in view of the lamentable state of political
culture, whether the influence of the estates of the realm would not
prove rather a hindrance than a help. From the gentry which,

according to Stein's proposals, was to constitute the most powerful element of the united diet, the free assent to a juster system of taxation and to the other innovations proposed by the minister, was hardly to be expected. Even the towns and the peasants showed only too often how little they were able to follow the reforming ideas of the crown.

If, however, Stein's own vigorous personality were to remain in control, if the reform were to proceed as he planned, step by step, if, first of all, by the abolition of the territorial police, the dominant position of the country gentry were to be destroyed, and if then the district assemblies and the provincial diets were to spread through the liberated areas, he might hope to bring the king to understand that the summoning of an assembly of the estates of the realm was necessary on behalf of the unity of the state, as a counterpoise to the centrifugal forces of the provincial diets. In this way, by the free choice of the crown, might be effected the transition from absolute monarchy to a representative system, and the Prussian state might perhaps be spared a whole generation of tentative proceedings. Stein was prepared to build upon the awakening insight in the loyal and good-hearted people. He did not fail to recognise the deep chasm which existed between the over-refined and unworldly culture of the men of learning and the esential roughness of the masses ; but he hoped to bridge this chasm by the reconstitution of the educational system, and it was only his sudden fall which prevented these plans from coming to maturity. Years before, in Münster, he had shown that this branch of internal administration was within the purview of his free and comprehensive spirit, for in Münster he had fought Jesuitism at the University, and had awakened a new life in this ossified institution.

Hand in hand with administrative reform, there proceeded the reorganisation of the army, this also being effected under Stein's personal supervision. The king himself gave the first impetus. In this department, which he regarded as peculiarly his own, he always retained the immediate direction, and never failed to display an apt power of judgment and a penetrating knowledge of affairs. As early as July, 1807, he appointed Scharnhorst to the presidency of a commission for army reorganisation, and submitted to this commission an autograph memorial in which he clearly pointed out all the defects of the existing military system, and rightly indicated the means for its improvement. There were associated with

Scharnhorst in this work a number of younger men of talent, who followed with a lively understanding, as did Scharnhorst himself, all the intellectual work of the time, men of statesmanlike intelligence who regarded the army as a popular school, and the art of war as a branch of politics. Their quiet activity served, not merely to sharpen the weapons for the War of Liberation, but also to bring the Prussian army once more into harmony with the new culture, and to endow the German military system for all future time with the characteristics of serious culture and intellectual freshness and alertness.

These officers were united from the outset with the leading statesman by a remarkable and instinctive agreement of moral and political conviction. It sounded like one of Stein's own utterances when Gneisenau, apropos of the French Rights of Man, exclaimed, "First make the human race enthusiasts for duty, and only after that for rights!" Just as the disciple of Adam Smith was unwilling to apply the principle of the division of labour unconditionally to the national administration, esteeming the skilled business ability of the professional official less highly than that popular maturity which is acquired in self-government, so also did these military experts cherish the belief that it is moral force which ultimately proves decisive in war. However highly they esteemed the essentials of technical training, they regarded as still more important, to use Scharnhorst's own words, "the intimate union of the army with the nation." Scharnhorst wrote soon after the peace: "The sense of independence must be instilled into the nation, which must be given an opportunity of becoming acquainted with itself, of standing on its own feet; then only will it respect itself, and learn how to gain respect from others. All that we can do is to work towards this end. We must loosen the bonds of prejudice, guide the rebirth of the nation; care for its growth, and not hinder its free development; more than this it is not in our power to do."

Scharnhorst had long been recognised as the first military writer of his country, as the most brilliant authority among the German officers, but after an extremely varied life he also had at his disposal an exceptional wealth of practical experience. He had seen service in every arm, in the general staff, and in the military colleges. During his training at the military college of Wilhelmstein, he had become acquainted with that exemplary little troop which the talented old warrior Count Wilhelm von Bückeburg had formed out of the young men of his own petty territory; next as a Hanoverian officer, in the Netherlands theatre of war, he had become closely acquainted with the English Army, which among all the armies of Europe still preserved most faithfully the characteristics of the ancient mercenary system ; he had seen active service against the loosely organised militia of the Republic and also against the well-trained conscripts of Napoleon, and in the war of 1806 he was sufficiently near to the leadership to have learned completely to understand the errors of the Frederician army and the ultimate grounds of its overthrow. To the simple Saxon, that stiff military conduct which the king demanded from his officers was repugnant. He went about in an inconspicuous, and almost untidy, dress, with his head hanging down, and his deep-set thinker's eyes turned quite inward. His hair fell in disorder over his forehead ; his speech was gentle and slow. In Hanover he was often seen knocking at the doors of the baker's shop, and then sitting quietly with his wife and children at supper under the trees of the Eilenride. Thus he remained throughout life, straightforward and unadorned in all things. The simplicity and tenderness of his private correspondence reminds us of the men of antiquity ; in his writings, as in everything else, matter is everything and form nothing. But the superiority of a powerful, continuously productive and thoroughly independent spirit, the nobility of a moral disposition which simply did not know what self-seeking is, gave to this unpretentious man a natural charm which, repellent to men of common mind, slowly and surely attracted magnanimous spirits. His daughter, Countess Julie Dohna, owed everything to her widowed father ; she was spoken of as a royal woman, and was accepted in distinguished circles as if she had indeed been of royal blood.

The equable temperament of the general was more agreeable to the king than was Stein's stimulating and stimulated nature ; none among his counsellors was so near to Frederick William. Scharnhorst returned the confidence of his royal friend without restraint. It would have seemed to him base to think any longer of past errors ; he admired the moral strength of the unfortunate monarch ; and he never swerved in his loyalty, not even when, in their patriotic impatience, many of his friends became disaffected towards the over-cautious prince. A true Low German, he was of a retiring disposition, quiet, and reserved by nature. Praise sounded to him almost like an insult, and a gentle word as a profanation of friendship. His life led him along a rough road, always among enemies. In Hanover, the plebeian had had to contend with the ill-favour of the nobility ; whilst in Prussia the innovator had to fight against the arrogance of the old generals. When now, by the confidence of the king and by the general acclamation of the army, he was placed at the head of military affairs, for five years he had to carry on the obscure activity of a conspirator, preparing for the War of Liberation under the very eyes of the enemy. He thus learned to control every word and every gesture, and the simple-minded man who despised on his own account every kind of duplicity, became, for the sake of his country, a master in the arts of concealment, unrivalled in the faculty of holding his tongue, cunning and world-wise. With a rapid and searching glance he read the thoughts of those with whom he came in contact ; whereas, when on his side he had to conceal one of the king's secrets, it was necessary for him with ambiguous phrase to lure friend and foe alike upon a false scent. The officers said very truly, that his soul was as full of furrows as his face ; he reminded them of William of Orange, who long before in a similar situation, quiet and self-contained, had prepared for the struggle with the world-empire of Spain. And just like William the Silent, Scharnhorst hid within his bosom the lofty passion, the love of struggle, characteristic of the hero, and during the last war these traits had acquired for him the friendship of the active-minded Blucher. He did not know fear, he would not admit how stultifying can be the anxiety that follows a defeat ; in the courts-martial his sentence was always the most severe against cowardice and breach of faith. In a strange and yet harmonious manner there were combined in this great soul a petty-bourgeois simplicity, and a world-embracing breadth of view ; a yearning for peace, and courage in war ; philanthropic tenderness of heart, and the elemental energy of the national hatred. Perhaps no one suffered so bitterly from the distresses of the time as did this man of silence ; day and night he was never free from the thought of the disgrace of his country. Everyone approached him with reverence, for all felt involuntarily that upon him depended the future of the army.

Among the men who assisted him in the work of army reorganisation, four proved equally the heirs of his spirit, so that each one of the four received a portion of the comprehensive talents of the master. These were Gneisenau and Grolman, the born commanders ; Boyen, the organiser ; and Clausewitz, the man of learning. All four of them were, like Scharnhorst himself, poor and temperate, men of few needs, free from all self-seeking, looking only to the end which had to be gained, and with all their candour, men of profound modesty as is natural to the gifted soldier—for whilst the solitary poietic activity of the artist and of the man of learning very readily leads to vanity, the soldier works only as a member of the great whole, and is unable to show what he is worth unless an inscrutable destiny leads him to the right place at the right moment. With an excess of modesty, Gneisenau declared himself to be merely a pigmy beside the giant Scharnhorst. He lacked the profound erudition of the master, and like so many men of action, he felt the gaps in his knowledge as if they were a lack of capacity ; on the other hand, he possessed in a far greater measure the inspiriting confidence of the hero, that joyful fatalism which makes the great commander. How proudly and securely did he now spread his sails when he at length emerged from the erroneous wanderings of a passionate youth, and when after the long and dreary calm of a subaltern service, he had attained to the high seas of life. Every task that destiny offered him he undertook with a happy facility and readiness ; unhesitatingly the infantry soldier took over the command of the engineers and the supervision of the fortresses. Whilst Scharnhorst was cautiously weighing the dangers of the immediate future, Gneisenau always looked forward with ardent yearning to the hour of the uprising, and suffered even fools gladly if they would only take part in the great conspiracy.

A kindred nature was that of Grolman, magnanimous, serene, and happy, incisive and unsparing in act and speech, created for the melée, for the bold seizure of the fortune of the moment ; yet he was to experience to the full the cruelty of the soldier's destiny, and never in war was he to occupy the first place. In his general demeanour, Boyen appeared to resemble the general most closely ; he was a serious and reserved East Prussian who had sat at the feet of Kant and Kraus, and who, as a poet, was also in close touch with the new literature. It was only the ardent eyes under his bushy eyebrows which betrayed the stormy courage that slumbered in the simple and silent man. After his quiet manner he had turned over in his own mind the organising ideas of Scharnhorst, had developed them further, and after the wars he helped to give its permanent form to the new people's army. Finally, the youngest of this circle of friends, Carl von Clausewitz, was more than any of the others the trusted pupil of Scharnhorst, deeply initiated into the new scientific theories of war to which Scharnhorst was devoted. Subsequently Clausewitz developed these theories independently, and in a series of works, which in respect of classic form greatly excel those of the master, he secured for the theory of war its place among the number of state-sciences. His was a profound intelligence, and he was a master of historical judgment; but he was perhaps too critical and too cautious to grasp, as did Gneisenau, the fortune of battle at the propitious moment; yet he was far from being simply a man of books, for he was a practical and valiant soldier, looking with wide-open eyes upon the tumult of life. He had just returned with Prince Augustus from duress as a prisoner of war. While he was in France, his love for the youthful candour and freshness of the Teutons had risen to the point of enthusiasm. He returned home with the conviction that the French were still in essentials as unmilitary a people as they had been formerly in the days of the wars of the Huguenots when they trembled before the German infantry and cavalry. How can the primitive character of nations alter in ten years? How could those who had been conquered one hundred times permanently control Germany mighty in arms?

It was with the aid of such forces as these that the king undertook the work of reconstruction. The whole army was formed anew. Six brigades, two Silesian, two Old Prussian, one from Pomerania, and one from the Mark, were all that still remained of the Frederician army, and constituted the last anchor for German hopes. The troops were given more practical weapons and clothing, the pigtail was done away with, the arts of the parade-ground passed into abeyance, and their place was taken by the strenuous work of field service. All the stores had to be provided anew; Napoleon's marshals had carried out their work of plunder so thoroughly that the Silesian artillery was unable for many months to undertake any practice for lack of powder. A commission of inquiry made a thorough examination of the conduct during the war of individual officers, and pitilessly cashiered all who were blameworthy or suspect. In the newspaper *Der Volksfreund*, edited by the valiant Bärsch, Gneisenau demanded the abolition of flogging in the army, asking bitterly whether the Prussian soldier was to continue to seek the stimulus of good conduct in the cane instead of in the sense of honour. His views found acceptance, the new articles of war abolished the old and cruel corporal punishments. How changed was the world when Prussian officers could now venture to discuss in the press the defects of the military system!

In another article, Gneisenau sarcastically alluded to the convenient system by which the sons of the Junkers could, while still children, exercise a hereditary right to command the soldiers of the king. In these words he merely gave open expression to what all intelligent officers were thinking. The abolition of the privileged position of the Junkers, and of all the other military privileges of the gentry, was a necessary consequence of the spirit of the new legislation ; and since the Prussians had taken practical note of the efficiency of Napoleon's youthful commanders many Hotspurs demanded that the renowned free promotion of the French should be imitated in Prussia. Scharnhorst, however, went his own way ; he saw the moral evils which had resulted from the adoption of the Napoleonic principle, "young generals, old captains"; he saw how many rough and unwholesome elements had found their way into the lower strata of the French officers' corps, and how seriously in the French army unbridled ambition had loosened the bonds of true comradeship. The son of the German peasant was well aware why Washington had exclaimed to the Americans, "Take only gentlemen for your officers." He understood why King Frederick William I had allowed his officers to disobey orders when these orders touched their honour. It was not his desire to destroy the ancient aristocratic character of the Prussian officers' corps, but only to substitute the aristocracy of culture for the aristocracy of the privileged nobility.

The regulation of August 6, 1808, concerning the appointment of ensigns, established the principle that in time of peace only knowledge and culture, and in time of war only distinguished bravery and intelligence, could give a claim to officer's rank ; no Junker could now become an ensign simply on the ground of hereditary right, for the position of ensign could not be attained before the age of seventeen years, and only then after a scientific examination ; whilst not until a second examination had been passed, and upon a proposal from the officers' corps, could a young man win his epaulettes. The king impressed it upon the officers that they should never cease to realise their honourable position as educators and teachers of a noteworthy portion of the nation. In the lower grades up to the rank of captain, promotion usually occurred by seniority, but in the selection of the staff-officers and in the filling of the higher posts of command, service was alone determinative. Through these inconspicuous proposals, the officer's position acquired a new character which to us to-day seems a matter of course, since it constitutes a distinctive national feature of the German military system. Now for the first time did the officers' corps gain an inner correspondence with the civil officialdom, now first did it acquire a definite intellectual superiority over the rank and file. The prospect of rapid promotion was open to talent ; and yet the slowness of promotion in the lower grades, the general similarity of culture and of manner of life, resulted in this, that every member of the officers' corps had a definite sense of his position, and that an aristocratic class-consciousness permeated the whole body. The social barrier which in France separated the officer promoted from the ranks from his more cultured fellows, could not here exist.

For no one was the transformation of the military system so momentous, as for the older generation of the landed gentry, whose members still continued to form the majority of the officers' corps. Many years passed away before the actual favouring of the nobility in the army ceased to exist. But the principle was none the less firmly established that even the noble must acquire his commission by the proof of scientific knowledge, and only men of a considerable degree of culture could show themselves adequate for the new and more severe ordering of the service. No longer did the state service offer an asylum for the ignorant, and the reformers already began to speak of the new Prussia as an intelligent state. It was by Scharnhorst that the excessive roughness of the eastern German Junkerdom was first smoothed away, for the house of cadets instituted by Frederick William I had but half succeeded in effecting this change. The old generation, which had despised the quill-drivers, died out, and their youthful successors recognised and revered the power of knowledge.

The fundamental idea of all these reforms was that henceforward the army was to consist of the people in arms, it was to be a national army, to which everyone capable of bearing arms must belong. Recruiting was abolished, the enlisting of foreigners was forbidden ; only a few volunteers of German blood were still admitted. The new articles of war and the ordinance concerning military punishments started with the premise that in future all subjects, even young persons of good education, should serve as common soldiers, and this established the need for a gentler treatment of the rank and file. All thinking officers were at one as to the need for abolishing the old exemptions from military service. The idea of the general liability to service had even before the war been defended by Scharnhorst himself, by Boyen, by Loussau, and by other officers, and it was fully considered by the king. During the unfortunate campaign, this idea had quietly been gaining ground, and it was now clear to every intelligent soldier that the unequal war could only be resumed through the utilisation of the entire energy of the nation. Immediately after the peace, Blucher begged his dear Scharnhorst, " to provide for a national army ; no one must be exempt on any account, it must be a disgrace to anyone not to have served." Prince Augustus, while still a prisoner of war, transmitted a plan for the reconstitution of the army, in which universal military service was the leading idea. Scharnhorst knew, however, what most of his contemporaries had completely forgotten, that this was merely the revival of an ancient Prussian principle. He reminded the king that his ancestor Frederick William I had, first of all the princes of Europe, introduced general conscription ; it was this principle whose application had once made Prussia great, and here Austria and France were merely imitators. It now appeared to be necessary to return to the old Prussian system, and straightway to abolish the misuse of exemptions. Thus only could be constituted a true standing army, an army which would be of equal strength at all times. Almost with the very words of the old soldier-king did Scharnhorst begin his proposal for the formation of a reserve army. The first section opened with the words : " All the inhabitants of the state are by birth defenders of the state."

From the first, the Prussian officers conceived the ideas of universal military service in a freer and juster sense than did the bourgeoisie under the French Directory. The conquered were too proud-spirited to imitate the institutions of the conqueror. It had been bearable that the king's command should except from cantonal duty certain classes of people, either on account of class-privilege or else for economic reasons. But the proposal that a man of means should be able to buy himself exemption from military service, that one subject should sell his skin to another, was utterly un-Prussian, and in conflict with all the traditions of the army. The French system of substitution was indeed recommended by a few civil officials, but not by any single officer of note. Here ideas were more democratic than among the heirs of the revolution ; in plain terms it was demanded that all should be liable to military service, and this demand was made, not simply as a means to the ends of the War of Liberation, but as a permanent institution for the education of the people. Notwithstanding his contempt for military superficialities, Scharnhorst was ever a trained expert ; he was well aware to how small an extent unaided enthusiasm was able to replace the staying power, the skill, and the discipline, of the trained soldier. With his rich historical knowledge he had attained to the conviction that the gentler the manners of the times, the more necessary for the nation was a military education, so that the civilised world might retain the virile virtues of simpler times, so that the vigorous energy of body and soul should not be lost by culture. Gneisenau joyfully acclaimed this manly view of historic life ; it was his desire that military training should begin even at the elementary school, for was the heroic glory of the Spartans no longer attainable to modern humanity ? From his soul, Boyen wrote for all friends of Scharnhorst the verses :

> "Valiant men throughout the country wield ye every one the sword ;
> Let all classes, as is fitting, fight for hearth and sov'reign lord ! "

Thus there was no dispute about the principle. But how were the enormous difficulties in the way of its execution to be overcome ? To this age, which had so recently emerged from the barbarism of the ancient military discipline, it seemed an intolerable severity that the sons of the cultured classes should be enrolled straightway in the standing army ; moreover, in September, 1808, Napoleon forced the acceptance of the Treaty of Paris, in accordance with which the ill-used state was forced to pledge itself not to keep an armed force larger than forty-two thousand men.

Thus the only thing that remained, was to overreach the conqueror by cunning, to find a way round the treaty, and to create, beside the standing army, a reserve army, a Landwehr, for use in case of war. And yet even for this end the direct road was closed. Scharnhorst at once recognised that the simplest plan would be to provide the Landwehr through the school of the standing army, to constitute the reserve army out of the trained soldiers who had served their time. Yet for the moment this was impossible. The calling up of so great a number of recruits would at once have aroused the suspicions of Napoleon ; and moreover, a Landwehr constituted in this way would obviously not attain a notable strength until many years had passed, whilst month by month a fresh outbreak of the war was anticipated. For this reason, the Prussians must content themselves with a militia without any apparent connection with the standing army, ostensibly intended only for the maintenance of internal peace, but trained for military purposes by repeated drills, and with a sufficient supply of arms to be able to take the field as a reserve army immediately after the outbreak of war. Four times during the years 1807 and 1810 did Scharnhorst resume these Landwehr plans, and confer upon them with the monarch. His first proposal came into effect on

July 31, 1807, quite independently, and long before the Austrian Landwehr came into existence.

The earlier plans pursued as their main purpose the preparation for military service of the sons of the well-to-do classes, who would be able to provide their own arms and uniform ; this force was to be drilled in time of peace under the harmless name of a " burgher guard " or of the " national watch." In the summer of 1809, the restless military reformer gave a wider scope to these proposals, in which could already be recognised the elements of the organisation of 1813. He set a high value upon the heroic energy of a wrathful people, but he also had a sober vision of the length of time that would be requisite before he could transform an armed mob into troops ready and fit for war. His plan was that the standing army should begin the attack ; meanwhile the reserve army was to be constituted out of the soldiers that had served their term, out of the supernumeraries, and also out of all the younger men liable to cantonal service ; the well-to-do were to join as volunteer yagers. This Landwehr was to take over service in the fortresses, and was to effect the investment of places garrisoned by the enemy ; as soon as it was sufficiently developed, it was to follow the army, and its place was to be taken by the militia, or Landsturm, which had meanwhile been assembled and was to comprise all those still fit to bear arms. Scharnhorst knew how disagreeable to Napoleon were his memories of the campaign of La Vendée, and how greatly he dreaded a popular uprising. It was Scharnhorst's hope to open the War of Liberation with a small army which should base its actions upon a few fortresses or entrenched camps, and with such an end in view, he had an extremely careful study made of the unfavourable ground of the North German plain. When Gneisenau learned of Wellington's Portuguese victories, he even hoped to reconstitute a Torres Vedras upon this plain, out of the little town of Spandau.

All these hopes came to nought. As soon as Napoleon was informed of the Prussian plans for a new Landwehr, he at once uttered masterful threats. His detested opponent was not to go a single step outside the provisions of the Treaty of Paris—while he reserved to himself the right to trample these provisions under foot. At length it became clear that the constitution of a Landwehr remained impossible so long as Prussia was not yet in a position to declare war against France. Until then, all that could be attained without arousing the suspicion of the Imperator, was to undertake a more rapid training of the men of the standing army.

The Rise of Prussia

The legally established age for the service of those liable to military duty was twenty years, and this was left unchanged ; but as many of them were called up as possible, and were sent home again in a few months when they had received a tolerable training. The strength of the army allowed by the treaty was not observed with undue strictness. For years, the bodyguard in Berlin, whenever the force went out into the field for manœuvres, left a portion of the men in barracks, so that Napoleon's spies could not ascertain the strength of the battalions. It was impossible to avoid that many of those fit for service should evade the more severe levies by flight, whilst on the other hand many conscripts entered Prussia from the territories of the Confederation of the Rhine. On the whole the people showed a self-sacrificing loyalty towards the king. It happened on one occasion that the peasants of the neighbourhood stole a cannon during the night from the ramparts of the West-phalian fortress of Magdeberg, and brought it by boat to Spandau—their tribal lord needed weapons to use against the Frenchmen. Through this system of partial training Scharnhorst gradually succeeded in building up a force of 150,000 soldiers. It was a tragical spectacle, that of this great man endeavouring year after year to elude the notice of his omniscient enemy by a thousand wiles and tricks. His soul longed for the joy of battle ; he was willing to sacrifice the last man and horse in the country so that Germany might once more be free ; yet ever again and again the watchful opponent rendered vain his plans of military preparation. It was not until the hour of open battle struck that in a moment there sprang to life all that had been quietly prepared in five years full of arduous labour, full of nameless anxieties. Scharnhorst and no other was the father of the Landwehr of 1813.

Meanwhile hatred and poverty brought about a profound transformation in the mood of the cultured classes of North Germany, a transformation for which the way had long been prepared by the ideas of the Romantic literature. After great tribulations of popular life there always ensues a storm of complaints and accusations, the tormented consciences endeavouring to lay upon the shoulders of isolated individuals the blame which belongs to all ; invectives and foul lampoons crawled like loathsome worms out of the corpse of the fallen old order. Thus there threw themselves upon the humiliated Prussian state a number of miscreants, for the most part the same persons who had before the war been loud in their advocacy of an alliance between North Germany and France.

Cölln's *Neue Feuerbrände*, Massenbach's *Historische Denkwürdigkeiten*, Buchholz's *Galerie preussischer Charaktere*, and similar writings, busily unearthed all the garbage that could be discovered in any neglected corners of the old monarchy, down to the domain-purchasers of the days of Frederick William II.[1] That conceited and barren precocity, which since the days of Nicolai had persisted in the circles of the half-cultured of Berlin, had now found its political expression. Just as those of this way of thinking had formerly contested, in the name of enlightenment, everything that was free and vital in the new poetry, so now was the war against Napoleon censured in the name of freedom. It was only the mercantile egoism of England, and the arrogance of the Prussian officers, which had forced war upon peace-loving France ; and there was nothing that Buchholz was less willing to pardon to the state of Frederick than the unworthy alliance with Russian barbarism against French civilisation.

The authors of these libels were the intellectual forefathers of a new political tendency which has since that time, under manifold shapes and names, continued to flourish secretly in the soil of Berlin, and to be a cancer in the Prussian state. This takes the form of a professional desire to criticise, of an unwearied search for scandals, infinitely conceited, and yet utterly under the dominion of phrases, flourishing great words of freedom and progress, and yet continually failing to understand the signs of the times. In all these writings there was also a genuinely German characteristic, a national weakness, of which but a few of our publicists have remained altogether free. I refer to the peculiar incapacity for rightly judging the dimensions of men and things, the failure to distinguish the great and the genuine from the small and the ephemeral. Just in the same tone as Lombard and Haugwitz had been blamed were Hardenberg and Blucher now abused by these perpetual critics, and the readers of their works were left with the despairing impression that in the rotten wood of this state no nail could any longer obtain a hold.

The needs of the moment, however, were all too pressing ; the sense of the people was too honourable for them to be satisfied with nothing more than retrospective blame. Whoever among them was a man, looked forward towards the day of liberation. The lampoons had comparatively little effect ; even in Berlin the

---

[1] No one acquainted with Buchholz's other writings can doubt that the *Galerie* is the work of his pen. We have in addition the testimony of Gentz (Ompteda *Nachlass*, I, 362).

criticisms received scant attention. A profoundly earnest sentiment prevailed ; it was as if all men wished to be purer and better,
as if rage concerning the overthrow of the fatherland had completely overcome all mean and base inclinations of the spirit.
Never before had so lively a sentiment of equality united high and
low in the German north ; people drew sadly together, like the
members of a bereaved household. There had been enormous
losses of property, the whole wealth of the Prussian gentry had
disappeared ; the arbitrary new territorial divisions had annihilated
the customary channels of intercourse of whole regions ; the
mutilated state could no longer furnish occupation for thousands
of its faithful servants. Those among the younger members of
the community who would not follow the star of disloyalty which
flamed over the Confederation of the Rhine, found nowhere scope
for their activities. As Dahlmann, thinking of his own youthful
days, expressed it, in these Napoleonic times no one knew what
to do. The sense of bitterness grew and grew, and the longer the
decisive issue was postponed, the more powerful and the more
passionate became the belief that the ephemeral structure of foreign
dominion could not and must not continue, that this dissolution
of all German life was a sin against God and against history, that
it was the febrile dream of an insane criminal.

It was during these days of convulsive excitement that there
first awakened in North Germany the idea of German unity. It
was in truth the child of sorrow, of historic yearning ; but no less
was it the child of poetical and political enthusiasm. How firmly
did the eighteenth century believe in the eternity of its Roman
Empire. With what docility, content, and affection had the generation of the nineties still adhered to its principles when George
Forster in his memorials of the year 1790 described in moving
terms " the amiable behaviour of a German prince," and when
Chodoviecki immortalised Archduke Max in an engraving as a
great friend of humanity, showing how he helped a market woman
to lift her basket on to her head ! Now the empire had perished ;
the Germans were no longer a people, merely comrades in speech.
How soon was even this last bond of community likely to be torn
asunder, since the left bank of the Rhine seemed for ever handed
over to French civilisation, and in the kingdom of Westphalia, the
French official speech was dominant as far as the Elbe. All but
two of our princes now wore the chains of the foreigner. Yet amid
the destruction of their old nationality, the Germans were still
inspired by the proud sentiment that the world could not do without

them, that in spite of all, through their poets and thinkers, they had done more for humanity than ever had done their conquerors. Amid the sorrows of the present, they yearningly looked back into the remote periods of German greatness; the empire which so recently had been a mock for children, now seemed to them a glory of the nation. In all the moving letters, speeches, and writings of this period of oppression, the two bitter questions recurred again and again : Why is it that individually the Germans are so great whilst as a nation they count for nothing at all? why is it that those who once gave laws to the rest of the world are now beneath the feet of the stranger ?

Poets and men of learning were accustomed to speak of an ideal Germany, to turn in imagination to all the sons of German blood, ignoring the territorial divisions of German soil. Now that literature was filled with political passion, these views were transmitted to the state. Fichte directed his admonitions as a German to Germans, refusing to recognise, and simply putting on one side, all the distinctive divisions which unhappy experience had for centuries made in the one nation. Germanism, the genuine ancient and uncorrupted German kind, should once more attain to honour. A magnanimous enthusiasm celebrated the inborn nobility of the German nature, and did so in terms of exaggeration, for only through hyperbole could so unpolitical a race once more attain to a right esteem for the concerns of its own home, to natural consciousness of self. The old, endurable resignation was replaced by a bold radicalism which despised all the structures of our recent history as works of chance and crime. What was there that was worthy of veneration, what was there that was worth sparing, in this Germany of the Confederation of the Rhine ? If only the foreign tyrants could be overthrown, if their voluntary slaves could be chastised and their reluctant slaves liberated, there would reconstitute itself a new and powerful Germany, brilliant with the adornments of clear thought and military glory. No matter what precise form it should assume, so long as it was unified and was derived from the primitive spirit of the nation. Then would the Germans, if they were left free to develop, win also in art and science the laurels which had once decked the foreheads of the Hellenes and add them to their own crowns of victory. People were loth to speak of the man of might, who had once before led our nation upwards along the road to political power. It seemed that what this generation required was the very opposite of the Frederician idea. The work of Frederick appeared to be destroyed, and many of the young enthusiasts could never forgive him for having raised his sword against the anointed imperial majesty. A magnanimous oblivion for the old fraternal strife, a true harmony between all of German stock, this was what was necessary for the common struggle ; it must not be directed from any one chosen political centre, but the world empire must be overthrown by the uprising of the whole nation, and then everything would come right of itself.

It was of great moment for our political life, and continues to influence us at the present day, that in the case of Germany the idea of national unity was not, as it had been in France, the outcome of the slow ripening of centuries, the natural fruit of a continuous monarchical policy directed always towards the same goal, but that it reawakened suddenly after a prolonged slumber, amid passionate tears, amid dreams of times that had passed away. Hence arose that touching characteristic of idealist enthusiasm, of loyal inspiration, which makes the German patriots of the following generations so lovable. Hence also its morbid bitterness, for even after the rude hatred of the French which was the issue of that tormented time had passed away, there still remained in the hearts of the spirited Teutons a profound rancour against the foreign world. It seemed impossible to dream of Germany's future greatness without railing at the foreign nations which had sinned so often and so grossly against Central Europe. Hence, also, the remarkably confused nature of the political aspirations of the Germans. An enthusiasm inflamed by indefinite historical images led to an intoxication for the idea of a great fatherland in the clouds which in one way or another was to renew the glories of the Othos and the Hohenstaufen, and animated all who were able to join in the same complaints and the same yearning, men of the most varied political tendencies, who united voluntarily as party comrades. These enthusiasts hardly noticed the while the living forces of genuine German unity which were actively at work in the Prussian state. From this, finally, came the weakness of the German national feeling, which even to this hour has not yet attained to the invaluable certainty of an automatic instinct. Very slowly did the dream of German unity pass from the cultured classes into the masses of the people, and even then the great name of the fatherland long remained an indefinite word to the common man, a miraculous land of promise, and the honourable love for a united Germany was often led astray into a narrow-minded, grasping particularism.

In Prussia the old loyalty to the king was too firmly established for it to be possible that the hopes of the patriots should be so completely diverted towards the realm of the indefinite. It was not by mere chance that none among the publicists and popular orators of the time displayed so much sober insight as did Schleiermacher, a Prussian by birth. If he spoke of the liberation of Germany, it was always on the understanding that the restoration of the old Prussian power was a self-evident pre-condition. When Schenkendorf preached of emperor and empire in inspired verses, when Heinrich Kleist urged Germans to draw " first of all the emperor into the holy war," they tacitly assumed that in this new empire, Prussia must occupy a worthy place. Upon the athletic ground on the Hasenheide, in the circles of Jahn, Harnisch, and Friesen, there was already to be heard the confident prophecy, that Prussia had always carried Germany's sword, and that in the new empire Prussia must bear the crown. It was, however, very gradually that Fichte came to accept these Prussian views, and it was not until 1813 that he recognised that no one but the king of Prussia could be " the despot to impose Germanism." Arndt, also, first learned through the victories of Prussia to understand the necessity of the Frederician structure of the state. Common, however, to all the youthful patriots, even to those of Prussia, was the childish belief in some miraculous good fortune to be realised only when Germany should once more belong to herself. The whole energy of luxuriant sentiment which had been accumulating throughout the classical period of our poetic literature, now streamed into political life. Never had the youth of North Germany had such large and proud ideas of themselves and of the future of their nation as now when this country seemed to be annihilated. They had no doubt whatever that the whole great land of Germany which had as a single community hearkened to the words of its poets must necessarily re-enter the ranks of the nations as a single united power. Nowhere, however, was any attempt made towards the formation of a political party with clearly restricted and attainable ends, nowhere was there any intelligent discussion of the question in what forms the rejuvenated fatherland was to be reconstituted. Out of the abundance of anticipations and hopes which moved impatient spirits, there emerged only one palpable political plan, and this plan was indeed conceived with serious earnestness, the resolution to undertake a fight against the dominion of the foreigner.

The enemy continued to occupy the country for a year and a

half after the declaration of peace ; and even for a long time after this, when the French troops had at length evacuated Prussia, the whole of Germany was closely watched by Napoleon's spies. All the French diplomatists and those of the Confederation of the Rhine must continually send reports as to the feeling among the people. Bignon in Stuttgart, and Linden, the Westphalian envoy in Berlin, were particularly zealous in this unsavoury occupation ; Napoleon's envoy in Cassel, Reinhard the talented Swabian and friend of Goethe, utilised his relationships with the German world of letters in order to keep the Imperator informed regarding all the movements of German thought. For this reason it was necessary that the patriots, altogether in opposition to the tendencies and gifts of the German nature, should meet in secret societies. Hardenberg himself, in his Riga memorial to the king, declared that at such a time as this, secret societies were indispensable, and especially recommended the freemasons' lodges to diffuse sound political principles, since Napoleon knew how to utilise for his own purposes the still considerable influence of the freemasons, and had his brother-in-law, Murat, appointed Grand-Master.

So long as the enemy continued to occupy the country, very few among the Prussians inspired with a genuine German sentiment held altogether aloof from this subterranean activity. Schön relates that even Stein had profoundly secret interviews in Königsberg with Gneisenau, Süvern, and other friends, in order to discuss the position of the fatherland and the possibility of its restoration. So intense was the excitement that even those with clear heads could not completely abandon the groundless hope that perhaps some fortunate *coup de main,* some sudden uprising of the people, might lay the French spectre. In the circles of the nobles of Berlin there were some, and especially women, who were moved by the enormous vigour of their hatred for the French to loud complaints against the men of half-measures and the weaklings ; by outsiders these extremists were spoken of as the Tugendbund [League of Virtue] ; everyone knew when they met in secret, for the German sense of honour lent itself very badly to the obscure arts of the conspirator. More serious plans were pursued by a number of other amorphous patriotic clubs, to which Lützow and Chasot, Reimer, Eichhorn, Schleiermacher, and a number of valiant soldiers, burghers, and men of science belonged. They bought arms, in so far as their scanty means allowed ; they endeavoured to get into touch with men of the same way of thinking elsewhere in Germany, to exhort them, to encourage them. How often did Lieutenant Hüser ride from Berlin to Baruth, in order to commit to the Saxon post, letters to the fellow-conspirator Heinrich Kleist. Subsequently Jahn and some of his gymnastic friends constituted a German league. Like the Swiss Confederates in the meadows of Rütli, the conspirators assembled at night in the woods near Berlin and consecrated themselves to the struggle for the fatherland. As the outbreak of the war was further and further postponed, the word was sometimes passed round among the Hotspurs that if this procrastinator Frederick William could not make up his mind, his brother, the knightly Prince William, must ascend the throne.

The epoch was one of fever. Among the patriots there was an everlasting secret coming and going. They went about in disguise, carried news about the position of the enemy, about the strength of the fortified places, even the open-minded must learn to write with sympathetic ink, and to travel under a false name. How profoundly transformed was now the quiet world of North Germany ; what savage elemental passion now flamed in these once so peaceful hearts ! The whole new order of things was in suspense ; involuntarily the thought found expression, Is this to go on for ever ? Countess Voss, praying in her own chamber, besought God to remove the man of ill-omen from the world. Among the young people in Magdeburg, among the friends of Immermann, it became a common subject of discussion as to how it might be possible to get rid of the Corsican, and no one took the discussion amiss. More serious natures embraced the thought in deadly earnest ; for months Heinrich Kleist had it as the dominant idea in his obscured soul. Subsequently Napoleon learned with horror, from the murderous attack of the unhappy Staps, how profoundly hatred can transform even pious and straightforward natures. It was a matter of course that the university students should, after their manner, take part in these forbidden societies. Even before the disaster of Jena, the students of Marburg, influenced by the murder of Palm, had constituted a secret league to preserve Germany and German freedom. The most celebrated among these secret societies, the one whose name the French employed to denote them all, the Tugendbund of Königsberg, never contained more than three hundred and fifty members, of whom four only belonged to Berlin. A few well-meaning but uninfluential patriots, such as Bärsch, Lehmann, Mosqua, and the young lawyer Bardeleben, had founded this society with the king's permission, to encourage moral and patriotic sentiments, but had obediently dissolved it as soon as the legal state-authorities returned on the withdrawal of the French, and when the old prohibition of secret societies came once more into operation. Neither Stein nor Scharnhorst were members of the Tugendbund ; and of their intimate friends two only belonged to the society, Grolman and Boyen.

In general, the effectiveness of the secret societies was far less considerable than the anxious French were inclined to believe ; there were those in France who after the fall of the Napoleonic dominion could explain this only as the outcome of secret influences. Many fine fellows were won over to the cause of the fatherland by this life of secret societies ; some of the best of the younger generation who, at a later date, took leading places in the administration, Eichhorn, Merckel, and Ribbentrop graduated in this school. Scharnhorst, who saw everything and knew everything, now and again entrusted some of the conspirators with dangerous duties, as for instance when it was necessary to bring arms across the frontier. In the year 1812, the secret activity took a new direction ; aid was given to the German officers who desired to enter the Russian service ; in the rear of the *grande armée*, news of defeat was disseminated, and once a French courier was cut off. On the whole, however, the immediate result was trifling ; but all the stronger was the repercussion, and it was by no means one for rejoicing. Through the secret societies that fantastical tendency, already natural to Young Germany, gained new energy. A portion of the young men became accustomed to play with impossibilities, to despise the hard facts of the existing relationships of power, and after a fortunate peace had been secured by hard fighting they continued to carry on an activity which could only have been justified under the pressure of foreign dominion. Among the Governments, on the other hand, when subsequently disaffection began to spread among the liberated peoples, a pusillanimous sentiment of anxiety was strengthened by the recollection of these days of fermentation.

In any case, even in this time of stress, the Prussian state remained true to its monarchical character. Whatever plans individuals might make on their own initiative for the liberation of the fatherland, their most daring hopes went no further than to carry the monarch with them ; even if they should take up arms without the king's orders, it was for the king that they wished to fight. The loyal people, however, could never repose confidence

in attempts at an independent drawing of the sword ; the movement succeeded only when the king himself called his subjects
to arms. The lack of freedom that lies in the very nature of every
secret society was antipathetic to the bold sentiments of the
Germans. It was the best and the strongest who therefore refused
to tie their hands, who said with Gneisenau : " My league is
of another kind, without signs and without mysteries ; it is in
harmony with the sentiments of all those who will not bear the
foreign yoke." Far more powerful than the activity of the secret
societies, was that great conspiracy under the free air of heaven
which wove its threads everywhere where loyal Prussians were
living. Everyone who was inclined to despond could find a
comforter who urged him to put his trust in the fulfilment of time.
But there was no one in the whole country who looked for the day
of decision with more invincible and brilliant confidence than
General Blucher. With profound insight he knew how to discover the essential amid all transitory phenomena, and the
internal weakness and impossibility of the Napoleonic world-empire
was to him unquestionable. Timorous natures regarded him
as mad when in his rough way he bluntly ejaculated concerning
the ruler of the world : " Let him do what he likes, he is only a
fool."

In the old days of the intellectual enthusiasts, a highly
cultured inhabitant of Berlin could not easily accept the idea
that it was a matter of duty to abandon the delights of intellectual
society for the salvation of the dull and ossified state. But now
everyone felt that the wealth of culture could secure peace of soul
for no one, that the disgrace of the fatherland disturbed the joy and
quiet of everyone's existence, and Schleiermacher's sermons found
a powerful response in the heavy-laden hearts of all. He more
than all others was the political teacher of the cultured people of
Berlin. The devout crowded into the narrow little church of
the Holy Trinity when Schleiermacher was expounding in his
sonorous and truly eloquent periods new and ever new applications
of moral ideas to the needs of the time ; when he insisted that all
human worth was to be found in the energy and purity of the will,
in a free self-surrender to the great whole ; that now more than
ever was applicable the scriptural exhortation, that we should
possess as if we did not possess, that we should regard our goods
and our life merely as things held in trust which must lead us
towards higher things, and that we should not fear " them which
kill the body, but are not able to kill the soul : but rather fear him

which is able to destroy both body and soul in hell " ; that the moral value was incomparably greater of those who lived for the love of their country, whereas those who thought only of themselves degenerated into a weakly sensuality ; how fine an object for love and loyalty was this state which had once been an example to other Germans, and which had ever remained a place open for every creed, the embodiment of justice and honourable candour. All this was said with such simple piety, in a way comprehensible to the most ordinary intelligence, and yet was put so spiritually, and was drawn from the very source of the new culture ; was at once so accordant with religious faith and so brilliantly adapted to the political needs of the moment. Practical theology, which had so long stood in the background, remote from the intellectual struggles of the time, now once more advanced into the very foreground of German culture, and the enheartened hearers realised that amid all the changes of history Christianity was able to remain ever new and vigorous, ever fit to exercise an influence upon contemporary life.

The enormous change in opinion, the forcible turning of the age from self-satisfied culture to the exercise of political will, is perhaps shown more clearly in Fichte's essay on Machiavelli than in any other writing of the period. The Icarus of the German idealists, the despiser of reality, now extolled the hardest of all the apostles of matter-of-fact politics, because in the strong-willed Florentine, Fichte recognised the prophet of his fatherland. Whilst the drums of the French garrison were sounding beneath the windows of the Academy, Fichte gave his lectures to the German nation. Remorseful and profoundly stirred, touched in conscience, was the assembly when the fierce-eyed man unsparingly passed judgment upon the profoundly debased time, in which excessive egoism had wrought its own destruction. But he restored hope to the discouraged by describing for them the invincible energy and majesty of the German nature in terms of such grandeur, of such boldness, of such conscious understanding as during these last two centuries of cosmopolitanism no one had ventured to use to our people—doing all this with the extravagance of the national pride characteristic of the new literature. The Germans alone, he said, were still men of primitive strength, not enthralled by arbitrary phrases, the people of ideals, of true force of character ; if they were to perish, the whole human race must perish with them. If any hope were still left for mankind, a new German race must be brought to life, a race which should honour its fatherland as the bearer and the security of earthly immortality, and which in that faith should take up the battle against the irrational and detestable idea of universal monarchy.

Schleiermacher's sermons aroused the suspicions of the French spies. The foreigners did not know what to make of the lofty emotion of this orator who postponed the fulfilment of his dreams to a future age ; they did not understand how irresistibly the emotions of this philosophical generation were affected precisely by such exaggerated idealism. The youth of the time assented whole-heartedly to the doctrine that it was the triumph of culture and the happiness of the individual ego to sacrifice oneself on behalf of the species. Fichte referred with philosophical condescension to " the rare case in which government and science are at one " ; his audience felt that the restoration of the German state was even more a moral task than a political one ; they felt that there was nothing more urgently needed than that " firm and conscious spirit " which the orator attempted to awaken. When faced by the masterful nature and the crushing moral severity of the philosopher, his hearers involuntarily thought of Baron von Stein.

It was in the same sense that, during and after the war, Arndt wrote new volumes of his *Geist der Zeit*. He took the field against our polyarchy which had become a universal servitude, against the unpolitical fair-mindedness of the Germans which conscientiously spared the obsolete until foreigners cleared it away for them ; and, above all, against the over-spiritualised and over-delicate culture, which fancied that fame in war was a trifle, that valiancy was too venturesome, that manliness was defiance, and that firmness was more trouble than it was worth. " Advance to the Rhine," thus ran his conclusion, " and then call out : ' Freedom and Austria ! Francis for our Emperor, not Bonaparte ! ' "

In the blustering activity of the valiant Jahn, there were manifest some of the most ludicrous traits which marred the new Germanism : rough and arrogant hatred of the foreigner, noisy boasting, contempt for all that was graceful and refined. This was a man of uncouth nature, whose influence upon our young people was necessarily all the more harmful in that the Teuton is spontaneously inclined to mistake coarseness for frankness. It was most unfortunate that the sons of a richly endowed nation should honour a noisy barbarian as their teacher. Nevertheless, during these early years of Jahn's activity, the preponderant result was good. His crude peasant's understanding was competent to grasp the one idea which was then of importance, the need for resolute fighting; and he possessed a rare gift for disciplining young men, for instilling into them an honourable hatred for all slackness and softness. The new athleticism did not merely serve to strengthen the bodies of those belonging to a slack generation. It was soon noted that the morals of the youth of Berlin became purer and more manly after, in the year 1811, the *Turnplatz* or open-air gymnasium had been opened on the Hasenheide; and this gain was of more importance than the ill wrought by the confusion which the *Turnvater* had introduced into many a youthful head. His book, *Das deutsche Volkstum*, amid an extraordinary jumble of whimsical conceits, contained many vivid descriptions of the energy and soundness of ancient Teutonic civilisation.

Horrible, indeed, was the way in which the rough primitive, always in honour of the true Germanism, kneaded with his hard fists the delicate leaves and blossoms of our speech. Everything was to be rubbed off which German had acquired in the interchange of ideas with other nations. It sometimes happened to him to coin a new primevally German word out of Romance roots—as in the case of his beloved *Turnen* (gymnastic exercises). But, like Luther, he made many fortunate ventures in speech; for instance, the good word *Volkstum* (= nationality) was discovered by him. So all-powerful, moreover, was still the idealistic tendency of the time that even this buffoon sought the true grandeur of his nation in its spiritual activity; he extolled the Greeks and the Germans as the sacred peoples of humanity, and termed Goethe the most German of all the poets. Like many a greater one among his contemporaries, and as harmlessly as they, he could see nothing in the great struggles between Austria and Prussia beyond a scrimmage between two vigorous young fellows who sparred at one another for a while in their exuberance of spirits, and then behaved themselves as soon as they had come to their senses. Yet he had enough mother-wit to recognise the profound difference between the two powers. The great jumble of people which was Austria could never be completely Germanised; it was from Prussia that the rejuvenation of the old empire had proceeded, and it was Prussia alone which could rouse Germans to become once more a great nation. We must get rid of the German national cancer, the childish petty territorialism, the patriotism of the small districts; there must be one single supreme authority in the empire, one national capital, unity of customs, coinage, and weights and measures ; there must be Reichstags and provincial diets and a powerful Landwehr composed of all fit to bear arms, " for it is an essential principle among the Teutons that he who is weaponless is without honour ! "

Such were the ideas which, with a berserker confidence, he threw into the world as if moved by an irresistible inner impulse, such were the ideas which were greeted by our young men with jubilant enthusiasm. And this was at a time when Prussia contained a population of little more than four millions, and when no one had given a thought to the question as to how the Austrian jumble of peoples could be brought into harmonious union with the true Germany ! How painfully must these proud dreams conflict with the hard reality of the particularist state authorities. Even if liberation from the foreign dominion could be effected, there still remained a cruel disillusionment for this hopeful generation, for it was inevitable that there should be a long period of bitter civil struggle.

It was not the publicists alone whose writings displayed the national passion, for this affected the whole of our literature. To the scions of the Romantic school, Achim von Arnim proposed the task of breathing the fresh morning air of the old German life, of entering devoutly into the glories of the sagas and chronicles of their ancient homeland. Thus should we learn to understand how we had come to be, and thus could we gain new confidence for the struggles of the present. It was in the consciousness of a lofty patriotic call, and with all the overstrained self-consciousness peculiar to our nineteenth century literature, that the young poets and men of learning set to work. Just as happened at a later date in the case of the orators of liberalism and the writers of Young Germany, they always retained the firm, conviction that the new order of German affairs was in reality created by themselves ; that the statesmen and the soldiers had merely carried out what they had themselves conceived in thought much more finely and far more grandly. Once more there came to German literature a period of youth. As formerly the generation of 1750 had discovered the world of the heart, and with naive wonderment had dug into its treasures, so now the new Romanticism greeted with intoxicated delight the even more joyful discovery of the ancient glories of the fatherland. They contemplated German antiquity with the wondering, wide-open eyes of childhood ; through all which they thought and dreamed there flowed a sentiment of historical affection, a feeling of deliberate 'contrast to the recent culture and to the fostering of the exact sciences characteristic of the Napoleonic empire. Out of the ferment of the New Romanticism sprang the great epoch of the historical and philological sciences, and these sciences, outwinging poetry, now assumed for a long time the foreground of intellectual life.

For some years, Heidelberg was the favourite assembling place of the young literary world. How painfully had the noble Charles Frederick of Baden suffered all through these evil years from the disgraceful position of the German petty princes ; but now in his old age he could once more display his love for the fatherland by a good action. He restored the University of Heidelberg, which, under the Bavarian rule, had fallen into complete decay, doing so from the first with the intention that it should be something more than a mere provincial university ; he provided on the Neckar a free city for the young literature, almost the only one in the desolated Germany of the Confederation of the Rhine ; and was able to delight in seeing how, for the third time, the ancient Rupertina, [Heidelberg University], as of old in the days of Otho Henry and of Charles Louis, was able to intervene in the course of German life with new creative ideas.

Here, in the most delightful corner of our Rhenish land, was the cradle of the New Romantic school. The castle, ivy-clad and hidden among the blossoms of the trees as if covered with snow, the towers of the ancient cathedral in the sunlit plain beneath, the ruined baronial castles which seemed to cling to the rocks like swallows' nests, everything here aroused memories of a high-spirited earlier time, which to the yearning imagination of the day seemed far more agreeable than the insipid present. Achim Arnim and Clemens Brentano met here ; here too came Görres, no longer able to endure existence on the French side of the Rhine, so close to the French inferno. The poets of the eighteenth century had felt at home everywhere on German soil, wherever they found warm-hearted friends and could live undisturbed their lives in the ideal ; now the North Germans began to look with longing towards the beautiful lands of the vines and of the traditions. How delighted was Heinrich Kleist when from his poor Bradenburg he found his way into the mountains of South Germany. It was first in these romantic circles that the land and people of our south and west once more found honour. The love for the Rhine, which is characteristic of all of German blood, became a cult of enthusiasts now that the river was in the hands of the foreigner. How often, when friends touched glasses, was repeated the complaint of Frederick Schlegel :

> "Wave so lovable and mighty,
> Fatherland upon the Rhine,
> See how fast my tears are flowing
> Since the stranger now has all."

The Rhine was now Germany's sacred stream, over every one of its churches there hovered an angel, round every ruin there played the nixies and the elves, or the heroic shades returned to visit the great scenes of history. A number of poems and romances endeavoured to reproduce these images. The ballads of the classical poetry had for the most part dealt with the grey primeval time, and their figures had moved upon an indefinite ideal stage ; now the poet must give, even to his shortest pieces, a definite territorial background, and must clothe his figures in historical costume. As the poet's images moved through the mind, people hoped to hear the roaring waters of the Rhine and the Neckar, and in his heroes they wished to rediscover the vigorous simplicity of their German forefathers.

That portion of the history of our country which alone continued to live in the memory of the common people, the last hundred and fifty years, was repulsive to the patriot as the time in which Germany had been torn asunder, and was horrible to the poet through the prosiness of its vital forms. It was only in the Middle Ages that the unbroken energy of German nationality was supposed to have displayed itself, and when they spoke of the Middle Ages people referred chiefly to the period from the fourteenth to the sixteenth century. The merry guild customs of the old manual workers, the secret rites of the operative masons, the love of wandering of the travelling scholars, the adventures of knightly brigands—such had been the true German life, and its theatre was to be found in the artist's country of the south-west, in the true ancient empire. But in all this enthusiasm there was no thought of a subdivision of German culture. The North Germans, with some of the Protestant Swabians and Franconians, continued to set the tone for the whole of Germany ; even the born Rhinelanders among the Romanticists, Görres, Brentano, and the Boisserées (the first Catholics who counted in the history of our new literature), owed the best values of their lives to that common German culture which was derived from Protestantism. Whoever still felt and thought as a German, was seized by the historic yearning of the time ; even the unæsthetic nature of Baron von Stein was not altogether untouched by this influence. A national feeling and national confidence built themselves up upon these pictures of the early days of our homeland. Only among the Teutons, of this the young generation felt assured, could individual originality thrive ; in France, as A. W. Schlegel said mockingly, nature had provided thirty million examples of one single original human being. Only upon German soil did the spring of truth well forth ; among the French, the spirit of lies was dominant—for to the youth of the new romantic epoch, all was classed as lying which seemed to them to lack freedom, to be dull, to be unnatural, and they included in these categories the academical regulation of art, the mechanical ordering of the police-ruled state, and the sobriety of the severe culture of the understanding. Among the writings of this circle at Heidelberg, none were so momentous as *Des Knaben Wunderhorn*, the collection of German folk-songs made by Arnim and Brentano. The figure of the vigorous youth upon the title-page, riding along upon a bare-backed steed, swinging the horn of his songs in his raised hand, seemed like that of a herald summoning all to the joyful struggle against the spirit of lying. It was not without misgiving that the friends sent out into the world of culture these ill-written poems, and they begged Goethe to cover them with the mantle of his great name. It seemed to them of profound importance that the gifts of old German life should not be squandered as had been the forests of the stripped mountains along the Rhine ; they hoped for the coming of a new time full of song and gamesomeness and cordial joy of life, in which training to arms would once again become the chief pleasure of the Germans, and in which everyone might range the world as happily and freely as " the glorious students," the last artists and discoverers in this prosaic age.

The collection of verses appeared at the appropriate hour, for just at this time Schiller's *Wilhelm Tell* began to exercise an influence through wide circles, awakening everywhere an understanding of the simple energy of our ancestors. There was no end to the delighted admiration of the readers when the bells of the *Wunderhorn* related with sweet sound how richly endowed had been this old Germany with the divine gift of poesy, with abundance of love and longing, of courage and roguery ; thousands of nameless students, lansquenets, hunters, and beggars moved through its artless songs. Herder's great revelation that poetry is a common heritage, now first received general understanding. Subsequently von der Hagen published the *Nibelungenlied ;* however bungling the mode of treatment, the mighty figures of Hagen and Kriemhild aroused in the minds of the readers the joyful conviction that even six hundred years before Goethe our people had known a great epoch of poetry. Yet dilettantism still predominated. Mediævalism and Germanism were regarded as practically synonymous. Fundamentally divergent epochs of mediæval civilisation were uncritically confused, and the enthusiasts were quite unable to dream that in the blossoming time of the days of chivalry the detested French had really been the pioneers of civilisation. Fouqué, the weakly visionary (who, nevertheless from time to time succeeded in producing a fable full of meaning, recording the secrets of the forest and of the water, or who could now and then write a powerful description of some old Norse hero) was for some years the fashionable poet of the world of good society. The ladies of Berlin were enthusiasts for his graceful, modest, and lovely maidens, for the incomparable virtue of his knights, and they adorned their dressing-tables with iron crucifixes and silver-mounted devotional books.

Teutonic philology had hitherto been a mere accessory to other sciences, the supplementary study of certain historians, jurists, and theologians. Now at length it endeavoured to stand upon its own feet, and to realise for German antiquity Herder's bold anticipations, and F. A. Wolf's views as to the origin of the Homeric poems. It was the brothers Grimm who first gave to German philology the character of an independent science. Little attention was paid to these two retiring men when they wrote in the *Einsiedlerzeitung* of Heidelberg ; but soon they were to prove themselves the finest and the strongest among their fellows. It is through their work, above all, that the genuine and fruitful nucleus of the romantic view of the world-order was subsequently handed down to an entirely transformed world and became part of the spiritual inheritance of the nation. They took quite seriously the old article of faith of the Romanticists that everything flows out of the ocean of poetry ; and in every domain of folk life, in speech, law, and custom, they endeavoured to demonstrate how culture and abstractions have everywhere been formed out of the sensual, the natural, and the primitive. How condescendingly had the writers of the eighteenth century spoken to the people when they troubled themselves at all about the common man ; but now the experts of science went to school to the common people, listening diligently to the chatter of the spinning-room and the shooting-gallery. An old peasant-woman helped the brothers Grimm in the collection of the German folk-tales, and thus there came into existence a book like Luther's Bible, a glorious common heritage of the European peoples, compiled so sympathetically as to retain its permanent national characteristics. The ancient Aryan figures of fable, Hop-o'-my-Thumb, Lucky Hans, Snow White and Rose Red, seem such essentially German figures, and the simple serenity of spirit which had clung to them in their wide wanderings through the nurseries of Germany spoke in so homely a manner from the unadorned and faithful narrative, that even to-day we can think of the darlings of our childhood only in these particular forms, just as we can listen to the Sermon on the Mount in no other words than those of Luther.

At this same period, another and even more grossly neglected treasure of the nation's early days was rediscovered. How terribly had our ancient cathedrals had to suffer for the self-satisfaction of the last century ; the glorious frescoes on their walls had been covered with stucco, and corkscrew columns and trumpet-blowing angels with puffed cheeks defiled the Gothic altars. Now the hatred for the Church and the hard utilitarianism of the Frenchified bureaucracy of the Confederation of the Rhine brought a new wave of iconoclasm over Bavaria, Swabia, and the Rhineland. A number of venerable churches were despoiled and came under the hammer ; deplorable was the sight when, during the breaking down of the walls, the stucco fell away, and for a moment the beautiful old frescoes were displayed once more to the light of day, then to crumble away for ever. Thereupon the brothers Boisserée resolved to save what it was still possible to save out of the great destruction. Their quiet and faithful activity was the first sign of the reawakening of the German spirit on the left bank of the Rhine. Indefatigably they endeavoured from amid the lumber-rooms of the houses of the Rhenish patricians to collect the forgotten old German paintings. Their aged mother gave her blessing to this pious work, and their Romanticist friends elsewhere gave faithful help. What a joy it was to Görres and Savigny when a fine sculptured altar-piece could be picked up for a few kreuzer from some peasant or second-hand dealer, and sent along to the brothers. Everything was welcome and everything was admired so long as it displayed the true characteristics of the old German spirit, the idealistic softness of the Cologne school of painters no less than the profundity of Dürer and the powerful realism of the old Dutch painters. Then Sulpice Boisserée found one of the old sketches for the cathedral of Cologne, and with joyful courage projected the designs for his great work on the cathedral. In these weary days when Napoleon once visited his good town of Cologne and after a few minutes hurriedly left the most beautiful cathedral of the Germans in order to inspect a regiment of cuirassiers, every true son of the Rhineland was already dreaming of the re-establishment of the Cologne building works, which had formerly for centuries been the living focus of German art on the Rhine.

The same firm faith in the immortality of the German people inspired also the creator of the history of our politics and jurisprudence, K. F. Eichhorn. The old dominion of the common law seemed for ever broken, the domain of the code Napoleon extended up to the shores of the Elbe, and the jurists of the Confederation of the Rhine regarded the German law as already fit for burial. Eichhorn showed, however, how the law-making spirit common to the whole German nation had ever remained active throughout the many transformations in the constitution of the state, and how the origin and growth of German law was explicable solely out of this persistent natural energy. The historical view of the nature of law, for which the way had been paved by Herder and the earlier Romanticists, now suddenly matured. It was so necessary a corollary of the view of the world-order characteristic of the new age, that it was simultaneously advocated by men of the most different outlooks. Among these were Savigny, the legal teacher of the brothers Grimm, who in Landshut had already awakened the suspicion of the Bonapartist-Bavarian bureaucracy by his doctrine of the law-creating energy of the folk spirit. Above all there was Niebuhr, whose *Roman History* speedily aroused general admiration as the greatest scientific achievement of the day. To him also it seemed that the spirit of the Roman people (and this was an idea altogether unknown to the pragmatical historians of the eighteenth century) had been the driving energy, the formative necessity of Roman history ; and at the same time he indicated new paths for historical research by a keen criticism of historical sources, which with a sure sense rejected as fit only for the dust-heap all the old traditions of the Seven Kings of Rome. Yet he also was of opinion that " the historian needs a positive spirit." Before his eyes, the dead letters of the historical sources came to life, and through his truly creative faculty he was able to erect upon the vestiges of a destroyed tradition a picture of real happenings. With how restrained a freedom did he exercise political judgment, quite in Stein's distinguished manner. He found just praise for the moderation of the plebs, severe criticism for the arrogance of the patricians, and at the same time he drew the genuinely Prussian conclusion that under the rule of a strong throne such manifestations of class arrogance would never have been possible. Thus in almost all branches science showed itself even more vigorous and more productive than were most of the younger poets. This, too, was a sign of the times that Alexander von Humboldt's *Ansichten der Natur* first made available for the whole German nation, in a simple and classical form, the acquirements of profound scientific and geographical research.

It was a crepuscular time. A fresh wind, as of morning, announced the approach of a beautiful day, but in the half light the forms and masses of the youthful world could not be clearly distinguished. Fundamentally contrasted opinions, which before long were to be in passionate conflict, still proceeded harmoniously hand in hand. Fouqué, the reactionary, lived with Fichte, the radical, as a son with a father. Of the Romantic poets, some held piously to the old faiths, whilst others were merely playing ironically with mediæval ideals. In the domain of history there appeared, side by side with the strictly methodical investigations of Niebuhr and Eichhorn, such fantastical works as Creuzer's *Symbolik*, the first attempt to understand the secret night-side of classical culture and the origin of the mysteries of the ancients —a book full of talented foreshadowings, but obscure and full of arbitrary caprices. The scientific contemplativeness of the historical school of jurists was not free from timorousness and fear of action ; in essentials those of this school had little in common with the hopeful, undismayed freedom of spirit of Arndt, and they betrayed much more kinship with the views of F. Gentz, who now, exhausted by excesses, cold and blasé, tended more and more amid the dull and unreflective life of Vienna to become an unconditional admirer of the good old time. The inexhaustible pageant of German history made it possible for everyone, whatever might be his own shade of opinion, to be an enthusiast for some particular epoch of the history of the fatherland. Some were charmed by the strange magic, and others by the fresh and vigorous folk-characteristics, of mediæval life. Whilst Fichte drew the attention of his admirers to the magnificent civic life of the Hansa towns, and to the faithful who fought in the League of Schmalkald, Frederick Schlegel condemned Frederick the Great as " a hereditary enemy," and the boastful visionary Adam Müller glorified the Holy Roman Empire as an incorporation of Christ.

Even more confused was the motley of religious sentiment. It is true that men who were Protestant through and through, such as Schleiermacher, Fichte, and the brothers Grimm, never vacillated in their evangelical conviction. Savigny, on the other hand, was brought nearer to the views of the pre-Lutheran Church by the brilliant Catholic Sailar. Schenkendorf sang enraptured songs to Mary, Queen of Heaven; the conversion of F. Schlegel and F. Stolberg to the Roman Church threw a strong light upon the moral weakness of the æsthetic views of life which were still predominantly characteristic of the age. A gloomy hatred of the Jews replaced the broad-hearted tolerance of the Frederician days. Many among the enthusiasts of mediævalism believed themselves able to see plainly sculptured on every Jewish face the instruments of Christ's passion. Political hatred played a part in the production of these sentiments, for Napoleon was endeavouring with considerable success to secure the aid of European Jewry on behalf of his world empire. All these different tendencies were for the moment in tolerable harmony, and the aged Voss found very little approval when, with a sound understanding and with unrestrained roughness, he attacked the dream-world of the Romanticists in the name of Protestant freedom of thought. In this chaotic activity no one found himself more at home than the noisy Görres, the honourable Jacobin in the monk's cowl, who found it possible to be at one and the same time a radical and an admirer of the Middle Ages, a Germanist and a venerator of the Roman papacy, always brilliant, stimulating and stimulated, overflowing with æsthetic, historical, and natural-philosophical instances, and yet always subject to a sort of rhetorical and poetical intoxication. All these different minds were at one in a single resolve: they all desired that it should be possible for them once more to experience a heartfelt joy in their German nature; they wished to maintain their native peculiarity and to develop it further in complete freedom, without any regard for foreigners who desired to make the world happy by the imposition of a foreign dominion.

The political passion of the time found its mightiest artistic expression in the works of Heinrich von Kleist, that profoundly unhappy poet who surpassed all other poets of the younger generation. In the primitive force of his dramatic passion, and in his power of vigorous characterisation, he exceeded even Schiller, but the wealth of ideas, the lofty culture, the wide outlook, and the adequate self-confidence of our greatest dramatist were denied to this son of ill-fortune. Hardly noticed by his contemporaries, and robbed by a cruel destiny of all joy in his own creative work, he seems to us who look back upon him as the one truly apt poet of this time of oppression, as the herald of that elemental hatred which foreign injury had poured into the veins of our good-natured people. His *Penthesilea* was the most savage, his *Käthchen von Heilbronn* was the tenderest and noblest, among the twilit dream-figures of German Romanticism; but his *Hermannsschlacht* was a lofty song of revenge, a mighty hymn of the lust of reprisal—as true, as vivid, as full of life in every characteristic as formerly Klopstock's songs of the bards had been indefinite and confused, every feeling pouring directly from the heart of one thirsting for revenge. Not like the patriotic men of learning had Kleist found it necessary to acquire the idea of the fatherland by a reflective process; he experienced the naive and natural hatred of the Prussian officer; he saw the ancient and glorious flag which had been the pride of himself and of his house trampled in the dust, and he longed to chastise the being responsible for this insult. Everywhere this rolling stone passed, he was followed, as if by the call of the Erinyes, by the wild question: " Art thou yet on thy feet, Germania? Is the day of thy revenge at hand? " Stormily, dreadfully, as never before from a German mouth did there spring from his lips the poetry of hatred:

> " Rescue from the yoke of serfage,
> Which, from iron-ore fast-forged,
> Hell's own first-born son the tyrant
> Rivets fast upon our necks !"

This was the same unrestrained natural force of national passion as had once sounded in the wild strains of the March of the Marseillaise, but incomparably more poetical, more truthful, more deeply felt. Subsequently, in his *Prinz Friedrich von Homburg*, the unhappy poet created the one artistically complete specimen of our historical dramas which drew its materials from the recent and still vividly remembered German history; this was the most beautiful poetic celebration of Prussian glory-in-arms. When this work also was ignored by his contemporaries, and when the situation of the fatherland seemed to become ever more hopelessly tragical, the impatient man died by his own hand, a victim of inborn morbid dispositions, but also a victim of this gloomy despairing time. It was characteristic of the great transformation that had taken place in the national life that a man belonging to the old Brandenburger race of soldiers should glorify Prussian militarism with all the brilliancy of colouring characteristic of the new poetry ; this Prussian militarism which had so long been without understanding and misunderstood, which had remained remote from modern German culture. How actively now was the stiff and arrogant Junkerdom of the Mark taking part in the intellectual activity of the nation : a whole series of its sons, Kleist, Arnim, and Fouqué, the Humboldts and L. von Buch, stood in the first rank among Germany's poets and men of learning. The philistine nature of the old Prussianism had at length completely passed away.

Strangely enough, no one contributed more powerfully towards this great transformation in the emotional spirit of the German people, no one did more to strengthen the happy feeling of self-satisfaction, than Goethe. He did it almost against his own will by a work which originally belonged to quite a different epoch. It remained as ever his destiny to find the right word for the most peculiar and most secret sentiments of the Germans. In the year 1808 appeared the first part of *Faust*. Goethe was now almost sixty years of age, and for nearly forty years had been a recognised force in German life. A pilgrimage to Weimar to see the dignified, cheerful, serious-minded master, had long been regarded as a necessary duty of all young authors. No one expected from Goethe yet another creative act, participating in the struggles of the new Germany ; everyone knew with what cold and distinguished reserve he refused to have anything to do with the Hotspurs of Romanticism. It was true that he had accepted the dedication of the *Wunderhorn* in a friendly spirit, and that he gave his good wishes to the collection, hoping that it might find a place in every German home. He himself, in his happy days at Strasburg, had sounded, in a way understood by but few, the praises of Gothic architecture. When now, after long years, he saw the seed thus sown springing to life, saw the whole world filled with enthusiasm for ancient German art, he expressed the opinion that humanity is first truly human when united, and he delighted in the amiable enthusiasm of Suplice Boisserée. None the less, the stimulated and fantastical nature and the defiant national emotion of the younger generation remained repugnant to him.

His own culture was rooted in the cosmopolitan century that had passed away. Never could he forget what he and all his contemporaries had in youth owed to the French. The elemental unrest of Kleist aroused horror in his contemplative mind. In his letters to his old comrade Reinhard, he expressed sharp criticism concerning the grotesqueries of Arnim and Brentano, and defended the old and honourable rationalism against the two-faced younger natural-philosophy. There even were moments in which he roundly declared that Romanticism was morbid, in contradistinction to the healthiness of the classical spirit. Least of all could he forgive the young people for the way in which their literary movement was directed towards political ends ; every immediate translation of art into the prosy life of the state seemed to him a desecration. He regarded as an inevitable destiny the great disturbance which had burst over Germany. The natural elective affinity of genius led him to believe firmly in Napoleon's fortunate star. What did he know of Prussia and the deadly injury that had been inflicted on Prussian pride ? How could the son of the good old time, who lived in Frankfort, Strasburg, Leipzig, and Weimar, among a harmless and peaceful people, regard a war waged by the German nation as possible ? Even to Goethe's contemporaries it seemed painful, and for all time to come it will be a distressing memory to the Germans, that our noblest poet could see nothing more in the enemy of his country than a great man, that he was too old to understand fully the wonderful and saving transformation which had come over his compatriots. He had felt so solitary since the death of Schiller. Meditating with a heavy heart upon the dear shadows of happier days, he let the greatest work of his life pass out into the hands of the unknown crowd. When fifteen years earlier a few fragments of this work had appeared, no one had taken much note of the matter.

And yet this poem now attained a success as flaming and as irresistible as had once his *Sorrows of Werther*, as if these lines, over which the poet had grown old, had been now first conceived, and were written for the day in which they appeared. The painful question whether old Germany was really done for, was on every-one's lips ; and now, in the decline of the nation, suddenly there came this work, beyond comparison the crown of the whole of the modern poetry of Europe ; and people felt a joyful certainty that only a German could have written thus, that the poet was ours, and that his figures were one flesh and blood with us ! It was as if destiny had given a sign that the civilisation of the world could not after all dispense with us, and that God still had in His mind a great destiny for this people. Schiller, already, had imposed upon the drama, greater tasks than had been imposed by Shakespeare, although Schiller had not attained to the grand power of delineation possessed by the Englishman ; the tragedy of passions was not enough for Schiller ; he wished to make men realise through their senses that world-history is the world court of justice. But now, with the appearance of *Faust* there was something yet greater ; now for the first time since Dante the attempt was made to incorporate in poetry the whole spiritual heritage of the epoch. Such from the first had been the poet's conception, as he himself has told us ; but when year after year he continued to carry these beloved figures in his heart, when again and again in all happy hours he returned to dwell with them, they grew with him and he with them. The old puppet-show, with its compactness and its thoughtfulness, its carnival jokes and its distasteful horrors, became expanded into a great world-picture which simply disregarded the ancient forms of dramatic art, to produce a picture of the promethean urge of humanity. In this poem the writer exposed the entire philosophical content of his age. It was not possible for Goethe, the modern, as it was for Dante, the child of the thirteenth century, to pass judgment upon the world from the altitude of an unquestioning and complete view of the world-order. He made no attempt to conceal that he was a striver, that he could never bring this poem to an end, and for this very reason his writing had so powerful an influence upon the fermenting time because he issued an invitation to further poetic activity and to further reflection. The fundamental idea of Goethe's view was, however, firmly established. To him humanity remained always a means for creation, and only for the sake of humanity did the world exist. Man's salvation by deed, by the loving self-surrender of the ego to the all, the triumph of the divine over the spirit of renunciation which always wills evil and always creates good—this was the joyful belief of the greatest of the optimists, this was the poetic theme of his whole life.

If ever a poem had been lived it was this one. Everything which had ever seized and moved the poet's protean nature was incorporated in this work : the cheerfulness of the days of Leipzig, the happiness in love of the Strasburgers, Merck and Herder, Spinoza and Winckelmann, the earth-friendship of the man of science and the experiences of the statesman, the intoxication with beauty of the Roman elegies, and the mature wisdom of the life of the old man. But *Faust* fascinated the Germans by an additional charm, by one reminding them intimately of home, one which even to the present day no foreigner has fully understood. To them the poem seemed a symbolical image of the history of the fatherland. One who entered deeply into its spirit was able to overlook the whole wide way which the Teutons had ranged since the mysterious days when they still lived in trustful communion with the gods of the forest and of the field, down to those joyful times when the folk had emerged " from the pressure of gables and of roofs, from the churches' venerable night," issuing forth from our ancient towns in search of freedom. Here was to be found the exuberance of German life : the wild and devilish frolics of our folk-superstition, and the tender profundity of the German love of women, the humour of the students, the war-lust of the soldiers, and the sunward aspirations of German thought —almost all which combines to make up our life. In none of his greater works since *Goetz von Berlichingen* had Goethe written in so national a spirit. The simple rhymed couplets of the ancient merry tales of the carnival rendered with wonderful energy and clearness every changing aspect and mood ; to the plain reader everything seemed comprehensible, and to the man of talent everything seemed unfathomably profound.

The younger poets esteemed *Faust* as the perfection of Romantic art ; they felt themselves to be strengthened and encouraged in their own activity now that the prince of classical poetry plunged into the quiet world of Romanticism and made his witches dance upon the Blocksberg. But the old master soon showed how high he stood above the literary parties of the day. Soon after *Faust*, he published his *Elective Affinities*. Everyone admired the psychological profundity and the magnificent artistic understanding of the master, for he had never before produced so perfectly finished a composition ; yet people felt uneasily that this discussion of sensibilities had nothing in common with the time ; it seemed to be written for a generation which no longer existed. What matter ? To the young people Goethe remained the divine poet of *Faust*, and since now for the first time Schiller's works also gained complete recognition, the common veneration for the heroes of Weimar became a bond of unity to all persons of refinement. This cult was also favourable to the self-esteem of the unhappy nation.

Even in the fine arts there at length re-awakened a happy delight in activity ; the beginnings of our new school of painting were directly associated with the re-discovery of German antiquity. How solitary had Asmus Carstens remained in his talented movement towards the simplicity of nature and the greatness of the antique, the prophet of a more joyful time which he was never to see. But now, in the cloister of San Isidoro at Rome, there was a whole crowd of German painters assembled, an inspired and confident young generation, enthusiasts for Dürer, Memling, and van Eyck, who regarded themselves as predestined, for the glory of God and for that of the German fatherland, to overcome the academic art of the French by the faithfulness and the profundity of the ancient Christian-Teutonic nature. Among these young painters, the Catholics were from the first more strongly represented than among the poets and the men of learning. The greatest of them all, Peter Cornelius, was a Catholic, but he had drunk at the sources of North German culture and conceived his vocation in a wide and great sense. His soul was filled with a sacred ambition, and he prayed : " Mayest Thou make this heart strive ever towards divine deeds, great in humility and in unending love towards Thee." German painting was to show itself at once ardent and severe, after the manner of Dürer, for it was only through the Germans that art could attain to a new tendency ; and by the instrumentality of this nation, it was God's will to diffuse through the world a new kingdom of His power and glory. The travelling expenses to Rome which were offered him by the Prince-Primate Dalberg were bluntly refused by the young artist, because it was suggested to him that he should follow French examples. If was from the sagas of the fatherland, from *Faust* and the *Nibelungen*, that he took the matter for his first great works. His was a genuine German nature ; serious, profound, and great, inexhaustibly rich in ideas ; but hard and uncouth in form, almost more a poet's than a painter's. To him also would apply the name *poeta tacente* with which the peculiarities of Dürer were once aptly described.

When Cornelius at length reached Rome, he soon got beyond the one-sided Nazarene views of Overbeck and the brothers of San Isidoro, who could find the spirit of true Christianity in the work of the northern and of the older Italian artists alone. In his spirit there was room, not only for Siegfried and Faust, but also for the figures of the Iliad and the Æneid ; he was also able to enjoy with a profound understanding the pagan beauty of the works of the Renaissance. Thus it was that, cultivating his powers unceasingly, and growing and strengthening with every new phase of the Nibelungen cycle, he laid the foundation for the monumental style of German painting. Just as in former days in the case of our classical poetry, so now, this renascence of the fine arts took place in precious freedom, springing directly from the depths of the folk spirit, without any co-operation on the part of the courts. It was not until the new tendency had already become clear as to its own nature and its own aims, that the Mæcenas was to be found who would provide the means for extensive artistic creation.

§ 2. THE ALTENSTEIN MINISTRY. THE WAR OF 1809.

For some months Stein forcibly restrained his hot anger. He succeeded in forcing himself to negotiate with the French in a yielding and almost in a servile spirit, since the promised evacuation of the country must be secured at all costs. Napoleon, on the other hand, desired to prolong the stay of his troops indefinitely, in order to complete in time of peace that destruction of the Prussian state which had only been half effected at Tilsit. As early as November, 1807, he declared himself to be prepared to cede the Danubian provinces to Russia, if he could in exchange receive Silesia, and to leave to the king of Prussia no more than a domain with 2,000,000 inhabitants. To all the petitions of the Prussians the blunt answer was returned that the existing state of affairs suited the emperor, that he saw no reason to make any change, and again, that the king had plenty of money, that he needed no army since he was not waging war with anyone ! Daru expressed the dry opinion that this calculation of the costs of war was a question not of arithmetic but of politics ; for the rest, the will of the emperor was as unalterable as fate, and no one would believe how much a country could put up with. In vain did Prince William go to Paris, in vain did he offer that he and his wife should remain as hostages in French hands until the war indemnity had been paid. The Imperator said threateningly : " I know that all the Prussians hate me " ; and he ordered his officers in Prussia to conduct themselves as if they had been in a hostile country. During the two years of the occupation, a sum of 1,129,000,000 francs was extorted from the impoverished land, in contributions, charges for maintenance, and stores supplied to the army of occupation, a sum equivalent to sixteen times the entire gross revenue of the state.[1] The province of Prussia alone paid

[1] According to the calculation of M. Duncker, *Aus der Zeit Friedrichs d. Gr. und Fr. Wilhelms III*, pp. 505 et seq.

113,000,000 thalers. Never and nowhere was a civilised people more cruelly misused.

When at length, after many months, the conquerors sent in their final demands, there remained due, according to their calculations, a sum of 154,500,000 francs, whilst the Prussian authorities demonstrated that, in accordance with Napoleon's express promises, the cost of the stores for the army of occupation was to be deducted from the contribution, and that if this deduction were made the only remaining debt amounted to 19,000,000 francs. What did it signify, in consideration of so colossal an exaction, that the provincial diets all stood security for a portion of the war indemnity? The demand remained extortionate. At the same time, preparations for war went on unceasingly in Magdeburg; there were French army corps in Swedish Pomerania, in Warsaw, and all over the country on this side of the Vistula; whilst the Imperator sent repeated messages to the effect that he would regard it as a mark of confidence if the king would soon remove his seat of government from the safety of Königsberg to Berlin! To this was superadded an incredible piece of rascality. Napoleon, once more in direct conflict with the Treaty of Tilsit, confiscated the capital which had been lent in the Duchy of Warsaw by the Prussian banks and charitable institutions; he similarly confiscated the sums that had been lent by private Prussian individuals; and then, since stolen goods always depreciate in value, he sold his spoil somewhat below the nominal price to the king of Saxony, who expressed his humble thanks for the grace thus accorded to him in the Treaty of Bayonne. The Prussian national income was thus further diminished by 30,000,000 thalers and the bank alone lost 10,000,000.

Meanwhile the war between the Wolf and the Fish was proceeding with increasing fierceness. The British invasion of Denmark, which was contrary to international law, was cleverly utilised by Napoleon in order to arouse public hostility against this power which was treading under foot everything that men regarded as sacred. In actual fact, the fable that the new world-empire aimed only at securing the freedom of the seas, still found many credulous hearers. But among these there could not be reckoned the cabinets of the east. From the time of the Peace of Tilsit, not one of the three eastern powers, however vacillating their policy might sometimes be, regained complete confidence in the ruler of the world; below the surface the recognition that they would all of them have to fight against France, was steadily gaining ground. The Hofburg learned with consternation of the far-reaching oriental plans with which the Imperator entertained his friend of Tilsit. Stadion did not entirely reject the thought that if things came to an extremity it might be possible for Austria to take part in the destruction of the Turkish empire, and thus to secure for herself the western part of the Balkan peninusla as far as Salonica ; but he was much more closely concerned with the reflection that the way from Napoleon's Adriatic provinces to Turkey lay through the Austrian territory of Istria, and that therefore this region had to dread a new invasion. The state gradually recovered from its reverses, and re-armed itself with unwonted zeal : in the spring of 1808 the formation of a territorial militia was even undertaken, and Stadion was of the hopeful opinion that the Austrians were once more a nation.

The Franco-Russian alliance, too, was in a very unstable condition. Although the Russian generals had at first been strongly averse to the Prussian War, the court and the people learned with profound dissatisfaction of the dishonourable peace. The national instinct led to a speedy realisation of what the establishment of the duchy of Warsaw signified for Russia's future. Hatred of France gained ground, and seized even the army ; people began to murmur, saying that the czar was allowing himself to be misused by the Corsican. Alexander's sensitive nature was not unaffected by this popular mood. When he sacrificed his ally in Tilsit, it was by no means his intention to renounce permanently " doing the right thing." In the circle of his confidants he continued to utter assurances to the effect that, if the worst came to the worst, he would take up the war once more, even in the deserts of Siberia. At first, however, he desired to enjoy the fruits of the alliance of Tilsit, and to strengthen his empire by Finland and the Danubian provinces. Should fortune prove favourable, he believed, in accordance with the indefinite consent of Napoleon, that even the annihilation of the Turkish Empire was possible. Being a master in the art of deceiving himself, he found excuses enough to justify his deplorable course of action ; moreover, he feared lest a premature war with France might result in the complete reconstitution of Poland. For this reason he temporarily remained faithful to the French alliance, and entered upon the war against Sweden.

Napoleon willingly let him pursue this course, and seized the opportunity of the Russian invasion of Finland to push his own troops forward into Portugal, in order to bring under his own control this important bridge-head of England. His letters to Alexander were full of flatteries and vague promises. The world, he said, was big enough for them both ; there was nothing he had more at heart than the glory, the welfare, and the aggrandisement of Russia ; if the two friends should advance in unison to the Bosphorus, this blow would resound as far as India, and would force England to submission. But as soon as the czar expressed more clearly his hopes for the possession of the Danubian provinces, Napoleon's attention was aroused, and he demanded in exchange a further mutilation of the Prussian state. Alexander could not conceal from himself that these sinister plans were no less threatening to Russia than they were to Germany. Subsequently news was received in St. Petersburg concerning intrigues of the French agents in the east. In Teheran, no less than in Constantinople, France was secretly endeavouring to countermine the plans of her northern ally. The alliance of Tilsit was already being disintegrated by the very force which had brought it into existence, by reckless land-hunger.

The Imperator, however, now found it necessary to re-establish the tottering alliance, owing to the circumstances in which he was involved by his own fault. The world had long been accustomed to hear every month of some new arbitrary act. Now came news of one blow after another : that East Frisia had been united with Holland, that Tuscany had been included in the French Empire, and that the Adriatic provinces of the Pontifical State had been incorporated into the kingdom of Italy, that Napoleon's troops had entered Rome, that they had invaded Portugal, and that the House of Braganza had ceased to reign. But almost incredible even to this epoch accustomed to horrors, was the news which came in May, 1808, from Marrac Castle in the vicinity of Bayonne, that Napoleon had decoyed the Spanish Bourbon into his power, that he had then incited father and son to strive each against the other like raging beasts, had forced them both to abdicate, and had placed his brother Joseph upon the throne of Spain. He revelled in these acts of brigandage ; in this very place he effected the sordid transaction concerning the crown of Saxony and Warsaw. In six weeks he hoped to be free from his Spanish troubles, and that the old saying, " The Pyrenees no longer exist ! " would become an established truth. But punishment followed hard upon the heels of crime. The whole of Spain rose like one man for its independence, for the rights of its royal house for its ancient Church. The peninsula bristled with weapons.

The Rise of Prussia

The high-spirited nation had passed the last two centuries in a waking dream, hardly touched by the ideas of the new Europe : it rushed into the unequal struggle with measureless self-confidence, without an inkling of the enemy's strength, still imagining itself the mightiest and the most highly cilivised nation in the world, asking who dared touch the empire on which the sun never set. No one in the country believed in the abdication of King Ferdinand. All the noble and all the gloomy passions of the Spaniards broke out in wild ferment in this terrible revolt of royalists without a king : their patriotic pride, their loyalty, their heroic courage ; but also their fixed hatred of the foreigner, their bigoted intolerance, their inhuman cruelty ; and simultaneously there awakened in the inexperienced people, abandoned to its own devices, the obscure dreams of political radicalism.

English policy speedily recognised that the enemy could now be attacked at his weakest spot, whereas hitherto all the English attempts upon the Continent had met with ill-success. England supported the revolt, with British and German regiments. It at length became possible for the valiant Hanoverians of the German legion to wash out the shame of Suhlingen. Wellington's patriarchal and cautious conduct of the war (for he, like his army, held firmly to the traditions of the eighteenth century, and upon any other theatre of war would certainly have been out-generalled by the Napoleonic methods of fighting) here obtained a brilliant success. The circumspect Briton rarely ventured a battle, and never a decisive one. Again and again, after every struggle in the open field, he hid his little army in a well-protected fortress, and did not emerge from this place of safety for weeks or months, when he would suddenly break out of his hole. In this way it became possible for him to effect all that could be effected upon this subordinate area of the world war. He was able to keep open this wound in the Napoleonic empire, was able to keep alive the ultimate forces of resistance for five long years, while the French troops melted away in successive sieges, and in the exhausting little wars against the Spanish guerillas. Even in the first year of the war, the Napoleonic army received two defeats of a character hitherto unknown in its annals : Junot capitulated in Portugal, and Dupont and his army laid down their arms at Baylen.

Through this news from Spain, Austria was encouraged to more rapid military preparations. Stein saw that the fulfilment of his dearest hopes was approaching, and he abandoned his diplomatic reserve. It was to be expected that Napoleon would

379

either at once throw himself upon Austria, or that he would recall the *grande armée* from North Germany, in order that he might immediately get the upper hand of the Spanish revolt. In either case it seemed to the bold patriot that a sudden uprising of the German power would be possible. His noble passion led him to desperate and impossible flights of imagination. The troops were to take the field under the black, white, and yellow banner of the League, inscribed with the names of the liberators of the nation, Arminius and William of Orange. This at a moment when the Prussian army was still in French prisons ! Stein counted upon the healthy energy of the peasants and of the middle classes ; but he put little trust in the " softness of the upper classes, and the mercenary spirit of the public officials." To inflame the national ambition, the baron, who was so proud of his own ancestors, actually wished to abolish the old hereditary nobility and to create a new nobility out of all those who should play a prominent part in this holy war. Was it to be wondered at that the valiant man himself should seem a desperate adventurer to many honourable patriots in Königsberg, that they should regard him as one who wished to place the king and himself upon a powder barrel ? The narrow, harsh, and despotic soul of Emperor Francis had no inclination for such hyperbolical proposals, but since Napoleon's language towards the House of Lorraine grew more threatening and more inflammatory day by day, the Hofburg allowed the Austrian diplomats to enter into a secret understanding with the Prussian war-party. In Teplitz there was a circle of Austrian and North German patriots ; the Hanoverian diplomats, Hardenberg and Omptada, were engaged in busy secret activity. Upon the king's command, the restless count Goetzen now resumed in Silesia secret intercourse with the Hofburg, which he had already been engaged in during the war. However trifling were the results at the moment, with these confidential negotiations of the summer of 1808 the reconciliation of the two great powers began. It was at least recognised that an understanding was possible ; the ideas of the Treaty of Bartenstein began to gain ground.

The king was cordially upon the side of the minister. He spoke of the friends of Stein and Scharnhorst roundly as " the good party " ; in his eyes, also, the peace of Tilsit was no more than a truce. But he did not conceal from the war-party that he was prepared to take up arms once more only in alliance with Russia. Not even the breach of the Treaty of Tilsit had disturbed his confidence in the czar, for he knew how little inclined Alexander was to remain permanently in alliance with France. The terrible experiences of recent years had served merely to confirm his old view that the power of Napoleon could be resisted only by a coali· tion of the whole of Europe. The moral greatness of the national monarchy, the far-reaching outlook and the sense of duty of true kingship, had seldom been displayed so admirably as now, when Frederick William endured in silence the misunderstanding of the best of his people. The modest man realised only too vividly how little he could compare himself with the genius of Stein or of Scharnhorst ; and yet he had a clearer and a sounder judgment of the European situation than had they, because he was the king, because he felt himself to be at one with the state, because the consciousness of his responsibility before God and man animated his whole life. The mood of the war-party was voiced by Heinrich Kleist with the naive utterance of the poet in the following verses :

> " Not victory the Germans now demand,
> As helplessly the signal they await.
> Let war but light its torch throughout the land—
> Worth all the men that find death for their mate ! "

Involuntarily the love of posterity must be given to these high-spirited men who thought that with a population of scarcely 5,000,000 souls they could venture a struggle against the new Carlovingian empire, and who were willing, should the worst come to the worst, to be buried with the ruins of the state. But what they advised was a policy of despair. When to these passionate spirits the king repeated again and again that he would not draw upon himself the fate of the Spanish Bourbon, that a small political existence was at any rate better than none at all, it was by no means that he wished to express a personal reluctance to discard the glamour of the throne. He was a man of few wants, and his opinion was that of his minister, that the peace of private life is worthier than the burden of this crown of thorns. Yet he felt that with the discrowning of the Hohenzollerns, with the disappearance of the Prussian state, there would disappear the last hope of the Germans, and that a premature drawing of the sword would entail the inevitable destruction of the fatherland. The fateful experience of the year 1806, could not so readily be forgotten. As he himself subsequently admitted, he at times underestimated the energies of the Prussian people, failed to do sufficient justice to the profound change of mood which they had undergone, and held gloomily that the sun of good-fortune would never again shine upon him. On the other hand, he also remained free from those pleasing illusions which affected the fiery hearts of the war-party. Of a simple nature, like all the best men of his house, he could not believe that the nation would so readily abandon the ancient habits of the monarchical order. He hoped nothing from a rising in the lands of the Confederation of the Rhine. It seemed to him that salvation could be found solely in an orderly war, directed from above ; and he was resolved not to utter his royal " I will ! " until he saw that there was at least a possibility of victory, and until he was protected in the rear by Russia. The reasonable considerations of the king were ultimately justified. But to the hot impatience of his contemporaries they did not suffice ; and even posterity remained for long unjust towards the conscientious prince, because historians formed their judgments solely from a study of the private letters of the " good party," and repeated in cold blood everything that had been written long before, amid the stormy waves of a noble anger. The excitement of these terrible days was so colossal that even the self-contained Scharnhorst once gave utterance to the harsh complaint that the king built only upon Russia and had no longer any confidence in his own people.

An incautious step of Stein's, suddenly disturbed his warlike plans. A letter from the minister to Prince Wittgenstein, asking him to add fuel to the flames of dissatisfaction in the kingdom of Westphalia, fell into the hands of Napoleon's spies, and on September 8, 1808, was published in the *Moniteur*. This inevitably brought about the fall of Stein. The Imperator at once demanded the dismissal of the conspirator, as otherwise Frederick William would never again see his castle on the Spree ; and Napoleon also made use of the ill-advised letter to browbeat the Prussian negotiators who were now in Paris endeavouring to secure the evacuation of Prussia. His plan was determined : he wished to reinvigorate the Russian alliance, so that he could safely withdraw the *grande armée* from Germany and use it against Spain. For this reason he now showed himself prepared to agree to Alexander's oriental plans ; assured the czar that the intended evacuation of Germany was only a sacrifice to Russian friendship, and invited him to a ceremonial meeting. The awe-inspiring alliance between the rulers of the west and of the east was to manifest itself to the terrified world in all its glory and all its greatness. Alexander actually accepted the invitation, but the Hofburg was so much alarmed at the bold diplomatic evolutions of the Imperator as to promise to put the Austrian army once more upon a peace footing—although unobtrusive military preparations still continued.

Prussia was once more completely isolated and deprived of all means for resistance, and on September 8th Prince William signed the oppressive conditions of the Treaty of Paris. The arrears of the contributions due to France were fixed at 140,000,000 francs, and the French army was recalled. The king was once more to receive the revenues of his own state, but he must hand over to the French until the war-debt was paid off the fortresses of Stettin, Küstrin, and Glogau, on the Oder, and must pledge himself not to increase his army beyond a force of 42,000 men and not to form a Landwehr. Thus Napoleon acquired, in addition to the fortified places on the Elbe and the Vistula, also the line of the Oder, as well as seven military roads leading across Prussian territory, so that the right of entry always remained open for his Poles and his friends in the Confederation of the Rhine, and for the 70,000 Frenchmen whom he continued to maintan between the Elbe and the Rhine. He dominated Prussia in a military sense as completely as he had done before, and would continue to do so for an indefinite period, since the punctual payment of the exorbitant debt was altogether out of the question ; he secured that his two suspected allies should discontinue their military preparations, and he obtained, in addition, the free disposal of the *grande armée*, as well as the promise of Prussian accessory troops in case of a war with Austria !

The king hesitated long before he would accept this new ill-usage. He demanded that the debt should be reduced, was unwilling to hand over the fortresses on the Oder, or to permit that the strength of his army should be thus prescribed, whilst least of all was he willing to part with his minister. One last hope remained, the intermediation of Russia. Alexander, however, had now no eyes for anything but the acquisition of Moldavia and Wallachia ; not until this goal of his ambition had been attained could anyone talk to him of the liberation of Europe. Consequently he adhered firmly to the French alliance ; and when, on his way to meet Napoleon, he visited the court of Königsberg, he remained completely inaccessible to the exhortations of his Prussian friend. For good or for evil, he said, they must get along with France as best they could ; he would do his best to secure from the Imperator a mitigation of the severity of the Treaty of Paris.

In October, 1808, the two emperors met in Erfurt. For the second time, just as he had done four years earlier in Mainz, the Protector of Germany held a brilliant court among his German vassals. Talma played before an audience of queens. In every gesture of the Imperator's, in every formality of the court ceremonial, was manifest the contempt of the crowned plebeian for his high-born servants. *Taisez-vous! Ce n'est qu'un roi!* called out an officer of the body-guard to his drummer when the latter wished to beat his drum in honour of one of the kings by Napoleon's grace. The sole object of the presence of the German kings was to display to the eyes of the czar the might of his ally ; the vassals were altogether excluded from the negotiations. In a secret treaty Napoleon pledged himself to offer no obstacles to the conquest of Finland and of the Danubian princedoms, and in return Russia recognised Joseph Bonaparte as King of Spain. In a joint letter the two emperors demanded of the king of England his assent to these arrangements ; if this were not accorded the war would be pursued with the utmost vigour. All that the czar was able to effect for Prussia was a reduction of the contributions by 20,000,000 francs. Even this concession had to be purchased by consent to a further despicable infringement of the peace of Tilsit. At Tilsit the king had been promised as an indemnity a domain with 400,000 inhabitants in case Napoleon should annex Hanover ; now, with the assent of Alexander, this concession was withdrawn. Napoleon seemed satisfied, for he could proceed without anxiety to repress the Spanish revolt. His Russian friend and the well-armed states of the Confederation of the Rhine would see to it that Germany remained quiet. As a parting gift, the Imperator sent another threatening letter to Emperor Francis, telling him that he must not venture to offer any opposition, for, " What your majesty is, is by my will ! " The czar was profoundly uneasy and disturbed. He had been able to see, close at hand, the vulgar arrogance of the man who was intoxicated with his own good fortune ; he had seen with his own eyes how Napoleon had invited Prince William of Prussia to a hare-hunt upon the battlefield of Jena, and how in the presence of his Russian friend he had given the Cross of the Legion of Honour to the soldiers who had taken part in the war against Russia. Alexander began to doubt whether it was not after all absurd to propose to share anything with this man, and most absurd of all to propose to share with him the dominion of the world. When the Prussian ambassador Schladin represented to him that the occupation of the line of the Oder was obviously intended to prepare for a war with Russia, Alexander had no answer to make. His mistrust grew continually. But it was necessary that his eagles should first wave in Bucharest and Jassy ; and until this was effected, the distasteful alliance must continue.

No choice was now left for the Königsberg court. As late as October, Count Goetzen made confidential enquiries in Vienna whether Austria was willing to take up arms immediately ; it was time that Prussia should declare. Scharnhorst and his friends desired that the diets should be summoned in order to gain a little time. But the Hofburg refused its concurrence, and what use could an outbreak be since the French were still in the country and could at once suppress any hostile activity ? When with a heavy heart the king at length agreed to the treaty, he did what was inevitable. The hesitating and cautious withdrawal of the French troops showed once more what were Napoleon's expectations from the detested Prussians, and it was not until the beginning of 1809 that he at length liberated his prisoners of war. Stein could no longer be retained in office, and on November 24th he took his dismissal. The small French party at the court, the timorous old Kockritz and the conservatives, breathed more freely when the bold reformer departed ; yet Stein's dismissal had not been effected by internal enemies but by the power of Napoleon. Frederick William had ventured the utmost when he still retained the minister in power for three months, in spite of the threats of the Imperator. Stein subsequently reproached himself because he had not earlier resigned his untenable position, and Hardenberg expressed his astonishment that so talented a man could believe this detestable letter would ever be forgiven him ! [1]

In a letter of farewell, drafted by Schön, the dismissed minister reminded his officials once again of the extensive innovations which had been effected during the rich year, saying that the unshakable pillar of every throne, the assent of freemen, had been founded. The letter went on to describe in broad outline what still remained necessary : above all the abolition of the authority of the landed gentry, and the introduction of that of the estates of the realm, for, " every active citizen has a right to

[1] Hardenberg's *Journal*, January 6, 1809.

representation." Stein signed this letter unwillingly, since he had no love either for fine words or for indefinite generalities. Yet it was precisely the doctrinaire wording of this official document which at a later date pleased an epoch searching for a liberal system. The forgetful world had little esteem for the true intelligence of the great reformer and for his ideas on self-government ; whereas this so-called political testament remained high in honour as the programme of the constitutional parties. The departing minister took with him the thanks of his king for having "laid the first foundation, given the first impulse, to a renewed, better, and more powerful organisation of the state structure that had been lying in ruins." He hoped that as the elevation of the lower classes was effected, the new and freer ideas would remain and would develop.

The fall of Stein was an irremediable loss to Prussia's internal life, and for decades yet to come the state felt the consequences of this blow. Yet there was a tragical necessity in the mischievous chance which had brought this momentous letter into the hands of Napoleon. Among all the visitations wherewith the past sins of Prussia were chastised, perhaps the most serious was that the monarchy was no longer able to endure a statesman of such a recklessly lofty spirit. It was impossible for so volcanic a soul to hide permanently all his hopes for the fatherland. Such was his character and such was his destiny. It was impossible for him to carry through with cautious cunning the diplomatic intrigues of which the state had need, and it was therefore inevitable that sooner or later he should be overthrown by his watchful opponent. The official ruin of Stein did not satisfy Napoleon's desire for revenge. On December 16th in an imperial decree issued at Madrid, " le nommé Stein " was declared to be the enemy of France and of the Confederation of the Rhine, and his goods were sequestrated. " Henceforward you belong to history," exclaimed Gneisenau to the outlawed man. The nation was now aware who it was among the Germans whom the Imperator hated most bitterly. Stein bore his losses with equanimity, saying indifferently that he had already several times before lost his baggage. When he went alone in the wintry night through the Riesengebirge towards the protecting Austrian frontier, there occurred to his mind the consoling words of Schleiermacher's sermon, " What has man to fear ? " Invincible in his mind was the pious belief that God could not permanently tolerate this dominion of force and lies.

In Austria, however, they did not know what to make of such

energy as this. Emperor Francis was willing to believe all the fables circulated by the French police regarding the revolutionary plans of the Tugendbund, and had a secret watch kept upon the dangerous Jacobin. Only on rare occasions did Stein give any advice to the imperial statesmen. In Troppau he had much intercourse with Pozzo di Borgo, the personal enemy of the House of Bonaparte, whom the revengeful spirit of the Corsican vendetta pursued restlessly from country to country. This Corsican and the first man of the German nation met on a common ground of hatred. For three years the exile remained without political influence. It was at this time that Gneisenau wrote the terrible words : " We must not hide the fact from ourselves that the nation is as bad as its rule." Stein, too, during these years of tarrying, sometimes suffered from the bitterness of the emigrant. There came moments in which he despaired of the stubborn phlegm of the northern Germans, and thought that Prussia might just as well perish ! This imperial knight was not so profoundly united with the state of Frederick as were his king and Hardenberg, and in case of need, he could imagine his rejuvenated Germany without Prussia. He now saw in Europe but two great armed camps. On one side was the world-empire, and on the other the freedom of the nations. Should all the minor princes, and even the Hohenzollerns, go down to ruin, still let him wear the imperial crown who should bring freedom to Germany. It was not until the spring of 1813 that the hot-blooded Franconian once more became reconciled with the North German people, and was won over for ever to the cause of Prussia.

Immediately upon Stein's departure his work of reform became arrested. The notable men of talent who had worked under him proved unable to effect anything, once his animating and powerful will had been withdrawn. So long as the new organisation remained incomplete, the state had need of a leading statesman, to whom the other ministers should be subordinate. Since Hardenberg was still kept remote from affairs by the disfavour of Napoleon, and since no one else was capable of a decisive activity, the Government got along as best it could with a joint ministry. The new Minister of the Interior, Count Alexander Dohna, was a finely-cultured and honourable patriot. He resembled all the scions of that ancient and heroic Protestant race of whom in East Prussia it was proverbial to say " as good as a Dohna." But he was a man neither rich in ideas nor endowed with a power of far-reaching resolution. The king did not fail to recognise that the new organisation could no longer remain in a half-finished state. He even overcame his disinclination to the representative system, and commanded the Minister of the Interior that he should at once take in hand the reconstruction of the diets and also of the rural police-administration.[1] His sound understanding recognised that the police authority of the country gentry constituted the bulwark of the old feudal privileges.

Hardly had these intentions of the monarch made themselves manifest when there was once more displayed the opposition of the diets, and this opposition was now more forcible than it had been under the powerful rule of Stein. The estates of the Electoral Mark demanded finally that they should be summoned to take part in the deliberations on the proposal for a constitution.[2] The knighthood of Pomerania, at their diet in Stargard, made a formal protest against any alteration in the old territorial constitution, and they protested also against the plan for a general income tax ; whilst the towns throughout the country implored the king to hold fast to his plans, for only through the abolition of the old privileges could there be reawakened that active love for the fatherland which had now been undermined by discontent.[3]

The entire feudal world was in an uproar. The new Lord-Lieutenant of Brandenburg, Sack, and the members of the Potsdam Government, Vincke, Maasen, Beuth, and Bassewitz, all zealous adherents of the reform party, were in continuous feud with the estates of the Electoral Mark. All these able men, who subsequently acquired an honourable place in the Prussian councils, were accused by Marwitz of revolutionary inclinations. Sack, more especially, was considered by the diets as the pattern of bureaucratic Jacobinism. In actual fact, the antediluvian system of taxation, which was still in the hands of the diets, was quite out of harmony with the new and stricter organisation of the boards. The Potsdam Government was absolutely right in proposing a complete reformation of the provincial diets, and, above all, " the exclusion of the estates from all administration."[4] The old struggle between the monarchical unity of the state and feudal

---

[1] Cabinet Order, January 10 and March 4, 1809.
[2] Report of the Lord-Lieutenant Sack to Dohna, September 19, 1809.
[3] Petition from the Further Pomeranian towns to the king, Stargard, September 28, 1809.
[4] Report of the Potsdam Government, December 6, 1809.

particularism once more burst into flame, and Count Dohna was so profoundly discouraged by the passionate intrigues of the privileged classes that at the end of his period of office he roundly declared that in such conditions as these an assembly of the estates of the realm would be the destruction of the royal house. In no country of Europe, he concluded bitterly, were the sense and the culture of higher statecraft and, above all, were all the qualities necessary for an effective system of representation, so incredibly rare as in Prussia ; and yet, on the other hand, there was no other country in which there were such admirable energies for the details of business.[1]

In any case the time for the introduction of constitutional reforms had not yet arrived. The Prussian Reichstag, if summoned at the present time, would have threatened to throw all Stein's work once again into question, especially since the baron himself could no longer introduce the reforms with the force of his own personality. It was inevitable that in such an assembly of the estates the dissatisfied large landowners would have the decisive voice, and even the bourgeoisie gave no secure support to the reforming ideas of the king. The members of the town guilds soon recognised that the crown was aiming at introducing freedom of occupation, and for this reason they clung all the more closely to their old privileges. Again and again had the Government of the Electoral Mark to intervene against the magistrates of Berlin and Potsdam, when these latter endeavoured to re-apply the half-forgotten old penal laws against " bunglers and foreigners." But the new minister lacked the power to avail himself of that sense for the details of business which he ascribed to his own countrymen. Nothing was done to effect the abolition of the police powers of the country gentry ; and instead of resolutely getting to work upon the completed proposals of the new territorial ordinances, fresh plans were worked out, which were full of bold suggestions but ultimately remained altogether unutilised. Even Beyme, the Minister of Justice, who had recently been in the habit of speaking quite in the sense of the reform party, got nothing more done than this, that he at length abolished the old distinction between the bench of the nobles and the bench of the men of learning in the supreme Court of Justice. As far as patrimonial jurisdiction was concerned, he ventured nothing at all, notwithstanding the king's exhortations.

Moreover, how could the timid, quietly diligent man of learning,

[1] Dohna to Hardenberg, August 22, 1810.

Altenstein, bring order into the financial chaos? In addition to the ordinary expenditure of the state, he had to provide a sum of 4,000,000 francs monthly for the payments due to France, also to pay the debts of the last two years, the amount of which was not yet fully known, and finally he had to provide for the maintenance of Napoleon's troops in the fortresses on the Oder. Moreover, the implacable enemy found further possibilities for maltreatment. The garrisons along the Oder were much stronger than had been arranged for in the treaty, and upon orders from the Imperator they enforced a whole series of unlawful supplies, so that in the three years after the withdrawal of the *grande armée* an additional sum of 10,750,000 francs was extorted from the country in conflict with the provisions of the treaty.[1] Like France before the outbreak of the Revolution, so now, the Prussian monarchy had nothing before it but bankruptcy, unless a radical transformation of the whole financial system were, by utilising the taxable capacity of the higher classes, to relieve the burdens of the state. Altenstein feared, however, that new taxes would prove oppressive to the impoverished people. He endeavoured to secure help by the sale of some of the domains, by a voluntary forced loan, and by a high duty upon jewellery and gold and silver articles. All was vain, however, and whenever the attempt was made to float a loan abroad the endeavours of the Prussian agents were counteracted by the diplomacy of Napoleon. The Minister of Finance finally declared in despair, in the name of his official colleagues, that so long as this economic stress prevailed it was impossible to think of internal reforms. The government gradually came to accept the same conditions of benevolent inactivity as before the battle of Jena ; and the present arrest was much more dangerous, for recently a momentous evil custom which had grown up under the regime of Hardenberg, became even more general. Whereas formerly the legislator, following the proper practice of his office, had simply issued his commands, in the new laws it became customary to speak of the prospect of numerous future reforms, to give promises whose import no one could foresee ; all the more serious was the subsequent disillusionment when these promises could not be fulfilled.

In two branches only of the administration did the great

---

[1] According to the calculations of the Ministry of Finance, handed to the great powers in Paris by W. von Humboldt in the spring of 1814 (Humboldt's Report to Hardenberg, May 20, 1814).

spirit of the days of Stein still remain active, in the army and in the department of education. Under the leadership of Scharnhorst, the reconstruction of the army went vigorously forward, and the ministry let the unwearied organiser follow his own counsels. But when at length he disclosed his last and most cherished idea, and in February 1810, proposed a conscription law, in accordance with which everyone, without distinction, upon whom the lot fell was to perform his personal service, there broke loose in the Government a memorable conflict concerning the essential ideas of the modern German military system. On the one side there was the old and honourable zeal of the civil officialdom, desiring to spare the economic powers of the nation ; on the other side was a high-minded political idealism, the spirit of those who regarded the moral significance of the military system as greater than any politico-economical considerations. The Minister of Finance was afraid that the introduction of the universal duty to bear arms would give rise to extensive emigration, and he could not understand of what use would be the entrance into the ranks of cultured young men, since the vigorous people of the lower classes made the best soldiers. The officers on the other hand, Scharnhorst, Boyen, Hake, and Rauch, made appeal to the principle of equality before the law ; they found it to be unjust that the man without means should at the same time have to pay taxes and should stand quite alone in bearing the burden of military service ; they reminded those of the other party of the poverty of the two classes which had done most for the Prussian state, the nobility and the officialdom; they even ventured to maintain what at that time appeared heretical, that young men of culture made the most efficient soldiers, for they brought into the army a moral energy, the principle of honour, whereas the poorer classes could but rarely have a sentiment of permanent dependence on the fatherland. In France, according to Scharnhorst's declarations, the power of purchasing substitutes had introduced an immoral traffic in human beings ; on the other hand, among the virile people of ancient Rome, military service had been an honourable right of the higher classes. Neither the Dohna-Altenstein ministry, nor subsequently that of Hardenberg, could rise to the height of this ethical conception of the military system, of which Stein had fully approved ; and moreover, the calling to arms of all who were competent to bear arms remained impossible so long as the state could enrol an army of no more than 42,000 men. The great plan remained unutilised until a more fortunate hour should arrive, for war was declared, and the fetters of the September treaty were broken.

Meanwhile William von Humboldt was appointed to the head of the Department of Public Instruction. This was a statesman of the stamp of Pericles, the first to recognise clearly that it was Prussia's call to maintain the first rank in Germany by true enlightenment and by a higher intellectual culture. No other man of his age was so fully immersed in the ideas and intimate with the personalities of the classical poetry, and no other had drained so deeply the cup of beauty. Among all the countries of the north, there was no one whose spirit was so closely akin to the universal genius of the Renaissance as was this versatile spirit, a man equally at home in all the joys of material life and in all the domains of thought, accessible to every impression, yet always fully master of himself, a man who led a complete existence, one of genuine beauty, equally remote from frigidity and from excess of enthusiasm. In this aristocrat of the spirit there was incorporated in flesh and blood the ideal of free personality. To live out his life, to develop the rich abundance of his gifts in a fine harmonious experience of enjoyment and action, to gain security for all the chances of life, to make life itself a work of art—this was to him the climax of wisdom :

> "Suffering is not all misfortune, nor fortune ever joy :
> One who fulfils his fate can smile on both."

Never would he abandon the idea that contemplation and cognition, imagination and artistic activity, constitute the true content of human history, that in this phantasmagoria of the temporal, the only living thing is the idea—"the being of the spirit which, caught unawares, lives in the bonds of humanity." Quite frankly, and without any intention to exaggerate, when the star of Bonaparte began to rise, he wrote to Schiller : " My measure of things remains firmly fixed ; the highest things in the world are ideas. Even if I possessed a field of action as great as that of the man who now in truth rules Europe, I should still regard that field as merely subordinate to the higher world of ideas." In old age, after a long and abundant period of activity as a statesman, he once said to Gottfried Hermann, when wandering with his friend the philologist over the battle-field of Leipzig : " Look here, my dear fellow ! kingdoms and empires, as we see here, perish ; but a fine poem endures for ever."[1] To become

[1] From an autograph letter by F. G. Welcker.

a great author was not his desire, nor was it within his capacity. The energies of his spirit were so perfectly balanced that no one of these energies manifested itself as predominant ; and for this reason there were lacking to his style, as Schiller complained, a sense of proportion and adequacy of expression.

When still quite young he came into intimate contact with the Dioscuri of Weimar and with F. A. Wolf ; he was greeted by all three as an equal, and he became familiarised with the creative activity of the two poets. His refined intelligence found its way into the most hidden regions of their spiritual life, and thus what had hitherto been concealed from all critics was revealed to him, an understanding of the great riddle of artistic genius, the hidden union of feminine receptivity with poietic virile energy. His sympathetic understanding and fine judgment which subsequently made him the darling of the Roman people, when for years, in the position of Prussian ambassador, he lived as a Hellene among the Romans, and when in the mountains of Albano he translated Æschylus and Pindar. Gradually he also became aware of the productive energies of his own spirit, and with his Basque investigations began those studies in comparative language which served to lead him to an understanding of " the height, the depth, and the manifoldness of the entire world," which were to furnish him with the key to the understanding of the emotional life of the nations.

Very early in life Humboldt combined with his bold idealism a secure understanding for the hard facts of historic life. The French Revolution repelled him, for he considered it a crime to build the state out of reason alone ; he was not befooled by the pacifism of the epoch, for he regarded war as one of the most valuable means for the education of the human race. He considered it to be the task of the historian that he should always allow himself to be ruled by ideas, but that he should not allow himself to wander unguided in the domain of unattached ideas. Even amid the æsthetic enjoyments of his years in Rome, he was often seized with a yearning for the cordial tones of his mother-tongue ; he loved the German people as the God-endowed bearers of the new European civilisation, and prophesied for Germany a time of requital, " when Germany will illumine the path for the coming generation." It was thus by an internal necessity that he also was at length influenced by the powerful political currents of those days. By the sense of duty of the patriot, and by the impulse towards a many-sided utilisation of his energies, he was moved to serve the state which at one time had seemed to him no more than a system of oppression.

His nature was not created for all the tasks of practical statesmanship. A profound political thinker, such as Hugo Grotius, would have excelled Humboldt in the struggles of diplomacy, just as Humboldt would have been excelled in these matters by many smaller spirits than that of Grotius, for Humboldt lacked the crude ambition of the man of action, and found no pleasure in the thousand necessary trivialities of the ambassadorial profession. He was too great for the diplomatic career. Where politics passed over into the world of the ideal, there was displayed the serene loftiness of his disposition, the vigorous activity of his humanism. From a very different starting-point, he attained to the same view of self-government as Stein ; he venerated the creators of the state-order because in the free movement of the communes he saw the school for the education of moral and vigorous human beings. On the other hand, the dry prose of the questions of international power left him cold. His diplomatic memoirs are far too comprehensive, and too acute. His rich spirit often takes a profitless delight in its own clearness, turns the object under examination over and over, examining it unendingly without profit, failing to see the wood for the trees ; he completely lacked that pleasure in successful dialectic which forces the reader against his will to accept a determined conclusion. Not without reason did Talleyrand name him " le sophisme incarné." Of the insipid pleasures of the world of fashion he could enjoy only those things which charmed his Hellenic sense of beauty ; he would never learn the difficult art of searching out the secrets of the moment in decorous association with all kinds of insignificant people. His diplomatic duties, like all that he undertook, were fulfilled with painful conscientiousness ; but in this occupation there was unknown to him that passionate delight in results which is essential to all great human activity.

Yet no one was so well fitted as he for the management of the Department of Public Instruction, with which the king entrusted him in the spring of 1809. In his brief period of office of fifteen months' duration, he gave to the Prussian system of education that humane and idealistic tendency which it cannot altogether lose even among our weaker imitators. His universal spirit knew how to do justice to every branch of the sciences and the arts, each in accordance with its own peculiarities. Even in the case of the ecclesiastical life which lay most remote from his own æsthetic culture, he brought to bear so frank and humane a sentiment of benevolence, that it was possible to the strictly religious Nicolovius to co-operate harmoniously with this great pagan : religious service was sacred to him because it united as one man all the members of society. It was with awe that he approached the educational question ; he rejected the idea of founding *Realschulen* [Modern Schools], for it seemed to him that the whole future of the nation would be endangered if a portion of the cultured youth should grow up without the methodical discipline of classical studies. He was familiar with the irritability of men of learning, and humoured them not merely by his urbane mildness and patient consideration, but above all by his cordial liberal-mindedness ; for he was well aware that in the domain of genuine culture, the hard power of the state could serve merely to assist and to lead, but that it could here create very little, that, in a word, in this domain, everything depends upon the poietic energy of free thought. The whole secret of his greatness as an organiser is to be found in his simple words concerning the foundation of the Berlin University : " All that is necessary is to appoint first-class men, and then to leave the whole thing to look after itself." He knew but one fatherland, the land of German culture, and in his new office he made it a point of honour to reanimate the ill-used nation with the consciousness of its imperishable spiritual unity. For this reason he restored the old freedom of movement, which had formerly been the pride of our universities, and which first underwent atrophy in the eighteenth century through the jealousies of particularism, and he allowed the Prussian youth to attend any German university. The universities of Prussia were to exercise their force of attraction in free competition, were to prove their superiority by their own performances.

During the first years of the new century, the University of Halle had exhibited a most promising advance. Once more, as formerly under Frederick I, it had taken a place in the foreground of the scientific life of the nation. Here was found the realism of the old people of Göttingen, in conjunction with the idealistic culture of Jena and Königsberg. This young life was suddenly disturbed when the Treaty of Tilsit allotted the region of Madgeburg to the kingdom of Westphalia. Simultaneously Prussia lost the flourishing Erlangen, as well as the three recently-acquired endowed Universities of Erfurt, Münster, and Paderborn, as well as the decayed Duisburg. Directly after the peace, the professors of Halle petitioned the king to transfer their university to Berlin ; but the king replied that he desired to endow a new university in the capital city, and added the graceful words, that the state must replace by intellectual energies what it had lost in physical. The old Berlin plans which had been so often considered, were thus once more resumed, but Humboldt was the first to bring a fresh will and a wide vision to help on the arrested project. At the very time when the Prince-Primate opened a legal school on the Napoleonic model in Wetzlar, the ancient home of German jurisprudence, the Prussian idealist brought to his exhausted state the energy which enabled it to complete in Berlin what had been destroyed in Halle, and " to open for German science a free city of which perhaps there still existed hardly a hope."

The new foundation was to be " something altogether different from a mere provincial university." It was not to concern itself about preparations for practical professions, but was to seek in science itself the goal of scientific work, and therefore, especially as regards its philosophical faculty, was to attract to itself the best energies of Germany. " We wish to teach you how to learn," says Clemens Brentano characteristically, in the song he wrote for the opening festival. In the charter of the university, Humboldt, with a happy tact combining old and new, established those simple and free forms which have since then served as examples for all the universities of Germany. He did not give to the University of Berlin the dangerous position of a state within the state, but placed it as a state-institution upon the foundation of the common law. But the old faculties were preserved, and there was also preserved what Schleiermacher had recently described in a valuable essay as " the true nature of universities in the German sense," namely, unrestricted freedom of learning and teaching. The more radical plans of Fichte were rejected. Humboldt felt that the free spirit of the German youth could not endure the monastic compulsion of a new Platonic Academe, such as was proposed by the inspired philosopher. This was the first Royal Prussian University, and yet was at the same time a foundation for the entire fatherland, the work of a free and great national civilisation, such as was unknown in the case of the old endowed universities based upon Roman imperial privileges. When the new university was instituted in its stately princes' castle opposite to the king's own palace, Prussia recognised that henceforward she sheltered the spirit of German science within her own bosom and could never again be separated from that spirit. It was impossible to show her spiritual superiority over the boastful conqueror in a nobler or worthier manner. Where was there to be found in the great waste of the realm of the Imperator, such an assembly of thinkers as here crowded round the cradle of the new foundation : the theologians, Schleiermacher and Marheineke, the jurists, Savigny and Eichhorn, the physician Hufeland, the agriculturist Thaer ; in the philosophical faculty, Fichte, Boeckh, Buttmann, and, above all, Niebuhr, who, in his lectures upon Roman History, gave to the academical life of Berlin the characteristics of moral earnestness and scientific seriousness which could never pass away.

When Humboldt, embittered by the incapacity of the ministry, resigned his post and re-entered diplomacy, which offered him more leisure to live his own life, there still remained certain advisers who continued to work along Humboldt's lines, and especially the refined and gentle Suvern. The great fundamental principles for the conduct of higher education had been firmly established by the negotiations concerning the University of Berlin ; it was merely necessary to apply them, now that the rejuvenation of the Catholic educational institutions was also undertaken. The old Jesuits' Academy of Breslau was united with the rigid Protestant Viadrina of Frankfort-on-the-Oder, and from the two the new University of Breslau was constructed (1811). This new foundation was a further milestone in the history of our intellectual life. What fierce struggles it had been necessary to fight on behalf of the idea of the equality of religious beliefs at the German universities, since Count Palatine Charles Louis had in his University of Heidelberg first abolished the fossilised old principle of the unity of belief. Now the toleration of the new philosophy forced its way far into the minds of the cultured classes. Everyone found it perfectly right that in the secular faculties of the Berlin University free access should be given to those of all beliefs. In Breslau the state even went a step further, and founded two theological faculties, one for Catholics and one for Protestants. Thus there came into existence the first university to give parity to different religious beliefs—and this characterised the peculiarity of German life in a manner hardly comprehensible to foreigners.

How disastrous was it for Prussia that at the moment when its greatest statesman had to be outlawed, a new war storm should break over Austria. In the new year of 1809 the Prussian royal pair accepted the pressing invitation of the czar Alexander that they should visit St. Petersburg. The czar received his guests with unprecedented display, as if he wished to excuse himself for his disloyalty at Tilsit ; the nobility of the court also endeavoured by exaggerated marks of honour to manifest their hatred for the French. Thenceforward the two courts were united in a relationship of mutual confidence such as never before had existed between great powers ; the Prussian ambassador in St. Petersburg was in future treated as a member of the imperial family. As far as political results, however, were concerned, the journey completely miscarried. The czar had not yet brought the Swedish war to a conclusion, he was negotiating with Persia about the Caucasian frontier, and was about to declare war upon Turkey. As long as these three wars were not brought to a successful conclusion, as long as Finland and the Danubian provinces were not yet in his hands, he was unwilling to break with Napoleon. He assured his friend that should there be a war between Austria and France, he was pledged to give his assistance to the latter ; he urgently advised the king to follow a similar policy, and by removing his court to Berlin to give the Imperator a proof of his confidence and friendship. Frederick William returned home profoundly depressed, but by no means convinced ; on no account would he take part in the campaign against Austria, on the contrary he gave orders for secret preparations for war, so that in case of need he might come to the assistance of the court of Vienna. In March, he again vainly attempted to win the czar over to his plan (which seemed to him to offer the only hope of salvation) for an alliance between the three eastern powers.[1]

Meanwhile Napoleon had hastened to Spain, and in a rapid and triumphal campaign had overthrown the Spanish armies, which were incompteent in the field, and had driven back the English army to the coast. Directly the prestige of his eagles had been restored, he resumed his plans against Austria, which in the previous autumn had merely been postponed, and prepared to chastise the Hofburg for its military preparations. As early as January, 1809, he sent orders from Spain for the army of the Confederation of the Rhine to be prepared for the march, and had the forces of Davoust and Oudinot moved to the Upper Danube. At the end of this month he returned to Paris. He proposed to open the war in Germany with 260,000 French, Poles, and Rhenish Confederates, and in Italy with 150,000 men. He wrote mock-

[1] King Frederick William to Czar Alexander, March 24, 1809.

ingly to his vassals to ask them if they thought that the Danube had become a river of Lethe, since in Vienna all earlier defeats seemed to have been forgotten. It was, however, his intention to defer the outbreak of the war until the spring. His preparations would not be completed till then, and also he wished to appear as the attacked party, because Russia was pledged to help him only in a war of defence. " My quarrel with Austria," he said in a letter to Frederick of Würtemberg, " is the fable of the wolf and the lamb ; it would really be extremely amusing if they could cast us for the part of the lamb ! "

In Austria tremendous excitement prevailed ; everyone believed that the decisive moment had arrived. Certainly in the amiable and knightly nature of Count Stadion there was no trace of the greatness of the reformer ; and the class-pride of the mediatised imperial count played a great part in his hatred of the French. But under his ministry a somewhat freer and gentler spirit had been introduced into the administration. The army had gained even more under the leadership of Archduke Charles. Austria was in a position to take up arms in a state of better preparation than had existed for years. The men of the Landwehr hastened to join the colours with loudly expressed delight. Everywhere, and especially among the German stocks, there was firm confidence in the old imperial house and joyful readiness for all sacrifices. The year 1809 was the finest in Austrian history. The imperial army, whose annals were so rich in valour and so poor in genius and inspiration, was once more to exhibit some brilliant characteristics of genuine heroism. It was indeed unthinkable that this House of Hapsburg which had grown to power through the suppression of all truly national spirit, should conduct a campaign on behalf of the freedom of the nations. It was a cruel irony that Archduke Charles, in his moving appeal to the Germans, should give utterance to the extremely questionable opinion, " By joining with Austria, Germany would become independent and happy ! " In a similar spirit, his brother John said to the Italians that they were to-day no longer Italians, and that they could attain their freedom only through Austria. The holy anger of the patriots in the empire had no eye for such contradictions. The ancient loyalty to the emperor reawakened in our people ; they wished to forget that this same Emperor Francis three years earlier had coldly relinquished his high office, and that his new war manifesto said not a syllable of the re-establishment of the empire. It was enough that he was drawing the sword against "a system which would recognise in Europe no other law but its own." It seemed that the destiny of the whole fatherland was now associated to his banner ; to follow his military leadership appeared, even to the North Germans, to be a point of honour, to the North Germans who had hitherto hardly spoken of emperor and empire.

For Austria the war was unavoidable, but it was begun prematurely, with a light-minded excess of self-esteem, and without sufficient diplomatic preparation. Deceived by the confidential reports sent by Count Metternich from Paris, the Hofburg believed that the forces at its disposal were greatly superior to those of Napoleon. Disregarding the warnings of the czar, Austria assumed the dangerous role of attacking party, and announced its determination in London and Berlin at so late a date that, at the opening of the campaign it was impossible for England and Prussia to co-operate at all. Whilst the imperial diplomacy had thus been so presumptuous, Archduke Charles failed by an over-cautious hesitation. Since the main force of the French army was not yet on the scene, and since he was opposed, almost exclusively, by the Rhenish Confederates, it would have been possible for him, by a bold advance, to transfer the theatre of war into Swabia, but he lost invaluable days whilst he divided his assembled army. Meanwhile Napoleon arrived and took up his headquarters among the Bavarian regiments, as he had formerly done amongst his own guards. The valiant troops felt themselves highly honoured ; the ancient trival hatred once more flamed up when the Imperator assured them, in high-flown language, that he would lead them to victory against the eternal enemies of Bavaria. More servilely than ever did the princes of the Confederation of the Rhine follow the army of their Protector ; he had assured them that it was essential to prevent the restoration of the German emperordom of the Hapsburgs. Now for the first time did it become fully apparent what was the significance of the Confederation of the Rhine for the military power of France ; it was only the co-operation of the German south which assured the Imperator of victory in this campaign.

In a series of brilliant battles he defeated the isolated bodies of the Austrian troops upon the Bavarian plateau, between the Iser and the Danube, by a campaign of five days, compelling the archduke to withdraw to Bohemia with a loss of 50,000 men. The uprising that had been begun with such exaggerated hopes, opened as lamentably as the war of 1805 ; and just as had been the case four years earlier, the conqueror descended the Danube without pause, took the capital, and then dictated his command that the Pontifical State should be united with the empire. But when, within sight of the archduke's army, he now attempted to cross the Danube, the fury of the imperial soldiers inflicted upon him at Aspern his first defeat. Terrible was the impression produced by this mishap upon the child of fortune. Everyone felt that this world-empire was tottering. Whilst after the battle Napoleon lay for many hours in a heavy slumber, his generals were already taking counsel whether it would be possible to lead back the beaten army to France if the Imperator should never wake again.

The report of the victory of Aspern spread like lightning all over Germany ; everyone joined with Heinrich Kleist in rejoicing over the " conquest of the Unconquerable." There arrived also encouraging news from the Tyrol, how the brave and pious peasants of the mountains had four times within a year risen in revolt against the detested Bavarian masters, in order to re-establish the dominion of the beloved imperial house and to restore Catholic unity of belief. Here everything was united which could raise and inspirit this romantic race ; the savage beauty of the Alps ; the rude, heroic energy of faithful men living in close contact with nature ; the honourable struggle for the customs, the rights, and the belief of their ancestors, the artistic confusion of a free popular revolt—monks and peasants, mountain guns and Alpine dairy-maids, all working confusedly together. " His equal in honours never was nor shall be," thus runs the inscription beneath the picture of Andreas Hofer in his headquarters at the Adler in Innsbruck. The childish simplicity and loyalty of his race were embodied in the brave " Sandwirt von Passeier " [Hofer], and so completely did political anger drive out the old pride of culture, that the North German patriots greeted him with frank delight as the hero of the nation. One-sidedness is the right of every great passion : those who were now embittered would not and could not see that the monks and the peasants of the Tyrol were not for a moment dreaming of the German fatherland, that their revolt was directed just as much against the benevolent reforms as against the bureaucratic severity of the Bavarian government ; that the power of inconsiderate custom, the gloomy hatred against heresy, and the old particularist hostility towards the Bavarian neighbours, had a large share in the heroic courage of this peasants' war.

Now in one place, now in another, the long repressed wrath

surged up into bright flame upon the soil of Germany ; the conqueror could no longer recognise this patient people, and imagined himself surrounded by a thousand La Vendées. In the valley of the Tauber, the former subjects of the Teutonic Knights fought vainly against the troops of their new Würtemberger master ; they wished to return to the quiet happiness of the good old times. The faithful Prussians in the region of Ansbach received with open arms the flying corps which the Hotspur, Charles von Mostitz, was leading through Franconia against the flank of the enemy ; on the approach of the insurgents, the imperial town of Nuremberg joyfully tore down the Bavarian arms from the gates. From Bohemia, the son of the unhappy commander of Auerstedt, Frederick William of Brunswick, began a guerilla war against Saxony—this was a true Guelph, brave, severe, and masterful. Many of the best among the North German youth hastened to place themselves beneath his black flag. In the kingdom of Westphalia, arms were twice taken up, on one occasion by Dörnberg and on the other by Emmerich, both officers of Electoral Hesse, and in each case the rising was savagely repressed. The Prussian Lieutenant Katt vainly attempted a surprise attack upon the fortress of Magdeburg.

Among the patriots in the Prussian army and among the Prussian officials there was only one voice. All thought like Blucher, all wondered why the Prussians should not follow the example of the Tyrolese and of the Spaniards ; why they should not say : " Let him bear fetters who will, I will bear them no longer." Many of the discharged officers were already fighting in the ranks of the Austrian army. The mood of the Prussian army was so unmistakable, that Napoleon simply did not dare to remind the king of his promise to send accessory troops ; he was afraid of such allies. So stormily did the discontent flame that now, for the first time in the honourable history of the Prussian army, was disloyalty possible, though only a disloyalty which pursued the noble aim of " restoring to our beloved king the very last of his villages." Major Schill, the hero of Kolberg, as he was commonly called, had re-entered the liberated capital only after the withdrawal of the French, and had been received there with great rejoicing. His soldiers regarded him with unlimited confidence ; the burghers of Berlin were devoted to him ; and since the masses do not believe in ideas until they see them incorporated in flesh and blood, the bold hussar soon came to be regarded as the embodied representative of the old warlike

Prussianism. Countless people expected from him the restoration of the ancient greatness; people smoked [Schill-tobacco; in every farm of the Mark, there hung upon the wall a picture of this moustachioed hero, with Fouqué's apposite verses written beneath. This popular favour went to the honest swashbuckler's head; he now believed himself to be chosen for a wonderful destiny, and hardly had the war in the south broken out when he led his little troop, a few hundred men only, away from the drill-ground of Berlin to attack the kingdom of Westphalia. "Better a terrible end, than terror without end," he exclaimed to his unlucky followers. The faithful fellows followed him only because he represented himself as being in confidential relations with the king, and because he undertook to restore the former greatness of Prussia. Soon after he had started he received the news of the defeats of the Austrians on the Upper Danube; the senseless undertaking collapsed in the very beginning, and there was no longer any talk of a great popular uprising. Not only did the king, as was his duty, set the serious forces of the law at work against the deserters, he also expressed in strong words his personal detestation of Schill's "incredible action," and he did so with full justice, for what would remain for this unhappy state if the obedience of the army were to be shaken? The foolhardy troop, after aimless wanderings, found an honourable end beneath the walls of Stralsund, and Napoleon did his best to consecrate the memory of the lost sons of the German people. What a profound impression was produced when it was learned that Schill's body had been decapitated; that those of his officers who had been taken prisoner had—unquestionably in accordance with the letter of international law—been treated as highway robbers, some being shot and others sent to the galleys. Greatly moved, thousands repeated the verses of Schenkendorf:

> "Steel alone, by men well wielded,
> Rescue brings to this our race!"

In his heart, the king was strongly inclined to take part in the struggle. He was determined to strike, and yet he kept cool amid the general fever, for the consciousness of a terrible responsibility was a heavy burden to his soul. If he should vainly draw the sword upon this occasion Prussia would be destroyed, and destroyed for ever, as far as man could foresee. The mad daring of a declaration of war, when the well-equipped forces of the enemy occupied Danzig and Magdeburg, and when the Prussian state was cut in two by the garrisons along the Oder—such a venture as this would have been utterly wrong if there had not been at least some possibility of success. Frederick William would not for a second time do what he had done in the days of Austerlitz, would not a second time, through the vacillation of Austria, be handed over to the revenge of the conqueror. He demanded guarantees that Emperor Francis would continue the war, even in the event of disasters, until Prussia should be in a position to participate in the struggle. He further demanded money and arms from England, and the landing of a British force in Germany. His state was utterly without means. In order to be able to do something towards the work of military preparation, the payments to France demanded by treaty had already been discontinued, with considerable lack of foresight ; and how was the little army, held in check as it was by the fortresses of the enemy, to maintain itself in the field unless it received some support from the coast ? The most important of all was the danger which threatened from Russia, the ally of France. It seemed to the king that only if he were secure against attack from the east, the undertaking would not be utterly hopeless. Napoleon thoroughly understood the desperate position of his secret opponent, and indifferently expressed the opinion : " Prussia to-day counts for very little ; I have sufficient means at my disposal to keep it under."

The king had very rightly understood the conditions indispensable to a Prussian declaration of war, and he soon had to learn that not one of these conditions was to be fulfilled. Even before the outbreak of the war, he had written urgently to the czar, begging for a definite undertaking that Russia would support him, or at least would not attack if he entered into an alliance with Austria. Alexander made answer that if Prussia failed to fulfil its pledges towards France, he himself could not quarrel with Napoleon. On May 12th the king wrote once more, saying that an unfortunate appeal to arms would readily lead to the destruction of Prussia, and he must at least have a pledge that Russia would not tolerate the destruction of his state. On this occasion, also, the czar's answer was a rebuff. Notwithstanding moving words and ardent assurances of friendship, the essential meaning of his reply was that Russia could not at present do anything in the matter, even if the Prussian state were to be effaced from the map. What this meant was that the Russian friend wished the Prussian sword to remain in the scabbard until he himself had got safe possession of the strongly desired Danubian provinces. Here he was quite in earnest ; the auxiliary army which the czar had promised his French ally actually advanced through Warsaw against Galicia. Although it conducted the war with the greatest possible caution, and almost as a mere pretence, and although it seemed to dread the revolted Poles in Galicia much more than the Austrians themselves, the effect of the move actually was to withdraw a portion of the Austrian army from the decisive battles on the Danube. A Russian army corps was close to the East Prussian frontier, and could cross that frontier at any moment if Prussia should join in the war. This attitude on the part of Russia was decisive as far as the king's conduct was concerned.

For months, too, England did nothing which could help the Prussian court. Finally, the Hofburg continued to exhibit the old arrogance of the Ferdinands. Whilst the negotiations concerning the alliance were still in progress, the Austrian court sent a military plenipotentiary, Colonel Steigentesch, to Königsberg, in order to unmask Napoleon's designs to the king. Steigentesch was extremely presumptuous in his demands, insisting, even before the negotiations were concluded, that the supreme command over the Prussian army should be given to Archduke Charles, and subsequently, while in Berlin, he betrayed the confidential announcements of the king to the Westphalian ambassador Linden, who faithfully reported everything to the Imperator. In Prussia itself, the embitterment against the royal hesitation was so strong that certain patriots advised in all seriousness that the Austrian troops in Poland should march through Silesia, so that the court might thereby be forced to declare itself! All that Emperor Francis could hold out in prospect to Prussia for this struggle of despair was a simple military convention and a pledge for the preservation of the *status quo !* Frederick William, however, demanded, as was just, a formal treaty which should guarantee his monarchy the restoration of the old power, with tenable frontiers. In all other questions of German policy, the views of the two powers were profoundly divergent. Austria was inclined, in the event of victory, to restore Warsaw to the crown of Prussia, but the king, having been convinced by the great disloyalty of 1806 that this possession was valueless desired for his state only so much of Polish territory as was indispensable in order to secure the union between Silesia and Old Prussia. Out of the rest of the country he would gladly have constituted a national Polish dukedom, under the common protection of the three eastern powers, were Prussia guaranteed compensation for this in Germany, perhaps in Saxony. Emperor Francis, however, was by no means inclined to allow any increase of Prussian territory upon German soil ; and when late in the summer, after Austria's defeats, the Prussian negotiator Knesebeck brought up for discussion the old plan of Bartenstein for a twofold hegemony in Germany, he was met by a cold refusal. Not even the experience of misfortune had lessened the arrogance of the House of Lorraine. The warm friend of Austria wrote sadly home that it was no longer possible to deceive oneself, that the Hofburg would not recognise the Prussian state as an equal power.

Consequently, the arrogance of Austria, the incapacity of the English policy, and the ambitious designs of the czar, combined to make it impossible for Prussia to enter the war. Moreover, the calm soldier-vision of the king enabled him to form a better judgment of the course of the war than was possible to his excited entourage. He regarded the battle of Aspern as no more than the brilliant repulse of an attack, and not as a decisive battle, and the result proved that the king was right. Archduke Charles did not understand how to make the best use of the victory of his soldiers ; he remained for several weeks almost inactive in the field, whilst Napoleon called up with unceasing energy reinforcements from all the corners of his extensive empire, and even summoned the sailors from the channel ports. In July the Imperator felt strong enough to attempt once more the crossing of the Danube; on July 5th and 6th, the archduke was defeated at Wagram, chiefly through the fault of his brother John who did not support him at the right moment with the troops from Hungary. Once more, as after the battle of Austerlitz, the cowardice of the imperial court prevailed. Six days later the Peace of Znaim was concluded, and the archduke threw up his command in a fit of temper.

The world had long been aware that Napoleon only agreed to a truce when he was certain of peace. Nevertheless King Frederick William continued to cherish his warlike designs, and collected his army in fortified camps. Blucher's army corps was ready in Pomerania to advance upon the line of the Oder at the first sign. Once more, on July 24th, the valiant prince wrote to his Russian friend that the day of Wagram had not, after all, been decisive ; that if Russia and Prussia should now sumultaneously declare war, the liberation of Germany was still possible. His ambassador Schladen proved to the czar in an urgent memorial that if Austria fell, Russia would have to pay for it. But Alexander remained silent ; it was not until after the peace had been concluded that an answer came from St. Petersburg. Meanwhile Gneisenau was sent on a secret mission to London, and adjured the British cabinet to transport to the German coasts the military force which was already prepared for this expedition, so that the English could give assistance to the Prussian army. George Canning agreed to the fiery German's proposals, for the talented young statesman had already come to the conclusion that the insular policy of England was narrow-minded and petty. But the mediocrity of the other ministers was such that they had eyes only for mercantile interests. The expedition was sent to the Netherlands, in order to provide for the British fleet a bridge-head upon the Continent, and before the walls of Antwerp and in the swamps of Walcheren came to an ignominious end. Moreover, it was no longer possible to reckon upon Austria's staying power. In the military headquarters the bold plans of the spring had long been abandoned, for the enemy, who had meanwhile received reinforcements to the number of 80,000 men, was now of over-powering strength.

Napoleon next effected a masterly diplomatic evolution. The old imperial house had been sufficiently weakened. Were he now to reconcile himself with the conquered, the plans for that great onslaught upon Russia which the indefatigable man had most at heart might he allowed to ripen undisturbed. His attitude towards Austria became more friendly. In the Peace of Vienna, October 14th, he gave the House of Hapsburg somewhat milder terms than had been expected a little while earlier. It was true that Austria would have to abandon her last position on the Adriatic, to cede to the Imperator the whole coastland as far inland as the Save, hand over to Bavaria in the west and to Warsaw in the north-east extensive domains ; but there was still left to Austria a position as a great power, and the nucleus of her military forces, the land of the crown of St. Stephen. For her services as a faithful member of the Confederation of the Rhine, Bavaria received Bayreuth and also the completion of the plans of exchange which had been so earnestly cherished in Munich for many years past—the central state of the Confederation was given the whole of Prussian Franconia, in place of the remote Rhenish provinces, which were now in the hands of Murat.

The war was finished. The valiant Guelph made a venturesome march across the kingdom of Westphalia, receiving the cordial greetings of the loyal inhabitants in the town of his fathers, to find at length with his troops an asylum on board English ships. Emperor Francis sacrificed his loyal Tyrolese with the same indifference with which he had at an earlier date discarded the duties of the German emperorship, and indeed this popular uprising had always been a matter for suspicion to the distrustful despot. The betrayed men could not believe that their Francis could abandon them. How solemnly had he declared that he would not sign any peace that was to separate the land of the red eagle from the monarchy! They resisted to the utmost, and it was only with the execution of Andreas Hofer that the deplorable tragedy came to a close. The revolt of the people of Austria ended in blood. Betrayed in their dearest hopes, inspired with a loathing for all ideals, the light-minded people returned once more to the joys of the life of the senses. The congential disease of modern Vienna, the pessimistic mood, gained the upper hand. Who could dream of glory and honour since Austrian stupidity was predestined to misfortune? Subsequently the disgraceful state-bankruptcy brought confusion and dishonour into every household; in gaming and dancing and drives in the Prater, people forgot the distresses of the time. The disillusioned victors of Aspern recreated themselves in the pornographic stories of the *Letters of Eipeldauer*: they knew nothing of Fichte, Kleist, and Arndt. The war of 1809 had once again set in motion the German blood of the Austrians; but a year later they were more inaccessible, more remote than ever from the life of our nation.

Thus was the ground prepared for the autocracy of Emperor Francis. The crafty old fellow had now sufficient confidence in himself to take the reins of the state into his own hands; after all, he had always been wiser than all the ideologues who had prated to him about the liberation of Europe. With a self-satisfied narrowness of mind, he now restored the ancient Hapsburg system of government, as it had existed for centuries before the days of Maria Theresa. In internal affairs nothing was changed in essentials. A suspicious police diligently suppressed all ideas of political innovation, just as in former days they had suppressed the doctrines of the heretics; prevented the awakening to national self-consciousness of the extensive national contrasts in this polyglot confusion of peoples; and secured for obedient subjects the Phæacian good-fortune of a waking dream-life.

The activity of the national authority was once more entirely directed towards European affairs, and to this system of fruitless love of ease, was admirably adapted the policy of the new Minister of Foreign Affairs—Count Metternich, the Adonis of the drawing-rooms, past-master of all pettiness and cunning trickery. At the end of his career, he summed up his own experience of life by saying : " I have often ruled Europe, but never Austria." All his activity was devoted to diplomatic intrigue. Utterly ignorant of political economy and of internal administration, he left all these bourgeois affairs, in accordance with the old Austrian custom, to the privy councillors and the secretaries. Like his emperor, he hated and feared the elemental energy of the national idea which was so active in Germany ; he dreaded no less the Russian neighbour, whose power he always over-estimated. He knew the world too well, and calculated with too much sobriety, to believe in the eternity of the Napoleonic empire ; if the favourable moment should arrive, he was ready to overthrow this oppressive power. So long, however, as the glories of the world-monarchy were still undisturbed, its friendship should bring advantage to the House of Austria. With shameless coldness of heart Emperor Francis wooed the grace of the conqueror. In the spring of 1810, even before the execution of Andreas Hofer, he gave the Archduchess Marie Louise in marriage to Napoleon. The daughter of the last of the Roman Emperors became the spouse of the new ruler of the world, and she dishonoured her ancient house by an open levity of spirit, by unworthy flattery of the French. The same Archbishop of Vienna who had, shortly before, consecrated the banners of the Landwehr, now gave his blessing to that union of the two imperial houses which in accordance with Catholic ideas was unquestionably adulterous. The favourite newspaper of the Viennese described with humble gratitude, how God had given His only-begotten Son for the salvation of mankind, and how the good Emperor Francis in accordance with this example had offered up his daughter for the salvation of the fatherland. Such was Austria in the year 1810. Never has a high-spirited uprising been succeeded by a more humiliating fall.

For good reasons did the leading princes of the Confederation of the Rhine hasten to Paris immediately after the declaration of peace, in order once more to assure themselves of the grace of the Protector, for everywhere had the war brought to light the inner hollowness of the rule of the Confederation. How much discontent

and hatred had there been displayed among the peoples of Franconia and Westphalia ; what weakness of the state authority
in Saxony, whose king had left the country even before the entrance
of the enemy, to attend in the security of the old imperial cathedral
of Frankfort the Te Deum which was sung in honour of the defeat
of his Austrian brother-in-law ! The Prussian patriots were
infuriated because the great hour had been allowed to pass
unutilised. The queen complained pathetically : " Austria is
singing her swan song, and then it will be Good-bye to Germania ! "
Yet the king had done only what he had clearly recognised to be
his duty. Napoleon was perfectly right when after the peace
he said dictatorially to the Prussian ambassador : " You have
not done me any service by keeping quiet; it would have been the
climax of lunacy if you had declared war against me with the
Russians at your back ! " He knew very well that in case of need
it would have been easy for him, first of all by a new battle, to
force Emperor Francis to make a separate peace, and then with
crushing force to give the death-blow to the isolated Prussians.
We who come afterwards also know what those of that day neither
would nor could see, that even the improbable event of an Austrian
victory could have brought no salvation for our fatherland. For
in that case, a new age of Wallenstein would have dawned for
Germany, and the foreign dominion of the Hapsburgs would have
replaced that of Napoleon.

The man, however, who was chiefly responsible for the great
disillusionment, was soon to reap the fruit of his fine calculations !
Alexander dreaded nothing so much as the re-establishment
of Poland by Napoleon. " If you are thinking of that," said he
to Caulaincourt, " the world is not great enough for an agreement
between us two "; and again and again he declared to the French
ambassador that Galicia must be allotted to Russia if it did not
remain Austrian. Now he was to learn that in the Peace of Vienna
Napoleon arbitrarily gave the whole of New Galicia, containing
one and a half million inhabitants, to the Duchy of Warsaw,
together with the important places of Zamosc, Lublin, and Cracow
—regions which Russia had recently conquered and still occupied.
All that was thrown to the czar as a scrap out of the booty, was
the strip of land at Tarnopol ; and this was done merely for show,
that the world might see that the czar was after all the ally of
France ; it was an accessory motive that this Greek gift was to
sow hostility between the court of St. Petersburg and that of
Vienna. The re-establishment of the ancient crown of Poland

was threateningly near; the relations between the allies of
Tilsit became cooler day by day, since Napoleon had concluded
the new alliance of friendship with Austria. Alexander felt that
a struggle for very existence was now in his own case at hand.

Next Prussia had to pay severely for the warlike intentions
of the past year. Now that the Imperator was secure of the
alliance with the House of Austria, he cared for nothing. He knew
the most secret thoughts of the royal court, partly through the
treachery of the Austrian diplomats, and partly through the
reports furnished by his own spies, and he had reason for his
complaints, since Prussia had put herself in the wrong by ceasing
the payment of the contributions due to France. If the king
now confiscated the Silesian possessions of the suspect Brunswicker, Napoleon was well aware that this zeal was exhibited
only to save the possessions of the Guelph from French avarice.
With fierce impatience he demanded the payment of arrears,
with usurious interest on account of the delay. When the king
alleged the complete exhaustion of the finances, and declared that
he had already sold his jewels and his gold plate in order to pay
the debts of the state, the mocking answer came : "What
pitiful means are these to employ while useless camps are being
occupied, whilst horses are being bought, whilst needless expenditure upon the army is being incurred."

In order to assuage Napoleon's anger by a proof of confidence,
at Christmas, 1809, the king removed his court to Berlin, amid the
French garrisons. How often in former days, in the time of
Frederick, had a dashing entry been made into the capital. And
now the conquered man must pass through the new Königstor !
The beautiful queen sat weeping in the carriage which the impoverished town had given her ; the king came on horseback ; behind
him Scharnhorst, pale and gloomy, surrounded by the generals ;
then the young princes leading their regiments. Several hundred men had hastened from the lost provinces in order to greet
their tribal lord on his return ; Arndt and Jahn also stood among
the crowd, greatly moved by the expressions of love which broke
simultaneously from thousands of hearts. Not an eye was dry.
It was as if the princes and the people and the army assured one
another that now all the old blames had been forgotten and
forgiven. Kleist greeted the king as the victor who was greater
than the triumphant Cæsar.

To the gentle spirit of Frederick William it was a joy to
exhibit on his side, after the patriarchal manner of the day, his

love for the faithful people. In the following month he celebrated for the first time the Ordensfest, the democratic festival of a bourgeois military monarchy, and invited all who had distinguished themselves in the performance of their duties, down to the very letter-carriers, to come to his castle as guests. Characteristically enough, in the general joy which greeted the returning prince, few took part more heartily than the French ambassador, Count St. Marsan. The honourable ultra-Conservative Savoyard had had to say to the king the worst and most contumelious things which had ever been said to a Prussian ruler. In this he had fulfilled the duties of his office, but he noted with quiet admiration the moral grandeur of this oppressed state, and soon learnt to feel a profound esteem for the character of Frederick William. Between the unhappy monarch and the ambassador of his deadly enemy there came into existence a firm relationship of mutual respect ; many years later, when the count was minister in Piedmont, the king repeatedly gave him assurances of his confidence.[1]

But of what value was the good-will of the ambassador, since his master remained relentless. More and more threatening and stormy became the messages of Napoleon. It was true he did not at present intend to make war upon Prussia, for had he done this the decisive struggle with Russia would have been prematurely begun. But it seemed a favourable opportunity for detaching in time of peace yet another province from the detested state. It was soon learned that the Imperator would renounce his further monetary claims in exchange for the cession of Silesia ! Even the ministers saw no other way out, and they came to accept that despairing idea of a yet further diminution of territory which Schön had already expressed three and a half years earlier. On March 10, 1810, Altenstein assured Prince Wittgenstein that the state would be lost unless it were prepared to renounce a portion of Silesia. Two days later the ministry unanimously declared to the monarch that if the worst came to the worst, it would be necessary to buy off Napoleon by a cession of territory. To this had Prussia come, that even Scharnhorst advised a cowardly action which would rob the unhappy country of its last shreds of prestige. Prince Wittgenstein was a courtier of the ordinary kind, timorous, smooth-tongued, sly, and frivolous, a sworn enemy of Stein. The detestable nature of this proposal, however, roused

---

[1] For example, in a letter from the king to King Victor Emanuel of Sardinia, dated March 15, 1821.

even Wittgenstein, and wrathfully reporting everything to his royal master he made urgent counter-proposals. The king, who had never had much respect for this incapable ministry, lost patience, and immediately made up his mind to dismiss his advisers. He never forgot the patriotic deed of his High Chamberlain ; henceforward Wittgenstein possessed a powerful if quiet influence, which was often to be exhibited, and in most cases to the detriment of the monarchy. Frederick William now came to an understanding with Hardenberg, and after prolonged negotiations in Paris, Napoleon agreed to permit the return of the outlawed statesman. Napoleon could not fail to see that in view of the firm attitude of the king the peaceful acquisition of Silesia was impossible ; it would suffice for the moment if a capable man should undertake the conduct of the Prussian finances, and should guarantee the punctual payment of the contributions. In the beginning of June, 1810, Altenstein was dismissed, and Hardenberg took over his office. The second epoch of Prussian reforms began.

§ 3. THE CONFEDERATION OF THE RHINE. HARDENBERG'S
ADMINISTRATION. THE RUSSIAN WAR.

Whilst the Prussian people was waiting with passionate impatience for the hour of liberation, in the Germany of the Confederation of the Rhine it was only in a few areas and in isolated patriotic circles that the disgrace of the fatherland was profoundly and bitterly felt—especially in the Protestant north, and above all in the provinces that had been detached from Prussia. In the County Mark, under the rule of the grand duke of Berg, the loyal people held together like one man ; while doing what they were forced to do, they never paid flattering homage to the stranger. Everywhere throughout these regions there were to be found a few faithful nobles of the old days, who at the bottom of their hearts still regarded themselves as servants of the Prussian state, and considered that the new order was no more than a transitory episode. Such men were the able lawyer Sethe in Münster, and young Motz at Eichsfelde. In Celle, the old president Rumann did not enter upon his Westphalian office until his king, George III, had given him formal permission. Very few among the higher Prussian officials entered the service of the Princes of the Confederation of the Rhine except on compulsion, and those who did so were regarded with general contempt, as for example the minister

Schulenburg-Kehnert. Dohm, too, the talented publicist, who had so often drawn up for the crown of Prussia plans for a league of princes, now atoned for his earlier views by suddenly losing faith in his state and taking service under King Jerome. Here and there a defiant nobleman of the old breed carried on a petty warfare against the foreigner after his own manner. Baron von Wylich, in Cleves, carried off the archives of the old diet to his castle, and was regarded everywhere as the one rightful representative of the land of Cleves, since his knightly comrades had died out ; and when the Prussians at length returned, he confidently demanded that they should at once re-establish the old diet with all its ancient rights. How greatly amused were the nobles of Magdeburg on one occasion when the turbulent Heinrich Krosigk locked up the gendarmes of King Jerome in the fire-station, and then contentedly endured a period of imprisonment in a fortress. As long as the " French episode " endured, the wild young fellow always had loaded pistols lying upon his table, and as soon as his former king summoned him, he hastened across the Elbe to the beloved flag.

In Saxony and in South Germany there was much complaint regarding the widespread poverty of the time ; but owing to the alienation from public life which had endured for many hundred years, and to the atrophy which had resulted from particularism, it was seldom that a sustained hatred was manifested. The Prussians did not believe in the endurance of the world-empire, but in the petty states hope was gradually abandoned. German patience made a virtue of necessity and honoured the Confederation of the Rhine as the last bond which still held the nation together. The weakling Dalberg was not alone in his enthusiastic appreciation of how the love for the fatherland had been awakened in his pure soul by the Confederation of the Rhine. Hans Gagern, too, hoped that a new and improved German Carlovingian empire would arise out of the state-structures instituted by the Imperator. Smidt of Bremen, a thoroughly patriotic and sober-minded young statesman, adjured his Hansa towns to join the Confederation of the Rhine, since this Confederation would soon become a general federation of Germany ; so only could the Hanseatics once more become German !

Yet anyone who closely studied the commands of the all-powerful ruler, could not fail to recognise that all these vassal-lands were intended before long to be directly incorporated " into the great family " of the empire. Hardly had the old princes been dethroned than the insatiable man began to rob his own brothers and to destroy the newly-created states. Not a year went by in which the states of the Confederation of the Rhine failed to experience new changes of frontier. To the heir of the Revolution, just as to the cabinet policy of the previous century, it seemed that his ownership of land and people entailed one-sided responsibilities alone—on his dependents and loyal subjects. When he enlarged the Grand Duchy of Berg, he stated officially that this was effected in order to do Princess Caroline an agreeable and advantageous service. What was there to prevent his destroying as new caprice might dictate these ephemeral structures of political caprice? It was not by chance that Napoleon retained in his own hands the important fortress of Erfurt in the heart of Germany, and would never entrust its possession to any of his satraps. In the salons of Paris there was never any doubt as to the destiny of the states of the Confederation of the Rhine, and the subjects of King Jerome, when they visited the Seine, were sportively greeted as " Français futurs."

The peoples of southern and western Germany would not allow themselves to be troubled by such fears. It was quite in order that the *code Napoleon* should be scientifically expounded by able German jurists such as Daniels and Strombeck; but the state law of the Confederation of the Rhine, which always remained a dead letter, occupied the perspicuity of servile German men of learning such as Winkopp and Karl Solomo Zachariä. Whilst Napoleon rejected all the federalistic schemes of the faithful Dalberg, remarking dryly : " I place no value in the Confederation as such, and my concern is only with individual princes and their dependents," there arose in Germany a whole literature which devoted itself with amiable diligence to this controversy of the undiscoverable federal law.

It was indeed with complete justice that the patriotic youth of the north raged against the lying spirit of the new time, for never before among the petty German states had there been disseminated such a wealth of detestable falsehoods concerning " Borussianism " as in the days of Stein and Scharnhorst. The hatred of Prussia assumed new forms. Formerly the Prussian state had found its most passionate enemies amongst the adherents of the Catholic imperial party, and even now Münster rejoiced at the fall of the regime of the Prussian heretics. But now, and especially in the circles of Bavarian officialdom, there were found even modern men of culture who, from the brilliant altitude of French enlightenment looked arrogantly down upon the obscure night of Slavonic Junkerdom in Prussia, and urged the Imperator to make what remained of Austria and Prussia happy with a constitution upon the Gallic model. The poisonous libels of Christopher von Aretin, the Bavarian, were the first phase of that new Napoleonic particularist literature which subsequently was for many years a great power for evil in the German south. The adroit world-ruler understood very well how to stimulate against Prussia the old Bavarian hatred of heresy and the enlightened arrogance of the new bureaucracy. The state of Frederick was the land of heresy and of noble privileges, whilst Napoleon was the hero of freedom and of the Roman Church. Such fables found belief, for the miserable newspapers of the Confederation of the Rhine said nothing of Prussian reforms, and wrote with contemptuous scorn of the lunatics of the Tugendbund and the Teutonomaniacs Stein and Scharnhorst. Suddenly there appeared simultaneously in German and in French, at two separate publishing houses in the Confederation of the Rhine, the Memoirs of the Margravine of Bayreuth, and this work was certainly not published without the co-operation of one of the petty royal courts. What a stormy and malicious delight now arose in the camp of particularism. A most trustworthy witness, the darling sister of the great Frederick, confirmed everything which had been said among the South German peoples concerning the intolerable severity of the Prussian state, concerning the military stiffness of its government, and the heartless cruelty of its royal house! Wilhelmina's French outpourings were far more dangerous to the good repute of Prussia than had been any of the lampoons of its enemies, and it was long before historical criticism succeeded in demonstrating the untrustworthiness of the embittered but talented princess. Napoleon noted with satisfaction : " All the German courts, and especially that of Saxony, desire the partition of Prussia."

The Wittelsbachs had long forgotten that it was to the Hohenzollerns that they owed the possession of their hereditary dominions. Frederick of Würtemberg, and several other princes of the Confederation of the Rhine, never wearied of warning the Imperator of the dangerous intentions of Prussia. The Saxon minister Senfft, drew up with the superficial hastiness of particularist ambition plan after plan for the destruction of Prussia, and for the erection upon its ruins of a great Saxon-Polish central realm. The old erroneous tradition, according to which the Bavarians were the descendants of the Celtic Boii was now revived by Pall-

hausen and others. Many zealous Bavarians were gratified to feel
assured that their stock was blood-kin to the French, as could indeed
be recognised in the national military moustachios. Nicholas
Vogt, however, in his book *Die deutsche Nation und ihre Schicksale*,
proved how the Germans for two thousand years had been playing
the drama of "the Hostile Brothers," until at length Napoleon
had established in new forms the ancient German constitution.
Since the marriage of the Imperator to Marie Louise, "the union
between beauty and heroism" had founded a permanent peace
among this quarrelsome people. The Confederation of the Rhine
had brought three great blessings : the disappearance of the feudal
monarchy and of religious dissension ; the certainty that in
the interior of Germany a war would never again be fought ; and
finally, the restoration of the national independence. For this
reason, "let the Germans kiss the hand which teaches them to
be united, as if it were the hand of God !" The peoples of these
petty states had long been accustomed to accept "with the most
humble and obedient pleasure," as the customary phrase ran in
the proceedings of the diets, every caprice of their tribal lords.
Never before, however, upon German soil had there been exhibited
such hypocritical flattery as was now shamelessly manifested
towards the foreign tyrant. With unshaken enthusiasm the
professor of oratory in Göttingen celebrated the services of Napoleon
and Jerome, and this professor was the very man who had
previously delivered patriotic discourses on the birthdays of George
III. and Frederick William III. Wherever the Imperator made
his appearance, communes and corporations must pay him homage,
and the officials of the Confederation of the Rhine understood
extremely well how "to stimulate the free expression of public
love and gratitude." Byzantine addresses celebrated Napoleon's
invinciblity, his wise justice, and, above all, his philanthropic love
of peace. "On every occasion," said to him the estates of the
Grand Duchy of Berg, "on every occasion when you were compelled
to take up arms, you seemed in principle to be waging war against
war !"

In the Confederation of the Rhine, just as in imperial France,
genuine conviction was to be found almost exclusively amongst
the troops. There was an end of those philistine-minded peace-
officers of the old imperial army, who amid the turmoil of camp
life yearned dolefully for the pigs and fowls of their farmyards.
A new generation grew up, full of boastful military self-confidence,
enthusiastically inspired for the glories of the imperial eagles. A

bold Bavarian officer must every day for breakfast consume at least a dozen Austrians, for what was there in the warlike history of Bavaria more glorious than the brilliant battle at Ratisbon ? Napoleon omitted nothing which might nourish the unpatriotic soldier-spirit of these fire-eaters. They were to sign away their souls to him, and for this reason he gladly employed them in the occupation of the Prussian fortresses, and against the revolted Tyrolese ; moreover the troops he sent into the field were mainly derived from the Confederation of the Rhine, from Bavaria, and from Saxony.

The Napoleonic prefectural system of administration found nowhere a more grateful soil than in the new middle states of the south, states without a history. Here there was no end to organisation and reorganisation. In Baden the administrative districts were completely remodelled thrice within seven years. The aim was to make it at length possible to rearrange the confused and variegated fragments of states in accordance with the course of the rivers, and to cut them up into regular departments. The Protector carefully guarded himself against stimulating the arrogance of his loyal subjects by needless interference in their territorial administration, but it was taken as a matter of course that his ambassadors took precedence of the princes of the vassal states. If he required new troops, he simply examined the budgets of the kings and grand dukes, and decided according to his own pleasure. Moreover, as Protector of the Roman Church, he laid great stress on seeing that there were plenty of Catholics in the state service, and everywhere he ordered strict watch to be kept on the enemies of France, especially among the nobility. In other matters the petty despots might rule undisturbed.

Most strongly and most enduringly did the Bonapartist methods of promoting popular happiness prevail in Bavaria; during the last three generations no other part of Germany has encountered such profound transformations. Since that unhappy year 1524, when the old Wittelsbachs arbitrarily excluded the evangelical doctrine from their hereditary dominions and thus laid the foundation for the ecclesiastico-political subdivision of the German nation, the valiant and loyal old Bavarian stock, which in energy of body and will was equal to the best of the Germans, had been rendered as foreign to the intellectual life of the German nation (based upon parity in matters of religious belief) as had been the Austrians. At the end of the previous century, there were living in Munich three Protestants, who were scheduled officially as Catholics, and went over to Augsburg to take the Lord's Supper.[1] Step by step the wanderer in Bavaria encountered memorials of militant enthusiasm. At the foot of the Mariensäule in the Schrannenplatz stood the genius, the conqueror of the dragon of heresy. The people firmly believed that a Protestant was something altogether different from an honourable Christian. In the carnival processions of the Bavarian peasants, Luther was represented with his Kathi beside highway robbers, the Bavarian Hiesel, and the Rhinelander Schinderhannes. Even during the Napoleonic compaigns the old Bavarian battalion made an image of St. Peter run the gauntlet, because the saint had refused to his flock the fine marching weather for which they had prayed. To these backwoodsmen all the new literature was " Lutheran-German," and was therefore prohibited and ignored.

What a change now took place when suddenly a whole bundle of Protestant territories was united with the lands of the cloister and of the church schools, and when at the same time the dynasty of Zweibrucken was installed—that accessory line of the House of Wittelsbach which had indeed returned to the Roman Church, but which was profoundly hostile to the bigoted ancient line owing to its Swedish-Protestant traditions and in consequence of a persistent family feud. It is true that the dull and uninspired good-nature of the new king, Max Joseph, remained as utterly inaccessible to great political ideas as were the bureaucratic severity and authoritative disposition of his minister Montgelas. No one took up the obvious idea to transfer the centre of the young kingdom to one of the territories where equality of beliefs prevailed, to Nuremberg or Augsburg. The royal residence remained in Munich, and the capital exercised a harmful influence upon the provinces. Beer, which to the old Bavarians, according to the testimony of their strict criminal lawyer Kreittmayr, constitutes the fifth element of life, made its victorious campaign throughout the country ; the emotional Swabians and Franconians soon adopted much of the easy-going and careless sensuality of the Bavarians. These richly-endowed stocks gradually underwent deterioration of their spiritual life, and under the Bavarian rule they have never done so much for German civilisation as they did in the brilliant days of their life under the empire. For old Bavaria, on the other hand,

[1] My authority here is the account given by the Bavarian Chief Ecclesiastical Commissioner von Schmitt, which his son, Pastor Schmitt, communicated to me in Heidelberg.

it was an immeasurable benefit to have a common life with the intellectual and more enlightened neighbours.

From remote times the personality of the ruler of the country had been a living force to this patriarchal people ; cordially had the burghers of Munich greeted the agreeable new ruler with the twinkling eyes, saying, " Now, Max, it is all right as long as you're there ! " How greedily did the people listen when it was reported that Max's wife, Princess Caroline of Baden, was a heretic ; that the court preacher Schmitt held Protestant services, at first on the quiet in the Castle of Nymphenburg, and afterwards openly in the capital, and that he offered the sacrament in common to Lutherans and to members of the Reformed Church. Nothing of that kind had happened since the conqueror Gustavus Adolphus had lived in the palace of the Wittelsbachs. A great number of Protestant officials came into the country, and among these many Hotspurs of enlightenment, such as Anselm Feuerbach. Parity of belief was decreed, and, most important of all, the educational system was to be placed under the supervision of the state. To the fiery zeal of Montgelas, formerly one of the Illuminati, even this was not enough ; he detested the " Shamanism " of the Roman Church and the pious simplicity of the people of old Bavaria, to whom he always remained a foreigner. A number of cloisters were closed, hundreds of churches were dismantled and their old finery was brought under the hammer. It was a radical transformation, heartless frivolity and brutal arrogance were in command ; and yet in milder hands, the curse of the unity of belief under which the country lay would not have been broken. The other great curse of Bavaria, serfdom, was abolished by a comprehensive law ; the burdens and tithes imposed upon the peasants were abolished ; but for the present, thanks to the feverish haste of the government, most of these reforms, introduced with loud boasting, were not carried into effect. The mistrustful minister never even ventured to summon the new diet, although the only right allotted to this peculiar parliament was to express its views through the mouth of three commissaries and thereafter to assent without a word to the proposals of the government. Of the new institutions, nothing was firmly established beyond the conscription army and the omnipotence of the officials, who remained just as negligent, rough, and corruptible as they had been in the good old days.

The young crown delighted in a ludicrous haughtiness. In official documents people spoke of the " Empire of Bavaria " ;

and it made no difference to the royal self-satisfaction that the Protector always began his commands to Max Joseph with the simple " Il faut," and ended in like words. Bavaria was to become the fortunate heir of the Prussian monarchy ; of all its power, its glory in war, its enlightenment. To outshine the brilliancy of Berlin, the academy of Munich and the University (removed from the old Jesuit fortress of Ingolstadt to Landshut) were richly endowed ; but what could the able professors who were summoned from the north do here in the stifling air of this Napoleonic satrapy where there was completely lacking the moral energy of Prussian life ? The murderous attack of a Bavarian student upon Thiersch, the philologist, showed with what difficulty and slowness the delicate plant of culture struck roots in this hard soil ; the bigoted Bavarian was unable any longer to endure the sight of the North German heretic. All the ancient routine had been disturbed, and no one any longer felt secure in the possession of acquired rights. At the same time the financial need increased from year to year, and the unconscientious administration did not itself know the amount of the state indebtedness. None the less, the vigorous rule of the semi-French Montgelas prepared happier days for the Bavarians. So little does man foresee the ultimate consequences of his own creative work that this despiser of everything German unwittingly led the Bavarians from their three centuries of separate life back once more into community with modern German civilisation.

The ancient prophecy which had promised the ambitious little House of Würtemberg the royal crown of Swabia, had now at length been fulfilled ; but another proverbial saying was also to prove true, a saying which the Würtembergers were accustomed to repeat with naive self-satisfaction : " Our princes have always been a bad lot." King Frederick was a highly talented man, next to Duke Charles Augustus perhaps the most brilliant intelligence in that generation of German princes, but he had early destroyed within himself the sentiment for noble culture, regarding all learned men as merely quill-drivers, ushers, and hairdressers. Since he had dutifully followed Napoleon's order, " Chassez les bougres ! " and had got rid of the diet, the arrogance of the autocrat knew no bounds, and he began a reign of sin such as the long-suffering German soil had never witnessed. His arbitrary will displayed itself as openly and audaciously as the new kingly crown was flaunted upon the roof of the castle of Stuttgart. The king did not conceal his admiration for Tarquin and Nero as the masters of the art of government. In two thousand three hundred rescripts of the *Sacra Regia Majestas* he threw on the dust-heap the entire substance of the historical law, and amalgamated in a single whole the bourgeois-Protestant Old Würtemberg with the ecclesiastical imperial-urban and noble territories of New Würtemberg. According to the modest phrase of official speech, the will of the king and of his twelve high-bailiffs prevailed without restriction in the northern as in the southern provinces of the realm ; the king appointed the officials in all the communes. People shook in their shoes when the fat profligate drove by ; his daily associates were the instruments of his unnatural lusts, these and a few greedy Junkers of Mecklenburg. It was by forced levies that he obtained all the labour power that he required, even his lackeys ; in a single bailiwick more than twenty-one thousand men were summoned for the royal corvée on a hunting expedition. A rigid prohibition of emigration robbed the despairing people of their last hope. It was with especial joy that the king exercised his autocratic powers over the distinguished members of the imperial nobility ; for him were hardly necessary the exhortations of the Protector, who continually warned his vassals against the intrigues of the mediatised princes and nobles. The old family laws of the princes, counts, and knights, were abolished in a single moment ; a new order of precedence at court gave the landed gentry a place behind the pages and stable-boys, and anyone who failed to appear at court lost a fourth of his income.

Beyond question this sultanism, as Stein was accustomed to call the proceedings of the despots of the Confederation of the Rhine, did not arise solely from personal caprice. The king pursued and attained the aim of the unity of the state of Würtemberg, and an iron hand was needed to introduce, in this classic land of parochialism, some idea of wider circumstances. Wherever the bureaucracy of the Confederation of the Rhine encountered the heritage of the petty imperial princes, they came upon utterly rotten and ludicrous conditions. When the states of the two Houses of Leiningen-Westerburg were annexed to the Grand Duchy of Berg, the cash available in the common district treasury of these two countries amounted to forty-five gulden, and this was advanced by the accountant out of his own pocket. The destruction of such state-structures as these, could not be any loss to the nation. But in Würtemberg the inevitable revolution was carried out with such cruel roughness, with such cynical contempt, that the masses could feel only the severity and not the necessity of the change. Whilst the muzzled press was silent, among the people there gradually gathered a silent rancour against the king. The inhabitants of the imperial towns, of the Hohenlohe territories, and of the ecclesiastical lands, simply would not adapt themselves to the new order of things. Even the original Würtembergers, under the oppression of the present day, forgot all the sins committed by the fathers and forefathers of the present generation of nobles, and yearned for the "good old times" of the feudal constitution. The circle of vision of this particularist world remained, indeed, so narrow, that even the most intelligent and passionate southern stock was almost unaffected by the savage national hatred which moved the hearts of the Prussians. The Swabians had a grudge against their domestic tyrants, but they thought very little about the ultimate cause of their sufferings, about the shame of the foreign dominion. It was only a few men of highly sensitive nature, such as young Ludwig Uhland, who perceived the full significance of the time.

In Baden, so long as the gentle and just Charles Frederick was alive, the severity of the Rhenish Confederate rule was not felt very severely. It was only under his successor, Grand Duke Charles, that the savage arbitrariness of Bonapartism came to affect this land. The Alsatians and the Lorrainers rejoiced in the glories of the empire, and proudly enumerated the long series of heroes which their country had sent to serve beneath the banners of the invincible Kleber, Kellermann, Lefebvre, Rapp, and Ney, the bravest of the brave. The other lands on the left bank of the Rhine remained in profound slumber. As far as many of them were concerned, they were still under the influence of the thoughtless sensuality of the episcopal days ; while the young men, adorned with the broad Bonapartist hat, migrated to the French *Lycées*. If in these regions a German book ever ventured into print, it was encountered by the mistrust of the imperial censors, who understood not a word of German : an objection was made to the publication of a work by the natural-philosopher Treviranus upon the organisation of the aphides, because "organisation" reminded the censor of the Tugendbund. The last traces of German culture seemed about to disappear. Above all, the frivolous Palatiners adapted themselves rapidly to French ways ; among the officials good form demanded that they should speak their halting French, even in their own houses. Even among the Prussian patriots many doubted whether it would still be possible to reconquer this bastard people for German civilisation! In Darmstadt, in Nassau, everywhere, the same thing was to be witnessed : fawning servility towards the Protector, and inexorable severity towards everything German. Even Hans Gagern, an ardent admirer of particularism, could no longer endure the profound immorality of such manifestations ; the patriotic current of the new literature carried him away, he left the service of Nassau, and in his confused manner he wrote *Die Nationalgeschichte der Deutschen* [The National History of the Germans].

The retired life of the little territories of the north offered the sharpest possible contrast to the revolutionary policy of the states of the south and of the west. In the north, even in the Confederation of the Rhine, the ancient institutions remained as completely unaltered as were the princely houses and the old territorial boundaries ; the only change was that everywhere conscription had to be introduced. In the kingdom of Saxony, even this one innovation was not carried out, and the ruler was content to secure a better military conduct for troops enlisted in the old way by the introduction of a new French regimental system. Here the ancient social order continued to display remarkable powers of resistance. Napoleon did not disdain the most petty means to secure for himself the obedience of the Saxon court ; for years he stimulated the Albertine vanity by indefinite suggestions that he might perhaps marry the king's daughter. Frederick Augustus fulfilled the Protector's demands almost more submissively than his comrades in Munich and Stuttgart, and in Warsaw he introduced the *code Napoleon* and the whole mechanism of the French prefectural administration. But he ventured no innovations in the matter of the estates of Saxony, daring neither to abolish the privileges of the nobility, nor yet to effect the legal union of his hereditary domains with Lausitz and the adjoining ecclesiastical territories. The amorphous structure of the ancient feudal state-system persisted without change ; and there persisted also the world-famed stiff etiquette of the court, so that Jerome, the parvenu, gave orders to his ambassador Dohm, that here in Dresden he should study the secrets of ceremonial at the source, and furnish detailed reports. One alone among the old-established lords of the north transformed his state in accordance with the Napoleonic model, the foolish Duke of Coethen. He could not rest until he had divided his realm into two departments, each blest with a council of state, a prefect, sub-prefects, and the "salvation-bringing" code. All these glories were announced in the new *Bulletin des lois de l'Empire Anhaltin-Coethien.*

To the two Napoleonides who established their thrones amid this highly conservative North German world, a revolutionary policy was forbidden by the nature of things. Here, in "states without a past" (as the Westphalian minister Malchus pleasantly put it), there was no reason for sparing ancient traditions, and here, therefore, everything that was desired could be transformed in accordance with the rule of thumb method of the Napoleonic *constitution régulière.* In Westphalia, as in Berg the transformation was begun under the immediate supervision of the Imperator. He impressed upon both his vassals that by the destruction of all privileges they should endeavour to secure that their North German neighbours, especially Prussia, should yearn for the Napoleonic rule. In actual fact, the constitutional law of the kingdom of Westphalia was regarded as exemplary, not only in the Confederation of the Rhine, but also by a portion of the Prussian patriots. In how stately a manner did the crown, with its pseudo-Parliament, rise above the carefully levelled society, free from all class privileges. In addition, there was to be admired the readiness for action of the prefects, the more speedy administration of the law, the unaccustomed politeness of most of the officials, the abolition of the internal tolls, the abolition of serfdom, patrimonial jurisdiction, and the legal authority of the gentry! The new regime prided itself upon its friendliness to the peasants. It abolished the very names of the ancient class divisions which had prevailed in the rural districts; to the enlightened counsellors of the king, it seemed that the old German name of *Kotsass* [Low German for *Kossat*, a crofter or peasant proprietor] was to be rejected, because they derived it from *Kot* [dung]. Anyone who lived in the country was *paysan.* The much commiserated country-folk were in many respects better off than they had formerly been under the rule of the Hanoverian Junkers and of the Hessian soldier-merchants. Among the smaller folk of the rural district of Göttingen, the name of *Pisänger* has persisted even to the present day. The peasants felt themselves honoured when their representatives appeared among the quality at Cassel, the guard presenting arms to the peasant-deputies as they went by. Many years afterwards the tenant farmers in the Magdeburg region honestly assured the Prussian minister Klewitz that they would much like to have as good a government once more.[1]

Notwithstanding this, there was no question of any real loyalty among the country-folk. Their fidelity to the ancient lords remained unshaken, and how could the peasants repose confidence in officials whose speech they could not understand? Although a few fell away, and although in Westphalia, as in Berg, several noble houses disgraced their old names through disloyalty, the enormous majority of the people regarded with increasing detestation the rule of the foreigner. The orgies of the dull, light-minded Jerome, the effrontery of the French sharpers and adventurers who exploited his extravagance, the terrible human sacrifice in the incessant wars, the base flattery of " the man before whom the world stands silent " (as Johannes Müller said in one of his parliamentary addresses), the malpractices of the secret police, the prosecution of those inclined to German sentiment, and the contempt displayed for the native language " which isolates you in Europe "—to a people German to the core everything in these foreign institutions seemed detestable and contemptible, like a mad carnival dream which must soon disappear without leaving a trace. Jerome soon perceived clearly enough how the ground was shaking under his feet ; but all the more severely did Napoleon order him to draw the reins tight. The well-meaning minister Bülow, a cousin of Hardenberg, had to quit office on account of the dislike of the French party. He was replaced by Malchus, able, and apt for business, but a hard and unscrupulous man, a fitting tool in the hands of his ruler, and, in general, an ideal official of the Confederation of the Rhine.

Moreover, the Napoleonides were themselves never safe for a moment from the blows of the unwearied crown-robber and crown-giver. Murat had from the first regarded his Rhenish dukedom as merely a transitory possession, and gave it up willingly enough when his brother-in-law ordered him, a few years later, to make instant choice between the crown of Naples and the crown of Portugal, saying, " You must settle it in one day " ! The little German territory was now bestowed upon the son of Louis Bonaparte King of Holland, who was a minor, so that this was tantamount to giving it to the Imperator himself. The northern part of Hanover had meanwhile remained, since the Prussian war, temporarily under French administration, nor had Napoleon

[1] Report of Klewitz relating to his journey through the province of Saxony, July 29, 1817.

yet decided the destiny of the Hansa towns. He had for them a fierce hatred as the faithful clients of England. During the last three years he had extorted from Hamburg alone 14,000,000 francs; and when the town complained of the decline in trade, he replied mockingly: " So much the better, for then you will no longer be able to do England's business!" In the autumn of 1809 he negotiated with the three towns at Hamburg through the intermediation of his capable agent Reinhardt. They were to combine to form a semi-sovereign state of the Confederation of the Rhine, under the supervision of three imperial officers. The Hansards, however, instead of jumping at the idea, as their prudent countryman Smidt had advised them, raised objections. They desired complete sovereignty and also the right of free diplomatic intercourse; they desired to compound by a monetary payment for the obligation to furnish a military contingent to the Confederation of the Rhine; and for a time they hoped all the more confidently for the fulfilment of their wishes since in the meanwhile (March 1, 1810) North Hanover had " for ever " been united with the kingdom of Westphalia.

Soon, however, the Imperator had another plan in view. A new sand-castle was to be constructed out of the ruins of these states. Napoleon dethroned his brother Louis of Holland, detached the region of Münster from the Duchy of Berg, retook from Jerome the recently bestowed North Hanover, and united all this region, together with Oldenburg and the Hansa towns, to the French Empire, December 10, 1810. All this had simply been " dictated by circumstances." To the seven German departments of the left bank of the Rhine there were added five Low German departments. The boundaries of the immediate dominion of the emperor now extended southward beyond Rome, and in the north, by way of Lübeck, as far as the Baltic. Through his possession of the entire coast of the North Sea, it seemed as if the carrying out of the Continental System would at length be secured. A canal, to be completed within five years, was to connect the shores of the Baltic with the capital of the world. If fortune remained kind to the Man of Destiny, the annexation of yet other German territories was merely a question of time. In the Confederation of the Rhine, the Imperator already possessed a number of domains, partly in his own hands and partly distributed as gifts among his high officials. Several times before had Fate reminded him of the limits imposed upon all earthly will; at Eylau, at Aspern, and in Spain; he paid no attention. His empire was now greater than ever, his dreams extended beyond the bounds of humanity. He complained bitterly that it was impossible for him to do what Alexander had once done, and declare himself to be the son of a God, saying, " Every fishwife would laugh at me if I did ; the world is to-day too enlightened, and there are no more great things to be done ! " The annexation of Spain and Italy had long been determined. All that was needed was a last victorious advance on the part of Massena to Lisbon ; then an imperial decree, which was already drawn up, was to announce to the peoples of the Iberian Peninsula that they also belonged to the great empire, and that their emperor was lord of all the coasts from the Sound to the Dardanelles : " The trident shall be united with the sword, and Neptune shall join with Mars in the construction of the Roman Empire of our days. From the Rhine to the Atlantic Ocean, from the Scheldt to the Adriatic, there shall be but one people, one will, one speech ! "

Such was the situation of the world when Hardenberg assumed the conduct of Prussian policy. A few weeks after Hardenberg's assumption of office, the monarch received a shattering blow ; Queen Louise died, broken-hearted, fading like a flower which lacks light. Her last care had been given to the fatherland, for Hardenberg's return was to a considerable extent her work. The widower was left with a nameless anguish in his heart ; never could he forget the lost one, never again could he rediscover a true joy in life. His loyal people mourned with him. So much robbery, scorn, and disgrace had been endured ; and now she also was gone, tortured to death by the rude conqueror, she the kindest and noblest of German women ! The pious veneration of the Germans for the dignity of woman once again became active ; with enthusiastic devotion this generation contemplated the image of the enlightened woman, and to all the angry sentiments which stirred the hearts of the Prussian youth there was now superadded the determination to avenge the shade of the queen. Upon all lips was the proud saying to which she had herself formerly given utterance in the days of greatest need : " We perish with honour, respected by the nations, and shall ever have friends because we deserve them ! "

Hardenberg was already sixty years of age. He could no longer bring unbroken energy to his difficult task, and yet he entered upon his office with the confident courage of a youth. Like Stein, a man of good family, belonging to an ancient and wealthy house, he differed widely from Stein in character, views of life, and education. The weaknesses in one were conspicuous precisely where the other displayed his strength, and it was not by chance that there gradually came into existence between the two reformers that mutual disinclination which was first expressed by Stein with passionate violence and was subsequently returned by Hardenberg with somewhat more amiability. Less thoroughly experienced perhaps than the imperial knight, and yet with a more many-sided culture, Hardenberg had in his life as a student, and in his years of travel, learned to know the world from all sides, and had come into fruitful contact with men of all kinds and also with young Goethe. He had been much more strongly influenced by the philosophy of enlightenment of the eighteenth century than had been the pious primitive Teuton, Stein ; Hardenberg's religious sentiment remained always weak, his tolerance honourable and unbounded. His outlook on life was that of a cheerful and refined *Marquis* of the good old Bourbon times. Money always ran through his fingers, and his great inheritance was soon spent. Even as an old man he continued to suffer from domestic scandals and from frivolous adventures with bad women. In physical appearance he displayed nothing of the overwhelming energy and greatness of Stein ; yet he was always a fine-looking man, with clear, good-natured blue eyes, with a winning smile, an expression seductive to every woman ; pleasing and adroit in all his movements, always serene-spirited and witty, a master in the art of managing men. And this compelling amiability was really derived from a good philanthropic heart. His own description of himself in his diary bears the stamp of perfect truth : " I sigh for my weaknesses, but if they deserve blame I console myself with the sentiment of benevolence which lies at the basis of my character."[1] He approached all from the best side. To the king he drew near with a respectful tenderness which was profoundly agreeable to the afflicted monarch ; and when with the progress of years his unfortunate deafness increased, his friendly heart remained altogether free from the natural error of the deaf, mistrust. True hatred he felt towards one man only, William Humboldt, who seemed to him a suspicious character, " false as hell ! " and never would he abandon this strange suspicion which must have had some personal grounds hitherto undiscovered.

He was but a little affected by the aristocratic prejudices

[1] *Journal de Hardenberg*, New Year, 1810.

of his Hanoverian home. He claimed as a self-evident right his place in the upper levels of society ; but in daily intercourse he loved a plebeian environment among whose members were some men of talent, like Rother, but among whom were a majority of unworthy companions, who took an unfair advantage of his open-handedness ; here he was master and could let himself go. In his political convictions, also, Hardenberg did not disavow the school of the French enlightenment. From the beginning, his heartfelt desire was a night of the fourth of August for Prussia, attained not through the stormy passions of the nation, but imposed from above by the deliberate will of the crown. In the new kingdom of Westphalia, it seemed to him that his ideal of the state was almost realised, only that in Prussia everything was to be done in a more just and equitable manner. The genuinely German fundamental idea of Stein's reforms, the idea of self-government, always left him cold. Indeed as the years passed this idea aroused in him positive repugnance, since he could not admit that the embittered opponents of his social reforms, the Junkers of the Mark, could possibly possess the capacity for the administration of the rural districts. A well-ordered bureaucracy, limited and advised by an assembly of the estates of the realm, not unduly powerful, was to restrain the social forces from which the old checks had been removed.

First in the Guelph state service, and subsequently in Franconia, Hardenberg had for many years conducted a difficult territorial administration ; when he was willing to trouble himself about affairs he soon found himself at home in the most difficult matters. He worked with astonishing ease ; his decisions, which he wrote in the margins of the documents, in a clear and elegant handwriting and in bold and thoroughly modern German, were always to the point. Yet he never attained to that delight in detail which characterises the great administrator, and he found much more pleasure in distinguished dilettantism. He was glad to hand over current affairs to the enlightened younger officials, whom he had himself trained in Franconia ; financial matters, alike in domestic and in public life, were treated by him with the indifference of the man of culture. His strength lay in diplomatic activity. Few have understood as did he how to await with certainty the right moment, how in the most perplexing situation to discover a hopeful way out, how through all the deviations of a policy of finesse to keep the same goal ever in view. Even in this occupation, for which he was most eminently fitted, he often betrayed an easy-going levity and good-natured generosity, which led him to think it was not worth while to maintain with pedantic exactitude a line of conduct which was in reality urgently demanded by the circumstances of the case.

Greatly had he sinned formerly through his confidence in the friendship of France. Now, thoroughly cured of his old illusions by cruel experience, he directed the whole of his energies into the struggle for liberation. How often did he say plainly to Count St. Marsan that Prussia was determined to conquer or fall sword in hand. But the desperate war could only be risked at a favourable moment, and after sufficient diplomatic preparation. Hardenberg was magnanimous enough to endure silently for years, " a colossal misunderstanding " on the part of the best of the nation ; and he adds with justified self-satisfaction that " more courage is required for this than to march against a battery."

He was a Prussian through and through ; far more profoundly than Stein did he become inspired with a national sentiment for his adopted fatherland. Even in the days of his Napoleonic dreams, the greatness of Prussia remained his highest aim, and without the least remorse, he advised the annexation of his Guelph homelands, because they were indispensable to Prussia. Yet however profound his love for the great fatherland, he would not begin the struggle against the hard reality of the Napoleonic empire with the ideal greatness of the German national spirit ; all imaginative Germanism was remote from his level-headed mind. More dispassionately than Stein did he calculate, holding ever that only with this existing Prussian state, only through an alliance between the Prussian monarchy and Austria, could the world-empire of France be destroyed ; he had been certain of this since the days of Bartenstein.

In Brunswick and Franconia, and subsequently as cabinet minister during the East Prussian campaign, he had been an almost absolute ruler. Thus through the habit of command there had been introduced into his character an authoritative tendency which harmonised little with his serene amiability, and yet became accentuated as the years passed. It was natural enough that he felt it necessary to justify himself to posterity on account of past errors, and that in his memoirs he should endeavour, not always quite honourably, to transfer to other Prussians the whole responsibility for the catastrophe that had befallen the old state. But even in his diaries, which were intended for his own eyes alone, we hardly ever find the admission of an error ; whoever dissents from him is harshly censured ; even the king does not escape his blame, though in these differences the sober sense of Frederick William was almost always in the right ! Hardenberg remained through life faithful to the groundless illusion that his Riga memorial of the autumn of 1807 had really been the starting-point of Prussian reform ; he often complained bitterly that others had deprived him of the well-deserved glory. Stein's greatness of soul kept him always far from thoughts of this kind.

When Hardenberg was now recalled to public affairs, he stipulated for an authority which was indeed partly necessitated by the difficulties of the state, but which went far beyond what was truly essential, and conflicted with all the traditions of Prussian officialdom. He became chancellor, received supreme charge of all the affairs of state, directly assumed the offices of Minister of the Interior and of Finance, and since the Minister for Foreign Affairs, Count Goltz, had in everything to follow the commands of the chancellor, the only offices that remained independent were the Ministry of Justice and the Ministry of War. The chancellor did not receive a fixed income ; the general treasury paid what he needed. As things were, it was fortunate for Prussia that this man, whose nature was in every respect a light one, now assumed the heritage of Baron von Stein. More boldly than the imperial knight was the disciple of the new French philosophy able to draw the necessary consequences from the law of the year 1808 ; the astuteness of the diplomat was better fitted than the elemental passion of Stein for steering a middle course in German affairs until the open struggle became possible.

The first care of the chancellor was naturally the payment of the contribution and the rehabilitation of the finances of the state, and in these technical questions it immediately became apparent how completely he lacked the more secure business-knowledge characteristic of Stein. After the manner of talented and sanguine dilettantists, he was extremely receptive for far-reaching projects when they claimed theoretical infallibility. Since at that time the world was filled with enthusiastic admiration for the wonderful doings of the Bank of England, he imagined that in this unhappy Prussia, where for the moment all the necessary conditions for a great credit-institute were lacking, a national bank could be founded, and that with its help the entire debts of the state and of the provinces might be consolidated. In addition, two loans, one at home and one abroad, together with the issue of treasury notes to the amount of 26,000,000 thalers, were to provide the state with the necessary cash for the payment of the war debt ; certain new taxes were also proposed, but not an income tax, because " public opinion " was too strongly adverse. Niebuhr brought forward decisive grounds to show the futility of this plan ; it would be a misfortune to dream of increasing the amount of the treasury notes and would invalidate the sacred pledges of the crown ; and whence were to come the fifteen millions which the chancellor expected his loans to provide ? Niebuhr himself had, after long and difficult negotiations and under humiliating conditions, just succeeded in floating a small loan in Holland—the only one which the monarchy without credit was able to place abroad during this whole period ! The refined man of learning was profoundly wounded at conscience by the giddy superficiality of Hardenberg's plans ; he was unable to see that the happy-go-lucky chancellor attached no importance to the details of the proposal, and angrily handed in his resignation. Schön, too, refused co-operation, since he shared Niebuhr's technical objections, and would work only as an independent minister, not under the control of the chancellor ; moreover, the logical Kantian hoped to realise in its completeness Stein's political testament, and was wrath with the " Hanoverian Junker " when Hardenberg cautiously raised certain objections.

Thus immediately the new chancellor entered office there was a passionate struggle in the circle of the high officials, such a struggle as from that time until the death of Hardenberg so often endangered the secure progress of the state. Harshly and severely did these rich natures come into conflict ; all men of first-class ability and all essentially desiring the same things, but each in his own manner. Since Stein's departure there had been lacking a personality of outstanding character, who could control the unruly. Those of conspicuous talent gradually withdrew from the head of the government into the provincial boards ; the only financier in the monarchy who might have been competent to deal with the colossal difficulties of the situation, Maassen, was not yet valued according to his true worth. Hardenberg soon found it convenient to employ submissive tools, such as Scharnweber and Jordan, and for a time he also allowed the valiant young professor F. von Raumer to play a part which went far beyond the measure of his talent and of his practical experience. Meanwhile he had accompanied the king on a journey to Silesia, there, in a secret meeting with Stein on the Bohemian frontier, to discuss his financial plans, and to gain fresh confidence from the enthusiastic joy with which the monarch was everywhere greeted : " A word from your majesty will have more effect than all else put together."

Returning home with renewed vigour, he displayed an astounding activity. First, by the decree of October 27, 1810, the supreme authority of the state chancellor was legally established. The five ministries remained in existence, but were subordinate to the chancellor ; the council of state planned by Stein was at length brought into existence, at least on paper, but in so modest a form that it could not threaten the chancellor's omnipotence ; the recently-created office of lord-lieutenant was abolished, for the local governments were, like Napoleon's prefects, to stand under the immediate control of the central administration. Here was already displayed a markedly bureaucratic tendency, for the chancellor had little regard for the independent life of the provinces. On the same day appeared the edict regarding the state finances. This was a law such as the Prussian monarchy had never before seen, alike in form and content a memorable testimony to the enterprising levity of the talented nobleman who now held the reins. Whereas Stein's laws were always concerned with some definite question alone, which was considered from all sides and in accordance with far-reaching and thorough prescriptions the new finance edict provided for the nation a shower-bath of splendid promises. The chancellor had indeed abandoned the idea of the national bank, of the treasury notes, and the other glittering projects of the previous summer ; but in place of these he displayed a programme of extensive reform of taxation " for the salvation of the country." He promised that henceforward all financial burdens should be borne by everyone upon equitable principles, promised a new cadaster, and undertook that land taxation, which was now different in different areas should be placed on an equal footing throughout the country ; he promised complete freedom of occupation, the secularisation of ecclesiastical goods, the amalgamation of the entire war debt of the state and of the provinces, the introduction of general taxes on articles of consumption and luxury ; and finally, after all these assurances, made the king declare that it was his majesty's intention " to give the nation an appropriate system of representation, at once in the provinces and for the state as a whole. In this way the bond of love and confidence between ourselves and our loyal people will be tied fast for ever ! " What levity of mind was this to make the crown give these solemn promises whose meaning and import, as was soon to be seen, it was still quite impossible to judge ! The only excuse that Hardenberg could bring forward for such frivolity, hitherto unheard of in Prussia, was that it was necessary to outdo the dangerous Westphalian neighbour in the acquirement of public favour !

Some of these promises the chancellor did in fact immediately fulfil. On the very next day, a general tax on luxuries was introduced, a tax on servants, horses, dogs, and carriages ; also a tax on ten commodities in everyday use, meat, flour, beer, etc., applying equally in the towns and in the rural districts. The intention was in this way to get rid of the old octroi which cut off the towns from the villages ; but the tax on flour, in especial, encountered invincible resistance from the country people. Since Stein had abolished thirlage, the peasants of Old Prussia had built a great many new windmills, and had accustomed themselves to the use of handmills ; they obstinately maintained their new freedom, and in many places there was resistance and rioting ; the poorer people in Lithuania and West Prussia ate dough instead of bread, in order to save the cost of the flour tax. The chancellor had soon to recognise that here his commands could not possibly be carried out. On October 30th there followed the secularisation of all ecclesiastical goods, a necessary *coup de main* which the legislator justified by " the general spirit of the age," by the example of the neighbouring states, and more especially by the demands of justice, since the means of the loyal subjects must not be unduly strained. The new measure had little effect in the old Protestant provinces, where the goods of the Church had for centuries past been reduced to a minimum. All the more powerfully, however, did it affect Silesia, where the bishopric of Breslau, the cloister of Grüssau, and other foundations, had since the Austrian times preserved a princely inheritance. A portion of the secularised goods was employed for the purpose of education, especially for the University of Breslau ; what was sold brought in very little, since the excess of supply depressed the value of the goods, and in the exhausted country there were very few buyers to be found. Finally, on November 2nd, a general system of trade licences, on the Franco-Westphalian model was introduced : every adult with an unblemished record could, on payment of the legally established tax, secure a trade licence, and only in the case of thirty-four occupations was there still demanded, for motives of public safety, a proof of special capacity. This was the first beginning of freedom of occupation. Soon after there appeared new regulations for servants, a humane law which even to-day largely corresponds to the profoundly altered relationships of the serving classes, but which at that time, when the harsh compulsory servitude had only just been abolished, appeared to be a radical innovation of unprecedented boldness.

Thus did the Hardenberg legislation open its cornucopia, to furnish, in addition to some barren fruits, a few gifts of permanent value. However unsteady was the chancellor's hand in financial matters, his resolution was fixed to carry through to the utmost the bourgeois institution of equality before the law and the liberation of all the economic forces of the nation. Stein's creative ideas were in advance of the day, and were fully understood by a small circle alone. Hardenberg's ideas lay nearer to the broad road of the Age of the Revolution, and for this reason he obtained from the newspaper press of his day a lively support, which Stein had always lacked. Among those who sang his praises, it was said that by the laws of these seven great days had been accomplished that which revolutionary France had required two years to perform—praise which subsequently was incorporated in all the historical works of the school of Schlosser.

In actual fact, the most important of the proposed reforms, the equal taxation of all classes, was for the moment merely promised and was not put into operation. But the mere promise sufficed to set the whole feudal party in an uproar. The gentry of the Electoral Mark had at first hailed the nomination of the chancellor with joy, for it was expected of Hardenberg that he would remedy the results of the excessive haste of Stein. As soon as the new ruler displayed his true intentions, a storm of discontent raged in the circle of the landed gentry, and before long Hardenberg was even more passionately attacked by them than had been Stein. A flood of petitions and of grievances poured in to the throne. " We have no longer any mortgages, we have no longer any property at all," complained the East Prussian von Domhardt, amid violent invectives against the new Leveller and Jacobin.[1]

Brandenburg was the classic land of the ancient feudal system. Nowhere else were the feudal institutions more corrupt, and

[1] Petition of December 4, 1810. Similar petitions were presented from Old Prussia by von Hülsen, von Brederlow, and others.

nowhere else were they dearer to the estates. In the eyes of this proud and vigorous nobility, the Pomeranians and the Silesians were still foreigners. Once more the ancient feudal particularism broke into open feud against the equality before the law and the unity of the state characteristic of the monarchy. As the spokesman of this tendency, a spokesman as violent and insolent as had once been Conrad von Burgsdorff against the Great Elector, Baron von der Marwitz, now took the stage. He was the archetype of the Brandenburg Junker, one of the bravest officers and wildest horseman in the army, rough, surly, and gnarled, a German to the marrow, with a keen understanding and an unlimited frankness, full of ardent love of the fatherland, but full also of harsh prejudices, so simple in his pride of caste that it was hardly possible for him ever to understand the opinion of an opponent. For long he had been in fierce conflict with the government of Potsdam, because this government wished to deprive the Brandenburg diet of a portion of its prerogatives, namely, its neglected system of poor relief. Ultimately, since the defiant man would not surrender the key of the treasury of the fund for poor relief, it was necessary to break open the treasure chest and to remove the contents to Potsdam. It seemed to him that the new schemes of taxation were a criminal breach of the ancient territorial rights which had been given a written form and sealed by the diet of the Electoral Mark in the year 1653. Unceasingly did the landed gentry besiege the chancellor with protests and appeals for justice, now individually, now combined in whole territories ; but among them none were more urgent and more frequent in their complaints than the estates of the regions of Lebus, Beeskow, and Storkow, where Marwitz lived. The romanticist Adam Müller also placed his pen at the disposal of the advocates of feudal licence. When the chancellor asked, after his bureaucratic manner, whence these ground landlords had obtained the right to term themselves estates, Marwitz answered : [1] " The quality of territorial privilege is as much our birthright as is our family name, and we can therefore just as little explain to you why we are estates as we can explain to you why we possess our family names ! " The gentry of the Priegnitz district, especially von Quitzow and von Wartensleben declared : [2] " The Electoral Mark and the New Mark of Brandenburg, which together form the nucleus of the entire

[1] Petition to Hardenberg, January 30, 1811.
[2] Petition to the king, Perleberg, January 24, 1811.

Prussian monarchy, have ever constituted a peculiar state, distinct from the other provinces, a state which possesses its own special constitution " ; for this reason they demanded that no tax law should be passed without the assent of the estates.

The undaunted reformer did not allow himself to be disturbed. These questions of law, which at best were extremely dubious, troubled him little ; the whole constitution of the new Prussian monarchy had proceeded out of struggles of the ancient feudal privileges. It sufficed him to recognise that the summoning of the old provincial diets would assuredly lead to the destruction of the new laws. In order to convince the nation of the necessity of what had happened, and to prepare them for further reforms, on February 23, 1811, an "assembly of territorial deputies"[1] was opened in Berlin : this consisted of one official from each of the eight provincial governments, eighteen knights (*Ritter*), eleven representatives from the towns, and eight peasants—all nominated by the crown. Since the embittered estates of Brandenburg and Pomerania made loud complaint, and without being asked sent representatives of their own body, the chancellor admitted also some of these "accessory deputies." Thus for the first time since the monarchy had come into existence, representatives from all parts of the country were summoned, simply according to the judgment of the crown, without reference to feudal rights and to the demands of the territories. In the old caste circles, the entrance of the eight peasant deputies was regarded as the first signal of a terrible revolution. Many contemporaries recalled the assembly of the notables at the outbreak of the French Revolution ; but the repute of the Prussian crown was incomparably higher than the power of the Bourbons, and from the outset they allotted to their notables very modest functions, giving them only the right of deliberation, and not of decision. Stein's legislation had already a long while before laid secure foundations for the great work of reform, and the laws which Hardenberg laid before the territorial deputies were in part accomplished facts.

The chancellor assembled the deputies in his dwelling, and at once greeted them in the paternal manner of the ancient absolutism. The king's demand from his beloved people was like the demand made by a good father of his children, not blind obedience but free assent to his benevolent commands. There-

---

[1] I utilise here, among other sources, the reports preserved in the Berlin archives of the assembly of the territorial deputies of 1811, and of the interim national representation from 1812 to 1815 (von Riedel, 1841).

upon four sections were constituted under the presidency of the four presidents of the local governments. Each section deliberated separately, transmitting its reports to Hardenberg, who then sent for individual members at his own discretion, and finally himself reported to the monarch. The assemblies seemed like a confidential discussion with the personality of the highest official, and yet they soon became extremely inconvenient to the chancellor. A whole world of threatened economic local interests arose in alarm ; justified and unjustified complaints were rife ; there was no trace of any formation of parties, only a general confusion of territorial and class groups. The representatives of the rural districts were all agreed about the severity of the new flour tax ; the proposed consolidation of the war debts aroused stormy opposition, since the Electoral Mark was deeply indebted, whilst Old Prussia had covered a considerable proportion of its war burdens by taxation.

Loudest of all were the complaints of the representatives of the nobility and gentry. They were familiar with the new English theory that a land tax has the character of a rent, and they maintained stiffly and firmly that the proposed equalisation of the land taxes was open spoliation. Side by side with an honourable respect for law, there was at work the crudest egoism. The representative chamber of the Electoral Mark, whose spokesmen held so tenaciously to the legal ground of their ancient charters, unthinkingly expressed to the chancellor the opinion that the complaints of their creditors might be temporarily suspended by a royal decree ! [1] Meanwhile the uncontrollable estates of Lebus, Beeskow, and Storkow appeared with a new demonstration of their " established exemptions and freedoms." With rude and unseemly words they insisted that the new laws would destroy the fundamental state law, and they asked whether it was proposed to transform the ancient and honourable Brandenburgish Prussia into a Hebrew state after the new model. Among the signatories to this document, the first was naturally that of Marwitz ; close by his name was that of Count Finkenstein, one of those faithful judges who in the trial of the miller Arnold had incurred the undeserved displeasure of King Frederick. The chancellor now lost patience ; without legal procedure, and in defiance of legal right, he had the first two signatories brought to the fortress of Spandau. On September 16th,

[1] Petition of the Representative Chamber of the Electoral Mark, October 10, 1810.

he then closed the assembly of the territorial deputies, and once more enumerated the essential ideas of the new system : everyone was to be free to utilise his energies, no one was to bear inequitable burdens ; all were to be free before the law ; there was to be a free path for every service ; unity and order were to prevail in the administration ; thus would there be awakened in all a national spirit, a single interest, and a community of sentiment. He concluded by saying : " Now you will return to your provinces and there diffuse the good spirit which animates you all. Strengthen the confidence in the government whose intentions are so honourable ! " His real opinions were by no means in accordance with these friendly expressions. He rather, and with him the king, derived from the chaotic deliberations of this assembly of notables the just conclusion, that a general diet, if one were now summoned, would necessarily hinder the progress of the reforms. Such was the state of affairs : only the omnipotence of the absolute crown could prepare for the Prussian people the way to freedom.

Almost simultaneously with the dismissal of the territorial deputies there appeared the second great forward wave of Hardenberg's legislation. The edict of September 7, 1811, concerning the finances fulfilled some of the wishes of the territorial deputies, abolishing the prohibition of handmills, and for the most part abolishing also the tax on articles of consumption in the rural districts, imposing instead a poll-tax upon the country people. The law, however, concerning the regulation of occupations was in flat conflict with the views of the assembly of notables : the crown here again hastened greatly in advance of the views of the people, establishing complete freedom of occupation, in such a way that everyone who possessed a trade licence could keep apprentices and journeymen, every craftsman could abandon his craft, every guild could be dissolved by a majority vote or upon the order of the local police authorities. This step was one of radical audacity. Not without reason did Stein and Vinck complain that instead of dissolving the guilds these should rather have been transformed in a free sense. None the less, the advantages of this bold innovation greatly predominated. The common man henceforward enjoyed in Prussia an economic freedom which existed nowhere else in Germany, and although the relationships of the minor industries, thanks to the tenacity of our daily habits, underwent far less change than had been expected, it was in essentials owing to the freedom of occupation that the population of the capital continued to grow during these years of bitter poverty.

Just as this law first brought the Towns-Ordinance of Stein to an issue, so also was this the case in respect of the agrarian laws of the imperial knight, which were first completed by the two edicts of September 14, 1811, concerning the regulation of the affairs of the peasantry and concerning the advancement of agriculture. In these laws, the skilled hand of Thaer had co-operated. The hereditary owners of peasant properties without full proprietorship, were to acquire this right in return for the cession of a third of their property, or the payment of a corresponding rent ; those who enjoyed only the non-hereditary usufruct of peasant property could become free owners by the cession of one-half. The law cut deeply and even cruelly into the customary relationships ; some intelligent men among the officialdom such as Hippel, regarded the step as too venturesome. The knighthood of Pomerania owned about 260 square miles [German] and of these 100 was land in peasant occupation ; now 70 square miles of this became the free property of the peasants. It can readily be understood that the landed gentry murmured, and was supported in its complaints even by Stein. The position of the ground landlord had long been so desperate that in the year 1810 the wealthiest female land-owner in Prussia offered to cede her property to the state in return for a yearly rent of two thousand thalers ; a Silesian landlord went bankrupt although he still possessed land valued at three hundred thousand thalers. The peasants also made loud complaint. On several occasions there were open disturbances, especially in Silesia, for the common people erroneously imagined that they had now been discharged from all duties. The redemption payment, which to the landed gentry seemed unjustly low, was regarded as excessive by those who had to pay it. None the less, the valuable reform went forward. Notwithstanding all outward similarities, it was strongly contrasted with the laws of the French Revolution, since honourable compensation was paid to those who were justly entitled to it. The carrying out of the law was notably assisted by the agricultural edict, which permitted of the free alienation and subdivision of country estates. It was considered that this constituted " the best means for preserving the land owners from indebtedness, and for giving them a permanent interest in the improvement of their property and in favouring the culture of the land." The king concluded by saying, with strong feeling :

"It is a matter for rejoicing that we have at length found it possible to raise to freedom all the members of our loyal nation, and to open even for the poorest classes the prospect of happiness and well-being." It was especially against this edict that Stein's anger was directed. He stormed (not without the embittered feeling characteristic of the statesman out of office) against this bureaucratic· levelling, and expressed his dread that the power of freely subdividing landed property would lead to the expropriation by purchase of his beloved peasantry, and to their consequent destruction—an apprehension which has proved exaggerated.

To these reforms there was finally added the emancipation of the Jews, who had hitherto been known officially as " Jewish villeins." By the edict of March 11, 1812, the Jews who adopted permanent family names and accepted the duty of military service became, as in the lands of the *code Napoleon*, burghers possessed of full civil rights, admitted to every occupation in town and country, and also to office in the universities, the schools, and the communes. Amid the loud lamentations of the feudal-minded, there now ensued a great renaming of the Prussian Jews. The Levis, Cohns, and Jacobsons retained their Semitic names, the Wolfs and the Kuhs remained contented with the nicknames which they had been given by the savage popular humour of the Teutons, and the Zwickaners and Bambergs simply called themselves after their homes ; but those of sentimental nature who had been affected by the spirit of the time chose more high-sounding names, which were faithfully to express the beauty of their souls, so that the doors of our stock exchanges are even to-day freely inscribed with the names of the Blümchens, Veilchens, Nelkens, and Rosenzweigs.

It was in these necessary social innovations that there was to be found the greatness of Hardenberg's reforms. In his financial measures, on the other hand, he remained unfortunate. He vigorously proceeded with the sale of the domains, partly because he was in urgent need of money, and partly because his doctrinaire advisers had convinced him that all state-ownership of land was a mistake. F. von Raumer wrote in round terms that in the matter of the domains we have only to learn from the British that the most important thing is to have none at all ! But in this impoverished country where were the buyers to be found ? After five and a half years, in June, 1813, for the sale of state lands there had been received in cash no more than 786,000 thalers, and, in addition, six and a half million of worthless paper. Since the taxes on articles of consumption also brought in very little, and since some of them were soon repealed, Hardenberg, who had begun with such hopeful financial schemes, was no better able to pay off the French debt than had been his dull predecessor Altenstein. In April, 1811, almost half the contribution, about fifty-nine million francs, was still undischarged. The new and heavy war burdens of the year 1812 finally made it necessary for the chancellor, in opposition to his theoretical convictions, to impose a severe property and income tax, amounting to three per cent. on property and from one to five per cent. on income. But in this matter also, he failed to make due allowance for the extreme economic exhaustion of the country. In the case of Old Prussia the tax had to be suspended after a few weeks, for this province had been completely sucked dry by the passage of the *grande armée*, and instead of the anticipated twenty-five million thalers, only four and a half million were received, the net yield being four million.

Although Hardenberg's social reforms could be carried into effect only through the will of the absolute monarchy, the crown was not in a position to dispense altogether with the co-operation of popular energies. As early as October, 1810, in the edict concerning the finances that was so full of promises, the crown had undertaken that a general commission, strengthened by representatives from the communes and the provinces, should give advice concerning the regulation of the war debts. The territorial deputies, and especially the representatives of the burghers and of the peasants, urgently demanded that the promise should be fulfilled. For this reason the king declared : [1] " It has always remained our intention to provide the nation with a suitable representative system, but since the preparations for this still require time the representatives summoned for the general commission will for the time being constitute the national representation." Consequently, on April 10, 1811, there met in Berlin a second assembly of notables, consisting of thirty-nine members, to which was given the high-sounding name of an interim national representation. This time the nation was given the vote. The eighteen knights were elected by the district assemblies, and the twelve burghers and nine peasants were chosen by indirect suffrage from the towns and the rural districts respectively ; the presidents of the local governments were to examine the elected persons, to determine

[1] Cabinet Order, September 6, 1811.

whether they were intelligent, patriotic, and " free from prejudices "—a definite hint to the feudal party !

The most notable point about this extremely tame attempt
at a representative system was that the newly-created estate of
peasants now came to participate in the deliberations concerning
affairs of state, through representatives of their own choosing.
The estates of the Mark murmured on this occasion also. They
referred to the " general lack of confidence " in the country in
the matter of the new plans of taxation, [1] and succeeded once
more in securing that out of their number a few accessory deputies
should be admitted. Hardenberg now again appeared as the
advocate of the new unity of the state. He regarded the estates
in the modern sense as a representation of interests, and he
insisted that the representative should recognise " no other judge
than his own conscience." Anyone who in the old feudal manner
regarded himself as bound by the instructions of his electors, must
be excluded from the deliberations.[2] In the provinces the
" electoral deputies," who had been chosen by national representation, assembled frequently on their own initiative (and regularly
so in Upper Silesia),[3] to discuss public affairs, and to carry on
regular intercourse with their representatives in Berlin. Everywhere among the people a sense of political life began to awaken.
In the national representation there were sometimes heard speeches
which aroused memories of the catchwords of the year 1789. On
one occasion in an address to the king, it was even demanded
that the right should be admitted to deliberate upon all new
laws.[4] Nevertheless the effective work of the new assembly
remained even more trifling than had been that of the first
assembly of notables. Its frequently interrupted negotiations
were concerned chiefly with the regulation of the question of the
war debt, and even here but little was effected. When other
questions came up for discussion there was almost always manifested a strongly conservative spirit and one hostile to reform ;
the chancellor was soon convinced that he could not for the
present carry through the equalisation of the land tax in face
of the passive resistance of the landed gentry. The zeal of
the representatives and of their electors soon evaporated, and

[1] Petition of the Estates of the New Mark, December 4, 1812.
[2] Instruction issued by the chancellor to the provincial governments, February
11, 1812.
[3] Report of the Provincial Government in Oppeln, October 14, 1816.
[4] A. Stern, *Abhandl. und Aktenstücke z. Gesch. der preuss. Reformzeit*, pp.
190 et seq.

the indifference extended so far that the estates of Hither Pomerania refused to pay their representatives the daily allowance any longer. Almost unnoticed by the nation, the assembly prolonged its fruitless existence until July 15, 1815 ; its last work was an ordinance of March 1, 1815, concerning the payment of supplies for the war.

The longer the chancellor occupied the saddle, the more manifest became his bureaucratic tendencies. Being, as always in administrative questions, altogether without fixed principles, he soon found the continued struggle with the defiant country gentry inconvenient, and resolved to destroy the juridical powers of the land owners, which constituted the chief source of their influence, yet not to do this by the founding of a just system of self government in the country districts, but to effect it in the Napoleonic and Westphalian manner, by increasing the power of the officialdom. In this undertaking, his most active coadjutor was Scharnweber, a strict bureaucrat and a deadly enemy of the nobles of the Mark. On June 30, 1812, was issued the edict upon the constitution of the gendarmerie. It was the worst misdeed of Hardenberg's administration, a complete falling away from the lofty ideas of Stein. The traditional office of Landrat, so closely associated with the life of the state, was abolished. The Landrat was replaced by a circle director, appointed by the crown, entirely at its own discretion, a salaried servant of the state, who was allotted a residence in the circle town, and was simply a tool of the central state authority, not as had formerly been the Landrat, a man in the confidence of the estates of the circle. Under his supervision, a circle brigadier, with four or five officers of the gendarmerie, were to undertake the management of police affairs in the circle, and were at the same time to engage actively in the control of the business of the circle directory, in such a way that this board acquired a purely bureaucratic character. The circle treasury became a state treasury, and a circle communal treasury was to continue to exist only as a trifling supplementary fund. Since the focus of self-government is found above all in financial matters, it followed that the circle assembly, consisting of two representatives of the knighthood, two town representatives, and two peasant representatives, and summoned from time to time by the circle director, could have very little significance. The land owners were deprived of their police authorities, retaining merely the right of supervision over the local police of the village courts, whilst they were entirely subordinated to the disciplinary authority of the circle director.

In his gendarmerie edict, Hardenberg started from the sound view that it was necessary to secure more efficiently than hitherto the carrying out of the will of the state in the rural areas, and to do away with the preponderance of the landed gentry in circle administration, " for experience showed that this preponderance had no longer any meaning since the introduction of freedom of occupation and identity of interests for all classes." And yet his remedies were worse than the disease. His circle director and circle assembly were nothing more than the sub-prefect and the council of the arrondissement of Napoleonic France. By this edict, which was promulgated under so harmless a name, the chancellor took the momentous first step for the introduction of the prefectural system. He had already abolished the lords-lieutenant, and he now promised to divide the state domain into " new governmental and military departments." He was by this time so completely convinced of the excellence of the prefectural system, with its readiness for action, that even his devoted adherent F. von Raumer found it necessary, in a moving letter, to lay before him the advantages of the old Prussian *Collegial System.*

Fortunately the talented man lacked the energy of will which was necessary to carry into effect the un-German and disastrous innovation which he planned. At first a portion only of the determinations of the gendarmerie edict were to come into force, " provisionally." This mischievous innovation of provisional legislation, had been altogether unknown to the strict old absolutism, and was now introduced only because the leading statesman moved unsteadily to and fro between projects and experiments. Provisionally, therefore, the pre-existing Landrats were to take over the business of the new circle directory, but before this was done, a thorough purge was made of their ranks, and a great number of those with feudal sentiments were dismissed. Yet even in this provisional form the new ordinance encountered an enormous and completely invincible resistance. The landed gentry, threatened in its holy of holies, complained more loudly than ever ; and the national representatives in Berlin protested against the infringement of ancient rights. Several of the warmest personal adherents of the chancellor joined in the just objections which were made by Stein, Vincke, and the other advocates of the idea of self-government. The talented Hippel broke completely with his old friend Scharnweber. It was only in a few governmental areas that the edict could be carried incompletely into effect, and in the Electoral Mark it could not be applied at all. Shortly afterwards the storm of the war of 1813 broke over the country, and swept away for the most part even these trifling beginnings ; and in the year 1814 its further execution was postponed. The only sound fruits of the unhappy law were the circle assemblies. It was in the quiet work of these bodies that the country people first learned to know and to love the new time. Wherever they came into existence, everyone was full of praise for the conduct of the peasants ; they furnished a proof that Stein's work, the liberation of the peasantry, had not been premature. All the reports of the boards related with naive astonishment how willing, efficient, and intelligent, was this new estate.[1]

But what a contrast there was between the laws of Stein and the experiments of Hardenberg. Stein's thought and activity always remind us of the ancient heraldic motto of his beloved County Mark : " A stone cube, whatever way it falls, falls always on one side." In Hardenberg's spirit, thoughts and fancies came and went like the cloud-pictures in a magic mirror. On the one side everything was full of design, profound, solid, and for these reasons was soon carried into effect ; on the other side there was an insecure oscillation between radical doctrines and despotic inclinations, a series of unlucky financial laws, extensive and dangerous promises for the future, rash beginnings abandoned after the first step, everything without plan and hasty ; and yet amid these inchoate and dilettantist activities, were nevertheless highly important reforms worthy of the greatest of statesmen, an unfettering of economic forces which subsequently made it possible for the state to find balm for the wounds inflicted by this terrible war. That tendency to levity which so often led Hardenberg's protean nature into error, was nevertheless closely connected with the best energy of his personality, with his inexhaustible and sanguine joyousness. Whilst Stein often gave up the Prussian state for lost, and continued to count upon the miracle of a general uprising of the German people, the levity of Hardenberg found ever new means and new hopes for the country, and after every fresh failure he quickly and vigorously recovered his footing.

Amid all the stimulating work of these internal party struggles, Hardenberg continued to reserve his best energies for foreign

[1] Many proofs of this are afforded by the report of the minister Beyme, April 1, 1818, concerning his official tour through Pomerania and Prussia.

policy. It was his wish to store for several years the economic and military forces of the exhausted country, and meanwhile to come quietly to a good understanding with the two other eastern powers, until, after the complete evacuation of the fortresses on the Oder, the right moment should arrive to take up arms. Until then, the suspicions of the Imperator must not be aroused. For this reason, Scharnhorst was apparently removed from the conduct of the war department ; but in actual fact he continued in charge of military affairs. Count Goltz, a well-meaning but timid man, to whom the French offered no objection, remained nominally at the head of foreign affairs; whilst behind his back Hardenberg negotiated with the English agent, Ompteda. The police superintendent of Berlin, Justus Gruner, a passionate patriot, deeply initiated into the plans of the secret leagues, was deprived his position. Friendly warnings were given to the excited professors and authors not to expose their designs to the enemy. A careful censorship supervised *nos deux gazettes :* thus in the language of Prussian diplomacy were termed the patriotic *Spenersche Zeitung*, and the characterless *Vossische Zeitung* which was secretly supported by Count St. Marsan. The chancellor was unwearied in the offer of conciliation and excuse whenever St. Marsan in Berlin, or Davoust in Magdeburg, complained of the intrigues of Fichte, Schleiermacher, and Schmalz.[1] Meanwhile events moved faster than Hardenberg's cautious wishes. Soon after the Peace of Vienna it became apparent that the decisive war between the allies of Tilsit was at hand ; not suddenly, like most of the other wars of this breathless time, but step by step, plainly visible two years in advance, did this new peril manifest itself.

The decisive cause was once more found in the untamable character of the world ruler. Just as the lion kills, not merely from hunger, but simply because he cannot help doing it, because it is his nature to tear other animals to pieces, so this omnipotent man could not rest for a moment after he had attained any success. His avaricious dreams were illimitable ; he had not yet been able to equal the fabulous glories of Alexander's campaigns. Hardly had Austria been subdued with Russian aid, when he proposed to humiliate the czar with the assistance of the Hofburg. But it was not merely the destructive ardour of a raging ambition which drove the Imperator forward, but also an inevitable political necessity ; it was impossible for his world-empire to exist unless

[1] Hardenberg's Diary, November 6, 1811.

he exercised unconditional control over all the coasts of Europe. More passionately than ever was he now carrying on a commercial war against inaccessible England ; by the edict of the Trianon he hoped to complete the closure of the Continent. When he united the North Sea coast with the empire he declared bluntly to the representatives of the Hansa towns : " The edicts concerning the Continental System are the fundamental laws of my Empire ! " On the Spanish peninsula, the horrible war seemed likely to continue interminably ; from the radical decisions of the Cortes of Cadiz there spoke the despairing resolution of a heroic people. Stringent political reasons demanded that the Imperator should first close this open wound ; but he would not and could not allow for the collossal force of national passion. As soon as Russia had been subdued and the English flag had been excluded from all the harbours of the Continent, as soon as the French custom house officers were in St. Petersburg, the Spanish rebellion would disappear like snow before the sun of the empire. The insatiable man was already brooding over more venturesome and more wonderful designs ; after the fall of Moscow, a new campaign was to be started from the shores of the Volga, outrivalling the glorious deeds of Alexander, a campaign to the Ganges, which was to destroy for ever this " platform of English commercial greatness."

The czar could no longer conceal from himself the dangers of the alliance of Tilsit. The whole of Russia learned with profound dissatisfaction how Napoleon had presented to Warsaw the greater part of Austrian Poland, which had been conquered by the Russians, without even consulting his ally about the matter. In St. Petersburg it was known that secret negotiations were going on between the Polish nobles and the Tuileries. Through the intermediation of Napoleon's aides-de-camp, the re-establishment of Poland by the grace of France, which in Alexander's opinion was the greatest of all dangers, seemed ever nearer at hand. To meet this danger the czar laid a proposal before the French ambassador whereby the two allies were to pledge themselves mutually never again to re-establish the Polish state, and never even to tolerate that the name Poland should be used. The Imperator gave an evasive reply ; his pious disposition made him shun " using the language of the Godhead " and the giving of a promise for all future time. It was not that he had already taken up in serious earnest the idea of the re-establishment of the Polish kingdom. The formation of national states conflicted with the nature of his world-empire. Moreover, the revolutionary ideas which were part of the twofold nature of Bonapartism had in the course of years passed into the background. Just as the enslaved peoples now saw in Napoleon nothing but the despot, so had he come to regard himself simply as the subduer of the Revolution, and once more he boasted, as he had boasted after the 18th Brumaire, that upon his shoulders rested the ordered prosperity of bourgeois society. The revolutionary spirit of the Sarmatians was antipathetic to him. He was disturbed by the thought that from a semi-republican Poland there might issue a " devilish propaganda " which could unite with the Hussitism of the neighbouring Bohemia. Yet he was unwilling to tie his hands, since the national aspirations of the Poles might perhaps serve as a valuable weapon against Russia. Moreover, the usurper could not venture openly to offend the enthusiasm of the French for the re-establishment of the kingdom of Poland, France's ancient ally. In any case, the negotiations between Paris and St. Petersburg fell through, and the embittered czar declared to the French ambassador, " I now know that you wish to re-establish Poland ! " But to the accusation that he was engaged in secret intrigues, the Imperator was to give the unambiguous answer : I am not intriguing but am waging war with 400,000 men.

Step by step accumulated the proofs of Napoleon's hostility. Shortly before his marriage to the archduchess he had been in treaty for the hand of Alexander's sister ; he calculated that Emperor Francis would rather offer his own flesh and blood to the crowned plebian than endure a family union between the Bonapartes and the House of Gottorp. The plan was completely successful, but the czar, in a very bad humour, accused Napoleon of duplicity. Next came the annexation of the German coasts. The world-empire stretched its tentacles round the Prussian state as far as the Baltic, coming ever nearer to Russia ; and the Imperator expressly declared that these annexations were merely the first ! Thus, also, duke of Oldenburg, France's ally and Alexander's near relative, was robbed of his hereditary dominions without Napoleon's Russian ally being given any information beforehand of this arbitrary exercise of power. Then Napoleon made a preposterous demand, that the czar should lay an embargo upon neutral shipping. This amounted to forbidding to the Russians all consumption of colonial produce. Alexander answered by a ukase which seriously affected the import of French manufactured articles. An angry correspondence gave lively expression to the bitterness of the two emperors. Napoleon wrote in February, 1811 :

"Your Majesty has no longer any friendship towards me; in the eyes of England and Europe our alliance no longer exists."

Meanwhile, with customary circumspection, Napoleon was engaged in the preparations for an unprecedented war. As long before as the spring of 1810, he had accumulated in the Warsaw region enormous stores of arms, and had had the fortresses in the duchy prepared for war—all this "as a mere precautionary measure," as he wrote to Frederick Augustus of Saxony. In April, 1811, the princes of the Confederation of the Rhine were ordered to hold their troops ready for the march. Magdeburg was occupied by the French, the garrisons in Danzig and in the fortresses on the Oder were doubled, and on the Lower Elbe there was assembled an army of 200,000 men. It was perfectly plain that Prussia was either to be annihilated by a sudden invasion, or was to be forced by threats to join France; then the Russian campaign was to begin immediately from Warsaw. On August 15, 1811, on a public occasion, Napoleon overwhelmed with hateful abuse the Russian ambassador Kurakin, and the world was well aware that it was by such scenes as this that the Imperator was accustomed to herald his wars.

If Alexander were to undertake the unequal strife it was indispensable that he should hold his entire forces in readiness, and that he should come to an understanding with the German great powers. Of the two golden fruits which he had promised himself to secure by means of the alliance of Tilsit, one had already been obtained. Conquered Sweden had ceded Finland to the Russians; and in the Danubian provinces Alexander's troops maintained their position. But the Porte still opposed an obstinate resistance, and was secretly encouraged in this resistance by Napoleon, who foresaw that the fight for the mouths of the Danube would render nugatory all attempts at reconciliation between Russia and Austria. The Hofburg was full of rancour against the czar, ascribing to him above all the misfortunes of the last war. None the less, as early as 1809 Emperor Francis was secretly attempting a reconciliation with Russia, since he had little confidence in French friendship. Alexander met the advance gladly. At this time he still believed in the permanence of the alliance of Tilsit, and coquetted with the plan for a league of the three emperors which was to lead to the partition of Turkey. But the sobriety of Vienna remained inaccessible to such dreams. Archduke Charles, in particular, showed, as always, an open understanding of the oriental interests of the monarchy; he rejected any friendship with Russia so long as the Lower Danube was in the hands of the czar; and Metternich finally declared to the Russian ambassador, " Have done with Turkey, and then we shall first be able to negotiate with you ! " As soon as Alexander recognised that the Treaty of Tilsit had been torn up, in the soul of the fickle-minded man new fantastical dreams sprang to life, plans which were to be as fortunate for the liberty of the world as they were to be advantageous to the land-hunger of the House of Gottorp. He returned to those Polish projects which he had in earlier years discussed with Czartoryski, and in December, 1810, wrote to his Polish friend that it was his intention to forestall the Imperator, and immediately after the beginning of the war to proclaim the freedom of Poland—freedom of course under Russian dominion. As the autocrat of all the Russias and as King of Poland he wished to rule despotically in the east and through parliament in the west; to live in the memory of remote centuries as the restorer of Poland; to give an exemplary constitution to the liberated neighbour-land, for " you know that I have always preferred liberal forms." If the Poles would respond to the appeal of their liberator, it would be possible for him to advance to the Oder " without firing a shot " As a matter of course Prussia would join him, and with a decisive superiority, with a force of 230,000 men which would before long be increased by several hundred thousand more, the conflict for the liberation of Europe would be begun. Napoleon could not put more than 155,000 men into the field against him, and among these only 60,000 were French ! So greatly did the old powers under-estimate the force at the disposal of the world-empire, and even far-seeing officers were not free from the universal error. In the year 1810 Radetzky had calculated that only 60,000 Frenchmen could march against Russia; and a year later than this Gneisenau had reckoned the entire forces at Napoleon's disposal for a war against the east to be 200,000 men.

The czar built with joyful confidence upon these thoughts of salvation. It seemed to him that it would not even be very difficult to secure Austria's assent, and he wrote to the emperor Francis that the Hofburg might have the Danubian provinces, and even Serbia, if only Austria would join the great coalition and agree to the re-establishment of Poland. It will readily be understood, however, that to the court of Vienna these Polish plans were almost more unacceptable than had been the attacks of Russia upon the mouths of the Danube. All understanding on these lines was rejected. The Austrian statesmen said openly that Russian policy was like that of a child who did not know what he wanted. In actual fact, the Sarmatian plans were soon to disperse into thin air. Czartoryski refused to accept Alexander's suggestions, for his Polish blood was stronger than his friendship for the czar. The prudent Pole at once recognised that his countrymen, faithful to the national traditions, would remain in the French camp, and he hoped for the re-establishment of his fatherland from Napoleon's victory. He wished to unite " tout ce qui est Pologne," including, that is to say, Danzig and West Prussia, once more under the banner of the white eagle, and became cool as soon as he noted how far these modest claims exceeded the intentions of the czar.

In May, 1811, Alexander at length recognised that should he invade Warsaw he could not reckon upon the Poles taking up arms on his behalf ; and he finally determined, now thoroughly sobered, to await the enemy's attack in his own country. He knew his Russians. He was aware that it was only half-heartedly that they would ever conduct a war on foreign soil, for they would regard this as a war on behalf of the heathen ; whereas the threatened soil of Holy Russia they would defend just as valiantly and joyfully as they had ever before defended it against Tartar and Turk. He no longer thought of yielding ; a war seemed to him unavoidable, and financial difficulties made a condition of armed peace unendurable for any long period.

Thus, as the newspapers phrased it, there now threatened an encounter between the two colossi of the east and of the west, and unhappy Prussia was likely to be crushed in the first violence of the onslaught. Neutrality was impossible, were it only that Napoleon must lead his army through Prussia. The Prussian generals foresaw that he would use this road in order to strike at the heart of Russia, and in order to separate the north of the extensive empire from the south. All his personal feelings, his hatred for the oppressor, and his friendship for the czar, impelled the king to take the side of the state which he had ever regarded as his natural ally. Should Russia be conquered, it was certain that the victorious Imperator would annihilate the detested Prussian state. His anger against these tenacious North Germans increased from day to day, and he continued to speak of the Prussians as the Jacobins of the north. The court-journals were always relating stories of the great anarchistic conspiracy which had its focus in Prussia ; they gladly repeated the prophecy of Bonald, the clerical, that this state, the work of the atheist Frederick, was hastening down to destruction.

But what would happen if Alexander should come to an understanding with France, over the head of Prussia ? Thrice already, in Tilsit, in Erfurt, and during the Austrian war, the czar had cynically abandoned his German friend. If Prussia should take up arms alone, it was almost certain that the small army, outmatched sevenfold by the forces which everywhere surrounded the frontiers and occupied the fortresses along the Oder, would be immediately overwhelmed. How could it be hoped that the troops could be assembled quickly enough on the coast, in the camp at Kolberg, since the neighbouring Saxon-Polish army could immediately cut off the Silesian troops from the main force of the monarchy ? A sudden attack by the garrisons of Danzig and Stettin would suffice to close the bridge over the Vistula at Dirschau and the new bridge across the Oder at Schwedt, the only two ways which still remained open between Old Prussia, Pomerania, and the Mark. There was no longer any doubt as to Napoleon's intentions. When half the contribution had been paid, he had, in accordance with the treaty, restored Glogau to the king ; but despite two reminders, he refused to evacuate the country. The prudent Talleyrand, who still sometimes advised moderation, had long ceased to control foreign affairs : his successor Champagny, and subsequently Maret, slavishly followed every caprice of the autocrat. In December, 1810, there was sold to the Prussian ambassador in Paris a forged memorial of Champagny, which expressly developed the plan for the annihilation of Prussia. It is doubtful whether Hardenberg saw through the trick ; but he became all the more anxious in proportion as the Napoleonic diplomats obstinately denied that there was any danger of war; as late as April, 1811, Lauriston assured him that the Russo-French dispute was only a harmless quarrel between husband and wife.[1] It was clear that Prussian watchfulness was to be put to sleep ; the Imperator was still uncertain whether he should give the *coup de grace* to the Hohenzollerns before or after the Russian war. But to take up arms in so deplorable a situation would be suicidal, unless the czar determined to open the war upon Prussian soil.

It was in this sense that Frederick William wrote to his friend, repeatedly, openly, and in most moving terms. Alexander long

[1] Hardenberg's *Journal*, April 20, 1811.

remained silent. At length, towards the end of May, he answered that it was not within his power to prevent the overrunning of Prussia by a great army, and that he would only begin the war in his own country. For the fourth time he abandoned his friend to a sinister destiny. Meanwhile Hardenberg had endeavoured to ascertain whether in Paris an alliance could be effected under honourable conditions ; he offered an accessory corps, in return for the restoration of Glogau, in return for a remission of the contribution and permission to increase the army. Napoleon rejected the proposal ; Prussia was to give him military aid, not as an ally on equal terms, but under compulsion. Thus, whichever way Prussia might turn, there loomed nothing but disaster and destruction.

Then, in the moment of greatest need, the hot passion of the war party broke out into flame. Even Hardenberg went over to the side of Scharnhorst. In the council of state, Gneisenau was appointed to the conduct of the military preparations, and thus there originated in the summer of 1811 those grandiose plans for a mass rising of the Prussian people, the most madly daring perhaps that modern statesmen have ever conceived, an imperishable monument of the greatness of soul of Scharnhorst and his friends. Just as they were, immediately under the fiery cannon of the *grande armée* which increased day by day, they ventured to believe in their own power to anticipate the all-powerful enemy by a sudden rising ; in every village the pastor was to summon the Landsturm ; everyone who could possibly wield a weapon was to join. In secret, the partially trained reservists had already been summoned, as many of them as could be called without arousing the suspicion of the French : towards the end of August, 75,000 men were ready. The generals in command of the provinces received extraordinary powers to enable them to strike on a given sign. Berlin had been almost entirely depleted of troops ; from all sides the regiments went to Kolberg, where Blucher was in command ; there and in Spandau was the people's war to find its chief foci. Gneisenau rejoiced, saying that the world was to be astonished by the Prussian strength ! One who saw the high-spirited man in these days, never forgot him ; it seemed as if enthusiasm radiated from him. His friends proposed for him the supreme command in Silesia, where he knew every bush and every road, and Clausewitz already greeted him prophetically as the marshal of Silesia. He had put into these plans for war all the ardency, all the nobility of his soul ; his whole nature was in a ferment when he went to the king with the poetic exhortation :

> " Trust in fortune, trust the Parcae,
> Move amid the stormy waters
> Calm as Cæsar in his ship ! "

And yet all these heroic plans were nothing more than a noble delusion. Gneisenau announced his own condemnation when he recognised that he now had only the courage of Curtius. A glorious destruction, destruction without any visible possibility of re-establishment, was the certain fate of Prussia if she were thus to rush into battle. Even before the people's war was really ready to start, Napoleon, whose eyes were everywhere, would have filled all the land with his armies ; and where did this open plain offer any opportunity for guerilla warfare after the Spanish model ? It was the salvation of the monarchy that even in this hour of temptation Frederick William never ceased to recognise his highest kingly duty, and that he would not sacrifice the existence of his state for a surge of heroice sentiments. He examined the plans after his profound and thorough manner, and in his marginal notes he gave expression to certain good ideas which two years later were to come to life—for example, the first proposal for the order of the Iron Cross. In many respects his view was too gloomy ; it was of such men as these that he enquired with discouragement, "Where are to be found the leaders for a people's war ? " But more accurately than his generals had he estimated the strength of Napoleon and the weakness of the Russian army, and he was too well acquainted with his Markers accustomed to orderly military service, to expect much from an irregular popular uprising. " Good as poetry," he wrote in one of his marginal comments ; and again, " if a single preacher were to be shot, the whole thing would be over." For a long time the king was prepared for the worst. For weeks his carriage stood in the castle court, ready for the journey, in order that at the first suspicious movement of the neighbouring French, he might take refuge in Königsberg. Again and again he wrote to Alexander how ready he was to lead his army to the Rhine, but he declared that the liberation of Germany was possible only if the three eastern powers were united in opening the campaign upon the German theatre of war.

In October Scharnhorst visited St. Petersburg in profound secrecy, and by his intellectual superiority succeeded in gaining a small but genuine concession. Alexander promised that if Napoleon should occupy Prussian territory, or should strengthen his forces on the Vistula, the Russian main body should advance upon the Vistula through the Duchy of Warsaw, and at the same time that for the defence of Königsberg an army corps of twelve battalions should be sent to East Prussia. Should the king content himself with these paltry proposals ? Could he venture to begin the desperate struggle in the most remote eastern corner of the state, upon the same area where the war of 1807 had ended so disastrously ? Immediately afterwards Scharnhorst hastened to Vienna ; not even the ambassador Humboldt (so strong was Hardenberg's mistrust) was to know anything of his arrival. Metternich received the confidential envoy in a friendly spirit. The Austrian minister continued to keep in mind the possibility of an alliance of the three eastern powers, although Emperor Francis had no less detestation for the military Jacobins in Berlin than had his son-in-law ; but Metternich considered that the time was not ripe for a revision of the alliances, and he thought very little of Alexander's force of will. It was impossible to draw from him any definite undertaking ; he would not even promise assistance in case of the annihilation of Prussia ; but at the same time (November 28th), in a secret memorial he declared to the emperor that to Austria the only choice now open was between neutrality and the French alliance ; if the monarch should choose the latter alternative, he might demand, as a reward for his assistance in the war, the frontier of the Inn, Illyria, and Silesia, since the disappearance of the Prussian state was now almost unavoidable.[1]

England also refused effective help. Prussia demanded merely what was indispensable ; subsidies and a landing on the German coast. The British government, however, was still unable to see that the decisive issue of the world struggle lay in Germany alone. Proud of her Iberian successes, England thought that she was doing sufficient in the vigorous continuation of the Spanish war. Even at the present day the general opinion of the English remains that it was Wellington's Spanish victories that destroyed the Napoleonic empire. The oppressed court of Berlin asked of England no more than a supply of weapons, and yet the Guelph statesman Count Münster ventured to ask Scharnhorst, Blucher, and Gneisenau whether they would not venture to take up arms against the will of their king ! The humiliated Frederician

[1] Posthumous papers of Metternich, II, 426.

monarchy had lost all prestige throughout the world; it seemed to be nothing more than a heap of ruins, without power of will, and no longer counted among the ranks of the powers.

Thus Prussia once more stood alone. A declaration of war in such a situation must lead to the annihilation of the state before a single Russian sabre could be drawn from the scabbard. What wonder, then, that in view of all this, in January, 1812, the French party at the Prussian court once more gained the upper hand. The chief spokesman of this party was Ancillon—the court parson, as Gneisenau called him—a submissive, shallow phrase-maker, cowardly by nature, always inclined to the pettiest of resolutions. With his unpleasant theological unction, he declared in a memorial that Napoleon cherished friendly intentions towards the Prussian monarchy, as otherwise he would long ago have destroyed it, and he urgently advised adhesion to the side of France. The king thought otherwise. Not for a moment did he doubt the ambition of the Imperator. From the fate of the duke of Oldenburg he had just learnt that even an alliance gave no security against the arbitrary exercise of power on the part of this friend. But he saw the situation as it actually was. If war were to be begun on behalf of Russia, and without Russian help, Prussia would sacrifice herself inevitably and uselessly. If Prussia went over to the side of the detested enemy, the state's existence would indeed be guaranteed only for a year, but a year was much in so desperate a time, and perhaps in that period of respite some other way of salvation would be disclosed. Profoundly disheartened, almost desperate, did the unhappy prince stand between his dearest inclinations and the interests of his state. Once more he endeavoured to find a way out. Colonel Knesebeck, an enlightened adherent of the peace party, was sent to St. Petersburg in order to adjure the czar to despatch a negotiator to Paris in order to avert this war, which must in any case be disastrous to Prussia; if it came to blows the king was not in a position to avoid forming an alliance with France. Even this last attempt, the outcome of hopeless perplexity, was unavailing. Alexander could answer only that he desired peace as earnestly as the king, but that in case of need he would defend himself bravely "against an attack at once unjust and groundless, and induced only by the insatiable ambition of Napoleon."[1] Now, therefore, the alliance with Napoleon was inevitable.

Meanwhile the Imperator had made his own resolves. In

[1] Emperor Alexander to King Frederick William, February 22, 1812.

order to be able to open the Russian war on the Niemen without delay, he thought it advisable to content himself for the moment with the peaceful subordination of Prussia. Owing to his threats, the Prussian preparations for war had, in the previous autumn, been partly discontinued. Now he had a force of nearly 300,000 men hard by the borders of the state. Even before the negotiations were concluded, the French troops crossed from Magdeburg and Swedish Pomerania into Prussian territory. The commander of the artillery of the *grande armée* received secret instructions to hold ready the siege trains for Spandau, Kolberg, and Graudenz. The king would have been lost if he had not agreed to Napoleon's terms. Thus came into existence the alliance of February 24, 1812. Prussia supplied an accessory corps of 20,000 men, so that the half of the Prussian army disappeared in the twenty-seventh division of the *grande armée*; what remained hardly sufficed to garrison the fortresses, for the king had to pledge himself expressly not to increase the number of his troops. The whole country, with the exception of Upper Silesia and Breslau, lay open to the armies of Napoleon, for their passage on the way to Russia, and had to provide for their maintenance. All that was obtained in exchange for these new sacrifices was the promise that the cost of supplies would subsequently be allowed for, and that the arrears remaining due of the contributions should be allowed for in the settlement! Now, as before, the occupied fortresses remained in Napoleon's hands; even the capital must be open to the French troops, for Napoleon dreaded a rising of the Berlin mob. Potsdam alone remained free; there the king now lived, surrounded by a few hundred men of his guard, yet he did not refrain from appearing sometimes in Berlin, among the soldiers of Napoleon. In a despairing letter Frederick William displayed to his Russian friend his determination that, since Russia had refused all active and speedy help, he must now think only of the salvation of his own monarchy; but at heart he still remained the friend and ally of Alexander, and hoped that they would both carry on the war in this sense. Immediately afterwards Austria also adhered to the French side, voluntarily and under far more favourable conditions, for to Austria was held out the prospect of the reacquirement of the Illyrian provinces, should it be necessary to unite Galicia with the re-established Poland.

Thus the whole Continent was allied in the war against the empire of the czar, and the *grande armée* passed ravaging across the fields of Prussia—about 650,000 men, the most enormous army that the world had seen since the days of Xerxes. The best energies of the European youth, from the Ebro to the Elbe, from Taranto to the North Sea, was under arms. There was no longer any talk of treaties. Contrary to the agreement, Pillau and Spandau, the citadels of Berlin, as Napoleon himself called them, were occupied by the French. Anything that the French had forgotten to steal in the year 1807, and everything in the way of warlike stores which had been provided anew during the subsequent four years, fell into the hands of these friends as they marched through the country. Through the passage of the *grande armée* Prussia lost at least 146,000,000 francs over and above the remaining dues of the contribution [1]—a sum that was never made good. It was Napoleon's intention to make this dangerous ally in his rear altogether harmless ; in case of need, by a *coup de main* at Potsdam, he could gain possession of the person of the king.

Horrible, overwhelming, was the impression produced by these occurrences in the circle of the Prussian patriots. The higher had been their hopes in the previous summer, the stormier was now their indignation. It was obvious that those who had been most active in the military preparations of 1811 could no longer retain their positions after the complete change of system. In the previous autumn, on the urgent representations of Napoleon, Blucher had been deprived of his command, consoled by the monarch with cordial words. Now Scharnhorst also was dismissed, but retained the king's confidence as before. Ostensibly Gneisenau, too, was given his congé, and travelled with secret proposals to Austria, Russia, Sweden, and England. Boyen and Clausewitz went to Russia. The last-named, on his departure, sent yet another ardent exhortation to his pupil, the young crown prince, and in his *Bekenntnisse* he laid down the programme of the war party. This is a classic memorial which even to-day must profoundly move every German heart. Once more he endeavoured, proudly and grandly, and with stimulating words, to prove that it must be possible in this ill-treated country, to beat 750,000 men to their knees if only all false prudence could be abandoned and if people would abandon their dull trust in the

---

[1] Such was the reckoning of the Minister of Finance, which was sent to Paris on May 17, 1814. But unquestionably the estimate is far too low. At the second Peace Congress of Paris, Hardenberg, in September, 1815, submitted another calculation, according to which Prussia had paid 94,000,000 francs over and above the remnants of the contribution, and had further suffered, through the passage of the *grande armée*, damages to the extent of 309,000,000 francs.

uncertain future. Never was a great-hearted error more beautifully and more worthily defended.

Of the other officers, there were some, like the fiery and high-
spirited Count Chasot, who had left the country during the
troubles of 1809 ; these were now offered an asylum by the czar
in his newly-formed German legion. Other valiant men, such as
Grolman, Oppen, and the brothers Hirschfeld, were fighting in
Spain. They thought with Gneisenau, " the world is divided into
the enemies and the friends of Bonaparte, and the essential matter
is not so much one of country as one of principle." The enormous
majority of the officers' corps, however, gave to their war-lord
a proof of German loyalty which outweighed many a brilliant
deed of warlike courage. There was not a single man in their
ranks who did not detest the war on behalf of Napoleon, and yet
there were only twenty-one active officers, and among these not
more than three staff-officers, who took their voluntary dismissal
in consequence of the French alliance, most of them to enter
the German Legion of Russia. [1] The others controlled their hot
hatred, and thereby were enabled to effect greater things than
those who were more impatient. It was quite otherwise than
Gneisenau believed in his holy zeal. The war for the nation's
rights demanded national armies ; the bastard structure of the
German legion of Russia remained a mixture of noble and common
elements, and played no notable part either in the Russian or in
the German war. The king accepted with great displeasure the
resignations of those officers who wished to leave. Subsequently
Clausewitz and several of the others found it very difficult to obtain
re-entry into the army ; how often in later years, too, did the
opponents of the reform party diligently remind the monarch
that some of the nearest friends of Scharnhorst and Gneisenau
had not remained with the colours.   .

Napoleon had still no inkling of the enormous hatred of the
German people. Vainly did Davoust and Rapp, and even his
invariably cheerful brother Jerome, warn him. He answered
contemptuously : " What on earth is there to fear from so dis-
creet, so reasonable, so cold, so patient a people, from a people to
whom all idea of outrage is so alien that not once during the
war has one of my soldiers been murdered ? " Count Narbonne,
however, who even in his allegiance to the Imperator continued
to retain a sense of justice and shame, declared at the outset that
this enforced Prussian friendship could not endure ; how could

[1] Reported by Max Lehmann, Knesebeck, and Schön, p. 57.

anyone possibly demand loyalty from an ally who was being watched in his own capital ? In actual fact, the cordial under- standing between the king and the czar remained undisturbed, even after the treaty of February. Alexander did not indeed renounce the opportunity of writing an unctuous letter to complain of the behaviour of the Prussian court, although he was himself in Prussia's debt ; but at the same time he confidentially explained to the chancellor, through Count Lieven, that his friendship persisted without change.[1] Both parties hoped for the day when their natural alliance would be resumed. Even the Hofburg gave pacifying assurances to the court of St. Petersburg, saying that in this war, Austria was actually more friendly to the czar than she had previously been in time of peace, because Alexander had temporarily abandoned his Polish plans ; the diplomatic relationships between Vienna and St. Petersburg were never completely broken off. The two German courts, more- over, remained in lively secret intercourse with one another and with England.

In May the successor of the Carlovingians held his third great court upon German soil, more brilliantly this time even than in Mainz or Erfurt. Whilst the regiments of the *grande armée* passed in an unending series across the Elbe, the princes of Germany assembled round their ruler in the palace at Dresden, and among them the former German emperor and the successor of Frederick the Great. What pleasure did it offer to the plebeian thus to rub the necks of his highborn servants beneath the yoke until they became sore ! He played in person the part of host in the house of his Saxon vassal, inviting his imperial father-in-law to dinner every day, but the king of Prussia and the master of the castle only every other day, since these were persons of inferior rank. Whilst the conqueror was at table the dukes of Weimar and Coburg, with a swarm of German princes, must stand in the ante-room. Even honourable Frenchmen regarded it as a wanton affront that the King of Prussia should have been forced to take this journey ; the Imperator denied his guest the customary salute of artillery, and greeted the king with the question : " You are now a widower ? "[2] Frederick William was profoundly enraged ; he knew only too well who it was had broken his wife's heart ; in the mind of the crown prince, who was present, there remained throughout life a profound hatred for the family of Bonaparte. Even the servile populace of the beautiful town on the Elbe was

[1] Hardenberg's Diary, March 11, 1812.　　[2] Ibid., May 26, 1812.

enraged by the cruel roughness of the Corsican, and honoured the quiet greatness under misfortune which ever displayed itself in the king of Prussia. Meanwhile Hardenberg and Metternich sat together in intimate confidential intercourse, and formed a sound friendship even though the intentions of the two powers were still widely divergent. Since his daughter's wedding Emperor Francis no longer desired the annihilation of Napoleon, and Metternich was only prepared to effect the limitation of the intolerable excesses of the French power. So much at least had the Austrian statesman learned from the terrible lessons of recent years, that he saw that a moderately strong Prussia was desirable, although he accepted this with many tacit reservations; and since, by forming an alliance with France, Prussia had once more saved itself from annihilation, he began to believe again in the vital energy of this state. The two ministers mutually disclosed their secret relationships with England; they promised one another that the confidential intercourse which had been carried on between them for years should in future be continued even more vigorously than before; and they agreed that in a spirit of cordial mutual understanding they would await the hour which would render possible a change in the present alliance.

But it still remained profoundly uncertain when this long-desired hour would strike. At the moment it seemed that hope could be placed only in some quite unforeseen occurrence, such as the death of Napoleon. The initiates did not believe the victory of Russia to be possible. It soon became apparent with what levity Alexander had overestimated his strength. He put into the field not more than 175,000 men against the forces of Napoleon, by which his were three times outnumbered. It was only when the campaign had actually begun that he made up his mind to put an end to the Turkish war, and in the peace of Bucharest to surrender the greater part of the Danubian provinces. Consequently his southern army could not participate in the war until quite late. Since the death of Suvòroff Russia had had hardly any notable generals, and in view of the capricious character of the czar, it seemed extremely probable to the courts that he would once more, as after Austerlitz and Friedland, give up the game after the first lost battle.

The people thought otherwise. During the last summer, which had been very hot, a magnificent comet had appeared nightly in the skies. The masses were certain since then that something great, something unheard of, was imminent. When now the savage foreign warriors from all countries streamed through the Prussian villages—the little frugal, brown Spaniards, the tall figures of the insatiable Bavarian drinkers, the slowly-moving Dutchmen, and the lively boasters of Gascony—they all seemed to the common man like a wild rabble of spectres ; he considered that this mad business would come to a bad end, and he was strengthened in this belief, when, with rage in his heart, he saw the undisciplined hordes in their quarters ; how in wild arrogance they trampled the fresh loaves of wheaten bread in the dung, how they smashed the full bottles against the wall. The policy of the un-ideal lust of conquest had ultimately demoralised its own armies ; the ancient discipline of the Napoleonic troops had disappeared, and an impudent masterless spirit, like that of the old mercenary soldiers, had gained the upper hand. Moreover, the old joyful confidence in victory had departed. The soldier himself had at length begun to weary of the eternal fighting, and he dreaded the snowy deserts of the east ; in the Italian and German regiments there was even manifest a dull rage. The cavalrymen complained that in the earlier wars their horses had neighed lustily when starting on the campaign, but that this year they were silent.

And, as is rarely the case, on this occasion the popular belief embodied a sounder judgment than had the calculations of the cabinets. The statesmen in their melancholy forebodings overlooked the one essential point, namely, that Alexander was forced to persevere in this war. The news of the campaign of the heathen against holy Moscow roused the whole Russian people in an uproar, and when under despotism the generally slumbering public opinion at length awakens, it carries all before it with irresistible force. Alexander dared not yield under risk of losing his throne. He knew this. In these days of trial, the unstable boy grew to manhood, so far as his character was capable of manly virtues. As the ivy clings to the oak, so clung he to the iron courage of Baron von Stein. The great German hastened to Russia, accompanied by the faithful Arndt, and stood by the side of the czar, a power in himself, filling the Russian ruler with the breath of his own passion. The nearer the danger approached, the more joyfully and the more confidently rose all the vigorous and heroic energies of his soul. The struggle was to be continued in Kazan, even in Siberia, for this war was decisive for the future of the world.

A profound stillness brooded over Europe when the last

columns of the *grande armée* had disappeared beyond the Russian frontier. In North Germany the blunt question was formed upon a thousand lips whether the stormer of the heavens was not at length going to meet his fate. In this time of expectant stillness, there sounded like a strange and harsh discord a great poem of Goethe's upon Marie Louise. The old man was out of place in this transformed time, and he hailed the Cæsar who was at that moment leading to the slaughter the finest blossoms of European manhood, with the verse :

" He who can will all, wills also peace ! "

Napoleon had passed through Warsaw almost without pause, for " the boundless future does not permit even to bivouac in Poland." He already entertained the plan, as Hardenberg learnt from Maret,[1] of making his brother Jerome king of Poland, and he allowed a general confederation in Warsaw to issue an appeal for the re-establishment of the kingdom of Poland. But he would not yet give the unhappy people any definite assurance, telling his ambassador in Warsaw to " encourage the national tendencies without awakening those of the liberals." He stormed onward ; but even before the enemy was in sight, the order of his army began to dissolve. This brilliant army perished above all through its lack of discipline. The plundering of Prussia, ordered from above, had accustomed the troops to rapine. The soldiers were continually at war with the provost-marshals ; a cloud of marauders hovered around the flanks and followed the rear of the army. Only the German and Polish regiments held well together. The administration of the army, which had hitherto been so admirable, now showed itself thoroughly dishonest and neglectful ; the greater proportion of the enormous supply of stores disappeared on the outward march. When Napoleon entered Russia he left in his rear, as had long ago Charles XII in the march to Poltava, Poland torn by factions, and the utterly devastated region of Lithuania.

Scharnhorst had advised the czar to conduct the war after the Parthian method, to use the vast spaces of his country as a weapon, and to lure the enemy far into the desert interior of the Russian empire. The pride of the Russians spurned this wise counsel, which Gneisenau and all the noted Prussian officers also gave. It was rather the hope of the czar that the enemy would

[1] Hardenberg's *Journal*, May 30, 1812.

break his teeth against the entrenched camp of Drissa; the brilliant example of Torres Vedras still dazzled the eyes of the world. It was only the feeling of their own weakness which compelled the commanders of the Russian army, against their plans and their desire, continuously to retreat. Meanwhile the peasantry began a Parthian war on their own initiative; they anticipated everything that was horrible from the heathen enemy, concealed their flocks and herds and all their stores of provisions in the forests, and abandoned their worthless, empty wooden huts; and whenever any isolated soldier fell into their hands they killed him as if he had been a mad dog. The rage of the superstitious people increased yet further when the sacred town of Smolensk, with its churches and wonder-working eikons, was occupied by the enemy after fierce fighting. Further and further did the conqueror advance into the evacuated country; day by day the ranks of his army grew thinner. The passion of the masses at length compelled the Russian Commander-in-Chief, Kutusoff, to venture a battle at Borodino for the possession of Moscow; the advantage of numbers and the valiancy of the French army, and above all that of the Saxon cavalry, gave the Imperator the victory, the bloodiest he had yet fought. Once more he hoped to do what he had so often done before, to dictate peace in the conquered capital; and although his campaign had in any case been begun too late in the year he wasted five invaluable weeks in fruitless negotiations for peace. Meanwhile the ancient Russian fanaticism did its worst; the burning of Moscow showed the world of what a semi-barbarian people is capable when its most sacred feelings are injured. The army lost its last moral standing through the horrible plundering of the unhappy town. The conqueror was to learn in the case of his own troops the truth of his oft-repeated declaration that bravery was only the second of the military virtues, discipline and staying power being the first.

When the retreat from the devastated town became unavoidable, Napoleon's pride—he himself termed it his greatness of soul —made it impossible for him to determine to take the open northern road; the consequence was that he withdrew from Moscow in front of the Russian army, which lay to the southward of the city. He thought that he would defeat the enemy and force an open line of retreat by the southern route. The presumptuous undertaking miscarried; by the battle of Malo-Jaroslawetz the *grande armée* was forced back into the intermediate road which it had employed for the invasion. Thereby its fate was sealed. The swarm of locusts had to return along the same road which they had already stripped bare to the last blade of grass. The weather remained tolerable for a time, and even when the frost set in, later than usual, the cold was hardly more severe than that which had been experienced six years earlier in the Polish-Austrian campaign. But in front of the army lay a snowy desert of immeasurable extent. As far as the eye could reach, there was no village, no hearthside ; the stores had been lost, the repute of the leaders had been destroyed, all around were the swarming Cossacks and in the forests the infuriated peasants. The greatest misery which can possibly visit mortal men now affected the unhappy army ; it was as if the horsemen of the Apocalypse were storming across the snow-fields. With the ghastly passage over the Beresina all order was dissolved ; the poor vestiges of the proud army made their way forward in irregular masses, barely 30,000 men in all, staggering hollow-cheeked figures of misery, many of them blind and deaf from cold, gnawing with wolf-like hunger at any offal they could find, weaponless, looking like the participators in some horrible masquerade, so that in Germany they were mocked by the popular rhyme :

" Drums without a drumstick, Curassiers in petticoats ;
  Thus has God stricken them, Horses, men, and chariots ! "

But the victor also had lost the greater part of his army through hardships and disease ; barely 40,000 Russians reached the frontier, all utterly exhausted and dispersed over wide distances, completely incapable for the struggle with the fresh troops which Napoleon still possessed garrisoning Prussian territory.

The first uncertain reports of the catastrophe reached Denmark, and were thence transmitted by Dahlmann to his German friends in the interior of Germany. Subsequently it was learnt that the Imperator, who with Caulaincourt was hastening alone in front of the army, had appeared in Glogau on December 12th, and how subsequently in Dresden, indifferently humming a popular song, he had communicated the terrible intelligence to his dismayed vassals. On December 17th the *Moniteur* published the Twenty-ninth Bulletin, with the news : " The *grande armée* is destroyed ; his Majesty's health has never been better." A few days later the Imperator appeared in person at the Tuileries. Not long afterwards the first columns of the French army crossed the Prussian frontier. With a sacred horror the people contemplated the living witnesses to fallen arrogance, and from a million lips there sounded with one voice the exclamation, "Such are the judgments of God!"

The hour of Germany's liberation had struck. No one recognised this earlier than Stein, who had from the first regarded the Russian campaign as merely a prelude to the uprising of Germany. During the war he stood at the head of the German committee in St. Petersburg, arranging for the equipment of the German legion, which according to his plans was to constitute the nucleus of the future German army, and he did not hesitate to disseminate among the troops of the Confederation of the Rhine appeals suggesting that they should desert their colours. What did he care for the oaths which the slaves of the despot had sworn? At the same time, Arndt wrote his catechism for the German warrior (*Katechismus für den teutschen Kriegs- und Wehrmann*), an invaluable popular work which was diffused in many thousands of copies; and in its simple truthfulness, its pious biblical language, moved the faithful people to the soul :—

"He who fights tyrants is a holy man, and he who humbles pride is in God's service.
This is the war which is pleasing to the Lord, this is the blood whose drops are numbered by God in Heaven"

At the court the German baron was at first received with mistrust; but since from the first he had unfailingly predicted the enemy's defeat, and since in his delight at the loyalty, the self-sacrifice, and the religious enthusiasm of the Russian people, he became ever more cheerful and more amiable, all the finer spirits were turned towards him, and above all from the women did he experience that sentiment of natural kinship which women's intuition leads them to feel for genius.

Long before the destruction of the *grande armée* was effected, as far back as September, he had drawn up plans for Germany's future constitution—the most ideal and the most venturesome conception which had ever been applied to German policy. Next to his participation in the transformation of Prussia and in the liberation of Europe, this constitutes his third great service which gives him a rank in world history. Earlier and more acutely than any other statesman had he, without phrase or reservation, placed the unity of Germany before his eyes as the highest aim of German statecraft. When anyone spoke to him about sparing the ancient and traditional fragmentation of the country, he answered that to re-establish such a condition would be just as if one were to endeavour to set a dead man upon his legs, because the man had been well able to stand as long as he was still alive. It seemed to him that all consideration for the dynasties was unworthy. What did it matter to Germany whether Mecklenburg or Bavaria existed, when the real thing of importance was that there should be a strong and vigorous German people, ready for battle, glorious in war and peace ? Was this war to lead merely to a revival of the old quarrels of the German Montagues and Capulets ? If so, the great struggle would end in a ridiculous farce. His aim was " unity, and if unity is not possible, some expedient which shall be a transition to unity." Now, when the whole territorial distribution of Europe was undergoing changes, he considered that the highest possible was attainable. There could be established one great monarchy from the Vistula to the Meuse. In the same way, Italy could be united to form a closed mass. The whole of Central Europe could be led back into a state of " energy and capacity for resistance." If this were impossible, Germany should be divided between Austria and Prussia by the course of the Main ; the princes of the Confederation of the Rhine should be treated as titled slaves and subjects of the conqueror ; whilst the princes who had been dispossessed by Napoleon should not be restored to their dignities. If this also was unattainable, then, as a last resort, some of the smaller states should be subjected as vassals to Austria and Prussia ; Bavaria, Würtemberg, and Baden with a reduced territory, passing to the southern power ; Hanover, Hesse, Oldenburg, and Brunswick to the northern.

Thus, for good or for evil, he endeavoured to bring his ideas on the subject of unity into harmony with those of the Treaty of Bartenstein. In any case the War of Liberation was to be conducted with radical boldness, and whatever German land was conquered was, for the time being, to be ruled as a masterless region by an administrative council of the allies. Among the allies he thought first of Russia, Austria, and England ; it was their business to carry with them hesitating Prussia. Thus profound was his antipathy to the wily policy of Hardenberg. The angry man could never regard as valid the compelling reasons which had determined the conduct of the king in 1809 and 1811, and although the ardent patriots who surrounded him in St. Petersburg were every one of them North Germans he was still unable to believe in the warlike passion of this cold and sluggish stock.

The imperial knight regarded it as a matter of course that it was altogether indifferent which portion of the fatherland should rise first, for when this happened the war must necessarily flow like a raging stream over the German frontiers. He endeavoured to win the czar for these ideas, and he found it quite easy to do so. Alexander had been moved to the soul. In the intoxication of victory all the noble and all the imaginative traits of his nature came to light. A short while before he had had to bear a terrible burden of care ; the news of the burning of Moscow had turned his hair white in a single night. Now Russia had been freed as by a miracle, now he felt himself to be chosen by God's grace as one who would save the world from its yoke of slavery ; nothing then could be more right than a rich reward for this liberator of the world. He immediately resumed his Polish plans, although secretly ; his German adviser heard not a word of them. The liberation of Germany was to bring to the czar the crown of the Jagellons ; the interests of humanity at large were once more in harmony with the dynastic aims of the House of Gottorp ! As early as November, Alexander had practically determined to continue the fight in Germany. The chancellor, Rumjanzoff, lost all influence ; the German baron maintained himself in the czar's favour, and in a memorial showed the Russian government the means which afterwards enabled that government to realise in Germany, paper money to the value of forty million roubles, and thus to secure cash for the prosecution of the war.

It is, however, remarkable to see with how secure an insight the great patriot recognised the decisive point in the world situation, the necessity that Germany should take up arms, and how grossly he erred in all matters of detail. He understood neither the weakness of the Russian military power, nor the cautious anxiety of the court of Vienna, neither the incapacity of the English tory cabinet, nor yet the dull particularism of the little peoples in the German petty states, to whom it never occurred to set themselves in opposition to the will of their rulers. Least of all did he understand the sacred anger which was boiling in the hearts of the Prussians, or the still hopes that were cherished by the king ; yet this very state, which the baron could think of only as towed along by the other powers, was to give the impetus to the European war. During the summer Hardenberg had been careful to consolidate the understanding with Austria, and had for this reason in September sent an aide-de-camp, von Natzmer, to Vienna. Here the plentipotentiary found a thoroughly friendly reception. In his answer, Metternich warmly assured Hardenberg that it was impossible to separate the interests of the two states ; but he gave no definite promise. As the war dragged on, the king began to hope that his Russian friend would on this occasion at length hold out to the end. As early as October 29th, before the news of the burning of Moscow had been received, he declared himself to be prepared for a change in the political system, but only in alliance with Austria. New confidential enquiries in Vienna had but little success. The Hofburg maintained the same attitude as in the crisis of 1811. It offered no objection if Prussia wished to try its own fortune, but would not itself abandon its far more secure position. In Berlin, as everywhere else, a profound impression was produced by the incredible news of the conspiracy of General Mallet—how by the fable of Napoleon's death this madman had taken by surprise the highest authorities, and for some hours had been master of Paris. So treacherous already was the ground on which the world-empire stood ! Then came the news of Napoleon's return, and soon afterwards (December 16th) there arrived from Dresden a letter from the fugitive to the king, which nonchalantly, as if there could be no question about the matter, demanded that the Prussian auxiliary corps should be strengthened. Not a word about compensation, not a word about the payment for the Prussian supplies in the previous spring ! The Imperator regarded Prussia as firmly enchained, and did not anticipate any refusal. In fact, Hardenberg did not over-estimate the significance of the Russian catastrophe. He perceived that Napoleon's unknightly flight had been just as much a matter of political consideration, as had formerly been his secret withdrawal from Egypt ; Hardenberg knew what this one man signified, and foresaw that before long the Imperator would return with a powerful army.

An immediate and open defection was impossible, not merely because the king's conscience would not allow him to break even an enforced alliance without thoroughly sound reasons in conformity with international law, but also because the French forces in the Marks were quite sufficient to stifle a sudden revolt in the germ. On the other hand, all vigorous men at the court were agreed that the favour of the moment must be utilised, and that immediate preparations must be made for an alliance with Russia and Austria. The cautious and conservative cabinet-councillor Albrecht declared, on December 17th, in a memorial which was thoroughly approved by the monarch, that now or never, by the uprising of the three eastern powers, must the intolerable foreign yoke be shaken off, unless "independence was to be renounced for the present generation, and perhaps for ever." Even Knesebeck, the man of peace, now said emotionally, "the moment has come!"[1] Even the rugged Junker Marwitz hastened uninvited to his deadly enemy Hardenberg, to place himself at the latter's disposal.

The king required an even longer period before he fully grasped the unique greatness of these days. Irresolute by nature, profoundly depressed by the sorrows of recent years, still lacking a cordial confidence in his people, he was not yet aware how completely the sentiment of his Russian friend who had once sacrificed him in so cold-blooded a manner, had now been transformed. He wished to venture the colossal undertaking only in alliance with Austria, and under the protection of secure diplomatic treaties. Hardenberg saw further from the first. He at once declared that in case of need the attack must be made without Austrian help, since in any case Austria would not take the field against Prussia.[2] On the day after Christmas, the Chancellor submitted his programme. He advised that preparation should immediately be made under the very eyes of the enemy, and therefore ostensibly on behalf of France. "It is of the utmost importance," he wrote, "to display at first the greatest possible dependence upon the Napoleonic system, and to take all our measures in such a way as if they were done on behalf of France, thus representing even the concentration and increase of our military forces as a consequence of the French demands."[3] His plan was that Austria and Prussia should appear as armed mediators between the belligerent powers. If, as was to be anticipated, Napoleon's pride should lead him to reject the conditions proposed by the intermediaries, a legal ground for declaring war would be given. Meanwhile the king should remove to the security of Silesia, and thence, at the right moment, should summon his people to arms. The king agreed to everything. It could not for the moment be foreseen where the new campaign would begin. The chancellor believed that it would be on the Rhine ; the king, in Poland and Lithuania. Frederick William's view was : "We must strike and must annihilate the enemy ; but that would be done much more confidently in the north than on the Rhine, for Russia could never advance her full force to the

---

[1] Albrecht's memorial, December 17th. Knesebeck's memorial, *Es ist Zeit*, December 23rd. King Frederick William to Hardenberg, December 25, 1812.
[2] Hardenberg's notes on Albrecht's memorial, December 26, 1812.
[3] Hardenberg's report to the king, December 26, 1812.

Rhine, and indeed could hardly get there at all. [1] As the sinister year was drawing to a close, in Berlin the men on furlough were being recalled, orders were being issued for the formation of a reserve battalion, and instructions were given to Knesebeck who was to go to Vienna as negotiator. The ice was broken, and the liberated floods of the popular anger broke forth so stormily that the crown could no longer withdraw. Anxious weeks had still to pass before the mask could be thrown off in face of the out-witted enemy ; many a weak hour of hesitation, of doubt, and of fear, had to be overcome. But neither the king nor his chancellor ever again proved unfaithful to the saving idea once it had been grasped.

This change in Prussian policy was of course concealed from the people, who waited with rising impatience the king's summons. It was therefore fortunate that from another side a deed was ven-tured which served as a beacon to announce to the people that the time of waiting was at an end. The determinism of the great transformation of historic life is most conspicuously mani-fested when it is brought about through unwilling instruments. Who would have regarded it as conceivable that General York, the commander of the Prussian accessory corps, should ever strain the interpretation of his military oath ? Many years before, when quite a young man, he had been dismissed from the Frederician army on account of disobedience ; but when, after long and adventurous wanderings, he was restored to his military rank, he seemed to the soldiers to be the incorporated spirit of the ancient Prussian discipline. The rankers shook in their shoes when the lanky, severe figure of the old Isegrimm, with his furrowed face and aquiline nose, appeared upon the scene. No error could escape those severe and piercing grey eyes ; abusive language was easier to bear than the measured and yet so dreadful, so profoundly humiliating blame uttered by these scornful and domineering lips. The officers did well to say that his words cut like a knife ; from the restlessly changing play of the gloomy features they learned how much ambition, how much hot passion, laboriously controlled by an iron will, was at work in the taciturn and unamiable man. The troops trusted him whole-heartedly, for they knew his valour and circumspection, having witnessed it in the battles of Altenzaun and Lübeck ; and they knew how zealously this thoroughly practical officer cared for his men

[1] King Frederick William's notes on Hardenberg's report, December 28, 1812.

in matters of clothing, provisions, and quarters. Just as in Marwitz was incorporated the caste sentiment of the landed gentry, so in York was incorporated the rigid pride of the old officers' corps. He never could find scorn enough for the new-fashioned follies of the reformers. He hated the French, who had dishonoured his flag and had destroyed the glorious structure of the ancient Prussian order—hated them with all the fierceness of his volcanic nature ; whilst for the comrades who had left the service of the king in order to go to Russia his only words were those of bitter contempt, for he regarded them as traitors and deserters.

During the war, the Prussian division belonged to Macdonald's corps, and marched into the Baltic provinces on the extreme left wing of the *grande armée*. However great the reluctance with which the troops obeyed the orders of the French supreme military staff, they burned with eagerness to display beneath the eyes of the victor of Jena what Prussian bravery could do. York could pride himself that his force was in warlike efficiency behind no other corps of the *grande armée* and that in strictness of discipline it excelled them all. He held them apart, guarded them against all intercourse with the foreign warriors, which was favoured on principle in the armies of the world-empire, and by his rigid and forbidding pride, he showed the French that his men were not vassals belonging to the Confederation of the Rhine but the accessory corps of a free king. The experiences of the last six years had made the feeling of the troops gloomy and bitter ; but this sentiment gave place to a vigorous and defiant sense of self-satisfaction when in the brilliant battle of Bauske and in many other celebrated fights, they displayed the old Frederician audacity, and at the same time exhibited their skill in the arts of the more mobile modern tactics. The brigade-unions, composed of a mixed force of all the different arms, proved no less admirable than did the new army-regulations of January, 1812. Throughout the autumn York maintained his dangerous position in Courland ; it was only the destruction of the main army which forced the left wing to withdraw. Macdonald's corps was ordered to protect from the rear the ruins of the *grande armée,* and to prevent the oncoming Russians from invading East Prussia.

For some weeks the cunning Italian Paulucci and other Russian commanders had endeavoured to persuade the Prussian general to change sides, but always in vain. Moreover, the patriotic appeals of the brave patriot Garlieb Merkel, who was an onlooker in Riga, left the despiser of the men of literature cold. But it did not escape the keen soldier's vision of York that his well-trained little corps, numbering now about 13,000 men, had acquired a quite unanticipated value after the catastrophe that had befallen the *grande armée*. If he should obey the orders of Macdonald, the few Russians who had advanced into East Prussia, to the south of his present position, would be unable to maintain themselves there ; the French remained strong enough to close the Prussian frontier against the Russian corps of Prince Wittgenstein ; and as far as human foresight could tell, the Russian war would end with a useless Cossack raid along the Niemen—but all this would take place only if, with superhuman self-denial, the Prussian corps was to sacrifice itself for its detested ally. Should the Prussians retire from the war, the Russian army would cross the German frontier, and the king, it might be anticipated, would be stimulated to the great resolve which York had longed for for years. A whole world of contradictory ideas were storming in the mind of the iron man. Cold and secure of himself during battle, he was before the battle always excited and gloomy. Was he to sacrifice his faithful troops, the nucleus of the Prussian army, in order to rescue the deadly enemy of the Germans, or was he by an arbitrary exercise of his own authority to endanger the throne and life of his king, who still remained within the power of the stranger ? Was he now, when he had grown grey in honour, once more to refuse his obedience to the stern laws of war as he had of old when, as a precocious boy, he had been drummed out of the army ? Was he to close his life in dishonour—or was he to allow to pass unutilised this great hour of God's judgment ? In answer to his repeated enquiries, Berlin made answer that he might act according to circumstances ; and this reply could be interpreted only to mean that the king would not for ever bind himself to the French alliance.

His course was decided by a letter of Alexander's, dated December 18th, which definitely stated that the czar was prepared to conclude an alliance with the king and not to lay down his arms until Prussia had reacquired her power of the year 1805. Thus on the one hand were the king's old friend, and the prospect of the re-establishment of ancient glory ; on the other hand the evil enemy, who, as York was well aware, thought only of the annihilation of Prussia. As greatly moved as a man can be, the general announced to his officers the determination at which he had arrived, saying : " Thus with God's approval let us begin and complete the work of our liberation." His faithful followers acclaimed his decision with delight. On December 30th, in the mill of Poscherun, near Tau-roggen, York met the Russian negotiators (they were all Prussians by birth, Diebitsch, Clausewitz, and Frederick Dohna) and signed a convention in virtue of which his corps was withdrawn to the strip of land between Memel and Tilsit, there to await the king's further commands. This dutiful soldier would venture nothing more. It was for the king to command an alliance with Russia. York, in a letter written with his heart's blood, laid his head at his king's feet, saying : " Now or never is the moment to regain freedom, independence, and greatness. The destiny of the world depends upon your majesty's decision ! "

The Convention of Tauroggen did not produce the effect which its bold negotiator had hoped, of inciting the king to ally himself with Russia. The monarch had already, though still hesitatingly, chosen a new way. To the chancellor, York's action was even extremely disagreeable, for it might very readily render it necessary to show his game too soon. York had opened the German frontiers to the Russians, had rendered it possible for the East Prussians to rise on behalf of Germany's freedom, and had given to the masses the first joyful certainty that the die had at length been cast. When the morning of this year of 1813 dawned, the most blood-stained year of the whole epoch, there awakened everywhere where Frederick's eagle was waving the ancient joy in arms of the Teutons, and far and wide over the Prussian land sounded the summons of the iron York, " Now or never ! "

CHAPTER IV.

THE WAR OF LIBERATION.

§ I. ITS PREPARATION.

THERE is nothing more sinister in the life of a nation than the need for the gradual repayment for past errors. How much arduous work had now to be undertaken by the best men of the German north in order to atone for the sins of omission of the unhappy decade before 1806. More firmly established than ever was the old loyalty of the Prussians to their king, and a new, free spirit animated the army and the administration. But what in the days of Frederick had been the finest and most peculiar advantage of Prussian policy, the proud and courageous openness of negotiation, was denied to the oppressed state. When the throne at length resolved to defend itself with the sword against violence and disloyalty, to begin the venturesome struggle for the re-establishment of Germany and for the freedom of the world, it was unable to do what was just and necessary in a well-balanced and dignified manner. It was forced into an ambiguous game which was distressing to thousands of honourable consciences, and which compelled many of the most loyal of Prussians to procedures which were characterised by arbitrary independence and were extremely dangerous for the existence of the monarchical order.

At the beginning of the year there were in East Prussia about 40,000 men of the Napoleonic troops, in Poland 10,000, and in the fortresses on the lines of the Vistula and the Oder, 70,000. Augereau occupied the Marks and the passages across the Oder with the still perfectly intact eleventh army corps, which contained more than 20,000 men ; and every day fresh supports arrived from the west, so that the Berlin garrison alone soon numbered 24,000 men. This was enough, more than enough, to hold in check the weak Prussian army, dispersed in four widely separated sections. York's corps had just crossed the Lithuanian frontier ; on the Vistula, Bülow was forming a reserve corps ; at

Kolberg, General Borstell commanded the Pomeranian regiments ; whilst a fourth section, which was subsequently placed under Blucher's command, was assembling in Silesia. When the deplorable ruins of the *grande armée* came into the country, many Hotspurs implored the king that he would allow them to wage a guerilla warfare upon these fugitives. Frederick William refused his permission. The people obeyed him silently, although the hasty innovations of the chancellor had evoked much indignation, justified and unjustified, against the government. The consequence was that these troops of disarmed and deadly enemies passed safely across Prussia, a fact which serves to show at once the compassionate nature and the legal sentiment of this valiant generation, and redounds to its honour. Here and there the mob exulted in savage, malicious joy ; the school-boys could not refrain from alarming the fugitives by the cry of " the Cossacks are coming." It even happened that in the case of some of the officers of the Confederation of the Rhine, the red ribbon was torn from their breasts, for the people detested these traitors even more ardently than they hated the French themselves. But the great mass of the unfortunates were left unmolested, and found shelter and care in Prussian houses ; they were still our allies. The sight of the horrible misery they were suffering moved even rough spirits ; to the common people it seemed as if it would be sinful to strike a blow in the back against those whom God had smitten. Amongst the thousands who thus escaped were the majority of the generals and colonels of the Imperator ; the German good-nature saved for him the leaders of his army. But what was the significance of the king's conduct ? Unquestionably it was not merely his painful conscientiousness which led him even now to refuse to begin the holy war of self-defence without thoroughly valid legal grounds, but it was also his accurate understanding of the military situation. A premature uprising of disorderly masses would have involved the certain destruction of the state. Under the very eyes of the enemy there had first to be marshalled the army by which the enemy was to be defeated ; the military forces were to be increased sixfold ; and meanwhile an alliance was to be formed with the two other eastern powers. All this could be effected only through cunning, such as was possible to the resourceful intelligence of the chancellor. He played the part of Napoleon's faithful ally, earnestly asseverating that his preparations were intended for the carrying on of the Russian war.

But even if the secret negotiations were to have a fortunate issue, and if a coalition of all the old powers could be effected, Prussia's political situation would still remain extremely disadvantageous, and almost desperate. Beyond doubt, Russia had need of Prussia's help. If the king remained faithful to the French alliance, the weak and ill-equipped army of the czar would unquestionably be annihilated by the returning forces of Napoleon before reinforcements could be called up from the remote east. The conqueror, taught by the misfortunes of the previous winter, would not again have risked a rash advance into the interior, but would have contented himself with detaching the Baltic provinces and the Polish-Lithuanian lands from the empire of the czar. Nevertheless, the prospects for the old powers were very unequal. During the last decade Russia and England had notably increased their strength, the former in Poland and Finland, and the latter in the Franco-Dutch colonies ; Austria, too, despite its serious losses, still occupied the position of a great power. If the work of liberation miscarried, England had nothing to fear ; and Russia and Austria need fear only a loss of territory. Should victory be gained, England would have to be compensated by transatlantic dominions, Russia by Polish territory, Austria by the re-establishment and enlargement of her Adriatic possessions. This was in the nature of things ; the entire diplomatic world was in agreement about it ; and the three powers, thanks to their geographical position, could rest assured that no one could rob them of these fruits of victory if the world-empire should be overthrown. For Prussia, on the other hand, this war was a struggle for existence or non-existence. If Napoleon were victorious, the plans for Russia's annihilation, which in Tilsit had merely been postponed, would inevitably be carried out. The Prussian state was absolutely compelled to demand, in case of victory, an incomparably greater reward than was demanded by its allies ; it must insist upon regaining the lost half of its dominions, and upon re-entry into the ranks of the great powers. The struggle for the liberation of the world remained, therefore, in the first place, a struggle for the re-establishment of Prussia. It was easy to foresee that the decisive battles would have to be fought upon Prussian soil, or in those North German territories which were to serve for the indemnification of Prussia ; every scrap of German land which the king asked for himself had first to be won by common efforts, and would rest by rights at the disposal of the coalition. The Prussian state was in the most unfavourable diplomatic situation it is possible to conceive, one whose disadvantages could be compensated neither by the courage of the army nor the adroitness of the statesman. Prussia had for the most part to expect the reward of her exertions from the goodwill of those courts whose interests and traditions were opposed to the establishment of a strong Central European power.

But what attention could be paid to such considerations in this hour when Germany's future was at stake? Step by step, with admirable circumspection, Hardenberg approached his two-fold end, the strengthening of the army and the conclusion of the great alliance. On all the roads could be seen the *Krümper* (half-trained reservists) returning to their regiments; the loyal men dimly recognised for what purpose the preparations were being made. The French troops became extremely uneasy when they encountered these remarkable military allies on the march; they could not fail to notice the fierce glances of the Prussians, and to perceive the threatening tones of the German war songs. The excitement increased from day to day. In the court of the castle at Königsberg an insolent French gendarme was killed by Prussian recruits under the very eyes of the king of Naples. Two French officers endeavoured to intervene on this occasion, but their swords were broken and they were chased away by the Prussians. Murat did not venture to demand the punishment of the offenders.

On January 2nd Knesebeck received his instructions for a secret embassy to the court of Vienna. Frederick William declared himself to be prepared to fight France, but not to tolerate Russian dominion in Germany. For this reason Austria should appear as an armed intermediary to demand the independence of Germany as far as the Rhine, and the destruction of the Confederation of the Rhine; and in case of refusal should take up arms against Napoleon. The king thought that he would himself immediately go to Silesia, where he could freely carry out his resolves. Liberated Germany must receive the constitution which had been first agreed upon in Bartenstein. There was to be a Prussian hegemony in the north, an Austrian in the south; an appeal was to be issued to the Italians, and the re-ordering of affairs in the Italian peninsula was to be left to the discretion of the Hofburg. At the same time Scharnhorst, who, since his dismissal, had been living in Silesia, was informed about everything that was in progress. On the same day, the news of the Convention of Tauroggen reached Potsdam. This news was welcome because it showed that York's corps was now out of the French power; but at the same time it threw the chancellor into some embarrassment because York "had staved in the cask too soon." The king resolved that in public he would censure the general's bold step, but would approve it in private.

Almost more important than the news of the Convention itself, seemed the letter of the czar to Paulucci, dated December 18th, which York reported to the king. In Potsdam there had hitherto been no clear understanding of Alexander's intentions, either as to the advance of the Russians or concerning Polish affairs. Now at length the king learnt that his friend was in fact prepared to carry on the war upon German soil, and he therefore immediately added to Knesebeck's instructions, that he was to declare for Russia, if the Russians should cross the Vistula. Next the aide-de-camp, Major Natzmer, was despatched to Murat, to announce the dismissal of the general who had acted on his own initiative, and thence Natzmer was to travel in secret to the czar. Meanwhile Hardenberg lived on the most friendly terms with the French generals and diplomats, inviting them again and again to dinner, fervently asseverating his indignation at York's unprecedented conduct, and evading the issue with courteous words when Count Narbonne announced to him that the Imperator would be pleased if the crown prince of Prussia were to marry one of the Murats or one of the Beauharnais.[1] Krusemark, the Prussian ambassador in Paris, was ordered to make an urgent demand for the repayment of the sums advanced by Prussia for the march of the *grande armée* through the country, and to say that the government had made a very low estimate of the sum in stating it at 94,000,000 francs. To complete the deception, Hardenberg made use of an ancient trick of the old cabinet policy, sending to Paris the most incapable of his diplomats, Prince Hatzfeldt, a declared friend of France, who had not the least conception of the chancellor's plans, to offer an excuse for York's actions, and once more to give a reminder about the repayment of the advance. "This embassy is a mask," were Hardenberg's own words.[2]

So intimate was the Imperator's knowledge of Prussian affairs that the personality of the negotiator could not but lead him to understand that this embassy was intended to fail. He had, however, no eyes for little Prussia, since he was living and working amid schemes for a second Russian campaign. Whilst brilliant fêtes at Fontainebleau were to deceive the world regarding the

---

[1] Hardenberg's *Journal*, January 7, 1813.
[2] Ibid., January 10, 1813.

increasing disaffection of the French people, a new levy of 350,000 men was ordered, and in France a further conscription of 180,000 men. Since the year 1793, more than 3,000,000 Frenchmen had been called to the colours, and the majority of these had perished in war ; and yet the minister Montalivet declared in an enthusiastic parliamentary speech, that conscription had led to an admirable increase in the population. It was the Imperator's plan to start the second war against Russia from Magdeburg in the spring, with the Saxons upon his right wing and the Prussians upon his left. In June, Danzig was to be relieved, and in August the Neiman was once more to be crossed. He had no thought of yielding. Everywhere, so he assured his father-in-law, the Russians had been beaten in the open field ; the czar was not to retain a single village in the Duchy of Warsaw. The constitutional limits of the empire, which included Rome, Amsterdam, and Hamburg amongst its towns, remained fixed for all eternity ! He once more assured his German vassals that he was waging war on behalf of the glories of German particularism ; it was for them to fight, not merely the foreign enemy, but also a more dangerous enemy, that spirit of anarchy which was cherished by the revolutionists Stein and company ; it was the aim of the German revolutionists to dethrone the dynasties of the Confederation of the Rhine and to create a so-called Germany (*créer ce qu'ils appellent une Allemagne*).

It was his intention to make himself secure of Prussia—if not of its faithfulness, at least of its powerlessness. Even in March he wrote contemptuously to Eugene Beauharnais that the Prussians could not possibly provide more than 40,000 men, and of these 25,000 only for the open field. He had at the beginning of the last campaign admired the excellent military bearing of York's corps ; he had been warned a hundred times over by the diplomats of the Confederation of the Rhine ; he knew that the dangerous German revolutionists were nowhere more powerful than in Prussia, and yet he could not bring himself to admit that this detested power could ever threaten him. He made a parade of his contempt for Prussia, as if he hoped thereby to deaden his secret cares, saying, " The Prussians are not a nation, they have no national pride, they are the Gascons of Germany ! " It would have been for him a matter of simple prudence to hold strictly to the treaty of 1812, and not to give the crown of Prussia any excuse for abandoning the enforced alliance. Yet from his solitary height he no longer regarded it as worth while to enquire about the sentiments of those upon whom his feet were trampling. He replied with empty words to all the demands of the Prussian negotiatiors, and they could never secure from him any examination of their accounts. Simultaneously the commanders of the fortresses on the Oder received orders, in conflict with the terms of the treaty, to provide for all their needs by means of requisitions. Thus the Imperator did precisely what Frederick William in his conscientiousness secretly desired. Napoleon put himself in the wrong ; he himself tore up the treaty ; and in accordance with international law the king was unquestionably entitled to disregard a treaty whose clauses had all been contemptuously ignored by the other party.

Hardenberg built high hopes upon the embassy of Knesebeck. Whilst the king in his heart recognised the czar as his nearest friend, the chancellor had for years past been chiefly endeavouring to bring about an alliance between the three " German " great powers—for England, too, was reckoned among the German powers on account of her possession of Hanover. His lofty expectations were to be disappointed. The immediate entrance of the imperial state into a war-alliance was out of the question, if only for the reason that if this should happen, Napoleon would once more take the well-known road of victory along the Danube, and, in view of the miserable condition of the Austrian army and the Austrian finances, would speedily make his third entry into the imperial capital. This was precisely what Emperor Francis wished to hinder at all costs. Count Metternich, pacifist by nature, a friend of gentle methods and petty schemes, considered that the situation of the world was unripe for a great decision. How should a decisive success be obtained—this was how Gentz represented the matter— since all the powers of the Continent were utterly exhausted, and even England's energies might readily be depleted by the payment of subsidies for a European war. In addition, there was the instinctive dread of the national passion of the North German patriots. In Vienna—this will remain a glorious tribute to the sobriety of Austrian statesmanship—in Vienna, from the days of the Great Elector down to the year 1866, there has never for a moment been cherished the good-natured illusion that the strengthening of the North German rival could possibly be in Austria's interest ! Even if there was some desire that Prussia should regain her forces to a certain extent, the last thing that the Hofburg wished was that a power of strength equal to her own should be reconstituted in the north—now least of all when every day fresh news came of the stormy uprising of the North German people, when the Prussian state was a prey to the elemental forces of the revolution, when the king of Prussia seemed to stand merely " by the side of," not at the head of, the nation. In these respects the emperor Francis was in complete understanding with his son-in-law, holding that only revolutionaries could desire the creation of a so-called Germany. He gladly believed all the fables of the Napoleonic police concerning the revolutionary activities of the Prussian secret societies ; in March his ambassador had begged the king of Prussia, it need hardly be said in vain, to dissolve the secret societies. He had indeed little to fear from the German sentiment of his own people ; the noble intoxication of the year 1809 never recurred ; the Germanism of the North-German poets and popular orators aroused only scorn and mockery among the jaded Viennese. Even the most isolated traces of patriotic sentiment were alarming to the despot. He did not forget that a few Austrian officers had also entered the Russian service. The dangerous Prussian conspirator, Justus Gruner, had long been confined in a fortress ; and when, in the spring, Hans von Gagern endeavoured with a few patriots in Vorarlberg and Tyrol to bring about a popular uprising, the emperor immediately initiated arrests and expulsions.

Another leading idea of the Hofburg was the fear of Russia. In later years Metternich admitted to the Prussian chancellor that from the moment when the Napoleonic power began to totter, he had been himself principally occupied by a new care : " the impossibility of preventing an enormous increase in the power of Russia as an inevitable outcome of the destruction of the French colossus."[1] On the other hand, how advantageous was it to have so mighty a son-in-law, a man so well-disposed, who had overthrown the Revolution, and who spoke of the Jacobin Stein with the same detestation as did Metternich ! In addition, personal considerations played a part. Metternich had attained to his position through the French alliance ; should there be a sudden change of system, it was almost inevitable that his opponent, Stadion, would assume the leadership of affairs. In addition, the intentions of the Hofburg for Germany's future were very different from the ideas of the Prussian chancellor. Hardenberg took his dualistic plans very seriously, desiring for Austria a secure foothold on the Upper Rhine, and for Prussia a similar position on the Middle and Lower Rhine, so that a common defence of the future Germanic Federation was to be possible. Unquestionably had the German alliance with Austria, for which that epoch hoped, ever been viable, it could

[1] Metternich to Hardenberg, January 9, 1818.

have been maintained only through a loyal understanding between the two leading states, and through the equitable delimitation of their spheres of influence. It is for this reason that at a later date, the ideas of a peaceful dualism were again and again revived at the court of Berlin, as long as there still remained some hope of the Germanic Federation. During recent years the chancellor had repeatedly expressed these ideas to his Austrian friend, and from a few words of half assent lightly uttered by Metternich, Hardenberg had assumed that the latter was in complete harmony with his own views. Yet Hardenberg and the trusty Hanoverian Ompteda were well aware that the Hofburg was by no means inclined to concede to its rival the hegemony of North Germany.

Metternich recognised that Austria could not reacquire the imperial crown which had been fooled away by a dishonourable policy. All the middle states would have been rendered hostile to Austria by a hereditary emperordom of the House of Lorraine. Since the old and loyal spiritual electors no longer existed, an electoral crown might very easily fall into the hands of the Hohenzollerns. It was necessary therefore, to gain the dominant influence in Germany by a prudent safeguarding of the dynastic interests of the middle states. For this reason Metternich not only renounced Belgium, which from old times had been regarded by the Hofburg as an extremely burdensome possession, but he renounced also the reacquirement of the Hither-Austrian territories. Through these advanced outposts the imperial house had of old continually threatened the South German courts, and had thus frightened them, now into the arms of Prussia, now into those of France. It was Austria's wish henceforward to maintain an honourable peace with her old enemies Bavaria and Würtemberg ; Austria was to be *primus inter pares*, with her possessions well rounded-off along the Adriatic ; above all Austria would secure for Bavaria and Würtemberg the costly gift of sovereignty which they owed to the grace of Napoleon. In his conversations with Knesebeck, Metternich gave certain indications of these political principles ; subsequently he declared himself even more definitely in a despatch to Lebzeltern (March 23rd), saying that for the states of the Confederation of the Rhine, the *status quo*, their sovereignty, and their independence, must be completely preserved.

From all this it necessarily appeared that Metternich was utilising the crisis in order to realise " the great plan of general pacification," as Gentz expressed the matter in a confidential letter to the hospodar Karadja. During the spring, by secret negotiations with Russia, he was able to secure the return home of the Austrian accessory corps which still stood beside the French in Poland, and thus in actual fact to liberate Austria from the French alliance. Austria was now free, occupying a dominant position on the flank of the belligerent powers, and could hope to give a decisive turn to affairs by her intermediation. Whilst Metternich urgently exhorted Paris to peace, to the Prussian negotiator he expressed himself just as warmly in favour of Prussia's adhesion to Russia ; Knesebeck even returned with an autograph letter from the emperor to the king, in which it was expressly declared that if Prussia should go over to the side of the Russians, this would in no way shake the confidence of the Hofburg. The intention was clear: should Russia be strengthened by Prussia's adhesion, the prospects of the new war were comparatively equal, and it would be all the easier for Austria to intervene with proposals of peace.

The cunning calculator overlooked one thing alone, the moral forces, the irreconcilable contrasts, which presided over this struggle. He allowed neither for Napoleon's unmalleable Cæsarian pride, nor for the natural energy of the national hatred which had awakened in Prussia. His exhortations to peace in Paris were uttered in perfect earnest, although to the czar he represented them as a comedy he was playing, nor could anything be more honourable than the assurance which Emperor Francis subsequently gave to the king of Bavaria that : " If France had desired peace, she could have had peace." For a long while Metternich continued to hope that the war could be altogether prevented, and when on February 12th Alexander demanded that in case of need Austria should support by force of arms her proposals for intermediation, the minister returned an evasive answer. Meanwhile the cautious man was prepared also for the undesired issue, should the Franco-Russian war once more break out. In that case, Austria was to save up her well-preserved forces until those engaged in the conduct of the war had been exhausted by a severe and indecisive struggle, and had become receptive for the intermediator's proposals. In this way the imperial house, without any sacrifices perhaps, and in any case without any immediate danger, would once more hold the balance in Europe, would become the peace-bringer and the mediator on the continent ; at the same time the power of the emperor's son-in-law would not be annihilated, but would simply be kept within certain bounds, and the leadership of the alliance of the sovereign German states would spontaneously fall to the House of Austria. Radetzky, the keenest intelligence upon the imperial general staff, issued a military memorial as late as March, in which he showed how Austria must hold a great army prepared in order to overthrow whichever party might reject her proposals. He placed himself above the contestants, devoid of love and hatred, venturing merely to suggest that France seemed the most likely opponent. To sum up, the embassy of Knesebeck had no more than a partial success. The enthusiastic admirer of the imperial magnanimity brought back from the Hofburg nothing more than the assurance that Austria would not take the field against a Prusso-Russian alliance.

The negotiations with Russia were far more successful. On January 13th Major Natzmer met the czar at Bobersk in Lithuania, and in the name of the king offered him an offensive and defensive alliance should Russia cross the Vistula and decide to carry on the war with all her energies. The czar was full of confidence ; the king alone could save Europe or destroy it for ever. He agreed cheerfully to everything that was suggested ; promised to send a force of 10,000 to 15,000 men towards the Oder at once, and estimated the troops that were soon to follow at 100,000 men. Not till January 20th did Natzmer rejoin the chancellor by a circuitous route, since Eugene Beauharnais had become suspicious, and had ordered his soldiers to arrest the aide-de-camp of his royal ally.

Immediately after the negotiator's return, the preparations were begun for the king's journey to Breslau, and orders were at the same time issued that all cadets who were fit for war should go to Silesia. The old commander of the nursery for the officers' corps simply did not know what to do in this time of wild excitement. Throughout the Christmas holidays, his young pupils had been carousing and rejoicing in an uninterrupted festival of victory on account of the news from Russia. Now the older ones among them set out joyfully over the frozen roads for the Silesian mountains ; the younger ones, remaining sadly at home, saved up all their pocket money for the holy war, for no one was in doubt as to who was now to be the enemy. On January 21st the royal house celebrated the confirmation of the crown prince. What glorious expectations, hopes destined to bitter disappointment, were then reposed upon the richly endowed young man of blooming intelligence ! There was not a dry eye in the assembly ; it seemed to all as if the shade of the enlightened queen was moving among her children, when the significant declaration of the heir to the throne was read, saying : " Firmly and quietly do I believe in Him Who advises us to keep our courage high, saying to arrogance:

> "Hitherto shalt thou come, but no further: and here
> shall thy proud waves be stayed."

The red dawn of a better day shows itself in the sky." Two days later the king suddenly departed for Breslau, and, here once more upon free Prussian soil, no longer exposed to a *coup de main* by French troops, he could act somewhat more openly.

The chancellor was once more unfortunate in his financial measures ; an endeavour to force the acceptance at par of the depreciated treasury notes had to be abandoned in a few weeks. The preparations for war went forward more speedily. The king formed a " Committee for the Strengthening of the Army," appointing on this committee Hardenberg, Hacke, the war minister, and Scharnhorst, whose name alone sufficed to tell all intelligent persons that the matter was now one of serious earnest. The talented Hippel, whom the chancellor transferred to the military department, carried out the general's proposals with fiery zeal. The artificer of German freedom at length saw his work bearing fruit ; his energies seemed to be doubled, his whole nature was elevated and illumined by a proud confidence. He was active day and night, now in councils and conversations with the king, now at home at his own writing table. He continually urged, " that we must be prepared to hazard all, that without such a venture no great ends can be attained in this world, and that those who do not trust in fortune, are never favoured by fortune." Boyen, too, who had just returned from Russia with a momentous letter from Alexander, reminded the still hesitating king of a bold change of political front of the Great Elector.[1] Decisive commands followed one another day by day. On February 3rd the king signed an appeal to the young men of the classes exempt from service to enter the army as voluntary yagers. A day or two afterwards Scharnhorst drew up the plans for the Prusso-Russian army. On February 9th there followed the edict which for the duration of this war suspended all exemptions from military duty. A few days later still, the general handed to the faithful Hippel an autograph proposal for the Landwehr law.

Meanwhile Knesebeck was recalled from Vienna ; he returned with empty hands, and the king said sadly : " All reports and news from the interior of the country show that the mood is every-

[1] Scharnhorst to Hardenberg, January 30th ; Boyen's memorial, February, 1813.

where the same ; but it appears that in Vienna they are all asleep.'[1]
This spirit throughout the country urged him forward ; he resolved
to go beyond his earlier plans, and to venture the struggle even
without Austria. Yet it was only human that his hopes should
sometimes flag. Privy councillor Ancillon, who was ever timid,
had in December sent warning as to the revolutionary principles
of many of the patriots ; he feared, above all, Stein's " republican "
sentiments, and now sought to prove in a lengthy memorial that
without the assistance of Austria and of the German states, it would be
very difficult to gain anything beyond the reacquirement of Altmark
and of the Polish provinces. In a weak moment the king accepted
this view. But his faint-heartedness did not last long. Hardenberg
declared himself strongly opposed to Ancillon, and soon drove the
unctuous talker into such a corner that he was forced to excuse
himself, saying that he had wished merely " to speak of the possible
maximum and minimum outcome of the war."[2] Ancillon's
memorial had no permanent influence. Knesebeck was sent to the
Russian headquarters to conclude the war-alliance, receiving his
new instructions on February 8th. On February 13th instructions
were sent to Paris which must necessarily lead to an open breach
with France. The king demanded the immediate payment of half
of his monetary advances, and demanded also a truce on such lines
that the French were to withdraw behind the Elbe and the Russians
behind the Vistula, so that the whole of Prussia, with all its fortresses, was to be garrisoned by Prussian troops alone. Frederick
William declared in advance that the Imperator would never agree
to these proposals.[3] If Napoleon refused, war was inevitable.
At the same time the king subscribed a cabinet order declaring
York's conduct to have been justified.[4]

In this way, quietly and unostentatiously, the throne prepared
for the struggle. As to its ultimate intentions, however, there
existed an unbroken secrecy. Even the committee of the supreme
government, which the king had left in Berlin under the presidency
of Count Goltz, received no information about the diplomatic
negotiations, and had been instructed to remain upon a friendly
footing with Marshal Augereau and the French military authorities.

---

[1] King Frederick William to Hardenberg, February 3, 1813.

[2] Ancillon to Knesebeck, December 27 ; to Hardenberg February 9 ;
memorial, February 4, 1813.

[3] Memorial by the king, January 26, 1813.

[4] Orders of the king to Krusemark, February 13 ; Hardenberg to St. Marsan,
February 15 ; cabinet order to York, February 12, 1813.

Intercourse was necessarily slow and was almost completely interrupted by the movement of the French troops. In the provinces for a long time all that had been known was that the king was no longer free, that he was surrounded by French bayonets. What was to be the issue ? Was it not time that the nation should take action without the crown and yet on behalf of the crown, and by a heroic resolve restore its own liberty and that of the king ? The desperate question was on everyone's lips, and nowhere was the torturing uncertainty felt more bitterly than in loyal Old Prussia. Here was the ancient borderland of the Teutons, where the red walls of the fortresses of the Teutonic knights spoke of the wonders of a great history. Were they to look on idly whilst the Muscovites were hunting the Frenchmen ; and perhaps in the end to see the beautiful province, which during the Seven Years' War had for five years passed under Russian dominion, become united once more and for ever with the empire of the czar ? Everyone felt that something must be done, that the province must use its own energies in order to deserve its freedom. Even in the beginning of January some of the members of the Prussian estates came to General Wittgenstein offering to raise troops which should fight under York's leadership on the side of the Russians.

York himself was in an extremely difficult situation. He had hoped that his desertion of the French would enable the Russians to pursue the enemy without pause, that it would stimulate the king to a rapid resolve, that everywhere throughout the German north it would light up the flames of a people's war. For a few days his troops nursed the most joyful hopes. In Tilsit, the furthest eastern frontier of German territory, Colonel Below promised his Lithuanian dragoons that he would not lay down his sabre until they had seen the towers of Paris. Wittgenstein, however, pursued the French so sluggishly that Macdonald was able to form a junction in Königsberg with the remnants of the *grande armée*, and then to withdraw across the Vistula unmolested. To avoid allowing the movement to be completely arrested, York found it necessary to undertake a second step upon his own initiative, and on January 8th he came to Königsberg and assumed the command of the province. He was received with indescribable rejoicing ; the student Hans von Auerswald gave him a formal assurance that the youth of Prussia were prepared to give their lives for king and fatherland. The feeling was excellent throughout the province, which was prepared for every sacrifice, although it had suffered terribly, and quite recently had lost over 33,000,000 thalers through the passage of the *grande armée*.

But what could be done without the assistance of the throne? This people was monarchical to the very marrow of its bones. Who could issue orders here except in the name of the king? Opinions and proposals were bandied to and fro. Some of the deputies of the estates issued a petition to the king urging him to join the side of Russia, to prevent the destruction of the glorious German name ; others loudly demanded that the diet should assemble on its own authority, and should order the levying of the Landwehr. Many loyal officials were troubled by a fear of the land-hunger of the Russians, who were still enemies, and who therefore in accordance with international law might seize the country. Yet everywhere the Russians behaved with discretion ; the czar's ambition was directed towards Warsaw, and at that time nothing was further from his mind than a cunning attack upon Old Prussia. When the hot-blooded Bärsch wished to have printed in Königsberg an appeal to the people to take up arms, the Russian commander conscientiously refused his endorsement, saying that such appeals as this could be issued only in the name of the prince or of one of his plenipotentiaries. But how long was this gentle attitude of the Russians likely to last unless Prussia declared openly on the side of Russia ?

President Wissmann hastened to Berlin with a few other officials, to beseech the chancellor that for God's sake the king should speak the decisive word, as otherwise a rising or even a Russian conquest might ensue. York wrote to Bülow, endeavouring to persuade him to move with his corps against the Oder and the Elbe : " The army desires war against France. The people desires it, the king desires it, but the king's will is not free. The army must free this will for him. We wish to fight in order to gain our national freedom. To receive independence as a gift means to expose the nation to a contemptuous position in the pillory ! " Meanwhile the man of iron actually grew uncertain when no answer came from the court, and when finally the Berlin newspapers brought the overwhelming intelligence that the Convention of Tauroggen had been rejected by the king and that he himself had been deprived of his command. None the less the general ventured to continue to exercise his powers as commander, since his dismissal had not been officially communicated. But his ignorance of the true intentions of the crown was a keen distress to the strict royalist. He had never thought of setting himself against the king's will ! He went about feeling like a criminal, tortured by gloomy anticipations. He saw his honourable life ending in undeserved shame, and wished at least that he should not have to bear the blame of a new act of disobedience. He therefore contented himself with strengthening his corps by summoning to the colours all who were liable for military service, and no longer thought of levying the population *en masse*. It was a touching spectacle, the uncertainty of this monarchist without a monarch ! Notwithstanding all its self-sacrificingness and lust for activity, the loyal people ran the risk of losing invaluable time, unless will could be found to complete by a bold resolve what thousands were yearning to see achieved.

This powerful will came with the baron von Stein. As early as December 16th the great patriot had announced from St. Petersburg to President Schön that he hoped soon to enter Old Prussia accompanied by Arndt. " Now it is time for Germany to rise, for her to struggle once more for freedom and honour ; for her to show it was not the people but only the princes who voluntarily placed their necks beneath the yoke." To the proud German, nothing could be more horrible than the idea that his fatherland was to be liberated by the Russians. Although he did not himself feel any doubt as to the good intentions of Alexander, he none the less cherished a profound mistrust of the plans of the old-Russian party. Subsequently he earnestly warned the chancellor that he should on no account open any of the Prussian fortresses to the Russians. When he now noted how the people of Old Prussia were tearing themselves to pieces in their impatience, he secured full powers from the czar to take over the leadership of the provincial authorities and to utilise to the best of his powers all the resources of the country. This was to be no more than a temporary measure, until the Prusso-Russian alliance had been formally concluded. It was expressly communicated to the king that these powers, which were necessitated by the urgency of the circumstances, were to be entrusted not to a Russian, but to one of the most faithful of Prussian subjects. On January 21st, Stein came to Königsberg, and the situation immediately underwent a change. All valiant spirits were reinvigorated at the sight of this powerful man. He himself seemed to move in an unknown country, since he encountered everywhere nothing but loyal self-sacrifice and valiancy, not a trace of the old slackness ; and he honourably recognised that in earlier days he had done the North German people an injustice. He gave definite assurance that the purpose of the Russian army was not conquest, but the restoration of the independence of Germany and of Prussia ; but he demanded from his fellow-countrymen that " in view of the greatness of the matter and the purity of the sentiments of those concerned," they should look beyond considerations of form. The country was immediately treated as though it were in fact allied with Russia ; the opening of the harbours and the repeal of the Continental System was ordered ; a loan was secured from the merchants of the seaports ; payment for all deliveries was to be made with Russian paper money.

Simultaneously Stein negotiated with York, Schön, and the provincial authorities regarding the arrangements for arming the people ; Clausewitz, who was in the country with his Russians, received orders to draw up proposals for a Landwehr Law. The diet was summoned—or rather an informal assembly of the deputies of the estates, since the conscientious president Auerswald hesitated to encroach upon the rights of the crown. Schön cautiously refused the presidency. On February 5th began the unpretentious and yet momentous proceedings of the diet of Königsberg, in which the colony of mediæval Germany splendidly repaid its debt to the great fatherland. Briefly and well, in accordance with the ancient Prussian manner, without oratorical arts, and without ostentation, all that was necessary was decided. Count Alexander Dohna was the leader of the nobles ; the good man was now to learn for himself and for his province how wrong he had formerly been when as minister he had denied to his countrymen a capacity for constitutional government. At the head of the bourgeois section was Heidemann, the burgomaster of Königsberg. York appeared in person, and laid before a committee of the estates the Landwehr Law which the favourite pupil of Scharnhorst had drawn up, following the ideas of his master, and in essentials agreeing with the plans of 1811. Thus resulted the remarkable phenomenon that East Prussia, on its own initiative, adopted the same ideas which at this identical time Scharnhorst was laying before the king in Breslau. Not in all respects, indeed, could this well-meaning representative of bourgeois interests attain to the bold proposals of the military organiser. At the desire of the towns, the diet agreed to the right of substitution in military service, whereas in Breslau it was decreed that all exemptions from military service were to be abolished. Again, the East Prussian Landwehr was to be no more than a provincial army, levied exclusively for the immediate defence of the country on the hither side of the Vistula ;

the battalion commanders must be domiciled in the province, and a general commission of the estates assumed the command of the forces as a whole.

Scharnhorst's idea that the army must be the people in arms, a regular school for the nation, had not yet permeated public opinion. In this war, but only in this war, all those capable of bearing arms were to serve, since this was a holy war, for all that is most valued in life. After the victory, however (for such was the natural hope of a generation sickened by endless fighting), the nation was to be rewarded for its sacrifices by a notable reduction in the army. Even Arndt, who had recently, acting under instructions from Stein, issued his fiery essay, *What is the meaning of Landwehr and Landsturm?* was in advance of the general view. In eloquent words he showed how, in a degenerate time, the peasant had become afraid of bearing arms, and how at length he had regained the ancient Teutonic belief " that the entire people must be equipped with arms and practised in the use of arms, unless it be prepared to lose freedom, honour, happiness, goods, and hardihood." Yet at the same time he guarded himself against the view that the Landwehr was to be looked upon as a sort of conscription, saying, " It is instituted for the war only." It would be possible, he considered, that subsequently as much as two-thirds of the standing army might be abolished.

In any case, the sacrifices which were made by the exhausted land were astonishing. This single province, containing one million inhabitants, furnished, in addition to thirteen thousand men of the reserve for York's corps, twenty thousand men for the Landwehr, and an admirable national cavalry regiment of seven hundred volunteers for the officers' corps. On February 8th, as soon as the diet had adopted the Landwehr ordinance, Stein hastened back to the czar. He saw that everything was in good hands, and he did not for a moment wish to give colour to the impression that the Prussian uprising was the work of the Russians.

The ancient Ordensland resounded once more to the clash of arms, as in the old days when the war-cry of the German lords had stimulated the dwellers on the frontier to hunt the heathen. Any man who could wield a sabre hastened to the service ; there was no distinction either of class or age. Alexander Dohna was the first to enter the Landwehr as a ranker. The university was empty ; the upper classes of the gymnasia were closed. What an impression was made when in Königsberg the honoured rector Delbrück, taking leave of his first-form youths who were going to the front, read to them Klopstock's ode *Herman and Thusnelda*. How often did this sentimental race listen with streaming eyes to the moving verses about the ancient warlike renown of the Teutons. Now it appeared vividly before the eyes of all, that the new Germany, grander and more glorious than the dream-picture of the poet, but no less strong and terrible, demanding the highest from its sons, was to drive its car of victory over thousands of young bodies. Yet all this took place only under the express understanding that it was to receive the king's approval. At the close of the deliberations, the estates wrote to the monarch : " We desire only what the beloved father of our country desires ; only under his sublime leadership to avenge the shame of Prussia and of Germany, to conquer or to die fighting for the independence of our dear fatherland." Then they adjured him once again to allow the enthusiasm of his faithful people its free course : " It is impossible that the destruction of the Prussian state can be a part of the great Providential plan. This state is necessary to the world and to true enlightenment." It was with these messages from Old Prussia that Count Ludwig Dohna entered Breslau on February 21st.

Here news of Knesebeck, who was treating in Kalisz with Alexander concerning the matter of the war alliance, was being awaited with tense expectation. The king had written to inform the czar about the Viennese negotiations, and had honourably explained that he hoped to put Napoleon altogether in the wrong : " Thus I shall be able to act consistently and in accordance with my character."[1] The aim of Prussia was naturally to reacquire its old position, and further, to do away with the Confederation of the Rhine and to liberate Germany as far as the Rhine. But now the unhappy Polish problem, which had so often proved a difficulty in negotiations between the three eastern powers, became a source of contention between the friends. The czar was prepared to agree to everything except that he did not wish to discuss the destiny of the duchy of Warsaw before the victorious end of the war. He suggested that his ally might find ample compensation for his Polish possessions in the North German states of the Confederation of the Rhine and, above all, in Saxony, if the king of Saxony should remain faithful to the French alliance.[2]

For some time past Alexander had been again in secret intercourse with Czartoryski. Hardly had the Napoleonic dreams of

---

[1] King Frederick William to Czar Alexander, February 8 and 17, 1813.
[2] Knesebeck's report, February 18, 1813.

the adroit Pole been consumed in the flames of Moscow, when he turned once more to his imperial friend with that happy nonchalance which had become second nature to the heroes of Sarmatian freedom in the course of their Jesuit training. At length he came to an agreement with the czar as to the establishment of an independent constitutional Polish kingdom under the sceptre of the autocrat of all the Russias. For a time the czar hoped that upon his appeal the Poles would voluntarily adhere to his side. But not a hand was raised in the country. In the overwhelming changes of fortune of recent years, the mass of the people had lost all will and all hope. The German immigrants, the Jews, and those among the Poles who were quietly engaged in industrial occupations, looked back with regret to the order and legal security of the Prussian rule. The great majority of the nobility remained in the French camp, as did their duke, the king of Saxony. No one trusted Russia, the hereditary enemy, and it was soon learned that a great conspiracy was on foot against the Muscovites. The consequence was that, after a brief fight with the southern army of Napoleon, the duchy of Warsaw fell into the hands of Alexander as conquered territory.

The Russians immediately regarded their booty as a newly won province. No one among them would have considered it possible that the conquered should henceforward enjoy greater freedom than the conqueror. Resistance, however, served only to strengthen the political enthusiast in his dreams. The czar had never paid much attention to the sentiments of his Russian subjects ; his chosen associates were talented foreigners. Nor was he troubled about the mistrust of the Poles, for he considered that the overwhelming good fortune which he proposed to bring them must overthrow their obstinacy, even if he wished to separate from Russia the Lithuanian province which had so long been united with that empire, and to overthrow the constitutional crown of the white eagle. It seemed to him that the might of his empire was now boundless. "I am well aware," he said later in his own justification, "that Russia's excess of power appears to be dangerous to Europe : in order to allay this danger I propose to make Poland an independent state." For the moment, however, these brilliant plans must be kept secret from all the world. His Polish friend must not appear at the imperial headquarters, for, so the czar wrote, "the news of our plans would at once drive Austria and Prussia into the arms of France."

Several months later, when the two monarchs had for

many weeks been together in camp, Frederick William complained that despite repeated questions he had never been able to obtain from Alexander any definite information about his political intentions. Ompteda, a keen observer and one well acquainted with courts, wrote, as late as the end of June, that Prince Anton Radziwill and the other Polish patriots who surrounded the czar would certainly have a bad reception. The secret was well kept. The Prussian court had no prior knowledge at all of the threatened re-establishment of Poland. From the news which was received as to the course of the negotiations at Kalisz, Prussia could only infer that the czar desired to incorporate a portion of the duchy of Warsaw with the Russian empire. The question at issue seemed to be whether war against Napoleon could be ventured in view of the danger that when peace was made Russia would have advanced further towards the west, and a badly secured eastern German frontier would have to be accepted.

To the plain understanding of the king, this problem had long ceased to be a problem. He was well acquainted with Polish faith, and was accustomed to say angrily, " Many thanks ; I have had enough of it already." At the moment when the Germans were issuing an appeal for the liberation of the fatherland, rational Prussian statesmanship could not honourably demand a complete restoration of the undesirable Slav possessions. Every acre of North German land which was exchanged for Warsaw, Pultusk, and Plotsk, would be an obvious gain for the national policy which had at length been resumed. The only part of Poland that was indispensable was the strip of land containing Posen and Gnesen, the only link of connection between Silesia and West Prussia. But if Warsaw were renounced, the question how far eastward the Prussian domain was to extend became of trifling importance, since westward from Warsaw, neither the Prosna nor the line of the Warthe offered a strong natural frontier. An eastern frontier which would at once secure the Prussian state from a military point of view, and preserve it from too strong an admixture of foreign nationality, was simply impossible of attainment. It was necessary that courage should be found to admit this unpleasant truth, and if the central lands of the Vistula were to fall into Russia's hands, military considerations must be sacrificed to those of national policy. It was unquestionable that the Russian state would be a less troublesome neighbour for Prussia than had of old been the Polish Republic. Russia was not, like Poland, hostile to the Prussian people in virtue of an ancient tradition of hate, was not like Poland forced by a demand for self-preservation to aim at the conquest of Old Prussia. The extensive empire which already possessed so many other harbours could, in case of need, dispense with the possession of the mouths of the Vistula, just as Germany could get along without the delta of the Rhine, and Austria without the mouths of the Danube. If Warsaw and Masovia should come under Russian rule, it could be foreseen that the commercial interests of Old Prussia, as well as those of Russian Poland, would be seriously affected ; and yet the new territorial distribution might be permanent, for a tolerable and neighbourly relationship between Russia and Prussia was not impossible. All the defects of the eastern frontier would be liberally compensated, if the Prussian area were to be well rounded-off by new acquisitions of territory upon German soil.

Hardenberg in fact recognised that some sort of concession to Russian wishes was unavoidable, and he instructed his negotiator in case of need to sacrifice to the czar the former territory of New East Prussia. Colonel Knesebeck thought otherwise, and arbitrarily disregarded his instructions. The learned and much experienced officer had once joyfully greeted the ideals of the Revolution, and even in his later years had not become so re-actionary as was commonly asserted ; nor had he ever freed himself completely from the fundamental ideas of the old diplomatic and military school. After the manner of the eighteenth century, it seemed to him that every neighbouring power must be a natural enemy. Just as in the field he continually studied the map and expected decisive results in war from the possession of dominant plateaus and spurs, so also in the study he carried ever in his mind a picture of the European balance of power, designing in accordance with this idea, and with doctrinaire self-confidence, a new map of Europe. Subsequently he formulated three leading ideas for the new distribution of territory, as follows : The west must lose its predominance, the centre must once again become the centre of gravity, and the east must not be allowed to follow the errors of the west.[1] For this reason he considered that the Prussian state must reacquire the frontiers of 1805, as otherwise Prussia would be outflanked by Russia and would become dependent upon the east : " The qualities and alliances of individuals may temporarily modify such circumstances, but cannot abolish them." Knesebeck returned obstinately to these favourite ideas. Like almost all his contemporaries, he overestimated the aggressive

[1] Knesebeck's memorial to Hardenberg, Freiburg, January 7, 1814.

powers of the "Russian colossus." With enthusiastic delight he valued "the writing of nature, which with a maternal hand cares for the protection of her children," for he considered that the morasses of the Narew were designed by nature as the frontier of the Prussian state. In addition, Colonel Knesebeck harboured a profound mistrust of Alexander. Just as hopefully as he had gone to his beloved Hofburg, no less suspiciously did he encounter the czar, and he considered it his duty to avoid the diplomatic blunder of the year 1806. Not a second time should Prussia conclude a Russian alliance without having imposed binding conditions upon her ally. The negotiations between the czar and the hypochondriacal, painfully considerate, immeasurably vain man, came to a standstill. Vainly did Hardenberg exhort Knesebeck to haste.[1] Whilst the yager volunteers were streaming to the colours, all the East Prussian Landwehr was assembling, and it seemed as if the work of the liberation of Germany was once more to come to naught in its very inception—because Knesebeck had discovered the handwriting of mother-nature along the Bug and the Narew.

The situation was all the more serious because in the Russian headquarters hardly anyone besides the czar seriously desired the German war. The Russian generals, above all the narrow-minded old Kutusoff, were a prey to immeasurable self-satisfaction. The wonderful successes, which were for the most part due to the errors of Napoleon, were attributed by them to the superiority of the Russian arms, and they regarded the war as completely finished. It seemed to them that there was no danger whatever of a new attack on the part of the profoundly humiliated French. Warsaw, and perhaps Old Prussia as well, would fall of themselves into the hands of the Russian conquerors. Unless the Prussian court went some way to meet the czar, the alliance could not come into existence, and Germany's hopes would once more fall to the ground.

At length Alexander lost patience, and sent the Alsatian, von Anstett, one of the most alert of his diplomats, to Breslau, to treat with the king directly. Anstett was accompanied by Stein. The czar counted upon the right feeling of his friend, nor were his hopes to be frustrated. Hardenberg, also, regarded it as folly to dispute with too much particularity about the skin of the bear which had not yet been killed. The generals at length came to a speedy determination. Scharnhorst said in his grand manner to Hippel: "Our task is to secure victory, and a peace congress will decide about the division of the spoil." The king adopted Alexander's

[1] Hardenberg to Knesebeck, February 20 and 21, 1813.

proposals without any alteration; Scharnhorst went to Kalisz with a favourable report, and on February 28th the treaty of alliance was signed. The czar pledged himself not to lay down his arms until Prussia had reacquired the power she had possessed before the war of 1806; he guaranteed to his ally the possession of Old Prussia as well as of the strip of Polish territory which constituted the link between Silesia and West Prussia; finally, he promised that the conquests which were to be expected in North Germany should, with the exception of the possessions of the House of Hanover, be applied to the indemnification of Prussia, to the constitution of a well-rounded and coherent Prussian state. In an affectionate letter, Alexander sent thanks to his friend, saying that in this frank and speedy understanding he had learned the heart of the king.

The Treaty of Kalisz was thoroughly justified by the situation; Russian help could not be obtained at a lower price. Just as Cavour did what was indispensable when he surrendered Savoy and Nice for the liberation of North Italy, so, and with far better reason, in a similar situation, did King Frederick William sacrifice for the liberation of Germany a portion of his Polish claims, which he himself regarded as a burden for Prussia. He thus acquired that western portion of Poland which was indispensable to his state, and a firm assurance of complete indemnification on German soil—a promise which was kept by the czar in knightly fashion. It was greatly to Prussia's disadvantage that the treaty did not definitely specify either the future eastern frontier of Prussia or the North German territories which were to be given in compensation; but this defect was unavoidable, for who at that hour could foresee what countries would be acquired by the good swords of the allies? In order that Prussia might not be put off with empty hopes, the two allies subsequently agreed by word of mouth to what was actually carried out, namely, that all the former Prussian domains in Germany which were reconquered should at once pass under Prussian administration.

The Alliance of Kalisz led to a firm community of interests between the two courts. The further westward the armies of the allies might advance and the greater the extent of German territory which should thus be liberated for the compensation of Prussia, the more definitely would Russia be forced to increase her Polish demands; nothing else could be expected in view of the tradition of Russian policy, nor could it be blamed after a victorious campaign in which the flags of Russia were to pass from Moscow to the

Rhine. It was not merely by the eloquent exhortations of Stein (whose influence upon Alexander's emotional nature was indeed very high), nor was it simply the lofty dreams of world-liberation, but above all it was his Polish plans, which determined the czar to conduct the German war with vigour. He was fighting on the Rhine for his Polish conquest, and it was in pursuit of his own interests that he became a true ally of the German patriots. The only weak spot in the Treaty of Kalisz was constituted by those plans for the re-establishment of Poland which the czar obstinately concealed from his Prussian friend. Not only was Alexander's secretiveness hateful when compared with the magnanimous frankness of Frederick William ; it soon displayed itself as a political error, for when the secret at length came to light confidence between the two powers was destroyed, and for a time the Prusso-Russian alliance was in danger of dissolution.

After no less than before the treaty, the situation of Prussia remained extremely insecure. The czar hastened to take complete possession of the duchy of Warsaw. Prussian engineers and Prussian artillery co-operated in the siege of Thorn and Modlin. This Polish campaign of sieges weakened the Prussian forces available for field operations, and, as the Prussian officers angrily observed, contributed notably to the failure of the spring campaign in Saxony. Thus Prussia made severe sacrifices on behalf of the conquest of Poland, and then placidly looked on while the provisional government instituted by the czar administered the whole duchy. The Russians had their booty secure ; Prussia could merely hope for the future. Nothing was said as yet concerning Germany's future constitution. Whilst outwardly Alexander appeared to agree with Stein regarding the formation of two German great powers,[1] he already knew that neither Austria, nor England, nor Sweden, was in agreement with such dualistic plans. Moreover, the provisions of the treaty regarding the military forces to be supplied by the allies respectively were extremely disadvantageous to the Prussian state. In February the government could not fail to see that enormous forces would be furnished through the incomparable self-sacrifice of the nation. Prussia had magnanimously determined to do all that was possible, but would not promise more than was certainly within her power. Czar Alexander, on the other hand, estimated his available forces at almost fourfold their momentary strength, partly because he wished to appear as the leading power of the coalition, and partly because in the intoxication

---

[1] Stein to Hardenberg, April 13, 1813.

of his Cæsarian pride, he really deceived himself. With Alexander it was impossible really to know where self-deception ceased and deliberate deception of others began. Friend and foe alike still believed in his exaggerations. In the beginning of February, in a conversation with Knesebeck, Metternich reckoned that Prussia would be able to reinforce the 150,000 Russians by 50,000 or 60,000 men. The Treaty of Kalisz imposed upon Russia the duty of putting into the field 150,000 men, while Prussia was to send 80,000 men. But for a long time the actual forces engaged exhibited, as between the allies, a ratio the reverse of this. From the first Prussia supplied far more than the treaty demanded, whilst it was not until the autumn that Russia's army attained the promised strength. When the terms of the treaty were drawn up, Hardenberg attached little importance to the figures, but in the subsequent treaties with England, they formed the measure for the subsidies. Hence for the Prussian finances, which were apart from this in a very depressed condition, the matter proved extremely harmful, and, further, an impression was created in the diplomatic world that Prussia was merely an accessory to Russia.

A number of trifling circumstances contributed to produce this unfortunate impression. At the head of the Russian army there was an excess of generals, glittering with orders ; impoverished Prussia had its brigades led by colonels, its regiments by majors. The consequence was that whenever the allies were engaged in joint operations the supreme command was almost always in Russian hands. Again, the shy reserve of the king, who so gladly retired into the background, was contrasted with the brilliant appearance of the czar ; and even Frederick William's noble soldier-like simplicity, was extremely disadvantageous to Prussia in the diplomatic field. What bathos it seemed when the king's light carriage drove by, with but few attendants, and shortly afterwards there passed the colossal equipage of the czar, or there came the thousands of mules carrying the baggage of Emperor Francis, together with the imperial and royal string quartette of the guards ! The state in whose army was really incorporated the moral energy of the great war, seemed to the eyes of diplomacy no more than a power of the second rank when compared with the two imperial courts, and in the complicated relationships of a coalition war the appearance of power is almost as valuable as power itself.

It was time that vacillation should come to an end. Whilst Knesebeck was hesitating in Kalisz, the Prussian generals who were

hemmed in between the two belligerent powers passed from one
false situation to another. The Russians pressed westward very
slowly indeed, for the insufficiency of their military forces became
more apparent day by day. It was not until the beginning of
February that the first Cossacks appeared in the New Mark. Everywhere the people received the semi-savage allies with open arms.
What delight was felt when the Bashkir allowed his bow and arrows
to be handled, when the bearded Cossack, his cloak decorated with
crosses of the Legion of Honour and the rags of French uniforms,
displayed his horsemanship. Happy was every German boy whom
the good-natured child-lover would allow to sit upon his horse.
All the world was singing the new song, " Lovely Minka, I must
leave thee," which a sentimental son of the steppes was said to
have written by the waters of the Don. Careful mothers, indeed,
thought it necessary to give their children a bath after they had
been kissed by these foreigners ; and when people became somewhat better acquainted with the thievish tendencies of these
grown-up children, enthusiasm cooled.

It was with great anxiety that York watched the advance of
the Russians. He felt that it would never do to leave the liberation of the Marks entirely to foreigners, and moved with his corps
to cross the Vistula. General Bülow was troubled with similar
doubts. For several weeks he had cleverly steered a middle course
between the demands of the Russians and those of the French,
and though the belligerents were on either hand he had strengthened
his reserve corps and had remained completely independent.
Urgently had he implored the king to speak the word of liberation
for which all were yearning : " Voluntarily all will make the greatest
sacrifices, and springs will again flow which have long been thought
dry ! " When a definite answer still failed to arrive, he at length
determined to act on his own initiative, and in concert with York
and Wittgenstein (February 22nd) resolved upon a united advance
towards the Oder. General Borstell, a strict man of the old school,
a declared enemy of Scharnhorst's reforms, began at length to see
that blind obedience was no longer sufficient in such a situation.
He, too, implored the king to give the word, wrote to England for
money and arms, and ultimately, on February 27th, announced to
the monarch that he was going to advance with his Pomeranians
into the New Mark, in order, in conjunction with York and Bülow,
to advance upon the capital. During these days also, Gneisenau
returned from England, making a joyful entry into Kolberg, which
was the cradle of his renown, firmly resolved to lead his troops

against the enemy without delay. Never before had the discipline of the army been put to a severer test. All felt enormously relieved when York received from Breslau orders to join Wittgenstein, and when, soon afterwards, he was publicly acquitted from blame. On March 2nd Wittgenstein crossed the Oder, and the Prussians followed on the 10th. The war alliance became effective.

What a chaos meanwhile prevailed in the capital! Goltz was still there with his unhappy governmental committee, still without any knowledge of the plans of the chancellor, unceasingly occupied in issuing strict prohibitions against tumultuous assemblies in the wildly excited town. The timid man, whose desire it was to be nothing more than " a simple agent of the royal will," hardly knew what to do when the appeal to the yager volunteers was issued. A few inquisitive people enquired " For and against whom ? " The great majority at once recognised the king's intentions, and volunteers pressed forward in crowds ; the municipal authorities made collections on behalf of those soldiers who were without means ; thousands of young men walked beside the last troops of the line which left Berlin for Silesia, singing warlike songs. On February 20th a small troop of Cossacks made a raid through the eastern gate. Several Germans had joined them ; one of these, young Alexander von Blomberg, fell as the first victim of the German war. It was difficult to hold back the masses from a premature outbreak of street fighting. Goltz was in open conflict with Prince Henry and the patriotic circle which surrounded the sick prince ; he even allowed himself to be persuaded by Augereau temporarily to forbid the departure of the volunteers. For this he received a sharp reprimand from the king. It was not until the war alliance had been actually concluded that the perplexed man was at length informed by Hardenberg as to the situation, although still in profound secrecy.[1] Napoleon at length began to be seriously alarmed when he heard of the constitution of the detachment of yagers. He at once ordered his stepson, who was commander-in-chief in the north-east, to tolerate no further levies in Prussia ; the position in the Marks was to be maintained with all the force at his disposal ; and in case of need Berlin was to be burned. Eugene Beauharnais was in fact still strong enough to make head against the forces of Wittgenstein and the three united Prussian generals. But the ground was burning under the feet of the soldiers, they were terrified at the suppressed intensity of this furious popular

---

[1] Goltz's reports, January 31, February 11, 17, 19, and 25 ; cabinet order to Goltz, February 23 ; Hardenberg to Goltz, February 28, 1813.

movement ; they considered that in Berlin the armed Prussians would soon outnumber the French. On May 4th the enemy evacuated the capital, and the pursuing Russians forced a skirmish at the very gates of the town. On the 11th, Wittgenstein made his entry, and on the 17th the man of Tauroggen rode along the Linden, glancing severely and gloomily over the heads of the shouting masses. On the same day, Lieutenant Bärsch and his Cossacks took possession of the quay of Hamburg ; almost immediately afterwards the valiant hussar Tettenborn, who had meanwhile persuaded the prince of Mecklenburg to join the coalition, occupied the old Hansa town with his light troops, and the people, intoxicated with delight, tore down the accursed French vultures from the walls. For a few weeks the Germans enjoyed the happy illusion that without a single blow the country had been freed as far as the Elbe.

The chancellor continued to meet the French ambassador with friendly words ; the longer an open breach could be postponed, the more securely could the equipment of the armies of the line be completed. St. Marsan had followed the removal of the court to Breslau, and after a few protests had even allowed himself to be pacified regarding the appeal of February 3rd, for Hardenberg proved to him that the state, being utterly impoverished, could not continue to exist without the voluntary sacrifice of its citizens. Even on the 27th he paid a friendly visit to the chancellor. This is no doubt the " extraordinary visit " of which Anstett speaks.[1] He saw how from all quarters the troops and volunteers were pouring into the Silesian capital ; how the king, in order to provide " an emblem for the general manifestation of loyal love for the fatherland," had ordered the wearing of the national cockade ; and how on the birthday of Louise he carried out his old plan of the foundation of the order of the iron cross. The well-meaning St. Marsan could not believe that little Prussia would venture upon the unequal struggle, and did not really grasp the situation until the entry of the czar into Breslau (March 15th) made all further deception impossible. Even when he took his departure, he implored the chancellor not to lead to destruction this prince and this country to which he had become so greatly attached ; all these boys and youths could not protect the king against the power of his emperor. On March 16th Hardenberg officially announced to him that Prussia was in alliance with Russia. War was declared.

[1] St. Marsan to Hardenberg, February 27, 1813.

2 K

On the following day Frederick William signed the Landwehr Law and the *Appeal to my People*. This was the return to truth and to open dealing, as Schleiermacher joyfully declared in a sermon. The people breathed once more, since now all doubt was over and the undue trial of their patience and their obedience was at an end. Never before had an absolute monarch spoken thus to his people. A breath of freedom, such as that which of old had animated the Æschylean war-songs of the Hellenes, breathes through the straightforward and impressive words which the talented Hipple had written in a good hour. With cordial confidence the king appealed to his Brandenburgers, Prussians, Silesians, Pomeranians, and Lithuanians, speaking to each separately by their ancient tribal name and summoning them to the holy war : " There is no other way, and we must either secure an honourable peace or go down gloriously to destruction. This latter even you will go confidently to meet, for the Prussians and the Germans cannot live without honour ! " Now did the people arise, the Prussians great in arms, the people of the fights with the Slavs, of the battles with the Swedes, the fighters of the Seven Years' War, and there happened what had happened in the case of that hero of the Teutonic saga whose wrath flamed up so highly at the sight of his fetters that the chains were molten. There was no doubt or hesitation, no deliberation concerning the overpowering strength of the enemy. All thought like Fichte : " It is not for us to conquer or to die, but simply to conquer ! " Scharnhorst wrote : " However often Napoleon may win battles, the whole situation of the war is such that in this campaign we cannot fail to conquer." The appeal of February 3rd had already produced results which no one except Scharnhorst had regarded as possible. It was the proudest moment of his life when in Breslau he led the king to the window and showed him the rejoicing crowds of volunteers, how in picturesque medley, on foot, on horseback, in carriages, an endless train, they pressed onwards towards the ancient gabled houses of the Ring. Tears stood in the king's eyes. Faithfully and conscientiously had he discharged his difficult duty in this long time of trouble, and often had his judgment been a sounder one than that of the war party ; what he had lacked was a belief in the sacrificing powers of his Prussians, but this he was now to recover.

Since May 17th the general masses of the population had also been entering the army. The competitive zeal of the various estates rendered possible the greatest yield of soldiers ever known in the history of civilised nations. The impoverished little country increased the 46,000 men of the old army of the line by 95,000 recruits, furnishing in addition more than 10,000 voluntary yagers and 120,000 men of the Landwehr, comprising 271,000 men in all. This was one soldier for every seventeen inhabitants, incomparably more than France had formerly produced under the pressure of the Reign of Terror. All was done in a single summer, to say nothing of the strong reinforcements which were subsequently sent to the army. It need hardly be said that the retired officers at once pressed forward in order to restore the honour of the old flag. As soon as General Oppen, at his home in the Mark, heard of the approach of the army of the fatherland, he took down his old sabre from the wall and, like a knight of the old days of the Wendish wars, rode in hot haste with a single squire to join Bülow, his ancient companion-in-arms. Bülow smilingly presented to his officers the Herculean man with the flashing eyes, saying, " This is one who understands how to cut the enemy down," and gave him command of the cavalry. Oppen, once he was at work again, remained happily engaged, never wearying of war, until the entry into Paris. Next to the old soldiers, it was the educated youth who grasped most vividly the seriousness of the time. There glowed in them an enthusiastic yearning for the free and only German fatherland. Not a single student who could wield a weapon remained at home. Professor Steffens left his professorial chair, after an enthusiastic recommendation to his audience to present themselves on the recruiting ground of the yager volunteers. The king also summoned the lost provinces to the colours, saying, " You are no longer bound by an enforced oath from the day when I summon my loyal people to take up arms." Although a mass uprising was as yet out of the question in those unhappy territories, the East Frisians and the Markers at the University of Göttingen hastened to the Prussian regiments ; so also did all the students from loyal Halle, which had not forgotten under Westphalian rule its memories of the Old Dessauer and of the good Prussian days. The same spirit animated the schools. From the gymnasia of Berlin alone 370 lads went to the war. Many a young fellow who was physically a weakling, wandered sadly from one regiment to another, rejected again and again, and happy was he who at length secured acceptance from an indulgent commander. The officials reported themselves for military service in such numbers that the king ultimately found it necessary to issue a proclamation to the provincial governments to insure the retention of enough men to carry on the work. In Pomerania, during the summer, the royal authorities had almost completely disappeared, and every circle and every village ruled itself, for good or for evil.

The common people, too, had, amid need and suffering, rediscovered their love for the fatherland. Their souls were stirred by the great passions of public life, stormily moved as never before since the days of the wars of religion. The peasant left his farm, the manual worker left his workshop, making up their minds in a moment as if it were a matter of course ; the time had come, and what must be, must be. The king, too, with all the princes, had gone into camp. In a thousand moving traits the loyalty of the common people was displayed. Poor miners in Silesia worked for weeks without receiving pay, in order that their wages might equip a few comrades for the army. A Pomeranian shepherd sold his little flock, his only possession, and then went, well-armed, to join his regiment. It was with admiration that the older generation contemplated all such manifestations to which the universal liability to military service has long accustomed us of a later day. Hundreds of betrothed couples went before the altar to unite their lives a moment before the young husband passed away to battle and death. It was only the Poles in West Prussia and Upper Silesia who did not share the devotion of the Germans ; and in a few towns which had hitherto been free from liability to military service the new laws encountered resistance. The German and Lithuanian country people of the old provinces on the other hand, had been accustomed to military service since the strict days of Frederick William I. At the same time, public collections were held everywhere, such as had hitherto been customary only for benevolent ends : this poor quarter of the German nation offered, together with the flower of its young men, also the last poor remnants of its property, for the re-establishment of the fatherland. Of actual cash there was very little available, but what still remained of old ornaments and plate was freely given. In many regions of the old provinces it was regarded as a disgrace, after the war, if any household still possessed silver plate. The common people brought their wedding rings to the mint, receiving iron rings in exchange, with the inscription : " Gold gave I for iron " ; many a poor girl sold her hair in order to get money for the war.

A marvellous and thoughtful silence brooded over the people, which was moved to its profoundest depths. This epoch knew nothing of the noise of the press and of the clubs ; but even in private circles boastful speech was rarely heard. In the days of their quiet domestic life, the Germans were inclined to use exaggerated expressions about trifling circumstances ; now life itself became rich and earnest, and everyone recognised the greatness of action, the poverty of speech. Everyone felt, as Niebuhr expressed it, " the delight of sharing one feeling with the whole nation, the man of learning together with the common man," and of becoming " loving, friendly, and strong in unison." Speaking to the very heart of his people, the pious sense of Frederick William had given to the Landwehr the motto, " With God for king and fatherland," and had ordered that the newly levied soldiers should immediately after enrolment attend a religious service. In every church through-out the country, a memorial tablet was to record the names of the sons of the commune who had fallen on the field of glory. Heavily had the hand of the living God pressed upon those who were proud of their culture. With humble resignation the new generation once more raised its eyes in firm confidence to " the old German God," exclaiming with the poet :

> " Who falls, he well can bear it,
> Exchanging earth for heaven."

When the first volunteers reached Breslau, they were still singing the *Reiterlied der Wallensteiner*. Soon, however, the army composed its own songs. Irresistibly, as once of old in the case of the pious lansquenets, did the source of songs flow from the new men at arms. On the march out they sang : " The Prussians have sounded the alarm ! " there followed a whole series of artless popular airs dealing with every experience of the prolonged war, until at length there came the cheerful tattoo, " The Prussians have taken Paris ! " Here we have once more a testimony to the warlike, and yet at the same time profoundly peaceful, mood of this people in arms

Soon there was great activity upon the heights of the German Parnassus. It was only the old Goethe who could take no pleasure in the new time ; depressed and hopeless was he, as he turned away from the stir of war, saying : " Shake your chains if you will ; the man is too strong for you ! " But everyone else in the north who had poetic fire in his veins rejoiced at the " outbreak of his fatherland," as Fichte said. Everything that politically mature nations express in newspapers, in conversation, and in publicist correspondence, immediately found poetical form in this generation to whom poetry was still the crown of life. Thus there came into existence the most beautiful political poetry on which any race can pride itself. We of a later age would sin deeply were we to contemplate this inheritance of a heroic time simply from the æsthetic outlook. The poets of the War of Liberation did not attain to Kleist's splendid richness of portraiture ; but all who saw in poetry the manifestation of the nation's heart, turned away with a breath of relief from the elemental strains of hatred to the clear and fresh songs which expressed the joys of open battle. What a blessing it was for our people that its oppressed heart could once more freely rejoice, that after a long and dull period of endurance, the oaths of freemen could rise once more to heaven :

> " Lift up your heart in joyful cry,
> To Heaven raise your hand,
> Swearing each man to God on high
> This slavery shall end."

Joyful as the sounds of the bugle were the tones of Fouqué's verses : " Up, up, to the joyful hunt ! " In Arndt's song : " What are the trumpets blowing ? Hussars to the front ! " was resounded the crashing " March ! March ! " of the German riders No one more happily expressed the sense and tone of the enthusiastic youth of those days than Theodor Körner, the knightly young man of the *Lyre and Sword*. Now it first became apparent what was the significance to the Germans of Schiller's muse. Its lofty moral emotion was displayed in patriotic passion ; its moving rhetoric became the natural prototype for the young poetry of this war. Körner, the son of Schiller's most intimate friend appeared to the younger generation to be the heir of the great poet. They saw how he went forth to battle with Lützow's Black Rifles, confident of victory, animated through and through by the German spirit of freedom, altogether careless of the petty troubles of life ; they saw how at every halt and in every bivouac he sang his ardent songs of the glories of war ; and how at length, with the *Sword-Song* still upon his lips, he displayed in a glorious death the sacred earnestness of what he had written a few hours before. In word and in deed he was a true representative of that warm-hearted manliness which is characteristic of the talented Saxons, when they have succeeded in breaking loose from the tame sobriety of their home life.

> " Arise, arise, the beacons flame !
> Clear from the north shines freedom's light ! "

Such were the words with which Körner himself described the origin and character of the great movement. It remained limited to the German north. Lützow's troop was expressly intended for non-Prussians; it was to incorporate the idea of the unity of Germany. Many a young man from the petty states entered his name at the "Sceptre" at Breslau, where the Lützowers had fixed their recruiting ground; two South German poets, Rückert and Uhland, joined in the loud chorus of patriotic poetry. But the masses of the people outside Prussia had little sense of the heroic fury of this war. Stein's hopes for a unanimous uprising of the whole nation were disappointed. It was only in those provinces which had already belonged to Prussia, and in a few regions of the north-west which had been directly under the rule of the Napoleonides, that the people voluntarily rose in arms as soon as the victorious columns of the liberators drew near. Everywhere else the people quietly awaited the commands of their territorial sovereigns and the logic of completed facts. The dukes of Mecklenburg and Anhalt joined their Prussian neighbours, with whom they were on old terms of friendship. A battalion from Weimar allowed itself to be taken prisoner by the Prussians immediately after the outbreak of the war, in order subsequently, like the valiant hussars of Strelitz, to join York's corps. The other members of the Confederation of the Rhine followed the orders of the Protector, most of them still animated by the ardent zeal of the Napoleonic army. In its first and more difficult half, the German War of Liberation was a war of Prussia against the three-fourths of the German nation that were ruled by France.

Just as had formerly happened in the beginning of the modern German state-building, so now did the re-establishment of the national independence proceed from the north alone. The new political and moral ideals of the awakened youth bore the stamp of North German culture. The old German God, to whom they prayed, was the God of the Protestants; all their activities and all their thoughts were based, consciously or unconsciously, upon the moral ground of the strict Kantian doctrine of duty. It was of momentous importance for many decades of German history that it was only the North German stocks that played any serious part in the finest happenings of this new Germany, whereas it was not until two generations later that the south had the happiness of taking part in the struggles and the victories of the great fatherland.

Soon became manifest the prophectic truth of the hard words of Fichte: " In war also does a people become a people; but those who do not co-operate in this war cannot by any decree be incorporated among the German nation." The new Prussia, its state and its army, had constructed itself in conscious opposition to all foreign characteristics; the states of the south owed to French dominion their existence, their institutions, their military memories. For this reason, in the north, the love of fatherland was a strong and secure national feeling; whereas in the south, French ideas long remained predominant, and the name of Germany was no more than an empty word. The peasants of the Electoral Mark and the weavers of Silesia struck shrewd blows, but only for wife and child and for their tribal king; Blucher, York, and Bülow, on the other hand, whom these men honoured as Prussian heroes, were in reality the heroes of the new Germany. The South German countryman knew nothing of them. Yet something of the German-patriotic ideas which filled the minds of the armed youth of the cultured classes gradually came to permeate the lower strata of the Prussian people. During this war, there occurred a notable increase in that democratic tendency which had been manifest in the Prussian state since the firm establishment of absolute monarchy. Just as in former days a common delight in the works of German poetry had done something to bridge the difference between the classes, so now did all classes find themselves at one in the incomparably more effective community of the fulfilment of political duty. The work of the committees of the Landwehr, the drilling of the Landsturm, the public assemblies, and the work done for love in the hospitals, brought nearer together even those who remained at home. The rough Junker learned to live in friendly intercourse with the burghers of the circle town. Whoever came to the front in this time remained a respected man throughout his life.

To crown all, the army became a single great community; and after the peace, the old and loyal brotherhood-in-arms persisted in clubs and in public festivals. The peculiar sharp and incisive characteristics of the Frederician army were preserved, and so was the proud sense of aristocratic caste-honour among the officers. But the old professional soldiers had to habituate themselves to quiet and friendly intercourse with the educated young men of the rank and file. The best among them willingly recognised how much sound energy had streamed into the officers' corps from the ranks of the yager volunteers. With cordial delight Gneisenau praised the young volunteers, saying: " I find it difficult to restrain my tears when I behold this nobility of spirit, this lofty German sentiment." Since most of the volunteers consisted of students and of educated people, the youthful tone of university cheerfulness persisted in the camps, and had only to be subordinated to the strictness of military discipline. How often did Lützow's yagers sing the *Landesvater;* the old song had become doubly dear to them since in sacred earnest they had now drawn their good swords for the fatherland, for the land of glory. As Scharnhorst had prophesied, the young volunteers became the best soldiers of all ; the conduct of the whole army was freer and more moral through its association with young men of education. Even the rough peasant-lad learned some of the ardent songs of the volunteers. When the days of victory came, and the Prussians again and again made their joyful entry into liberated German towns, when at length the German Rhine lay at the feet of the conquerors, even the common man felt that he was not fighting merely for his own farmyard. The idea of a fatherland sprang to life in these valiant hearts, the Prussians felt themselves proud to be fighting on behalf of Germany. Not since the days of Cromwell's ironsides had the world seen an army which was so permeated by a sacred moral earnestness ; and it was not, as it had been in the case of Cromwell's army, a mere fanatical party, but an entire nation. All the old separations of political life disappeared in the unity of this struggle. Marwitz, the declared opponent of the national army, gladly accepted the command of a Landwehr brigade, taking delight in the firm courage of his Markish peasants.

All the hot passions which alone can inflame a virile people to the highest deeds, were now awakened, and yet the colossal movement was held within civilised limits. There was nothing here of that gloomy ecclesiastical and national fanaticism which made the uprising of the Russians and the Spaniards so sinister. This Young Germany, which was now shaking its spear with flaming eyes, bore upon its forehead the garlands of art and of science, and with justified pride Boeckh could exclaim at the opening of this summer of battles : " See how Germania is here, is well equipped with weapons and with thoughts ! " Those who were consciously engaged in the struggle felt themselves to be chosen by God's grace to destroy the kingdom of craft and of material coercion, to establish a permanent peace, once more to allow all the nations to develop each after its own kind, to live out their lives in fruitful rivalry. The German war was regarded as the salvation of the ancient national forms of western civilisation, and when it attained its victorious end, Benjamin Constant, though a Frenchman, declared : " The Prussians have restored the human countenance to honour ! "

But the future constitution of liberated Germany had not as

yet been envisaged by this childlike and loyal generation. If all who spoke the German tongue were now to be at one, it could not fail to happen that a strong, united, national, and free kingdom should once more come to life. No one asked about ways and means ; every doubter was accused of cowardice ; it was the war and the war alone which occupied everyone's thoughts. Apart from those rough, abusive attacks upon the enemy which are never lacking in any fiercely contested war, there appeared in this spring only those political writings calculated to stimulate the lust of battle, such as Arndt's valuable booklet, and Pfuel's story of the retreat of the French from Russia, the first true account of the great catastrophe, a little book of far-reaching influence. Nor did the only North German newspaper which had a definite political tendency, Niebuhr's *Preussische Korrespondent*, concern itself about the great question of the future of Germany.

Fichte alone insisted upon clearness. In the joyful excitement of these days so full of hope, the majesty of the idea of the state had come home to the philosopher. He thankfully recognised that the rebirth of Old Germany had followed sooner than he had antici-pated in his speeches ; with delight he saw his audience depart to battle ; he himself took up sabre and pike and joined the ranks of the Berlin Landsturm. And since he now grasped, from personal experience, what sacrifices a loved and respected state-authority may demand of its people, he learned to think greatly of the nature of the political community, and in his *Staatslehre* he described the state as that which educates the human race for freedom. It was for the state to realise the task of morality upon earth. Thus, shortly before his death, he enunciated for the first time with absolute definiteness the opinion that the leadership of Germany was for the Prussian state alone. The petty princes continued to think of nothing but their own dynastic interests, and Austria used the energies of Germany for personal ends. Prussia alone was a genuine German state, and as such had absolutely no interest in injustice or in the subjugation of others. The Prussian state was the natural ruler of Germany ; it must expand to become a realm of reason, or else it would perish. This fragmentary work of Fichte's was a valuable heritage which the valiant and influential teacher of the North German youth left for his pupils, constituting also a significant indication of the aspirations which were now fer-menting in patriotic circles. And yet to the idealist the idea of intervening in the politics of the day was remote. He merely wrote down his prophetic thoughts, " in order that they may not perish from the world"; they were not published for several years after his death. This epoch had as yet no understanding of the arduous duties of political party-life. The single aim, to destroy the foreign dominion, was the only thing that was clear to the vision of the patriots; all that lay beyond consisted simply of lofty dreams, as indefinite, as formless, as those of the song which was written in that winter at Königsberg: " What is the German's fatherland ? "

The Russian headquarters staff and the Hofburg at Vienna could not master their astonishment at the incredible speed with which the work of Prussian equipment proceeded. In the hands of Scharnhorst were united all the threads of the colossal network, and he was operating in accordance with a firmly conceived plan, which had been thought out years before. Since the desire was to begin the attack speedily, with a numerous army, and since it was further hoped to manifest the high functional capacity of Prussia by the speedy placing in the field of strong forces, the first task was considered to be the increase of the troops of the line. For this reason as early as December the formation of the reserve battalion was undertaken and completed. The levying of the volunteer yagers was directed for the most part towards the same end ; they were to constitute the cadre for the officers and non-commissioned officers of the army ; and in actual fact a great preponderance of the generals and staff-officers who subsequently throughout the weary years of peace preserved for the army the sentiments of a great epoch, were derived from the school of these volunteers.

The levying of the volunteers also made it possible to cloak the state of affairs from the French, to avoid completely raising the diplomatic mask. It was effected with a prudent regard for the rooted prejudices which still opposed the universal obligation of military service. It was simply impossible to enrol the sons of the higher classes as ordinary rankers. For this reason, the volunteers who equipped themselves at their own expense, constituted special detachments of yagers attached to the regiments, and were distinguished from the mass of the men by the green yager uniform. They received a treatment corresponding with their class customs, were specially trained, and had the right, after some months, of choosing their own officers. All exemptions from military service were now cancelled, and the decree of February 22nd established that every evasion of military service should be severely punished. Even this step could, in case of need, be excused to the French ambassador. It aroused considerable discontent amongst the people. Why, they asked, should there be all this compulsion, when as many more volunteers could be provided as the king might demand ? And yet the compulsion was inevitable. The state must perforce be able to reckon, for the line and for the Landwehr, upon all those competent to bear arms, even in the regions where very little zeal was displayed.

Not until the diplomatic negotiations had been broken off, not until the cadres of the line regiments had been already constituted and very nearly filled, was the Landwehr Law promulgated, and this was tantamount to an open declaration of war. Scharnhorst's plan for the Landwehr was from the first conceived in a greater sense than had been the proposals of the diet of Königsberg. Like the East Prussians, he counted first upon the activity of the estates in the various circles and provinces, applying to the military system the principles of the new self-government. In every circle a committee was to be formed, to consist of two deputies from the gentry, one from the town, and one from the peasantry, in order to select the men for the Landwehr, which was to comprise all those between seventeen and forty years of age who were not serving in the line. Two commissary generals, one appointed by the crown and one by the estates, conducted the levies and the equipment in each province. The men wore upon their collars and their caps the colours of their province, whilst the officers wore a distinctive uniform. The formation of the battalions and of the companies followed as far as possible the boundaries of the circles and of the communes, in such a way that, as a rule, neighbours were incorporated in a single military unit. Up to the rank of captain, the officers were elected ; the staff-officers were appointed by the king, in part upon the recommendation of the estates. Nevertheless this *armée bourgeoise*, as Napoleon mockingly termed it, was by no means a purely provincial army intended solely for the defence of the immediate home. On the contrary, the Landwehr was sworn to the articles of war, and had imposed upon it all the duties which were imposed upon the standing army. It wore uniform, a simple one it is true, with the service cap and the blue *Litewka*, which could readily be adapted from the Sunday coat of the peasants ; and the king reserved the right of summoning individual Landwehr men, and even whole battalions, for service in the field. Thus the entire male population up to the age of forty years, in so far as not already under arms, now became available for the strengthening of the offensive forces of the state ; upon the king's command, the East Prussians had to modify their more narrowly conceived previous proposal, and had to impose upon their Landwehr the like duty of serving outside the province. The majority of the rank and file consisted of peasants and men of the common people, especially in Silesia, where almost all the young men of education had joined the voluntary yagers. The officers were for the most part landowners, but in part officials or young volunteers ; only a few of them had received military training. For equipment, the impoverished state could make no more than an inadequate provision ; the first section of the infantry carried pikes, and only in the course of the war did it become partly armed with fire-arms taken from the enemy.

Months had yet to pass before such troops as these could be employed in the field. During the spring campaign, the Landwehr could receive no more than an exiguous drill, or be employed in siege operations. Not until after the truce was declared did great masses of them enter the field. Even then, the line, to which all the higher leaders and all the skilled troops belonged, necessarily remained the nucleus of the army. Among the forty-one battalions of his corps, Kleist von Nollendorf had only sixteen Landwehr battalions ; in the same number, Bülow had only twelve ; it was in York's corps alone that the Landwehr was in the majority, constituting twenty-four battalions among forty-five. The men of the Landwehr had for some time to contend with the natural difficulties of untrained troops. At the first onslaught it was not easy to keep them steady when an unexpected fire alarmed them. In hand to hand conflicts, the long-restrained rage of the peasants took the form of a horrible lust of murder. After the victory they were hard to hold in check, for they always wished to follow the beaten enemy to the other end of the world. After a few weeks their conduct became steadier, and towards autumn Napoleon's joke concerning this " mob of bad infantry," began to lose its meaning. Those battalions of the Landwehr which grew accustomed to battle, gradually became as fit for war as the standing army, even though they were unable to compete in respect of discipline or in respect of military appearance with the troops of the line ; and though they continued to sustain comparatively high losses (an unexampled fact in the history of war, rendered possible only by the moral impetus of a struggle for national existence). More difficult, of course, was the formation of the Landwehr cavalry ; but even this force, under skilled leaders, did much excellent work. Marwitz allowed his young peasants of the Mark to ride their ponies

on the snaffle, without curb or spurs ; he did not interfere with
their bucolic horsemanship, asking merely that they should learn
to use their horses and their arms with security ; and after a little
while he brought this natural cavalry to such a degree of excellence
that he could ask anything of them in service in the field.

After the levying of the Landwehr five weeks elapsed until
on April 21st the Landsturm Law was signed. The cadres of the
Landwehr battalions had first to be established before the final
step was made in calling up the ultimate forces of the people.
Scharnhorst was now in camp, far from Breslau. The general
never became completely acquainted with the form and content
of this law, drawn up by Bartholdi, a civilian official. It demanded
the impossible of a civilised people, and if completely carried into
effect would have impressed a stamp of fanatical barbarism upon
the conduct of the war by both the contending parties. Here was
given direct expression to the terrible principle that in this war
need was to justify every means. As soon as the enemy approached,
on the sound of the alarm bells, all men of fifteen to sixty years of
age were to take the field, equipped with pikes, axes, scythes, pitch-
forks, with any kind of weapon which can either pierce or cut—
for in the long run the defenders always have a preponderance in
every country. The Landsturm had to undertake espionage and
guerilla warfare : the enemy was to learn that all its dispersed
sections would be immediately cut off. Cowards and laggards were
to be treated as slaves, and to be flogged. Upon the orders of
the military governor, whole districts were to be laid waste, cattle
and stores were to be removed, the springs were to be filled up,
standing harvests were to be burnt. Should a region be taken by
surprise, all the local authorities were to be immediately dissolved
—this being plainly a fruit of the tragi-comic experiences of 1806.
Anyone who was forced to swear an oath to the enemy was not
considered bound thereby. The faithful people gladly did their
best to meet even these enormous demands. In every circle a
protective deputation was constituted for the leadership of the
Landsturm. Weary old men and beardless youths zealously
exercised themselves in the use of their rough weapons, as well as
in the free art of whistling, which was recommended to the men
of the Landsturm. It was with especial delight that this people's
army practised itself in the storming of unoccupied heights, thus
doing honour to its name. In the Berlin Landsturm the professors
of the university drilled together, forming a well-equipped troop,
which was indeed distinguished more by scientific repute than by

warlike skill. It even happened in Berlin that the ladies were summoned for the construction of trenches to the south of the capital. The institution of the Landsturm effected the great military advantage that, in course of time, the entire strength of the line and of the Landwehr became available for the field and for siege operations. From the Baltic to the Riesengebirge beacons were erected on every height and were guarded by men of the Landsturm.

These popular levies proved useful as watchmen and in the messenger service, and also for the capture of marauders and small isolated detachments. But it was only in exceptional circumstances that the Landsturm was used in open fighting. For example, during the first days of April, even before the Landsturm Law had been promulgated, the alarm bells were sounded in all the villages on the Havel, and armed troops of peasants voluntarily joined the soldiers who were advancing upon Magdeburg. In the large towns, the fanatical severity of the law gave rise to well-grounded complaints. Since, moreover, there was considerable danger of anarchical lack of discipline, since bourgeois life could not dispense with labour power, and since the officials of the old school had an instinctive dread of armed masses of the people, in the course of the summer the excessive stringency of the edict was mitigated by fresh enactments. The Landsturm remained under the articles of war, and served chiefly to form a reserve battalion for the Landwehr ; in the large towns it ceased entirely to exist, burgher-companies for local defence being constituted out of the most efficient third of its members. None the less, the institution of the Landsturm was of momentous importance It educated the people in the idea that this holy war was the common affair of all. How many fine old fellows found it a consolation to the day of their death that they also had taken up arms for the fatherland. Even more powerful was the effect upon the enemy, who, after their experience in Spain, dreaded nothing so much as a war of all against all. The very name of this popular levy, so happily chosen, aroused alarm in the camp of the Rhenish Confederates ; sinister to them seemed the sounds of the song of the Landsturm :

> " Ha ! hurricane be welcome,
> Welcome be God's good storm ! "

The premature evacuation of the Marks in the spring, and the subsequent vacillating operations of the marshals against Berlin, can be explained only by their indefinite uneasiness as regards a popular uprising.

It was wonderful to observe how this state, deprived of all financial resources, re-entered in a moment the ranks of the great military powers. Only a master could have given form, measure, and direction, to all the turbulent forces which so suddenly surged up from the depths of our folk-life. Undisturbed by opposition and misrepresentation, Scharnhorst carried out his military and political plans, and succeeded in doing what had been regarded as impossible in modern history, in transforming an entire people into an army ready for war. To him came the greatest happiness which is allotted to great men, he could at length show all that he was capable of doing. He knew that the fate of his country rested upon his shoulders, and once at least a word of pride was uttered by this man who never made claims. He wrote to his daughter : " I am acting despotically, and am taking a heavy responsibility, but I believe that I have been called to do this."

The diplomatic arts of Hardenberg, the vacillation at the court, and the waiting upon Austria, had delayed the outbreak of the war for several weeks. None the less, Napoleon was taken by surprise. Maret himself admitted to Krusemark when taking leave, that his emperor had not believed the danger to be so near.[1] Prussia's action altered the Imperator's plan of campaign. For the moment he could think no longer of an attack upon the empire of the czar, for the first task before him was the annihilation of Prussia. As early as March 27th, Napoleon proposed to the Hofburg the partition of Prussia, suggesting that Silesia should be allotted to Austria, that Saxony and Westphalia should each be increased by a million of Prussian subjects, and that there should be left to the House of Hohenzollern no more than a petty state on the Vistula with a million inhabitants. The Prussian declaration of war was answered with sanguinary threats ; if Prussia demanded back its inheritance, the world was well aware that this state owed all its acquisitions in Germany only to an infringement of the laws and interests of the Holy Roman Empire. In a published report sent to the emperor, Maret made complaint that the Prussian court was collecting round itself the members of that fanatical party which was preaching the overthrow of the throne and the destruction of the bourgeois order. He scornfully concluded by saying that this declaration of war was " Prussia's gratitude for the Treaty of Tilsit which restored the king to his

[1] Krusemark's Report, March 13, 1813.

throne and for the Treaty of Paris of 1812 which accorded to him the French alliance ! ''

In such a struggle, no thought of compromise was possible. How uncertain, too, were the prospects for the great venture ! The allies could get no further in negotiations with Austria. In answer to repeated and urgent appeals, Metternich finally stated on April 2nd that there could be no question of an immediate breach with France, but that Emperor Francis was prepared to co-operate with the allies if Napoleon should reject the peace proposals which Austria intended to present. Even young Count Nesselrode, who at this time began to play a considerable part in the councils of the czar, and who was always a warm friend of Austria, found this declaration vague and insufficient.

Nor was help forthcoming in Great Britain. English subsidies were as indispensable for the war as was the goodwill of Hanover indispensable for the existence of the future Germanic Federation ; for this reason the restoration of the Guelph possessions in Germany was made an express condition in the Treaty of Kalisz. The fortunate island, which alone among the states of Europe had consistently refused recognition to the Imperator, was regarded by all the German patriots as the citadel of freedom, and its cunning and arbitrary commercial policy was regarded as a heroic struggle for the highest good of humanity. With ardent enthusiasm pæans were sounded in honour of the high-minded House of Guelph. Count Münster dreamed of a free Guelph realm of Austrasia, which was to embrace all the country between the Elbe and the Scheldt, and this mad plan received support from many German patriots. How often in Pitt's lifetime, had England promised great things to the Prussian state, and especially the possession of the Netherlands, if Prussia were to join the league against France. Now Prussia was at length in arms, and nothing seemed more certain to the chancellor than that England would immediately come with full hands to the help of the new ally.

But the ministry of the mediocrities which had taken over Pitt's inheritance, had received from its great predecessor nothing more than the tenacious hatred of the Revolution, it had not acquired Pitt's far-reaching political grasp. These high-tories constituted the nucleus of the European reaction ; as Lord Castlereagh once dryly put it, they expected from the great struggle nothing more than the " re-establishment of the old conditions " ; they watched with anxious mistrust every manifestation of youthful energy in Europe ; they looked down with boundless arrogance upon the peoples of the continent who were predestined to enslavement. "A constitutional government," said Castlereagh, "is not suited for countries which are still in a condition of comparative ignorance ; the extremely venturesome principle of freedom must rather be checked than favoured." The rise of the Russian power had already for a long time been regarded as a sinister event by the cabinet of St. James's, and the prince regent contemplated with hardly less alarm than Emperor Francis the passionate enthusiasm of the North German youth and the fine courage of the Prussian generals. Wellington wrote with serious alarm of the feverish excitement of the Prussian army, where discipline was certainly not enforced, as it had been in the peninsular regiments of the iron duke by the idealism of the cat-o'-nine-tails.

Since the old weakness of English statesmen, their ignorance of continental conditions, was exceptionally marked in this tory cabinet, England's German policy was in reality directed by Count Münster, the confidential Hanoverian counsellor of the prince regent. The days were past in which Count Münster had earned the respect of Baron von Stein by his tenacious hostility to the Napoleonic world-empire. After the uprising of Prussia there were manifested only the petty traits of his political character ; the Guelph envy of a strong neighbour and the detestable old prejudices against "the Prussian cudgel and ramrod." Hardenberg's moderate dualistic plans seemed to Münster almost more alarming than Stein's dreams of unity. Never should the crown of the Guelphs bend its head before a higher power. Since his cherished ancient plan to limit Prussia, as a power of the third rank, to the region between the Elbe and the Vistula had been rendered nugatory by the force of circumstances, and since the Guelph kingdom of Austrasia had unfortunately become impossible, the Prussian state should at least pay dearly for the English subsidies ; not only was Prussia with her good sword to reconquer Hanover for the Guelphs, but Hanover, which after its liberation had done nothing on behalf of the German war, was to be increased by the addition of Old Prussian provinces. The Guelph statesman declared confidentially that without such an accession of strength Hanover could not live beside Prussia in peace and security. The prince regent accepted these ideas all the more gladly since his daughter Charlotte was heir to the throne in England, and consequently the Guelph male line must expect that it would soon be restricted to the German hereditary dominions. In his letters, it is true, he gave unctuous assurances that he was not acting as he did from personal interest, but that he merely regarded it as his duty to repay his electoral dominions for the distresses of the French rule. Sir Charles Stewart, who came to Germany in the beginning of April, was instructed to demand for the Guelph realm the territory of Hildesheim which the Guelphs had unwillingly ceded to the Hohenzollerns in the year 1802, and also the old Prussian domains of Minden and Ravensburg.

The ageing chancellor, though he still had the pen of a ready writer, was no longer equal to the oppressive burden of official work ; yet he was unwilling to give up his dominant position over the ministers. In the vortex of affairs and of frivolous dissipation, he saw his royal master too seldom, and the course of business in the chancellery began to be neglected. He could not indeed be accused of a ready compliance to the Guelph demands. For nearly three months he carried on these wearisome negotiations, at first through Niebuhr and afterwards in person. What a spectacle was this. Wealthy England, having proudly declared herself to be fighting for the freedom of Europe, left her most valiant ally, who had fiercely thrown herself into the desperate struggle, month after month in a condition of intolerable need, haggling about souls and shillings—and all this on behalf of the dynastic caprice of an incapable prince who did not care a straw for the well-being of the English state ! In a word, when the campaign began no definite arrangement had been made, and the Prussian state was in urgent need of money.

Not even Sweden, which was already in alliance with Russia, had concluded any treaty with Prussia. When the Swedes had chosen the artful Bernadotte for their future king, they had definitely expected that the Napoleonic marshal would, in accordance with the ancient traditions of Swedish policy, adhere to France, and that with the help of Napoleon he would win back from the Russians the lost land of Finland. But the prudent crown prince chose another course. He saw that Sweden, an agricultural country, could not endure the Continental System, and he recognised also that the reconquest of Finland was extremely improbable. He therefore resolved to idemnify his new fatherland by the acquisition of Norway and to establish his youthful dynasty in the hearts of the people. He had been in alliance with the czar since the beginning of the Russian war. Thereafter the court of Copenhagen was urgently summoned by Russia, England, and Sweden to give up Norway and to join the great alliance ; it was taken as a matter of course that the Danes should make their loss good in that great area of universal compensation which was known as Germany. The Russian ambassador in Stockholm promised the Danish chargé d'affaires, Count Wolf Baudissin, in the name of England, that Denmark should receive the two Mecklenburgs, Swedish Pomerania, and perhaps also Prussian Pomerania— "two villages in Germany for every one in Norway." Bernadotte himself went even further, promising Mecklenburg, Oldenburg, Hamburg, and Lübeck. Fortunately for Germany, Frederick VI of Denmark trusted in Napoleon's star, and for many months took no definite side. To the well-balanced mind of King Frederick William these detestable northern negotiations were utterly repulsive from the first. He hoped to win over Denmark for the coalition by honourable means, would not consent to the robbery of his smaller neighbours, and when his ambassador in Stockholm had agreed to an alliance warranting the Swedish conquest of Norway, the king refused to ratify it. Thus the remarkable thing happened that in the spring Bernadotte landed at Stralsund, with a small Swedish army, in order to conquer Norway in Germany, and yet was not in alliance with Prussia. England free-handedly provided this ambiguous ally with subsidies to the amount of one million pounds sterling in return for its weak army.

Last of all, what was to be expected from the states of the Confederation of the Rhine? Since January, the chancellor had been eagerly negotiating with Bavaria. The court of Munich had been profoundly moved by the loss of the 30,000 Bavarians who had perished in the snow-fields of Russia. Although Montgelas had a passionate hatred for the North German patriots, and had instructed the ambassador Hertling to follow the removal of the court to Breslau and to hold fast to St. Marsan,[1] he began to be weary of his sacrifices for the Protector, since they no longer brought any return. The queen, the crown prince Louis, Anselm Feuerbach, and several other men of influence, were actively at work for the good cause. Hardenberg cleverly removed a serious obstacle to an understanding. He was aware that King Max Joseph attached much importance to the possession of the Franconian margravates, and that for this reason the king had a year before regarded with great anxiety the conclusion of the Prusso-French alliance.[2] Quickly making up his mind, he agreed that

---

[1] Royal despatch to Hertling, January 27, 1813.
[2] Dépeches royales (King Max Joseph and Montgelas) to the ambassador von Hertling in Berlin, April 30 and June 11, 1812.

the royal House of Prussia would not demand the return of its Franconian tribal dominions ; it was agreed between the parties that Prussia should be compensated by the former Lower Rhenish province of the Bavarian Palatinate. Montgelas was already prepared to sign a treaty of neutrality when he heard of Napoleon's enormous armaments, and of the hesitating attitude of Austria. It seemed to him, in view of such an inequality of forces, that the destruction of Prussia was inevitable. He broke off the negotiations and once more with accustomed zeal fulfilled his duties as a vassal towards the ruler of the Confederation of the Rhine.

Whilst the allies were thus vainly endeavouring to win over by friendly negotiation the powerful state of the south, they adopted sharper measures in the case of the North German states. The Treaty of Breslau of March 19th, quite in the sense of Stein's St. Petersburg memorial, threatened with the loss of their states all the German princes who did not within a definite time determine to join in the struggle for the freedom of the fatherland. A central administrative council, under the presidency of the baron, was to establish provisional governments in all the North German territories (Hanover and the former Prussian provinces alone excepted), was to supervise the military equipments, and was to receive the state-revenues on behalf of the allies. The south was tacitly left out of consideration, for Hardenberg held strongly to his dualistic plan, and was therefore unwilling to put pressure upon the Austrian court in the matter of South Germany. Alike in Vienna, in London, and in all the courts of the Confederation of the Rhine, this first attempt at a practical policy of German unity aroused stormy discontent. It was angrily asked whether this Jacobin Stein wished to become German emperor. Metternich and Münster instantly determined to restrict the powers of the sinister unified authorities.

Still more severe was the language of the proclamation of Kalisz, issued by the Russian commander Kutuzoff on March 25th. This expressed the hope that no German prince would fail to put himself on the side of the German cause, and would thus " insure himself against an otherwise well-merited destruction by the force of public opinion and by the just power of arms." A young Saxon, Carl Müller, had drawn up this emotionally worded proclamation. Just as confused and untenable as the patriotic dreams of this enthusiastic youth were the promises for a German constitution which the field-marshal made in the name of the allied monarchs. He declared that the renascence of the venerable empire was left entirely at the discretion of the princes and of the peoples of

Germany, that the czar would merely extend his protecting hand. " The more definitely in its foundations and in its outlines the work is the spontaneous issue of the primitive spirit of the German people, the more rejuvenated, the more vigorous, and the more firmly unified will Germany reappear among the peoples of Europe ! " These were high-sounding and well-meaning words, and the only misfortune is that they conveyed no definite meaning. Subsequently, in a time of embitterment and depression, they were to carry a quite unanticipated significance. It was to these words that disillusioned patriots chiefly made appeal in order to prove that the nation had been betrayed by its princes—whereas it was unfortunately true that the primitive spirit of the German people had at that time just as little understanding of the prerequisites of German unity as had the princes themselves.

The threats of the allies were dictated by the just recognition that the satraps of Napoleon were now amenable to the language of force alone. But if strong words were to have the requisite effect, deeds must be ready to follow them. And the deeds were not forthcoming. The king's natural good-nature and his quiet consideration for Austria, prevented him from giving a well-timed example of warning to the German princes by the dethronement of his Saxon neighbour. When the demand was sent to Frederick Augustus of Saxony that he should repeat for the sake of Germany the breach of faith which in the autumn of 1806 he had made for the sake of his own house, the position of the weakly prince was certainly a difficult one. He was forced to come to a decision earlier than the other kings of the Confederation of the Rhine, at a moment when the issue of the war was still uncertain, and he could not hope to regain Warsaw, which had been conquered by the Russians. But it was within his power to secure compensation for his Polish possessions by a well-timed desertion to the cause of the allies ; the czar had long before given his consent to this. The indemnification for so uncertain a crown would certainly not have been considerable. As everyone knew, Warsaw had been but temporarily placed in the hands of Frederick Augustus until the Imperator could make further arrangements for its disposal. The duke of the House of Wettin had never understood how to deal with the distinguished Polish royal electors or with their savage hatred of Germany ; he had never ventured to give any kind of orders to his Polish troops. Nevertheless Frederick Augustus was unwilling to abandon this Polish crown whose possession had already brought so much misfortune to Saxony, and he moreover regarded the defeat of his " Great Ally " as unthinkable. When the allies approached, he did what he had done in the danger of the war of 1809 : he fled the country. Upon the urgent demand of the king of Prussia whether he wished to remain " an adversary of the noblest things," he returned an unmeaning answer and referred to his existing alliances.

His minister Count Senfft, one of those inflated mediocrities of whom there are so many in the diplomatic history of the middle states, put forward the childish plan of a Central European alliance, which was to humiliate France and Russia alike, and to reduce Prussia to the level of a third rank power. Yet he felt that some protection was needed, and therefore endeavoured to adhere to the waiting policy of Austria, a policy of neutrality. This was not merely an impossible course, since Saxony must inevitably be the theatre of war, but it was also an infringement of international law. Saxony was still in a state of war with Russia, and therefore with Prussia also ; Saxon troops were at the moment fighting in the streets of Lüneburg with the brave soldiers of Dörnberg. It was a necessary rule of international law that a belligerent power could not declare itself neutral without the consent of the enemy, for otherwise anyone who was conquered could immediately save himself from the consequences of a defeat. Neutrality was allowed to the Austrian court since Napoleon and the allies alike wished to spare Austria and hoped for its assistance ; but both parties demanded an immediate decision from the king of Saxony.

Almost the whole of the Saxon army was in Torgau, under the command of Thielmann, whose instructions were that he was to open the important passage over the Elbe to neither of the contending parties. The general was a valiant soldier, but vain, boastful, and immeasureably ambitious. Hitherto a zealous servant of Napoleon, he had recently, and quite suddenly, come over to the German side. It was within his competence, by a bold and arbitrary resolve, in pursuance of the example set by York, to save throne and army for his king, and to make the opening operations much easier for the allies. But he did too much for a Saxon general and too little for a German patriot. Secretly negotiating with Prussia, and even surrendering to the Prussians some of the ferries which rendered the passage over the Elbe possible to the allies, he did not venture to unite his forces with the German army. In such circumstances the allies were unquestionably justified in treating Saxony as a hostile country. Yet they behaved with unseasonable gentleness, simply taking over the country in the name of the fugitive prince. Scharnhorst was chiefly responsible for this error. He had formed a false judgment as to the sentiments of the Saxon court, accepting the descriptions of the friend of his youth, General Zeschau, one of the most intimate confidants of Frederick Augustus. Stein, too, still hoped for the voluntary adhesion of the Albertines. It is true that he used hard words regarding the cowardice of "this soft Saxon dealer in words," who was so completely unaffected by the enthusiasm of the Prussian people, and he censured the dullness of the Dresden philistines, to whom, amongst all the happenings of this tremendous time, nothing seemed so important as the destruction of their bridge across the Elbe. But instead of acting in accordance with the Treaty of Breslau and immediately subjecting the occupied country to the dictatorship of the central administrative council, Stein quietly allowed it to be taken over by the governmental commission appointed by the fugitive king, and disdained even to lay an embargo upon the state treasury.

Thus the proposed German centralised authorities never came into existence on the radical lines which had originally been planned ; the first attempt at a unified policy was arrested in the germ. Even before the great war had actually begun, it was possible to recognise how great was still the force of particularism in the people and in the dynasties. Foreign dominion was ripe for destruction, but the foundation was still lacking for the construction of German unity.

§ 2. THE SPRING CAMPAIGN. THE TRUCE.

In times of difficulty the right man speedily rises to the right place. Since the king in his modesty did not venture to follow the example of his forefathers and lead the army himself, there was only one man fit for the Prussian supreme command, the leading German campaigner of the day, General Blucher. What had now become of the dreams of perpetual peace cherished by cultured philanthropists ? The Germans had been ripened and fortified by hard trials, and had now regained faith in the God who made iron. Those simple virtues of primitive humanity which to the end of time will remain the firm foundation of all national greatness, had once more attained to honour ; courage in war, the fresh energy of the inspired will, the frankness of hatred and of love. In these lay the strength of Blucher, and this nation which had been so glad to call itself the people of the poets and the thinkers, bowed before the spiritual greatness of this uncultured man. They felt that he was worthy to lead them; that in him were embodied the heroic wrath and the joy in victory of the million. How much had the old man gone through in the half century since the hussars of Belling had first received the Swedish cornet, and old Belling himself had instructed the unruly Junker in the arts and practices of the Frederician cavalry. At Peene he had fought against the Swedes, at Freiburg against the Imperialists, in Poland against the Confederates; during the bloodless but victorious campaign in Holland he had everywhere been a well-wishing protector of the burghers and peasants; and during the Rhenish campaigns he had been admired by friend and foe. The incisive daring, the nimble cunning, and the unwearied staying power of old Zieten lived once more in the new king of the hussars. Throughout life he held to the view that for the infantry leader enduring courage suffices, but that the cavalry leader must have a naturally gifted inspiration. This alone will enable him to seize, instantly and impetuously, those rare and fugitive moments which endow cavalry with its striking influence.

Since the year 1806 and the bold campaign at Lübeck, he had been the hope of the army. Scharnhorst had then learnt by Blucher's side that with courage and force of will anything in the world can be effected, and he said, " You are our leader and our hero; in you alone do we find resolution and good fortune !" It was far more than the valiancy of the broadsword which so irresistibly attracted the loyal and the fearless. From Blucher's whole nature there radiated the inner happiness of the born hero; that invincible confidence which seems to master a hostile fate. To the soldiers he appeared as glorious as the very God of War, this handsome, tall, old man, sitting his grey charger with youthful energy and grace; there was a force of command in the high forehead and in the large, dark, flaming eyes; on the lips beneath the thick moustache was an expression displaying the hussar's cunning and a cordial love of life. When he went into battle he loved to deck himself with all his orders, as if for a wedding, and never in all the dangers of his warrior's life did he once have the misfortune to be struck by a bullet. Notable was the impression he produced when he rose to speak with his fine and powerful voice, a God-given orator, always sure of producing the highest effect, equally when he was good-humouredly encouraging the wearied troops with guard-room jokes and rough phrases, or when he was giving his officers clear, concise, and expressive orders, or, finally, when in a formal assembly he was pouring forth eloquent words in honour of some national festival. Whoever was in daily association with him became devoted to him. His beloved red hussars were under his influence to the last man, so that after the unlucky capitulation of Ratkau, not one of them could be taken to France; all escaped from the victors, most of them finding their way to the king in East Prussia.

Blucher knew the land and the people of the German north as did none other among the Prussian generals. During his long and varied service, he had become familiar with all parts of the country, from the Rhine to the Polish frontier, and as a farmer he had been initiated into the conditions of bourgeois life. Everywhere he went he won all hearts, living happily and allowing others to do the same, drinking and playing cards familiarly with high and low, always frank and outspoken, and yet never unbending unduly. Thus the school of life strengthened in him the sentiments of German patriotism which the odes of Klopstock had long ago awakened in the soul of the youth. However strongly he cleaved to his Prussian flag, he still, like Stein, always felt himself to be a German nobleman. Limitless was his confidence in the inexhaustible energy and loyalty of his compatriots. His heart rejoiced whenever he encountered the primitive freshness and freedom of the Teutonic nature; hence his preference for the free people of Frisia and for the proud burghers of the Hansa towns; hence, too, his detestation of the class arrogance and the unpatriotic sentiments of the gentry in the Münster region. In old age he often complained that in the rough-and-tumble life of a hussar, his education had been almost entirely neglected. Yet an inborn freedom of spirit and the secure instinct of a magnanimous and kingly heart, led him to advance with the advance of the times. Long before the reforms of 1807 he had practically abolished the use of flogging among his red hussars. The pedantic enforcement of useless drills was to him an abomination, and at quite an early date he had declared his conviction that the army must become a national army. He was altogether free from the Junkerdom of his co-estates in Mecklenburg. Since he owed his successes solely to his own valiancy, he gladly welcomed everything which awakened in the nation personal energy, free activity and self-confidence. He was an eloquent defender of Stein's reforms, and more especially of the Towns' Ordinance. Profound was his hatred of the foreign dominion; he felt it to be a personal humiliation that French authorities should do as they willed upon German soil, declaring : " I was born free and must die free."

The old warrior belongs to those genuinely great figures of history which grow in grandeur the better we know them. What a keen political insight is displayed in the barbarous German of his private letters ! In every political situation he sees quickly to the heart of matters, at once recognising the essential point in all the confused phenomena, and prophesies with firm security the ultimate outcome. He was never deceived by the excessive elaboration of the policy of Haugwitz, and never believed in the possibility of an honourable understanding between Prussia and Napoleon. In the spring of 1807, after a single conversation with Bennigsen, he knew at once what his state had to expect from the Russians, exclaiming angrily : " We are betrayed and sold ! " During the long years of servitude he was often near to despair, and yet always returned to the happy belief that his Prussia would rise once again to its ancient brilliancy, that Napoleon would necessarily be overthrown, and that to him it was predestined to co-operate in this work, saying : " German courage is merely slumbering, and its awakening will be terrible ! " Doubtless during this time of weary waiting, even Blucher shared many of the fine illusions which led astray the members of the war party. He was ever willing to attribute to all Germans the heroic sentiments which animated his own soul, and believed that it would be possible to reconquer the western province with a force of 16,000 men. Yet however hasty the plans of uprising which he then unweariedly drew up in conjunction with his darling son Francis, he was perfectly right in the essential point, in his recognition of the inner weakness of the Napoleonic world-empire. The *petits-maîtres* were disgusted with the grey-headed youngster who still sometimes at the court balls danced a quadrille with the elegant young officers of the guard ; but those of deeper nature soon felt that this unlimited activity was no more than the natural expression of the unrestrained fervour of vital energy. The patriotic party regarded him as their securest support. For many years Stein had been his intimate friend, esteeming most highly the apt judgments of the general, which were always the fruit of an abundance of actual experience, and recognising in Blucher the same boldness of soul, the same courage of truth, which were deep-rooted in himself.

Fearing no one, with unshaken frankness, Blucher always said exactly what he thought ; and yet even in his roughest phrases there was nothing of Stein's painful severity. His words of anger flowed so frankly forth that very rarely was anyone hurt by them, and even the king allowed him to say what he liked. Despite all his impetuousness he was thoroughly prudent. Not merely in war was he so careful and crafty that Napoleon angrily spoke of him as *le vieux renard ;* but he was also endowed with a thorough knowledge of men which enabled him always to place his instruments rightly. He had a perfect grasp of the art of command ; of his men he could ask the impossible, if his eyes flashed when giving the order to advance ; even from the defiant spirits of his generals he enforced obedience, for he never thought of anything but the matter in hand, after every misfortune he took all the blame upon his own shoulders, and in the case of disputes among his subordinates, always played the part of a good-natured intermediator. In him, as in Stein, the inexhaustible energy of hope and confidence was rooted in a straightforward piety. Although after his hussar's manner, he sometimes treated God as a good fellow, and detested all cant, he still, in the depths of his soul, remained happy in the simplicity of his faith ; in difficult hours, this man with a firm belief in the Bible gladly encouraged himself with some brave word from the gospels. How remote, too, was the love of battle of this good-natured lover of men from the heartless roughness of the mercenary soldier ! It was to him a sacred Christian duty to care for the sick and wounded. The young crown prince never forgot how on one occasion upon the battlefield the old hero, profoundly moved, had taken him by the hand and shown him all the horrible distresses round about, saying that this was the curse of war, and calling down woe upon the prince who from vanity and arrogant pride should bring such misery upon his brother men !

Blucher had long been aware " that the confidence of the nation and the love of the army were given to him," that the leadership of the army was in his hands. When at length the longed-for hour struck, and the regime of the accursed " commissaries of safety and lazy-bones " had come to an end, he felt himself to be once more a young man despite his seventy years, calling gladly to mind the long-lived heroic energy of Derfflinger, the old Dessauer, and the many glorious grey-heads of Prussian military history. With what joy did he place himself upon the crest of the wave of this turbulent popular movement. How delighted was he that the fresh air-current of truth once more blew through German life, and that every man could now speak boldly what was in his heart. "Sing away," he once said cheerfully to a patriotic poet ; "in such times as these everyone must sing after his own heart, one with his mouth and another with his sword!"

Such was the hero chosen by the voice of the nation to be its leader—a true Teuton, whose rough greatness could be comprehensible in its entirety only to men of Teuton blood ; for they alone could understand the rough-hewn primitiveness of his nature. The French have never given him that qualified recognition which persistent success is apt to enforce even from the conquered. For his part, he could see nothing at all in the refined Romance nature, and even after the rage of the conflict had long passed away he said : "This nation is disagreeable to me!" On the other hand, the noisy frankness and the rough humour of "the crazy nation" of the English, were thoroughly congenial to him. As soon as the war began he devoted himself with all his energies to his task, and even laid aside the playing cards of which he was so fond, not to touch them again until he had entered Paris. He knew the defects of his education, and was aware that he had need of a man of methodically trained intelligence who should give him ideas for the conduct of the war. Thus in the campaign of 1806 he had carried out the ideas of Scharnhorst ; utterly without envy, in upright modesty, he recognised the intellectual superiority of his friend, and rejoiced that Scharnhorst was now once more at his side as quarter-master-general. He believed that with Scharnhorst's clear vision and his own boldness working in unison, they could defy the world, for the old man had never liked a many-headed council of war.

Temporarily, however, he himself still remained under the orders of the Russian supreme command. After the death of the incapable old Field-Marshal Kutuzoff, General Wittgenstein undertook the leadership of the allied armies. He was a valiant and well-meaning soldier, but without the gifts requisite for the commander. The Russian headquarters-staff, proud of the successes of the previous year, was little inclined to heed Prussian advice. On the day after the issue of the king's appeal, Blucher left Breslau, crossed the Elbe at Dresden, subdued almost the whole of Saxony including the fortresses, and in the first days of April advanced into the district of Altenburg ; his lighter troops moving on far to the west beyond Gotha. Simultaneously, in the north, York and Bülow approached the Elbe, defeated the viceroy Eugene in the brilliant battle of Mökern (this being the first great encounter which showed the French that they had no longer to do with the army of 1806), and in Anhalt crossed to the left bank of the stream.

Whilst Scharnhorst and his friends had at first hoped that before Napoleon's arrival they would succeed in occupying a large portion of western Germany, and would everywhere effect the arming of the people, they had soon to recognise that the forces immediately available were insufficient for such far-reaching plans. A fortunate attack upon Lüneburg, made by the little corps of Dörnberg, did indeed bear striking witness to the bravery of the young army. The soldiers extolled the first cavalryman to win the iron cross, Major Borcke, and the poets sang the heroic girl, Johanna Stegen, who brought the troops powder and shot under heavy fire. But this was an isolated affair and had no permanent results. A rising of the patriots in the district of Bremen was rapidly suppressed and cruelly punished by Vandamme, the roughest and most savage of Napoleon's generals. The fortresses eastward of the Elbe, with the exception of Thorn and Spandau, were still in French hands at the end of April. A bold conduct of the war, such as was demanded by Scharnhorst, could none the less have annihilated the army of the viceroy in the territories of Magdeburg before Napoleon's main body could arrive. But for many weeks the Russian headquarters-staff remained inert in Poland. The czar needed a longer time for the reinforcement of his army, whose weakness was in ludicrous contrast with his boastful promises. Moreover, he himself was unwilling to leave Poland before peace had been established in the greatly excited country by the presence of a sufficient force of troops. There also came into the question the unwillingness of his generals and the painful doubt regarding Austria's intentions, for Austria, being in a strong position on the flank of the allies, might easily be an extremely dangerous adversary. Not until April 24th did the Russian main body enter Dresden, subsequently to make a junction with Blucher to the south of Leipzig after a very slow march.

Meanwhile Napoleon had greatly increased his military strength. It was true that thousands of his tried veterans lay beneath the Russian snows. The young conscripts were far inferior to the veterans, and many of them had been brought to the regiments in chains ; even the marshals began to be weary of the unceasing wars and longed for the peaceful enjoyment of their booty. The superiority of moral energy and of warlike ardour which had hitherto been the privilege of the Napoleonic armies, was now entirely transferred to the side of Prussia. Nevertheless, the world-empire, which for years past had not known the tread of an enemy, was enormously superior to the allies in its immeasurable resources. Whilst Bertrand marched from Italy through Bavaria, the other corps of the French and the Rhenish Confederates assembled on the Lower Rhine near Frankfort and in the neighbourhood of Würzburg. In the last days of April, Napoleon himself, with the main body, passed eastward through Thuringia on the Frankfort-Leipzig road, and on the 29th formed a junction at Naumburg with the army of the viceroy. He had at his disposal a field army of at least 180,000 men without counting the garrisons of the German fortresses, whilst for the moment the allies could place in the field against him not more than about 98,000 men.[1] Scharnhorst at first wished to fight upon the open plain of Leipzig, where the superior force of the allied cavalry would have had free play. The Russian headquarters-staff, however, determined to venture an attack upon the right flank of the enemy which was advancing towards Leipzig to the southward of the old battle-field of Lützen, in the marshy meadow-land at Grossgörschen, intersected by dykes, hedges, and sunken lanes, and this was a region which gave little scope for the deployment of large masses of cavalry. Scharnhorst first gave the simple and bold advice that the superior force of the enemy should be attacked by surprise, while on the march, in the hope of breaking the lines by a flank onslaught. This bold plan could succeed only through the greatest swiftness and simplicity of execution. General Diebitsch, to whom by Wittgenstein's orders the arrangements had been entrusted, led the attack so unhappily that the corps of Blucher and York got in one another's way.

It was not until noon on May 2nd that the Prussians could begin the attack upon the four villages of Grossgörschen, Kleingörschen, Rahna, and Caja, concealed amid copses, and held by Ney with a greatly superior force. The regiments advanced to the attack with loud hurrahs, and never before had the French legions been encountered with such turbulent and warlike enthusiasm There was no sign of the natural unsteadiness of inexperienced troops ; a storm of rage seemed to carry everyone forward ; so great was the bravery of all that no one could distinguish himself beyond the others ! After a murderous fight of two hours, three of the four

---

[1] Even C. Rousset, who everywhere conscientiously gives the lowest possible figures, reckons the strength of Napoleon's and Eguene's united army at 170,000 men (*La Grande Armée de* 1813, p, 113) : and of these, three-fourths (that is, six army corps out of eight) took part in the battle of Grossgörschen [Lützer].

villages were taken from the French. Napoleon therefore hastened from the Leipzig road, endeavouring to turn the fortune of the battle with fresh troops. It was under his eyes that the Prussian guard took possession of the last of the villages, in a second fierce attack ; had the allies' reserves come up at the right moment, the French line of march would have been broken, and a severe defeat of the main body would have been inevitable. For a moment the Imperator wavered. " Do you think that my star is declining ? " he asked doubtfully of Berthier ; and when he witnessed the bravery of the Prussians he exclaimed : " These beasts have learnt something." But Wittgenstein's reserves did not put in an appearance. Miloradowitsch's corps was kept away from the field through an unfortunate misunderstanding, and the Russian guards did not appear until as night fell the fight was ceasing. The allies' cavalry was unable to effect a decisive intervention, for Wittgenstein proved himself altogether incapable of maintaining the conduct of the army in his own hands, and there was really no supreme commander. The infantry was wasting itself in the bloody struggle for the villages, and in view of the superiority of the enemy's infantry no certain issue could be promised. Meanwhile Napoleon brought up fresh reinforcements from the north, and towards seven o'clock he felt strong enough, following his usual practice, to venture a decisive attack under cover of powerful artillery fire. When it became dark the Prussians were still maintaining themselves in Grossgörschen alone, the other three villages having been won back by the French, and the enemy had partially surrounded the allies in a wide curve. A last despairing attack made by Blucher's cavalry, hoping for good fortune in the darkness, failed, owing to the unfortunate character of the ground.

Yet the battle was not yet entirely lost. Everyone in the Prussian camp expected that the struggle would be renewed on the following morning. But whilst the allies had in the evening with their 70,000 men been engaged with a hostile force nearly double their own, on the following day, when Napoleon had brought up all his forces from the neighbourhood of Leipzig, they had a far more unequal struggle in prospect. They therefore withdrew to the Upper Elbe, and were not pursued. At least 10,000 men among the allies, and a far larger number of the French, remained dead upon the field. The troops felt themselves unconquered ; they had secured several trophies, and had left nothing of their own in the hands of their opponents ; everywhere where they had met the enemy in equal force, they had proved themselves superior.

The War of Liberation

During the retreat, the Cossacks were joyfully shouting " Pascholl ! The French are done for ! " In the Prussian army there prevailed the proud conviction that, even under foreign and incapable leaders, they had restored the honour of their flag, and had proved themselves equal to the victors of Jena. Carried away by the view of the re-established German renown in arms, Arndt sang his song of the day of Grossgörschen :

> " Valiant Prussians, valiant Prussians,
> Greeting to you, heroes bold !
> Best of Germans shall men name you
> When the new league is enrolled ! "

Among the victims of this bloody day was Scharnhorst. In the Seven Years' War a cruel fate had removed almost all the Prussian commanders. During the War of Liberation, on the other hand, they almost all escaped. Only this one man fell, the mighty spirit from whose clear intelligence the German national army had sprung fully armed, as Pallas sprang from the head of Zeus. He had received a slight wound at Grossgörschen, and would not give it a chance to heal quietly. Since the weakness of the Russian army and the lukewarmness of its leaders were obvious, the Prussian headquarters-staff had become firmly convinced that victory could be assured only through the help of Austria. Soon after the battle the king issued a *mot d'ordre* to his troops saying : " In a few days we shall receive fresh and powerful aid." Scharnhorst was well aware upon what weak grounds this hope was established, and therefore resolved, notwithstanding the warnings of the surgeons, that he would himself go to Vienna, in order by personal persuasion to induce the Austrian statesmen to take a decisive step. Upon the journey his wound grew worse. Whilst in Bohemia he lay alone upon a bed of sickness, his thoughts turned always towards the army of the fatherland. So much magnificent energy had been wasted by the mistakes of the Russian commanders. He had himself armed the Prussians, and felt that he could lead them to victory if he were only allowed a chance to act freely at Blucher's side. The dying man could no longer conceal the great ambition which tore him, and he wrote to his daughter (for her eye alone, that she might know how her father's thoughts had run when he should no longer be there) saying : " Distinctions are of no importance to me. If I do not secure the one which I have earned, all others would be an insult to me and

I should despise myself if I thought otherwise. All orders and my life would I give for one day of supreme command ! " It was not to be. On June 28th he died of his wound, with his last words prophesying the freedom of Germany. Of the great creative spirits of our history, none has had a more tragical end. Without Scharnhorst there would have been no Leipzig, no Waterloo, no Sedan, and he who had sowed the seed of so many victories was never himself to see the Prussian flag borne to victory ! To those who survived, the great riddle of human destiny now seemed to press with overwhelming force ; always when they thought of this dead man the conviction was impressed upon them that our life does not end with out last breath. How often did Blucher after a victory appeal in ardent language to the shade of Scharnhorst, begging him to look down upon the completion of his work. But to the poet the fallen hero seemed an envoy of victory sent by the liberated Germans to greet their ancestors in Walhalla :

> " The heroes' envoy must a hero be.
> Hence is it that Germania's greatest son,
> Scharnhorst, shall tidings bear (and who but he ?) :
> From foreign yoke soon shall the nation free
> Herself ; revenge be proudly won ! "

Although the battle of Grossgörschen brought much honour to the young Prussian troops, it was none the less a defeat, and its political consequences were momentous. The Napoleonic repute for invincibility was re-established ; there was no longer any thought among the Rhenish Confederates of abandoning him. Frederick Augustus of Saxony was the first, on April 20th, to adhere by a secret treaty to Austria and to a policy of armed intermediation. Upon receiving the news of Napoleon's victory, he immediately returned, even before a threatening message from the Protector hastened his movements—returned to the colours to which in his heart he always adhered. Several weeks before, he had sent Colonel Odeleben to the French headquarters to serve the Imperator as a guide through Thuringia ; Senfft, the advocate of the policy of neutrality, was dismissed, the army and the country was placed at the disposal of his great ally. General Thielmann received orders to open Torgau to the French, and since his troops gave unconditional obedience to the king's orders, he himself went alone over to the side of the allies, accompanied only by the talented Aster, the German Vauban. The possession of the Saxon fortresses enabled the French to prolong the war for months. Severe punishment was allotted to the loyal Prussians in Kottbus, where, in March, when Blucher's army entered, the people had gone over with delight to the German side, numerous volunteers placing themselves at the disposal of their old territorial lord. As soon as the Saxon dominion was restored, the land of Kottbus was declared by the French to be in a state of siege, and a number of the most distinguished patriots, and first of all the brave Landrat von Normann, were thrown into prison upon the denunciation of the Saxon officials, whilst the families of the volunteers were ordered, under pain of confiscation of property, to command their sons to return home. This cruel persecution filled the inhabitants of the country with such deadly hatred, that after they had once more been liberated they begged the king to unite them to the Electoral Mark, and not to the province of Saxony, saying : " It is our desire that we shall never again come into any close relationship with the Saxon authorities, not even if they should become the subjects of the kingdom of Prussia.[1]

In accordance with the Protector's orders, Frederick Augustus himself hastened from Prague, in order to pass through the French lines into the Saxon capital, and the neutral land of Austria permitted the disloyal ally to pass freely back into the Napoleonic camp. The Imperator received him all the more gladly since his coming afforded evidence that Emperor Francis had by no means determined to go over to the side of the allies. Now once more the Saxon court moved along the narrow path of the French alliance. The king of Saxony hoped that he would secure aggrandisement at Prussia's expense, and begged the Protector that when peace came he would give him Glogau and a strip of Silesia, so that Electoral Saxony might unite with Warsaw to form a compact domain. King Frederick William however said already in May to a Saxon noble, that the inevitable consequence of such a breach of faith would be the destruction of the crown of the Albertines.

Meanwhile the allies had withdrawn across the Elbe into Upper Lusatia. Napoleon followed. His army was spread along the wide line from Dresden to Wittenberg. He now for the first time conceived the idea of an attack upon Berlin, a thought that recurred again and again in the calculations of this campaign. Whilst he himself followed the army of the allies eastward, Ney

[1] Petition of the deputies of the Kottbus circle to the king, Berlin, August 25, 1814.

was to make a rapid march northward, to threaten the most detested and most dangerous of the enemies of his capital. The Prussian headquarters-staff was prepared for the worst, and had already made all preparations to defend Berlin in case of need by street fighting and with the Landsturm. But the army remained united with the Russians. The king wished to maintain his position in the neighbourhood of the Austrian frontier, hoping that by a victory of the conjoined army he would move the hesitating Hofburg to a decision. Success would in fact have been possible if Wittgenstein had at once ventured an attack upon Napoleon with the united army, before Napoleon had got his forces together. The Russian leadership however, which was at this time chiefly guided by the dilettantist suggestions of the czar, determined, in opposition to the advice of the Prussian generals, to wage a defensive battle at Bautzen, and this gave the Imperator, who immediately saw through the plans of his opponent, sufficient time to collect his forces and also to recall Ney's army. Whilst the main body of the allies remained inactive at Bautzen, the two corps of York and Barclay de Tolly were by a direct attack to defeat the oncoming armies of Ney and Lauriston, by which they were three times outnumbered. York endeavoured with the utmost courage to carry out this impossible demand. Through the sanguinary forest fight at Königswartha (May 19th) he first gained the name of the fighting general, and secured for his old Prussian regiments a dreadful respect alike from friend and foe. With wonderful tenacity and boldness did he conduct the unequal struggle, and brought back his little army to the main body in good order. The Prussians, however, had had to pay for the folly of the czar with terrible sacrifices ; more than one half of Steinmetz's brigade lay upon the field of battle, and yet the junction of Ney with the French army had not been prevented.

Thus, on May 20th, Napoleon was able to lead his entire force of 170,000 men against the 80,000 allies. The latter awaited the onslaught in a widely extended position upon the steep right bank of the deep valley of the Spree, fronting the west. Their left wing spread over the wooded heights of the Lusatian mountains, from which long before Loudon had attacked the camp of Hochkirch ; the right wing was unprotected in the open plain. In the first day of the battle Napoleon attacked his enemies' left wing, crossed the river, occupied Bautzen, and this led the czar to believe that the French sought a decision on the left of the allies, wishing to cut off the allied army from the mountain. The intention of the

Imperator, however, was rather to overthrow the exposed right wing of the allies, then to surround the centre, and to force the defeated army to undertake a dangerous retreat southward into the mountains. Whilst the Russians were still further strengthening their well-protected left, on the second day of the battle Napoleon threw himself in force upon the weak right wing under Barclay de Tolly, inflicted a complete defeat here, and then advanced upon the heights of Kreckwitz which Blucher held with the centre. After a long and murderous struggle this position too had almost been won, the lines of the allies forming a deep curve. Knesebeck, thereupon recognising the danger of a complete defeat, insisted upon breaking off the battle, and thus saved the army. Towards three o'clock Blucher withdrew in exemplary order ; and when evening fell the conqueror had won nothing more by the bloody work of two days than the possession of the field of battle. "What," he exclaimed fiercely, "is there no decisive result ; are there no trophies and no prisoners after such a slaughter ? " Forty thousand men had fallen, and of these twenty-five thousand were French ; the horrible place of decision was illumined by the surrounding villages in flames.

Immediately after this fruitless victory, Napoleon resumed his old plans, and sent Oudinot's corps against Berlin, but after a savage struggle, this force was driven back by Bülow and Oppen in the burning suburb of Luckau (June 4th). This was the first of four bloody battles by which during the summer the Prussians safeguarded their possession of the capital. In these very days, however, Hamburg was once again lost to the French. The unwarlike customs of the rich trading town had now to be atoned for in the day of need. The slow-moving and cautious senate did not know what to make of the grave burgher Mettlerkamp and of the many other valiant patriots who offered themselves for the defence of the town. Tettenborn had done little for the defence of the threatened city. Bernadotte, since he was not joined in Pomerania by the promised Russian accessory corps, did not wish to risk his little Swedish army, and made no attempt to relieve the place. On May 30th, Davoust was able to re-enter the rebel town. A reign of terror broke out such as had never before been known upon German soil. Courts-martial and extortionate monetary levies showed the German burghers what it signified to disobey the emperor of the French. The open city was speedily surrounded with fortifications which the unlucky inhabitants had themselves to construct, and twenty-five thousand were expelled as

a prepration for a prolonged defence. The fortified line of the
Elbe from Dresden to the sea was once more in the hands of
the French.

In a council of war held by the monarchs at Lauban, Hardenberg, supported by the Prussian generals, put forward the view that
the allied army, instead of withdrawing directly towards the east,
ought rather to move southwards towards Schweidnitz, in the
lower slopes of the Riesengebirge. [1] In this way, staking everything on a single card, the greater portion of the Prussian monarchy
would be abandoned to the enemy, but communications would be
maintained with Austria, and therewith would be kept open the last
possibility of victory. This counsel was followed. Thereupon
Blucher, in the plain of Haynau, suddenly made an attack from an
ambush upon the advance-guard of the pursuing French army
(May 26th), and pushed the enemy back so far that they lost touch
with the allies, and did not notice the changed direction of the
retreat. It was with astonishment that Napoleon discovered some
days later that the allies were on his right flank. How glad did the
grey-headed Prussian hero in later days think of the first cheerful
reception which he had prepared for the enemy upon Prussian
soil. For the first time in this campaign, fortune smiled on him,
and the brilliant success was due solely to his favourite arm. As
confidently as its leader, did the entire Prussian army now look
forward to fresh battles. In all the obstinate struggles of this
campaign, the German soldier preserved an invincible cheerfulness
and freshness. More than twenty minor battles and two great
battles were fought ; fifty cannon and a number of prisoners were
taken from the French, whilst Napoleon had not a single trophy in
his hands. Very different was the mood in the Russian army.
The generals, at first no more than lukewarm, now became cold when
they found themselves pressed back into the uttermost eastern
corner of Germany. As they had done six years earlier, they asked
themselves the disagreeable question, why they were sacrificing
themselves for foreign purposes. Barclay de Tolly, who had meanwhile taken over the supreme command, definitely declared that his
exhausted army had need of rest, and that it must be re-established
and reinforced in Poland. Blucher then wished to separate himself
from Russia, and to resist the enemy to the southward, at the foot
of the hills round Glatz.[2] The withdrawal of the Russians across

[1] Hardenberg's *Journal*, May 23, 1813.
[2] Blucher's Report to the king, June 1 ; Gneisenau to Hardenberg, June 3,
1813.

the Oder had already been ordered ; the alliance of Kalisz threatened to break up. Then came a serious mistake on the part of Napoleon which secured a truce for the allies and was to prove their salvation.

However loudly he might crow in his bulletins, Napoleon did not underestimate the dangers of his position, which to outward seeming was so brilliant. It was true that he held all the country on the right bank of the Elbe ; and that, in addition, Lusatia and a portion of Silesia were in his power, but he recognised the increasing disorder of his army, and dreaded the incalculable forces of a desperate national war. If now, with the laurels of two new victories on his brow, he were to offer peace, the outcome might perhaps be that the empire could secure its constitutional frontiers, and that the war of annihilation against Prussia might be resumed at some later date and under more favourable circumstances. The best ally of the French empire, the divergency of the eastern powers, might once again do good service. The Imperator expected nothing from his father-in-law's attempts at intermediation ; he had not forgotten that Schwarzenberg had recently said to his very face, that politics had been the cause of this marriage-alliance and that politics might also dissolve it ! He wished no good to the treacherous Hofburg which endeavoured to secure accessions of territory but lacked the courage to fight for them. He hoped rather, for a time, to gain something from the vacillations of Alexander, whom even before the battle of Bautzen he had vainly endeavoured to influence by alluring proposals of peace. The trusty Caulaincourt should conduct the negotiations with Russia. Perhaps the happenings of Tilsit would be repeated if the czar had " a golden bridge " built for him, if Warsaw could be divided between Russia and Prussia, if the Prussian state could be pushed back across the Oder and thus completely subordinated to the czar. Should this hope prove fallacious, it was true, as Napoleon and his marshals were well aware, that the allies would secure greater advantages from the truce than the Imperator himself. But it seemed to him that a truce was indispensable even for the continuation of the war. He needed time to strengthen his army, and especially the cavalry ; and he desired by pressing forward military preparations in Illyria to guard himself against the falling away of Austria. These were the two reasons which he gave to his generals as decisive. On June 4th he accepted the truce of Pläswitz.[1] However keen his calculations, he deceived himself

1 Cf. *Zeitschrift für Geschichte und Altertum Schlesiens*, pp. 38, 362.

regarding the energies of the Prussian state, and regarding the significance of this war in which any half-solution was impossible. He did not know that the allies accepted the truce in secret understanding with Austria, and that they hoped with increasing confidence that the Hofburg would join the coalition. As early as May 16th, Knesebeck had drawn up plans for a new campaign in conjunction with the Russians Toll and Wolkonsky, and these plans were based upon the idea of Austrian co-operation.

Count Metternich stood at the goal of his desires. A rare chance of fortune fulfilled everything in accordance with his hopes and threw into the hands of the state that had done nothing whatever towards the liberation of the world an opportunity for pronouncing a decision. As in Vienna had always been anticipated, the contending parties were equally balanced ; notwithstanding Napoleon's unwillingness, they would be forced to accept the mediation of the Hofburg. Now Austria could either impose peace on conditions in accordance with her own ideas, or else, if contrary to the wishes of the Hofburg the fight should be resumed, Austria could, with well-preserved energies, enter the coalition as leading power. Stein, Arndt, Blucher, and the whole Prussian army received with extreme ill-humour the news of the suspension of hostilities. After such sacrifices, nothing seemed more detestable to them than an easy-going peace. Their anger grew even hotter when it was learned that Lützow's volunteers had been treacherously attacked by the Rhenish confederates during the first days of the truce and had been almost annihilated. The king regarded it as necessary to pacify his loyal people by a proclamation. The truce, he said proudly, had been accepted in order that the national energies might be fully developed ; the ancient glory in arms had been regained, and soon the nation would be strong enough to fight for its independence. At the same time he ordered that an entrenched camp should be constructed at Spandau, so that in case of need, in accordance with the plans of the war party of 1811, Prussia might be able to continue the desperate struggle single-handed. At the wish of Gneisenau, Clausewitz composed his valuable work upon the spring campaign, and in this he proved that during the truce the military forces of the allies would increase enormously. Such also was Hardenberg's view of the situation ; in his diary, after the record of the fact of the truce, we find the laconic remark, " the best thing after all." Intimately acquainted as he was with the pride of Napoleon, he regarded it as altogether unthinkable that the still unconquered Imperator would accept the Austrian proposals of peace ; his confidence was the greater since he received from Stadion reassuring reports as to the friendly intentions of the Hofburg.

Whilst Austria was endeavouring to intermediate in securing the peace of the world, the chancellor continued to negotiate with England, and on June 14th accepted the treaty of Reichenbach, in virtue of which the two powers mutually pledged themselves to restore the independence of the states that had been subdued by France. He had had to struggle step by step with Guelph greed, and if at length he partly yielded, it was because he was in the position of the man who in great pecuniary need must pay enormous interest to a usurer. Without subsidies from England it was impossible for Prussia to carry on the war. In February, Hardenberg had himself declared this to the British cabinet. The tory government could absolutely rely upon a submissive majority in the two houses ; what use would it have been for the Prussian chancellor to ask for the support of the opposition ? When on one occasion he suggested to General Stewart that parliament and the English nation would assuredly not approve of such pettiness in so momentous an affair, Stewart answered with involuntary humour : " I have not been sent here by the nation or by the parliament, but by his Royal Highness the Prince Regent " ! Stewart and his colleague, the wooden, stiff, and pedantic Lord Clancarty, displayed the superior strength of the paymaster, and all the inconsiderateness characteristic of their nation. In addition there came into the question the fathomless ignorance of these tories. It was evident to Hardenberg from Clancarty's letters that the Englishman had either not read the treaty of Kalisz, or had totally misunderstood it. It was taken as a matter of course that Prussia would receive in subsidies only half what was given to Russia, and that in addition, thanks to her geographical position, she was to be immune from Guelph demands for territory ; the unlucky figures of the treaty of Kalisz now showed their practical significance. At length an agreement was arrived at for the payment of £666,666 sterling, for which Prussia was to put 80,000 men into the field ; and this pitiable sum, less by a third than the subsidies to Sweden, was paid in such a way that, allowing for the deduction for exchange, which was almost thirty per cent., Prussia received no more than three and a half million thalers. It was only after the most nauseous negotiations that Jacobi, the ambassador in London, succeeded in securing an agreement that the cost of the arms that were delivered was not to be deducted from the subsidies.

The king's sense of duty revolted against the idea of ceding Old Prussian territories. In case of need, he was willing to hand Hildesheim over to the Guelphs, for this had been Prussian for only four years; but he would not give way about loyal Ravensberg, nor yet about the strong position of Minden which, in accordance with the art of war of the day, was regarded as the key of the line of the Weser. When the Guelph negotiators demanded instead of this the cession of East Frisia, the king also remained firm; there even occurred a violent dispute between him and the chancellor. The Guelphs had at length to content themselves with the promise that Prussia would part with an area containing a population of 260,000 to 300,000 souls inclusive of Hildesheim. The prospects of Prussian diplomacy became gloomier day by day. The country had assumed new and far-reaching duties, and in exchange for these had acquired no more than a general assurance that Prussia should become once more " at least " as powerful as before the war of 1806. A day later Russia concluded her war alliance with England. The czar was altogether inaccessible to the desires of his generals for peace and also for Napoleon's offers. The reputation of the liberator of the world and the glory of the royal crown of Poland were now so tempting to his mind, that he hardly needed the exhortations of Stein; and the chancellor Rumjanzoff, the old opponent of the coalition, resigned his post. After a brief period of disheartenment, the Prussian patriots soon found themselves once again in the happy community of the invisible church, as Niebuhr used to say; they soon realised how greatly the truce would redound to the advantageous development of the Landwehr. In Silesia, Gneisenau, in conjunction with the president Merckel, conducted a splendid work, so that when the truce came to an end, sixty-eight battalions of the Landwehr had been constituted. Blucher wrote to him contentedly : " Go on doing the best you can with the Landwehr, but when the war is resumed you must come to me ! "

All these military preparations, and the peace proposals brought forward by the czar and the king, showed that the allies were not inclined to half measures. They demanded the restoration of the ancient power of Prussia and Austria; the dissolution of the Confederation of the Rhine, and the suppression of the duchy of Warsaw; the return of the North Sea coast; and, finally, the independence of Holland, Spain, and Italy. In most important respects these were the plans of Bartenstein; they could be realised only through a terrible war. The emperor Francis took a very

different view of the situation. He shuddered at the prospect
of this war and at the enthusiasm of the North German youth ; in
the bottom of his soul he had wished luck to his son-in-law in the
battle of Grossgörschen, and had expressed the hope that this
first meeting would have led to the cooling of many passions and
would have destroyed many chimæras. Terrible to him was the
thought that he might have to abandon the unsoldierly habits of
his sedentary life, and that it would be necessary for him, like the
two allied monarchs, to go into camp. The hard-hearted man
was not indeed troubled with any sentiments of tenderness for his
daughter in Paris, and the diplomats were accustomed to say of
him that his viscera consisted entirely of politics. But what was
the use of a hazardous war when it was possible by peaceful measures
to put some restrictions upon the superiority of France, and to
acquire a brilliant position by the side of his powerful son-in-law ?
Among the Austrian statesmen, the peace party was even more
strongly represented. Their most zealous spokesman was Gentz,
now completely plunged in blasé stupidity ; though when subsequently the war party proved victorious, he maintained with
astonishing coolness that the saving resolution was his work. On
June 24th he wrote confidentially to Karadja that the Hofburg
considered the time still unripe for the overthrow of the
French power ; he found it remarkable that the allies, whilst
they were demanding Austrian intermediation for peace, were
simultaneously concluding a war alliance with England. On this
occasion, Metternich saw further ahead than his emperor. He
recognised that Austria must necessarily become involved in a
Prussian defeat, should Prussia carry on the struggle until her own
annihilation had been effected ; moreover, he considered that the
elemental revolutionary forces in the Prussian army could only be
held in check if Emperor Francis joined the coalition. But he had
not yet formed a definite resolution, had not yet overcome his
inborn preference for crooked methods. On May 30th he assured
his confidant the Hanoverian Hardenberg that a permanent peace
was for the present impossible ; it would suffice if for the moment
a temporary peace could be patched up, which should secure for
the three eastern powers a basis of operations from the Baltic to
the Adriatic and which should render possible a decisive war at
some future date.

Such, then, was the sense of the peace proposals which the
mediator laid before the allies. These proposals showed unmistakably that the Hofburg was still a long way from a warlike

resolution, and that the Austrian negotiations with Napoleon had been no mere comedy. The wishes of Austria were restricted to four points : the abolition of the duchy of Warsaw, which was to be divided among the eastern powers ; the strengthening of the Prussian state by this partition, by the restoration of Danzig, and by the evacuation of the fortresses ; the restoration of the Illyrian provinces to Austria ; the restoration of Hamburg and Lübeck, and (in the improbable case that England should agree to a general peace) the surrender of the German North Sea coast. In this programme all the deepest desires of the Hofburg were displayed. With Illyria, Austria would regain her power on the Adriatic ; the suppression of the duchy of Warsaw would lead to the disappearance of that focus of Polish conspiracies which Metternich had always regarded as extremely dangerous for the three eastern powers ; by the new partition of Poland, Prussia would receive back those provinces to which the king of Prussia attached very little value, and would thus be made a power of barely the second rank ; finally, the Confederation of the Rhine was to be preserved, in accordance with Metternich's old principle that the smaller courts must be gained over by a yielding disposition.

What demands to make of the allies ! They hesitated for a considerable time, negotiating from June 10th onwards with Stadion in the headquarters at Reichenbach, and having at the same time repeated personal interviews with the imperial court, which had removed to the castles on the Bohemian and Silesian frontier. Hardenberg remained confident that Napoleon would never agree to these modest terms ; for they asked him to surrender what he still held by the strong hand ! At length, on June 27th, Stadion, Nesselrode, and Hardenberg signed the treaty of Reichenbach, which approved the Austrian proposals, but at the same time imposed upon the Hofburg for the first time a partial pledge of duty. Austria had to promise that if Napoleon would not accept the peace proposals before July 20th, she would immediately take up arms, would join in the campaign with at least 150,000 men, and would carry on the war on a plan concerted with the allies. If the war were to be resumed, the original idea of the allies of a thorough reconstruction of Europe was to be accepted as the goal of the common campaign, and the allies pledged themselves mutually to carry out this plan in the widest possible sense. Thus the Hofburg was bound in at least one eventuality. For themselves, the allies retained a free hand, declaring plainly that without the dissolution of the Confederation of the Rhine and the restoration of the ancient power of Prussia, they would not make peace, and to this the Austrian plenipotentiary offered no objection.

Meanwhile Metternich had gone to Dresden in order to win over Napoleon on behalf of the preliminaries to the peace proposals. Here they were holding high festival in the Marcolini Palace ; the whole imperial court was assembled, Talma and Mars acted before the Imperator. The French nation was to believe that their ruler really desired peace, and that arrangements were being made for the prolonged negotiations of the great European Congress. In reality his intention was wholly directed to the resumption of the war ; all peaceful thoughts had been dissipated since he had noted the satisfactory progress of his powerful equipments, and since he had come to recognise the unswerving determination of Alexander. In a prolonged private interview with the ambassador of the intermediating court, his injured pride and his repressed anger on account of all the disappointed hopes which he had at one time placed upon his alliance with the House of Austria, led him to use such passionate and insulting language that Metternich now began seriously to doubt whether an understanding was possible with such a man. To the experienced Austrian diplomat, the vanity of the Imperator, who had long accustomed himself to deal with the Hapsburg-Lorrainers as " refractory vassals of the crown of France," seemed akin to madness ; moreover, the man of the world said to himself with a quiet smile, this unruly and storming autocrat is, after all, only a plebeian. Nevertheless the two at length parted on the understanding that a formal peace congress should meet at Prague, and that the term of the truce should be extended from July 20th to August 10th. Napoleon had not yet completed his equipments, and to the Hofburg every postponement was welcome, for the Austrian army was still unready.

Meanwhile there were new and distressing problems to consider in the headquarters of the allies, to whom neither the congress nor the prolongation of the truce was convenient. On July 4th, Hardenberg met Nesselrode, Metternich, and Stadion in the castle of Ratiborschitz. There was a long and stormy discussion. Nesselrode declared that in the whole course of his long diplomatic career he had hardly ever attended a more lively sitting. Ultimately the allies trustingly left the conduct of the Prague negotiations in Austrian hands, because Metternich threatened that unless this were done, it was likely that his emperor might persist in armed neutrality ; but at the same time the allies declared with unflinching resolution that in case of need they would continue the war without Austria. Thereby Austria's entry into the struggle was rendered almost inevitable. It was obvious that Metternich's plans could prove successful only if he did not completely separate himself from the allies. If the fight were resumed and the Austrians remained neutral, he would have to fear being excluded from the advantages of a victory of the coalition, whilst he would be involved in the consequences of their defeat. It was by a political necessity stronger than human will that the Viennese court was forced to abandon its expectant attitude. Yet even in July, even down to the hour of the ultimate decision, there were grave moments of doubt. In the Prussian headquarters, Ancillon, after his cowardly manner, spoke in favour of peace, while Knesebeck declared in a memorial[1] that it was no longer possible to hope for the dissolution of the Confederation of the Rhine ; that in case of need, the Prussian state could continue to exist without Madgeburg, if well rounded off on the right bank of the Elbe by Mecklenburg and Swedish Pomerania, and should secure a strong position on the Vistula ! The king took a more courageous view, and wrote an autograph letter to Emperor Francis to the effect that the Prussian state must be notably enlarged in Germany if Austria were to find in it a strong and satisfactory neighbour.

The negotiations with Sweden had at length been brought to a successful conclusion. Since Denmark had once more formally returned to the French alliance, Frederick William's scruples fell to the ground, and he agreed by the treaty of July 22nd that the crown of Sweden should now join the league of Kalisz and should acquire Norway. By a secret article it was arranged that in case of need the Danes should receive compensation for Norway on German soil. To Hardenberg's levity of mind this seemed a matter of no importance. He considered that the compensation could, at most, take the form of a small strip of land, since Denmark was to be overpowered by force, and he considered it certain that in no event could Swedish Pomerania be the price paid for Norway. Bernadotte gave him a verbal assurance that Sweden was prepared to cede to Prussia the last remnants of her German possessions,[2] but what confidence could be placed in such indefinite assurances from a man so untrustworthy ?

Day by day the hopes of Austria's accession to the side of the allies became stronger. The news, too, of Wellington's brilliant

---

[1] My copy is undated. It is clear, however, from the form and content that the memorial must have been written during the truce.

[2] Hardenberg's Diary, January 24, 1814.

victory at Vittoria and of the complete liberation of Spain, had an encouraging effect upon the Hofburg. After the conversation of Ratiborschitz, Metternich came to the conclusion that the role of third party could no longer be sustained. On July 13th he for the first time disclosed his warlike plans to his imperial master ; even if the allies were to reject the peace proposals whilst Napoleon were to accept them, Austria could no longer remain separate from the coalition without exposing herself to public contempt. The emperor, who still remained whole-heartedly for peace, would not yet admit this unwelcome possibility, and he merely promised to do his utmost on behalf of the proposed peace programme, although certain parts of it seemed to him very extreme ; meanwhile Napoleon had gone to Mainz, to " the classic soil of France," as he was accustomed to term the left bank of the Rhine. Once again he held high festival in this town. Thither came Dalberg and the princes of Baden, Darmstadt, and Nassau, to pay their personal congratulations on the victories of the previous spring. He rejoiced at the sight of his fine troops, and returned to Dresden with the proud conviction that he was once more strong enough to impose laws upon the world. In the intoxication of his pride he did everything which was calculated to annoy and to injure the intermediating court, so that Emperor Francis was at length compelled by mortified pride to break with his son-in-law.

Anstett and Humboldt, the ambassadors of the allies in Prague, had extremely restricted powers, and had both secretly resolved to throw every possible obstacle in the way of the negotiations. No one was better fitted for such a task than Humboldt, a master of all dialectic arts. He, too, had been seized by the enthusiasm of the time, so far as this was possible to his cool nature, and he gladly laid aside his learned labours to devote himself for once entirely to politics. Napoleon's arrogance, however, rendered it unnecessary for Humboldt to do anything. He and Anstett had to wait several days before the French plenipotentiary arrived. Narbonne at length appeared upon the scene, but with insufficient credentials. Some days more elapsed until Caulaincourt arrived on July 28th. There then began an exchange of diplomatic notes concerning the form of the negotiations. The French plenipotentiaries made all sorts of malicious remarks, and continued the obstinate struggle upon matters of form until the last days of the truce, so that this most wonderful of all congresses came to an end without a single common sitting of the plenipotentiaries.

The open scorn displayed by the French, was sufficient for

the Austrian minister. He felt that his court could no longer hold back, and quietly prepared measures to secure a large war loan for the imperial house. Even during the congress, on July 27th, a secret understanding was concluded with the allies, in accordance with which Austria was to receive Illyria and northern Italy ; the king of Sardinia was to be restored to his inheritance, and Central Italy with Genoa was to be divided among the archdukes related to the Austrian imperial house ; Sicily was to be left to the Bourbons, who were under England's protection. Indeed, the allies even promised in advance to approve of anything that Austria should do in the Italian peninsula.[1] A few weeks later England also adhered to this treaty. The intention of the British cabinet was simply to overthrow French rule in Italy ; the tories would not recognise an Italian nation, and they were altogether indifferent to the claims of the Pope. The Russian court, the old well-wishers of Piedmont, who under Emperor Paul had so vigorously opposed Austria's Italian plans, now departed from its ancient traditions, since the friendship of the cabinet of Vienna was more important than any other considerations. To the Prussian statesmen, however, the demands of Metternich seemed unobjectionable. The chancellor regarded it as a matter of course that the Hofburg should revive the ancient plans of Thugut. He even asked Austria to incite the Italians to a war of liberation. In Knesebeck's memoirs we find in plain terms : " What Austria demands from Italy is in the very nature of things."

The position of the mediator, who had now abandoned impartiality through two secret treaties, became daily more untenable ; the farce of the congress was drawing to a close. Four days before the end of the truce Napoleon once more despatched a confidential enquiry to Austria, obviously doing this merely in order to prove to the peace-loving French nation his own freedom from responsibility for the war. When Metternich replied by an ultimatum, a somewhat more definite restatement of the proposals of Reichenbach, the Imperator sent a reply whose general sense was one of refusal, and with intent despatched this from Dresden too late, so that it could not reach Prague before August 11th. The truce had come to an end without France having accepted the conditions of peace. At midnight on August 10th, Humboldt and Anstett

---

[1] The actual wording of this treaty is still unknown. Its essential contents are manifested in a note from Metternich to Castlereagh, dated at Paris, May 27, 1814, and discovered by Farini in the archives of Turin (*Storia d'Italia dall' anno 1814*, I, 27). Much in this affair still appears puzzling (the alleged note of Metternich is a forgery. Cf. A. Stern, *Geschichte Europas* I, 275).

declared that their powers had expired and that the congress was at an end. The pledges of Reichenbach now came into force, and Napoleon's defiance had driven Austria into the camp of the coalition.

That great European league, for which statesmen had vainly been working for eighteen years, was now at length in arms. It comprised the four great powers, and with them Sweden, and, in addition, the liberated states of the Iberian peninsula. This time, moreover, it was not the chances of diplomatic negotiations which brought the congress together, but an absolute necessity. It was essential to re-establish the freedom of the world, to reintroduce that vigorous neighbourly association of the nations upon which depends the greatness of western civilisation. It is true that with the adhesion of England and Austria to the league, it was joined by two powers which were absolutely without understanding of the yearnings of the North German people. Strange enough was the difference between the involved terminology of the Austrian war-manifesto and the invigorating tone of the Prussian appeal. To what an extent had the talented spirit of Gentz undergone ossification and corruption in Vienna, that he could now glorify in Byzantine periods the Imperator's father-in-law, who, elevating himself above everyday circumstances, had given up for the sacred interest of humanity all that was dearest to his heart ! The bitter remarks in the manifesto regarding the impatient desire of the nations to anticipate the regular progress of the governments, sufficed to show that Austria's adhesion would lead to a change in the character of the war, and to the disillusionment of many of the hopes of the patriots. But this could not be helped, for the coalition could not maintain itself against the world-empire without the assistance of Austria. The issue of the congress of Prague was a great diplomatic success, and Frederick William was aware that he owed this success in large measure to the adroitness of his chancellor. With a lightened heart, on this momentous midnight of August 10th, Humboldt hastened to the Hradschin to give the pre-arranged signal, and soon there flamed the beacons on the summits of the Riesengebirge, so that in the same night the news was flashed to Silesia, and the delighted Prussian army received the joyful intelligence that in six days the war would recommence.

§ 3. THE PERIOD OF VICTORIES.

Through the fortunate progress of the Prusso-Russian military preparations and through the accession of 110,000 Austrians, the numerical balance between the two contending parties was now made approximately equal. The coalition had at its disposal a field army of over 480,000 men, of whom 165,000 were Prussians, and nearly as many were Russians ; the allied army was much stronger than the enemy in cavalry and artillery. Napoleon had increased his army to the strength of 440,000 men. The princes of the Confederation of the Rhine gladly furnished military aid, especially since the Protector was once more playing the part of the sustainer of particularism, and painted to them in the gloomiest colours the dangers of the restoration of the old German empire and of the loss of their sovereignty. It was the court of Munich alone which displayed a suspicious hesitancy, making the Austrian declaration of war a pretext for retaining the principal part of its military forces in its own country, and sending no more than one weak division to the North German theatre of war. If fortune should desert the French flag, Bavaria was prepared to go over to the other side. Among the unhappy troops of the Confederation of the Rhine, discontent had been gaining the upper hand since the dearly bought and fruitless victory of the spring. Napoleon did not trust them, and least of all did he trust the Westphalians. Nevertheless, he looked forward confidently to the war. The slight excess in numbers of the field army of the allies was largely outweighed by the French possession of the fortresses in the north-east, the siege of which occupied nearly half the Prussian Landwehr and also a great portion of the Russian army ; especially advantageous also to Napoleon was his favourable central position on the line of the Elbe, which he held from Glückstadt and Hamburg as far as Dresden and Königstein. Almost in the same place, Frederick the Great had for six years been able to hold his own against a far greater discrepancy of forces ; why should not the war-lord of the new century also succeed by skilful utilisation of the short inner lines of operation which were entirely within his control, in taking his enemies by surprise and in destroying separately their widely dispersed armies ?

The accession of Austria brought no increase to the moral energies of the coalition. The imperial troops fought bravely, as they had always done ; but they knew little of the stormy enthusiasm of the North German people, less even than the Russians, for these latter had not merely regained their ancient renown for an invincible passive contempt for death, but also by long association with the Prussians and by the favour of fortune, had gradually learned to delight in the German war which they had begun with great unwillingness. The spirit of 1809 was not revived. The people of Austria were unwillingly stirred out of the comfortable quiet of the last four years, and expressed with such vigour their dread of a new invasion by the French conqueror that Archduke John had to bespeak more courage from the men of Graz ; they were compassionating the soldiers on their way to the front, recalling nothing of the great days of this war, whilst the memories of Aspern and Wagram were still vivid in all their hearts. The great gulf between the mental life of the Austrians and that of the other Germans, was not bridged over by the War of Liberation. It was only for the sake of decency, only lest Austria should seem to lag too far behind Prussia, that Emperor Francis arranged for the formation of a legion of volunteers from the empire, a corps that never attained to any importance. The traditional hopeless inertia in the leadership and administration of the Austrian army, once more aroused the mockery of the French soldiers ; not one of the Austrian generals, with the exception of a few cavalry officers, acquired any renown in this war.

Since the Hofburg was carrying on the war in a half-hearted way, continually alarmed about the national enthusiasm of the Prussians and the Polish plans of the czar, it could not make use of its finest commanders. Moreover, Archduke Charles was an object of suspicion to his mistrustful imperial brother, and was unwelcome to the court of St. Petersburg as an old opponent of the Russian alliance. The supreme command was given to Prince Schwarzenberg, a brave cavalry leader and an honourable cavalier, who knew well, being possessed of fine diplomatic tact, how to hold the balance between the powerful conflicting interests in the great headquarters-staff, and how in the most difficult circumstances, notwithstanding the presence of three monarchs, to maintain a tolerable harmony in the medley of the allied armies. But he was no match for the genius of Napoleon, and he lacked the great ambition of the born commander. Radetzky, his admirable chief of general staff, had but little influence ; as a rule the generals Duca and Langenau had decisive influence in the councils of war. These were two theorists of the cautious and methodical school of Lloyd, to whom nothing seemed more terrible than to stake everything upon the open field. The magic of the Napoleonic name was still unbroken. Even Alexander began to believe that the new French art of war could be overthrown by its own pupils alone ; he placed his confidence chiefly in Bernadotte and two other deserters from the French side, Moreau and Jomini, and he even expected that these renegades would be able to bring about differences and party struggles in the Napoleonic army—a hope which was bound to be frustrated by the praiseworthy patriotism of the French. It was only in the Prussian camp that there prevailed the passionate demand for a great and decisive resolution, there alone was manifest that proud self-confidence which brings victory. It was however only in the course of the war, after some successes had been gained, that the Prussian commanders, who were the most notable military talents of the coalition, gained power and repute.

Metternich's intention to secure for his court the leading position in the alliance was completely fulfilled. Just as the supreme command of the united forces was entrusted to Prince Schwarzenberg, so also the new plan of campaign, which was based upon the conversations of May, was mainly conceived in the Austrian interest. General Toll, the most capable general staff officer of the Russian army, came to an understanding with Knesebeck and the Swedish crown prince at Trachenberg on July 12th for the formation of three armies, each of which was to consist of troops of the different nations, whereas Blucher desired to unite all his Prussians under his own command. A main force of 235,000 men assembled on the northern frontier of Bohemia, under the immediate leadership of Schwarzenberg ; thereby Emperor Francis was relieved of his chief anxiety, for a shift of the theatre of war into the interior of Austria was now hardly to be feared. In the Marks and on the Lower Elbe was the northern army under Bernadotte, numbering more than 150,000 men ; in Silesia was Blucher with 95,000 men. All three armies were to assume the offensive and to find their place of junction in the enemy's camp. If Napoleon should leave his central position at Dresden, and should attack one of the three armies with a superior force, this army was to retire and the other two were to threaten the enemy on the rear and flanks. This old Europe had at length learnt something of the new and bold methods of warfare. The aim of the operations was no longer conceived as the occupation of individual geographical points, but had become the conquest of the enemy. It is true that the cautious prescriptions for the carrying of this idea into execution, harmonised badly with the boldness of the fundamental strategical idea. The Silesian army was allotted by the headquarters-staff no more than the modest task of a great observation corps, for this army was the weakest of all, and was opposed to the strongest position of the enemy ; it was with difficulty that Blucher secured permission to venture upon a battle in exceptionally favourable circumstances. His officers complained of the modest role which was assigned to them, and envied their companions who were marching to Bohemia to join the main army ; but the old hero proposed to put the widest possible construction upon his powers. By good luck, too, in the headquarters-staff the enemy's forces were under-estimated by no less than 100,000 men, so that the cautious-minded were given a certain amount of courage.

Napoleon on his side was ill-informed regarding the strength and position of the allies ; he believed that their main army was in Silesia, and estimated the strength of the northern army at far too low a figure. His immediate goal remained, as always, the annihilation of the Prussian power. Whilst the Imperator himself undertook the difficult task of keeping in check, from Dresden, at once the Bohemian and the Silesian armies, Oudinot was to conquer Berlin, to disarm the Landwehr, and completely to repress the Prussian national uprising. If this should be successfully effected, it might be possible to reinforce Stettin and Küstrin, and perhaps even to relieve Danzig ; Bernadotte the irresolute would then certainly retire to the coast, whilst Prussia and Russia would have to throw their entire military forces into the threatened north-east, and would be forced to separate themselves from Austria. Thus would the forces of the coalition be dispersed, and perhaps it would then be possible for Napoleon's diplomatic arts to detach them completely one from the other. Since he did not even yet believe altogether in the earnestness of the Hofburg he intentionally avoided the campaign against Bohemia ; Emperor Francis was not to doubt the benevolent moderation of his dear son-in-law. The dread that he might be surrounded and cut off from the Rhine, was rejected by the experienced warrior with a smile, for he said : " An army of 400,000 men is not surrounded." He was well aware what an advantage was placed in his hands by the unity of the supreme command and the concentrated position of his army, and all the forces still available were collected by him in Upper Saxony. Only Davoust's corps was retained on the Lower Elbe for political reasons, for the strong position of Hamburg must on no account serve as a bridge-head for the landing of an English army.

Whilst Oudinot advanced towards the Marks, Napoleon himself turned first against the Silesian army, in the hope that he might induce the active Blucher to give battle. The Prussian commander retired in face of superior force, and did not venture upon an attack for several days, when Napoleon had hastened back to Dresden with a portion of his army in order to repel the advancing Bohemian army. Macdonald, who had remained in Silesia, imagined that the allies were already in full retreat, and on August 26th marched towards Jauer, not expecting any battle. His troops drove back the Prussian advance-guard, passed over the Katzbach, which was greatly swelled by the rains, crossed the raging Neisse, and then carelessly mounted the steep banks of the valley on to the plateau which rises above the confluence of the two mountain streams. There, however, York was awaiting him, hidden behind gentle undulations, with the centre of Blucher's army. He allowed a portion of the enemy to make its way on to the plateau, and then suddenly broke forth with a crushing impetuosity from his ambush, powerfully supported on the right wing by Sacken's Russians. A terrible slaughter began. The enemy, taken by surprise, was pressed into the corner between the two mountain streams ; the infantry could fight only with bayonets and with clubbed muskets, for their fire-arms would not work in the rain. As night fell, Katzeler's cavalry drove the broken remnants of the hostile army into the valley and the raging Neisse, and thousands were drowned in the wild waters. It was only the dilatoriness of Langeron, who remained at a distance from the battle with his Russian corps on the left wing, that saved Macdonald's army from complete destruction. Gneisenau bore in mind the night of terror after the battle of Jena, and commanded that all possible forces of horse and men should be sent in pursuit. Exhausted by the battle, and by the forced marches of recent days, the victorious troops were encamped during the night upon the sodden ground, without fire, hungry, and cold, in thin and torn clothing, most of them without shoes, and many of them succumbed to their inhuman exhaustion. Then they were started in pursuit of the conquered ; on the 29th, Puthod's division was overtaken by the pursuers at Plagwitz and was completely overthrown before they could cross the savage waters of the Bober ; the Irish legion, which was fighting under the French flag against its English enemies, here found a grave in the waves of the German river. The savage pursuit continued for days, always under heavy rain, involving serious losses for the victors and absolute destruction for the routed, until at length on September 1st, Blucher was able to announce in triumph to his army that the whole land of Silesia had been freed from the enemy.

The battle of Katzbach was the first really fruitful victory of this campaign. It freed Silesia, raised the confidence of the allied army, and provided a brilliant justification for Scharnhorst's work, for the new Landwehr showed itself a match for the best troops of the line. It awakened what is absolutely essential to every national war, a delight in a national hero, to whom the common man can look up with admiration. Blucher's name was in every mouth.

Those who stood nearer to the centre of affairs knew, indeed, that the old hero's plan of campaign had actually proceeded from the head of Gneisenau. Thus Gneisenau had now become marshal of Silesia, as Clausewitz had prophesied. It was he who formerly in terrible times had upon the walls of Kolberg first restored to honour the disgraced flag of Prussia. Now he was able to permeate the Silesian army so completely with the fiery energy of his heroic spirit, that the smallest army of the coalition soon became the focus of its finest energies—for to him it was an unquestionable fact that a man of courage can create courage for others. There soon came into existence between him and Blucher that admirable relationship of invincible mutual confidence which was to be as fruitful of blessings for Germany's destiny as had formerly been the friendship of Luther and Melanchthon, or the friendship of Schiller and Goethe. The veteran general gladly accepted the ideas of his quartermaster-general, doing justice to them as effectively as if they had been his own thoughts. The younger man, however, used all possible tact to maintain the prestige of the commander, issuing orders always in Blucher's name, keeping himself modestly in the background, so that not even Gneisenau's wife was aware for a long time of the true efficiency of her husband ; he accepted without a murmur that the rank and file should know little of him.

At the outbreak of the war he had taken with him into camp the maps of West Germany and France, and no others, for he counted with absolute certainty upon a speedy victory. Now his destiny brought him back into this eastern Mark of Germany where he had passed his best years in the monotony of subaltern's service. The dullness of that weary time now turned to his advantage ; he knew every nook and cranny of the country, and was well aware that the mischievous little brooks of the Riesengebirge quickly swelled in bad weather to become raging torrents, and it was upon this that he had built his plan. Nothing seemed to him more contemptible than to rest upon acquired laurels. Hardly had Silesia been liberated, than he conceived it as his aim to unite the three armies. Only in this way could a decisive issue be forced, and the bold man felt so sure of this ultimate success that as early as September, at a time when most were hardly venturing to hope for the conquest of Dresden, he declared to his officers that this very autumn they should pluck grapes along the Rhine. He was willing to speak of Napoleon as his teacher, for he had learned from Napoleon to despise the arts of the old military school, and he hoped to lay down his arms only when he had reached the enemy's capital. Thus to many of the leaders of the allies he was the pathfinder of victory, as he has been represented by the chisel of Christian Rauch, standing with extended arm pointing to the ultimate goal of victory, the only man who felt himself a match in greatness for the military genius of Napoleon. *Fortiter, fideliter, feliciter*—thus runs the motto of his coat of arms.

The serene energy and freshness of the man of genius attracted the enthusiasm of youth and the favour of women ; but among his old comrades-in-arms Gneisenau had first to justify himself by success. The three commanders of the Silesian army were loath to accept the directions of the young major-general, but the egoism of Sacken and the unruliness of Langeron were easier to bear than the captious censures and complaints of York. This ultra-conservative had not yet overcome his ancient hatred of the reform party. He spoke of Blucher as a rough hussar, and of Gneisenau as a fantastical war genius ; he complained of the destroyer of armies who demanded of the exhausted troops impossible deprivations and forced marches, and he repeatedly sent in his resignation. Blucher's magnanimity was not disturbed by all this. He said equably : " York is a poisonous fellow ; he does nothing but argue, but when he really gets to work he bites harder than anyone."

Gneisenau went his own way, equally undisturbed by Blucher's impetuous desire to press forward and by the anxious warnings of the generals. Through the victory on the Katzbach he disarmed opposition. Censure could no longer speak in so loud a tone, although it was not completely silenced. As in the subsequent course of the war almost all the finest laurels fell to this little army, the prestige soon seemed rightly to belong to the Silesian army as a whole. A glad feeling of self-satisfaction united all its parts, for they knew that they were in reality as Clausewitz said, " the steel pointed head of the heavy iron wedge of the coalition." Even the Russians were influenced to some extent by the peculiar joyful confidence of victory which radiated from Blucher's headquarters. Some of their leaders, such as Sacken and the daring cavalry general Wassiltshikoff, lived in friendly comradeship with the Prussians ; the Cossacks greeted the grey-headed commander with hurrahs whenever he showed himself, and told one another that the old man was really a Cossack himself, born on the shores of the blue Don.

The heart of any young German might well rejoice in the circle of heroes which surrounded Blucher. Besides York, there was the brigadier-general Steinmetz ; Horn, to whom years before the French had given the name of the Prussian Bayard ; Queen Louise's brother, Carl von Mecklenburg ; the bold cavalry leaders Jürgass and Sohr ; Katzeler, a favourite of Blucher's ; and the mad fellow Platen, with his eternal pipe ; among the younger men were Schack and Count Brandenburg, the minister of 1848, of whom York was glad to think as Prussia's future commanders-in-chief ; besides Gneisenau, there was the sober-minded Müffling, almost the only one to whom the youthful tone of this circle was unsuitable ; there was Rühle von Lilienstern, the friend of Heinrich Kleist, a highly-cultured and talented officer, who had always to be on hand when it was necessary to influence the other head-quarters-staff by personal persuasion ; there was Major Oppen, the hero of Spain, Fehrentheil, who subsequently succumbed to the demagogic phantasies of Teutonism, and young Gerlach who later became the leader of the ultra-conservatives ; besides these there were " the men of letters," as Blucher jestingly called them, the amiable and pious natural-philosopher Carl von Raumer, Steffens the philosophic enthusiast and, finally, Eichhorn, who preserved the memories of these rich months in his heart as a sacred inherit-ance, and who subsequently endeavoured to complete the work of the War of Liberation by the construction of the customs-union. It was like a microcosm of the New Germany, containing repre-sentatives of almost all the parties of politics and literature which were to animate German life during the following decades. Here there was no longer any trace of the rough hatred of culture charac-teristic of the old army. On unoccupied evenings the officers sometimes read Shakespeare's plays together, each taking a separate part ; or Oppen played German and Spanish songs on his zither. Everyone of them spoke his thoughts with unrestrained frankness, just as did Blucher himself ; nowhere else was the criminality of the German princes more sharply condemned, nowhere was the destruction of the Rhenish confederate sovereignty and the strength-ening of the Prussian power more frequently demanded, than in the environment of the Prussian commander-in-chief. " If I can get my way," said General Hünerbein to the electoral prince of Hesse, " your father will not get back as much land as I have dirt under my finger-nails ! "

What a contrast to the headquarters of Napoleon ! What a stillness brooded round the Cæsar since his luck had turned. He sat gloomily over the bivouac fire, his train whispering nervously at a distance, till suddenly, issuing his commands in a harsh and bearish tone, and with a flood of abusive language, which he showered on the heads of all from marshal to stable-boy, he would set the army once more in movement. To the diplomats and to the learned strategists of the headquarters-staff of the three monarchs, the Silesian army seemed like a closed political party. Metternich and Langenau heard with disgust of the delight in battle and of the loud candour, of the Prussian pride and the national passion, that characterised the camp of Blucher. Even in Frederick William's entourage anxious voices were already heard warning the king of the dangerous plans of the Silesian Hotspurs. Amid whispering and tale-bearing there was manifest the beginning of a party struggle which in years to come was to have momentous consequences for Prussia. Stein alone stood unmoved upon Blucher's side, and gave the czar his approval for every blow struck by the old hero. It was from the Silesian army that proceeded all the great resolves of the alliance, and Gneisenau said, with perfect justice, that posterity would be astonished when it came to learn the secret history of this war.

Meanwhile Napoleon's third attempt upon Berlin had come to nought. The natural inertia and dissension of all coalition armies was nowhere so conspicuous as in the northern army. What had this Napoleonic marshal, Bernadotte, in common with the sacred wrath of the German people ? He had abandoned his own father-land, but had not abandoned French conceit. Seven years before he had met as conqueror these same Prussian generals to whom he was now issuing his commands ; he had a poor opinion of their talents, and asked contemptuously if these were the men who were to defeat the great Napoleon. He expected nothing from the ragged and badly-equipped Prussian troops, who had to get along with five different kinds of small-arms, and with badly-made iron cannon. He knew so little of their sentiments that he held up before them as a shining example the great deeds of the French in the year 1792. He had always been a cautious commander, and now least of all did he wish to undertake any great venture, since a defeat might readily deprive his house of the still insecure Swedish throne. Urgent political grounds demanded of him that he should spare his Swedish troops. The war was not popular in Sweden ; the fine plan of conquering Norway in Germany remained incomprehensible to the people, and how was thinly populated Sweden to replace a lost army ? He said openly that it was the business of the Prussians to defend their capital with their own blood. Since his vanity was such that he imagined himself to be the most dangerous of Napoleon's opponents, he confidently expected that the Imperator would employ the best forces of the French against himself, and he declared an advance against Upper Saxony to be extremely precarious. The position of the northern army to the southward of Berlin was unquestionably difficult, for it might be attacked in the rear from Hamburg, might be threatened on the flank from Magdeburg, and had in front of it the fortresses of Wittenberg and Torgau. Other profoundly secret political plans imposed caution upon Bernadotte. The sly Béarnais had already learned in France to play the part of the free-thinking man of opposition, and was now once more in confidential intercourse with Lafayette and other dissatisfied spirits in France. It did not seem impossible to him that the will of the French and the favour of the great powers might place him upon the throne of France if his personal enemy Napoleon were overthrown. But if he wished to avoid inflicting a deadly wound upon the pride of the French who were already sufficiently embittered against him as a renegade, he must avoid giving the decisive blow in this war.[1]

The Prussian officers were at first pleased with the winning amiability of the talented and eloquent southerner, but they soon became estranged when they learned that their commander, even now when he was at the head of a great army, was just as hesitating and cautious as he had been in the spring when he let Hamburg fall into the hands of the enemy. A serious quarrel broke out. Generals Bülow and Borstell, both of them known to the Prussians as inconvenient subordinates with an obstinate belief in their own opinion, felt themselves conscientiously compelled to lay before the commander-in-chief certain advice and ideas, and it will be readily understood that the two valiant warriors, in the heat of their anger, were sometimes unjust to the suspected foreigner.

Oudinot's army advanced out of Saxony, 70,000 strong and composed of troops of the most diverse nationalities : French, Italian, Croatian, Polish, Illyrian—and in addition, the ill-famed division of Durutte, with its crowd of pardoned deserters and criminals. The principal part of the force, however, was made up

---

[1] I cannot find that G. Swerderus (in his rancorous book *Schweden's Politik und Kriege in d. J.* 1808-14) has brought forward any important data in favour of his hero.

of Germans from Saxony, Westphalia, Bavaria, and Würzburg. It was expected that a glorious entry into Berlin would once more firmly attach the Rhenish Confederates to the French side. The semicircular line of defence which is formed by the marshy waters of the Nuthe and the Notte, about fifteen miles to the south of Berlin, was crossed by the French after vigorous fighting, for Bernadotte had occupied the marshy forest land with an insufficient force. The French advance-guard was already moving through the woods and had reached Grossbeeren. Should it succeed in maintaining itself there, the hostile army had merely to cross the open plain to Teltow and could then immediately enter Berlin. The crown prince of Sweden cared little about maintaining possession of the Prussian capital, and had long made all necessary preparations for the evacuation of Berlin and for the retreat across the Spree. It was in a feverish tension that the inhabitants of the town listened to the thunder of the guns which were heard to the southward. They knew the fate which threatened them, for Napoleon had issued orders to burn the detested city.

On August 23rd, in the afternoon, Bülow determined on his own initiative to attack Reynier's corps at Grossbeeren, before Oudinot and Bertrand could bring up their supports. Whilst Borstell attacked the right flank of the enemy, Bülow directed his own advance against the centre in Grossbeeren. On this occasion, as in the case of almost all the battles of this autumn, a thick mist enveloped the countryside. The troops advanced dripping with rain. Among them were many men of the Landwehr. All were longing for the battle, none more so than the men of the Mark, who were here, in truth, fighting for wife and child, for house and home. Their flintlocks were useless as fire-arms, so they seized them by the muzzles and with loud shouts they dealt crashing blows with the butts upon the enemies' heads. Towards evening, Grossbeeren had been taken, notwithstanding the heroic defence of the Saxons, and Reynier was forced to retreat through the woodland with heavy losses. His corps would have been absolutely annihilated had it not been for the crown prince of Sweden, who, deaf to Bülow's requests, would allow only one Swedish battery and a portion of the Russian artillery to take part in the battle, instead of, by a well-timed attack upon Reynier's left wing, completely crushing the beaten enemy. Here, as in Silesia, the heaviest part of the work fell to the Prussians, and not by chance, since for them only was this war a struggle for existence. Oudinot gave up the game for lost, and returned with his army to Wittenberg.

On the following days the Berlinese hastened in crowds to the battle-field to greet their saviours; there was a long train of loaded carts bringing bedding for the wounded, food and wine for the weary. What outbursts of joy and sorrow; there was no end to expressions of thankfulness and to embracing; in a thousand moving lineaments was displayed the holy power of love which a just war awakens in noble nations.

The best of all was that the Prussians henceforward learned to love one of the heroes of their own fatherland, the ever-fortunate Bülow—for such was he named after the victories of Luckau and Grossbeeren. In the war of 1807 his comrades had indeed praised his efficiency, but had lamented his unending misfortune. Moreover, like York, he was a soldier of the old school, unfriendly to the aims of the reform party. But when the struggle began his level soldier's sense and his native courage induced him to make war boldly and in a manner concordant with the theories of Scharnhorst; moreover, Boyen was by his side as quartermaster-general. Bülow was talented and highly cultured. In youth he had been an ornament of the salon of Prince Louis Ferdinand, a connoisseur of the arts, and a talented composer. In his outward aspect he showed nothing of that stimulating and inspiring power which flamed from the eyes of Blucher. Who would have believed the inconspicuous little man to be a great commander, riding quietly along on his small and hardy roan, in overcoat and forage cap. But the officers knew how just and well-meaning he was, and, as a leader, genuine and level-headed. To his men he was a careful father, so that they swore by him and believed that under his command nothing could go wrong. Nor was the fear lacking which is essential to the command of an army; the quiet man could sometimes flame out in fierce wrath, when he held up before some captured Rhenish Confederate officer in unsparing words the disgrace of his employment as a catch-poll, or when from one of Bernadotte's aides-de-camp he received an order to retreat. After the success of Grossbeeren he encountered the crown prince with straightforward self-satisfaction, and even ventured to contradict in the newspapers the partisan and coloured reports of the battle which were issued by the commander-in-chief. The Prussian generals determined that they would not again obey the dilatory waverer, if he should once more in the fortunate hour refuse to attack—a dangerous resolve which could be justified only by the unnatural circumstances in which was placed this coalition army.

Simultaneously with Oudinot, Davoust had advanced from

Hamburg against Berlin, but retired upon receiving the news of
Grossbeeren. Girard's corps also, which from Magdeburg was to
have attacked the northern army in the flank, retreated upon hearing of the disaster ; on August 27th the retiring force was attacked
by the Landwehr regiments of the Electoral Mark under the
leadership of General Hirschfeld, in their camp on the Zauche
sand-hills near Hagelberg. Hirschfeld, a fine old fellow, who had
rejoined the army as a veteran of the Seven Years' War, led the
attack in accordance with the rules of the Frederician linear tactic ;
he did not expect too much from his rough and inexperienced troops,
and Marwitz, the leader of the reserve brigade, took the same view.
In actual fact the young soldiers did not at first hold their ground
in face of the unexpected fire of the French batteries ; but as
soon as their first alarm had been overcome, the Brandenburger
peasants, encouraged by the firm behaviour of a tried regiment of
the line, stormed forward irresistibly, and then there broke loose
the old *furia tedesca*, that savage wrath of the northern berserkers,
of which since the days of Varus the sagas of the Romans had so
many horrors to relate. What a wonderful sight it was when the
peasants rushed upon the compact square of the French infantry
at Hagelberg, advancing silently, pitilessly, in unspeakable wrath ;
when the dull crackling of the musketry at length ceased, there
lay a horrible heap of corpses piled up to the level of the top of the
wall, with the brains oozing out of the smashed skulls of the dead.
Girard brought off in safety only 1,700 of his 9,000 men out of the
horrors of this Landwehr battle. Such was the cost at which the
Mark was freed. Many an old burgher of Berlin took part in this
affair, as for instance, the bookseller G. A. Reimer, the friend of
Niebuhr and Schleiermacher, the unwearied patriot. He was a
captain in the Landwher of the Electoral Mark ; after the battle
of Hagelberg he hastened home on furlough, to hold his youngest
daughter at the font, and then returned to his battalion.

Less fortunate was the advance of the Bohemian army upon
Dresden. This helpless mass slowly crossed the ridge of the Erzgebirge, passing at first north-westward in the direction of Leipzig,
and then turning eastward towards Dresden. Fatigued by the
difficult marches in the mountains, on August 25th one-third of
the army, numbering about 60,000 men, reached the heights which
surround the town on the left bank of the Elbe. Had they had
the courage to deliver an immediate attack upon the greatly outnumbered corps of St. Cyr, which had been left for the defence of
the place, the most important supporting centre of the Napoleonic

army would have been taken by a *coup de main*. The inhabitants, who concerned themselves little about the great significance of this war, had already given up everything for lost ; and the alarmed king fled into the new town upon the safer right bank. In the many-headed council of war of the three monarchs, however, a cautious mood prevailed, and it was decided that the attack should be postponed until the whole army had been assembled. This was an unlucky hesitation, for meanwhile Napoleon's army came by forced marches from Silesia upon the Bautzen road. On the grey and gloomy morning of August 26th the Imperator reached the height of Mordgrunde just above the stream, where the view opens upon the charming basin of the Elbe, and looked long upon the majestic spectacle, how in the distance, upon the left bank of the river, the dark masses of the allied army surrounding the town in a wide semicircle and touching the river with both wings, slowly came down from the hills.

Once more, and for the last time upon German soil, the fortune of victory shone upon Napoleon. It was true that at the moment his army was still weaker by half than that of the allies, but as every hour passed new supports came up, and it was absolutely essential that the inadequately fortified town should be held until they all arrived. He was certain of success, rode with a loose rein into the town, and then remained for hours in the castle square across the bridge, quietly giving his orders, whilst the regiments of the guard passed by him at the double towards the western gates. The valiant grenadiers in their bearskin coats hailed their little corporal with loud shouts of acclamation, for wherever his eye watched, victory and plunder were certain. A Saxon officer upon the summit of the Kreuzturm, at whose feet the wide battle-field lay like a carpet, reported the advance of every section of the allied troops. In the monarchs' council of war the news that the invincible man was himself upon the spot aroused alarm and even terror. In the Austrian headquarters-staff, the men who were so learned in the art of war thought of retiring without a battle, and it was only the decisive opposition of the king of Prussia which forced them to venture an attack. Schwarzenberg, instead of collecting his best forces upon the left wing and advancing with these into the unfortified Friedrichsstadt, sent his centre and right wing against the suburbs of the old town, where the fortifications at the gates and the high garden walls of the palaces and country houses, facilitated the work of defence. After bloody but altogether random fights, the Austrians in the centre of the demi-lune advanced to storm the Falkenschlage ; on the right wing Kleist with his Prussians occupied the Grosser Garten just in front of the gates of the town, and endeavoured thence to enter the town itself, under a fierce fire from the guns which were concealed behind dangerous embrasures in the wall of the Rococo Garden.   When evening came, Napoleon himself felt strong enough to assume the offensive, and suddenly advanced simultaneously from all the gates powerful masses of fresh troops, snatching from the allies the few parts of the town in which they had already secured a footing, and ultimately pressing them back along their whole line into the villages upon the heights.   The attack had been repulsed.

Confusion and disappointment prevailed in the headquarters-staff when during the night the disastrous intelligence further arrived that the great army was already threatened in the rear. During recent months thousands of Saxon country-folk had been engaged in constructing a broad artillery road, leading upon the right bank of the Elbe over the Ziegenrücken through the rocks of Saxon Switzerland, bridging the river beneath the defiles of the Königstein, and opening beyond into the great Teplitz road.   Along this way was now hurrying Vandamme's corps, numbering about 40,000 men, in order to cut off the allies' retreat.   To the council of war it seemed that in such a situation victory was impossible, and the battle was renewed on the morning of the 27th only in order to safeguard the retreat.   Even this modest aim was not attained. Whilst the allies' right wing was in the course of the day gradually pressed back from the river and from the Teplitz road, the left wing sustained a crushing defeat.   Here the Austrians occupied the heights between the Elbe and the Plauen gorge ; on the right they were separated from the rest of the army by this precipitous gorge, and had failed to extend their posts leftward to the river.   Consequently Murat, under the guidance of Saxon officers, was able to lead a powerful force of cavalry through the narrow gorges which ascend from the valley of the Elbe, and to attain the plateau unnoticed.   Several squares of Austrian infantry were now cut down, taken by surprise in the rear and in the flank, and a whole division, hemmed in between the enemy and the deep rocky valley, was forced to pile its arms.   The Plauen gorge and therewith the road to Freiburg was in the hands of the French.   In the afternoon the beaten army retreated.   There were 20,000 prisoners in the churches of Dresden and in the Zwingerhof, and thirty captured guns stood in the castle court.   The servile Saxon ruler expressed delight at being delivered from the Russian plunderers, and in the palace wonderful fables were current of the great Saxon artilleryman who was said, by a well-aimed shot, to have killed the traitor Moreau at Alexander's side.

If the outward march of the Bohemian army had been laborious and disordered, what was now to be expected of its retreat ? A beaten army of 200,000 men, and only one road, that leading by Altenberg to Dux in the Teplitz valley. Those who could not find room on this main road must, for good or for evil, take the by-roads running along the mountain torrents through narrow rocky valleys, gradually rising to the crest of the Erzgebirge, and thence winding down on the steep southern spurs in numberless tortuous routes. The gorges were soon blocked by the immovable masses of the heavy baggage trains ; the rain was pouring down, everywhere disorder, anxiety, and hunger prevailed; and there was no longer any thought of a common leadership of the dispersed fragments of the army, penned in the narrow passes. The reins fell from the hands of the commander-in-chief, and in his anxiety he demanded of Blucher that he should bring help from Silesia to the great army. The diplomatists of the headquarters-staff began to despair, and it almost seemed as if the coalition were likely to dissolve after the first reverse. Who was to guarantee that Emperor Francis would not once more give up the game as he had done after the days of Austerlitz ? The definite treaty of alliance with Austria was still unconcluded. Had a vigorous pursuit been undertaken by the conqueror, its results would have been brilliant. Fortunately, Napoleon meanwhile received news of the battle of Grossbeeren, and hastened back to Dresden with the nucleus of his army, in order there to prepare a fresh campaign of annihilation against Berlin, for this was the aim he had nearest at heart. Even now the situation of the Bohemian army was a very dangerous one. If Vandamme, by the shorter route, should reach the valley of Teplitz before the allies, he could easily attack with superior forces the isolated corps as they laboriously emerged from the narrow mountain defiles.

Young Prince Eugene of Würtemberg who, with a Russian corps, stood in opposition to Vandamme's troops, near Königstein, recognised with secure insight all that was at stake. He threw himself into the great Teplitz road, from which the mass of the allies had been driven away, dispersed Vandamme's advance-guard, and thus reached before the French the crest of the mountains at Peterswalder. On the morning of August 29th, when the

Russians were attacked by the enemy, they slowly ascended the southern spur of the mountains towards Kulm. In opposition to the opinion of the prince, their generals had already resolved to evacuate the field and to retreat further southward across the Eger. But there then came from the king of Prussia, who had meanwhile reached Teplitz in advance of the army, the reiterated command to stand firm at all costs ; only if this corps in the east was able to check Vandamme's advance would it be possible for the Bohemian army further to the west to reach the valley of Teplitz without danger. Frederick William showed that he was a thorough soldier, now that he made up his mind to take command. He hastened to the Russians, encouraged the generals to desperate resistance, sent his messengers to the outlets from the mountain to summon all the troops that could emerge from the blocked passes, and himself issued orders to Archduke John's dragoon regiment to advance at once into the fighting line. The Russians offered battle ; the pride of their army, the carefully preserved guard, was on the spot. The valiant force, comprising 15,000 men, preserved its position throughout the day with invincible firmness against the stormy onslaught of an army twice as large. But the guards had suffered terribly ; what was to happen on the following day ?

In the evening the king sent to General Kleist, who was still high in the mountains at Zinnwald, ordering him to attempt to make his way eastward over the crest towards the Teplitz road, and thence to attack the French in the rear from the heights of Nollendorf. When the order arrived, Kleist had already on his own initiative after consultation with his quartermaster-general Grolman, formed the same lucky determination. The general, a quiet self-possessed soldier of the old school, could no longer advance with his corps through the blocked mountain ways, and had decided that the most venturesome course was here the only salvation. Whilst the Russians in the valley beneath, now considerably reinforced by the Austrians, recommenced the battle on the morning of August 30th, Alexander was upon a hill at Kulm overlooking the decisive spot. To the southward was the picturesque cone of the Mittelgebirge, northward the extended line of the enormously steep wall of the Erzgebirge, and between the two, in the luxuriant plateau, was the raging battle. Then he saw with astonishment how, up there at Nollendorf, artillery appeared, and thick masses of troops were descending the mountain upon the French. These were Kleist's Prussians, who, hungry and exhausted by a difficult nocturnal march, had reached the heights in the rear of the enemy. Thus hemmed in between the two attacks, Vandamme's army was completely defeated after a long and severe fight. More than 9,000 men were taken prisoner, and among them the rough leader himself, the executioner of Bremen. It was with difficulty that he was rescued from the hands of the German soldiers.

The laurels of Dresden withered on the day of Kulm. The tottering coalition once more became firmly re-established. Depressed as had been the spirits of the allies in recent days, the more jubilant were they now over this fine victory. The three allied nations had vied with one another to do their best : Eugene with the Russian guard ; the valiant Austrian cavalrymen ; Frederick William and the heroes of Nollendorf. In addition came the reports of the victories in the Mark and Silesia ; even the strategists of the great headquarters-staff, who had had nothing to do with these successes, began to believe that an ultimate victory might be possible. Within a week Napoleon had lost an entire army, nearly 80,000 men, and was again in the position he had occupied at the beginning of the autumn campaign.

A week later he sustained a new and more severe defeat. As soon as he heard of Blucher's successes, he abandoned the intention of himself leading the attack upon the Prussian capital. Advancing in person into Lusatia against the Silesian army, he entrusted to Marshal Ney the conduct of the fourth campaign against Berlin. The doughty marshal, who from the first had little confidence in this undertaking, assembled his army at Wittenberg, fought a sanguinary fight, in which he pushed back an isolated Prussian detachment, and marched on September 6th, without being aware of the neighbourhood of the enemy, across the sandy plain towards Jüterbog. Here Bertrand with the advance-guard encountered Tauentzien's Prussians, and whilst a fierce struggle was taking place Bülow attacked the left flank of the French columns on the march at Dennewitz. There thus ensued an unexpected and widely extended battle. Bülow, with a force of 40,000 Prussians, ventured to attack an enemy which outnumbered him by more than half, counting on the intervention of the crown prince, who was advancing with the principal forces of the northern army. The French were placed in a wide curve, with their right directed northward towards Tauentzien, and their left westward towards Bülow. The marshal was upon the right wing, with eyes only for what was going on in his immediate neighbourhood. As soon as he saw the forces under his immediate command beginning to waver, he sent orders to Oudinot's corps to hurry to his support from the left wing. Thus the left wing was greatly weakened, and Bülow succeeded in driving the Saxons out of Göhlsdorf, and in advancing as far as Dennewitz. The Prussians were everywhere advancing, when clouds of dust announced the approach of the crown prince with his seventy battalions. The sight of this reinforcement aroused a panic, and Ney's army fled in wild disorder.

Napoleon's most cherished plan had thus been annihilated. To the Prussians alone belonged the honour of the day. Once more had the Landwehr rivalled veteran troops, and once more had Germans striven with Germans in fierce fight. In the army of Würtemberg, whose best troops had been on Ney's right wing, the soldiers continued to tell as late as the year 1866 with tenacious anger, with what pitiless fierceness the Prussian Landwehr, and above all the stalwart Pomeranian cavalrymen, had swept away the Swabians at Jüterbog. The valiant Saxons fought in a manner worthy of their ancient warlike renown, and in return for this were accused of cowardice in Napoleon's bulletins. The unhappy little army began to feel the shamefulness of service for the Confederation of the Rhine, and after the battle of Dennewitz a battalion of the bodyguard went over to the Prussians. Frederick Augustus, however, at once discarded the uniform of the dishonoured troop and remained inalterably devoted to the great ally who had slandered his army.

After the exertions of these wild days, the Bohemian army needed a period of repose. Whilst the weapons rested, the diplomats were all the more zealously at work. Since the victory of Kulm Emperor Francis had no longer shown any inclination to listen to the affectionate protestations which his son-in-law continued to send. On September 9th, at Teplitz, three almost identical treaties of alliance, which replaced the temporary agreement of Reichenbach, were signed by the allies. They established what Prussia had demanded from the first. The Confederation of the Rhine was to be dissolved ; the dominion of France and of the Napoleonides upon the right bank of the Rhine was to be completely abolished ; for Austria and Prussia the *status quo* of 1805 was to be re-established. The powers mutually pledged themselves in the most solemn manner that they would not listen to any peace proposals on the part of France without communicating them to one another. Nevertheless, an unconditional agreement was by no means attained. The czar continued to veil his Polish plans in profound obscurity. In Reichenbach he had agreed that the duchy of Warsaw should be divided among the three eastern powers. Literally interpreted, this promise did not exclude the possibility of a kingdom of Poland under the Russian sceptre, on the condition that Prussia and Austria received certain portions of Warsaw. In the treaty of Teplitz the pledge was further weakened, for it was merely arranged that a friendly understanding should be arrived at between the three courts as to the future destiny of Warsaw. Thus the fortunate possessor of Warsaw undertook no definite duty in respect of the duchy.

Henceforward the Polish question hung like a thundercloud over the great alliance. All those who were well-informed knew how Count Münster in his reports to the prince regent continued to explain that it was especially anxiety regarding the future of Poland which was responsible for the hesitating course of Austrian policy throughout the war. As things were, Prussia and Russia could hope to acquire considerable gains only through the complete humiliation of France, whereas England knew that the colonies she had seized were well secured, and Austria might hope to obtain a dominant position in Italy after a partial victory. In addition, there came into the question the anxiety of the Guelphs and the Lorrainers regarding the ambitions of Prussia, for Prussia became more ominous to them after each fresh victory. Thus there ensued a schism in the camp of the allies which became more marked from day to day. Austria and England hesitated, while Prussia and Russia pressed forward ; this remained the essential characteristic of the diplomatic negotiations of the great war, although even the czar and the king experienced momentary hesitations. Schwarzenberg's slack circumspection and Gneisenau's brilliant boldness gave contrasted expression to the Austro-English policy on the one hand and the Prusso-Russian policy on the other. Openly and angrily did the Prussians and the Russians express their discontent concerning the lamentable performances of the great headquarters-staff. The king was himself extremely dissatisfied. Even before the advance upon Dresden, he had vainly proposed that the supreme command should be entrusted to the czar, who, through his imperial prestige and with the assistance of the talented Toll, might perhaps be able to carry something through.[1] When the event showed that his mistrust had been only too well justified, he no longer concealed his anger, and, greatly to Hardenberg's vexation, he decisively refused to gratify the Austrian commander-in-chief by the customary politeness of bestowing an order upon him.

[1] Hardenberg's Diary, August 18, 1813.

The most notable point about the treaty of Teplitz was its first secret article, which assured to the states lying between Austria, Prussia, and the Rhine " full and unconditional independence." If this clause were to be strictly interpreted, every subordination of the princes of the Confederation of the Rhine to a national centralised authority, and every serious attempt to construct a united state-constitution for Germany, would be rendered impossible, and such were Metternich's secret intentions. Hardenberg, on the other hand, understood by these momentous words no more than the abolition of the Napoleonic protectorate, and he subscribed the treaty unreflectingly, trusting blindly in Austria's patriotic intentions. He was not in the least inclined to admit sovereignty to the princes of the Confederation of the Rhine. To him, just as to Stein and Humboldt, the moment seemed propitious for a union with Austria in order to establish the elements of a strong federal constitution.

Stein sent to the monarchs a memorial which he had composed in Prague in the last days of August, one of the most eloquent and powerful productions of his pen. He solemnly adjured his distinguished readers that the contemporary world and posterity would condemn them utterly if they failed now to undertake with full seriousness the reordering of the German nation. " We have here the greatest opportunity in the world. There are fifteen million cultured and moral human beings, worthy of all respect through their inherited acquirements and the degree of development to which they have attained, and these by their frontiers, their speech, and their moral aptitudes, as well as by an innate and indestructible national character, are closely akin with two other great states." He thereupon went on to describe in his lapidary style how in the old empire, thanks to the imperial courts and the diets, everyone was secure in person and property, and he proceeded to levy a terrible accusation against the Confederation of the Rhine which had exposed these fifteen millions to the arbitrary procedures of six-and-thirty petty despots. " A lust for innovation, an insane self-conceit, a boundless extravagance, and a bestial voluptuousness, have succeeded in destroying every possibility of happiness for the unfortunate inhabitants of these once flourishing countries." Were this dismemberment to persist, Germans would continually become worse, more crawling, and more ignoble ; the mutual estrangement of the different countries threatened to increase year by year ; the influence of France would tend to become ever more firmly established. For this reason there must disappear with the Confederation of the Rhine, also "the despotism of the six-and-thirty petty chiefs." The writer then returns to his St. Petersburg plans, and demands, since the complete unity of the old and grand days of the empire is impossible, that there should be constituted two great federal states : that Prussia strengthened by the addition of Saxony, Mecklenburg, and Holstein, to attain 11,000,000 inhabitants, should rule the north ; and that Austria should control the south, with a German possession of 10,000,000 inhabitants. In this dualistic community all the workable institutions of the ancient empire were to be revived. The mediatised territories of 1806 were to be restored (the baron gave up for lost the victims of the Diet of Deputation) ; the middle states, which had been enlarged by France at the expense of the empire, were to be reduced in size, for they were far more dangerous to the fatherland than the powerless particularism of the petty states. For this reason, also, the emperordom was to be revived for Austria ; this half-foreign state must be bound to Germany by its interests, whereas in Prussia the German blood spontaneously flowed more freely and purely. Military matters and foreign policy were to be under the control of the empire, so that a German diplomatic corps was to come into existence distinct from the Austrian ; similarly there were to be imperial coinage, customs, and law courts. There was to be a Reichstag in Ratisbon, with three benches as of old ; its members were not to be envoys but representatives ; the bench of the imperial towns was to be increased by the deputies of the provincial diets which were to be summoned in all the German states. In the opinion of the imperial knight, such a league could ultimately take away from the French the country between the Rhine and the Scheldt—for not even Stein ventured at this moment to hope for the immediate liberation of the left bank of the Rhine.

Great ideas, which were to bear rich fruit in the future, were contained in this memorial, such as the twofold demand for provincial diets and a German parliament ; but everything was still fermenting and inchoate. The true nucleus of the German question still remained completely obscured from the leading man of the nation. In his magnanimous enthusiasm for the greatness of the Othos and the Hohenstaufen, he desired to restore that foreign dominion whose miseries had been endured for three centuries, and which had led to the destruction of the old imperial realm. How the Prussian hegemony of North Germany was to be harmonised with the Austrian emperordom and with the Reichstag of Ratisbon, whether Prussia was to renounce an independent

European policy and to renounce also its own military supremacy in favour of this imperial crown—all these momentous questions were left untouched by the imperial knight.

The chancellor showed himself to be in agreement with several of the fundamental ideas of the memorial. Like Stein, he regarded the middle states as the worst enemies of Germany, and proposed to take away from them the shameful acquisitions of the last seven years. The *status quo* of 1805 was to form the criterion, not only for the re-establishment of the two great powers, but also for the other German states. Hardenberg, however, did not wish to restore to the mediatised states the territories which had just been won, but wished to use these to strengthen Austria and Prussia. Just as much as Stein, he was convinced of the necessity of dualism. So seriously and so disinterestedly did he pursue these old Bartenstein plans, that he repeatedly and urgently begged the Austrian statesmen to reunite with the imperial state the hither-Austrian lands on the Upper Rhine. Thus only could Austria become in reality the lord of South Germany, and thus only, compelled thereto by her own interests, could Austria make head against any attack by France. The safeguarding of German soil against new abuses of power on the part of the western neighbour, appeared in Hardenberg's eyes to be the most important aim of the future Germanic Federation. On the other hand, he decisively rejected the restoration of the emperordom. Except Stein, Humboldt and all the other Prussian statesmen were in agreement with the chancellor. So strong had grown the sense of independence of the North German power, that even a formal subordination could no longer be endured ; it was only in complete equality that the two great powers could stand at the head of the minor states. Among the North German patriots, since the victories of the last few weeks, the question was voiced ever more frequently : Why should not this Prussia, who is leading the armies of Germany, take over for herself the leadership of the empire in place of Austria ?

If it had been possible for Metternich's dread of the North German Jacobins to be increased, such an increase must have been the outcome of this memorial. In every sentence he found the exact antithesis of his own opinion. Which was worse : Stein's unceremonious language about the Confederation of the Rhine, the demand for the annexation of Saxony, or the demand for a German parliament ? The timorous Gentz, who had long cast aside all memories of his more energetic years, complained in moving terms that this War of Liberation was beginning to resemble a war for freedom, and threatened to end with a revolution instead of with a restoration ! The offer of the imperial dignity tempted the Austrian statesman as little as it had done in the spring. England, Russia, and Sweden had also in recent weeks repeatedly spoken of the renewal of the emperordom. Since the glories of the revolutionary world-empire had begun to wane, a conservative tendency grew continually stronger at all the courts ; involuntarily there manifested itself everywhere the desire for a simple restoration of the ancient conditions. Austria, however, held firmly to a refusal. Never again should the House of Lorraine be burdened with the empty vanities of a crown which could now only secure the hatred of France and of the middle states.

Metternich wished to spare at all costs even these French vassals who had incurred Prussia's contempt and anger. He thought of defeating Napoleon's German policy with its own weapons. He played the part of the well-wisher of the Rhenish Confederate courts, declaring himself prepared in case of need even to mediatise some of the petty princes for the advantage of the kings. Since he was well aware of the hatred of the middle states towards all strong federal authority, he declared that the German problem could be solved only in a free understanding with the Rhenish Confederate princes. He even surprised the Anglo-Hanoverian statesmen with the question : " Why, after all, should we have a German federal constitution which could only make bad blood ? How much simpler would it be if we were to content ourselves with an extensive system of treaties and alliances, which would pledge the sovereign German states to mutual help in case of war ! " For this reason he refused to have any intimate discussion with Hardenberg, and actually managed to secure that nothing should be arranged at Teplitz about the German constitution. His confidant, privy councillor Binder, said good-humouredly that just as the constitutional work of the peace of Westphalia had originated directly out of the chaos of the great war, so also the constitution of the Germanic Federation would, when the time was ripe, be the spontaneous creation of circumstances. Meanwhile, Humboldt, the old friend of Gentz, the daily companion of Metternich's adventures and pleasures, was maligned to the chancellor. Next to Stein, Humboldt was hated by the Austrians as the chief originator of the Prussian federal plans ; it was considered that there would be little difficulty in proving to the already prejudiced chancellor that the suspected man was endeavouring with the help of " political enthusiasts " to grasp the helm of the state.

Metternich's attitude did not arise merely from his natural love of ease, nor was it solely the outcome of the poverty of his intelligence (for despite all his cunning, his infertile spirit was incapable of grasping the idea of a great creative plan for a constitution) ; it was due also to a sound appreciation of the capacities of his own state. Just as Prussia had always suffered more from its weakness, so had Austria suffered from its strength, from that excess of fundamentally differing political aims which were imposed upon the country by the extraordinary complexity of its confused territorial possessions. This ancient curse of the imperial state was now renewed by the blind greed of a cunning and arrogant statecraft. The new Austria wished to rule Italy, to maintain at the same time the leadership of Germany, and to hold together the dissentient national masses along the Danube. These were three difficult tasks which no state in the world, and least of all a state whose spiritual forces were so inadequate, could permanently succeed in fulfilling. The time was to come in which the shortsighted folly of this policy was to be cruelly punished, but as yet no one had seen the profound immorality and the inner impossibility of Metternich's designs. It was not without envy that the cabinets contemplated the good fortune and security with which this skilful man approached his goals. He recognised with justice that Austria possessed its chief force in inertia, and that it must necessarily reject all bold innovations. A state in such a situation had no more dangerous enemy than the desire of the nations for unity and freedom, and on the hither side just as much as on the further side of the Alps, Austria must support itself solely upon the dynastic interests of the courts.

This Austrian statesman wished to be content in his wary fashion with an indirect dominion over the whole of Germany, without injuring the kings by Napoleon's grace through the establishment of the pretentious forms of imperial majesty. All the less had he in view a joint dominion with Prussia, since he was well aware that the middle states were united in fearing the hegemony of the rising Prussian power in the north far more than they dreaded the Austrian emperordom. All instructed diplomatists were well acquainted with Metternich's view. Even Hardenberg could not have failed to recognise it if he had kept his eyes open ; for why should Austria have so persistently refused to renew its rule over the Upper Swabian territories ? Here, however, began the long series of diplomatic failures of the chancellor. His treaties with England and Russia were, apart from isolated defects, certainly

justified by the demands of necessity. His behaviour to Austria
was the outcome of an error weighty with consequences. He lightheartedly assumed that Austria was animated by a friendly and
neighbourly sentiment, of which in actual fact the Hofburg displayed no trace. It is however probable that this opinion of his
was intentionally strengthened by his cousin Count Hardenberg,
the Hanoverian agent in Vienna, a double-tongued man of ill
repute who for long played the part of intermediator between
the two German great powers but who was in reality a mere tool
of Metternich.

Austrian policy knew how to make a clever misuse of this careless confidence of the allies. Metternich in later years, when he
became more serious and hard-working, sometimes carried out an
artfully planned game of sowing discord. At this time he was still
the light-minded, frivolous man of the world, and often reduced to
despair the passionate Gentz, who carried on the struggle against
Prussia and Russia with grim seriousness, while Metternich was
carelessly spending his time in amorous intrigues. So childlike,
however, was Hardenberg's ingenuousness, that an easy-going
delay, and at times even a friendly lie, were sufficient. Since Austria
refused all discussion of the problem of the German constitution,
the Prussian statesman obstinately continued to believe that the
Hofburg would in the end allow itself to be persuaded to undertake
the dangerous office of guardian on the Upper Rhine. Hardenberg, moreover, acted as if his dualistic plans had already received
the assent of the court of Vienna; and full of confidence he approved
that Austria, as the leading power of South Germany, should treat
with the southern states regarding their adhesion to the coalition.
It seemed to him a matter of course that this should be done when
the Austrian troops were already at the Bavarian frontier. Thus
was the fate of the German constitution left in Austria's hands,
and this at a moment when the falling away of the Rhenish confederates from Napoleon could no longer alter the course of the war!
The form of the future Germanic Federation depended exclusively
upon the negotiations with the southern kings. In North Germany,
in the Prussian sphere of influence, no negotiation was necessary;
there the only thing of immediate importance was to rid the land
of King Jerome and the Napoleonic prefects. What sanguine
patriots had really to expect from the Hofburg was shown in
October by a cynical utterance of Gentz in the *Prager Zeitung*,
to the effect that victory was the transition from a state of self-
denial into a state of peace and enjoyment! What was to be

expected was shown even more clearly by the interminable negotiations about Stein's central administrative council.

Ill-fated from the first was this creation of the baron's. For months the council had really nothing to do because there had been no conquests to speak of. All the foreign powers which were still reckoned as German, England, Sweden, and Austria, repeatedly manifested their mistrust. The dethroned petty princes, on the other hand, pressed forward, and naturally the irrepressible Gagern was not lacking. This old and tried saviour of particularism produced full authority from the elector of Hesse and the prince of Orange, demanding a seat and a vote for these two landless lords. As soon as Austria had joined the alliance, Metternich demanded that the suspect authority should be completely transformed, insisting that it was to be nothing more than a military victualling office. The Russian envoy Alopeus, who had hitherto carried on the provisional government in Mecklenburg, and was a trusted friend of the Prussian patriots, was recalled at the desire of the Hofburg. In Teplitz, Humboldt brought forward a modified proposal, but to Metternich's horror, this contained an article to the effect that the central administration should summon diets in the conquered territories. There was fresh deliberation and fresh procrastination. Nesselrode, too, Alexander's new adviser, who always eagerly accepted Metternich's views, showed himself lukewarm. Matters remained in abeyance, and it was not until October 21st, after the battle of Leipzig, that a new agreement was signed, by which the authority from which so much had been expected was robbed of all political significance. Stein and his faithful collaborator Eichhorn wished that the petty princes who might join the coalition should be given no more than temporary charge under the supervision of the central administration, for they ought to regard all suzerain rights restored to them by the future charter as a gift from the Germanic Federation. Metternich, on the other hand, wished to win over the petty princes by securing for them the continuance of the suzerainty bestowed upon them through the robbery of the old empire. The central administration seemed to him all the more dangerous because he feared that it might pave the way to a union of Saxony with the Prussian state. Metternich's view prevailed. The efficiency of the central administration was restricted to the conduct of military equipment and to the provisioning of the army in the conquered territories. Stein, with a council of agents from the allied governments, received the supreme supervision. The military governors appointed by him

were to have their commands carried out only through the intermediation of the existing authorities. Whoever voluntarily joined
the coalition might by agreement preserve his territory from the
interference of the central administration. Within the sphere of
activity thus limited, the central administrative council did very
valuable work in Stein's vigorous hands, although it was continually
at war with the ill-will of the Rhenish Confederate sovereigns,
but the original bold plan to deal with the domains of the petty
princes as masterless goods, was brought to nought by Austria.

Meanwhile Metternich had made use of his valuable authority,
and had come to terms with Bavaria. Notwithstanding the favourable military situation of the allies, in the timorous headquarters-
staff, three weeks before the decisive battle, there still prevailed
so little confidence of victory that even the czar regarded the little
Bavarian army as an extremely valuable reinforcement. Metternich attached yet more importance to the accession of Bavaria.
It was his hope, by a speedy understanding with the court of
Munich, to win back without delay the western provinces lost during
the last eight years, Tyrol and the surrounding region, and thus to
open the gate of Italy to the Austrian army; he hoped further by
his understanding with Bavaria, to prove to all the Rhenish Confederate kings that in the Hofburg they had a far-seeing well-wisher.
In September, the cabinet of Munich at length came to the conclusion that it was time to abandon the sinking ship. Both the
emperors encouraged the king of Bavaria by friendly letters ;
privy councillor Hruby, one of the cleverest of the Austrian diplomats, through whose activities the Prussian state was often to
suffer greatly in the future, travelled busily to and fro. On October
8th Austria and Bavaria concluded the treaty of Ried. Both
parties could claim a considerable diplomatic success, but the
greater gain was that of Austria. The Hofburg acquired Tyrol,
Salzburg, and the region of Inn and Hausruck, and at the same
time delivered three shrewd blows against Prussia. The leading state of the Confederation of the Rhine entered the coalition
as a power of equal rank with the others, securing a formal exonera-
tion of all past errors. Now it became apparent what sense was
attached by Austria to the momentous words of the treaty of
Teplitz. The " complete and unconditional independence " there
spoken of, was interpreted in such a way that Bavaria, freed from
all foreign influence, was to " enjoy her absolute sovereignty."
In this way the federal plan of Prussia had its edge turned. Bavaria
received further the recognition of the *status quo*, this meaning that

Hardenberg's plan to deprive the Rhenish Confederate states of the spoil of recent years fell to the ground, and Ansbach-Bayreuth was lost to Prussia. Finally, the court of Munich received, in return for the provinces ceded to Austria, the territories of Würzburg and Aschaffenburg, as well as the secret promise of other German territories which were supposed to be inseparably dependent upon Bavaria. In this way the House of Wittelsbach was firmly cemented to Austria for the immediate future.

The secret articles of the treaty of Ried were long kept concealed from the Prussian cabinet,[1] and when they at length came to light they aroused lively anger. In Teplitz, Hardenberg and Humboldt had proposed an article for the Bavarian treaty in accordance with which Bavaria was to be subjected to the Germanic federal authority, but they did not succeed in inducing either the czar or Metternich to accept this, and now they were to learn that Austria agreed that the most dangerous and inimical state of the Confederation of the Rhine was to be discharged from all duties towards Germany. Montgelas did not even think it necessary to conceal his Bonapartist inclinations. In the public declaration which announced the complete change of colours, he openly expressed the hope that there would soon be renewed those friendly relationships which the king had renounced only at the last moment and in consequence of urgent need. And this was the state to which Austria had surrendered the ancient tribal lands of the Hohenzollerns !

At the beginning of the year, at a moment when the detachment of Bavaria from France might have altered the whole course of the war, the chancellor had indeed been prepared to renounce the Franconian margravates. Now, when the circumstances were completely changed, no one thought any longer of making such sacrifices for so trifling a gain. On the contrary, Frederick William had at this very moment commissioned Colonel Krauseneck to undertake from Bohemia a raid into Ansbach-Bayreuth, to summon the Franconians to rise on behalf of their old prince. Now it was learned that Metternich had misused the authority given him by Prussia, to bring about what the Hofburg had vainly sought since the days of the peace of Hubertsburg, to drive the North German state out of the south, and to deprive it of its position on the flank of Bohemia. The king was no less embittered than were the people of the margravates. The childlike political culture of the time is manifested by the fact that as soon as the fetters of the Confedera-

---

[1] Hardenberg's Diary, November 17, 1813.

tion of the Rhine had been broken, all the German stocks without exception desired to return to their ancient princely houses. Nowhere was this legitimist sentiment so manifest as among the Franconians. By Hardenberg's administration they had once been relieved from a position of intense economic embarrassment, and had subsequently suffered severely under the arbitrary rule of the prefects of Montgelas. They implored the king not to sacrifice them, and subsequently sent a touching address to the Congress of Vienna, asking to be restored to their former prince, whose wise administration had alone enabled the country to make head against the troubles of the last eight years. In the Fichtelgebirge the memory remained vivid for many decades of the good old time, when Queen Louise with her young consort had wandered through the rocky chasms of the Luxburg. In the forests, the children sought for the bracken which when the stems were cut across showed them the Brandenburg eagle. It was hard for the king to be forced to repel so much heartfelt loyalty, but as soon as the terms of the treaty of Ried were made known it was necessary for the chancellor to make a formal renunciation of Prussian claims upon Ansbach-Bayreuth. But the precaution came too late. Soon after the battle of Leipzig, Prussia, to avoid remaining quite empty-handed, occupied the duchy of Berg, and retained under its own administration this region which in Munich had always been regarded as the equivalent of the Franconian margravates.

In this way it was decided that Austria was to hold in her own hands the arrangement for the future of Germany. Meanwhile the Imperator's need was increasing. New and extensive levies were demanded from exhausted France. The nation must take example from the enormous exertions of little Prussia, and must stake everything in this war against England ; it was only on this account that the war continued, because the irreconcilable English enemy insisted that the French should work like the Hindus for England alone. The wretched woman who was carrying on the regency in Napoleon's name, the daughter of the last German emperor, was shameless enough to say in the senate : " I know more than anyone else what our people has to expect if it ever allows itself to be conquered." Surrounded by three hostile armies, Napoleon still endeavoured several times to gain air for himself by an attack. Twice he turned against the Silesian army, which had pressed forward into Lusatia, and once against the Bohemian army. Blucher, however, cleverly eluded him, and when on September 10th the

Imperator looked down into the valley of Teplitz from the summit of the Geiersberg, he could not summon up resolution to offer battle to the Bohemian army. As Napoleon said, it was nothing but an everlasting *va et vient*. The useless game threatened to continue for ever. The great army did not move from its position. Bernadotte made no use of the victory of Dennewitz, and would not cross the Elbe as long as Wittenberg was still in French hands. Wallmoden's corps did indeed, by a fight on the Göhrde, frustrate an attempt of Davoust's to reinforce the garrison of Magdeburg. The military adventurers Colomb and Thielmann obtained many fine successes in the rear of the enemy. Czernitsheff's Cossacks were even fortunate enough to occupy Cassel for some days, and to chase King Jerome out of his capital. But what bearing had all this upon the course of the great war ? Clausewitz said mockingly that both parties remained opposite one another like a setter and a partridge, until the sportsman gave the word.

The word was at length given by Blucher and Gneisenau. They had disregarded the repeated order to withdraw to Bohemia, because they wished to retain freedom of movement for the Silesian army. When the war seemed completely arrested, they determined on their own initiative to move north-westward across the Elbe, and to carry with them the hesitating Bernadotte. If they were successful in this, the great headquarters-staff would be forced at length to pluck up courage to cross the Erzgebirge, and the three armies could unite somewhere in the neighbourhood of Leipzig. Should Napoleon in the meanwhile move towards Silesia, it would be all the better for the allies, for their united forces would then forbid his return, since Gneisenau's aim was not to safeguard the province, but to gain the enemy's camp. He wrote proudly : " Let us open the scene and play the leading part, since the others will not do it." The king fully approved of the bold resolve, but the Russian plenipotentiary in Blucher's headquarters entered a formal protest.

On September 26th Bennigsen with the Russian reserve army entered the valley of Teplitz from Poland ; could Schwarzenberg only see his way to unite the armies he would have control of a decisively superior force. On the same day, Blucher advanced out of Lusatia, and this was the turning point of the campaign. On October 3rd he crossed the Elbe at Wartenburg, in that marshy depression where the black Elster joins the Elbe. On the left bank was Bertrand's corps, consisting of Frenchmen, Italians, and Rhenish confederates, between Wartenburg and Bleddin, completely hidden from the eyes of the Prussians, protected by lofty embankments and by the marshy old channel of the Elbe. Blucher sent York's corps against this almost impregnable position. York was enraged at the madness of Gneisenau's plans, but he undertook the venture and after repeated attempts, his troops, with incomparable courage, actually succeeded in mounting the dykes and forcing the enemy to withdraw. Once more a brilliant victory was gained by the Prussians alone, and once again the unfortunate Würtembergers had to learn the sharpness of the Prussian swords. The struggle was so furious that the black hussars on one occasion forced the Italian artillerymen who had been taken prisoner to direct their guns against their comrades. General Oppen fought happily amid the *mêlée*; he had ridden over from the neighbouring northern army, and could not be prevented from going under fire as an ordinary cavalryman. It was horrible to see the poor linen-weavers of the Silesian Landwehr lying in masses shot through the heart on the wet ground beneath the fruit trees on the Elbe dykes ; before the battle they had shaken down the plums at their ease. When Eichhorn contemplated these lamentable corpses, which had been animated by so much devotion and so much heroic fire, pious thoughts came to his mind, and he recognised the meaning of the text, "The Lord is mighty even in the weak." The greatest sacrifices of all were made by the Kolberg bodyguard, that brave regiment which had been at the side of Gneisenau when the star of this hero was first in the ascendant ; before this troop the severe York uncovered his head, as had once King Frederick before the dragoons of Ansbach-Bayreuth. In the evening in the castle of Wartenburg, when the wine was going round, Blucher summoned Scharnhorst's son to his side, spoke of the father in moving words, and modestly described himself as merely a handicraftsman who was carrying out what the ever-memorable man had planned.

The Elbe had been crossed. In a personal interview Blucher urged the crown prince of Sweden to follow his example. When Bernadotte wasted time in courtly compliments, old Blucher called out to his interpreter, "Tell the fellow the devil shall have him if he won't do what I want." Already on October 8th the Silesian army was in the neighbourhood of Düben, a few miles to the north of Leipzig ; and behind this army was the northern army at Dessau. Blucher's advance had set everyone moving. Whilst the Bohemian army at length addressed itself to the march on Leipzig, Napoleon withdrew his troops from the right bank of the Elbe, ordering them before leaving to destroy everything down to the last fruit tree ;

he left a strong garrison in Dresden, and himself hastened north-westward to meet the two united armies. But Blucher evaded him once more, moving westward across the Saale so that the road to Leipzig was open, and the diplomatic arts of Rühle von Lilienstern succeeded in persuading the crown prince, who was already wishing to withdraw across the Elbe, to march over the Saale. Napoleon recognised too late that he had been striking blows in the air. Now in the greatest need, he once more returned to his cherished plan, and thought of making a fifth attack upon Berlin, so passionate was his desire to chastise this focus of the German national movement. His advance-guard was already crossing the Elbe ; Tauentzien made an extremely hasty retreat with his corps, and on October 13th the Prussian capital had once more to dread a hostile attack. Meanwhile, however, the Imperator had again changed his plan, and returned towards Leipzig. His pride scorned to retreat openly towards the Rhine. He hoped to offer battle before the walls of Leipzig to the Bohemian army advancing from the south before the other two armies could arrive. The chase stood at bay ; the hunting of this autumn was drawing to a close.

On the morning of October 18th, Gneisenau's eyes flashed when he looked out over the immense battle-field, how from the north-west and the north, from the south-west and the south, the columns of the allied troops advanced towards Leipzig in a wide semicircle. He knew that the hour of fulfilment had struck, and how ready was the people. How often had the Germans been delighted by the descriptions given by merchants of the polyglot crowd which, in fair-time, bargaining and chaffering, thronged the high-gabled streets of the ancient town. Now once again the people of all nations, from the Ebro to the Volga, were assembling in the Upper Saxon plain, so inured to battle. The great week of reckoning was approaching, when payment must be made for two decades of disaster and turmoil. After the battle, the people of the Palatinate told how the eight emperors had risen from the vaults of the cathedral of Spires, and by night had crossed the Rhine, in order to join in the fight at Leipzig ; when the work had been completed they rested once more peacefully in their graves. The allies had the threefold advantage of superiority in force of men and artillery, of a concentrating attack, and of a secure support on the wings. Napoleon occupied a semicircle upon the plain to the east of Leipzig ; at his rear were the town and the Auen—those rich, wild, and leafy woods which extend for miles between the Elster, the Pleisse, and their numerous marshy arms. This forest and marsh-land was altogether unsuited for the deployment of great masses of troops, and both wings of the allies were thus safeguarded against all flanking movements. Should the attack prove successful, it was possible that the Imperator might attempt to break through the iron ring of the allied armies in one direction or another, to cut his way eastward towards Torgau ; but this would have been a mad venture, which due watchfulness on the part of the allies would necessarily have rendered vain. Otherwise his only line of retreat would be to the west, at first through the narrow town, then across the bridges of the Elster, and finally upon the high embankment of the Frankfort road, through the damp meadows of the Auen, the most unfavourable route conceivable for a beaten army.

On the 15th, Rühle von Lilienstern had arrived with a message from the Silesian headquarters-staff to the commander-in-chief at Pegau. Gneisenau proposed on the first day of the battle to postpone the decisive onslaught, for at least 80,000 men of the allied army were not yet on the spot. As soon as these reinforcements arrived, the attack was to be resumed with a decisively superior force upon all parts of the semicircle, and meanwhile a corps was to be despatched to Napoleon's rear, to cut off the only road of retreat. This would render possible, not merely a victory, but a battle of annihilation, a surrender unexampled in history. The flight was too high for Schwarzenberg's imagination. For a time, indeed, he hoped that the battle might be altogether avoided, and that the mere appearance of the three allied armies would make it necessary for the Imperator to retreat. When he was at length convinced that Napoleon could not be driven away so easily he decided upon an extremely unfortunate plan of battle. Since the Bohemian army was advancing from the south and the other two armies from the north, the commander-in-chief, in the opinion of the Silesian headquarters-staff, must seek the decisive action upon his right flank, forming a junction upon his right with the northern army, in order to surround the enemy completely. Instead of this, he massed a force of 35,000 men, consisting entirely of Austrians, upon his extreme right wing, and sent them through the pathless bushland of the Auen towards Connewitz, in the extraordinary hope that there, upon this quite inaccessible ground, they would drive Napoleon's right wing away from the town. General Langenau had agreed to this unfortunate proposal. The ambitious Saxon who, with Senfft, the minister, had entered the Austrian service in the spring, burned with eagerness to gain the emperor's favour, and wished, for this reason, to deliver the principal attack with Austrian troops alone, and to leave for the Prussians, whom he detested with all the fierceness of the particularist, an altogether subordinate role. This mean-spirited idea was to be cruelly punished.

The principal mass of Napoleon's force was assembled at Wachau, eight miles south-eastward from the town. Since he had no fear of the irresolute Bernadotte, and since the Silesian army was still far away to the north-west at Merseburg, the Imperator issued orders to Marshal Marmont, who was in the north at Möckern, to unite with the main army in order to ensure the complete defeat of the Bohemian army. Bernadotte did in fact act as the Imperator had expected. On the 16th the northern army did not appear at all upon the battle-field, so that the allies had only a slight advantage in numbers, 192,000 against 177,000 men. There was a wide gap between the two halves of the allied armies, and the struggles of the first day consisted really of two distinct battles, at Möckern and at Wachau.

Blucher did not take the devious road by Merseburg, but went direct from Halle, by the main road, along the eastern border of the Auen, and by his unexpected appearance forced Marmont to stop at Möckern. How joyful had been during the last few days the life of the valiant Silesians, when they had entered Halle, and had been received with ardour by the citizens of the loyal town now at length liberated, when in the evenings they had clinked glasses and sung patriotic songs in accordance with ancient student custom. To this intoxication of youthful life there now followed serious work, the bloodiest of all the war, for the hardest task was once more allotted to York's corps. On the morning of the 16th, in Schkeuditz, when York heard beneath his windows the bugles calling the hussars to horse, he opened the casement and spoke in the pithy words of his beloved Paul Gerhardt :

> "From now till comes the end
> May God advantage send ! "

He might well commend himself to a higher hand, for the enemy's position seemed once more as unassailable as it had seemed at Wartenburg. Marmont's left flank was protected at Möckern by the steep bank of the Elster ; he had prepared the walls of the village for defence, and further to the right, upon the flat-topped heights, he had placed a battery of eighty guns. The Prussians advanced across the gently rising, treeless plain, to take this little fortress by storm. Six times they made their way into the village and had again to give ground. A feeling of the unique great-ness of the day inspired both sides with energy. At length York himself led his cavalry to an attack upon the heights, with the cry " Forward, long live the king," and after a fierce fight among the houses, the infantry drove the enemy out of the village. In the evening Marmont had to fall back upon the town, leaving fifty-three guns in the hands of the Prussians, and around the watch-fires of the victors there resounded hymns of praise to God, as in the winter night of Leuthen. But what a terrible sight it was the next morning, Sunday, when the troops assembled for divine service. Twenty-eight commanders and staff officers lay dead or wounded ; of his infantry force of 12,000, York had hardly 9,000 left ; the Landwehr had entered the field in August with 13,000 men, and of these only 2,000 remained. But at this place the allies had been able to push forward to within a couple of miles of the gates of Leipzig.

The failure of the northern army to arrive had as its unfor-tunate consequence that Blucher dared not weaken his own army, and could not carry out his first intention of sending a corps west-ward through the Auen to cut off Napoleon's retreat. To the west was Gyulay with 22,000 Austrians, opposed to no more than 15,000 men of Bertrand's corps ; since Gyulay had not sense enough to take advantage of his superior force, the high road to Frankfort remained open for the Imperator. Nor did the allies fight with good fortune at Wachau, the principal theatre of the struggle. Here, two days earlier, there had been a magnificent prelude to the national battle, a great cavalry fight, in which Murat had with great difficulty escaped the sabre of Lieutenant Guido von der Lippe of the New Mark dragoons. To-day Napoleon in person, with the guard and the nucleus of his army, held the eight miles line from Dölitz to Seifertshain in a superior position to the allies, outnumbering their forces, having 121,000 against 113,000 men. Upon the allies' left wing, between the two rivers, the unhappy victims of Langenau's art of war wasted their energies in a brave but hopeless struggle. Confined in the woodland it was impossible for them to use their forces. General Merveldt and a portion of his corps were taken prisoner. It was with great difficulty that the reserve of this Austrian force was able to escape from the Auen across the Pleisse rightwards into the open plain. It was full time, for here in the centre Kleist's Prussians and Prince Eugene's Russians could not permanently maintain themselves in a desperate struggle against a greatly superior force, which was delivering its attacks under the protection of three hundred heavy guns. A full half of the heroes of Kulm lay upon the battle-field. Napoleon already believed the battle won, ordered peals of rejoicing to be sounded in the town, sent news of a victory to his vassal Frederick Augustus, who was anxiously awaiting the result in Leipzig. "The world is still turning with us," he called out joyfully to Daru. A last crushing attack of the whole of the cavalry was to break through the centre. Once more the earth was shaken by the fire of three hundred guns and then 9,000 cavalrymen rode furiously, in closed order, across the plain, an impenetrable thicket of horses, helmets, lances, and swords. At this moment the Austrian reserves came out of the Auen, and whilst the enemy's cavalry, breathless from their mad charge, were gradually pressed back, the allies re-established themselves once more in the villages they had lost, and in the evening they held almost exactly the same positions as in the morning. Schwarzenberg's attack had failed, but the conqueror had not even secured the possession of the battle-field.

Had Napoleon now retreated, he could have conducted his army in good order to the Rhine, for the Silesian army, the only one that had been victorious in this first day of battle, was far away from the Frankfort road, and was, moreover, greatly exhausted by the struggle in which it had sustained such heavy losses. But the darling of fortune could not endure misfortune. He no longer displayed his customary coldness and certainty of political calculation ; his arrogance would not allow him to recognise the full seriousness of the situation ; and he could not abandon impossible hopes. The Imperator took the worst possible course, endeavouring through the intermediation of his prisoner Nerveldt to open negotiations with his father-in-law, and this gave the allies time to bring up all their forces. On October 17th both sides rested upon their arms, except that Blucher, unable to deny himself the joy of battle, pressed the French right back to the northern side of the town.

On the 18th, early in the morning, Napoleon withdrew his army closer to Leipzig, so that its semicircle was now only about two and a half miles from the gates of the town. This force of 160,000 men was now attacked by 225,000 of the allies. Anything more than an orderly retreat was now impossible for the Imperator, but he continued to hope for victory, absolutely rejecting the idea of a defeat, and disregarding all precautions which might have made somewhat easier the difficult withdrawal across the Elster.

The nature of things at length brought matters to an issue which the keen insight of Gneisenau had from the first recognised as the only one possible. The decisive struggle was fought on the right wing of the allies. From the height of the Thonberg, Napoleon looked down upon the Austrians, on the left wing of the allies, opening the struggle for the villages on the Pleisse at first with scant success ; subsequently he saw the allies' centre advance across the battle-field from Wachau. These were the veteran troops of Kleist and Prince Eugene. The army moved over the unburied corpses of their comrades who had fallen two days before, and the bones of the dead could be heard grating beneath the hoofs of the horses and the wheels of the cannon. In front of the attacking force were extended the high mud walls of Probstheida, the key of the French centre, protected on both sides by artillery. The attack began under the cross-fire of the batteries. Six times was the attack renewed across the open field, but in the end Napoleon's guard maintained its position in the village ; and after repeated onslaughts and murderous fighting among the houses, Stötteritz also remained in the hands of the French. After the battle, in the gardens and in the houses, there were to be seen lying side by side the bodies of Frenchmen and Russians who had run one another through with their bayonets. Even to-day, under the immediate eyes of the Imperator, the allies had not a decisive success, although they advanced close to the key of his position. Meanwhile upon their right wing, the northern army entered the line of battle, filling the gap which separated the Bohemian army from the Silesian, thus closing the great ring of battle which surrounded the French. It had taken trouble enough to persuade Bernadotte, who on the 17th had at length arrived at Breitenfeld the old ground of Swedish military glory, to take an active part in the fight. To induce the cautious man to enter the struggle, Blucher had made a severe sacrifice of his own fighting force, detaching 30,000 men from his army to the northern army, and thus depriving himself of the glory of a new victory. Once Bernadotte had made up his mind, he displayed the circumspection of the experienced commander. Whilst Langeron's Russians on the extreme right of the line of attack endeavoured by repeated onslaughts to drive the enemy out of Schönefeld, in the course of the afternoon the principal force of the northern army drew near to the eastern side of

Leipzig. Bülow led the advance and drove Reynier's corps out of Paunsdorf.

Thus the old enemies of Grossbeeren encountered one another once again, but how greatly since the former meeting had the mood of the Saxon regiments altered. For a wonderfully long time the German fidelity to the military oath had held together the troops of the Confederation of the Rhine, keeping them faithful to their duties as soldiers ; except in the case of a few isolated battalions, two only of the Westphalian cavalry regiments had gone over to the side of the allies. But with the vanishing of good fortune there vanished also the self-satisfaction of the Napoleonic mercenaries ; they began to feel ashamed of the war against Germany, and felt the truth of what their countryman Rückert said to them :

> "An eagle, may be, still can glory gain,
> But ye, his robber train of crows,
> Win nought but shame, for all the days to come!"

Moreover, the Saxons felt that their military honour was affected by the lies of the Napoleonic bulletins ; they saw with anger how their homeland was being plundered, and how their king was moved about from place to place behind the Protector ; and they asked themselves whether they were to withdraw to France if Napoleon should lose the battle and Saxony should fall entirely into the hands of the allies. Even the French felt compassion for the unnatural position of these comrades-in-arms. Reynier had ordered the withdrawal of the Saxons to Torgau, when the approach of the northern army prevented the carrying out of this well-meant command. Frederick Augustus alone showed no understanding either of the distress of his army, or of his own disgrace. His confidence in the fortunate star of his great ally remained unshaken, and even while the battle was in progress he coldly referred his generals to their military duties when they begged him to allow the Saxon contingent to be separated from the French army. German good-nature rendered it impossible for the Saxons to believe that their hereditary monarch was as infatuated as he appeared. The officers imagined that their king was not free to express his real opinion. It was not with the deliberate intention of breaking their military oath, but simply in order to preserve their small army for their king, that they made up their mind to commit the greatest crime possible to the soldier, to change sides during the actual progress of a battle. In the neighbourhood of Paundsorf and Sellerhausen about 3,000 men of the Saxon troops went over to the northern army, and with them a cavalry troop from Swabia. The Prussians and Russians received the deserters joyfully, and it was only General Normann, who at Kitzen in former days had treacherously attacked the Lützowers, who was repelled by Gneisenau with contemptuous words. The honourable feeling of Frederick William, however, made it impossible for him to refrain from reproach. How much noble blood the Saxons might have spared to the fatherland if they had made up their minds to this course before the opening of the decisive battle! This tragical incident had no influence upon the course of the national struggle, but it threw a horrible light upon the profound moral corruption of particularist life. The conscience of the nation at length sickened of the Napoleonic particularism, and notwithstanding all the false-hoods which prevailed in the petty states, these began once more to perceive that even after the destruction of the old empire the Germans possessed a fatherland, and that they were bound to this fatherland by sacred duties.

Towards five o'clock, Bülow united his whole corps for a common attack, took by storm Sellerhausen and Stüntz, and in the evening pressed forward as far as the market-gardens just beyond the eastern gates of the town. Whilst upon the right, Langeron had at length occupied Schönefeld, after a hard struggle, and was also pressing forward towards the market-gardens, Ney, with the left wing of the French, was defeated along the whole line. Through this reverse, Napoleon's position in the centre became untenable. This very evening he ordered the retreat of the whole army. Now the thick masses of the beaten army pressed into the town simultaneously by the three gates, subsequently to join in terrible confusion upon the Frankfort road. It was due to the unhappy Gyulay that this way of retreat was still open, for even upon the third day of the battle he had done nothing from the west; Bertrand held the way of retreat open for the French as far as the Saale. The 100,000 men who camped upon the dearly-won battle-field by the light of twelve burning villages were profoundly impressed with the sacred earnestness of the day; involuntarily the Russians raised one of their pious lays, and soon in the tongues of all the nations of Europe there arose hymns of gratitude to heaven. The conquerer had now to bow beneath the powerful hand of God!

It was only the commander-in-chief, officially celebrated as the victor of Napoleon, who was unable to grasp the greatness of the success. Schwarzenberg refrained from sending in pursuit the still untouched Russian and Prussian guards—not from craft, as many of the angry Prussians assumed, but simply because in his pusillanimity he did not wish to drive the beaten army to despair. Owing to the late entry of the northern army into the field, Blucher had been forced throughout the day to hold his small army ready to repel a sortie in the direction of Torgau, which was still feared ; and consequently it was not until the evening that York was despatched after the retreating enemy by a wide detour through Merseburg. The consequence was that Napoleon was able to rescue 90,000 men from the battle, almost all of them Frenchmen. It was to his vassals, the Rhenish Confederates, the Poles, and the Italians, that he left the covering of his retreat and the defence of the town. Let them bleed on his behalf once again, for in any case they were lost to his empire.

Consequently on the 19th the struggle for the possession of the town itself had to be recommenced. Whilst Blucher in the north led his Russians to the Gerbertor, and was there for the first time greeted by the Cossacks with the honourable name of Marshal Forwards, Bülow's corps advanced from the market-gardens against the eastern side of the town. Borstell's brigade pressed into the Milchinsel Park, whilst Friccius with the East Prussian Landwehr stormed the Grimma Gate. The regiments of the Confederation of the Rhine were still crowding the old market-place, when they heard the bugles of the Pomeranian fusiliers coming down the Grimma Gasse, shouting at intervals, " Long live Frederick William ! " Soon in the narrow streets round the old townhall the bayonets were gleaming, the drums and the fifes were sounding. All were streaming towards the market-place ; the victors of Katzbach, of Kulm, and of Dennewitz greeted one another here with loud rejoicings in the presence of the captured enemy. There were reiterated and stormy shouts of joy when the czar and the king rode in. Even the Rhenish Confederates joined in these ; they all felt how out of the disgrace and horror of recent days the new Germany was rising in its glory. Whilst his valiant soldiers joyfully thronged round the king of Prussia, there stood near by, with bared head, amid the crowd at the gate of the palace, Frederick Augustus of Saxony, a pitiable representative of the old time that was now going down to its grave. During the last hours of the storm the terrified king had taken refuge in a cellar, deluded even till the last moment by the boastful assurances of the Protector, and hoping in the victorious return of his invincible ally. Now the conquerors did not deign to give him a single glance, his own people paid no attention to him, and before his very eyes his red guards were led by Natzmer, the aide-de-camp of Frederick William, to pursue the French. With the frank joy of a hero of antiquity, Gneisenau wrote news of the victory to his distant friends in all corners of the fatherland, saying : " We have drawn our national revenge in broad outlines. We have become poor, but we are rich in warlike renown and pride at the re-acquirement of our independence."

The victors took 30,000 prisoners. The town had been almost surrounded when the Elster bridge on the Frankfort road was blown up, and thus the last way of retreat was cut off. A whole army of 100,000 men were dead or wounded. What could the art of the surgeons, what could the philanthropic sacrifices of the noble East Frisian Reil, do in face of such a mass of misery ? The army medical service had made few advances since the days of Frederick the Great, and the good-hearted citizens of Leipzig were still influenced by the slumberous spirit of the old days of Electoral Saxony, so that they did not understand how to set to work vigorously when it was necessary. For days the bodies of the Prussian soldiers remained unburied in the court of the Bürgerschule, torn by carrion crows and gnawed by dogs ; in the concert room of the Cloth-workers' Hall, dead, wounded, and sick lay side by side upon dirty straw ; a pesitilential reek filled the horrible place, and a stream of filth slowly trickled down the steps. When the wagon to carry away the dead passed through the streets, it sometimes happened that to save time the body would be thrown into the cart from one of the upper storeys ; or the soldiers in charge of the wagon would notice among the rigid bodies someone who was moving, and would compassionately give him the *coup de grace* with the butt-end of a musket. Out in the open upon the battle-field the kites were feasting. It was long before the peasants who had fled from their homes returned to the devastated villages and disposed of the bodies by tumbling them into great pits. It was amid such misery that this epoch of wars came to its close as far as German soil was concerned, the horrible time of which Arndt said : " It had almost come to this, that there were now only two kinds of men, the eaters and the eaten ! " For the generation that had seen these things there remained an inextinguishable hatred of war, a profound need for peace, such as was hardly credible to less afflicted times.

On October 24th, Frederick William visited his capital. He

felt the need to pray beside the grave of his wife, for everywhere throughout this savage campaign her image had been by his side, and even among the troops the question was constantly asked why the queen had not been able to live to see these days. Then he made his appearance at the theatre, and *Heil Dir im Sie-gerkranz* resounded through the building, on this occasion more appropriately than when the presumptuous generation of the nineties had first delighted in the beautiful strains. Seven years earlier, on the very same day, Napoleon had ridden in through the Brandenburg Gate, and what a change had there been since then! How had this mutilated state, with its five million inhabitants once more risen to the heights of history! Even if the men of the war party of 1811 were mistaken in their choice of the moment, they had not had too high an opinion of the greatness of their nation. Now once more was applicable the old proverb *Nec soli cedit!* In those days an English newspaper wrote : " Who gave to Germany the first example of defection from Napoleon ? The Prussians. Who won the battles of Lutzen and Bautzen ? The Prussians. Who was victorious at Haynau ? The Prussians. Who at Grossbeeren, Katzbach, and Dennewitz ? Always the Prussians. Who at Kulm, Wartenburg, Möckern, and Leipzig ? The Prussians, ever the Prussians." How like a threat sounded this proud " the Prussians, ever the Prussians " to Emperor Francis and to the princes of the Confederation of the Rhine. What was likely to be the future of Germany if this state should regain its ancient power ?

The battle of Leipzig secured the original aim of the war, the dissolution of the Confederation, and the liberation of Germany as far as the Rhine. But hope grew with success. On the day after the storm, Stein and Gneisenau met in the market-place at Leipzig, and grasped hands in the undertaking that this struggle must not end except with the overthrow of Napoleon and the reconquest of the left bank of the Rhine. That which a few weeks earlier had seemed incredible even to these two bold men, now seemed in a moment to have become attainable. Upon Stein's orders, Arndt at once set to work. From the rich treasury of his knowledge he assembled all the historical recollections and romantic images which were at his disposal to influence the nation, thinking out a view which was then new, but was soon to become one of the driving forces of the century—the idea that, in the last resort, language and the historical peculiarities of the nations must determine the frontiers of states. Thus while still under the fresh impressions of the

" glorious battle," he wrote the most effective of his books, the happy watchword for the struggle of the subsequent months : *Der Rhein, Teutschlands Strom, aber nicht Teutschlands Grenze!* [1]

---

[1] *The Rhine, the German River, but not the German Frontier.*

CHAPTER V.

CONCLUSION OF THE WAR.

§ 1. LIBERATION OF THE WEST. PLAN OF CAMPAIGN.

Notwithstanding the sluggish pursuit of the beaten army, the battle of Leipzig brought freedom to all the German lands as far as the Rhine. To the Austrians also the victory which had been gained seemed almost too great as soon as its import was fully grasped. The inevitable annihilation of the Napoleonic power was in prospect, but it was averted by the fault of the great head-quarters-staff. Bennigsen's army withdrew to the Elbe ; the Bohemian army advanced slowly westward through Franconia and Thuringia ; the northern army returned towards Hanover and Westphalia. But Blucher, upon the Frankfort road, followed close upon the heels of the enemy, until, when only a day's march from the Imperator's headquarters, he suddenly received orders to turn aside from the direct road, towards Wetterau and the valley of the Lahn, because Emperor Francis with his Austrians wished to enter the old coronation town. Consequently with his rear unmenaced Napoleon conducted his troops through the difficult and narrow passes of the Rhöngebirge. Thousands had deserted, to live as marauders, and many had been slaughtered by the infuriated peasants, but the nucleus of the army held together, successfully reached the plain of the Main at Hanau, and there, breaking forth from the forest of Lamboy, defeated the Bavario-Austrian army under General Wrede, who endeavoured to bar its passage (October 30th and 31st). The Bavarian leader, the most outrageous boaster among the mercenaries of the Confederation of the Rhine, had expected by a brilliant victory to secure for his state the favour of the allied powers, but he had wasted valuable days before the walls of Würzburg, and did not attain at the favourable moment the advantageous position on the Kinzig passes, where the French retreat could have been easily cut off. He had supposed that the allies would be closly pursuing the enemy, and when he at length perceived his error, he did not decline battle, because Bavaria

598

had to earn the confidence of her new friends. Consequently the Imperator had the satisfaction of closing his German campaigns with the humiliation of an unfaithful vassal. A force of 70,000 men gained the left bank of the Rhine. Here, however, the last energies of the unfortunate men collapsed ; their ranks were thinned by terrible outbreaks of illness, and for some weeks France was without an army, defenceless against any attack. The 190,000 men who were still dispersed through the fortresses of North Germany and Poland were given up for lost by Napoleon. He offered to evacuate the lines of the Oder and the Vistula, on condition that the garrisons should be allowed to withdraw unmolested, but the allies saw through his design and refused to present the desperate man with a new army.

Bülow's corps had the delight of reoccupying the lost western provinces. As soon as the news of the battle of Leipzig arrived, the Westphalian director of taxes, von Motz, immediately brought out his old uniform, and made his appearance in Mülhausen as royal Prussian Landrat ; the people obeyed his orders as a matter of course. Everywhere the liberators were received with open arms, and nowhere with more loudly expressed delight than in East Frisia, the favourite country of the great king. The old flags and emblems of the Frederician days, which had been carefully hidden in the beautiful *salle d'armes* of the townhall at Emden, were once more brought to light when the hussars of Blucher made their entry, followed by Friccius with the East Prussian Landwehr. How much anger and sorrow had the faithful Vincke found it necessary to choke down during recent years, living quietly upon his property in the County Mark. The French certainly had an inkling that his society in Hamm for the reading of political economy was not solely concerned with its ostensible subject. For a time they exiled him to the left bank of the Rhine, for Stein's friend and successor must not stay upon the right bank as long as the Russians were on the hither side of the Oder. When he was at length set free, he hourly expected rearrest. Then came an urgent message from the red hussars at Hamm. Vincke went there hot-foot, and immediately dictated a circular letter to all the burgo-masters as far as the Rhine, that they should once more submit themselves to their lawful masters. He took over the conduct of the administration in all the Old Prussian dominions of West-phalia, and extended his authority without ceremony over some of the enclaves, Dortmund, Limburg, and Corvey. A breath of delight ran through the liberated country.

The same moving manifestations of self-sacrificing upheaval which in the spring had been witnessed in the eastern provinces, were now seen in the west. Two of the most respected landowners issued an appeal, headed of course with the Prussian eagle, greeting the liberators in moving terms : " Who among you worthy landsfolk was not overwhelmed with a sacred wonder and delight when the first Prussians were seen as rescuers in our midst ? " ; and a demand was made of the men of the Mark that they should follow the example of these " true sons of Arminius " in enrolling themselves as volunteers and forming a Landwehr. In Cleves, too, there was the same joyful reception. It was a great domestic festival, a delighted reunion of long separated brothers, a plain contradiction of the view current in the petty states that this Prussia was an artificial construction. It was only among the gentry of the Münster region that there was once more seen the old religious hatred against the Prussian heretics. The young people hastened with delight to the colours, most zealously of all in the Old Prussian domains, for here, even to the present day, in these regions of Germany which passed through the severe school of King Frederick William I, do we find the greatest readiness for military service. In most circles of Cleves and of the County Mark, a formal levying of troops was unnecessary, for the supply of volunteers greatly exceeded the demand. Even the East Frisians, whom King Frederick had exempted from cantonal duty, overcame the hostility of seamen to military service, and offered themselves in great numbers The result was that a large proportion of the troops that were formed in such haste were able to be utilised advantageously for investing the French fortresses. To the religious Markers, the pastors preached of the Lord God of Sabaoth who summoned his people to the holy war ; when the war was over, a memorial cross was erected, bearing the inscription : " We raised our flags in the name of God ! " Even the Landsturm was utilised on several occasions, more frequently than in the east. The East Frisian Landsturm took part in the siege of Delfzyl, and that of Cleves was for weeks before Wesel. In the anciently celebrated village of Brünen, which had displayed its loyalty in the Seven Years' War, there was not a man without a war-medal.

It was very remarkable how strongly conservative this people showed itself to be, as soon as it regained control of its destinies. Everyone wished to return to the good old times, to enjoy ancient blessings, even the feudal order ; here, as in the east, it was committees of the estates which supervised the levying of the Landwehr under the supervision of one royal commissary and one commissary of the estates. It is not surprising, then, that the old diets immediately regarded themselves as the legal representatives of the country. Immediately after the liberation, the captain-general (*Landesdirektor*), von Romberg, summoned the diet of the County Mark, announcing that : " The excellent feudal consti-tution comes once more into operation." [1] The leader of the old feudal party, Baron von Bodelschwingh-Plettenberg, was sent to the king at Frankfort, in order to express the delight of the county at its reunion with Prussia, but also to convey the request that there should be no alteration in the ancient territorial constitution until the opinion of the diet had been heard. In a similar sense wrote the president of the knighthood of the estates of East Frisia, Baron Kuyphausen, upon the king's next birthday, express-ing in warm terms the delight of the country to be able once again to celebrate " its ancient and glorious festival," and how greatly it was to be regretted that only a portion of the Landsturm had come under fire, whilst the Landwehr had not been used at all ; at the same time the estates petitioned for the complete abolition of the French institutions, and for the restoration of the ancient constitution.[2] Hardenberg replied in cautious terms, saying that the king would be glad to establish the permanent happiness of a province so devoted to its liege lord and to its consitution. No definite promise was given, for what would happen to the reform plans of recent years if recognition were again to be extended to all these petty diets which had so long been abolished under the foreign dominion ? Thus in the very moment of the liberation there began that reversionary feudal movement which subse-quently, in association with the allied efforts of the Brandenburg gentry, was to threaten the national unity of the re-established monarchy.

Among the non-Prussian domains, the duchy of Berg showed the most pleasing patriotic zeal. For a very long time the country had been in friendly relations with its Prussian neighbours in the County Mark. Even in Frederician days, its Protestants had always belonged to the Prussian party. Now everyone was embittered against the Napoleonic prefects, who in the beginning of this very year had repressed an attempt at revolt with extreme severity. The whole country adhered to the German cause as soon as the

[1] Romberg's circular letter to the estates of the County Mark, dated Novem-ber 22, 1813.

[2] Kuyphausen's Petition to the king, July 25, 1814.

governor-general, Justus Gruner, made his entry, and after his impassioned manner exhorted the people in enthusiastic words to undertake military preparations. The youth of the region assembled almost as swiftly as in the Old Prussian domains. As early as January 3rd, at Mülheim and at the foot of the Seibengebirge, the Landsturm attempted to force its way across the Rhine, and the names of the two leaders of the unfortunate attempt, Boltenstern and Genger, were long preserved in the memory of the people of Berg. It was the first reawakening of a serious political will in these exhausted Rhenish territories. The embittered people desired to see the immediate abolition of all the institutions of the foreign dominion. "Away with the French laws!" they cried everywhere; on the anniversary of the battle of Leipzig, the guillotine, regarded as a symbol of foreign tyranny, was ceremoniously burned at Düsseldorf. Gruner, however, was content to reconstitute the military system, and to expel French methods from the schools (this is sufficiently characteristic of the idealistic tendency of the time); the ancient and honourable *gymnasium illustre* of Düsseldorf was at once re-established upon a German footing. The most severe of the Napoleonic taxes, the celebrated *droits réunis*, were also abolished, as well as the government monopoly of tobacco manufacture, which was especially hated by the German smokers. In other respects for the present the organisation of the administration and of the courts remained unchanged, except that for the circle-directors, as the sub-prefects were now termed, there was, after the German manner, secured greater independence.[1] On the whole, the inhabitants were satisfied and cheerfully bore the severe burdens of this provisional government which in one and a half years had to demand from the impoverished country an additional six and a half million francs in war taxes and forced loans.

How different was the sentiment, and how different were the conditions, upon the left bank of the river. When in December the allies entered Alsace, they were everywhere encountered with a gloomy and fanatical hatred. The people had been completely intoxicated by the warlike renown of the Napoleonic eagles, and the peasants believed, even more firmly than in the nineties, that the victory of the coalition would revive for them the vexations of the tithes and of the corvée. Lower down the Rhine, indeed, such open hostility was seldom displayed, but none the less, after two

[1] Gruner's Report upon the administration of the general government of Berg, January 24, 1814.

decades of foreign dominion, there remained a firm belief in the invincibility of France. However, a few of the inhabitants regarded the fall of the Napoleonic empire as now definitely decided, and no one desired the restoration of the old state of affairs. Manufacturing industry, which had flourished under the protection of the Continental System, dreaded the loss of the rich French markets. The women of the higher classes, who even in the interior of Germany had only too often yielded to the amiable advances of the French, here rarely concealed their preference for the gentle charm of French morals. The mass of the people were weary of the foreign system. Here and there the German troops were ceremoniously received ; pleasure was felt at the abolition of the detested *droits réunis*, and at the re-opening of intercourse with fellow-countrymen across the Rhine, so that here the people themselves helped to tear down the hated customs houses.

In those circles of the cultured youth who had been touched by the influence of the new Christo-Teutonic remanticism there was dominant a joyful enthusiasm. With delight did young Ferdinand Walter enter the field with the Cossacks of the Don, and some of the older men voluntarily joined the Prussian battalions. But there was no question here of a general uprising of the people. The conquerors themselves hardly dared to treat these German men simply as Germans. The *Courrier d'Aix-la-Chapelle* continued to appear in French for another year, whilst the *Journal du Bas Rhin et du Rhin Moyen* published its official notifications in both tongues. The new governor-general, the lord-lieutenant Sack, himself a native of the Rhineland, understood how to deal with these people ; he was, like them, a declared enemy of all feudal privileges, and had for years been regarded with suspicion by the Brandenburg nobles. As far as possible, he endeavoured to engage the people themselves in the work of administration. On several occasions the old general councillors (known here as territorial deputies) were summoned to Aix, in order to give advice concerning the war-taxes and the supply of military stores ; in every canton there was appointed an unpaid commissary from among the inhabitants of the district, who was to convey to the government the wishes and the grievances of the area.[1] But the new officials who replaced the departed French, together with the inevitable pressure of the war-taxes and the insecurity of the provisional conditions, soon awakened disaffection in the readily

[1] Sack's General Report upon the provisional administration of the Middle and Lower Rhine, March 31, 1816.

influenced population. It was not long before the saying, " Let us hope that this too will be no more than provisional," became a favourite malediction in the Rhineland. Already it was easy to recognise how much more severe would be the labour before it would become possible to incorporate into the new German life these half-Frenchified lands of the crozier. It was only the Old Prussian subjects in Cleves on the left bank, in Mörs and Guelderland, who with unmixed delight devoted themselves to the cause of the father-land, and upon Bülow's demand immediately began to constitute their Landwehr. But Bernadotte, the supreme authority, who still had hopes of the crown of France, suddenly intervened with a pro-hibition, declaring that French subjects must not fight against France !

Wonderful had been the revolution of destiny ! It was from these beautiful Rhenish lands that, a thousand years before, our history had taken its rise. Now the mighty stream of German life was flowing back westward into its disturbed ancient channel from the youthful colonial lands of the north-east. Not one among the sons of the Rhineland greeted the new day which was rising for the Western Mark with more enthusiastic delight than Joseph Görres. To this Hotspur there now came the most fruitful and happy time of his changeful career ; he returned from his remark-able scientific divagations to the publicist activity of his youth, and in the *Rheinische Merkur* began a war of the pen on behalf of the new Germanism. He wrote now on this side as stormily, as uncontrolledly, as forcibly, as years before when he had announced the saving truths of the revolution. He was a great orator, a master of language, unwearied in the use of powerful and grandiose images, an honourable and free-spirited zealot, a wakener of conscience—and yet with all this, an unpolitical mind, one without any pene-trating knowledge of affairs, devoid of understanding of the con-temporary relationships of political power. The *Rheinische Merkur* was not what he himself called it, a voice of the people across the Rhine who were now once more to become a bulwark of the father-land. Along the Rhine the exaggerated language of patriotic passion found an echo only in isolated circles. All the louder, however, was the response in North Germany. For two years remote Coblenz was the acropolis of the German press, for thus under the influence of chances and of personalities did the centre of gravity of political life change in this people without a capital city. The angry French spoke of Görres as the fifth among the allied powers, and the diplomats of the Hofburg trembled before him.

The *Rheinische Merkur* was soon more widely read than had previously been the *Staatsanzeigen* of Schlözer, and among the cultured classes it acquired a prestige which has since then been possessed by no other German newspaper—for when there is a well-developed party life, no one journal can possibly possess so much power. For the patriots of all colours the *Merkur* served as a parliamentary debating chamber ; everyone was welcome as long as his sentiments were not French, and even Stein and Gneisenau did not disdain to send contributions.

It was only in the polemic writing of the paper that a definite political tendency was displayed, for in truth Görres only knew what he did *not* want. When he was chastising the secret and traitorous intrigues of the princes of the Confederation of the Rhine, when he was thundering against the hired scribes of Montgelas and the superficial enlightenment of the *Aarauer Zeitung* of Zschokk, the old fighter was in his element. Unsparingly, with biting truth, did he describe the sins which had led to the destruction of the old empire, attributing to the fallen Napoleon the saying : " A people without a fatherland, a constitution without unity, princes without character or aims, a nobility without pride and without energy— all this must be an easy booty for me ! " His plans for the future of Germany, however, were not a whit clearer than the high-sounding words of the appeal of Kalisz. The Romanticist expressed his enthusiasm for the restoration of the throne of the Carlovingians, and endeavoured, for good or for evil, to fuse his imperial dreams with the dualistic plans which were communicated to him from the Prussian chancellery. Yet he could not cling firmly even to these tortuous ideas of a twofold hegemony under Hapsburg suzerainty, but exposed in his paper, for the choice of his readers, a variegated series of essentially different constitutional plans, as they were sent along to him by warm-hearted patriots. As long as the governments were animated by good intentions, it seemed evident to all that the reordering of the liberated fatherland would be child's play ; anyone who suggested that a return of the old struggles for power between Austria and Prussia could be possible, was regarded as a blasphemer. Every proposal for the political construction of the German future was gratefully accepted, so long as the proposer spoke with sufficient energy of the German nature, of the harmony between the two great powers, of unity and of freedom, and as long as he displayed the proud self-confidence which the nation demanded from its tribunes.

Those who were speaking here regarded themselves as the

representatives of the nation, and the nation, amid its hazy dreams, regarded itself as secure of the attainment of its aims, and as far wiser than the cabinet. " Something complete and just must be effected," exclaimed Görres to the diplomats, " and it is necessary to listen to the voice of the nation, which is speaking plainly everywhere ! " Nevertheless the *Rheinische Merkur* was the best that a newspaper can be, a faithful mirror of the present, honourable, talented, youthful, inspired like this whole generation, still quite free from the influence of those unavowed aims which the press is accustomed to pursue in times of more developed intercourse. The clerical tendencies of the fantastical editor had not yet seriously affected him. The respect he paid to the imperial archducal house, did not prevent him from singing the praises of the Prussian heroes. When he demanded of the Germans that they should complete the cathedral of Cologne as a memorial of the reconstitution of the fatherland, and when he declared that Pope Pius VII, the steadfast martyr of Napoleonic tyranny, was the greatest hero of this war of world liberation, the romantically-minded time took no umbrage. In Freiburg, Rotteck's *Teutsche Blätter* pursued a similar tendency ; this was a widely-read paper, which gave first-hand war-news obtained from the great headquarters-staff.

The Hanoverians, the Brunswickers, and the Electoral Hessians, were no less delighted than the Old Prussian provinces at the recovery of their former dominion. Before the gates of Brunswick there was erected a decorated temple upon the spot where " Brunswick's Guelph," Frederick William, had camped four years before with his black riders. The Hanoverians once more felt themselves proud to be Britons, and showed their enthusiasm for the insane English king, who during the fifty years of his reign, had never once deigned to visit their country. In Cassel, when King Jerome had for the second time taken to flight, the evil-minded elector William once more entered into possession ; the burghers took the horses out of his carriage, and themselves drew the father of the country, this man with a thick neck and a long pigtail, shouting with joy as they dragged him to the castle of his ancestors. The people was not indeed under any illusions as to his princely virtues, but he was their tribal lord, and when does love ask for reasons ? More apt than the servile words of the official newspapers was the expression used by an old peasant to describe the family feeling of this degenerate world of petty states, when he employed the memorable words : " Even if he is an old fool, we want him back again ! " During the years of exile, the great wealth of the electoral house, acquired by the blood of the purchased Hessian soldiers, had been preserved in Frankfort with the house of Amschel Rothschild, who used this money to found the world-wide power of his firm, and the avaricious prince had not given the least portion of his treasures towards the liberation of Germany. Notwithstanding this the allies received him as a new found friend ; King Frederick William, in his good nature, would not bear any grudge against his faithless neighbour for having played double in 1806 ; the Hofburg on principle was in favour of dynastic interests, and even Stein showed himself extraordinarily yielding in this case to the desires of particularism.

Immediately after the restoration there began in Hesse the senseless regime of "the seven sleepers" : the last seven years, with all that had been done in that time by "my administrator Jerome," were to disappear without leaving a trace. In the Guelph lands, too, a malicious restoration was in progress, aiming at the inconsiderate abolition of all the creations of the foreign dominion, whilst Prussia in her reacquired provinces was proceeding with a reasonable consideration for established institutions. It was with the greatest possible dilatoriness that the re-established petty princes of the north-west complied with the military demands of the coalition. From Oldenburg and Hanover, absolutely no troops were sent into the field ; the Göttingen students who offered themselves as volunteers were roughly repelled by the Guelph noble government. The ruler of Hesse, indeed, immediately recommenced his old playing at soldiers, and delighted the Hessians with his order of the iron helmet, since the Prussians had their order of the iron cross ; but the equipment of the Landwehr went forward very slowly, amid continuous quarrels with the central administration, so that Stein angrily exclaimed : "Send me cannon, I don't want any of your reasons ! " The Hessian Landsturm was not summoned until April, 1814, when Paris had already been occupied.

Among all the princes of the north-west, it was only the minor mediatised lords who showed any zeal for the German cause, and this was because they hoped to regain their crowns by their valour in war. In the castle at Anhalt the tender hands of the princesses were already working the flags which were to lead the warlike forces of the nation of Salm-Salm to battle and victory ; but thereupon General Bülow issued a threat that he would have all the petty princes of Westphalia arrested if they ventured to give themselves out as ruling princes. The Hansa towns were more fortunate than these mediatised lords. As early as November 5th, the ancient senate of Bremen asembled upon its own responsibility ; the re-establishment of the republic was formally proclaimed, and Smidt was sent to the headquarters at Frankfort. The adroit diplomat immediately urged the citizens of Hamburg and of Lübeck to send representatives to the monarch, and was able to influence the Austrian statesmen so cleverly that they overcame their mistrust of anything republican. In the peace negotiations at Prague, Prussia had already demanded the independence of the Hansa towns, and how could Hamburg be treated as a hostile town when the Hamburg militia, led by the valiant Mettlerkamp, had already been fighting for months in the ranks of the northern army ? The three towns received assent to their re-establishment, and by the fault of Stein, yet a fourth republic was introduced into the new monarchical Germany, the old coronation town of Frankfort. So entangled and hopeless was already the position of German affairs, that the ardent advocate of national unity devoted himself with vigour and success to the reconstitution of a town-state which was quite unfit for independent life. The imperial knight had always cherished a special fondness for the life of the imperial towns, and desired at any cost to rescue the beautiful town on the Main from the neighbouring princes of the Confederation of the Rhine, who were all stretching out their greedy hands towards the rich booty.

These Rhenish confederates, now that the issue was decided, all thronged busily round the allies. As had formerly happened at Rastatt, in Paris, and in Posen, the high nobility of Germany sued for the grace of the conqueror, and this time it was not necessary to come with hands full of money. When Emperor Francis entered Frankfort, he was greeted by the shouting people as the ruler of Germany ; the name " our emperor " once more exercised its powerful charm upon German hearts. But Francis wished to have nothing to do with this " unmeaning title." Metternich admitted, to one of the French negotiators, " in this way Germany belongs to us even more than it did before." The immediate aim of the German policy of the Hofburg was the control of the Germanic Federation by a majority of princes devoted to the House of Austria. For this reason, Metternich was irreconcilably hostile to the mediatised, for he recognised with justice that the friendship of these old allies of Austria was of little significance now that the spiritual princedoms had disappeared, and he turned his benevolence towards their fortunate inheritors, the Rhenish Confederate princes. The view of the foreign courts was similar, for they all desired Germany's weakness, and they were all connected by blood and marriage with the petty kings. Regarding these family connections among the serene highnesses, which to the present day constitute the strongest support of German particularism, the czar spoke openly in Frankfort, when once in an unguarded moment he said to Stein, "Where should I get wives for my great princes if all these petty princes were to be dethroned?" The baron answered angrily: "I was not aware that your majesty regarded Germany as a Russian stud-farm." Like Stein, all the Prussian generals anticipated a severe punishment for the "rabble of the Rhenish Confederates," as Blucher called them. When York entered Wiesbaden, he immediately had the guard-rooms of Nassau dismantled, and when a chamberlain asked him whether he wished to dethrone his majesty, he gave the rough answer, " I have as yet no orders to that effect."

In the headquarters at Frankfort they had upon their hands the repentant Rhenish Confederate princes, and fêted Wrede the Bavarian, on account of the defeat of Hanau, as if he had been a commander crowned with glory. Among the greater princes of the Confederation of the Rhine, with the exception of the two Napoleonides, it was only the prince-primate Dalberg who was dethroned, and this was in no way on account of his unworthy conduct, but because he was not of princely blood, and because Eugene Beauharnais had been destined to be his successor. With him fell his cousin, Prince von der Leyen, and the prince of Isenberg had to be sacrificed by Austria to the anger of King Frederick William, because he had formed a French regiment out of Prussian deserters and vagabonds. The minor Westphalian Rhenish Confederate princes, who had been dethroned by Napoleon three years earlier, did not regain their crowns, because no one advocated their cause. The watchword was the convenient *beati possidentes,* and all received grace who still reigned at the moment; by chance, favour, and caprice, two dozen of the innumerable state-structures of the Holy Roman Empire had lived through the storms of the Napoleonic epoch; it was a similar arbitrary decision which now led to their continuance. The Fürstenbergs and the Hohenlohes remained mediatised, whilst the Reusses and the Bückeburgs retained their thrones; those who had acquired their shameful booty as traitors to the fatherland, and in the service of the enemy of their country, were able to retain it.

Whilst still upon the march to Frankfort, Metternich had

come to terms with Würtemberg. The treaty of Fulda, of November 2nd, was similar to that of Ried, with the only difference that, out of regard for Prussia, a proviso was introduced in favour of the future Germanic Federation. King Frederick entered the coalition and retained his sovereignty and his possessions "under the guarantee of the political relationships which will arise out of the arrangements to be established in the future peace, for the maintenance and safe-guarding of the independence and freedom of Germany." The only clear point about this confused and inexpressive phrasing, was the admission of sovereignty and of the *status quo*. Upon Stein's demand, in the treaties of accession with the other middle states a somewhat more definite clause was inserted, although even this remained sufficiently obscure. Baden, Darmstadt, Nassau, and Electoral Hesse, had to pledge themselves to fulfil the duties which would be rendered necessary by regard for the independence of Germany, and to submit to any detachments of territory which might be requisite for this purpose, in return for full compensation. But what was the value of this pledge, since they also were promised preservation of the *status quo* and sovereignty ? Thus Hardenberg's dualistic hopes lost all foundation, as well as his plan to establish his friend Austria upon the Upper Rhine ; at the same time the German domain which remained available for the compensation of Prussia, was reduced by every new treaty of accession. The chancellor was profoundly displeased, but after he had once allowed the Hofburg to play a part in drawing up the South German treaties, he could no longer help himself. Notwithstanding so many bitter experiences, this man of unending trust was still far from clear as to the intentions of the court of Vienna. He complained strongly of " the defective, foolish, and hurried mode " in which the negotia-tions were conducted,[1] and did not recognise that Metternich was not acting as he did out of indifferent good-nature, but was adroitly and logically pursuing the aim which he had already announced in Teplitz, of securing the independence of all the German princes.

Six weeks after the decisive battle, the princes' revolution of 1803 and 1806 had been condoned, and by a great act of amnesty all the German vassals of France had been accepted into the great alliance. Some of the North German petty princes were honour-ably glad at release from the foreign yoke, and none more honestly so than Charles Augustus. During these sorrowful years, the court of Weimar had remained a centre of the German spirit. Napoleon himself had admired the regal demeanour of the duchess, when after

[1] Hardenberg's diary, December 1, 1813.

the battle of Jena she had encountered him in a proud and worthy spirit. She retained a profound detestation for the Imperator. With the unerring instinct of a noble-minded woman she sensed, like Louise of Prussia and Caroline of Bavaria, the strain of commonness in the great man's nature. Her husband had the same feeling, but the French could not believe that the light-minded, pleasure-seeking prince was doing anything seriously wrong, and never imagined that for years he was engaged in secret intercourse with the Prussian patriots. As soon as his hands were free, he entered the army of the allies as a Russian general, and regarding his old friend Goethe, whose mood still remained despairing, he said sadly : " Let him alone, he is grown old ! "

Very different was the mood of the South German courts. They did only what they could not leave undone, and left undone only what they dared not do. Montgelas expressed without concealment his aversion to " the fatal Germanism." The despot of Würtemberg prohibited, under pain of confinement in a fortress, all political discussions, immediately cashiered the general who had changed sides at Leipzig, and to one of his bailiffs who had given expression to German opinions, he said threateningly : " It is the duty of the good servant to advocate those causes only as truly good for which his sovereign has declared." It was in an extremely morose disposition that he returned from his visit to the headquarters at Frankfort. The allies had not vouchsafed him a scrap of his neighbours' territory as a reward for his change of flag. How much more remunerative had been the service of the Imperator ! He immediately resumed secret treasonable correspondence with the free-handed Protector. In Baden, too, it was a considerable time before the *Carlsruher Staatszeitung* began to speak of " Napoleon," and at length of " the enemy," instead of using the customary " his majesty, the emperor." When the change at length became unavoidable, the grand duke Charles expressed his most lively regret to the Protector. Napoleon, however, understood how to deal with his people, and swore that in case of his return he would lay their lands desolate, just as Louis XIV had formerly devastated the Palatinate. With clenched fist and an angry "You will have to answer for this, my prince ! " did Napoleon's envoy Vendeuil take leave of the grand duke Louis of Darmstadt when the latter announced his alliance with the conquerors.

The Imperator's threats did not fail of their effect, for they paralysed the energies even of the better disposed among the Rhenish Confederate princes. In any case, in most of these lands, the arming of the people after the Prussian manner was impossible, because the ruler did not trust his own people. In Bavaria the volunteers were sent home again by the authorities with contumely. In Würtemberg the king would not tolerate either volunteers or a Landwehr, and he utilised the formation of the Landsturm merely as a convenient excuse for the disarmament of his subjects, and for the issuing of an order for the handing over of all fire-arms, under pain of imprisonment. At these courts no one was more vigorously abused than Stein, for they knew that at Frankfort the baron had just proposed the temporary suspension of their governmental authority. Even the excellent men he had appointed to serve in the German central administration were soon all termed " Muscovite Jacobins "—such was the abusive cognomen of the Prussians Friesen and Eichhorn and the Russian Turgenieff, of Count Solms-Laubach, the leader of the hospital service, of Rühle von Lilienstern, the organiser of the arming of the people. Day by day the particularist arrogance and meanness of the South German cabinets led them to undermine the efficiency of the central administration ; Montgelas threatened Stein's officials with expulsion when they wished to ascertain the condition of the Bavarian hospitals. Frederick of Würtemberg refused to admit " foreign " wounded into his hospitals. When the Austrians brought their sick from the overcrowded Villingen to Rottweil, the Würtemberg authorities left the sufferers lying in the streets until the doors of the hospital were opened by force. Thus were displayed the friendly sentiments of those allied courts to which Austria had unconditionally restored their sovereignty. Stein himself now held the gloomy opinion that it would be better to postpone negotiations concerning the constitution of Germany until the peace, as otherwise the loose coalition might easily undergo a spontaneous dissolution. In order, however, to keep the nation informed as to the mode of thought of its princes, he made Eichhorn publish a work upon the central administration, which, without circumlocution, exposed the sins of the petty kings. After this had been done, the hatred of the Rhenish Confederate courts against Prussian Germanism knew no bounds.

The common people, too, of the south were but superficially touched by the storm of enthusiasm which had spread through North Germany, although everywhere an honourable will was displayed, and a number of young men of the cultured classes swore by Stein and Görres. The hatred of the foreign dominion had here in the south never been able to strike such deep roots as in Prussia, for here there was no lost glory to be regained. When the hour of liberation struck, it is true that most did their duty, but a strong and warlike desire for activity, which would have made short work of the disaffected governments, was nowhere displayed. Nothing could be more characteristic than Rückert's song for the Coburg Landwehr :

> "At first no summons came at all,
> But now we hearken duty's call,
> And ready are to go!"

After the distresses of this endless time of war, the universal wish was for quiet and for peace. In the theatre at Mannheim, at a ceremonial performance for the advantage of the national armament, Schiller's *Reiterlied* was sung, with a contemporary improvement, written by the valiant young patriot von Dusch :

> "Unless by force you peace attain
> For you 'tis hopeless peace to gain."

Unfortunately the further course of the war did not serve to bring North Germany and South Germany nearer together. In South Germany, the only general government of the central administration, that of Frankfort, was, in accordance with Hardenberg's dualistic plans, given over to Austrian officials and officers ; in Alsace, the Bavarians arbitrarily took control of the provisional administration, without asking Stein. The Russians and the Prussians were united by a true brotherhood-in-arms after so many common victories. The Russian troops had a hero-worship for King Frederick William, who knew how to speak to them in their own mother-tongue, and they had a similar feeling for their Marshal Forwards. The Prussian soldier, on his side, regarded with no more than moderate respect the Russian lieutenant who had to submit to a box on the ear from his major. But he had a high esteem for the bravery of the Russian rank and file. The Prussian soldiers, however, heard little of the Bavarian and Würtemberg regiments, for these, as was provided for in the treaty, were assigned to the Austrian army ; it was only the Badenese guard which fought side by side with the Prussians. Consequently, to Germany's misfortune, no living sentiment of comradeship could arise between the Prussians and the troops of the petty states, and the hateful memories of the bloody battles of the summer campaign remained unforgotten. By a disastrous fate it happened that the petty contingents played a small part in the acquirement of the warlike renown of the allies. A considerable proportion of them were used for the investment of Mainz, and for the Flanders sieges, which led to little glory ; the Saxon volunteers never even saw the enemy. It is true that the Bavarians and the Würtembergers went to Paris, and that they fought with their accustomed bravery, but they did not take part in any brilliant victory which might have obscured the triumphs of Ratisbon, Wagram, and Borodino. For this reason, the star of the Legion of Honour continued to retain its prestige among the veterans of the middle states. The peasants in Franconia and in the Black Forest, who even now continue to tell one another stories of the archduke Charles and of the campaign of the nineties, heard little of this war. Not even yet was there known to the Germans the reckless unanimity of a general uprising. It was in much later days that historical study and the slowly awakened impulse towards unity, aroused among the South Germans a belated enthusiasm for the War of Liberation which was unknown to any similar degree among the contemporaries of that war.

Whilst the powers were treating with the South German courts, they negotiated among themselves concerning the continuance of the war. France was defenceless at the point of their swords. As Ney later said jestingly, such was the actual state of affairs that "the allies could arrange their nocturnal halts beforehand all the way to Paris." In a luminous memorial Radetzky drew attention to the decisive fact that Napoleon no longer possessed an army, and that consequently the winter campaign had lost its terrors. Even Schwarzenberg was in favour of the invasion of France, if only for the reason that he did not see how this enormous army was to get along in the impoverished German territories. "My basis," he said confidently, "is Europe, from the frozen sea to the Hellespont ; must not Paris be its objective ? " Much more definitely did Gneisenau exhort the king to a rapid advance before the loose coalition should dissolve ; if the French were attacked simultaneously from the Netherlands and from the Central Rhine, in their weakest spots, the dreaded threefold girdle of fortresses on the eastern frontier could no longer serve as a protection for Napoleon, but would be a positive disadvantage, for the Imperator lacked the troops needed to garrison them. Finally, Blucher had never doubted from the first that this war could be ended only on the Seine. "The tyrant," he said, "has visited all the capitals, has plundered and stolen there ; we shall not behave in the same way, but our honour demands that we should pay him out by visiting him in his own nest."

To the straightforward understanding, the position seemed so simple that even the archduke John, who was by no means a hero, regarded the taking of Paris as certain. But in the diplomatic world for centuries the belief had been as invincible as an article of faith that France could never be conquered on her own soil. Even Charles V and Prince Eugene, the ever fortunate, had done no good when they ventured to press into the interior of the country, and how lamentable had been the course of the campaign of 1792, although France at that time possessed no army ready for war. The Frenchmen Bernadotte and Jomini depicted the dangers of the hazardous undertaking in the gloomiest colours. Knesebeck anxiously urged that the gods should not be tempted. York complained of the miserable state of his valiant corps, and demanded that there should be at least a brief period of rest for the exhausted troops. Even Frederick William was for some time affected by an attack of faint-heartedness. The purpose for which in the spring he had drawn the sword, the liberation of Germany as far as the Rhine, had been attained ; his slow-moving nature demanded a considerable time before he could gain a real understanding of the completely changed situation, and could recognise that all that had as yet been acquired could only be rendered secure by complete destruction of the French power. The Viennese court, above all, desired the speedy conclusion of this inconvenient war.

As early as the beginning of November, Metternich, in opposition to the letter and to the spirit of the treaty of Teplitz, had entered into separate negotiations with the captured French diplomat St. Aignan, and had assured him that no one contemplated the dethronement of Napoleon. If the Imperator would recognise the independence of Spain, Italy, and Holland, France could maintain her old position of power within her natural frontiers between the Rhine, the Alps, and the Pyrenees, and, without any formal suzerainty, could exercise over the petty German states that influence which every great nation necessarily possesses over its less powerful neighbours. Had an understanding been arrived at as to the boundaries of the Austrian dominion in Italy, all would in fact have been attained which Metternich desired. The liberation of the left bank of the Rhine was altogether outside his circle of vision; his views did not go beyond the mechanical doctrine of the balance of power characteristic of the days of the Barrier Treaty. He would have been fully satisfied if a handful of arbitrarily constructed petty states could have been introduced between quarrelsome France and the eastern powers, so that the chances of collision between the great political masses might be diminished by this buffer. But the House of Austria was the natural enemy of all powerful national states. The English plenipotentiary at the headquarters, Lord Aberdeen, blindly followed in all continental questions the views of Metternich, and was of opinion that enough would be done for English interests if only Hanover and the Netherlands should be re-established. By good fortune he lacked sufficient authority for a decision. Consequently Pozzo di Borgo was despatched to London, in order to secure the assent of the prince regent, whilst St. Aignan was to lay Metternich's peace proposals before the Imperator in Paris.

Meanwhile Stein, whom the Austrian statesmen had hitherto retained in Leipzig, came to Frankfort, and immediately threw himself with ardent zeal into the cause of the continuation of the war. He proved successful in winning over the czar, and subsequently the king as well. Napoleon's pride could not brook giving an immediate assent to the unduly favourable proposals of Austria. When he at length declared himself ready to undertake negotiations for peace, with the proviso that the petty states of Germany and Italy must in some way or other be subjected to his suzerainty, at the headquarters the decision had already been made, not indeed to break off the negotiations, but simultaneously to carry on the war. Thus Stein had won the game, for every new success of the allied armies must unavoidably render the peace conditions more onerous. Confidence grew from day to day, and soon without any formal understanding on the subject, it became the generally accepted view that a demand must now be made for at least a portion of the left bank, and perhaps the re-establishment of the frontier of 1792. The war party had triumphed. When Blucher took leave of the chancellor at Frankfort, in reply to the question " Where shall we meet next ? " he said with a happy laugh, " In the Palais Royal ! " [1]

The words and actions of the great headquarters-staff did not, indeed, render it possible to recognise the existence of any such fresh resolution. The manifesto of December 1st, which announced to the French the intended attack, seemed precisely calculated to increase to the utmost that French arrogance, which during the past two decades the world had never allowed to slumber. In flattering terms, such as had never before been employed in a declaration of

[1] Hardenberg's diary, December 16, 1813.

war, the allies excused their undertaking. It was not, they said their wish to make war against France, but against Napoleon's excess of power; they wished that France should remain great, strong, and happy; and they promised to the French state a greater extent of territory than it had ever had under its kings, for a valiant nation should not be forced down from the altitude to which it had attained because it had proved unfortunate in a heroic campaign!

As lamentable and mean-spirited as these words was the plan of campaign thought out by Duca and Langenau. Vainly did Gneisenau defend the view, which at that time was still a new one, that this centralised France could be conquered only in its capital. The Austrian war authorities had discovered upon the map the plateau of Langres, that modest elevation on the frontiers of the Burgundian highlands which constitutes the watershed of three river basins, leading to as many seas. They assumed that Napoleon in his campaigns would also allow himself to be guided by the considerations of geographical learning, and were prepared to demonstrate that " a winter campaign against this remarkable plateau would force the Imperator to make peace." In December, the great army slowly set itself in motion in order to make a wide detour, through Baden, Alsace, and Switzerland, to Langres. In pursuing this plan, the Hofburg was at the same time working with accessory political aims in view, intending to restore in Switzerland the old aristocratic regime, and to force the enemy to evacuate the Italian theatre of war, which was far more important to Austria than to France. The Austrian strategists justified the unnatural artificiality of this plan of campaign, which arbitrarily diverted the principal power of the allies from the direct and safe road to victory, by the extraordinary contention that in this way they would gain the support of Wellington's army, which was in the extreme south-west of France, near the Pyrenees. The leaders of the Silesian army wished to keep Langenau occupied in the investment of Mainz, far from the theatre of war. It was only after a long and violent struggle that Blucher secured permission to cross the French frontier on the Middle Rhine. Thence, by the territories of the Saar and Lorraine, he also was to gain the wonderful plateau.

Thus did the incapacity of an antediluvian policy and strategy give the Imperator another chance of rescue, furnishing him with three months' respite in which to create a new army, and formulating its plan of campaign upon the careful avoidance of any decisive issue. Although Lainé, and a few other men of courage in the tame legislative body, now raised their voices to express the discontent felt throughout the country on account of the unending wars, the despot brow-beat them with contemptuous words. The proverb of the empire still held, that the reign of talk was at an end! Napoleon pursued his military preparations with the old circumspection, counting upon the success of his diplomatic negotiations and upon the dismemberment of the loose coalition. Repeatedly did he assure the statesmen of the Hofburg that a great victory would be opposed to Austrian interests, for it might easily change the balance of power in Europe to Austria's disadvantage. There was no word of yielding. "The old frontiers," he wrote to Caulaincourt, "would be a humiliation for France; all our conquests do not balance what Prussia, Austria, Russia, and England have won during the last ten years." His negotiators were to word their proposals for peace "as indefinitely as possible, for time is on our side!"

Meanwhile some of the fortresses of the north-east, which were defended by the French with commendable tenacity, at length fell into the hands of the allies, and among these Danzig and Torgau. On January 13th, Wittenberg was taken by storm by Tauentzien's troops, after a fierce artillery attack which was ably directed by young Bardeleben; this was the only great siege in this war so full of battles. Far more important was the conquest of Holland. Since Bernadotte had in November proceeded from Hanover to Denmark, in order to secure his Norwegian booty, Bülow was freed from the detested commander-in-chief; he advanced from Westphalia into the Netherlands, and the world immediately learned once more what the northern army was capable of effecting, when it was allowed to act freely. General Oppen stormed the fortress of Doesborgh; the Kolberg regiment and the queen's dragoons, the old Ansbach-Bayreuths, added a new leaf to their laurels. Next Arnheim was taken by storm, the passage was forced across the Rhine and the Meuse, Herzogenbusch had to open its gates, and from now onwards, as in the days of the great elector, the predominant position of France in the Netherlands had been overthrown by the might of Prussian arms. Bülow's brilliant campaign of victory was first arrested under the walls of Antwerp. Here Carnot was in command; the steadfast republican had magnanimously controlled his party hatred for the sake of the fatherland, and in this important place he firmly maintained his position until the conclusion of the peace.

The prudent Dutchmen understood how to seize fortune by the forelock. The members of the ancient aristocracy had for years been preparing for the re-establishment of the state. At a sign from them, the people of Amsterdam rose in revolt, as soon as the first Cossacks appeared upon the frontier, and hoisted the flag of Orange (November 15th). The French officials fled, and the troops entered the fortress. The adherents of the old ruling-house formed " a provisional government," and recalled the prince of Orange. Everywhere was to be heard the old cry of *"Oranje boven,"* and the new *"Met Willem komt de vrede !"* Consequently the unwarlike commercial nation could maintain with some show of truth that the country had freed itself, although the bloody work of the conquest was left entirely to the Prussians and the Russians.

Since everyone knew that Austria wished to get rid of Belgium, it was proposed to unite the two halves of the Old Netherlands, this suggestion having been made several times already during the war of the coalition. Spiegel had even defended the plan as early as 1794. The notion was in the air, it was a spontaneous outcome of the ideas of that old school of diplomacy which was accustomed to the carving out of states solely with respect to questions of geographical situation, and to the rounding off of territory without any understanding of the principles of historical life. The commercial policy of England took up the idea with zeal. The British had conquered the Dutch colonial empire, and desired out of the rich booty to retain Ceylon and the Cape, which were so important for their Indian dominion, together with the Dutch fleet, and a portion of Guiana. According to the views of the eighteenth century, it seemed a matter of course that from masterless Germany should come compensation to the Dutchmen for this loss ; the consolidation of the English naval dominion was to be paid for by the Burgundian region of the German empire. Since the good old times seemed now everywhere returning, there were revived also the traditions of the days of Wilhelmina, the memories of the long-lived alliance between the two naval powers. England hoped to find a trustworthy ally in the strengthened Netherlands, and to obtain a well-protected bridge-head for her continental wars in the harbour of Antwerp ; there was hope also that by the marriage of the heir of the House of Orange with the heiress of the English crown, this alliance might be yet more firmly cemented. Anxiety regarding the Jacobin spirit of the Prussian army served to strengthen the English tory cabinet in such views ; " this headstrong " warlike power must, for the sake of the general peace, be separated from restless France by a peaceful commercial state.

Thus it happened that the English statesmen diligently advocated the re-establishment of the united Netherlands as an advantage to British policy, showing even more zeal for this step than for the enlargement of the Guelph realm in Hanover. Since the spring of 1813, the London cabinet had been in communication with the prince of Orange, and had been endeavouring to convince the European courts of the necessity of reconstructing the united Orange state. In the diplomatic world the new kingdom was regarded so completely as a British creation, that of every new portion of land which fell to the Netherlands it was accustomed to say bluntly " this domain becomes English." A skilful trader when he accepts a price somewhere near half of that which he first asked, is accustomed to assure the purchaser that he closes the bargain only out of personal regard for his customer. In the same way, the English commercial policy has always understood how to conceal its intentions behind lofty phrases about freedom and justice. England desired to retain one-half of the colonies of its Netherland protégé. Lord Castlereagh, however, declared proudly that his state was generously prepared to restore a portion of its conquests, but that this sacrifice could not be made unless the Netherlands should receive enlargement upon the Continent, and should thus be put in a position to defend against France the restored portion of its colonial empire. England robbed the Netherlands of those overseas possessions upon which the power of the country had depended, and then claimed the thanks of Europe for her generosity. The new Netherland realm was " an arrangement for a European object " ; it was only in order that the Rhineland might be safeguarded against France that Germany was once more to surrender a part of her old Reichslande. At the same time the heroic spirit of the Dutchmen was enthusiastically praised, and it was declared to be the duty of Europe to reward the *noble élan* of this nation. This English fable was repeated with such earnestness and persistency that in the great headquarters it ultimately came to be believed, and the phrase about " Holland's services to Europe " found a place in the diplomatic dictionary.

After Bülow's victorious campaign, Prussia was for the first time during this war in a sufficiently favourable position to enable her to offer and not merely to beg ; Prussia could now declare to the English cabinet that an understanding as to the disposal of these lands which had been reconquered by herself could not be arrived at unless England would give a binding assent to the annexation of Saxony. Yet this idea did not find open expression, for the Prussian cabinet was itself all the while dominated by that same policy of the balance of power upon which the Netherland plans of England were based. In all Hardenberg's proposals it was presupposed as a matter of course that Switzerland and the Netherlands must serve to preserve peace between Germany and France, and that in case of war they must bear the first onslaught of the French aggressor. Only in the second line were Austria and Prussia to take up the battle. All the more did the enlargement of the Netherlands seem to be a German interest, because Hardenberg still confidently hoped that Holland and Switzerland might be linked to Germany by a confederative bond—as " leagued allies " (*Bundesverwandte*) as the phrase ran. Moreover, the prince of Orange, so closely related to the Hohenzollerns, was regarded as almost a member of the Prusian royal house, although the military caste could not forgive him the shameful capitulation of Erfurt. It was by his participation in the war of 1806 that he had lost land and people ; it seemed to be an honourable duty that he should be richly rewarded. For these reasons Hardenberg was hardly less zealous than were the English statesmen on behalf of the Orange cause ; when the news came of the conquest of Holland, he embraced the Netherlands envoy, Gagern, with joyful tears. To the European courts it seemed that the formation of this buffer state was a success of Prussian policy, and by no means a step which entitled Prussia to make new demands.

Here we certainly find the second of the great errors of Hardenberg's policy ; and yet these Netherland dreams, like his plans for German dualism, were not the fault of the man but of the age. Long before anyone ventured to hope for the conquest of the left bank of the Rhine, Stein had demanded the strengthening of the Netherlands as a European necessity, and everyone had agreed. Subsequently when the land-hunger of the House of Orange became too plainly manifest, many doubts had indeed arisen. The *Rheinische Merkur* complained because " the least warlike German stock " was to be entrusted with this border country ; and even Castlereagh asked anxiously in his letters whether this commercial people would prove equal to its European task. Ludwig Vincke, who had long been watching the affairs of the Netherlands, declared in advance that this arbitrarily constructed state must necessarily perish. In the Netherlands, there at once reawakened the old hatred which for two hundred and fifty years had separated the

Catholic Belgians from the Protestant Dutchmen. German diplomacy, however, was uninfluenced by these considerations. Hardenberg had unlimited confidence in English policy. After the taking of Antwerp, he at once agreed to the proposal that the warships captured by the Prussians and Russians in the harbour, should be removed to England. German policy had as yet no understanding of the importance of sea power, and no one even raised the question whether this valuable booty might not form the nucleus of a Prussian fleet.

The prince of Orange, thus overwhelmed with gifts from a spendthrift hand, still regarded himself as inadequately paid for his recognised services to Europe, and unashamedly conceived further plans of aggrandisement. Now it was a kingdom on the left bank of the Rhine, a new Burgundy extending to the Moselle, now it was a kingdom on the right bank of the Rhine, a great Nassau, from Dusseldorf to Bieberich, which was to fall into the insatiable maw of his house. The people along the Rhine, wearied by the oppression of the Napoleonic prefects, cherished golden dreams of what they might gain from the wealthy Dutchmen, and dreaded the military strictness of the Prussians. The prince of Orange, like his British well-wishers, cherished a profound mistrust of these liberators of his country. Almost on every page of the despatches between England and the Netherlands we find anxiety expressed that Prussia should not acquire Luxemburg, and that Prussia should not gain a strong Rhenish province which would enable her to exercise " pressure " on the Netherlands, for, " Prussian craft cannot easily harmonise with the English sense of honour." Hardenberg knew nothing of these hostile sentiments of the Guelph and the Orange statesmen, doing his best for the Orange cause as if it had been his own, and he was even prepared to hand over to the Netherlands certain purely German territories on the Lower Rhine.

Not until after the conquest of the left bank of the Rhine had been determined could the Prussian cabinet bring forward a definite plan for the re-establishment of the monarchy, for now first had it become manifest that German domains would be available for Prussia. The chancellor immediately took full advantage of the favour of the moment, and began to treat with the allies concerning the Prusssian demands for territory. Since the battle of Leipzig, the allies had had the kingdom of Saxony in their control. On the day when Frederick Augustus had been removed from the captured town as a prisoner of war, no one could have ventured to believe that this most devoted of Napoleon's vassals would once more become a friend of the allies. The Imperator himself always felt for the king a well-earned gratitude, and on several occasions during this winter demanded the restoration to Frederick Augustus of the crown of Warsaw, because it would touch his honour to abandon this faithful ally. Frederick Augustus had hoped that Napoleon's victories would secure for himself the enlargement of Saxony, and must consequently be prepared to suffer in his own person for the results of the French reverses. In a just war his country had been conquered to the last village, and in accordance with international law it remained absolutely at the disposal of the conquerors. The change of sides of a portion of the Saxon army, which had been effected against the king's commands, and which from the political and military point of view had had no effect whatever, could make no difference to these facts. After the capture of Frederick Augustus, Hardenberg triumphantly greeted Frederick William as King of Saxony and Grand Duke of Posen.

The natural compensation for Prussia was offered by the conquest of Saxony. Through this, the Prussian state received the means of coming to a complete understanding with Russia concerning the Polish question. Prussia gained a well-secured southern frontier, which seemed all the more indispensable since the Prussian domain remained undefended towards the east ; and in this way a German province, which by race and culture, by religion and by trade interests, was closely linked with the northern neighbour land, now became associated to Prussia. For the well-being of the future Germanic Federation, it would be an unquestionable blessing to get rid of a princely house which in almost all crises of our recent history had sinned deeply against the great fatherland. Since unfortunately it was not possible to treat according to their deserts all the kings by Napoleon's grace, it seemed desirable to inflict a beneficial chastisement upon one at least of the Rhenish Confederate princes ; and the experience of the year 1866 proved how wholesome would have been the effect of such an example upon the mood of the German high nobility. But all the excellent reasons which commended the annexation of Saxony to the Prusso-German policy, could to the court of Vienna appear only as ominous warnings.

The conflict of interests between the two great powers was so decisively manifest in the Saxon question, that only the credulity of a Hardenberg could have been deceived in the matter. Gneisenau's penetration was such that he was never for a moment in doubt as to the simple truth. It was evident to him that the Hofburg must desire to push the northern great power as far as possible towards the east. It was not permissible for Austria to deliver over the passes of the Erzgebirge to the state which already threatened eastern Bohemia with the fortresses of County Glatz ; nor could Austria sacrifice the Catholic princely house closely related to the imperial court, and one which had for so long been a useful tool against Prussia. Moreover, how could Austria approve of the dethronement of one of the Napoleonic satraps, when she wished to form a devoted Austrian party out of the middle states ? On October 29th, Gentz wrote to Metternich in great anxiety, saying : " The plans of Prussia for territorial aggrandisement, plans which day by day come more plainly to light, will give us more trouble than the main negotiations with Napoleon." Radetzky, in a confidential memorial to Frankfort, said that it was urgently desirable that the Prussians " such as they are now displaying themselves to be " should have as few troops as possible once the peace was arranged.

The time did not yet seem ripe for the open expression of such opinions. Even among the Saxon people the general discontent with the sins of the Albertine court was still too loudly voiced; even the Guelph Münster was still of opinion that Frederick Augustus was worthy not of respect but of contempt. Anyone who saw through the specious frankness of the Austrian monarch could readily grasp the heartfelt wishes of the Lorrainers ; Emperor Francis demanded that the captured king should remove to Prague, and that his troops should join the Austrian army. Prussia and Russia, however, arranged that Frederick Augustus should be taken to Berlin, and that temporarily Saxony should be ruled by a Russian governor. The introduction of a Prussian administration, which would have served as an intermediate step towards annexation, was for the moment impossible, since the common conquest could not be thus dealt with without Austria's consent. The members of the Saxon ruling house remained in besieged Dresden under the protection of the French arms ; as soon as the capital capitulated Emperor Francis offered his relatives a residence in Austria. Prince Antony, the emperor's brother-in-law, began from Prague to carry on a vigorous secret activity for the deliverance of his imprisoned brother ; from the outset the entourage of Frederick Augustus set their chief hopes upon Austria's favour.

The chancellor saw nothing of all this. During the monarch's stay in Freiburg, Hardenberg trustingly communicated all his

Saxon plans to the Austrian minister, and since at a friendly dinner party the crafty Austrian replied to him with a few soft words, he lightly assumed that Metternich approved the Prussian designs.[1] Here in Breisgau, Emperor Francis was welcomed with joy as their ancient suzerain. This portion of Hither Austria had always been one of the best governed provinces of the imperial house ; the people still yearned for the easy-going rule ; the powerful Catholic nobility disliked the enlightened bourgeois Badenese bureaucracy, and could not forgive the loss of their old feudal constitution. Everywhere in the charming town the emperor encountered ancient Austrian memories. Here was the Dauphinenstrasse, down which had once passed the wedding train of Marie Antoinette ; there was the monument at the Martin Gate which recorded the battles of the Breisgauer volunteers in the nineties ; there, again, was the beautiful old Kaufhaus, with the statues of the Hapsburgs, which the town council had resolved to replace in honour of the imperial visit. Many of the men of Breisgau, despising the Badenese service, sent in their names for enrolment in the Austrian army. In confidential conversations the emperor was implored to gather his children once more to his fatherly heart, and indeed the die had already been cut for stamping a medal which was to commemorate the reunion. Emperor Francis was by no means disinclined to yield to the desires of these faithful ones, but Metternich adhered firmly to his own policy. He did not wish to irritate the Rhenish Confederate courts ; and although the cabinet of Carlsruhe was for two years longer rendered profoundly anxious by the Austrian sentiments concerning Breisgau, the Hofburg during the whole of this time never even attempted to negotiate with Baden regarding the restoration of the Hither Austrian territories. Hardenberg noted with concern that Austria herself manifested no inclination for the position of power in South Germany which he wished to assign to her.

After the vacillations of the Frankfort days had been overcome, the natural relationships of parties amongst the allies became speedily re-established. Prussia and Russia demanded a resolute prosecution of the war, whereas Austria and England wished to avoid a decisive issue. The tension in the great headquarters notably increased. Everywhere the two parties came into hostile contact. In Switzerland, Metternich endeavoured, through the intermediation of Count Senfft, to resestablish the ancient powers of the Bernese aristocracy, as well as their suzerainty over

[1] Hardenberg's diary, January 8, 1814.

Aargau and Vaud. Alexander, on the contrary, played the part of the well-wisher of liberalism, supporting the fellow-countrymen of his Vaudois tutor Laharpe ; arranging, in unison with Prussia, that the independence of the new cantons should be recognised, and also that some at least of the justified new formations of recent years should be carried over into the epoch of the restoration.

The slow march of the army gave the Prussian statesmen plenty of time to discuss conditions of peace. At Freiburg, Knesebeck drew up a memorial incorporating the demands which seemed to him still attainable in view of the sentiments of the Hofburg. Whilst in the Silesian headquarters the demand for the reacquirement of the Vosges, the German Thermopylæ, was put forward, the Austrian diplomats held strictly to the manifesto of December 1st, which in their view was already excessively bold. Thus Knesebeck was of opinion : " Since the view has been definitely expressed that France is to remain greater than under the kings, and that the Rhine is to constitute a portion of the French frontier, let the Rhine be the boundary from Basle to Landau."[1] It was only Strasburg that he hoped to regain for Germany, as a free town. For Prussia, he demanded Saxony, Westphalia, Berg, and the left bank of the Rhine, and, above all, the Polish territory as far as the Narew. The pedant could not get rid of his fixed ideas of Russophobia.

Hardenberg, for his part, wished first to gain clear ideas as to Russia's intentions. For this reason, in Freiburg, and subsequently in Basle, he did what Frederick William had so often done, and urgently begged the czar to state clearly how much Polish land Russia demanded for herself. It was not until Alexander had refused to give any definite answer before the conclusion of peace, that Prussia acted upon her own initiative. The chancellor made a precise calculation of the compensation necessary for Prussia, and sent a memorial upon the subject to the Austrian court during his stay in Basle in January, 1814. The Prussian demand was for Saxony, Hither Pomerania, the Rhineland from Mainz to the Netherland frontier, and Poland as far as the Warthe ; the population of the new monarchy was reckoned at from ten to eleven millions. The only answer Hardenberg received was a letter in French from Count Stadion.[2] In a tone of confidential

---

[1] Knesebeck's Memorial concerning the reconstruction of Prussia, January 7, 1814.
[2] Stadion to Hardenberg, Basle, January 21, 1814.

friendship, the Austrian remarked with the familiar national good-nature, that the Prussian figures were really too high, and that Prussia must not go beyond ten millions. He then ventured to make certain cautious " remarks in favour of the unhappy Saxon electoral house, whose complete expulsion from Germany seems to me to infringe too greatly the obligations of political morality." He suggested that Prussia might well content herself with Lusatia and the right bank of the Elbe, concluding in harmless terms : " Your excellency will excuse these frank observations ; I some-times allow myself such frankness in politics." Hardenberg immediately answered : [1] " Of all things that could happen to Saxony, a partition of the country would certainly be the worst." He definitely maintained his demands, referring in conclusion to the report which had just come to hand of the taking of Witten-berg by storm, and of all the other rights which Prussia had acquired by her warlike services. This was the end of the correspon-dence, for Metternich refused to give any assent until peace was concluded.

The exercise of a little caution would have rendered it impos-sible for the chancellor to deceive himself regarding the motives which had inspired Stadion's " frank observations." In these very days, he received definite news that the man who possessed the confidence of Emperor Francis and who had drawn up the plans of the great headquarters-staff, Langenau the Saxon, was in secret communication with the Saxon royalists. Metternich, when spoken to about these intrigues, immediately gave a con-ciliatory answer. Notwithstanding all these indications Harden-berg could not abandon his belief in the faithful friendship of Austria.

Another cherished hope of the trusting chancellor proved to be based on the customary insecure foundation. Bernadotte had brought the Danish war to a conclusion, and in the peace of Kiel had enforced the cession of Norway, January 14, 1814. In com-pensation, the very Swedish Pomerania which in the previous summer the crown prince had promised to the Prussian chancellor, was handed over to Denmark. Hardenberg gave vent to bitter complaints against Bernadotte's breach of faith, and resolved firmly that in no circumstances would he endure this blow. For his gratification he received shortly afterwards a communication from Prince Putbus, the chief landed proprietor of Swedish Pomerania, entering in the name of his fellow-countrymen a formal protest

[1] Hardenberg to Stadion, January 21, 1814.

against the cession to Denmark.[1] But all these considerations were still remote. When the war recommenced, Prussia was secure of victory, but not of the reward of victory.

§ 2. THE WINTER CAMPAIGN.

On new year's eve, 1814, at Caub on the Rhine, the officers of the Silesian headquarters-staff were seated with full glasses, engaged in lively and cheerful conversation concerning the great changes of the time. It was exactly a year since York, on the further side of the eastern frontier of Germany, had concluded the treaty which had announced to the Prussians the beginning of the decisive struggle. To-day, Blucher, with York's victorious troops, stood at the gates of the western march of Germany, on the very spot where, twenty years before, he had begun the first war for the liberation of the left bank of the Rhine. Outside, in the sharp frost, the Russians were building a bridge of boats across to the islet upon which stands the crumbling wall of the ancient Palatinate. Count Brandenburg with the Brandenburg volunteers, quietly crossed the pontoons, and at midnight there resounded the thundering hurrahs of the men who set foot upon the left bank. Silence had been ordered but the men were so happy that they could not but disobey ; their joy had to find vent, so glorious was the hour which brought fulfilment to the yearnings of so many weary years. Next day the joyful Palatinate celebrated its new year's festival. Music, song, and mirth broke out wherever the Prussians appeared ; the faithful Protestants of Hundsrück had always remained good Germans, and greeted their liberators with warm thanks as their neighbours in the lands of the crozier. Simultaneously General St. Priest entered Coblenz with his Russians, and when, near the Kastorkirche, he saw the new fountain, with the boastful inscription in honour of the taking of Moscow, it pleased him to write underneath " Seen and approved."

The Silesian army marched through Lorraine without encountering any serious resistance. The fortresses were poorly manned, and, as Gneisenau had foreseen, were in no way dangerous to the allies. From the extraordinary experiences of this campaign, the public at large soon drew the hasty conclusion that the day of fortresses had passed away. In Nancy, Blucher celebrated with lively satisfaction the Prussian coronation festival, in the very

[1] Memorial of Prince Malte zu Putbus, January, 1814.

town where many of his unlucky comrades had been kept for two years as prisoners of war. Thence he made a bold evolution to the south-west across the Marne, and in the last days of January was at Brienne on the Aube. He thus thrust his army between the Imperator, who was advancing from Châlons, and the great army of the allies, which after a march lasting more than a month had at length reached the plateau of Langres. It was the old hero's hope that he would incite the hesitating Schwarzenberg to advance with him to certain victory.

In the great headquarters-staff at Langres, dissension and uncertainty were once more dominant. The wonderful plateau, the possession of which according to Langenau was to prove decisive in the war, had been successfully attained, the fortress of Langres had opened its gates without resistance, but with all this nothing had really been effected. No unprejudiced head could fail to be impressed with the stupidity of this campaign, directed against mountains and rivers. All the more tenaciously did the learned strategists hold fast to their principles. In their view, through the advance from the Rhine to Langres, a second campaign had been concluded, and indeed it only remained to be considered whether a third campaign was still necessary. Knesebeck declared that the watershed of Langres was the Rubicon which must on no account be crossed. General Duca recommended that a methodical campaign of sieges should be begun by the investment of Mainz. Schwarzenberg observed with contempt the childish eagerness with which Blucher and Gneisenau, despising all the rules of the art of war, pressed on towards Paris ; in his view these Prussian heads " were too small for so great an emergency "—their only aim was, in truth, to make themselves at home in the restaurants of the Palais Royal ! His view of Alexander's zeal for the war was precisely that of the Austrian court : " Alexander's footsteps are guided not by reason but by greed " ; for every new victory could serve only for the aggrandisement of Russia and for the re-establishment of Prussia. The affectionate letters with which Marie Louise assailed her father's heart did not indeed affect the unsentimental disposition of Emperor Francis, but he saw with increasing uneasiness that he was expected to sacrifice the energies of his state and his own comforts for foreign ends. The re-establishment of the faithful spiritual princes was absolutely impossible ; how then could he be expected to reconquer the left bank of the Rhine for Prussia ? He demanded peace, that the war should be brought to a speedy close, with a recognition of those " natural frontiers " which in Frankfort Metternich had already agreed to recognise. His dislike to the war increased to the point of horror when he learned that Alexander was aiming at Napoleon's deposition. The overthrow of his son-in-law was not merely opposed to the interests of the House of Austria, but it was to be feared, whoever might succeed to the dethroned emperor, that Alexander would exercise a decisive influence upon the new French government.

Many of the Austrian statesmen had so thoroughly accepted the disgrace of these years that the deadly enemy of Old Europe seemed to them the prop of public order, whilst they regarded his deposition as a dangerously revolutionary and arbitrary act. Even Gentz, who nine years before had issued warnings against the recognition of the Napoleonic emperordom, now cried out in terrible anxiety that if the French were allowed to appoint another ruler this would involve " a recognition of the principle which in our times can hardly be uttered without trembling, that it depends upon the people whether they shall or shall not tolerate the actual ruling sovereign. This principle of popular sovereignty is the very pivot of all revolutionary systems." So greatly moved was Gentz that he could scarcely find words for the expression of his veneration for the stable and peaceful policy of the House of Austria, for his renegade's hatred for unquiet Prussia, and for his fears of Russia. When the enthusiasts of the Silesian headquarters-staff subsequently carried through the campaign against Paris, he exclaimed with anger that this march was " essentially directed quite as much against us as against the emperor Napoleon." During the advance of the Silesian Jacobins he had only one hope left, that the Imperator would make peace as soon as possible. " Every other issue will be regarded by the powerful party which has already forced us to give way, not merely as a victory over Napoleon but as a victory over ourselves. It would disturb me very little if the coalition which has now served its ends and more, should fall to pieces. But it cannot be a matter of indifference to us how the coalition ends."

To such a mood as this, the French capital, which lay immediately beneath the feet of the conqueror, must seem altogether impregnable. Metternich's sympathies were not quite so Napoleonic as were those of Gentz. Yet he dreaded " the Arndts, the Jahns," and all the other Prussian incendiaries who threatened to lay waste the capital ; he dreaded the revolutionary dreams of the czar, who was already proposing to appeal to the French nation to establish a new government ; he dreaded most of all the Polish plans of Russia. It was already reported that Alexander was thinking of bestowing Alsace upon Austria and then taking Galicia for himself. By the Austrian minister's adroitness, almost all the diplomats were soon brought over to his way of thinking. All the English statesmen, Castlereagh, Stewart, Cathcart, and Aberdeen, admired Metternich's wise moderation ; admired the manner in which the Austrian statesman (who was so soon himself to advocate active intervention) endeavoured to make the czar recognise that the veneration which must be felt for all truly national conditions forbade the dethronement of Napoleon. Aberdeen regarded it as positively unworthy to go beyond the Frankfort proposals, although Napoleon had himself rejected these. The English cabinet became more and more confirmed in the belief that the humiliation of Russia would be the next task of British policy. Metternich knew how to represent the renunciation of Belgium, which was a primary element of Austrian policy, in so clever a light as to suggest that Austria was making a great sacrifice for her dear friend England ; and in this he gained the complete confidence of the British. How was it possible for such intelligences to see through the specious mask of frankness worn by the good emperor. Quite carried away by his feelings, Castlereagh wrote about the pure character of this monarch, whose virtues were beyond all description. Nesselrode, too, inclined to the peace party ; Hardenberg complained of Stein's intrigues, and reposed such incautious confidence in the enthralling amiability of the Austrians that he could learn nothing from the most severe disillusionments. Even before a single battle had been fought upon French soil, the coalition was ready to conclude peace upon the Frankfort terms. This was in the most favourable military conditions conceivable, when the forces of the coalition were distant only eight marches from Paris !

Schwarzenberg's army numbered 190,000 men, and that of Blucher 83,000 men. This was a decisive superiority, although the troops were dispersed between Geneva and the Moselle. In November, according to his own admission, Napoleon had been unfitted for any kind of warlike undertaking, but this was no longer the case. Thanks to the hesitation of the allies, he had formed a new field army, but it contained 70,000 men only, for the most part untrained and spiritless recruits ; whilst the troops of the allies consisted of veteran soldiers confident of victory. The disgrace of making peace in such a situation was averted, with Stein's help, by Alexander and Frederick William. Alexander threatened that in case of need, he would carry on the campaign alone, and since Frederick William declared that he would not separate himself from his friend, Austria gave way in part, and a compromise was arranged. The war was to be continued, but at the same time a great peace conference was to be opened in Châtillon. The question of the deposition of Napoleon, and that of the internal condition of France, were temporarily shelved. Nor was any settlement to be made until after the war concerning the claims for compensation made by the individual powers. Alexander demanded this, not merely because he did not wish to disclose his own Polish plans ; but also because the coalition was in fact attached by such extremely slender bonds that it could not have borne the discussion of such thorny questions.

Metternich unwillingly accepted these determinations, and unwillingly did Schwarzenberg carry them out. On January 29th, at Brienne, Blucher had had a skirmish with Napoleon, with trifling success ; he burned with desire here, in sight of this place where the great war-lord of the century had once been at school, " to show the French that the Germans had also learned something in the art of war ! " Upon the urgent representations of the Prussian generals, the commander-in-chief at length agreed that on February 1st Blucher, reinforced by two corps of the great army, should descend from the heights of Trannes and should attack the Imperator in his widely extended position at La Rothière. Schwarzenberg himself, with two-thirds of the allied armies, idly looked on at the battle. But the forces actually engaged were already altogether superior to the 40,000 men whom Napoleon had under his command. In the centre, in a wild snow-storm, Sacken pressed forward against La Rothière with his Russians, and maintained himself there against the imperial guard. Then the right wing of the French was also defeated by Wrede and the crown prince of Würtemberg, and although Gyulay, the child of ill-fortune, had, as formerly at Leipzig, been able to do very little against the enemy's left wing, in the evening a complete victory had been gained. A large portion of the French army fled in wild confusion. If the victory had been rightly utilised by the overwhelming force of the allies, nothing could have saved the vanquished from annihilation. Sacken triumphantly exclaimed : " On this memorable day Napoleon ceases to be any longer a dangerous enemy of the human race." For the first time in open battle had Marshal Forwards stood independently face to face with the Imperator ; for the first time for centuries had proud France been defeated in a serious battle upon her own soil. Notable was the impression produced on friend and enemy alike. Napoleon now regarded the game as lost, and empowered Caulaincourt, his plenipotentiary in Châtillon, to save the capital at all costs and to conclude peace. It is true that, as he wrote to his brother Joseph, he regarded such a treaty as no more than a capitulation, and promised himself to renew the war two years later.

Thereupon the policy of Austria once more rescued the Imperator. Schwarzenberg, instead of pursuing the vanquished with all his forces, divided his army, ostensibly because he had not means for provisioning the whole, but in reality because the Austrians wished to dissociate themselves from the Silesian zealots. Whilst the great army marched along the Seine to deliver the main assault upon the enemy, Blucher was to move north-eastward to the Marne, and thence to outflank Napoleon's left wing. Cheerfully the old Prussian general took his way across the cold and treeless plateau of Champagne, bounded to the north by the vine-clad limestone rocks of the Marne valley, and to the south by the pleasant hills of the Seine. The wind whistled across the open country, the rain was pouring down ; laboriously the troops had to wade through the celebrated muddy roads of *la Champagne pouilleuse*, whose evil repute was known to the veteran officers of 1792. Then a severe frost set in, forcing the soldiers to burn the abandoned houses and barns if they were to find anything to warm themselves with in this treeless land. As ill-luck would have it, the army had found its way into the most repulsive region of *la belle France;* the Prussians considered that, compared with these weary wastes, the green plains of the Mark were like a garden ; they made a mock of the cave-like uninhabitable houses, with plastered rooms and smoky chimneys. Yet they remained cheerful, for they knew that their ever-victorious general was leading them direct to the capital, for the fortunate ending of all their sorrows and struggles.

In the valiant regiments of York's corps, there prevailed an invincible feeling of satisfaction ; in the whole of this war not one of the attacks made by the Lithuanian dragoons had miscarried. Who could get the better of these *Heurichs* of the old Isegrimm ? By this nickname, which the French could not pronounce, the men of York recognised one another on dark nights. At La Chaussée, York's cavalry had just attacked the columns of Macdonald's corps upon the march, and the soldiers long continued to tell one another how the iron riders of the Napoleonic cuirassier and carabineer regiments had proved unable to resist the onslaught of the light Brandenburg hussars, and how then the Lithuanian and Landwehr cavalry had captured the flag of the dreaded Polish lancers, Napoleon's best cavalry troop. Then York had forced his old chief Macdonald, to whom a freakish destiny again and again allotted the most unfortunate undertakings, to withdraw from Châlons, and York subsequently rejoined the Silesian army.

The individual corps moved westward, separated by wide intervals. Gneisenau had done nothing to safeguard the left flank, but had understood from Schwarzenberg that Wittgenstein's corps was to maintain the union between the two armies, and that he would cover the wide space between the right bank of the Seine and the Silesians' line of march. The commander-in-chief, however, did not keep his promise, but after slow marches and repeated rests, moved southward on the left bank of the Seine, so that a huge gap was left between his forces and Blucher's army. On February 13th, in consequence of a secret order from Emperor Francis, he remained upon the left bank of the Seine, and this order had a consequence which made it tantamount to treachery.[1] The good emperor, whose childlike innocence was the admiration of the British statesmen, desired to prevent a victory of the united armies which would have disturbed the wavering peace negotiations.

As if by miracle Napoleon perceived himself to be rescued from certain destruction. He at once advanced all his forces to Sezanne, midway between the two armies of the allies, suddenly attacked the left flank of the Silesian army, which was taken by surprise, and during the five days from February 10th to 14th, he defeated the isolated corps of this army with his combined and preponderant forces in a series of brilliant fights. At first he dispersed Olsuwieff's weak division at Champaubert and thus made his way between the columns of the Silesian army. On the following day at Montmirail, Sacken's corps escaped destruction only through York's heroic sacrifice ; the bold Lithuanians learned here for the first time the inconstancy of the fortune of war. On the 12th, the generals who, the day before,

[1] From the work *Oesterreich's Teilnahme an den Befreiungskriegen* (Vienna, 1887, p. 810) it would seem that no such order was issued. Cf. also Delbrück, *Gneisenau*, ii, 67.

had been defeated at Château Thierry, withdrew to the right bank of the Marne, after heavy fighting. On the 13th, Napoleon made his triumphal entry into the conquered town, in order to prepare an unexpected and bloody reception for the last, and still untouched, corps of the Silesian army, personally led by the field-marshal, who had no close knowledge of the mishaps of the previous days. This was on February 14th, at Etoges and Bauchamps, and on this occasion also fortune favoured the French. During the fight there came a terrible moment which might easily have led to a shameful end to the whole war. Blucher, Gneisenau, Prince Augustus, Kleist, Grolman, almost all the best men of the German army, in a square of Prussian infantry, were surrounded by greatly superior forces of hostile cavalry. Blucher himself sought death, for he would not allow the enemy to take him alive. But Grolman spoke to the troops in his powerful voice ; the assured repose of the majestic and heroic figure filled the hearts of the despairing with renewed courage ; they attacked the cavalry with the bayonet, and opened a way for the generals to the protection of the neighbouring woods. As unshaken as they had ever been in the days of good fortune did the regiments stand the test of these battles. Even that silent and long-visaged Englishman, who was accustomed to encounter Gneisenau with the same unmoved, dull, and stiff countenance, as he whipped the air with a riding-cane, even Hudson Lowe, hardly found words sufficient to express his admiration for the lion-like courage of these ragged and half-starved heroes. But however gloriously the men had fought, the best army of the allies had been beaten, had lost fifteen thousand soldiers and fifty guns. Nor were the leaders free from blame, but they had at least been forced to recognise the untrust-worthiness of their Austrian allies.

Once more the star of the French empire seemed to rise and to scintillate. With his 30,000 men, Napoleon had attacked an enemy which could dispose of almost double the number, and had yet been everywhere successful. Again, as in the days of Austerlitz, long trains of prisoners were conducted to the strains of martial music, were displayed to the delighted gaze of the Parisians as they were led past the Vendôme Column. Once again, as of old, the troops shouted with joy when they saw the splendid blue-clad aides-de-camp of the emperor spring on their richly caparisoned horses in order to carry some command of the invincible emperor. Even the weakest of the French arms, the cavalry, could once again tell of victory, for Schwarzenberg had not detached any portion of his powerful force of cavalry to join the Silesian army. Was it to be wondered at that the self-confidence of the army and of the people underwent a notable increase ? The out-wearied masses had at first looked on with astonishment and alarm when the long trains of tall, blonde men streamed into the country ; here and there they had even expressed their joy at the thought that the conqueror might abolish the oppressive taxation of the empire. But the honourable patriotic pride of the French showed itself stronger than party hatred. Never could the invaders find trustworthy guides and spies ; everywhere cavalrymen had to fear that the French blacksmiths would lame their horses in shoeing them ; throughout, the women displayed a worthy aloofness, never showing the amiable weakness of the Germans. As the war continued, the peasants became self-confident ; after the first news of victory they answered to the appeal of their emperor, who summoned all adult Frenchmen to arms, and they united everywhere against the foreigner. But this petty warfare was limited to the immediate neighbourhood of the desolate villages. No one knew better than Napoleon that his centralised official state offered no place for a popular uprising in the grand style. " In this country," he often said, " a *levée en masse* is a chimæra, for the nobility and the clergy have been destroyed by the revolution, and I myself have destroyed the revolution." None the less, the struggle with the countryfolk was vexatious to the conquerors ; both parties became savage in the unresting feud.

Subsequent to these days, there was displayed in the character of the French a trait of rough hatred of the foreigner which they had never known during the centuries of their excessive self-confidence, and this hatred was exhibited especially towards the Prussians. Napoleon made it a practice in his letters no longer to speak of Prussia ; his pride was in revolt against the admission of that which Maret had in September, 1813, confidentially admitted to the war minister Clarke, that France had suffered her severest blows from the sword of this despised little state. Yet he knew just as well as his people who was the most terrible opponent. To the wits of Paris *les Prussiens, les plus chiens*, were even more detestable than *les rustres* and *les autres chiens*. The victories of the Russians, the English, and the Austrians, were regarded as misfortunes ; those of the Prussians seemed an injustice, a thing altogether intolerable. It was inevitable that such sentiments should react upon the mood of the Prussian army. That good-nature which in past years the German soldier had preserved despite his embitterment was lost more and more. The prolongation of the war, for which Schwarzenberg's slackness was responsible, impaired the morale of the troops ; more especially the discipline of the Landwehr often suffered. Plundering became almost a necessity, for the villages had all been deserted, and the thievish Russians left very little for their Prussian comrades. Profoundly moved, York once reproved his valiant soldiers for their breaches of discipline, and pointed out to them the *suum cuique* upon the star of his order. Napoleon diffused among the people terrible fables of the horrors prepetrated by the foreign ogres ; he regarded the increasing savagery of the war with cynical contempt, saying it was all the better, for the peasants would then take up arms. It is true that the worst things done by the Prussian soldiers during these last wild weeks of the war fell far short of the misdeeds of the French in Germany ; whereas the Napoleonic marshals excelled their men in misconduct, the Prussian officers and the volunteers did their utmost to control the roughness of the rank and file. There was not a single one of the German generals who failed to return from wealthy France with clean hands.

In a word, at the first return of good fortune the old national hatred flamed up once again, and thoughts of peace fled. With good reason Napoleon felt that his throne was secure, no danger threatened him from within. The Bourbon name was completely decayed, except in a few royalist regions of the south and the west. The nation was modern through and through, and had no memory of anything which went back to days before the storming of the Bastille. If a word was ever uttered about the old royal house, the peasant thought with anger of the pressure of the tithes and of the corvée. Bernadotte was generally regarded as a miserable traitor, and who else was there to take over the Imperator's heritage ? If Napoleon had persistently pursued the beaten Silesian army, it was unquestionable that the great army would have withdrawn to the Rhine, and then a glorious peace could certainly have been secured for the empire. But just as Schwarzenberg had from timidity refrained from plucking the fruits of the victory of La Rothière, so now, in his arrogance, Napoleon failed to take advantage of success. "The Silesian army no longer exists," he cheerfully exclaimed ; he thought himself to be once more nearer Munich than Paris, and expected that before long he would regain the Vistula. He still had no grasp whatever of the moral forces of resistance which animated Blucher's headquarters. Instead of pressing upon this dangerous enemy until he had effected his annihilation, he suddenly moved his army southward to the Seine, defeated a few isolated corps of the great army, compelled the crown prince of Würtemberg to withdraw from the steep slopes of the Seine valley at Montereau, and actually forced the terrified Scharwzenberg with his enormous army to withdraw upwards along the Seine, and to send urgent demands to Blucher for assistance.

Never had Blucher and his brilliant friend shown themselves greater than in these days of distress. They candidly admitted past errors, and determined to make everything good once more ; they desired to forget that Schwarzenberg had by his march over the Seine been responsible for Napoleon's attack upon the Silesians, and that even later, when for two days the sound of the artillery at Champaubert and Montmirail had reached the great army, Schwarzenberg had refused to send any assistance. They thought only of victory. Four days after the battle of Etoges the army was once more in good order and again eager to enter the breach. In forced marches the Silesians now moved southward, and as early as February 21st, at Méry on the Seine, Blucher re-established a junction with the great army. The soldiers confidently expected a day like that of Leipzig, a great battle in which they would bring the war to an end with a single blow. They outnumbered the enemy almost threefold—150,000 men against 60,000.

Meanwhile in Châtillon the diplomats had opened peace negotiations. Only the great powers were represented, for after the decline of the world-empire, the aristocratic constitution which King Frederick had given to the society of states immediately returned. The power of the European pentarchy became more manifest day by day ; the states of the second and third rank had less significance than ever before, and it was Hardenberg's pride that he had reintroduced his own state among the leading powers. The allies demanded the frontiers of 1792, subject to a few rectifications, and at the same time put forward the condition that the powers of the coalition alone, without France having anything to say in the matter, should decide as to the distribution of the domains to be ceded by Napoleon and his allies. Prussia and Russia were absolutely firm upon this point ; harsh and mortifying as it was for France, the condition merely imposed upon the conquered a humiliation demanded by the profoundly moved public opinion of Germany and England. Hardenberg even wished to exclude France altogether from the general congress which was to be summoned, after the conclusion of the peace, for the final settlement of the new European relationships. He was under no illusions as to the deadly hatred felt by the French for the boldest of their enemies, and he foresaw that France, in conjunction with her former ally, would exercise upon the congress an extremely dangerous and intriguing influence. Metternich, however, was opposed to so profound a humiliation of his opponent, and only after vigorous resistance did he agree to the minimum condition that the distribution of the conquests was to be exclusively in the hands of the allies. At first, and as long as the alarm produced by La Rothière persisted, Caulaincourt showed himself conciliatory. On February 12th, in the headquarters at Troyes, Hardenberg, Metternich, and Castlereagh were prepared to concede the Imperator an immediate truce upon the basis of these peace proposals ; it was only Russia that demanded the march upon Paris.

At the very beginning of the congress of Châtillon, England took advantage of the monetary need of her allies to carry into effect a master-stroke of her commercial policy. If any of Napoleon's plans had ever been justified, certainly this was the case in respect of his struggle for the freedom of the seas. That balance of power for which the weary world longed, was not secure so long as one single state could act upon all the seas in accordance with her own arbitrary caprice, and so long as naval warfare, to the scandal of humanity, still bore the character of privileged rapine. Prussia and Russia, since the days of the league of armed neutrality, had always represented the principles of a humane sea power which could not be oppressive to neutral trade ; it was now their hope to see this idea of Frederick and Catherine recognised by a joint agreement of the whole of Europe. England, however, felt that this would threaten the very basis of her power. Lord Cathcart bluntly declared that if the English had ever recognised the principles of armed neutrality, French trade would not have been destroyed, and Napoleon would still have been ruling over the whole world ; never would Great Britain recognise any other law upon the seas than "the general rules of international law." As matters stood, other questions were far more pressing for the three continental powers ; moreover, they were all in need of new pecuniary resources for the war, and the rich ally was prepared to pay over the sum of five million sterling as additional subsidies. Consequently in the very first sitting, on February 5th, England maintained that the question of naval rights was not to be discussed. Caulaincourt did not offer any opposition, for he also had more pressing cares. The consequence was that the foulest spot of modern international law was not touched upon during the peace negotiations of Châtillon, Paris, and Vienna. The public opinion of Europe, blinded by its enthusiasm for glorious Albion, found nothing to complain of in this.

Once matters were in train, Lord Castlereagh simultaneously attempted to realise another cherished idea of British policy, and to secure a sufficient rounding off of territory for the Netherlands. No one offered any objection, although it had just been decided that all proposals for compensation should be postponed until after the conclusion of the peace, for no one wished to be on bad terms with the great money power, and all were agreed as to the European necessity of the joint state of the Netherlands. On February 15th, at the headquarters at Troyes, a proposal was carried to the effect that the old Dutch Republic was to be placed under the hereditary dominion of the House of Orange, and that it was to be enlarged by Belgium, as well as by a portion of the German bank of the Rhine, together with Cologne and Aix-la-Chapelle. Even Hardenberg agreed to this in essentials, making only a proviso in favour of the German north-west frontier; he did not wish to allow the Dutch to push so far into purely German territory.[1]

Meanwhile the first reports of Blucher's mishaps had reached the great headquarters-staff. Jesting observations were not lacking. The presumptuousness of the little men of the Silesian army had then been punished; why had they wanted to be wiser than the wisdom of Duca and Langenau? Yet stronger than malicious joy was the sentiment of alarm. In great anxiety Metternich demanded the speedy conclusion of this unlucky war, and matters went so far that Austria actually threatened to withdraw from the coalition.[2] Napoleon's obstinacy underwent a proportionate increase. Immediately after his first success he withdrew Caulaincourt's powers, and forbade the envoy to accede to any demand made by the allies. " It is not my custom," he

[1] Hardenberg's diary, February 15, 1814; Castleragh's Memorial on the Netherlands, January 25, 1815.
[2] Hardenberg's diary, February 14, 1814.

said, "to treat with my prisoners." The coalition seemed on the point of dissolution. The czar's arrogant and patronising manner offended Austrian pride. Hardenberg, too, became uneasy when he learned how the Russians had been establishing themselves in Danzig, and how they would hardly allow their Prussian companions-in-arms to enter the town. Nothing but a great success in the field could reconcile the jangled tempers. Even now, however, after his rejunction with Blucher, Schwarzenberg was unwilling to make use of his manifest superiority in force ; he once more abandoned the idea of a decisive battle, and gave orders, unquestionably under urgent instructions from the Austrian diplomats, to withdraw to the unhappy plateau of Langres. More violent than ever was the discord between the two factions. The king, after his honourable fashion, uttered the severest truths to the very face of the commander-in-chief, and the czar quarrelled vigorously with Lords Aberdeen and Castlereagh.

Then came salvation through the Silesian heroes. Colonel Grolman represented to his field-marshal that as long as they were linked to the Austrian council of war, they would never attain their goal. How would it be if the Silesian army were to detach itself from the main army, once more to march northward to the Marne, join there with the corps of Bülow and Wintzingerode, which were advancing from Belgium, and, thus reinforced, march directly upon Paris ? It was as if Scharnhorst himself had spoken through the mouth of his fiery pupil, so simple, great, and bold did the plan seem. Blucher gladly accepted the happy idea, wrote at once to the king and to the czar asking for their approval of the undertaking. On February 25th a great council of war was held at Bar, and after violent disputes, Blucher's proposal was accepted. That remarkable position of affairs, which in the previous summer had existed in actual fact, now received official recognition. The little Silesian army undertook to carry out the main attack, whilst the great army looked on. Frederick William wrote to his field-marshal : " The issue of the campaign lies henceforward in your hands."

Whilst Blucher, glad at heart, had begun his second march upon Paris without waiting for permission from the monarchs, in the great headquarters-staff the old game went on from day to day. "The embitterment and the mistrust of Austria are at a climax," complained the chancellor.[1] Unceasingly the

[1] Hardenberg's diary, February 27, 1814.

Imperator endeavoured to influence the Austrians by secret messages, and suspicious was the zeal with which Emperor Francis took part in these separate negotiations, which conflicted with the treaties entered into by the allies. "Do you still wish," asked Berthier of the allied commander-in-chief, "to pour out your best blood in order to satisfy the ill-conceived revenge of the Russians and the self-seeking policy of England?" Dread of the power of the czar pressed more and more heavily upon the Viennese cabinet. Gentz, in his letters to Karadja, declared that the principal task of the immediate future was to secure the balance of power in eastern Europe, and that a peace which should leave to France the left bank of the Rhine would in any case be less disastrous than the overthrow of Napoleon. But what else could happen than the dethronement of the emperor's son-in-law, if the campaign of the Silesians were to prove successful? The experiences at Châtillon made it perfectly clear that it was impossible to conclude an honourable peace with this man. "Down with Napoleon"—this cry expressed the universal spirit of the Prussian army. Moreover, his fortunate heirs were already appearing upon the stage. The count of Artois came to France, in the rear of the allied armies, and found his warmest advocate in Stein. The German statesman was well aware what a bold venture it was to restore a ruling house which belonged to a time long passed away. The czar detested the stiff arrogance of the Bourbons, the king had no love for them, among the allied monarchs it was only the Guelph prince regent who displayed himself as an unconditional supporter of the divine right of kings, and manifested a lively zeal for the old dynasty. Nevertheless the Bourbons won ground daily, for no one could suggest any other successor to Napoleon.

All the more anxiously did Austria avoid a decisive issue. While it had unfortunately been impossible to prevent Blucher's advance, steps must be taken to secure that Schwarzenberg at least should do nothing decisive. His troops were already utterly depressed by the eternal retreats and the aimless marchings to and fro. In the second half of December, the vanguard of the great army had entered France, and now, more than two months later, these enormous masses of soldiers had not yet fought a single battle. The neighbouring capital seemed to vanish before the eyes of the discouraged men like a mirage. "Now you can see what fear is," said Napoleon, with great satisfaction, to his guard. On February 27th, when Oudinot's corps, a ridiculously small number of men, appeared at Bar upon the heights above the Aube, Schwarzenberg once more avoided battle and evacuated Bar, allowing the enemy to diffuse themselves commodiously throughout the town and in the valley of the Aube. Frederick William at length lost patience, overcame his timidity, and once more, as at Kulm, showed sound military judgment. He compelled the commander-in-chief to order the attack. The soldiers received the greatly desired news with loud shouts of joy. Although the Austrian began the attack much too late and with only a portion of his army, a fine victory was won. This was a joyful day for the royal house, for Frederick William's second son, Prince William, rode in battle beside his father for the first time. The officers smiled with satisfaction to see how the fine stripling of seventeen performed his aide-de-camp's duty quite unconcernedly under heavy fire, and subsequently stormed the height of Malepin with the celebrated Russian regiment of Kaluga. In him, they considered, were the making of a second Prince Henry. Invidious comparisons were already being made between the fresh, heroic disposition of this youth and the æsthetic and altogether unsoldierly nature of the talented crown prince.

After the custom of the great headquarters-staff, the victory was not followed up, but none the less the courage of the coalition was to some extent restored. Just as the treaty of Teplitz had followed upon the battle of Kulm, so now the treaty of Chaumont followed upon the battle of Bar. On March 1st the great alliance was formally renewed for twenty years. Spain, Italy, Switzerland, and the enlarged Netherlands, were to receive complete independence upon the conclusion of peace ; the German sovereign princes " were to be united in a federative league which was to secure and guarantee the independence of Germany." Meanwhile Blucher had reached the valley of the Marne ; but since Napoleon, who speedily recognised that the capital was in danger, followed, the Silesians withdrew by forced marches to the north, and at Soissons formed a junction with Bülow's army. The conqueror of Holland was horrified when he saw beside his full complement of men, who had been well fed while wintering comfortably in Flanders, the weak battalions of York, these dirty, savage, and neglected soldiers. Involuntarily the generals thought of the days before the battle of Zorndorf, when King Frederick had joined his " snappy mudlarks " with Dohna's fresh troops. What a prospect for the future ! The Prussian army had done the greatest and suffered the worst, the finest blossom of the northern youth lay upon the battle-fields. Even Gneisenau, when he mustered the thinned ranks, sometimes lost his regal cheerfulness, and asked sadly how this state, with its exhausted purse and its weakened army, could persist in the severe struggle over the division of the spoil. Yet the hour was approaching. At Craonne, Napoleon, though he suffered heavy losses, had forced the Russians to withdraw; and on the foggy morning of March 9th, he advanced across the marshy flats of the Lette, to attack the rocky fortress of Laon, the main point of support for Blucher's army. On this day the battle was indecisive. Not until late in the evening did York and Kleist throw themselves upon Marmont's corps, the enemy's right wing, and here at Athis there occurred that extraordinary nocturnal battle which restored to the Prussians the joy of victory after so many disasters. First of all, Prince William led his East Prussian battalion to the storm, to the sound of intoxicating field music, carrying all before them through the village and out on the other side; then the Lithuanians, Sohr's Brandenburger hussars, and the black riders with the death's head, broke upon the terrified enemy. The whole corps was dispersed, leaving forty-five guns in the hands of the victors. In the wild fighting of these days, York had found a friend; his heart warmed within him when he saw the man of Nollendorf working beside him, always clear-headed, always sure of what he was about. But a little while and the *Heurichs* related to one another with astonishment that the hard old man had drunk brotherhood with Kleist after the ancient Teutonic warrior custom. Next morning the Imperator's fate was decided. After the complete breaking up of the right wing, there was no longer any possibility of withstanding the army of the allies, which outnumbered his own threefold; and, just as at Leipzig, there was only one road of retreat, through the marshy lands of the Lette! It seemed to all appearance that this old rocky nest, which nine hundred years earlier had been the sole possession and the last refuge of the young Frankish kingdom, must now witness the destruction of the new emperordom.

Now it became manifest what Blucher's flaming glance, his commanding will, were worth to the German army. The field-marshal was ill, exhausted in body and mind by the terrible experiences of these weeks, and since he was no longer in command, hatred and strife filled the headquarters-staff. That excess of rugged and strong personalities which constituted the strength of the Prussian army, now became dangerous. Neither York, nor Kleist, nor Bülow would subordinate themselves to Gneisenau's fancies. The old ill-feeling broke out once more, and went so far that York threatened to leave the army. But by this dissension Gneisenau was merely strengthened in the prudent considerations which had dominated him during recent days; after so many sacrifices he would not take over the responsibility for a new and sanguinary struggle. It was his patriotic anxiety for Prussia's future which was responsible for this one great failure of his life as a commander. Now that Napoleon's star was unquestionably setting, was it permissible to weaken the troops yet further? Nothing would please the House of Austria better than that when peace was concluded Prussia should no longer possess an army; and Radetzky had in Frankfort expressed a neighbourly desire to that effect. Boyen, in especial, expressly raised this political consideration, and convinced his ardent friend. Once more the Imperator was saved by the wonderful favour of fortune. He was able to withdraw without pursuit, and immediately, adroitly availing himself of the advantage of the inner line of operations, turned once more against the great army. Schwarzenberg, after the victory of Bar, instead of immediately advancing upon Paris, or threatening the Imperator in the rear, had once more withdrawn southward. The columns of his army were now dispersed as far as Sens, in the pleasant valley of the Yonne, far away from the open road to victory. The Prussians growled as they asked whether it was really against the nature of an Austrian general to seek the attainment of his aim by the shortest road. Subsequently the hesitator drove back a weak French corps from the Seine, and once more ventured to advance a short distance northward as far as the Aube. The miseries of this wretched campaign would never, it seemed, come to an end.

Then the policy of the court of Vienna underwent a sudden change. Whereas six weeks before, the disasters to the Silesian army had interfered with the course of the congress of Châtillon, now, conversely, the breaking off of the diplomatic negotiations had a strengthening and stimulating influence upon the conduct of the war. Vainly had the plenipotentiaries of the allies been waiting since February 17th for an answer to their ultimatum; vainly, as late as March 10th, did Emperor Francis in a letter of exhortation endeavour to overcome his son-in-law's obstinacy. Not until March 15th did Caulaincourt give a definite reply, and this conveyed a refusal in essential points, being even less acceptable

for Austria than for the other powers ; for whilst Napoleon at
length agreed to the cession of the Rhineland and to the dissolution of the Confederation of the Rhine, and wished merely to
retain for Berg and Saxony their previous sovereigns, he insisted
that the Italian throne should remain in the hands of his stepson
Eugene. Thus the purblind man deliberately opposed the only
one of the allied powers which definitely wished him well, and
Gneisenau said with good reason : " Napoleon has done us better
service than the whole army of diplomats." Metternich was
forced to recognise that the unhappy man was no longer to be
helped, and that the destruction of the empire was inevitable.
On March 19th, the allies declared the congress at an end, and the
change in Austrian policy was immediately manifested in the more
vigorous mood at headquarters. With unaccustomed resolution,
Schwarzenberg showed himself prepared on March 20th to venture
battle against the Imperator at Arcis-sur-Aube. It is true that,
as always, the execution of this happy thought was slack ; only
Wrede's troops took part in the battle. But in any case, on the
next day Napoleon was forced to abandon the field after severe
losses, and, best of all, the great army began once more to bestir
itself.

The defeated man now undertook a mad venture, based
upon his views of the character of his opponent ; in a wide detour
he surrounded the victorious right wing, and pressed eastward
towards St. Dizier, in order to gain the rear of the allies. It
was Napoleon's hope that Schwarzenberg, anxious about his line
of retreat, would immediately order a withdrawal to the Rhine.
This bold step, if undertaken a few weeks earlier, would certainly
have been successful. Now, however, all the powers, Austria
included, felt that the unworthy drama must be brought to a close.
As Gneisenau subsequently wrote to Rüchel : " Thus at length
we went to Paris, not because of a conviction of the force of the
reasons for this step, but simply because there was nothing else
to do, and because destiny drove the great army in that direction."
On March 24th, Blucher's Cossacks intercepted a letter of Napoleon's, and from this the czar, at Sommepuis, learned the enemy's
intentions ; thereupon Toll was the first to demand the self-
evident step which to Alexander had so long seemed impossible—
a march upon Paris. The road was almost open. The weak
opposing forces could easily be overpowered ; a strong body of
cavalry was to remain behind under Wintzingerode in order to
deceive the Imperator (whose name was now gradually losing its

old magic) concerning the movements of the great army. Alexander agreed ; he longed to revenge the entry into Moscow. On the same day Frederick William and Schwarzenberg, in a council of war at Vitry, expressed their consent.

It was with a deep breath of relief that Blucher received the decisive orders, and he exclaimed, " Now there is to be a general forward movement, it is no longer left to us alone ! " In Vitry the allies issued a manifesto, wherein they demanded of the French nation to put an end by its own free will to the destructive system of the empire ; thus alone could the peace of Europe be ensured. The last bridge had been broken, even Emperor Francis had abandoned his son-in-law ; he remained behind in Burgundy in order to avoid personal participation in the dethronement. Thus at length the army advanced westward, across the sinister battle-fields of February, and once more there passed across these blood-drenched plains all the horrors of war, when Pacthod's division, on March 25th, was driven back at La Fère Champenoise by a simultaneous attack from the Silesian army and from the main army. Though hopelessly lost, the valiant French general rejected the capitulation which Frederick William offered, so that nothing remained but a horrible slaughter. It was with shuddering that the king and his son William saw the cannon balls ploughing long furrows through the heaped masses of men, and subsequently the cavalry cutting them down with sabres. Finally, four thousand surrendered, and five thousand lay dead on the field. It was a veritable drama of annihilation, such as is often described in boastful reports, but such as is very rarely experienced ; veteran officers grew pale when this day was spoken of.

It was certainly time that the depressed troops should at length acquire the confidence that comes from success. To-day there was no Clausewitz who, after the lost battles of the campaign in the previous spring, had proved to the army the unavoidable necessity of what had happened. Reflective officers all knew that an incomparably slack conduct of the war had caused a needless outpouring of German and Russian blood ; the army was becoming sickened with the coloured official reports issued by the great headquarters-staff. Now at length the curse was broken, and all ill-feeling ceased in view of the happy certainty of the approaching final decision. For some days, indeed, Napoleon remained under the illusion that the great army was following him eastward ; when at length he recognised his error, and hastened back in forced marches, it was impossible for him to reach the threatened capital in time, and his fate could no longer be averted.

In front of the allies there now stood only the depleted corps of Marmont and Mortier. The slowness of Schwarzenberg's march gave these time to reach Paris. Although Marie Louise, with the king of Rome, had fled to the Loire, the two marshals determined to venture a last battle before the walls of the capital. Strengthened by the national guard, they occupied with 34,000 men the villages of the suburbs and the steep heights which encircle the town in a wide arch to the north and the east on the right bank of the Seine. Marmont held the right, as far as the Bois de Vincennes, close to the confluence of the Seine and the Marne; Mortier was on the other side of the Ourcq Canal, and his extreme left wing extended as far as the bluffs of Montmartre. The struggle against the 100,000 men of the allied army was useless from the first, notwithstanding the strong positions occupied by the French; none the less it was extremely sanguinary, owing to the unhappy dispositions of the great headquarters-staff, which did not bring its forces into action at the right place and at the right time. Already since the morning of March 30th, Prince Eugene and his Russians had been attacking the French centre; he took the village of Pantin and endeavoured to gain the plateau of Romainville, but was repulsed and hard pressed until at length the Russians and the Prussian guard, which had unfortunately been held back too long, came to his assistance. Under the command of Colonel Alvensleben, the guard stormed the batteries at Pantin whilst the Russians occupied the hill of Père-Lachaise at the point of the sword. Much later the struggle was opened upon the French right wing. The crown prince of Würtemberg established himself in the Bois de Vincennes, and maintained his position there until in the afternoon he pressed forward as far as the river. It was only just before noon, too, that the Silesian army joined battle with the enemy's left wing. Who would have been able to forbid the sick Blucher from taking part in the German advance on such a day? Protecting his inflamed eyes with a woman's hat and veil, he pressed into the *mêlée*, watching his well-tried Silesians fighting once again, as at Möckern, under the cross-fire of the hostile batteries. By the afternoon the allies were advancing victoriously along the whole line; the elder prince William had already reached the barriers of the town, whilst Kleist's troops, with fixed bayonets, stormed the hill with the five windmills at Montmartre, and on the left of the French Langeron's Russians pressed up the steep slopes of the Montmartre quarries to reach the batteries arranged in echelon on the summit. Thereupon aides-de-camp sprang forward waving white cloths. The battle was at an end. Paris had capitulated.

Long did the generals stand beside the mills upon the hill silently watching the conquered town, whilst the square towers of Notre Dame and the dome of the Pantheon shone in the evening light. Colonel Bülow climbed up there too, with his Lithuanians; he had to keep the promise that he had made in Tilsit and show his young fellows the enemy's capital. Nine centuries and a half had passed since our emperor Otho II had planted his eagles upon this hill, and had terrified the town beneath by the hallelujah cries of his warriors; since then Englishmen and Spaniards and a few cavalry troops of German mercenaries had pressed to the heart of the French power, but never since then had there been a whole German army in Paris. How terribly had Germany suffered from the power and the arrogance of this worst of neighbours, so that even the great elector had held the view that nothing but a campaign to Paris could secure the freedom of the European states, could restore a permanent balance of power. Now the new Rome was conquered, and it seemed that an unending future full of peaceful national happiness was unrolling itself before the delighted gaze of the war-weary world. The Germans believed that the wrongs of two centuries had been atoned when, on the following day, the czar, the king, and Schwarzenberg entered at the head of the allied armies, through the Porte St. Martin which still commemorated the German conquests of Louis XIV; then the train marched forward amid the joyful shouts of the assembled masses, along the great boulevard to the Place Louis XV, where the guillotine had once carried out its bloody work, and thence to the Champs Elysées. Who could ever have dreamed that within two generations the Prussian flags were again to follow the same route? No one was happier on this day than those two great Germans who had now gloriously fulfilled the compact over which they had shaken hands in the market-place of Leipzig. Gneisenau wrote: "What patriots have dreamed, and egoists have scorned, has come to pass"; but Stein said, in his blunt way, "The fellow is overthrown."

§ 3. PEACE AND THE RETURN HOME.

In the old home of Gallic inconstancy, in the town of Paris, the embitterment with the empire had become apparent earlier and more vividly than in the provinces. The desire for criticism and contradiction, which had so long been put to sleep, once more became active ; in the legislative body, the speeches of the opposition were loudly acclaimed ; the constitutional ideas of the early days of the revolution were revived ; the talented nation began to feel the dull quietude which enveloped its official life to be an unnatural oppression. With wonderful knowledge of the national character, the Imperator had firmly established the governmental forms of the new France ; had established the centralised official state upon a durable foundation. Yet the apex of this imposing structure remained insecure. As soon as luck deserted the ruler he had to learn that after all he was only the chosen of the people, and was personally responsible to the million ; a regime which in principle appealed only to common avarice could not reckon upon loyalty. Already in February, when the prisoners from the battle-fields of Champagne were led through the streets of Paris, they were no longer greeted, as formerly, with triumphant shouts, but were received with sorrow and compassion. Since the defeats of March the transformation of sentiment in the capital had been completed ; it was a change of mood as thorough, as comprehensive, as over-whelming, as that which had occurred long ago when Henry IV had made his peace with the Old Church and when Catholic Paris suddenly threw itself into the arms of the detested heretic.

The nation recognised with a sound instinct that now only the old dynasty was possible ; it was not royalists but men of the revolution and of the empire who raised their voices most loudly on behalf of the forgotten and despised Bourbons. When the allies entered Paris they noted with astonishment that the masses were endeavouring to remove the image of the glorious Imperator from the Vendôme Column, and that the men of the national guard had tied the much-coveted star of the Legion of Honour to the tails of their horses. On many hats were already to be seen white cock-ades. Everywhere were heard maledictions against the tyrant, and loud acclamations for the liberators. The vanity of the French led them to insist on believing that the white bands which the troops of old Europe wore as a sign of mutual recognition, were assumed in honour of the king of France ; the allies seemed to them to be royalist crusaders, passing judgment upon the tyrant in the name, and on behalf, of the French nation. In the theatre the king of Prussia was greeted by the song :

> "Vive Guillaume et ses guerriers vaillants,
> De ce royaume il sauve les enfants ! "

The straightforward Frederick William was, as Madame de Staël put it, quite astonished to find that these people were so pleased at being conquered. In his own army, the old national hatred was only increased at the sight of such disloyalty. The North Germans spoke with profound contempt of this most heartless of all the nations. They had no eye whatever for the indestructible and elastic vital force which is to be found in the mobile French character. It was a misfortune for both nations that there did not become established a peaceful relationship of mutual respect. This whole generation of Prussian statesmen and generals remained firmly convinced that a last reckoning with France was still to be made ; Gneisenau and Stein bore this conviction with them to the grave.

Meanwhile the conquerors could enjoy the luxurious life of the capital. The conquest brought no discomfort to the Parisians, for the allies, out of delicate deference to the feelings of the conquered, had their troops encamped for a long time in the open squares ; the conquest brought to Paris only the opportunity for easy gains. Many rich English families hastened to the Seine, to the long foregone enjoyments of the city of pleasure ; money flowed in streams. The cafés in the galleries of the Palais Royal and the gaming houses on the boulevards had occasion to rejoice at the good client they had found in the Prussian field-marshal who, now that the work of the war had been brought to a successful conclusion, returned to his old habits. Every evening he sat for hours over his beloved cards, coolly staking his money, as self-possessed and as fortunate at the gaming-table as in war. To the French, accustomed to the roughness of the conscripts, the character of the Prussian national army remained altogether incomprehensible. They shook their heads when the Prussian volunteers visited the art treasures of the Louvre almost as eagerly as did the crown prince. None of the Murillos and none of the Raphaels were so irresistibly attractive to the Teutonic youth as was Memling's " Last Judgment " with the terrible and earnest figure of the judging archangel—the " Danzig picture " which Napoleon had stolen from the Marienkirche ; here the young Germans were always thronged, as if amid the French splendours they had for the first time become really conscious of the nature of their own homeland. The Parisians, after their manner, sought relief in couplets and caricatures from the secret sense of shame from which they could not free themselves.

All their amiable sentiments were directed towards the czar.

The fortunate conqueror was intoxicated by the calculated flattery, and Stein's influence declined from day to day. Alexander lived in Talleyrand's palace, and his cunning host displayed unlimited admiration for "the first man of the century, who had alone completed the liberation of Europe." The authorities, the academicians, and above all the ladies, rivalled one another in swinging censers in honour of the gentle and amiable "angel of peace." Alexander's vanity was profoundly touched when the matron of a lunatic asylum for women told him that the number of young women who had become mentally afflicted from unrequited love had greatly increased since the arrival of the Russian autocrat. The czar once more plumed himself as the protector of national freedom, and imagined that he would astonish the world by his generosity, above all since Russia had nothing directly to gain from France. The English cabinet, full of jealousy towards Russia, now endeavoured to gain the friendship of the French by a carefully planned considerateness. Austria, which had long desired peace at any price, was influenced by a similar tendency. Consequently Prussia soon stood alone in her demand for a relentless utilisation of the victory.

The changed situation of parties in the coalition camp was already manifest in the negotiations with Napoleon. At length on March 25th, Caulaincourt had written to Metternich, still in extremely indefinite general terms, to the effect that he had received authority to sign the peace. The letter came too late, the decisive blow had been struck. Immediately after their entry into Paris, the allies declared that they would no longer treat with Napoleon, and demanded of the senate the institution of a provisional government. The actions of this government were guided by the simple principle of its leader Talleyrand : " It is not necessary for people to allow themselves to be buried in the ruins of a falling building," and with unworthy insults it expressed itself in favour of the deposition of the Imperator. In the new France it was a matter of course that the thousands of officials and chevaliers of the Legion of Honour should all so speedily forget their oaths. Talleyrand considered that his day had come, and hoped to carry on the regency in the name of the infant Napoleon II ; but as soon as he saw that this plan received no support from the victors, he at once went over to the side of the Bourbons, and came to an understanding with his imperial guest concerning the restoration of the royal house.

Napoleon, when he reached Fontainebleau after the fall of

the capital, was soon deserted by his marshals; although he had no longer any purpose in life, he lacked courage to seek a voluntary death, and on April 11th he signed his abdication. Vainly did Hardenberg advise the monarchs that the dangerous man should be sent into some remote place of exile, and vainly did the Prussian cabinet recommend on several occasions during the following months the island of St. Helena as the most suitable place of banishment. Emperor Francis was opposed to the complete destruction of his son-in-law, although he inconsiderately separated his daughter from the fallen man; the British counted upon the vigilance of their Mediterranean fleet. The decisive point was, that Alexander wished to display his nobility. The consequence was that the incredibly foolish determination was reached to send this powerful man, inspired by restless ambition, to the island of Elba. There he was to be peacefully housed between the excitable nations of France and Italy, to both of which he was closely akin—the Titan, who at this very moment said to Augereau: " Asia has need of a man ! " He was left the dignities and rights of a sovereign prince, including therefore the right of making war, and he fancied his career at an end, especially since upon his journey through the royalist regions of southern France he with difficulty escaped the rage of the mob.

Alexander now hoped, in conformity with his new liberal principles, to recall the Bourbons by a resolution of the French nation, and at the same time to pledge them to a constitution. The pretender had other views, and so had his brother of Artois, who simultaneously came to Paris under the style of *Monsieur, Fils de France.* Who among the House of Bourbon had ever doubted that upon the death of the unfortunate boy who was named Louis XVII, the crown of the Capets had passed by God's grace, to the Roy Louis XVIII? Louis did not forget that the czar had once expelled him from Mitau, and diligently displayed his preference for England, the rival of Russia; he felt at home with the reactionary prince regent and the high tories, who were all so firmly convinced of the divine right of the French royal house, and felt assured that to this great realm, under God, he owed the re-establishment of his house. He left England on board a British man-of-war, entering France immediately as the rightful king, announcing on the journey, notwithstanding the personal dissuasions of the czar, that it was his intention, in virtue of his kingly power, to bestow a charter upon his faithful subjects. He reached Paris on May 3rd. When he made his entry into the capital, this fat and gouty old man, with the still older dukes of Condé and Bourbon with him in the carriage, one of the two heavily wrapped up, the Prussian officers looking on in wonder asked themselves if all these dotards were to be the heirs of a Napoleon. What a wonderful contrast, too, was the review before the Tuileries, to the majestic festivals of victory of the soldier-emperor ; there upon the balcony was the old gentleman in his arm-chair, and down below were the troops, obediently shouting out their *Vive le roi*, and finally the gracious nodding of the king's head, and the sigh of relief as he said *Je suis content !* The Bourbon felt completely secure of his throne, encountered the allies with naive arrogance, and as the most distinguished prince of christendom he demanded in his own castle precedence over the three monarchs to whom he owed everything.

The victors on the other hand did not fail to recognise the serious dangers which threatened this regime resurrected from the tomb. With increasing anxiety they recognised that neither the servile behaviour of the Napoleonic marshals, who had immediately been converted to royalism, nor yet the playing at soldiers of the Duc de Berry, could repress the Napoleonic sentiments of the army ; they saw how resentful were the deposed officials, and how between the returned *emigrés* and the mass of the people an impassable gulf was fixed. From the very first days of the new regime, the allies had little confidence in its persistence. But instead of drawing from these sinister indications the conclusion that the neighbour of France must be strengthened, and must be placed in a position to confront the incalculable variations of this land, the statesmen of Russia, England, and Austria thought rather of alleviating, by mild conditions of peace, the thorny task which lay before the ancient royal house.

Meanwhile in Germany those tones which Arndt had sounded in his pamphlet on the Rhine, had found numerous echoes. The busy imperial patriot Gagern demanded in an extraordinary booklet, *Zur Berichtigung einiger politischen Ideen*, that the *avulsa imperii*, Alsace and Lorraine, should be returned to the realm ; this was the way in which the imperial crown might be restored to Austria. " In this way, too, the crown of Prussia might without injustice gain the space that appears essential to the stability of this realm, and would acquire a respect without which our future would be a gloomy one." Herman Teuthold wrote an *Appeal to the nation*, in which he expressed the desire to see the whole of the left bank of the Rhine united, to form a kingdom of Burgundy. The *Rheinische Merkur* and the *Teutsche Blätter* expressed similar opinions. Arndt, Görres, and their friends, all cherished Hardenberg's view, that Austria must guard the frontier in Alsace, and Prussia in the lands of the Moselle. A favourite song ran as follows :

> "Above by Austria's power guarded,
> Below by Prussia's heroes warded,
> On the Rhine, on the Rhine,
> Secure be our frontier-line."

During this year, however, there was not manifested any general and passionate desire to extend the German frontier to the Vosges. Yet there were many who felt with a learned poet of the year 1814 : *jam vicisse sat est, victor non ultor habebor.* The wonderfully victorious campaign from the Niemen to the Seine, had exceeded the boldest hopes. Many declared that they would be satisfied if only the old frontier of the north-west should be re-established and, the tyrant should be chastised. The Corsican's death was almost universally demanded, and the newspapers wrote at considerable length of Harmodius and Aristogiton.

After all that had happened it was almost impossible to render the conditions of the peace more stringent. The czar had recently declared, during his entry into Paris, that the allies desired to restore the ancient kingdom and the ancient boundaries of France. It was hardly possible to disregard this oft-repeated assurance, and to impose upon the friendly Bourbons harder conditions than had been imposed upon the hostile Napoleon. Consequently the Prussian diplomats did not venture to put forward a formal claim to Alsace and Lorraine, although the chancellor wished to press such a claim, and although the Prussian generals made urgent representations to the effect that the safety of South Germany would be imperilled if a great wedge of French territory were to thrust itself far into our highlands from Landau to Hüningen. Hardenberg, and even Stein, were content to demand the return of Strasburg and Landau ; for this claim did not conflict with the earlier promises of the coalition. At the outbreak of the War of the Revolution, a whole quarter of Alsace, comprising two hundred and forty five communes with 252,000 inhabitants, had indeed still been in possession of the German estates of the realm, although for the most part under French suzerainty. Should the Germans abandon this ancient claim, should they renounce the reacquirement of the beautiful territories of Saarwerden, Lützelstein, Rappoltstein, Mömpelgard, Dagsburg, and Hanau-Lichtenberg, they were certainly justified in asking for the two fortresses which constituted the key to the Upper Rhine. The three allied powers, however, were unanimous in resisting this modest demand of Prussia. Talleyrand gave unctuous assurances to the effect that the only means of preventing future wars would be to avoid dishonouring a great and strong nation, and these views obtained a hearing only too readily from the czar, Metternich, and Castlereagh.

A provisional treaty was signed with Monsieur as early as April 23rd, in virtue of which, the civil administration of all those territories which had been French on January 1, 1792, was to be immediately resumed by the French authorities ; it was also agreed that the allied armies should be withdrawn from these areas as soon as France had evacuated the fortresses which she still occupied in Italy and Germany. Stein drew the chancellor's attention to the point that this treaty by no means involved the sacrifice of the whole of Alsace-Lorraine and Burgundy to the French administration, for old German domains were interspersed throughout these regions ; as leader of the central administration he immediately issued orders that in the department of the Moselle, none of the districts which had first been conquered in 1793 should be handed over to the French. [1] But this honourable interpretation of the treaty found no acceptance among the allies of Prussia. During the multifarious changes of this eventful time, it had already been forgotten that this quarter of Alsace, which had remained German, had formerly given the first impulse to the revolutionary wars. It was generally believed in the diplomatic world, as the French persisted in declaring, that the whole of the Upper Rhenish land had been French for the past two hundred years. In any case, no one was concerned about these difficult historical investigations, and it was decided that the whole of Alsace and the whole of the department of the Moselle should immediately be restored to the French authorities. In this way the basis of the peace was already established before the peace congress was opened. The coalition, despite the Prussian objection, had already recognised the principle that the boundaries of January 1, 1792, were to form the general rule, but that in individual points alterations must be made in favour of the conquered. The pledge given at Frankfort, that France was to be greater than under her kings, was to be fulfilled.

The negotiations concerning the treaty of peace could not be begun until May 9th, when there once more existed in France a

[1] Stein to Hardenberg, March 11, 1814.

recognised national authority.[1] The plenipotentiaries met in Talleyrand's house. Metternich and Stadion, Hardenberg and Humboldt, Nesselrode and Rassumoffsky, and finally Castlereagh, Stewart, Aberdeen, and Cathcart, represented the coalition. Talleyrand, who had just been appointed Minister for Foreign Affairs, and Laforest, who up till 1806 had been in charge of Napoleon's interests in Berlin, negotiated in the name of the Most Christian King. With customary audacity, the French minister expressed his discontent that the same claims should be made of the unstained *fleur de lys* that had been made of the revolutionary tricolor. He pathetically reiterated the phrase which had so often of late been employed by Napoleon that all the other great powers had obtained immoderate enlargements of territory. Was France to return to the boundaries of 1792, thus seriously disturbing the European balance of power? The adroit Frenchman was in truth well aware that all important matters had already been decided; he knew that disarmed France could not, in the circumstances, wish anything better than the considerate offers of the coalition, and he therefore soon limited himself to the attempt to secure as liberal a rounding off as possible of the frontiers of 1792. The sittings of the congress were few and short, thrust hastily in between a number of dances, banquets, and pleasure-makings of all kinds, and they served merely for the discussion of questions of secondary importance; consequently, even from the archives very little information can be gleaned. In view of the favour which Russia, England, and Austria vied with one another in displaying for the French, there could no longer be any question of rendering the original conditions more severe; the only point left open was how much land Talleyrand's cunning would be able to secure in addition to the old dominions. French arrogance still occasionally manifested itself. On March 11th, in the council of state, the marshals demanded the recommencement of the war, open resistance to the shameful demands of the coalition, and for several days the Prussian generals dreaded the outbreak of street fighting in Paris.[2] But the clouds dispersed, for the sober sense of King Louis would pay no attention to the mad proposal.

Thanks to Hardenberg's firmness, the agreement of Châtillon, in virtue of which the disposal of the ceded provinces was left entirely in the hands of the allies, was maintained. Talleyrand, however, succeeded in securing that this stipulation should be

---

[1] Metternich to Hardenberg, May 8, 1814.
[2] Gneisenau to Hardenberg, May 13 1814.

hidden away in the secret articles of the treaty of peace ; the French were to learn nothing of the arrangement, which would have been intolerable to their pride. In the discussion of the individual details of the frontier-settlement, the yielding disposition of Prussia's three allies prepared for the French minister one triumph after another. Not only did he secure that all the dominions that were actually surrounded by French territory, Avignon and Venaissin, Mömpelgard and the Alsatian Reichslande should remain in the hands of France, but he also succeeded in obtaining certain valuable outposts beyond the old frontiers : Savoy and a strip of land on the Belgian frontier, with Givet, an important fortress on the Meuse. He chaffered about every fragment of land with the utmost tenacity ; it was only through Humboldt's decisive refusal that Kaiserslautern was saved to Germany.[1] But the old domains of the Palatinate, lying between the Weissenburg lines and the enclave of Landau, were handed over to France ; and in order to round off the frontier at Saarlouis, Saarbrücken, with its invaluable coal basin and the ancient burial-place of the princes of Nassau at St. Arnual, were sacrificed to France. The loyal German and Protestant town was in despair. It had trusted so long the assurances of Gruner, the governor-general, that whoever spoke German was to remain German. Now Stein, profoundly moved, received the touching complaints of these valiant Lorrainers as to their terrible situation, which necessarily aroused profound sorrow in the heart of every German, and he put in a good word for the petition of the Saarbrückers that they might at least be allowed to send their sons to serve under the German state.[2] Switzerland was better cared for, of course once more at Germany's expense : it seemed impossible to do enough to strengthen the famous buffer state on the German frontier. The confederacy received the bishopric of Basle, and Metternich declared himself prepared to hand over to Switzerland in addition the old Austrian domain of Fricktal, with Rheinfelden and Laufenburg.

Day by day the Prussian statesmen had to fight with the inexhaustible free-handedness of their allies, until Humboldt at length declared to Metternich and Nesselrode that it was enough and that not an inch more of German land should be ceded.[3] Talleyrand, however, could afford to regard his work with satisfac-

---

[1] Humboldt to Hardenberg, May 17, 1814.

[2] Petition of Chief-Burgomaster Laukhard to Gruner, Saarbrücken, June 7, 1814 ; Stein to Hardenberg, June 15, 1814.

[3] Humboldt to Hardenberg, May 20, 1814.

tion : after wars lasting a quarter of a century, in which France had arrogantly threatened the whole world, the country was enlarged by one hundred square miles [German] and by more than one million inhabitants.

In the intoxication of his generosity it was the wish of the czar, in contradiction to all the customs of international law, to excuse the vanquished the payment of the cost of the war ; he regarded it as ignoble to deprive this well-to-do country of France, enriched by the plunder of all lands, of a modest portion of her ill-gotten gains. Since Austria and England also shared this remarkable view, Prussia, after vigorous protests, found it necessary to give way, and was forced to renounce all recompense for the enormous contributions of Tilsit. It seemed as if there were a deliberate intention to strengthen in the minds of the French the arrogant delusion that for them alone international law did not exist. In addition, Prussia had to demand the repayment of advances made to France. The ministry of finance reckoned them at a very low rate ; frs. 136,000,000 for the march of the *grande armée* on the way to Russia ; frs. 10,700,000 for the supplies enforced contrary to treaty during the years 1808 to 1812 ; and finally more than frs. 23,000,000 of arrears of payments to the kingdom of Saxony and the town of Danzig, which were both already regarded as Prussian territory—in all frs. 169,800,000. The payment of this sum was a vital question to Prussian finance ; the unequal struggle had exhausted the economic resources of Prussia to such an extent that Hardenberg was at this very moment forced to make an urgent request to Castlereagh for an immediate cash loan—of £100,000 sterling ! All these millions had been expended for the maintenance of the French army, and there was no question as to the justice of the demand for repayment. Hardenberg considered that this was shown all the more unanswerably since, in the previous spring, the refusal of the payments demanded according to treaty had been the incontrovertible legal ground for the Prussian declaration of war. It was for this reason that, during the war, Hardenberg had not asked the allies to give any pledge in support of his claims.

This was a sin of omission weighty with consequences, although it was a mistake which a statesman less trustful than Hardenberg might very well have made, for who could have believed that such a demand, whose justice was so absolutely incontestable, would not receive the support of the allies ? When Prussia first laid her claim before the congress, no one offered any objection. Then, in the sitting of May 17th, Humboldt demanded a definite declaration from the French. Laforest thereupon answered that the king had unconditionally forbidden him to discuss the question, and had done so immediately after a conversation with the czar.[1] Subsequently the Prussian plenipotentiary learned in confidence from Metternich and Anstedt, that the two imperial powers had agreed that no monetary demands at all were to be made of France on their part—they, certainly, had no debts to claim from the French—and to leave the Prussians to their own devices. Thus Prussia was completely left in the lurch by the allies, in an extraordinary position, as Humboldt said, and he added, with an implied reproach against the chancellor, that the just claims of Prussia might have been established with somewhat less shamefacedness and somewhat more adroitness, *before* the entry into Paris. King Louis was well aware of his people's hatred for the Prussians, and for this reason, since he had nothing more to fear from the three powers, he made the arrogant answer : " It would be better to spend three hundred millions in fighting Prussia than one hundred millions in satisfying her claims ! " Was the North German power, devoid of financial resources and with a greatly thinned army, to resume the war single-handed ? There was nothing more to do ; the consequences of Hardenberg's mistake must be endured. By articles 18 and 19 of the treaty of peace, the European powers mutually renounced all pecuniary claims upon one another (with the exception of certain claims made by private individuals), and this was a renunciation which meant nothing to Austria and Russia, but which in the case of Prussia was a colossal sacrifice.

Throughout the deliberations of the congress, the Prussians had to play the part of the importunate members, and everywhere they came off badly. Frederick William, like his faithful people, assumed it to be a matter of course that the art treasures, which had been seized in defiance of all international law, would now be returned to their rightful owners. He demanded the restoration of everything which had been taken from Prussia in the way of books, works of art, and trophies, and actually secured a verbal assurance that this should be done. But when Humboldt came to discuss seriously with the French minister when and how the transfer should be effected, Talleyrand displayed obvious embarrassment, saying that he certainly believed that his master would restore everything, that Frederick William had better talk to the French

[1] Humboldt's Report to the chancellor upon the sitting of May 17, 1814.

king about it once more ; that it was probable that the *premier gentilhomme du Roy* would attend to the matter.[1] After repeated insistence, the Victory of Berlin was at length brought out of its shed ; how delighted was Jacob Grimm when one morning he seated himself in the brazen chariot, to eat his breakfast there. Frederick the Great's sword was also recovered, and with the sagacity of the collector, Grimm succeeded in unearthing some other treasures from the library of Cassel ; that was all. Baron von Oelssen, who late in the summer was sent to Paris by the king to fetch the Prussian works of art, was put off month after month with excuses and empty words.[2] Since the other three powers hardly raised a finger on behalf of the claims of Prussia, King Louis considered it unnecessary to keep his word. The whole nation stood behind him like one man. There was not a Frenchman who did not regard the demand for the return of the spoil as a crying injustice. This throws a painfully clear light upon the way in which the plunder campaigns of the empire had destroyed this nation's sense of justice, and how necessary it was that a stern chastisement should recall to its consciousness the fundamental moral ideas of the peaceful comity of nations.

In this posture of affairs how could it be hoped that the allies would immediately proceed to arrange for the territorial compensations demanded by Prussia ? Austria had already made sure of her own share of the booty. On April 20th, after a slackly conducted and inglorious campaign, the Austrians entered Venice ; on the same day a sudden rising of the Milanese overthrew the kingdom of Italy. In this way, almost without trouble, Emperor Francis was fortunate enough to gain possession of northern and central Italy, and was therefore less than ever inclined to undertake any duties in favour of the suspected Prussia. Nevertheless Hardenberg, as his duty demanded, made an unpropitious attempt, and on April 29th, in a detailed memorial, laid before the allies the demands which he had already expressed in Basle.[3]

This memorial opens with the upright assurance that Prussia cherished friendly intentions towards all the other powers, Denmark alone excepted, for Swedish Pomerania, which had been ceded to the Danes, must be regained by Prussia at all costs. For Germany he demanded a federal charter whose principal aims must be to

---

[1] Humboldt to Hardenberg, May 27, 1814.
[2] Report from the ambassador Count von der Goltz. Paris, October 30, 1814.
[3] Hardenberg *Plan pour l'arrangement futur de l'Europe*, April 29, 1814.

institute a vigorous military system, to regulate the relationships between princes and subjects, and to control the judicial system and the commerce of Germany ; it was " to take the place of a constitution." Holland and Switzerland were to conclude a perpetual league with the Germanic Federation. Russia was to receive the greater part of Warsaw, with 2,300,000 inhabitants ; Prussia was to receive Posen as far as the Warthe, including Thorn, comprising 1,300,000 inhabitants ; Austria was to receive only the regions of New Galicia, Cracow, and Zamoscz, ceded in 1809, with 700,000 inhabitants. In addition to these Polish territories and Northern Italy, Austria was to retain Breisgau, which was essential to the defence of the Upper Rhine ; this outpost must be directly connected with the imperial state, and for this reason Bavaria, Baden, and Würtemberg must cede certain parts of their highlands (such as Passau and Lindau) ; the princes of Hohenzollern and Liechtenstein were to be mediatised and their territories were to be utilised for the same purpose. In this way Austria would contain 1,700,000 inhabitants more than in the year 1801. Prussia was to renounce, though very unwillingly, a claim to loyal Ansbach-Bayreuth, and would demand, in addition to the two duchies of Westphalia and Berg, the whole of Saxony, and the Rhineland from Mainz to Wesel.

Thus the chancellor in no way underestimated, as he was accused of doing by the uninitiated, the military significance of the Rhineland ; the whole point of his plan was obviously directed against France. Hardenberg reckoned the inhabitants of the Prussian monarchy, thus re-established, at 10,500,000—600,000 more than in the year 1805—an estimate plainly too low. Just as in the case of Hither Austria, so also in the case of Prussia, were the western provinces to be united with the main body of the state by an " isthmus " ; the maps of the chancellery showed a portion of Hanoverian land, southward of Göttingen as destined for Prussia, in order to maintain a connection between the district of Eichsfeld and the eastern part of Westphalia. To the Netherlands were to be allotted a portion of the German Rhineland in addition to Belgium and Luxemburg ; but the cession now proposed was somewhat more sparing than before, and the House of Orange was offered no more than a strip in the extreme west, with the fortress of Jülich, in addition to the removal of the German cousins upon the left bank, upon the Luxemburg frontier. Hardenberg was determined not to allow the fortresses of the Rhine valley to fall into weakly hands. It was with great unwillingness, as he himself declared, that he demanded these dangerous outposts for his state. He felt that Prussia had here a duty to fulfil for the great fatherland. The mistrustful eye of Gagern, the Orange statesman, did not fail to observe how the Prussian provisional government in Aix-la-Chapelle was treating the reacquired Old Prussian territory of Cleves and Guelderland on exactly the same footing as the lands of the crozier, embracing Cologne and Treves ; quiet preparations were being made for annexation. Finally Bavaria, in return for the provinces to be ceded to Austria, was to receive the whole of northern Baden, with Mannheim and Heidelberg, together with a portion of the Palatinate on the left bank of the Rhine, with Spires. The court of Baden could find its compensation somewhere on the left bank of the Rhine ; the loose rule of the grand duke Charles was in general disrepute among the great powers, and besides, his dynasty seemed on the point of dying out.

Such were the hopes of Hardenberg. The memorial furnished Austria with a striking proof of the loyal friendship of the Berlin cabinet. How often in former days had the great king fought with the pen and with the sword against every step westward ventured by Austria ; now Prussia herself deliberately offered to the Hofburg, dominion over South Germany. The chancellor himself proposed to sacrifice the Swabian Hohenzollerns, the cousins of his monarch, to the idea of German dualism ; he even wished, in order to secure for the imperial power a firm position upon the Upper Rhine, to allow to the Bavarian state, of which he was still, as ever, suspicious, a very dangerous enlargement ; by the possession of the Badenese Palatinate, Bavaria would completely sever the small South German states from the north, and the south would become absolutely dependent upon Austria and Bavaria. The patriotic aim of these foolish plans was the hope that Austria might in this way be gained over for the reconquest of Alsace ; it was well known that the powerful nobles of the highlands on both banks of the Rhine were wealthy, and that they still lived among Austrian memories. The enlargement of Bavaria seemed free from danger if an Austrian spur could be thrust in between Bavaria and France.

Fortunately for Germany, Austria herself rejected the free-handed intentions of her Prussian friend. Metternich held fast to his view that the South German neighbours must not be alarmed. He found absolutely nothing in the Prussian memorial which corresponded with his own views ; it was neither his wish to allow Russia to press so far into Poland, nor to allow Prussia to advance so far southward across the Moselle ; least of all did he wish to sacrifice the Albertines to the Hohenzollerns. He therefore replied that the question could not find solution until the great congress which was to meet within two months. Beneath the surface, however, he went on with preparations in order to wrest the fortress of Mainz from the hands of Prussia, and on June 3rd, he agreed with Wrede upon a treaty for the carrying out of the terms agreed upon at Ried. Bavaria was to receive Mainz and as large a domain as possible upon the left bank of the Rhine, as well as the Badenese Palatinate and the territory that would be necessary to connect these with the main Bavarian possessions. Thus Germany's most important fortress, the key to the Rhineland, was promised to the state which was still guided by Montgelas, and which was rightly regarded in Berlin as the persistent ally of France. Of course Prussia was to learn nothing as yet of all this. But Metternich was quite open with his English friends, explaining that he desired to have as many German states as possible established in the Rhine-land, and thus to make them feel compelled to defend the river. Never again, he said, could Austria and Bavaria give to Prussia the fortress of Mainz, and therewith "the dominion over their one great river," the Main—to Prussia which already dominated the Rhine and the Elbe, the Oder and the Vistula! The tories, as was their custom, gladly accepted Metternich's views ; they accepted his assurance that the Main was an Austrian river, and they also were unwilling to engage in Paris upon any negotiations regarding the claims of Prussia.

The czar held the same view, although Stein ardently supported the chancellor's proposals, and made urgent representations to the effect that the Prusso-Russian demands must now be pressed, when France had not yet fully recovered, and when Austria had not reinforced her army. Alexander was still unwilling to disclose his Polish plans, regarding which Stein himself had as yet no definite information. There were other excellent reasons for the post-ponement of the decision until the congress which was to establish the structure of the new system of the states. It now became apparent that this tremendous war had primarily been a struggle for Prussia's existence. The re-establishment of Prussia required negotiations with Russia, Austria, England-Hanover, Denmark, Sweden, Holland, and a whole series of German petty states ; it involved the two questions regarding which opinions were most widely divergent, that of Saxony and that of Poland. To deal with these problems now, would simply mean to deprive the con-gress in advance of the most important tasks which it was called

upon to discuss. The new order of the society of states depended
chiefly upon transformations of Prussian territory; herein lay at
once the significance and the profound danger of our central position.

Stein subsequently blamed the chancellor because he had not
availed himself of this favourable moment, when the deeds of the
Prussian arms were still fresh in everyone's memory, to demand the
reward of victory. As if such good-natured considerations could
ever have had any significance in relation to the powerful interests
which determined the calculated reserve of the allies! In the eyes
of Austria and of England, the victories of Blucher and Gneisenau,
far from being a service, were simply an additional ground for
suspicion, and for imposing restrictions upon Prussian ambition.
The imperial knight was utterly wrong when he fancied that
at this time Metternich had been prepared to cede Saxony;
besides, what means did Hardenberg possess to force from the
opposing courts any binding promises? Since the allies had
mutually pledged themselves that they would not conclude peace
except in common (*d'un commun accord*), Prussia was indeed formally justified in giving her assent only upon conditions. She might
have declared that she would not agree to the destiny of the Netherlands and Italy being decided in the peace unless proper arrangements were made for her own compensation. But that last trump
card had already been played; Prussia had long before agreed to
the suzerainty of Austria in northern Italy, and to the strengthening of the Netherlands. A subsequent contradiction would have
been no more than a blow in the air, for its only effect would have
been the omission from the peace of the articles regarding Italy
and Holland. This would in no way have improved Prussia's
position, and would merely have increased the suspicion of the
allies.

For the moment there was nothing to be done. On May
31st, Prussia, with the three allied courts, signed a protocol which
referred to the congress all questions still in dispute. Until then,
Würzburg and Aschaffenberg were to be administered by Bavaria;
the duchy of Berg and the territories between the Meuse and the
Moselle by Prussia; the lands to the south of the Moselle by Bavaria
and Austria; and the Belgian territories by England and Holland.
Mainz was to be occupied by a mixed garrison of Prussians and
Austrians, this being done with the express intention to leave the
decision open. In his defeat, Hardenberg had as his only consolation, that his most dangerous opponent, France, was to have
nothing to say in the distribution of territory. But the practical

significance of this determination plainly depended upon the harmony of the allies. If they failed to come to an understanding, it was inevitable that a state with the power and the widely ramified associations of France, if it took part in the congress, would also interfere in the disputes concerning the distribution of territory, and might perhaps, notwithstanding all undertakings to the contrary, speak the decisive word. In Paris this was already obscurely foreseen. The czar and Stein soon learned that there was going on a suspicious secret intercourse between Talleyrand, Metternich, and Castlereagh ; as the coalition became looser, it was felt that England and Austria were seeking for allies in order to frustrate the Prusso-Russian designs.

Thus whilst Prussia's most irreconcilable enemy was being wooed by some of the allied powers, the friendship between the Prussian and the Russian cabinets began to cool. The cheap generosity of the czar had already put the chancellor greatly out of humour, and now something began to transpire as to the plan for the re-establishment of Poland. It was reported that in Talleyrand's house the czar had spoken enthusiastically of Poland's freedom ; the adroit Frenchman still had need of Russian favour in connection with the peace negotiations, and by harmless assenting remarks he strengthened his imperial guest's enthusiasm. On several occasions Alexander attended the festivities of the Polish emigrants, who thronged round him admiringly ; he at once took into his service the Polish regiments which had fought under Napoleon, and sent them home under the banner of the white eagle. Immediately after the conclusion of peace, the Russian army also returned hastily to Poland ; and at the same time the reserves from the eastern part of the Russian empire went to Warsaw. During the summer, on the Bug and the Narew, there assembled a force double the strength of the army which the czar had sent into the field against France ; the Russian generals said threateningly that they would like to see who was going to snatch away conquered Poland from such a fighting strength as this. It was said that the czar hoped to unite almost the whole of the duchy of Warsaw, and perhaps Lithuania as well, under his Polish crown ; that Austria was to receive only a small strip of land in the neighbourhood of Cracow, and the town itself ; that there would be ceded to Prussia no more than Posen as far as the Prosna, but without the old German town of Thorn. Alexander himself, however, now, as before, avoided any open declaration upon Polish affairs. It was only natural that this underhand conduct on the part of his affectionate friend should make Hardenberg extremely bitter, and that he should now lend an ear to the suggestions of the English and Austrian diplomatists. Yet the needs of the Prussian state made it urgently necessary that all such receptivity should be suppressed, and that an understanding should be arrived at with the czar, for how could the demands of Prussia receive honourable support elsewhere than from Russia ?

The treaty of peace signed on May 30th contained no more than a few brief sentences regarding the distribution of the conquered territory, all as to which an agreement had hitherto been secured. The territories on the left bank of the Rhine were to be utilised for the compensation of Holland, Prussia, and other German states ; the Italian possessions of Austria were to be bounded in the west by Ticino and Lake Maggiore ; the domain of the former republic of Genoa was to be united with the re-established kingdom of Sardinia. All other questions were left open. Thus Austria failed to secure the fulfilment of the whole of her excessive Italian hopes. The treaty of peace passed over the Pontifical State in silence ; but since the Pope, on May 24th, re-entered the eternal city, and the enthusiastic Latin world greeted him everywhere with delight, it was now obvious that there would be restored to him at least a portion of his territory. The handing over of Genoa to Piedmont, the ancient rival of Austria, was a severe blow to the Hofburg ; England had just conquered the town, and inconsiderately declared herself ready to give Genoa to King Victor Emanuel because he must be compensated for the cession of Savoy. Russia, true to her old traditions, espoused the cause of the Piedmontese ; and even France was favourable to this side, for Talleyrand, more far-sighted than the diplomats of the coalition, recognised that the strengthening of the intermediate states was advantageous to France rather than the reverse. Just as he had offered no objection to the constitution of the kingdom of the united Netherlands, so he now endeavoured to strengthen as much as possible the buffer which in the south was to separate the dominions of Austria and of France. Austria was forced to yield to the united veto of these three powers. It was with great moroseness that Emperor Francis suffered this defeat. He had definitely counted upon the possession of the Pontifical State ; as early as 1799, the secularisation of the *Patrimonium Petri* had been seriously planned by Thugut. Metternich transmitted to the English cabinet a formal protest, calculated upon the frank ignorance of the tories, reminding the British of the promises given at Prague in the previous summer, and referring to the incontestable rights over the Pontifical State which the head of the House of Austria possessed as king of the Romans as well as hereditary emperor and chief of the German imperial body. In any case the principal aims of Austria had been attained ; her Italian possessions had increased fourfold ; her cousins were once more domiciled in Florence and Modena ; and the peninsula lay henceforward open to her armies. The whole of Italy, with the solitary exception of Piedmont, was now under the dominion of foreign rulers, who were tied to the Hofburg by a natural community of interests. The ominous name of the kingdom of Italy was immediately abolished, and the fatherland of Machiavelli was in future to be regarded only as the family property of the kin of the House of Austria. For this reason the reconstitution even of the venerable republics of Venice and Genoa was not to be effected, for how readily might the national spirit of the Italians, which had been revived by Napoleon, have here found refuge.

This epoch of the commencement of restoration was hostile to all republics. Where there was no prince who could put in a claim of hereditary right by God's grace, there seemed to exist no rights at all. The new state system of Europe received the general character of a great league of princes ; and ever stronger in this monarchical society of states became the influence of the five great powers. They alone had determined the peace of Paris. It was only as a matter of form that they subsequently allowed the three states of Spain, Portugal, and Sweden also to make peace with France, so that the *puit puissances signatrices* combined to constitute a sub-committee of the pentarchy. The destiny of Switzerland was decided without even consulting the Confederacy.

With the customary official felicity, the chancellor notified Count Goltz, the minister for foreign affairs, who had remained in Berlin, of the conclusion of peace, whereupon Goltz, in a circular letter to all the diplomats of Prussia, declared : " We can rest in the confident expectation that our wishes for the glory and the power of Prussia will be completely fulfilled." [1] In reality the ruling circles were gloomy and depressed. The generals expressed their open anxiety regarding the still completely insecure position of the monarchy. Gneisenau wrote to the chancellor that without Mainz and Jülich, Prussia would be altogether unable to protect the western frontier of Germany. Müffling related that Wrede was already speaking triumphantly of Mainz as a future stronghold of the league, and he asked whether the miserable conditions

[1] Hardenberg to Goltz, May 31 ; Goltz to the ambassadors, June 8, 1814.

of the old imperial fortresses were to recur. " What sort of security shall we have ? " he continued. " What a tragical prospect it will be for us if the petty princes defy us and we—yield ! If we are not to receive enlargement in the same proportion as Austria and Russia, if we allow ourselves to be fooled by the Austrian system of family-appanages, and to be deprived of Mainz and Jülich, the nation, which has done so much, will never forgive it." Better a new war than so great a disillusionment as this ! [1]

The mass of the nation had no part in such fears, although a few thoughtful patriots uttered complaints as to the terms of peace. Throughout the summer the clear sunshine of grateful joy shone over the Old Prussian territories. How much had this nation suffered ! A few months before, the capital had heard the thunder of battle beneath its very walls ; the fields lay desolate ; the houses were bald and unadorned, and there was hardly one which had not to mourn the death of a son or brother ; but now the highest success had been achieved ; the French Babylon had been overthrown, although to those who had stayed at home this success had seemed altogether unattainable. Here was miracle enough for one short year ; who was going to utter complaints ? Since the days of Frederick, Berlin had never experienced such happy hours as upon that sunny April day, when the aide-de-camp, Count Schwerin, brought the first news of the battle of Paris. In accordance with the ancient Frederician custom, the bearer of the despatches rode through the Potsdam Gate, escorted by a squadron of trumpeting postilions ; then he passed down the Wilhelmsstrasse, passed the Dönhoff house, where his pretty young wife was at the window almost fainting with delight. Then he passed along the Linden, to the governor, Lestocq ; he was too old to follow the army any longer, and expressed his envious joy of the young man who had been so much more fortunate than himself long before at Eylau. Then the messenger went on to the palaces of the princesses, and to the ministers. Everywhere he was surrounded by rejoicing crowds ; everywhere resounded the cry : " The despatch-bearer, the despatch-bearer, Paris is fallen ! " And then they all said to one another : " That's Count Schwerin," for in those days people still all knew one another by sight. There was only one who failed to take part in the rejoicings of this great family feast at Berlin, the ill-tempered old field-marshal Kalckreuth of Tilsit memory ; he had remained fixedly French in sentiment,

[1] Gneisenau to Hardenberg, May 18 ; Müffling to Gneisenau, May 17, 1814.

and gave vent to his anger by frivolous jokes against the new Teutonism. The second day of rejoicing came in July. All Berlin was on foot; thousands of people remained for hours in the Tiergarten through the warm summer night, until at length amid loud hurrahs a heavy wagon came by, drawn laboriously by twenty horses; on this was a huge wooden crate, covered all over with writing, names, verses, mottoes, et cetera, all from the hands of good Prussians who had thus expressed their welcome to the remarkable freight upon its long journey. This was the Victory of the Brandenburg Gate. How often during all these evil years had the citizens of Berlin looked with anger in their hearts at the long iron stakes upon the gate to which the chariot had formerly been attached; people loved to tell one another how the *Turnvater* Jahn had once boxed a little boy's ear, because the lad did not know how to answer the question what he ought to think about when he saw the stakes. To the people it seemed that the removed goddess of victory had been the symbol of ancient Prussian honour; now after brave fighting they had got her back again and everything was as it should be.

Everywhere similar outbursts of joy were repeated. When the Prussians entered through the old gate of Hildburghausen, Rückert sang:

> "Through this gate faring
> Army was ne'er
> Gentler in bearing
> Braver in war."

What relief was now felt in unhappy Hamburg, which until the peace was signed had remained in the fierce grip of Davoust. Thanks to the compassion of the brave Danish colonel Buchwald, the thousands of poor people who had been expelled from the town had received gratuitous support in Altona; but five hundred of them had succumbed, and rested now in a dismal fosse in the cemetery at Ottensen. Nor were the millions that had been stolen from the bank returned, for the strict enquiry which in the peace of Paris King Louis had promised to undertake, naturally never took place: towards the Germans the Bourbons showed themselves in all respects to be Napoleon's heirs, regarding truth and honour as empty words.

But the rejoicings of those who had remained at home paled beside the inexpressible sense of proud delight which animated the returning warriors. The leaders took leave of their troops with a cordiality which had never been known to the rough Frederician army of former days. " I hope in the future to find a friend in every one of my brothers-in-arms," wrote the grey-headed colonel Putlitz, when he parted on the Rhine from his Landwehr brigade from the Mark ; " every one of you who gives me an opportunity to show him that I am his friend, will give me genuine pleasure." Before the departure from Paris, the dissolution of the yager detachment had been ordered. There followed the cabinet order of May 27, 1814, restoring the exemptions from cantonal duty which had been suspended during the war, " now that the purpose of our great exertions has been so happily attained," and commanding all officials and teachers to return to their duties. The needs of domestic life urgently demanded attention. How delighted were the volunteers when they returned from the rude turmoil of the camp to the holy calm of peace. There before their eyes, in the blossoming glory of spring, was extended the beautiful Rhineland ; it was once more ours, and the bells of its ancient cathedrals were celebrating the victory of Germany. Straight to the hearts of his comrades did Schenkendorf exclaim :

> "Summon now of joy the voices,
> Servitude and strife are past !
> Fatherland, my soul rejoices
> In thy splendour, won at last !"

What a change, too, had taken place in foreign judgments of Germany, since the compelling power of success now spoke on her side. Madame de Staël admitted sadly that it seemed as if the sun of freedom was now rising in the east ; Pozzo di Borgo and Capodistrias expressed the view that the centre of European civilisation was to be found in this old Germany with its loyalty, its courage, and its power for profound passion—everywhere else were rocks or sand, and here alone was fertile soil.

In England, too, when the king and the czar, accompanied by Metternich and Blucher, came over from Paris to visit the prince regent, the Prussians were the heroes of the day. The uncorrupted mass of the people thronged with primitive enthusiasm round Blucher and Gneisenau, whose life was even endangered by the mad outbreaks of turbulent joy ; the valiant Cossack captain, Platoff, was their only rival in popular favour. How many hundred times, as long as the field-marshal was alive, was the cry raised in English households : " Drink a cup for old Blucher ! " The arrogant nobility, however, was pleased neither by the straightforward conduct of the king nor by the soldierly bluntness of his generals. Metternich alone understood how to win the hearts of the quality; his relationship with the tory cabinet became daily more intimate. The disinclination of the court towards Russia was increased to a profound hatred on personal acquaintance. The utter futility of the Guelph ruler was repugnant to the czar; the liberal autocrat learned, with unconcealed contempt, that the prince regent hardly ventured to show himself in the streets, and how the London mob shouted invectives against the adulterer, saying: " Where have you left your wife ? " The tories upon their side, listened with horror to the big words of Alexander upon national freedom and national happiness; to them he was " half a fool and half a Bonaparte." Their rage increased yet further when, during these very days, a cherished wish of their court was frustrated. The young prince of Orange had come to London, and had concluded the long-planned engagement with the princess Charlotte; everyone hoped for the return of the days of William III, but the headstrong little princess had a word to say in the matter. With the loud exclamation: " I hate Oranges," she rejected, before the whole court, a dish of oranges, expressing her determination not to leave England. It was necessary to break off the engagement. The Guelph was furious. He imagined that Alexander's sister, the talented grand duchess Catherine had egged on his daughter,[1] found the arrogance of the Russians quite intolerable, and actually offered the Austrian minister a secret alliance against the czar, as Humboldt was told by Metternich himself shortly afterwards.[2]

In the beginning of August Frederick William re-entered Berlin. Meanwhile the troops had returned home. Blucher's grateful fellow-countrymen would give him no time to recover from the fatigues of the English demonstration of joy; almost in every town he had to speak to the people, always cheerful and high-spirited; but also pious and profoundly modest. He gave the honour to God alone, the new princely dignity made no difference to him. There was still further rejoicing in the capital when the Berlinese Landwehr arrived; it was impossible to keep the people in order, the battalions were broken up, the wives throwing themselves into their husbands' arms, the children shouldering their fathers' muskets, and in this way the long train of soldiers made its entry, the men decked with garlands, soldiers and citizens,

[1] Hardenberg's diary, June 29, 1814.
[2] Humboldt's Report to the king, Vienna, August 20, 1814.

men and women, all confusedly intermingled—in genuine truth a nation in arms. It was only the king who was displeased, for in matters of military parade he would tolerate no levity. Finally, on August 7th, came the formal entry of the army, the ceremony being rendered somewhat less striking than it would otherwise have been by the modesty of Frederick William. Not merely, as was becoming, did the considerate king arrange for the captured Frederick Augustus to be removed as speedily as possible to Friedricksfelde, in order to spare him the distressing spectacle of the festival of victory ; his gentle spirit was even affronted at the sight of the columns of victory and the trophies which had been displayed by Schinkel ; he would not allow any insult to be offered to the beaten enemy, and during the night before the display the French flags and weapons had to be concealed by thick garlands.

Whilst thus among the Prussian people joy was rising ever higher, the prospects of the congresss became daily more gloomy. The king, with his clear sense of reality, soon came to feel that his friend in Vienna was far from inclined to share with him the dominion of Germany. He said bitterly, " They wish to make me confidential adviser to the emperor of Austria." But the Prussian statesmen did not even yet abandon their dualistic plans. While still in Paris, Knesebeck composed a new memorial which once more offered to the House of Austria Breisgau, and in addition Mannheim, as the chief future military exercise ground of southern Germany.[1] Among the Viennese statesmen, Stadion alone was favourable to this idea ; he still retained the views of a Swabian imperial count, and said aptly to Humboldt that by the renunciation of her Upper Rhenish territory " Austria would also cease to be a German state." Metternich, however, stood firm, and finally, in August, declared to the Prussian ambassador with unusual definiteness, that the whole plan was inacceptable. Thus did Austria, to quote Stadion's words once more, "cease to be a German state" —and only through the free resolve of the Austrian court and in opposition to the urgent desire of Prussia.

In every one of the great territorial questions under discussion, Metternich was the decisive opponent of Prussia. Just as he had already promised Mainz to Bavaria, so also in the Polish question he was far from being in agreement with the unsuspecting chancellor, finding Hardenberg's demands far too low and desiring to press Russia farther back towards the east. The Hofburg had no

[1] Knesebeck's Memorial upon the Peace of Paris (undated, written in Paris).

illusions, either as to the inseparable connection between the Saxon question and the Polish, or yet regarding the natural community of interests between Prussian and Russian policy. In June, Emperor Francis said to General Zeschau, an envoy from the captive king, that he (Francis) regarded the dethronement of Frederick Augustus as improper and immoral : " For we have just been making war in order to restore everything to its old footing. The trouble is that Russia will not yield anything from Poland, and that therefore Prussia wishes to secure compensation in Saxony." For this reason, he went on, he had ordered his minister to avoid all discussion of these questions at the congress ; " because I hope that a better way may be found." The general could communicate upon the subject with his king by word of mouth : " I cannot write about the matter." [1] During the winter, a Saxon agent, Baron von Euchtritz, was captured by the Cossacks of the Saxon general government. From his papers it appeared that the dismissed Saxon minister, Count Senfft, was to be enpowered by Frederick Augustus to undertake secret negotiations regarding the re-establishment of the House of the Albertines ; the communications between Senfft and his imprisoned master were to pass through the hands of Count Zichy, the Austrian ambassador in Berlin ! During the summer, Emperor Francis vainly endeavoured to persuade the king of Prussia to hand his prisoner over to Austria. It was learned that Prince Antony of Saxony, at the invitation of his imperial brother-in-law, was going to Vienna in July, in order to influence the congress on behalf of his brother. Some weeks later, Metternich himself declared, to another Saxon agent, Count Schulenburg, that the interests of Prussia and Austria were absolutely opposed in the Saxon question, and that it would be best if Schulenburg himself should appear at the congress, as Saxon envoy, " with tacit powers," and that instead of acting in accordance with simple and precise instructions, he should in all respects follow the indications of Austria. Frederick Augustus hastened to follow this advice literally. The alliance between the Lorrainers and the Albertines was firmly established.

The English cabinet was at first quite indifferent towards the Saxon dispute, and knew nothing about the matter. A study of Castlereagh's letters forces us to ask whether the noble lord really knew where the kingdom of Saxony was. In so far as the tories had given any thought to the matter, they were, as sworn enemies of Napoleon, unfavourably disposed towards the Rhenish Confe-

[1] Cf. Zeschau's Memoirs, Dresden, 1866, p. 69.

derate princes. It was only the prince regent who felt the natural favour of the Guelph for the Albertines. The agents of Frederick Augustus knew how to foster such sentiments very adroitly. They represented to the court of St. James's that this conservative power had re-established the legitimate Bourbons and could not now possibly wish to dethrone the no less legitimate Wettins. In the end, England, as before, depended simply upon the advice of Metternich and Münster, and Hardenberg could all the less expect from the English ministers a firm support of his Saxon claims inasmuch as the interconnection between the Saxon question and the Polish could not fail, sooner or later, to become apparent even to these thick-headed tories.

Castlereagh threw himself into the Polish negotiations with all the ardent zeal of his stupidity. Both the western powers had formerly regarded the partition of Poland as a profound humiliation for themselves, because this partition had been effected by the eastern powers alone ; now the old disgrace was to be atoned. The will of England which, in accordance with ancient custom, was regarded as the will of Europe, was to be decisive upon the Vistula. In the summer of 1812 the tories had despised the prudent advice of Stein, when the latter recommended them to come to an understanding in advance with Alexander about the Polish frontier ; now there was much talk in London of an independent Poland under a national dynasty. The ministers themselves had certainly no clear ideas as to what they meant by such a phrase ; this much alone was certain, that Castlereagh, as the spokesman of Europe, wished to oppose the ambition of Russia. Especially sinister to the high tories seemed the czar's intention to give Poland a constitution ; " This would be a danger to the peace of Europe," said Wellington in Paris to the Prussian ambassador, Goltz, " especially now when in most of the nations of Europe a ferment has been initiated by the diffusion of unduly liberal ideas from above." [1] England had already gained all that she desired : the Cape and Ceylon, Malta and Heligoland, the enlarged Hanover, were hers ; and she had effected the construction of the strengthened Netherlands state. Except for the Ionian Islands, which the English still hoped to acquire by negotiations at Vienna, there remained nothing more in the whole world to desire ; consequently, with the approval of all enlightened spirits it was possible to assume the unselfish pose of counsel on behalf of the European balance of power.

Meanwhile Castlereagh was engaged in active correspondence

[1] Goltz's Report, Paris, September 2, 1814.

with the Tuileries. After a few weeks, the czar had withdrawn the light of his favour from the Bourbons ; Louis XVIII, offended by Alexander's pride, was joyfully prepared to support the cabinet of St. James's in the struggle against Russia. Castlereagh proposed to the Bourbons to communicate to the great powers their opinions regarding the Polish question, and at the same time asked his envoy, Wellington, to let him know whether France was in a position to support her views by force of arms. The iron duke replied : " The situation of European affairs must necessarily make the influence of England and France decisive in the congress, if these powers come to an understanding ; and such an understanding may lead to the preservation of general peace." It was by no means Castlereagh's idea to cut altogether loose from his old allies ; on the contrary, he was not free from suspicions with regard to the incalculable ambition of France. He was well aware how profound was the need for peace in this exhausted land, and he knew also that Austria would use no other weapons against Russia than those of diplomacy. But by his invitation to France to intervene in the Polish negotiations, he lightheartedly infringed the treaties of Reichenbach and Teplitz ; and in view of the cleverness of the French cabinet and the stupidity of the English, this thoughtless breach of the treaties might very readily have led to the destruction of the coalition.

Nor was England favourable to the Prussian plans in the Netherlands question. During the monarchs' stay in London, the union of Belgium and Holland had at length been recognised by the allies, but the perpetual league with Germany, which had been proposed by Hardenberg, was supported neither by the Dutch nor by their British protectors. The Orange ruler desired to be an independent prince, and to enjoy the protection of the Prussian arms without giving anything in return. His policy was henceforward animated by the twofold aim : to wrest from his Prussian liberator as much German land as possible on the left bank of the Rhine ; and to secure for the Guelph House the East Frisian and Westphalian provinces of Germany, bordering upon Holland, so that a closed Westphalian-Orange power could hold the balance against Prussia in the north-west. Count Münster worked towards similar ends. It was with horror that the Guelph diplomats heard of the Prussian " isthmus " which was to surround Hanover to the south ; never was the proud Guelph realm to become an enclave of the detested neighbour state.

Whilst victorious England was wasting her energies in the

artificial construction of the Netherlands state, which sixteen years later was once more to be broken up with England's own co-operation, the clever statecraft of the Bourbons completely restored humiliated France with astonishing rapidity to her old position in the system of states. Talleyrand guided France back from the dreams of Napoleonic world-dominion to those of national policy, which since the days of Henry IV had been firmly associated with all the prejudices and the customs of the French. France was to seek her strength in the building up of neighbouring powers and in showing favour to the petty states. Nowhere else has this policy, which persists to the present day, found so manifest and clear an expression as in the Memorandum which, in September, 1814, Talleyrand wrote for his own guidance. The treaty had hardly been signed by which France pledged herself to take no part in the decision of the territorial problems ; and immediately, as if no pledge had been given, with incredible unconscientiousness, the French statesman drew up a complete programme for the reorganisation of the map of Europe. Since this article of the treaty of Paris had been kept secret at the instigation of France, the general public had no idea of the incredible breaches of faith which the French cabinet was now undertaking. Talleyrand's memorandum coincides, point by point, with the confidential memorial of Paris in which Hardenberg had expounded the Prussian territorial claims, and deals with all German questions altogether in the sense of the Austrian cabinet. It is probable, therefore, that the Prussian proposal was betrayed by Metternich to Talleyrand, and that the matter had been discussed in detail between the two statesmen. Here we have an example of Austrian disloyalty which was repeatedly to recur subsequently in Vienna.

Louis XVIII was well aware that Prussia was suspiciously watching the Napoleonides, and that she had more than once proposed to the allies that Bonaparte should be removed from Elba ; but he knew also that the Prussian court was hardly less distrustful of the Bourbons than of the fallen usurper. For the moment, indeed, a friendly relationship between the two courts seemed to be established. The Duc de Berry hoped to win the hand of the beautiful princess Charlotte of Prussia, and on several occasions had this delicate question raised through the intermediation of Count Goltz,[1] but since Frederick William would hear nothing of such a family tie, a painful tension soon recurred. The Bourbon ruler felt, with good reason, that his nation demanded

[1] Goltz's Report of July 20, 1814.

from him a decisive hostility towards the growing German state.

Talleyrand's memorandum starts from the same idea. It shows first that France must everywhere support the small states, and then propounds three presumably incontestable rules of international law : sovereignty, which for public law is the same thing that property is for civil law, can never be acquired by conquest alone, but only by the renunciation of the existing sovereign ; it is legally applicable to those powers alone which have recognised it ; finally (with particular reference to the imprisoned king of Saxony), every renunciation of sovereignty is null and void unless it has been effected in complete freedom. The conclusion was, that Prussia had no right to reacquire the provinces ceded legally in the peace of Tilsit. The middle states, on the other hand, were justified in retaining the mediatised estates of the empire which had been given to them by Napoleon. For the mediatised were not sovereigns, but subjects of emperor and empire ; every attempt to reinstate them would be illegitimate and dangerous. " A moment's hesitation about this matter would suffice to excite the whole of South Germany, and to set it in flames." In this way it was proved, with marvellously bold logic, that the legitimate dynasty of the Bourbons must carry on the policy of the Confederation of the Rhine, and must protect the kings by Napoleon's grace ; Prussia's love of power threatened German freedom with the greatest danger. To the covetousness of this state every excuse seemed sound ; she was not restrained by any conscientious scruples. If the promised ten million inhabitants were allotted to Prussia she would soon have twenty million, and the whole of Germany would be subjected to her. For this reason the dominion of Prussia in Germany must be limited ; by a wise federal constitution, her influence upon the German states must be restrained, the federal authority being placed in as many hands as possible. For this it was necessary to preserve the smaller middle states and to enlarge the greater ones, and above all it was necessary to re-establish King Frederick Augustus, so closely related to the Bourbons. " By the acquirement of Saxony, Prussia would make an enormous and decisive step towards her goal of the complete subjugation of Germany." For this reason, too, Mainz must never again become a Prussian fortress, but must remain like Luxemburg a fortress of the Germanic Federation ; Prussia must not extend south of the Moselle. France must assist Holland to advance as far as possible along the left bank of the Rhine, and at the same time must support

the claims of Hesse, Bavaria, and above all Hanover, "in order
to diminish as much as possible the amount of territory available
for Prussia." Since the independence of Poland was unfortunately
impossible and would lead only to anarchy, here the *status quo*
of 1805 must be re-established; "This is all the more necessary since
by these means the claims of Prussia upon Saxony would be frustrated." The independence of Italy consisted in this, that upon
the Italian peninsula, several powers should always maintain a
balance among themselves; consequently the usurper, Murat,
celui qui règne à Naples, must restore the crown to the legitimate
Bourbon; Tuscany must fall to another branch of the Bourbons;
the Pope was to retain the legations, Sardinia was to be enlarged,
and the right of succession of the Carignano line secured. In this
way, in the south, France was to obtain next to Austria, the dominant influence. The best ally on behalf of these plans would be
England, which indulged her own land-hunger outside Europe,
but in Europe pursued a conservative policy.

In a masterly manner did Talleyrand draft his memorial with
an eye to its effect upon the personal inclinations of the most legitimist of all the kings. The man who had once said High Mass at
the festival of fraternity of the revolution, and who subsequently,
as Napoleon's minister, had, according to his own admission,
played the part of "the executioner of Europe," now defended the
right of the legitimate monarchs, with a ceremonious unction which
was most pleasing to the Bourbon, describing this conquered France,
which after the conquest could ask nothing for herself, as the high-
minded protector of the weak and oppressed; and going so far in
the end as to demand war "for the right" in Poland if Russia could
not be peacefully controlled. The court of the Tuileries alone
among the great powers was at this time not averse to warlike
ideas, as Wellington soon noticed. The veterans returning from
the German fortresses angrily demanded the reconquest of the
natural frontiers. The dread of "the dangerous lunatic in Elba,"
as Fouché said, and the increasing confusion in the interior of
France, thrust the idea upon the Bourbon that he should make use
once more of the oft-tried means of the clash of arms to control
the passions of party life. King Louis approved from the depths
of his soul his minister's memorial, which had so admirably wrapped
up the old traditions of the Bourbon policy in the fashionable cloak
of legitimacy. Especially was the king concerned about the fate
of his Saxon cousin; he wrote encouraging letters to the prisoner,
and when the minister came to take leave before his departure

to Vienna, Louis gave him formal instructions to rescue at all costs the hereditary dominions of this relative of the oldest and most distinguished of the dynasties.

Such were the views of Austria and of the western powers. Since all the smaller German courts were passionately opposed to the enlargement of Prussia, it was manifest even before the congress that the soil had been prepared for the Franco-Anglo-Austrian alliance which Talleyrand had for years desired. The Italian question, the only one which might have separated France and Austria, passed into the background beside the German. It was impossible for Prussia to hope to carry through all her claims, however reasonable they might be, before the high council of Europe. Unless, in the congress, Hardenberg was to conduct an altogether isolated struggle, he must make an inevitable sacrifice and come to a clear understanding with Russia. With goodwill on both sides, the Polish question was by no means insoluble. Without sacrificing any vital Prussian interests, the chancellor could hand over to Russia, Kalisz, Czenstochowa, and the land between the Prosna and the Warthe (which was worthless from a military point of view), if in return he could secure the German town of Thorn, together with the region of Kulm, and Russia's loyal assistance in all German territorial questions. On a sober examination, even the idea of Alexander's assumption of the crown of Poland would have lost its terrors. The czar's plans were unquestionably fantastic folly : but far more dangerous for Russia herself than for Prussia. The Polish crown would involve Alexander in negotiations without end, which for years to come must occupy and weaken the Russian state ; Prussia, on the other hand, might hope with some confidence to safeguard her own small Polish domain against Sarmatian greed by a strict and just administration. Amid the intoxication of victory, Alexander still sometimes had a keen sense of the dangers of his isolated position. Upon the return journey from London, he met Metternich at Bruchsal, and endeavoured there to come to an understanding with the Hofburg regarding the future of Poland ; but the Austrian statesman carefully avoided the momentous question. A skilful Prussian diplomat who knew how to flatter the czar's vanity, could therefore, in return for the offer of the crown of Poland, very probably have secured a reasonable delimitation of the eastern frontier ; a loyal mutual support on the part of the two old allies might be taken as a matter of course in respect of the questions of Mainz and Saxony, for Russia regarded the approximation of Bavaria and Austria with an extremely unfavourable eye, and had from the first offered Saxony to her neighbour as compensation for Warsaw.

It was the misfortune of Prussia that Hardenberg did not adopt this course, the only one which could have led to good results, until very late, after pursuing false routes for many months. It was long before he could overcome the overwhelming impression which the first sudden information of Alexander's Polish plans had produced in his mind ; he saw an incalculable danger threatening Prussia from the east, and wished, in alliance with England and Austria, to defend the so-called interest of Europe, to impose bounds upon the czar's lust of conquest, without abandoning the Russian alliance. The gratitude of the Hofburg and of the cabinet of St. James's was to secure for him the possession of Saxony. He failed to notice that in this way he was inevitably leading the state between two fires, and was cutting the ground from under the feet of his Saxon claims.

The chancellor was confirmed in his errors by the detailed report of Humboldt, dated August 20th, upon the sentiments of the court of Vienna—a remarkable document which proves with overwhelming clearness how grossly even a keen intelligence, one possessed of decisive political gifts, can misunderstand the diplomatic relationships of the moment, if he despises the minor duties of the ambassador.[1] Humboldt gave a masterly description of the internal relationships of Austria, of the corruptness of the administration, of the disordered economy, and of the increasing dissatisfaction of the Italians. Yet he had allowed himself to be completely deluded by the smooth tongue of Metternich as to the immediate aims of the Hofburg. With regard to the Polish negotiations, he said confidently that Metternich was firmly convinced that the czar would give way before the common opposition of England, Austria, and Prussia, since the Russians, like the Poles themselves, were opposed to the czar's designs. England and Austria were determined to resist Russia by peaceful means ; to perfect this understanding General Nugent had just been despatched to London, the same diplomat who in the year 1810 had brought about the friendly understanding between the two courts. Moreover, Austria wished to strengthen her army and to assume " an imposing attitude." In Humboldt's view Prussia must work towards the same ends, for the union of Poland with Russia would be extremely dangerous, and still more disastrous would be the re-establishment of the

Humboldt's Report to the king, Vienna, August 20, 1814.

Polish crown, under whatever name. In the Saxon question, Prussia had nothing to fear from Austria. It was true that the military party, headed by General Radetzky, was making a fuss about the surrender of the passes of the Erzgebirge ; and there were a few others who were demanding that Austria should herself effect enlargement in Saxony. "But Prince Metternich, whose counsels are alone followed by the emperor, regards this matter from the right point of view, and wishes Prussia to secure the necessary rounding off in Germany." Since the simple dethronement of the imprisoned Albertine seemed impossible to the legitimist sentiments of the time, it was suggested to the chancellor by Humboldt, that Frederick Augustus should be compensated out of the legations. In Germany, the Saxon house, deprived of its hereditary dominions, could only sow discord ; but as King of Romagna, Frederick Augustus could certainly have played the part of a devoted Austrian vassal as happily as did his cousins in Florence and Modena. But Metternich, so Humboldt innocently said, found that the proposal was involved in "the greatest difficulties." It was not as if Austria required the legations for herself ; on the contrary, Emperor Francis would most gladly see his relative established in the south. But the Pope would never agree to the cession, whilst the bigoted king, dreading excommunication, would never accept it. Thus Humboldt had absolutely no suspicion of the secret intercourse which was going on between the Lorrainers and the Albertines, and knew nothing of Austria's designs upon Bologna and Ferrara.

He was just as ill-informed in the Mainz affair. He dreaded, indeed, that this question might lead to serious complications, for Bavaria was stormily demanding the Rhenish fortress for herself ; but he believed that he could secure support from Austria. He had just had the privilege of seeing a map, which the Austrian statesmen had drawn up in order to quiet his mind, "probably based upon Stadion's proposals," and in this Mainz was indicated as a Prussian town ! Finally, in the German constitutional question, Metternich "was more willing even than in any other matter to trust himself to Hardenberg, in whom he had unbounded confidence "—it would certainly have been hardly possible to misunderstand the intentions of the Hofburg more grossly. Yet the memorial seemed all the more trustworthy to the chancellor because it corresponded with his own preconceived opinions. On this account he for once gave full credence to the views of his opponent, although suspicious indications regarding Austria's

Saxon plans were manifest, and although Goltz reported from Paris that it was plain from the utterances of the Austrian ambassador, Count Bombelle, that Metternich desired the re-establishment of the Albertines ; [1] and he took Humboldt's report as the basis of his diplomatic plan of campaign.

Thereupon Hardenberg sent to Colonel von Schöler, the chargé d'affaires in St. Petersburg, an official despatch and a letter from the king to the czar. [2] The king who, it is plain, was uneasy about the negotiations, contented himself with requesting, in cordial terms, that his imperial friend should observe moderation. The despatch, which was certainly based upon Humboldt's report, expressed the hope that the emperor would lay aside his Polish plans. " His intentions are pure, great, and magnanimous, but I must say frankly that I believe him to be wrong." The Poles were unteachable, and demanded the frontiers of 1772, and for this reason there must be no re-establishment of Poland under Russian guidance, but a repartition of the country ; Russia could annex the greater part of Poland, leaving only Kalisz, Czenstochowa, Thorn, and Cracow. Prussia then went on to demand that the administration of Saxony should be handed over as soon as possible, and asked for a free hand in the immediate institution of reforms in Saxony, since the maintenance of the old, impracticable laws was " welcome only to the oligarchs."

Colonel Schöler was a literary dilettante, as were many of the officers of that æsthetic epoch, finely cultured, well-meaning, and of agreeable manners. Receptive for liberal ideas, he had once celebrated the reforms of Stein and Schön in a brilliant acrostic. To him the partition of Poland seemed to be a political crime. " Providence had plainly determined the restoration of Poland as an eternal memento in politics." He lacked a secure, statesmanlike judgment and keen knowledge of men, He had learned to know the czar in a great time, about the year 1811, had studied Alexander's best side, and had formed a very favourable view of the monarch's character. Subsequently, during the war, he saw nothing of the czar, and for a long time after Alexander's return he had no confidential conversation with the monarch, because Alexander intentionally avoided all intercourse with the diplomatic corps. The colonel was suddenly disillusioned when Alexander's Polish plans were

---

[1] Goltz's Report, August 31, 1814.
[2] Hardenberg to Schöler, August 26, 1814.

revealed to him. He could hardly understand how the czar, who was in other respects so receptive for everything noble, could debase himself to this truly Napoleonic policy, and Schöler like his Austrian colleague, General Koller, was firmly convinced that these ambitions must be resisted.

On September 7th, he handed the czar the king's letter. Alexander apparently received it with satisfaction, but when Schöler proceeded to give him the ministerial despatch, the czar broke into a violent rage, saying that the ministers in Berlin were evidently following quite a different policy from their royal master. " I have conquered Warsaw, what I have I will hold, Cracow, Thorn, Czenstochowa, and Kalisz, and will defend them against everyone with 700,000 men." At the same time he made solemn asseverations that in all other questions he was at his old friend's disposal. He promised that as soon as the congress opened, he would hand over the kingdom of Saxony in its entirety to Prussia ; unquestionably Prussia had the right to organise her new province as she would, even though it might be desirable that the old Saxon name and territorial constitution should still be preserved for a time. Thus, even amid his royal anger, he gave a valuable and binding pledge, whereas Austria and England furnished the court of Berlin with nothing more than indefinite assurances.

A clever negotiator would have taken advantage of this concession to go further, and to bring about a definite understanding. Schöler, however, concerned solely about the Polish question, failed to avail himself of the favourable opportunity. On September 11th the czar summoned Schöler, and excused himself warmly on account of his violent expressions. The ambassador's answer was " a brief and edifying note, which he sent to the czar immediately after the interview. " It is only his sense of obligation " wrote Schöler, " which hinders your best friend, sire, from giving free expression to his own wishes. But it seems to me that there can be no stronger claim upon your imperial majesty than this noble forbearance on the part of the king, to lead you as far as possible to fulfil the desires of your friend. The modesty of the demands, your majesty, depends upon the advantages for which Europe should have, and actually has, to thank you, so long as the independence of the other states is not imperilled and so long as the recently acquired peace remains undisturbed. Russia's internal force and her consequent security are incontestable, but if Russia should secure excessive advantages whereby her power over her neighbours should be so greatly increased that the security of these neighbours should become endangered, the service your majesty has done to Europe would be completely annulled." [1] Such an utterance, in which no attempt was even made towards an approximation of views, could serve only to strengthen the czar in his masterful defiance ; he immediately broke off all negotiations.

In his reports to the chancellor, and in a detailed *Memoir concerning the demands of Russia*, the ambassador gave a sinister picture of Alexander's greed. True and false were here confusedly intermingled. He suggested that the czar thought of acquiring Memel, and even the whole of East Prussia, and issued a warning with regard to the Russian garrison which was still in Danzig under General Kuleneff. Since the peace of Tilsit, Alexander had taken pleasure in " an unrestricted veneration for the *zeitgeist* " ; it was possible that he would give even his own Russians a constitution, and in any case he would revive the oriental plans of his forefathers ; he was " Napoleon's pupil." The colonel felt that Prussia was too exhausted to think of driving the Russians out of Warsaw. First of all, peace must be preserved at any price, but the future would compel us to join with Austria in a contest with Russia.

Alarmed by this gloomy picture, and encouraged by Humboldt's sanguine report from Vienna, the chancellor determined to adhere to Austria and England, but without breaking openly with Russia. In his answer to Humboldt, he expressed this resolve,[2] and unfolded once more Prussia's claims for territory and his own dualistic plans. " We need Saxony (*Il nous faut la Saxe*). I should for ever reproach myself it I yielded an atom in this point. Prussia's exertions have played so important a part in the liberation of Europe, that we are justified in expecting that due regard shall be paid to our interests. The alliance between Austria and Prussia is essential to the maintenance of the independence of Europe ; statesmen who have had the excellent idea of freeing themselves from the unhappy prejudices of earlier times must recognise that the interests of the two great powers coincide, and that Austria can do nothing better than contribute to the strengthening of Prussia, just as Prussia would joyfully witness the enlargement and enhanced power of Austria. I know with pain, and I have proofs, that there are

---

[1] Schöler's Reports, St. Petersburg, September 7, 10, and 12, 1814.
[2] Hardenberg to Humboldt, September 3, 1814.

still men worthy of esteem who have failed to become permeated with these great truths, and who, on the contrary, still think and act under the influence of the political views of the last century."

The chancellor then expressed his views regarding Mainz. Never could Prussia hand over this place to Bavaria, and the Bavarian claims to Frankfort and Hanau must be strenuously resisted. In order to convince Metternich, a memorial of Knesebeck's was attached, wherein, with great parade of cumbrous military learning, the sound principle was established that Mainz was indispensable to the defence of northern and central Germany. Prince Metternich was wrong, Hardenberg continued, in hoping to win Bavaria by favours. "He will never satisfy this state. It is a power animated by insatiable land-hunger, like Würtemberg, and has become a threatening and harmful element in the system of German policy. In this system, in the present position of affairs, there can be but one aim, towards which Austria and Prussia must work together, in their several and common interests. This is to share between the two great powers, force and decisive influence, to exercise this influence in common, in complete harmony." For this reason also, the lands on the left bank of the Rhine, must come into the hands of Austria and Prussia. "Beyond question, this is the only way in which to make the German states of the second and third rank dependent upon our system, and to safeguard that system. Small states upon the left bank of the Rhine, would always remain under French influence, would always be making mischief, and would inevitably threaten to disturb the balance which we wish to establish."

There was not a word in these lines which did not directly conflict with Metternich's plans, and yet Hardenberg was under the illusion that he was quite at one with the Austrian. Utterly blinded, he threw himself into the arms of his false friend, and led the Prussian state towards a shameful defeat. The king had other views; he did not conceal his opinion that the czar was still the best ally of Prussia, and for this Hardenberg in his diary, writing with customary infallibility, accused the king of *pusillanimité*. With his usual undue indulgence, the king allowed the chancellor to do as he liked for the present, but he intended on no account to tolerate a breach with Russia, and by this saving resolution he was able before long to reguide the state into the paths of national policy.

Meanwhile the reordering of the administration was under-taken with vigour, even before the boundaries of the state had been established. The chancellor felt that his energies had begun to fail and had therefore, as early as November, 1813, handed over the ministry of finance to his cousin Count Bülow. On June 3, 1814, there followed a comprehensive change in the ministry. Hardenberg, while retaining the chancellorship, took over the immediate conduct of foreign affairs ; his old collabor-ator of Franconian days, Baron von Schuckmann, became min-ister of the interior ; the newly formed ministry of police was handed over to Count Wittgenstein ; whilst von Kircheisen continued to hold the position of minister of justice. Finally, at the head of military affairs was Major-General von Boyen, hitherto Bülow's inseparable companion-in-arms. Under his direction, Major-General von Grolman was in charge of the general staff, and being a man of incisive activity, he immediately gave to this authority the constitution which for the most part it retains to this day. The general staff was not, as in so many armies, to constitute an independent branch of the service whose members belonged to it once for all, but was to remain in inti-mate contact with the practical work of the troops of the line ; its officers were after some years to enter the line, and would return to the general staff, or not, according as their service might justify. At the same time the king appointed a commis-sion to draw up the foundations of the entire military organisa-tion : it comprised the minister of war, Hardenberg, Gneisenau, and Grolman.

Among the generals there was hardly any difference of opinion that the cabinet order of May 27th which had re-estab-lished the exemptions from military service had been merely a tem-porary step, intended to meet the crying needs of the national economy. Universal military service had proved a brilliant success ; what had been born of the needs of the hour, was now to become a permanent institution. It was in this sense that, at the king's table, Blucher proposed a toast to Hardenberg. The chancel-lor, he said, had awakened the new spirit of the monarchy, so that to-day in Prussia no one knew any longer where the citizen class ended and where the soldier class began. Yet more proudly did Gneisenau demand for his Prussians the best and most national military system in the world, together with the freedom of a thoroughly scientific culture, and a reasonable national constitution which would unite the state to form a living whole. "The threefold primacy, in arms, constitution, and science, can alone enable us to keep our place among our more powerful neighbours."

Nowhere, however, did the bold political idealism of the soldiers of the War of Liberation find nobler expression than in Colonel Rühle von Lilienstern's book *Vom Kriege*. This brilliant work, which to us of a later generation seems to constitute the scientific programme of the modern German military system, contradicted Kant's doctrine of perpetual peace, and more espe cially the fiction upon which that doctrine was based of a state of nature, by proofs drawn from the history of politics and jurisprudence, which was already becoming a common possession of well-educated Germans. It gave a victorious demonstration of the indestructible and blessed necessity of war, which served to educate the nations for peace, and it proposed for the new century the task " of nationalising the armies and militarising the nations." In a free state, every drop of blood must be intermingled with the iron of war ; the army must not be conceived as a weapon in the hands of the state, as a dead instrument which in time of need is taken out of a corner, but it must be conceived as the armed hand of the state, as a living member of the community, vitally associated with the communal life. All the institutions of the state, all science, and all sentiment, must be at once warlike and peaceful ; then only do the enduring moral energies of national life, courage, obedience, and a sense of honour, remain active. Whilst the whole of the foreign world, and sometimes even Prussian statesmen like W. von Humboldt, continued to revive the ancient fable of Prussia as an artificial state, this valiant soldier confidently expressed the view that amid the infective environment of expiring and desiccating petty states, the armed nation of Prussia alone preserved the sense of the fatherland and the proud resolution to remain a complete and living people. Thus did the seed sown by Scharnhorst spring up. A ripened sentiment led the Germans back once more to a manly conception of life, to a just valuation of the vigorous will-power of simple humanity.

Among the mass of the Prussian people, too, opinions regarding the military system underwent radical transformation. The once-dreaded blue coat was now a garment of honour, and most people recognised that neither birth nor wealth can be allowed to liberate anyone from the most arduous of all civic duties. In the circles of the patriots, people spoke with contempt of the old times in which people were afraid of arms. Rückert sang mockingly :

> "Still is the old rule pleasant :
> The soldier to the front !
> Still wields his flail the peasant
> While another bears the brunt."

It is true that the image which was formed by the public mind of the military system of the future had but little in common with the ideas of Scharnhorst. Even during the war, there came into existence among the masses a number of legends regarding the events of the wonderful year. As was natural, the Landwehr became the darling of the nation, for the ancient hostility towards the professional officers had not yet disappeared. A thousand stories were told of the dread felt by the French for the *peuple sauvage des landwères,* and it soon came to be imagined that this force had really done everything, and that the troops of the line had constituted merely a worthless appendage. Out of these popular imaginings, and out of the urgent need for peace, there now developed the view that the technical training of the soldier was a mere game, and that a militia army, of as short a term of service as possible, would best suffice to meet the needs of war and those of peace. This view found adherents even in the highest circles of the officialdom. President Schön was its its ardent advocate.

The task of the new minister of war was one of exceeding difficulty. Even before the war of 1806 he had defended the idea of universal military service, and desired now to preserve this great acquisition without lapsing into the dilettantist dreams of a militia system ; he desired to secure for the state a strong army, adequate to make front against the great neighbour powers without further disturbing the exhausted finances. During the last two decades, there had occurred a shifting of the relationships of military power, extremely unfavourable to Prussia. The Frederician army had been the strongest in Europe, thanks to the cantonal duty imposed by Frederick William I. Since then, however, all the neighbour states had imitated the Prussian system of compulsory levies, each after its own manner. The natural superiority of population came into operation ; the smallest of the great powers could hope for no more than not to fall too far behind her stronger neighbours, and must endeavour by the greatest possible tension of the moral energies of the army to compensate to some extent for the disfavour of numbers. Boyen was well aware that the Landwehr had won all its victories with a comparatively large expenditure of life, and he knew how defective its discipline had proved, especially in the terrible trials of the winter campaign. Scharnhorst himself was hardly prepared for so extensive a utilisation of the Landwehr in the open field. It was only through actual need, through the miscarrying of the spring campaign, and probably through the advice of Gneisenau, that the king had determined, during the truce, to enrol in the field army these troops with their motley corps of officers. It was solely in consequence of extraordinary circumstances, through the long and steady pressure of the foreign dominion, that there had become possible the glowing ardency of national hatred and patriotic passion which had rendered the unskilled force of the Landwehr capable of attaining such wonderful success. The minister of war knew the world too well to expect the return of similar self-sacrifice in the future, if a war whose purposes were not really understood by the masses should be forced upon the king. And yet Prussia, at once by her central position and by the proud Frederician traditions of her army, was always forced to assume the offensive. The state required a strong field army ; its Landwehr must be pledged to service beyond the frontier, so that hostile territory could be immediately overwhelmed by powerful masses of troops.

In view of these considerations it appeared necessary to affiliate the Landwehr closely to the standing army. The monarchy had now at its disposal many thousands of trained soldiers accustomed to battle, and also a large number of tried officers, who were returning to civic life ; this was the most favourable hour that could possibly be conceived for the constitution of a thoroughly efficient Landwehr. By the very nature of things, the reorganisers of the army were brought back to the simple and great idea from which Scharnhorst had started, and from which he had only been diverted by the necessities of his day ; they recognised that standing armies constitute the military school for the entire nation, and that the Landwehr must consist chiefly of men who have served their time. How often, in former days, had Boyen, Gneisenau, and Grolman discussed with Scharnhorst every possible method of arming the nation. All the questions now under consideration had long been threshed out ; Boyen had himself for years been the direct leader and organiser of the *Krümper* system. It is only through the preliminary work of years that we can explain how the commission could complete its difficult task in a few weeks, and that the king with equal rapidity could approve the proposals.

On September 13, 1814, was promulgated the law decreeing liability to military service, subscribed by the king and all the ministers. This is a fundamental law of the Prussian state, one of those epoch-making acts of legislation which prove with victorious eloquence that all history is in essentials political history, that it is not the task of history to watch a Volta experimenting with frogs' legs, or from the discoveries of those who dig up ancient pottery to trace the evolution of lamps and drinking goblets, but to study the deeds of the nations considered as persons endowed with will, as states. The army law of 1814 determined the moral and political views of the Prussians for generations, and graved itself more deeply in all their vital customs than could any scientific or technical discovery.

The law began, as did Scharnhorst's proposal, with a repetition of the monumental words of Frederick William I: " It is the duty of everyone born in the country to take part in the defence of the fatherland." This time, however, the old Prussian rule was to be applied with pitiless earnestness. The king did not forget how the universal efforts of his loyal people, without exception and without distinction, had effected the liberation of the fatherland and had acquired for the state its present honourable position. The institutions that had secured this happy success, and which the whole nation desired to preserve, were to constitute the basis for all the military institutions of the state, but were to do so in such a way that the progress of science and industry was not to be disturbed, for " in a legally ordered arming of the nation is to be found the best security for permanent peace." Instead of adopting the old twenty year term of service of the cantonists, the duty of bearing arms was imposed for nineteen years on all those who were physically fit. They were to serve five years in the standing army ; of this time three years being spent with the colours and two years as reservists on furlough ; and at the age of twenty-six they were to be enrolled for a term of seven years in the first reserve of the Landwehr. In time of war, this first reserve, like the standing army, was liable to foreign service ; on appointed days the men had to attend minor drills in the neighbourhood of their own homes, and once a year they united with divisions of the standing army for lengthy manœuvres. The second reserve of the Landwehr, whose members were also to be enrolled for seven years, was during peace time to assemble in its own native district and on isolated days ; in war time it was to serve in the first place for strengthening garrisons ; but the king reserved the right of employing this portion also of the Landwehr " for strengthening the army " in general, so that its use on foreign service was not excluded. Finally came the Landsturm, which was destined only for use in the last resort, in order to repel a hostile attack ; this was to embrace all those capable of bearing arms from the age of seventeen to fifty. Young men of the cultured classes who provided their own equipment were to serve only one year with the colours and to enter the Landwehr after three years ; they had the first claim to be appointed as officers in the Land-wehr. The separate yager detachments remained in existence, for it was not yet ventured to enforce to its logical extreme the democratic idea of universal military service. The cultured volunteers were to be assigned chiefly to the select corps of the yagers and riflemen, although it was left open to them to choose other regiments. Further experience was needed to show how valuable for the moral conduct of the troops was the intermixture of the more refined with the rougher elements. The circle committees, formed jointly from the army with the civil self-governing authorities, persisted in a changed form. In every circle the business of providing substitutes was to be in the hands of a commission composed of the Landrat, a military officer, and several property owners from the town and the rural districts.

Never before in times of peace had a modern state imposed such severe demands upon its people ; the blood-tax which Prussia now laid upon the citizens was unquestionably more severe than all the other taxes put together. Even the advocates of universal military service could hardly believe their ears when they learned that all men up to the age of thirty-nine, despite the preservation of completely free choice of domicile and occupation, were to hold themselves ready for military service. This was a radical breach with all the inclinations and prejudices of a peacefully developing society, a venture without precedent, which could succeed only because the skeleton of the Landwehr was already in existence, and because the high-minded excitement of war-time was still exercising its influence. The king was under no illusions as to the vigorous passive resistance which the new institutions would encounter, especially in the new provinces, and he therefore commanded that the carrying of the law into effect should take place by gradations and without undue pressure.

Moreover, everything was still in process of construction. The law itself recognised that it was impossible for all those capable of bearing arms to enter the standing army, and that a portion of these must immediately be assigned to the Landwehr; but at present no definite decision was reached regarding the extent of the annual levies. This much only was certain, that the unfortunate condition of the finances rendered it impossible to have a strong army of the line; the weighty military and economic considerations which militated against the excessive increase of the Landwehr, must for the moment pass into the background in face of these overwhelming financial troubles. Besides, nothing but experience could show whether the officers' corps of the Landwehr would really be capable, as this law assumed, of remaining completely independent of the officers of the line. Yet however inchoate the scheme still appeared, the die had at length been cast. The institution of this national army provided a grandly-conceived means for the moral education of the people, one admirably suited to develop the ancient virtues of the nation, courage, loyalty, and a sense of duty, and to overcome its natural weaknesses of stubbornness, particularism, and vagueness of mind. To this generation, which lacked the sense of the state, the state now for the first time became a living entity, as it had been to the citizen-nations of antiquity; now first with its inspiring majesty and its harsh strength did it extend its influence into every household. The short term of service rendered it necessary for the troops, and still more for the officers, to strain every nerve; the year of voluntary service offered a simple means for enabling the unaccustomed burden to be borne by the higher classes. The old idea of Frederick William I, which was so closely associated with the nature of the Prussian state, now at length took a form which corresponded to the democratic views of the new century, and was yet just towards the indestructible aristocracy of culture.

The army law furnished incontestable evidence of the peaceful intentions of the government; it was simply impossible that a policy of uneasy ambition should be carried out with a field army which for the most part consisted of a Landwehr. None the less the levying of the whole nation gave expression to the definite determination to uphold the regained position of the monarchy as a great power. For this reason there was lively uneasiness at all the neighbouring courts. Although a few generals of the old school spoke contemptuously of the Prussian " militia system," the warlike deeds of this army were still fresh in everyone's memory. Dupont, the French minister of war, at once anxiously asked for information of the Prussian ambassador, and received the dry answer : " We desire to have great fighting forces without having to maintain an excessive standing army." [1] Still more anxious was the Hofburg, which did not merely dread the strengthening of her old rival, but recognised also in the army law the triumph of the military Jacobins of the Silesian army, and scented sinister democratic aims.

Boyen, however, saw in this law the priceless inheritance of the War of Liberation. He recognised with joyful pride that the peculiarity of the Prussian state was incorporated in these institutions, that in the development of its military system, Prussia was superior to all other states, and that no other great power of that day, least of all Austria with its discontented Italian subjects, could dare to place arms in the hands of the whole nation. The great and free sense in which he conceived his work, the faithful manner in which in his fiery soul he had preserved the traditions of the days of Stein and Scharnhorst, were not disclosed by the modest man until many years afterwards when, at the silver jubilee of the Landwehr, he recalled in poetical form the saying of Gneisenau's regarding the threefold primacy, and wrote the verse :

> "Threefold the Prussian's saving grace :
> Right, light, and sword !"

This silent man loved Germany with the whole-hearted, profound, and restrained passion of the genuine East Prussian ; for the sake of his fatherland he had once been one of the conspirators of the Tugendbund, and had gone into exile in Russia. But he was unwilling to sacrifice the peculiar characteristics of his Prussian national army to the vague ideal of a German federal military constitution. In a detailed memorial,[2] he described to the chancellor the way in which in Germany there existed four fundamentally distinct systems of military constitution. These were the Austrian, the Rhenish-Confederate-French, the English-Hanoverian, and the Prussian. Never must Prussia sacrifice

---

[1] Goltz's Report, Paris, September 26, 1814.
[2] Boyen's Memorial upon the German military constitution. (Undated. Handed to the chancellor during the congress).

the German character of her army to a compromise with these foreign systems. " Because in the opinion of the respective countries it is necessary to deal with the servile people of Bohemia, of Rascia, of Bukowina, by strict laws, are the Pomeranians and the Brandenburgers also to be subjected to severe rules simply in order to secure harmonious treatment ? Prussia can maintain her position in Europe only if the greater harmony of her inhabitants and the higher culture of her nobles and burghers are utilised to the utmost in her military system. Anyone who should wish to sacrifice these natural advantages to some momentary philanthropic idea, would not merely be an enemy to Prussia but would annihilate the energy of will by which Prussia has maintained herself in Europe since the days of the Great Elector." Consequently the future Germanic Federation might entrust to the greater princes, the circle leaders, the military control of the circles, and might demand extensive military services from all the members of the League. " In this war, Prussia has provided sixty thousand soldiers for every million inhabitants. This is the measure ! Whoever will give more, will be commended ! " But the Federation must not be allowed to interfere in the organisation of the Prussian army. Anyone who should wish to impose more upon the German military constitution would injure himself and Germany as well.

Such was the opinion of the justified Prussian particularism which was at the same time a deliberately German sentiment. The petty states might still preserve for a time their French and English institutions, for the moment they lacked alike the energy and the will to return the gifts of the foreigners. In Prussia, meanwhile, Scharnhorst's work, the German military constitution, grew and ripened, and the day would inevitably arrive when the foreign system would have lived itself out in the petty states. Then the Prussian national army could be enlarged to become a German army. Its cradle had been at Grossgörschen ; who could venture to determine beforehand the proud and victorious paths of its future ? Boyen was firmly convinced that this national army would some day secure richer garlands than had ever been gained by the soldiers of Frederick.

Thus while in Vienna the great Peace Congress assembled, there arose in Prussia a new glory of German history : a people in arms.

END OF VOLUME I.

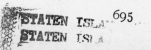

Printed by Jarrold & Sons, Ltd., Norwich, England

INDEX

INDEX

A.

Index

Index

Index

Index

Index

Index

Index

Müller, Johannes, 25, 80, 175, 185, 242, 292, 426
Münster, Count, 248, 302, 415, 457, 521, 525, 573, 624, 675
Murat, 263, 290, 353, 407, 426, 480, 568, 589
Murillo, 6

N.

NAGLER, 166
Nantes, Edict of, 34
Napoleon, 200, 248, 258, 265, 271, 280, 287, 295, 300, 322, 338, 341, 353, 368, 376, 386, 398, 410, 424, 449, 456, 465, 482, 495, 504, 516, 520, 526, 531, 536, 542, 551, 560, 567, 571, 583, 590, 596, 605, 611, 614, 630, 642, 652, 666, 674
Napoleon II, 652
Narbonne, Count, 461, 551
Nassau, House of, 315
Nassau, Prince of, 226
Nassau-Orange, House of, 270
Nassau-Siegena, Prince of, 157
Natzmer, 470, 481, 487, 595
Necker, 181
Nelson, 256
Nesselrode, 521, 548, 580, 631, 657
Netherlands, Republic of the, 37
Nettelbeck, 305
Ney, 423, 540, 571, 614
Nicolai, Frederick, 74, 118, 348
Nicolovius, 324, 395
Niebuhr, 225, 243, 294, 319, 324, 366, 397, 433, 509, 514, 523, 546, 566
Nollendorf, 517, see also Kleist
Normann, von, 539, 593
North German Federation, 210, 281, 285
Nostitz, Charles, 179
Novalis, 245
Nugent, 681

O.

ODELEBEN, 538
Oelssen, Baron von, 661
Oldenburg, Duke of, 450, 458
Olsuwieff, 634
Omptada, 380, 448, 485, 497
Oppen, 461, 507, 541, 561, 585, 617
Orange, House of, 289, 619, 640, 662
Orange, Prince of, 619, 672
Orange, William of, 339, 380
Otho II, 649
Oubril, 282
Oudinot, 398, 541, 557, 564, 571, 642

P.

PACHTOD, 647
Padau, Declaration of, 143
Pahl, 211
Pallhausen, 417
Paris, Academy of, 189
Paris, Treaty of, 265, 267, 276, 345, 383, 521, 677

Paul, Czar, 196, 208, 552
Paul, Jean, 224, 236
Paulucci, 474, 481
Peace of Amiens, 247
Peace of Augburg, 5
Peace of Basle, 160, 161, 276
Peace of Campo Formio, 192, 193, 195, 200, 211
Peace of Hubertusburg, 211
Peace of Jassy, 150
Peace of Lunéville, 200, 203, 211, 212, 260
Peace of Posen, 296
Peace of Pressburg, 262, 271
Peace of Tilsit, 307, 376, 384, 678, 685
Peace of Utrecht, 56
Peace of Vienna, 407, 410, 448
Peace of Westphalia, 6, 10, 19, 33, 34, 41, 69, 207, 218
Peace of Znaim, 405
Peasants' War, 137, 138
Peter Cornelius, 374
Peter the Great, 26
Pétion, 126
Pfaltz-Zweibrücken, House of, 211
Pfeffel, 268
Pfuel, 514
Philip of Macedon, 245
Philip the Fair, 46
Pichegru, 156
Pillnitz, Declaration of, 143
Pitt, William, 254, 265, 521
Platoff, 671
Poland, King of, 283, 452
Polish Nobles, Republic of, 130
Polish Rebellion, 298
Pope Pius VII, 606
Posen, Peace of, 296
Potsdam, Edict of, 34
Potsdam, Treaty of, 260
Pressburg, Peace of, 262, 291
Prince Antony of Saxony, 624, 674
Prince August, 290
Prince Augustus, 341, 344
Prince Eugene of Würtemberg, 569, 590, 615, 648
Prince Frederick Louis, 270
Prince Hatzfeldt, 481
Prince Henry, 504
Prince Hohenlohe, 287, 288, 289, 290, 293
Prince of Hohenzollern, 662
Prince of Isenberg, 609
Prince Karl Emil, 49
Prince Kaunitz, 77, 143
Prince von der Leyen, 609
Prince of Liechtenstein, 662
Prince Louis Ferdinand, 180, 227, 287, 294, 565
Prince of Löwenstein, 214
Prince of Mecklenburg, 505
Prince of Nassau, 226
Prince of Nassau-Siegena, 157

705

Index

Index

707

Index